ASHGATE
RESEARCH
COMPANION

THE ASHGATE RESEARCH COMPANION
TO POPULAR MUSICOLOGY

ASHGATE
RESEARCH
COMPANION

The *Ashgate Research Companions* are designed to offer scholars and graduate students a comprehensive and authoritative state-of-the-art review of current research in a particular area. The companion's editors bring together a team of respected and experienced experts to write chapters on the key issues in their speciality, providing a comprehensive reference to the field.

The Ashgate Research Companion to Popular Musicology

Edited by

DEREK B. SCOTT

University of Leeds, UK

ASHGATE

Published by
Ashgate Publishing Limited
Wey Court East
Union Road
Farnham
Surrey GU9 7PT
England

Ashgate Publishing Company
Suite 420
101 Cherry Street
Burlington,
VT 05401-4405
USA

www.ashgate.com

REPRINTED 2010

British Library Cataloguing in Publication Data
The Ashgate research companion to popular musicology
   1. Popular music – History and criticism 2. Musicology
   I. Scott, Derek B.
   781.6'4

Library of Congress Cataloging-in-Publication Data
The Ashgate research companion to popular musicology / [edited by] Derek B. Scott.
     p. cm.
   Includes bibliographical references and index.
   ISBN 978-0-7546-6476-5 (hardcover : alk. paper)
  1. Popular music—History and criticism. 2. Popular music—Social aspects.
3. Musicology. I. Scott, Derek B. II. Title: Research companion to popular musicology.

ML3470.A84 2008
781.64—dc22

2008049688

ISBN 9780754664765 (hbk)

Mixed Sources
Product group from well-managed forests and other controlled sources
www.fsc.org Cert no. SGS-COC-2482
© 1996 Forest Stewardship Council
FSC

PRINTED AND BOUND IN GREAT BRITAIN by TJI DIGITAL, PADSTOW, CORNWALL

Contents

List of Figures and Tables

Figures

Tables

List of Musical Examples

List of Contributors

Philip Auslander is Professor in the School of Literature, Communication and Culture of the Georgia Institute of Technology (Atlanta, Georgia, USA) and an Affiliate Professor in the Department of Theatre and Film Studies at the University of Georgia. He is the author of six books, including *Liveness: Performance in a Mediatized Culture* (Routledge, 2nd edn 2008) and *Performing Glam Rock: Gender and Theatricality in Popular Music* (University of Michigan Press, 2006), as well as numerous essays and reviews in the areas of performance theory, media, popular music, and visual art.

Alf Björnberg is Professor in Musicology at the University of Gothenburg, Sweden, where he received his PhD in 1987 for a dissertation analysing the songs in the Swedish preliminaries of the Eurovision Song Contest. His research interests include popular music, music and the media, and music analysis. He has published work on music video, music broadcasting and Scandinavian mainstream popular music.

Geraldine Bloustien is Associate Professor and Deputy Director of the Hawke Research Institute for Sustainable Societies, University of South Australia. She has published internationally, including a monograph *Girl Making: A Cross Cultural Ethnography of Growing up Female* (Berghahn, 2003), a co-edited book, *Sonic Synergies: Music, Identity and Communities* (Ashgate, 2008), and *Playing for Life: Local Music and Global Youth*, co-authored with Margaret Peters (forthcoming Palgrave, 2009).

David Cooper is Professor of Music and Technology at the University of Leeds and Dean of the Faculty of Performance, Visual Arts and Communications. He has written monographs on Bernard Herrmann's scores for *Vertigo* and *The Ghost and Mrs Muir* and is co-editor of the collection of essays *CineMusic? Constructing the Film Score*. He has recently completed a study of the traditional music of Northern Ireland.

Kevin Dawe is Senior Lecturer in the School of Music at the University of Leeds. His publications include *Music and Musicians in Crete: Performance and Ethnography in a Mediterranean Island Society* (Scarecrow, 2007), the edited collection *Island Musics* (Berg, 2004), and the co-edited collections *Guitar Cultures* (Berg, 2001) and *The Mediterranean in Music: Critical Perspectives, Common Concerns, Cultural Differences*

(Scarecrow, 2005). He is currently working on a book entitled *The New Guitarscape in Critical Theory, Cultural Practice and Musical Performance* (Ashgate, forthcoming, 2010).

Nicola Dibben is Senior Lecturer in Music at the University of Sheffield, UK, where she specializes in psychology of music and popular music. Her publications appear in edited books and journals, including *Music Perception, Psychology of Music, Popular Music* and *Journal of the Royal Musical Association*. She has two forthcoming books, *Björk* (Equinox Press) and *Music, Mind and Everyday Life* (Oxford University Press), and is joint coordinating editor of the journal *Popular Music*.

Susan Fast is Professor in the Department of English and Cultural Studies at McMaster University. She is author of *In the Houses of the Holy: Led Zeppelin and the Power of Rock Music* (Oxford University Press, 2001). Her publications include articles on Live Aid and cultural memory, constructions of authenticity in U2 and Tina Turner's gendered and racialized identity in the 1960s. She is currently researching issues related to gender, race and normative genre boundaries in rock music and is also co-editing a book entitled *Music, Global Conflict and the Politics of Identity* with Kip Pegley (Wesleyan, forthcoming).

Andreas Gebesmair is Director of Mediacult and Lecturer in Sociology of Culture and the Media at the Universities of Vienna and Linz. He is a specialist in the culture industries and has recently published *Die Fabrikation globaler Vielfalt. Struktur und Logik der transnationalen Popmusikindustrie* (Bielefeld, 2008). Together with Alfred Smudits he edited the volume *Global Repertoires: Popular Music within and beyond the Transnational Music Industry* (Ashgate, 2001).

Stan Hawkins is Professor in the Department of Musicology, University of Oslo. His main publications include *Settling the Pop Score* (Ashgate, 2002), *Music, Space and Place* (with Sheila Whiteley and Andy Bennett, Ashgate, 2004), *Essays in Sound and Vision* (with John Richardson, Helsinki University Press) and *The British Pop Dandy: Music, Masculinity and Culture* (Ashgate, 2009). He is the editor of *Popular Musicology Online*.

Antoine Hennion is Professor at the Ecole des Mines de Paris and former Director of the Centre for the Sociology of Innovation (CSI). He has written extensively in the sociology of music, culture and innovation and is currently working on amateurs, taste and the definition of new forms of attachments. He is the author of *La passion musicale. Une sociologie de la médiation* (Metaille, 1993, reprinted 2007), and his other publications include a book on music lovers, *Figures de l'amateur* (La documentation française, 2000, with S. Maisonneuve and E. Gomart) and a book on the use of J.S. Bach in nineteenth-century France, *La grandeur de Bach* (Fayard, 2000, with J.-M. Fauquet).

Ian Inglis is Reader in Popular Music Studies at the University of Northumbria. His books include *The Beatles, Popular Music and Society: A Thousand Voices* (Macmillan, 2000), *Popular Music and Film* (Wallflower, 2003) and *Performance and Popular Music: History, Place and Time* (Ashgate, 2006). He is currently preparing *The Words and Music of George Harrison* for Praeger's singer-songwriter series.

Freya Jarman-Ivens is Lecturer in Music at the University of Liverpool. She is co-editor of *Madonna's Drowned Worlds* (Ashgate 2003) and sole editor of *Oh Boy! Masculinities and Popular Music* (Routledge, 2007). She has also written on masculinity in rap for *Queering the Popular Pitch* (Routledge, 2006) and on cover versions and authorship for *Popular Musicology Online*.

Anahid Kassabian is Professor of Music at the University of Liverpool and author of *Hearing Film: Tracking Identifications in Contemporary Hollywood Film Music* (2001) as well as many articles on film music. Her research and teaching focus on music, sound and moving images, ubiquitous music, listening, sound studies, disciplinarity, and Armenian diasporan film and music. Her particular areas of theoretical interest are media studies, film theory, cultural studies, feminist theory, and postcolonial theory.

Adam Krims is Professor of Music Analysis at the University of Nottingham. He is the author of *Rap Music and the Poetics of Identity* (Cambridge University Press, 2000) and, most recently, *Music and Urban Geography* (Routledge, 2007).

Portia K. Maultsby is Professor of Ethnomusicology in the Department of Folklore and Ethnomusicology and Director of the Archives of African American Music and Culture at Indiana University, Bloomington. She specializes in African American popular music and is co-editor of *African American Music: An Introduction* (Routledge, 2006).

Miguel Mera is Principal Lecturer in Music and Performing Arts at Anglia Ruskin University. He is widely published in screen music studies from music in historical drama to the use of popular songs in contemporary cinema. He is co-editor of *European Film Music* (Ashgate, 2006) and author of *Mychael Danna's* The Ice Storm (Scarecrow, 2007). Miguel is also a composer whose work has appeared at film festivals and been broadcast on television throughout the world.

Allan F. Moore is Professor of Popular Music and Head of Music Research in the Department of Music and Sound Recording at the University of Surrey. He is the author of *Rock: The Primary Text* (Ashgate, 2nd edn 2001), *The Beatles: Sgt. Pepper's Lonely Hearts Club Band* (Cambridge University Press, 1997) and *Jethro Tull: Aqualung* (Continuum, 2004). His edited books include *Analyzing Popular Music* (Cambridge University Press, 2003), the *Cambridge Companion to Blues and Gospel Music* (Cambridge University Press, 2003) and *Critical Readings in Popular Musicology* (Ashgate, 2007). He is founding co-editor of the journal *Twentieth-century Music*.

Jason L. Oakes received his PhD in ethnomusicology from Columbia University. He has since taught classes at Columbia, Marymount Manhattan College, and the Cooper Union for the Advancement of Science and Art. His work has been published in anthologies, including *Queering the Popular Pitch, Bad Music: The Music We Love To Hate, Access All Eras: Tribute Bands and Global Pop Culture*, and in the journal *Current Musicology*.

Tarja Rautiainen-Keskustalo is a post-doctoral researcher in the Department of Journalism and Mass Communication at the University of Tampere. Her work focuses on popular music studies, transnationalism and relationships between culture and economy. Her contributions to the study of popular music, economy and transnationalism include the articles 'On the Articulations of the Popular Music and Creative Economy in Late Modern Culture' (*Popular Music Online*, 2008) and '"East of Rock" – The Developments of Finnish National Rock on the Edge of Europe' in *Rock 'n' Roll and Nationalism*, ed. M. Yoffe and A. Collins (Basic Books, 2004).

John Richardson is Professor of Ethnomusicology (ftc) at the University of Helsinki and Adjunct Professor of Music and Media at the University of Turku. He is the author of *How We See Music: Locating the Visual in Contemporary Music* (Oxford University Press, forthcoming) and *Singing Archaeology: Philip Glass's Akhnaten* (Wesleyan University Press, 1999). In addition, he is co-editor with Stan Hawkins of the collection *Essays on Sound and VIsion* (Helsinki University Press, 2007). He has published on popular music, contemporary avant-garde music, musical multimedia and Finnish music.

Anjali Gera Roy is Professor in the Department of Humanities of Social Sciences at the Indian Institute of Technology Kharagpur. She has published essays in literary, film and cultural studies, translated short fiction from Hindi, authored a book on African fiction, edited an anthology on the Nigerian writer Wole Soyinka and co-edited another on the Indo-Canadian novelist Rohinton Mistry. She has recently co-edited, with Nandi Bhatia, a volume of essays *Partitioned Lives: Narratives of Home, Displacement and Resettlement* (Longman Pearson, 2008) on the Indian Partition of 1947. Her book on Bhangra's global flows *Bhangra Moves: From Ludhiana to London and Beyond* is scheduled for publication by Ashgate in 2009. She has investigated the relationship between global musical flows and diasporic identity formation on a Senior Research Fellowship of the Indo-Canadian Shastri Institute in 2007 and is now researching Bollywood's transnational flows.

Derek B. Scott is Professor of Critical Musicology and Head of the School of Music at the University of Leeds. He is the author of *The Singing Bourgeois* (Ashgate, 2nd edn 2001), *From the Erotic to the Demonic* (Oxford University Press, 2003), and *Sounds of the Metropolis* (Oxford University Press, 2008). He is General Editor of the Ashgate Popular and Folk Music Series.

Nicola Smith is Lecturer in Sociology and Popular Culture at the University of Wales Institute, Cardiff (UWIC). She writes on popular music in relation to post-subcultural paradigms, ageing fandom and the performance, construction and prolongation of cultural identity. She is co-editor of *Authentic Artifice: Cultures of the Real* (University of Salford Press, 2007).

Timothy Warner is Head of Music at Salford University, Manchester. His research interests are in music technology, popular music and music video, and he is the author of *Pop Music – Technology and Creativity* (Ashgate, 2003).

Jacqueline Warwick is an Associate Professor of Music and Gender and Women's Studies at Dalhousie University, Canada. She is the author of *Girl Groups, Girl Culture: Popular Music and Identity in the 1960s* (Routledge, 2007) and articles on popular music's role in articulating gender and generation identity.

Sheila Whiteley was the UK's first Professor of Popular Music (University of Salford) and is currently Visiting Professor at the University of Brighton. She is the author of *The Space between the Notes* (Routledge, 1992), *Women and Popular Music* (Routledge, 2000) and *Too Much Too Young* (Routledge, 2005). Among her recent co-edited works is *Queering the Popular Pitch* (with Jennifer Rycenga, Routledge, 2006).

Peter Wicke is Professor for the Theory and History of Popular Music and the Director of the Centre for Popular Music Research at Humboldt University's Seminar for Musicology. In 1988 he was appointed as Adjunct Research Professor at the Department of Music at Carleton University in Ottawa, Canada. He has published numerous articles and books on theoretical, aesthetic and historical aspects of popular music, among them *Rock Music: Culture, Aesthetic and Sociology* (Cambridge University Press, 1990) and *Music and Cultural Theory* (Polity Press, 1997, with John Shepherd).

Introduction

Derek B. Scott

The seven parts of this book are allocated to different themes, but this is not to suggest that they should be regarded as discrete entities or separate areas of research in popular musicology; rather, they occupy parts of the same field, and this is evident in the overlapping of concerns and issues that is to be found in the topics of individual chapters. They consist of recent research, and the general approach is that of *rethinking* popular musicology, its purpose, its aims and its methods. Contributors were asked to write something original, while at the same time trying to provide an instructive example of a particular way of working and thinking. The *Companion* is aimed primarily at research students and scholars who need to familiarize themselves with the work of cutting-edge researchers, rather than to study textbooks that cover tried and tested methodologies from the past (the type of book that is more useful for undergraduate students). The essays here are intended to help graduate students with research methodology and the application of relevant theoretical models appropriate to popular musicology in the twenty-first century. To select one example, David Cooper's essay (Chapter 1) seeks to demonstrate how an analysis of sources throws light on both musical and technical processes in composition for film. He evaluates Trevor Jones's score to *In the Name of the Father*, in which Jones incorporates songs by Bono, and finds in it an interesting model for the composite soundtracks found so often in early twenty-first-century Hollywood cinema.

I am sure others will lay claim to coining the term 'popular musicology', although Stan Hawkins and I knew of no previous usage when we began editing and publishing a journal with the title *Popular Musicology* at the University of Salford in 1994.[1] The journal continues as *Popular Musicology Online* <http://www.popular-musicology-online.com>. We both felt dissatisfied with the lack of musicological engagement with popular music in the early 1990s, despite the significant work being done in the sociological field of 'popular music studies'. In 1987 Simon Frith had written with irony, but not without a measure of truth: 'Popular music ... is

---

1   The earliest usage of the term found in the RILM database is Stan Hawkins's article, 'Perspectives in Popular Musicology: Music, Lennox, and Meaning in 1990s Pop', *Popular Music* 15/1 (1996): 17–36.

taken to be good only for sociological theory.'[2] Popular musicology addresses this neglect and embraces the field of musicological study that engages with popular forms of music, especially music associated with commerce, entertainment and leisure activities. It is distinct from 'popular music studies' in that its primary concern is with criticism and analysis of the music itself, although it does not ignore social and cultural context. The time was opportune for this development, because an interest in critical musicology was growing (a Critical Musicology Group had been founded in London in 1993). Critical musicology and popular musicology share much common ground, and this overlap occurs because, by challenging the concepts of high and low art, critical musicology raises the status of popular music research. Many British critical musicologists (like Allan Moore) chose to focus on popular music. In the USA, the term 'new musicology' had come into being more or less simultaneously and provoked much vexation – especially from those who thought their work was suddenly in the process of being dismissed as 'old musicology'. Now, 'critical musicology' is gaining ground as a preferred term in America; it was, after all, an American, Joseph Kerman, who first called for a critical musicology.[3] American critical musicologists have not had the same urge to direct their attentions to the popular, and some (for example, Lawrence Kramer) have concentrated mainly on the classical tradition. Critical musicology, however, is driven by a desire to understand the meanings embedded in musical texts, whatever kinds of musical texts those may be. There are various theoretical models that popular musicologists and critical musicologists make use of, drawn from anthropology, sociology, psychoanalysis, semiotics, postcolonial studies, feminism, gender studies and queer studies. Given this diversity, it is not surprising to find that there is no party line to popular musicology; indeed, it may be thought of as a post-disciplinary field in the breadth of its theoretical formulations and its objects of study.

Popular musicology may be regarded as a branch or subset of critical musicology that has tended, for the most part, to interest itself in one particular area more than others, that of the music industry, its output and its audiences. In doing so, it has needed to be careful not to neglect those who, in reacting against the music industry and its products, nonetheless attempt to communicate with what might be termed a 'popular voice'. The music industry model, as distinct from the light entertainment or show business model began to solidify only in the 1960s. Some 1950s pop stars were rapidly absorbed into the previous model (for instance, Tommy Steele). This *Research Companion*, like most popular musicology, concentrates on the meaning of the popular within a music industry context from the 1960s to the present, and in Chapter 25 Andreas Gebesmair provides the reader with an overview of the various theoretical frameworks that have been employed by scholars in their attempts to understand the workings of that industry over the

---

2   Simon Frith, 'Towards an Aesthetic of Popular Music' in Richard Leppert and Susan McClary (eds), *Music and Society: The Politics of Composition, Performance and Reception* (Cambridge, 1987), pp. 133–49, at p. 133.

3   Joseph Kerman, *Contemplating Music: Challenges to Musicology* (Cambridge, MA, 1985).

years, and discusses its structural features. As the General Editor for the Ashgate Popular and Folk Music Series for ten years, I have found that proposals for books that concentrate on popular music prior to the 1940s are infrequent. For instance, in a list that now exceeds 55 publications, there are only two books on jazz. However, there is no convincing argument for restricting popular musicology in this way, and it is to be hoped that more investigative studies will, in future, be carried out into jazz and country, as well as into earlier popular music, such as that of the music hall, vaudeville show and cabaret.

In the Ashgate series, two areas of research have been given the most attention by contributors, and both in equal measure. One involves questions of identity, ethnicity, space and place, and the other focuses on albums, artists and particular musical genres (for example, blues, rock, heavy metal and indie). The next most popular topics are those that engage with politics or issues of gender and sexuality. After that, the interest is pretty evenly divided between screen music, technology, performance and the music business. An interest in popular music and education has been very much the province of Lucy Green.[4] Familiarity with the research pursued by scholars who have contributed to the Ashgate series has influenced the thematic structure of this *Research Companion*. The seven parts are given over to the following: film, video and multimedia; technology and studio production; gender and sexuality; identity and ethnicity; performance and gesture; reception and scenes; and the music industry and globalization.

Popular musicology may be a relatively recent domain of study, but there is already a history of theoretical models and analytical tools that it has employed. Cultural sociology dominated at first, revealing the influence of the New Left critics, writers such as Richard Hoggart, E.P. Thompson, and Raymond Williams, as well as influential theorists like Stuart Hall at the University of Birmingham's Centre for Contemporary Cultural Studies (CCCS). By the mid-1980s, however, a poststructuralist turn began to change the perception of key rock values. Dave Laing's *One Chord Wonders* (1985) was important for introducing many popular musicologists to the theoretical ideas of Michel Foucault.[5] Authenticity, in poststructuralist semiotics, was seen to rely on a number of signs brought together to construct, represent and valorize authenticity. Instead of being perceived as emanating from an honest, sincere, inner essence, it became 'authenticity' – the scare quotes directing the focus on to an assemblage of signs governed by particular conventions (moods, emotions, and as such, *re*presented). Moreover, performers with no personal commitment to authenticity were recognized as having within their semiotic power the ability to create an illusion of authenticity. There again, a performer might choose to reject notions of authenticity and, instead, deliberately

---

4   Lucy Green, *How Popular Musicians Learn: A Way Ahead for Music Education* (Aldershot, 2001); *Music, Informal Learning and the School: A New Classroom Pedagogy* (Aldershot, 2008).

5   Dave Laing, *One Chord Wonders: Power and Meaning in Punk Rock* (Milton Keynes, 1985).

emphasize a constructed persona – something glam rockers delighted in.[6] Arguably, Madonna's postmoderrn role-play rested on the instability and artificiality of personae created previously within glam rock. All that being said, authenticity has not disappeared from the critical agenda. Many people feel a need to *believe* in some kind of music-making – for example, in the sincerity of rock – and authentic music may be defined as the music that has the effect of making you believe in its truthfulness. If we believe in no music at all, then we can only feel fooled or dissatisfied by the emotions it arouses, for the self has been invested in a bewitching configuration of sound in which any apparent honesty of emotion is, at bottom, nothing more than a technique (even though this technique is, in most cases, not *consciously* employed as an artifice).[7] Nicola Dibben's essay (Chapter 16) focuses on the ideology of authentic emotional expression, asking how emotional authenticity is perceived and suggesting that answers may be found by exploring the aural intimacy of recordings and analysing bodily movements in live performance.

A few words are needed on areas of neglect. As already mentioned, popular musicology tends to focus on recorded music, but there is no reason why its remit should not be wider. What popular musicologists have tended to avoid like the plague is the stratum of taste often labelled 'middlebrow' (for example, lounge music and easy listening). It is into this vacuum that well-known figures like Cliff Richard disappear. There has also been an Anglo-American emphasis in the majority of studies, and the writing has been dominated by the English language (this would not be the case, for example, in Baroque musicology), although one of the notable pioneers in popular music research was Peter Wicke, Europe's first professor of popular music at the Forschungszentrum Populäre Musik, Humboldt University, Berlin.[8] I have tried to broaden the representation of scholarship in this *Companion*, and I have translated two essays myself – would that my language skills were more extensive! European scholars have so much of interest to contribute. In large part, the field has been occupied, to date, by what tends to be referred to as 'popular music studies'. Scholars from cultural and media studies have been most influential, but often have had little to say regarding musicological issues.[9] Popular musicologists seek answers to a range of questions. What are the significant events or facts of popular music history? What caused the shift in popular style between Frank Sinatra and Elvis Presley? Is there a popular music canon? Where do popular styles begin? Is everything always in a state of transition? Is it productive to trace

---

6   See Philip Auslander, *Performing Glam Rock: Gender and Theatricality in Popular Music* (Ann Arbor, MI, 2006).

7   This is not solely a musical problem: linguistic philosophers have so far found no means of establishing the certainty of a true utterance.

8   Peter Wicke's work became widely known following the publication of *Rock Music: Culture, Aesthetics, Sociology*, trans. Rachel Fogg (Cambridge, 1990; originally published as *Rockmusik: zur Ästhetik und Soziologie eines Massenmediums*, Leipzig: Reclam, 1987).

9   Keith Negus tells the reader frankly, for instance, that his book *Popular Music in Theory: An Introduction* (Cambridge, 1996) 'contains little direct engagement with formal musicology' (p. 4). It is an admirable introduction to cultural theory and popular music, nonetheless.

popular idioms back centuries, as Peter Van der Merwe attempts to do?[10] As popular musicologists became interested in world music, the work of ethnomusicologists exerted increasing influence. Kevin Dawe's essay in this *Companion* examines the links between ethnomusicology and popular musicology, while exploring the output of two Greek musicians whose music bears the stamp of innovation as well as locality.

Defining the popular was to be an initial hurdle, especially given the negative connotations it had acquired when theory was dominated by the mass culture model (in which a passive mass is assumed to contentedly consume the junk food of a culture industry). Richard Middleton considers the various meanings of the term in his influential *Studying Popular Music*, the first book-length study to take on board the upheaval in cultural theory during the 1970s and 1980s.[11] For me, 'popular music' is useful for designating a *third type* of music production, distinct from rural traditions and classical traditions. In the Anglo-American sense of the term that developed in the nineteenth century, it indicated a category of commercial entertainment music (in Germany, such music was, indeed, labelled *Unterhaltungsmusik*). Once over that hurdle, further definitional problems loom up in the shape of genre and style. In popular music, a genre is best conceived of as a category, such as blues, rock and country. Style can then be reserved for discussing the musical features that characterize different cultural features within a particular genre (for instance, psychedelic rock or hard rock). However, the issue can become very murky when trying to separate styles from subgenres. Is punk a style or a rock subgenre? Franco Fabbri has been influential in his thinking on the subject of style and genre.[12]

This *Research Companion* does not cover everything, or even most things. It does not deal with copyright, nor censorship, nor illegal downloading (for instance, the closure of Napster in 2000 or the *Grey Album* of DJ Danger Mouse, aka Brian Burton), nor music and violence, nor popular music education (for example, the founding of the Institute of Popular Music at the University of Liverpool in 1988, the pioneering Rockschool examinations developed by Norton York in the 1990s, and the innovative BA degree at the University of Salford that resulted in the UK's first cohort of popular music graduates in 1994). Music technology has been a neglected area in the past – one of first major studies, published in 1997, was by

---

10   Peter Van der Merwe, *Origins of the Popular Style: The Antecedents of Twentieth-Century Popular Music* (Oxford, 1989). For an overview of some of the problems facing popular music historiography, see Negus, *Popular Music in Theory*, pp. 136–47.

11   Richard Middleton, *Studying Popular Music* (Milton Keynes, 1990). Fifteen years on from Middleton's text, the editorial board of the journal *Popular Music* debated the adjective 'popular' and whether or not it still had meaning. 'Can We Get Rid of the "Popular" in Popular Music?', *Popular Music* 24 (2005): 133–45; reprinted in Allan F. Moore, *Critical Essays in Popular Musicology* (Aldershot, 2007), pp. 35–47.

12   His early thoughts were published as 'A Theory of Musical Genres: Two Applications', in David Horn and Philip Tagg (eds), *Popular Music Perspectives* (Göteborg and Exeter, 1982), pp. 52–81. More recent thoughts are in his 'Browsing Music Spaces: Categories and the Musical Mind' [1999], in Moore, *Critical Essays in Popular Musicology*, pp. 49–62.

Paul Théberge.[13] – but its importance is now recognized, and a strong case for analysing the techniques of sound recording is made in essays in this *Companion*. Both Tim Warner (Chapter 6) and Peter Wicke (Chapter 7) consider the sound recording to be the primary medium of popular music. Electronic manipulation of sound has been employed increasingly since the mid-1950s. Wicke pays specific attention to the way sound is conceptualized and organized in the recording studio.

One of the areas of study that has faded since the 1980s is that concerned with establishing a close relationship between social class and the political and moral meanings of popular music – although class has been brought back firmly on the sociocultural agenda by Beverley Skeggs.[14] Moral issues come and go, and often continue to reach back to the 'moral panic' model.[15] Moral outrage where popular music is concerned has a lengthy history stretching from the early waltz to gangsta rap. Popular music always seems to stir greater moral indignation than film. Much more fuss is made of rappers than directors of extreme violence on film (like Quentin Tarantino). Perhaps this is owing to the common perception that popular music is the culture of young people. David Hesmondhalgh has called for the link to be severed: 'the close relationship between the study of youth and that of popular music was the result of particular historical circumstances, and the privileging of youth in studies of music is an obstacle to the developed understanding of music and society.'[16]

Areas that have been debated regularly are, as to be expected, those that involve broad concerns about popular music and society. These include questions about how manipulative the industry is and whether or not artists have compromised their ethnic identity to appeal to a wider audience. The main theoretical concerns and issues from the 1970s onwards have included debates about essentialism, human agency and economic determinism. At times there have been changes of perception about popular genres that defied prediction: few in the 1960s would have thought the rise of lesbian country music ever possible. I will rehearse some of the past concerns of popular musicologists and relate them to present concerns, especially as revealed in the work of those who have contributed essays to this *Companion*.

Having emphasized the importance of studying the music itself, I ought to begin with musical analysis. The earliest work in the analysis of pop music was done by Wilfrid Mellers, but the analytical tools he used were those honed for use

---

13   Paul Théberge, *Any Sound You Can Imagine: Making Music/Consuming Technology* (Hanover, NH and London, 1997).

14   Beverley Skeggs, *Class, Self, Culture* (London, 2004).

15   Stanley Cohen coined the term 'moral panic' to describe the media reaction to mods and rockers in the 1960s, in *Folk Devils and Moral Panics: The Creation of the Mods and Rockers* (3rd edn, London, 2002; originally published MacGibbon and Kee, 1972).

16   David Hesmondhalgh, 'Subcultures, Scenes or Tribes? None of the Above', *Journal of Youth Studies* 8/1 (2005): 21–40, at 38.

in the classical repertoire.[17] Andrew Chester had already developed an argument regarding extensional and intensional structures in an attempt to make the case for popular music's need to be analysed on its own terms and not those of classical music.[18] However, Chester did not demonstrate in any detail how that was to be achieved. Dai Griffiths offered a somewhat scornful overview of popular music analysis in the closing decades of the twentieth century in 'The High Analysis of Low Music' (1999).[19] Pioneers of popular music analysis in the 1980s, who made an effort to analyse this music on its own terms without an unconsidered recourse to the tools of classical analysis were Walter Everett, Philip Tagg and Alf Björnberg (each using different analytical models). Some examples of their work are reprinted in Allan Moore's *Critical Essays in Popular Musicology* (2007). A range of insightful popular music analysis appeared in the early 1990s from the likes of David Brackett, Richard Middleton, Allan Moore, Rob Walser and Stan Hawkins. In his essay for this *Companion*, Allan Moore continues the search for 'useful and usable' analytic interpretations that has occupied him for many years, and offers interpretations of several songs using theoretical models from Peircian semiotics and the much more recent field of the 'ecological' perception of music (see Chapter 22). Tim Warner's essay (Chapter 6) puts forward persuasive reasons for analysts to take more interest in analysing the way popular music recordings have been made, and examines some of the investigative procedures that are possible. These may be undertaken with the aim of revealing a recording's aesthetic characteristics, or in order to explore the impact technological processes have had on listeners. Alf Björnberg's essay (Chapter 5) explores the reception of recorded music and its related technology over the years 1950–80, looking in particular at 'hi-fi culture'.

The study of popular music reception has shifted its focus over the years from the 'masses' to teenagers to subcultures to scenes and to neo-tribes. In the writings of Theodor Adorno, which still hold inordinate and, some would say, undeserving sway over popular musicology, a child-like, passive listener is manipulated by the culture industry. In the 1970s Adorno's ideas were countered by arguments about the possibility of new meanings being made in the consumption of popular music (suggesting activity rather than passivity on the part of consumers). The industry can determine its output, but not the way its products are used or the meanings that are made of them. It became common in the 1970s and 1980s to speak of 'relative autonomy' (although the extent of this autonomy, and just how relative it was, were issues never completely resolved). The relationship between popular music and audiences is no longer the straightforward affair it was once assumed to be (especially in the old days of mass-culture theory, with its idea of the passive audience).[20] There has been some interesting work on celebrity by

---

17   Wilfred Mellers, *Twilight of the Gods: The Beatles in Retrospect* (London, 1973).

18   Andrew Chester, 'Second Thoughts on a Rock Aesthetic: The Band', *New Left Review* 62 (1970), 75–82; reprinted in Moore, *Critical Essays*, pp. 111–18.

19   Dai Griffiths, 'The High Analysis of Low Music', *Music Analysis* 18 (1999): 389–435; reprinted in Moore, *Critical Essays*, pp. 63–109.

20   See Robert Walser, *Running with the Devil: Power, Gender, and Madness in Heavy Metal*

Chris Rojek, and fans have been the subject of much interest since Lisa Lewis's collection of essays in 1992.[21] Spectators are now often involved in performance: camera shots of audiences are common.

Among early formulations in the late 1950s and 1960s of the concept of subculture was Howard Becker's work on 'outsiders' like jazz musicians, whom he theorized in line with the sociology of deviance.[22] Writers in the late 1970s and in the 1980s – for example, Dick Hebdige and Iain Chambers[23] – emphasized that resistant meanings were made in the consumption of popular music. There may be meanings encoded, but the listener has room for negotiation in decoding and accepting meanings, although not any meaning can be made in the consumption. Popular music has frequently been seen as an arena of hegemonic negotiation (in line with Gramsci's argument that powerful social and political groups exercise cultural hegemony, persuading rather than forcing others to accept their values). The meanings that subordinate social groups, especially young working-class males, made of popular music were to be interpreted as resistant, transgressive or evasive of the dominant culture. This was the basic cultural studies theoretical framework. The 'spectacular' subcultural styles of teds, mods and rockers, or punks were analysed as reworkings of existing cultural artefacts, arranged to yield new, subversive, oppositional or otherwise challenging meanings (for instance, a hair comb sharpened as a weapon by some mods). Three problems were soon highlighted. First, where were the young women? Angela McRobbie was the first to intervene here.[24] Second, where was the cultural interaction with family or work colleagues? Subcultures, post-Becker, seemed to be exclusively about conflict between generations, and the semiotics of fashionable clothing and of leisure spaces outside the home or workplace. Yet music is often used as background to another activity. Third, what kind of resistance can popular music offer? Is it merely symbolic? There is evidence that it may be more than this (Rock Against Racism, Live Aid).

The debate about how much impact popular music is able to achieve politically has never gone away. Stung by Tory leader David Cameron's enthusiasm for the Smiths, John Harris penned an article in the *Guardian* in March 2008 with the exclamatory title, 'Hands off Our Music!'. Harris's recollection of the 1980s is of a decade in which popular musicians were untied in anti-Tory anger. He remembers fondly the bands who came together to support Labour in the Red Wedge tours, and especially the song 'Eton Rifles', in which Paul Weller and the Jam envisaged

---

    Music (Hanover, NH, 1993); and Nick Abercrombie and Brian Longhurst, *Audiences: A Sociological Theory of Performance and Imagination* (London, 1998).

21   Chris Rojek, *Celebrity* (London, 2001); Lisa A. Lewis (ed.), *The Adoring Audience: Fan Culture and Popular Media* (London, 1992).

22   Howard S. Becker, *Outsiders: Studies in the Sociology of Deviance* (New York, 1963).

23   Dick Hebdige, *Subculture: The Meaning of Style* (London, 2002; originally published Methuen, 1979); Iain Chambers, *Urban Rhythms: Pop Music and Popular Culture* (London, 1985).

24   Angela McRobbie, 'Settling Accounts with Subcultures: A Feminist Critique', *Screen Education* 34 (1980): 37–49.

a class war taking place at the gates of Eton College.[25] As the comments of various letter-writers revealed a few days later, however, the relationship of pop and politics is fraught. One of them pointed out that the Jam's bass player went on to send his own son to Eton; others remarked that lyrics of the past could not always be described as adopting a left-wing position; and another raised the matter of pop's being part of a multibillion-pound entertainment industry.[26] Yet this does not diminish the politically motivated and active support given to a variety of causes by bands during the 1980s – bands such as the Housemartins, who played to raise funds for the miners' strike, and the Smiths, who performed in aid of the Liverpool councillors who had been financially penalized for their opposition to the government's 'rate-capping' policy. The argument that popular music has no impact on politics is one that ignores the crucial importance of the way music is *used* in particular social and historical contexts. Rock Against Racism in the later 1970s, for example, certainly helped to stop a growing racist movement in its tracks, even if racism is still a problem we confront today. The *then* should never be conflated with the *now*, and the maxim 'eternal vigilance' needs to be kept in mind by all who share a vision of a fair and just society.

Popular music can be articulated to particular political meanings whatever the intentions of the creators of that music might be: consider, for example, the reception in some quarters of Springsteen's 'Born in the USA' or U2's 'Sunday, Bloody Sunday'. Even genres that are not normally thought of as allied to political causes can become so: a CD of electronic dance music, a type of music generally seen as non-political, was issued some years ago with the title *Loyalist Trance Euphoria* (thus linking it to Ulster Protestant political aspirations).[27] Articulation is a useful concept for understanding how a connection may be made between production and consumption in the absence of an obvious or direct link. In fact, there may be a series of links, forming a chain between production and consumption. There may also be a contingent link that nobody predicted. Thus, the concept of articulation avoids the idea in homological interpretations that the lives people lead explain their cultural preferences in a deterministic manner, or, at best, that people are driven to seek a symbolic cultural parallel to their social existence. Of course, this may happen; but it is only one possibility of what may happen.

Indeed, the theory of homology, taken from structural anthropology, and used by Paul Willis in his *Profane Culture* of 1978, was the first to cause problems in the poststructuralist climate of the 1980s.[28] The idea of arbitrary signifiers did not square with the notion that cultural patterns replicated, albeit symbolically, the

---

25 John Harris, 'Hands off Our Music!', *Guardian*, G2 supplement, 18 March 2008, pp. 4–7, at p. 6. Eton College, founded 1440, is the best known of the British independent schools, and has long been associated with the education of boys from the wealthiest and most privileged of families.

26 Letters and e-mails, *Guardian*, 22 March 2008, p. 43.

27 Numbered CD12, it was available until at least 2006 through the Orange Pages website ('The Burning Torch for Protestantism'): <www.orange-pages.tk>.

28 Paul E. Willis, *Profane Culture* (London, 1978).

social patterns of a person's life. While cultural sociologists emphasized mediation in communicating meaning, poststructuralists and semioticians focused on the importance of representation in the construction of meaning. Semiotics is not just about spotting an individual sign and deriving a meaning. Signs acquire meaning by being interrelated, or linked in a chain. An individual minor chord does not signify sadness outside of a certain context, any more than a train arriving at a station at 9:30 means it is the 9:30 train. According to the chain of signs known as a timetable, it could be the 9:00 train running half-an-hour late. Thus, the 'devil's interval', the tritone, in Robert Farnon's light orchestral piece *Jumping Bean* is perceived as funny, because the context in which it features rules out the possibility of its signifying evil or menace. Signs relate to each other in a particular context, but these signs also circulate in other contexts, often enabling unexpected connections of thought to be made. Intertextuality (Julia Kristeva's translation of Mikhail Bakhtin's term 'dialogic') acknowledges the circulation and interplay of meaning across numerous signifying practices (music, literature, film, the visual arts and so on).[29] Intertextuality does not mean simply quoting someone or something. My favourite example of intertextuality is the answer given by a young person to the question: 'How did Romeo die?' It was: 'He drowned on the Titanic.' The intertextual transposition of signs, here, occurs because Leo DiCaprio, who played Romeo in Baz Luhrman's film of Shakespeare's drama, also starred in the film *Titanic*.

Another question that emerged to challenge subcultural theory was: is everyone who is not part of a youth subculture a bland and undistinguished member of the homogeneous cultural mainstream? That possibility certainly does not square with Pierre Bourdieu's contention that culture is used by people to create social distinctions between themselves and others via judgements of taste.[30] By the turn of the century, subcultural theory was being replaced by scenes and neo-tribes as models for theorizing collective musical identities. The development of scene theory can be dated back to an influential essay Will Straw published in 1991, in which he described scenes as characterized by the 'building of musical alliances and the drawing of musical boundaries'.[31] These alliances are then maintained, as are their boundaries. Scenes are not necessarily marked primarily by class, although that might form part of the alliance, as might other characteristics (relating to gender, ethnicity and generation). Adam Krims (Chapter 21) surveys some of the literature on scenes, noting the sometimes vague definitions and meanings given to them. In advancing his own ideas, he stresses the overriding importance of the urban

29 For an informative discussion of various types of intertextual play in popular music, see Serge Lacasse, 'Intertextuality and Hypertextuality in Recorded Popular Music', in Michael Talbot (ed.), *The Musical Work: Reality or Invention?* (Liverpool, 2000), pp. 35–58; reprinted in Moore, *Critical Essays*, pp. 147–70.

30 Pierre Bourdieu, *Distinction: A Social Critique of the Judgment of Taste*, trans. Richard Nice (London, 1984; originally published as *La Distinction. Critique sociale du jugement*, Paris: Editions de Minuit, 1979).

31 Will Straw, 'Systems of Articulation, Logics of Change: Communities and Scenes in Popular Music', *Cultural Studies* 5/3 (1991): 368–88, at 373.

context and insists that we regard urban cultural intermediaries as pivotal figures. Ian Inglis's essay (Chapter 20) offers an account of popular music fans in Britain in the late 1950s and early 1960s, presenting evidence to support an argument that this was the first British popular music scene. He adopts a flexible and dynamic model of scene theory and stresses the role of human agency – especially the part played by the committed enthusiast. He counters the usual assumption that there was a sudden shift in popular taste and reveals that it was a taste that had been forming for several years.

The 'scene' was employed as the regular model for understanding popular music reception in the early years of the twenty-first century, and it was adapted to include translocal, global and virtual scenes.[32] Soon, the idea of neo-tribes began to gain ground, influenced by Michel Maffesoli's writing; Andy Bennett was one of many who found problems with subculture and began to accept the idea of tribes and scenes as a useful alternative.[33] Tribes prove to be unstable and provisional collectivities that no longer have a particular relationship to class, but the theory is not without its problems. Unfortunately, there is always an awkward group: for example, the fans of Northern Soul whose interests failed to wane. This begs the question of whether or not a scene can remain a scene when so much that was originally important to the scene has gone (not least the Wigan Casino), and whether pensioners (which many older 'soulies' now are) can be part of a neo-tribe. Nicola Smith's essay (Chapter 23) moves beyond subcultural models to theorize the 'ageing scene' of Northern Soul. She explains how the neo-tribe model might be adapted to account for its longevity, as well as for the continuing participation of its earliest devotees. She stresses that what is important here is a 'desire for the continuation of the collective'. Northern Soul does not fit satisfactorily into either the modernist or postmodernist perspectives on subculture given by David Muggleton.[34] Neither does it fit the epoch of the hypermodern that Gilles Lipovetsky argues we are all now part of, a time characterized by more autonomous yet more fragile individuals, by fashion, novelty, ephemerality, worries and alarms and by an 'unstable, fluctuating confidence'[35] – the latter exemplified, perhaps, by the global stock-market panic of October 2008. We are certainly in a period of fragility when it comes to confidence in existing cultural–theoretical models. David Hesmondhalgh, for instance, has rejected subcultures, tribes and scenes altogether. He sees 'no possibility of a return to subculture in any adequate sociology of popular music' and claims that 'neo-tribe' is too malleable a concept, while 'scene' has been used so variously and

---

32   Andy Bennett and Richard A. Peterson (eds), *Music Scenes: Local, Translocal, and Virtual* (Nashville, TN, 2004).

33   Michel Maffesoli, *The Time of the Tribes: The Decline of Individualism in Mass Society*, trans. Don Smith (London, 1996); Andy Bennett, 'Subcultures or Neo-Tribes? Rethinking the Relationship between Youth, Style and Musical Taste', *Sociology* 33/3 (1999): 599–617.

34   David Muggleton, *Inside Subculture: The Postmodern Meaning of Style* (Oxford, 2000).

35   Gilles Lipovetsky with Sébastien Charles, *Hypermodern Times*, trans. Andrew Brown (Cambridge, 2005; originally published as *Temps hypermodernes*, Paris: Grasset, 2004), p. 45.

imprecisely that it has lost meaning.[36] Brian Longhurst has made a case for 'spaces of elective belonging' as an alternative concept to that of scene: 'we belong to places and feel attachments to people, things and processes ... Attachments and modes of belonging are lived through globalized and mediatized processes.'[37] The idea of attachments has played a significant role in the work of Antoine Hennion, whose essay in the *Companion* (Chapter 19) examines the reception of rap and techno from the perspective of what they mean those who love listening to such music (thus avoiding the objectifying accounts found in much musicology and sociology).

The attention now given to questions of space and place reveals the influence of research in cultural geography. Applied to music, such questions become: how does music construct a sense of place? Why do people of one place sometimes respond very warmly to music of a distant place (such as Wigan's enthusiasm for the soul music of Detroit)? Music can, of course, mean something different in one place compared to another. In the 1970s there was a great deal of debate about cultural imperialism, whereas in the 1990s the term 'globalization' became more common.[38] World music has gone from being a term that excited critical irritation (as a media fabrication) to a term that has been widely accepted.[39] All the same, the interpretation of world music needs to remain responsive to postcolonial critique and debates about cultural otherness.

Today, however, the single mass-marketed global product is untypical, and far more diversity than might have been expected is found in the world's marketplaces, with the onset of flexible accumulation that has replaced the Fordist model of mass production. Post-Fordism and flexible accumulation – small batches, niche markets and so on. – have posed the greatest challenge to Adorno's arguments, since, as Adam Krims points out, 'the unprecedented concentration of the music-recording industry does *not* necessarily promote an increasing homogenization of the product (form or content) and does *not* necessarily entail ever more standardized, falsely differentiated musical forms of deadening similarity'.[40] Nevertheless, these represent what Krims calls mistakes about the particulars, rather than an error in Adorno's contention that music has become commodified. The *Pop Idol* format that has been ubiquitous for several years is, for example, local in content but global in format. It was conceived in New Zealand in 1996 by Simon Fuller and has since then spawned *Australian Idol, Canadian Idol, Indonesian Idol* and many others;[41] interestingly, the only show that failed was *World Idol*. In Chapter 26 of this *Companion*, Tarja Rautiainen-Keskustalo discusses the *Pop Idol* format as a

---

36 Hesmondhalgh, 'Subcultures, Scenes or Tribes?', p. 38.
37 Brian Longhurst, *Cultural Change and Ordinary Life* (Maidenhead, 2007), pp. 58 and 61.
38 A key text for popular music studies was Timothy Taylor's *Global Pop: World Music, World Markets* (New York, 1997).
39 Philip V. Bohlman, *World Music: A Very Short Introduction* (Oxford, 2002).
40 Adam Krims. *Music and Urban Geography* (New York, 2007), p. 99.
41 See Su Holmes, 'Reality Goes Pop! Reality TV, Popular Music, and Narratives of Stardom in Pop Idol', *Television and New Media* 5/2 (2004): 147–72, at 149; and Charles Fairchild, *Pop Idols and Pirates: Mechanisms of Consumption and the Global Circulation of Popular Music* (Aldershot, 2008), pp. 95–102.

transnational musical phenomenon and as an illustration of the interplay between global economy and local meaning. She challenges, as too simple, the idea that such formats colonize the local culture. For some global companies, however, the emphasis on local sensitivities in a global market may be more a question of promotional style than content: note that HSBC currently advertises itself a 'the world's local bank'.

The importance of branding grows rapidly after 1980. Branding aims to hold on to a particular image throughout a range of products – and a pop star is a very useful brand image. Bethany Klein writes of the disapproval felt by some fans at 'the increasingly comfortable relationships between artists and corporations' in the world of advertising. Yet there is no simple condemnation to be made, since it is clear that both popular music and advertising rely on commercial markets.[42] An appearance in an iPod commercial was key to the American success of the British duo, the Ting Tings, in the summer of 2008. Branding obscures the relationship between the musician and the product that was formerly easy to recognize in marketing and advertisements. Rautiainen-Keskustalo comments, 'the new formation of the popular does not maintain the sites (the forms of agency) that popular culture has traditionally offered to individuals (for example, popular culture as a countercultural or sub-cultural identity marker), but maintains rather different values, derived from both the ideological basis of late capitalism and the history of the popular, which are in the constant process of struggling for signification'.[43]

The 'cultural imperialism' model that focused on the corruption or degradation of existing local cultures has faded in the present century,[44] even though a mere four companies now dominate the popular music industry: EMI, Time Warner, Sony/BMG and Universal. In its place, there has been a move to examine issues of the local and global employing the model of transculturation. In this model, an artist such as Elvis Presley or Madonna is examined for an appeal across cultures (without, however, making a claim for universality of appeal). This avoids implying that millions of people have been manipulated and duped by American cultural imperialism. It recognizes that no power is capable of configuring global media into one pattern (a pattern sometimes termed a 'mediascape') while, at the same time, it acknowledges the imbalance of power between producer and consumer. Whatever room for manoeuvre a listener has, there are limits imposed on him or her by the power of the producer – even in such basic matters as what the producer chooses to make available to the listener. Rapid developments in digital technology and new

---

42   Bethany Klein, *As Heard on TV: Popular Music in Advertising* (Aldershot, 2008).

43   Tarja Routiainen-Keskusm 'Rocking the Economy: On the Articulations of Popular Music and the Creative Economy in Late Modern Culture', *Popular Musicology Online*, at: <http://www.popular-musicology-online.com>.

44   For a collection of essays that has moved away from arguments about American imperialist dominance, see Andreas Gebesmair and Alfred Smudits (eds), *Global Repertoires: Popular Music Within and Beyond the Transnational Music Industry* (Aldershot, 2001).

mobile media have triggered what Gerry Bloustien (Chapter 24) refers to as the 'creative knowledge economy' (fashion, games, film, television, telecommunications and so forth). She looks at how music underpins this, and speaks optimistically about 'rejuvenating the local in a global context', pointing to the important role that has been played by micro-businesses, small and medium-sized enterprises (SMEs), and not-for-profit organizations. Andy Bennett has suggested that the experience of popular music can be understood as occurring in a local space, but that this space can be connected to local spaces elsewhere.[45] Some theorists worry about *spaces*, which they see as controllable, and look more optimistically to *places* for evidence of autonomous assertions of identity. Adam Krims advises us not to be over-celebratory in ascribing an antagonism to the space–place relationship, where space 'represents coercive forces of social restraint' (he gives the example of the shopping mall), and place represents the way people 'reaffirm the importance of their specific and unique corners of the world'. He asks how such a distinction can be accepted when 'global forces of spatial reorganization demand that cultural products and practices be saturated with the symbolic content of place'.[46]

Debates about space and place lead us to ask what the characteristics are that define a nation, a region, a social group, or an individual. In early academic work on popular music there was often an unproblematized reference to 'black music' – as, for instance, in Simon Frith's *Sound Effects*.[47] David Hatch and Stephen Millward explained the difficulties in defining exactly who is (or was) black, and Philip Tagg bewailed the essentialism of arguments built on the idea that certain features formed a natural part of black music.[48] Paul Gilroy was originally in favour of retaining such terminology, but modifying it to embrace the black diasporic experience.[49] The difficulty is that arguments about black identity have too often rested on the fiction of race, instead of focusing on the cultural experiences and preferences that develop within social groups in particular locations. Portia Maultsby's essay (Chapter 13) presents findings drawn from in-depth ethnographic research into the way funk in the 1970s and 1980s constructed multiple layers of identity for the diverse black community of Dayton, Ohio. Despite the evidence showing that it is the way cultural features and devices are *used* that constructs identity and builds particular cultural competences, essentialism has not disappeared in journalism.

---

45 Andy Bennett, *Popular Music and Youth Culture: Music, Identity and Place* (Basingstoke, 2000). He provides a very useful account of arguments about space and place in the Introduction to Sheila Whiteley, Andy Bennett and Stan Hawkins (eds), *Space and Place: Popular Music and Cultural Identity* (Aldershot, 2004).

46 Krims, *Music and Urban Geography*, pp. 32 and 39.

47 Simon Frith, *Sound Effects: Youth, Leisure and the Politics of Rock 'n' Roll* (London, 1983).

48 David Hatch and Stephen Millward, *From Blues to Rock: An Analytical History of Pop Music* (Manchester, 1987); Philip Tagg, '"Black Music," "Afro-American Music," and "European Music"', *Popular Music* 8 (1989): 285–98, reprinted in Moore, *Critical Essays*, pp. 5–18.

49 Paul Gilroy, *The Black Atlantic: Modernity and Double Consciousness* (Cambridge, MA and London, 1993). He later attacked arguments based on race in *Against Race: Imagining Political Culture Beyond the Color Line* (Cambridge, MA, 2000).

Essentialist thinking often surfaces in opinions implying that certain cultural skills are biologically determined: 'The Latin American feel flows through their DNA' claimed the reviewer of a CD by young Venezuelan musicians in August 2008.[50] It needs to be stressed constantly that musical preferences are related to cultural and not biological factors. Music should no more be mapped directly on to ethnicity than on to social class, or you end up tying yourself in explanatory knots when encountering a middle-class Asian who enjoys both Bhangra and rap. Anjali Gera Roy, warns, in Chapter 14, about the simplistic view of Bhangra as signifier of South-Asian ethnocultural identity. New diasporic identities come into play here, as they have often done before: in the Al Jolson film *The Jazz Singer* (1927), the father of Jakie Rabinowitz cannot comprehend the Americanized musical taste of his son: '*you* from five generations of Cantors!'

What do we mean when we speak of a community? Is it a localized group, like a parish community? Is it a group of people defined by their ethnicity, class, occupation or sexuality, such as a Chinese community, working-class community, farming community or gay community? Is there an Internet community (as we often hear) or merely a lot of people using the Internet?[51] The word has been stretched almost to breaking-point. So, too, has the term 'hybridity'. Reggae is often seen as an example of hybridity. Rap is made up of stylistic elements associated with musicians from a range of ethnic backgrounds (African-American, Latino and white), so it also offers itself up to the label 'hybrid'. What is the difference between a mixture, or fusion, and a hybrid? In the work of Homi Bhabha and Robert Young, hybridity is used to indicate the political charge that is generated when cultural practices that have been brought together in hybrid form are denied any of the sense of uniqueness or purity they formerly may have been assumed to possess.[52] However, in the writings of many others, hybridity has become almost synonymous with the term it replaced: syncretism (in which disparate cultural elements are reconciled).

Gender, just like ethnicity, has often been interpreted as something natural. This is the implication of older arguments about some forms of rock *expressing* male machismo; but this music and its performance can also be analysed as a configuration of signs that *connote* machismo. Suzi Quatro was already challenging the stereotypical masculinity of rock in the early 1970s, and Riot Grrrl in the 1990s showed how an assertive femininity could be encoded in rock. Theories of sexuality followed a similar trajectory. They began with a focus on the gay eroticism of disco,[53] but were later followed by poststructuralist explorations of sexuality, initially much

---

50   Philip Clark, review of *Fiesta*, DG 477 7457GH, *Gramophone* (August 2008): 64.
51   Andy Bennett raised this issue at an IASPM UK conference in Newcastle-upon-Tyne, July 2002.
52   Homi K. Bhabha, 'Signs Taken for Wonders' in *The Location of Culture* (London, 1994), pp. 102–22; Robert J. C. Young, *Colonial Desire: Hybridity in Theory, Culture and Race* (London, 1995).
53   See Richard Dyer, 'In Defense of Disco' [1979] in Simon Frith and Andrew Goodwin (eds), *On Record: Rock, Pop and the Written Word* (London, 1990), pp. 410–18.

influenced by Foucault.[54] Queer theory began to develop in the 1990s, although it remains an unsettled question how far any one musical style can be queered. Despite k. d. lang's queering of country in the late 1980s, she subsequently moved away from that style to some extent. There is also the problem that if you break too many conventions, a style becomes lost or unrecognizable. To communicate meaning, you need to relate to style codes in some way.

Theorizing about the way the body (the larynx, tongue, teeth and lips) can be registered in the singing voice,took its departure initially from Roland Barthes and his use of Julia Kristeva's distinction between phenotext and genotext (where, to simplify, the former is perceived cognitively and the latter sensed physiologically) to distinguish between phenosong and genosong.[55] The shift to a consideration of performance and performativity has been a significant development from the 1990s onwards. A big influence was, and still is, Judith Butler, who argued in *Gender Trouble* (1990) for a theory of performativity in relation to the production of gender identity, claiming that this identity is produced through 'a stylized repetition of acts', which are performative rather than expressive.[56] Performativity is performance repeated over and over, so that it appears natural; it is not a performance in which you are consciously acting out a role. It is not a matter of 'I am *X*, so I do *Y*', but of 'I do *Y*, so I am *X*'. Sheila Whiteley, who has been engaged with questions of gendered identity for most of her academic career, offers further thoughts in Chapter 10 of this *Companion*, drawing upon Butler's theoretical model of performativity and gender construction. Some confusion was caused by Butler's simplified reference to drag as an example of performing gender. Her argument is much more nuanced than that suggests, although it is remarkable how closely at times she approaches Erving Goffman's ideas on performing the self in everyday life.[57] Philip Auslander, in Chapter 15, makes use of Goffman's frame analysis in exploring role-playing and the physical and gestural dimensions of performance. He considers how the visual dimension of performance affects the audience's musical experience and notes provocatively that 'the real person is the dimension of performance to which the audience has the least access'. In Chapter 18 Jacqueline Warwick speaks of the

---

54   Michel Foucault, *The History of Sexuality. Vol. 1: An Introduction*, trans. Robert Hurley (Harmondsworth, 1990; originally published New York: Pantheon, 1978; originally published in French as *Histoire de la sexualité*, Paris: Gallimard, 1976).

55   Julia Kristeva, *Revolution in Poetic Language*, trans. Margaret Waller (New York, 1984; originally published as *La Révolution du langage poétique*, Paris: Editions du Seuil, 1974); Roland Barthes, 'The Grain of the Voice', in Stephen Heath (ed.), *Image-Music-Text* (London, 1977), pp. 179–89. Geno-song offers another way of describing the problem raised by Wittgenstein concerning expression in music (see later in this Introduction).

56   Judith Butler, *Gender Trouble: Feminism and the Subversion of Identity* (London, 1999; originally published 1990), p. 179.

57   Erving Goffman, *The Presentation of Self in Everyday Life* (London, 1990; originally published University of Edinburgh, Social Sciences Research Centre, Monograph. no. 2, 1956); *Frame Analysis: An Essay on the Organization of Experience* (Boston, revd edn 1986; originally published London: Penguin, 1974).

'different masks of rock authenticity' and examines the anxiety caused when belief in an innate masculinity is threatened by imitations of 'rock authenticity'.

Stan Hawkins (Chapter 17) and Susan Fast (Chapter 8) also ask questions about how we interpret vocality, and what issues of subjectivity and identity are involved. Fast's topic is the gendered and racialized conventions of back-up singing in rock music (and how they relate to the soloist's identity). Hawkins concentrates on the style and function of the pop voice and how we link these two aspects of performance. His investigation proceeds by way of a close analysis of Prince's 'Chelsea Rodgers' (2007), in a sustained attempt to pin down the disco-funk style. Hawkins makes the point that disco 'was never meant to be performed live', which makes one wonder if, perhaps, the authenticity argument regarding liveness is designed to exclude genres like disco. Liveness plays a crucial role in John Richardson's essay (Chapter 4), which takes up the matter of visual authentication. He chooses to focus on KT Tunstall, a 'nu-folk' performer committed to live performance, in order to explore the complexities of the meaning of 'live' in the context of her use of digital looping technology to simulate multitracking (albeit achieved in 'real time' via a looping pedal). He also considers the gender issues raised by her 'mastery' of electronic technology.

The body or, to be more accurate, discourses of the body have acquired much more importance in popular musicology of the twenty-first century, and dance research has continued to grow as well (Sarah Thornton's 1995 study of dance culture was trail-blazing[58]). Music and queerness has become a whole field in itself,[59] but there are still bare patches to cultivate. The relationship between camp and queerness is one. Freya Jarman-Ivens offers, in Chapter 9, one of the first attempts to sketch out a musicology of camp, teasing out particular musical gestures that might invite camp interpretation. Masculinity did not receive as much attention as did femininity at first, but now it certainly does. Jason Lee Oakes's essay (Chapter 11) asks how popular music can help us understand what masculinity means and examines some of the recent ways in which this subject has been theorized.

The study of screen music has overlapped considerably with popular musicology. Roy Prendergast was highlighting the neglect of film music back in the 1970s, and Claudia Gorbman set the ball rolling for film music theory with her semiotic analyses in *Unheard Melodies* (1987), at the same time as Ann Kaplan was producing critical work on music video.[60] The critical tools of the 1980s, resting on the significance of the distinction between underscore and source music (expressed, not entirely without oversimplification, as a contrast between non-diegetic and

---

58   Sarah Thornton, *Club Cultures: Music, Media and Subcultural Capital* (Cambridge, 1995).

59   An enormous influence here was Butler's *Gender Trouble*. An informative book on popular music and queerness is Sheila Whiteley and Jennifer Rycenga (eds), *Queering the Popular Pitch* (London, 2006).

60   Roy M. Prendergast, *Film Music: A Neglected Art* (New York, 2nd edn 1992); Claudia Gorbman, *Unheard Melodies: Narrative Film Music* (Bloomington, IN and London, 1987); E. Ann Kaplan, *Rocking Around the Clock: Music Television, Postmodernism, and Consumer Culture* (London, 1987).

diegetic music) were soon enriched by a host of new terminology from Michel Chion – raising questions such as 'is this music empathetic non-diegetic, or anempathetic non-diegetic?'[61] In Chapter 2 Anahid Kassabian provides an overview of the rise of film music studies, before offering a theoretical and methodological guide to research in the wider field of music, sound and the moving image. In studying music video, a frequent problem has been to decide whether the image or the music dominates. George Martin remarked in a lecture given at the University of Salford in 1998, 'in the 1960s, we listened with our ears; today we listen with our eyes'. Early academic work on video concentrated on the image but, in the 1990s, Andrew Goodwin raised the stakes for music.[62] Carol Vernallis responded to Goodwin's call for more study of the music in music video by analysing Madonna's 'Cherish' and making the case for that video's having created its meanings 'within the flow of the song'.[63] In the twenty-first century consideration needs to be given also to websites such as YouTube.

Television has been largely ignored in popular musicology, despite the fact that during 1954–55 a TV series signature tune, 'The Ballad of Davy Crocket' (Blackburn/ Bruns) became the fastest-selling song in the history of the record industry (more than 20 versions were released).[64] Miguel Mera (Chapter 3) points to the neglect of television music and argues that study in this area 'raises new questions for screen music studies generally'. He shows how the transformations of a current affairs programme's theme tune over a period of nearly 30 years can be related to social, cultural and political changes. He also speaks of the 'democratization of the compositional process as mediated through technology', with reference to the production company Mcasso.

The final matters I want to consider in this Introduction concern taste and aesthetics. There was often a tendency in the 1970s and 1980s to map taste on to social class, and this is something Bourdieu does, too, in *Distinction* (1979). Bourdieu's idea of cultural capital and the *habitus* (the way a person lives, behaves and feels comfortable in particular social situations as a consequence of educational and family background) proved especially influential. It remained a puzzle, however, how a working-class person might break free of the constraints of his or her cultural capital and *habitus*. This raises the subject of human agency – a subject that has been much explored by Anthony Giddens, who defines it as 'the stream of actual or contemplated causal interventions of corporeal beings in the ongoing process of

---

61 It is very common to see 'diegetic' and 'diegesis' written incorrectly as 'diagetic' and 'diagesis'. The terms are taken from the Greek for narration: διήγησις.

62 Andrew Goodwin, *Dancing in the Distraction Factory: Music Television and Popular Culture* (London, 1993; originally published Minneapolis: University of Minnesota Press, 1992).

63 Carol Vernallis, 'The Aesthetics of Music Video: An Analysis of Madonna's "Cherish"', *Popular Music* 17 (1998): 153–85; reprinted in Moore, *Critical Essays*, pp. 443–75, at p. 459.

64 Joseph Murrells, *Million Selling Records from the 1900s to the 1980s: An Illustrated Directory* (London, 1984), p. 89.

events-in-the-world'.[65] More recently, an interest in the idea of social capital (never much expanded upon by Bourdieu) has deepened and prompted research into social networks, relations and contacts. Bourdieu's concept of the 'field' as an area of social and cultural production and practice has also been influential.[66] Different fields exist with different kinds of rules and values, but within each field there are partitions (in the artistic field one genre has a different status from another, for example).

The development of an omnivorous taste in culture, following a general collapse of the hierarchy of high and low art, was first theorized in the work of Richard Peterson and Albert Simkus, who argued that knowing about and consuming a wide range of cultural forms had become a new kind of high status marker in the 1990s.[67] Consequently, the 'univore' was likely to be at the bottom of the taste hierarchy. None of this means that everything is regarded as of equal value; indeed, *how* you consume (for instance, ironically) is as important as *what* you consume.[68] Incidentally, omnivorous taste offers evidence of the crumbling link between youth and pop (although some pop is undoubtedly aimed at, and appeals successfully to, a youth market). Aesthetic judgement has a habit of creeping into arguments as self-evident or correct – even in the work of sociologists. Negus remarks that Lennon's 'Imagine' has 'a rather lazy easy-listening quality'.[69] Bourdieu has claimed that bourgeois aesthetics can be summed up as driven by disgust at the 'facile'.[70] But this inclination to reprimand composers and listeners for laziness is a characteristic of a particular aesthetic disposition – one that believes culture should be hard work – and has a history stretching back to the rise of 'light music' in Vienna in the 1830s. This term was a translation of the German *leichte Musik*, and since 'light' in German means 'easy', it quickly antagonized the serious-minded.[71]

Ludwig Wittgenstein argued that aesthetic questions are conceptual and cannot be answered by empirical methods; what is needed, instead, is comparative study of artworks and an analysis of connections between genres and styles. He believed it was wrongheaded to imagine, for instance, that beauty might exist as an essential property of an artwork. He maintained that, instead of seeking inner essences, we need to investigate the *use* to which critical vocabulary is put. To describe this use,

---

65   Anthony Giddens, *New Rules of Sociological Method: A Positive Critique of Interpretative Sociologies* (Cambridge, 2nd edn 1993; originally published London: Hutchinson, 1976), p. 81.

66   Pierre Bourdieu, *The Field of Cultural Production: Essays on Art and Literature*, ed. Randal Johnson (Cambridge, 1993).

67   Richard Peterson and Albert Simkus, 'How Musical Taste Groups Mark Occupational Status Groups' in Michèle Lamont and Marcel Fournier (eds), *Cultivating Differences: Symbolic Boundaries and the Making of Inequality* (Chicago, 1992), pp. 152–86.

68   See Richard A. Peterson and Roger M. Kern, 'Changing Highbrow Taste: From Snob to Omnivore', *American Sociological Review* 61 (1996): 900–907.

69   Negus, *Popular Music in Theory*, p. 194.

70   Bourdieu, *Distinction*, p. 486.

71   I discuss this topic at various places in my book *Sounds of the Metropolis: The 19th-Century Popular Music Revolution in London, New York, Paris and Vienna* (New York, 2008).

or 'to describe what you mean by a cultured taste', he insists that 'you have to describe a culture' and to be aware that an 'entirely different game is played in different ages'.[72] We might argue, therefore, that authenticity, for example, has a meaning within a particular context, but that there are no essential properties in the adjective 'authentic'. Wittgenstein, in his later work, stressed that words did not merely name properties and that the meaning of words existed in the use to which they were put. In poststructuralist theory words are concepts, too. As Jacques Lacan pointed out, toilet doors might look identical, but will be conceptualized differently depending on whether they are marked male or female (we would not think of the door itself as a property labelled male or female).[73] Yet, if we had no experience of what might lie behind such doors, we could not interpret the signs correctly. Poststructuralists often took a hostile stance towards empiricism, none more so than Jacques Derrida, who, scorning its hypothetical propositions drawn from finite quantities of information 'subjected to the proof of experience' and ever ready for revision, accused it of being 'the matrix of all faults menacing a discourse which continues ... to consider itself scientific'.[74] The work of Sarah Thornton and Sara Cohen, however, shows that empirical work (especially the gathering of quantitative and qualitative data) can lead to valuable insights, and such research also reveals the errors that can be made when cultural formations are studied only as texts, ignoring the need for fieldwork. Antoine Hennion's essay (Chapter 19) asserts the value of empirical methodology in reaching a better understanding of how music 'presents itself' to the listener. It was empirical research, also, that led to the omnivore thesis concerning cultural taste. Ethnomusicologists, of course, find fieldwork absolutely necessary to their research. An area of neglect in the twentieth century was the study of music consumption in the context of everyday social interaction. This has been a concern in the work of both Tia DeNora and Dan Laughey.[75] Another area that Björnberg, Warner and Wicke reveal to be calling out for empirical investigation is that of listener response to different kinds of studio technological processes used on sound recordings.

I return, in my concluding paragraph, to the issue of why a popular musicology is needed, and I will give an example of how a problem of interpretation can occur when the music itself is not taken into account. Keith Negus takes issue with Sheila Whiteley's account of the psychedelic coding of 'Lucy in the Sky with Diamonds' and its hallucinogenic connotations.[76] His counterargument rests on an

---

72 Ludwig Wittgenstein, *Lectures and Conversations on Aesthetics, Psychology, and Religious Belief*, ed. Cyril Barrett (Berkeley, 2007; originally published Oxford: Blackwell, 1966), p. 8.

73 Jacques Lacan, *Ecrits: A Selection* (London, 1977), p. 151.

74 Jacques Derrida, 'Structure, Sign and Play in the Discourse of the Human Sciences' ('La Structure, le signe et le jeu dans le discours des sciences humaines', 1966), in *Writing and Difference*, trans. Alan Bass (London, 1978, originally published as *L'Ecriture et la différence*, Paris: Editions du Seuil, 1967), pp. 351–70, at p. 364.

75 Tia DeNora, *Music in Everyday Life* (Cambridge, 2000); Dan Laughey, *Music and Youth Culture* (Edinburgh, 2006).

76 See Negus, *Popular Music in Theory*, pp. 157–58; and Whiteley, *The Space Between the Notes*

interpretation of the lyrics alone, and this leads him to suggest that the song could easily be associated with Lennon's interest in the word-play of Edward Lear and Lewis Carroll. Yet Whiteley draws her conclusions from an analysis of the way the music works *together with* the lyrics, and she makes a persuasive case about how these words may be understood in the context of particular musical signifiers. Her thoughts on the psychedelic coding of music are drawn from musical analysis of semiotic devices for representing drug-induced trips in other songs of the period. Scholars in cultural and media studies have also thrown down a more general challenge to popular musicologists to define stylistically genres such as ragtime, blues, gospel, rock 'n' roll, or to accept that they all overlap so much with other styles that this is an impossibility. Lawrence Grossberg has claimed, 'rock cannot be defined in musical terms'[77] – a statement implying that there is a degree of futility in characterizing rock musically. He believes it has no really distinctive musical features that cannot be found elsewhere. Yet, as long ago as 1975, Ronald Byrnside made a strong argument for considering rock a new style.[78] Popular musicologists will never be satisfied with discussion of genres or styles that avoid reference to musical detail, and are therefore driven to make a case for the importance and relevance of musical terminology and analysis. Crucial to popular musicology is the desire to understand popular music qua music.[79]

(London, 1992), pp. 43–44. Naphtali Wagner also proposes a psychedelic reading of the music of 'Lucy' and even produces a 'psychedelic Shenkerian graph', in 'Psychedelic Classicism and Classical Psychedelia', in Olivier Julien (ed.), *Sgt. Pepper and the Beatles: It Was Forty Years Ago Today* (Aldershot, 2008), pp. 75–90, at pp. 84–89.

77 Lawrence Grossberg, *We Gotta Get out of This Place* (London, 1992), p. 131.

78 'The Formation of a Musical Style: Early Rock', in Charles Hamm, Bruno Nettl, and Ronald Byrnside (eds), *Contemporary Music and Music Cultures* (Englewood Cliffs, NJ, 1975), pp. 159–92; reprinted in Moore, *Critical Essays*, pp. 217–50 (see, especially, pp. 239–45).

79 Allan F. Moore, *Rock – The Primary Text: Developing a Musicology of Rock* (Aldershot, 2nd edn 2001; originally published Buckingham: Open University Press, 1993) was a determined attempt to put music in the primary position.

PART 1
Film, Video and Multimedia

Trevor Jones's Score for
In the Name of the Father

David Cooper

I've done a handful of films in my time that I feel are particularly significant. These are films that have commented on, and I believe contributed to, changing people's perception or understanding of particular subjects. One such film was *In The Name of the Father*, which, I believe, was screened for the House of Commons and the House of Lords. I feel that this did change the British government's attitude and their policies at that time with regard to the Irish question. Up to that point we were interviewing Sinn Féin people behind frosted glass and using actors' voices. I wanted to score this film because I felt I could contribute, in however a small way, to such an important issue. Other such films include Alan Parker's *Mississippi Burning*, which looked at the question of racial tension in 1960s America, and *Aegis*, the Japanese film which raised the question of the North Korean threat to Japan.[1]

This chapter considers how the various sources, both textual and auditory, can offer insight into the technical processes and musical judgements which go into the creation of a film's score. It also examines how film may use the meanings encoded in music to support the unfolding of the narrative. It is suggested that Jones's approach in his score for the film *In the Name of the Father*, directed by Jim Sheridan, which incorporates songs performed by Bono, Sinéad O'Connor and others, offers an interesting model of an integrated soundtrack employing composite sources in which the composer has moulded and influenced the popular.

Born in Cape Town, South Africa, in 1949, Trevor Jones has an extensive filmography that includes popular mainstream cinema for both Hollywood and independent studios, and work for television. As a postgraduate student at the University of York, his teachers included Wilfrid Mellers (1914–2008) and Elisabeth Lutyens (1906–83), and both of these were influential on his philosophy and approach to film-scoring. Mellers, a man of broad musical tastes that spanned art-

---

1   Trevor Jones, personal e-mail correspondence. The BBC ban on the broadcasting of representatives of organizations that were thought to be supporting terrorism was introduced by the Conservative government in 1988 and withdrawn in 1994 after the announcement of the IRA ceasefire

music, jazz and popular music, had established the York Music Department in 1964, and fashioned there a very liberal curriculum and a pedagogical approach that integrated analysis, performance and composition.[2] As well as being one of Britain's most successful women composers, Lutyens had a successful career writing for film with more than 20 pictures to her name. Her modernist language had found a particular home in the British horror genre, and she was able to communicate with Jones both as a serious art-music composer and someone familiar with the professional practice of film production. In her autobiography, Lutyens would remark of media composition that:

> Both films and radio music must be written not only quickly but with the presumption that it will only be heard once. Its impact must be immediate. One does not grow gradually to love or understand a film score like a string quartet.[3]

While it could be argued that changes in technology since the time of Lutyens' comments have transformed the relationship between film and its audience, and it has become increasingly feasible with media such as video and DVD to develop a fuller understanding of a film score and its relationship to the rest of the film's narrative elements over time, the importance of immediacy of film music's impact remains.

Jones completed his studies at York in 1977, and from 1979 his name began to appear in credits as composer or member of the music department for film releases. John Boorman's *Excalibur* (1981), which also drew on the music of Richard Wagner and Carl Orff, was an early success for the composer and in the subsequent two decades he became established as a figure who was both versatile and technically sophisticated, scoring a large number of mainstream films. His career has spanned the move from analogue to digital technology, and he is a representative of a generation of composers who are also very competent music technologists, at home with both the symphony orchestra and the electronic studio. At the time of writing, Jones has a list of more than 80 films and has worked for directors such as Jim Henson, Andrei Konchalovsky, Alan Parker, Michael Mann and Ridley Scott.

The Trevor Jones Archive of film music recordings was donated by the composer to the School of Music at the University of Leeds in June 2005. The archive consists of around 400 two-inch reels of 24-track analogue audio and associated paperwork including spotting notes, cue sheets and information about multitrack recording, mixing and effects. It embraces the analogue tapes of the scoring sessions from Jones's student work at the National Film School through television and advertising work to major movies such as *The Dark Crystal* (1982), *Runaway Train* (1985), *Labyrinth* (1986), *Angel Heart* (1987), *Mississippi Burning* (1988), *Sea of Love* (1989), *Arachnophobia* (1990), *Freejack* (1992), *Cliffhanger* (1993), *Richard III* (1995),

---

2   As a DPhil student at the University of York between 1978 and 1981, I observed Mellers' humane influence over the final three years of his academic career at York.

3   Elisabeth Lutyens, *A Goldfish Bowl* (London, 1972), p. 171.

and *Brassed Off* (1996).[4] Jones has also supplied more recent material created and stored digitally.

Session recordings and related documentation offer a rich resource that contains important evidence about the development of the film score. The multitrack recordings include both synthesized mock-ups and final mixes and provide data about balance, orchestration and synchronization, as well as the structure of recording sessions and deliberations made during mixing of the score. While the study of multiple recordings of a single cue can help to identify subtleties in the development of the score, and the examination of recordings of a sequence of cues can shed new light on the development and progression of the scoring process, these materials may also enable greater comprehension of a composer's overarching musical scheme for a film. Once recording and mixing are completed, the fate of a film score usually leaves the control of the composer, and decisions taken by the director on the dubbing stage can lead to a composer's carefully crafted musical structures being radically transformed. However, evidence for the putative larger-scale musical organization of a film score can be found in the various session recordings and notated score for a film. Consideration of the composer's apparent intentions and the influence of other members of the production team as documented in paperwork, such as spotting notes and track sheets, can enable scholars to more precisely contextualize the 'final' soundtrack (in as much as it is ever final) in terms of its importance in defining 'the film score'.

Documentation held in the University of Leeds archive varies from film to film, but includes:

- spotting notes
- 'sync pop' placements
- scoring log revisions
- multitrack sheets.

In addition, Jones has given researchers at the University of Leeds access to copies of short and full scores in order to reproduce them photographically. To illustrate the range and content of the archive, some of the materials associated with Jones's score for Geoff Murphy's *Freejack* (1992) are discussed below.

---

4   Around 15 per cent of the collection has currently been digitized in Pro Tools Session format as part of an Arts and Humanities Research Council project.

Freejack Musical Documentation

Music Spotting Notes of 11/10/91 (US Date Format)

Spotting notes derive from the post-production discussions held between the composer and senior figures involved with the production (generally the director). They indicate the position and length of scenes within a reel of film for which music is to be provided, as well as contextual information (for example, a description of the action or the kind of music expected) and are differentiated by a series of cue number codes. The numbering system generally adopted for cues indicates: first, the reel of film; second, the fact that it is a music cue; and, third, the cue number within the reel. Some cues also terminate with the letter 'S' to indicate a 'source' cue – in other words, one involving existing, rather than specially written, music.

The spotting notes for *Freejack* consist of 17 typescript pages numbered from 1 to 18, the fourth page being missing. It appears from the content of the remaining pages that page 4 was probably blank and separated the first three pages (which are titled 'underscore' and contain a list of cue numbers, titles, durations and very brief narrative descriptions) from the final 14 pages which have one or two pages of information per reel and include detailed typed notes about the narrative and the potential musical content. The first and fifth pages have the note 'Roger's copy' in biro, a reference to Jones's synthesizer programmer, Roger King. Pages 5 to 18 comprise very detailed handwritten information relating to cue locations, synthesizer patches, timings and general musical characteristics.

Cue 1M1 (Main Title) from page 5 is indicative of the approach. The descriptive text reads:

> MAIN TITLE. ENIGMATIC "TOOL KIT" CUE STARTS IN BLACK AT TOP OF SHOW AND CONTINUES OVER FADE UP TO EERIE LANDSCAPE AS BIZARRE CONVOY APPEARS ON SMOKE SHROUDED HIGHWAY. MAIN TITLE CARD WILL FOLLOW MUSHROOM SHAPED LAB TRUCK BREAKING THRU FOG. THREAD OF CUE SHOULD CONTINUE ACROSS SCENE IN JULIE'S APARTMENT: A SLOW PAN ACROSS MANTLE LADEN WITH PERSONAL EFFECTS TO REVEAL JULIE AND ALEX IN BED. THIS SCENE IS STILL TO BE CUT, BUT GEOFF [Murphy the director] SAID THAT IT SHOULD BE "EMOTIONALLY BRIGHT". ALARM CLOCK GOES OFF AND MUSIC IS OUT. NOTE: TIMING IS APPROXIMATE.

In the margins of the typewritten notes, a number of handwritten comments have been added in biro:

1:35

8:00 – 01:42:19

Atmos 1   Start Lo

Sting credit (Morgan Creek)

Swirly atmos (atmos 1)

Rhythm ⟵—— on truck lights

Build to main title (over vehicle)

Over cut to bedroom

(Romantic from "How Touching"

Strings and EWI*)

Stops on alarm clock

Bonejacker rhythm – rework (to 5/4 + thin out)

At the end of the notes for each cue, a very brief indication of the underlying expressive or affective content has been provided in a different hand to the notes on the left-hand side of the pages. Examples of these descriptions include: 'enigmatic, intriguing, towards ominous' (1M1), 'tension building suspended after chord' (1M5), 'disorientation – action' (2M2), 'celestial' (3M2), 'exotic' (3M3S), 'poignant – sad' (5M3) and 'melancholy' (6M3S).

'Sync Pop' Placements

These two pages consist of handwritten information faxed from 'Freejack editorial' on 17 and 19 December 1991. They involve a list of cue numbers, film position timings in both feet and frames, SMPTE timecode and a brief description of the visuals for the start-point of each cue. For example, the fifth item in the list sent on 19 December is given as follows:

5M2   248+8   02:45:19   A. [Alex] up stairs

The 'pops', 'pips' or 'beeps' listed on this chart indicate the placement of a brief burst (1/15th second) of 1000Hz tone which is used to synchronize (or lock together) sound and picture during editing.

Scoring Log 12/19 Revision

A two-page scoring log (or session report) is dated 19 December [1991]. This consists of a table of cues running from 1M1 to 12M4. For each cue in the table, the following information is supplied: cue number, title, audio cassette, start footage and timecode position, out footage and timecode position, length, synth/orch, status. For example, the first field appears as follows:

CUE	TITLE	CASSETTE	START FTG/SMPTE	OUT FTG/SMPTE	LENGTH	SYNTH/ORCH	STATUS
1M1	MAINTITLE	12:18	43+15/00:29:09	258+7/02:52:09	2:23	ORCH	A

Multitrack Track Sheets

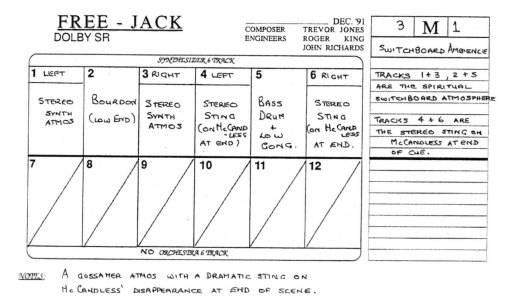

Figure 1.1   Multitrack sheet for cue 3M1

Each cue has an individual track sheet associated with it (see Fig. 1.1 for cue 3M1); these identify the names of the composer (Trevor Jones), the engineers (Roger King and John Richards) and technical/musical information. Many of the multitrack notes provide technical synchronization information (for example, in 1M3 the position of the 'sync pip' is given). However, others present more detailed expressive data, especially those found in relation to cues 3M1 ('Switchboard Ambience'), 3M2 ('Nun with a Gun') and 4M1 ('Brad's Place'). Tracks 1 and 3 of cue 3M1, are noted to contain the 'spiritual switchboard atmosphere', and 4 and 6 a sting occurring on McCandless's disappearance. In the notes, the cue is defined as providing a 'gossamer atmos'. The spotting notes for 3M2 report that the 'cue may be ecclesiastical but should not be mistaken for source organ', and this is reinforced by the multitrack notes which indicate that 'although not meant to sound like an organ source cue we are trying for an ethereal/celestial feel'.

The use by Jones of 'toolkits' of what he describes as atmospheres created on the Synclavier in some of his film work is of particular interest. The composer described the process to Ian Sapiro as follows:

> The idea of 'toolkits' originated at York when, as a student, I tried to compile a series of sounds harmonically and rhythmically which had specific relationships to each other and could be used in varying permutations. I had a 24 track tape [recorder] at the BBC and access to synthesizers so I set off a metronomic beat and built up different sounds on the 24 tracks. These sounds could be played in any permutation and played together as a composite track, constituted a piece. The original piece was very repetitive, very boring. But when I came to score Alan Parker's film Angel Heart, I set about choosing sounds which I responded to in a particular way: for instance a basic heartbeat rhythm with low end frequencies affected me physiologically. There were other sounds that were pertinent to that project – the sounds of New Orleans and the gospel choral sounds of the south gave resonance to the world that Parker evoked in the film. On Mississippi Burning another Alan Parker project, I explored this idea further and built up a 'toolkit' of over 96 tracks. I had a rhythm that went [sings] comprising 12 notes as I recall [demonstrates] and this rhythm was played on different instruments, different combinations of sounds. You could have a very basic [texture] and it would become more and more complex the more tracks you brought up.
>
> Introducing each track (sound) successively built up compound rhythms in addition to building the texture of the piece. Played as individual tracks, or in varying permutations or as a composite track resulted in pieces which had a common tempo and could serve the image in a multitude of ways.[5]

While Jones's explicit use of toolkits began to decline in the later films he scored, their influence is still heard in the complex textures that pervade his scores, and in particular that for *In the Name of the Father*.

The Documentation of the Musical Discourse in the Cue 'Brad's Place'

The most detailed scoring information for *Freejack* relates to the short cue 4M1 ('Brad's Place'). The typed spotting notes for this cue read as follows:

---

5   Interview with Ian Sapiro, 17 October 2007.

> Brad's place. Alex searches building for Brad. He knocks on first door and
> gets no answer. Music eases in as he moves away thru dilapidated hallway.
> Quiet cue should emphasize his loneliness, but in an eerie sort of way. Alex
> tries another door .... no answer .... door opens behind him and ... whap! Big
> sting as Brad grabs him and music tails for dial.

These are supported by technical notes on the musical material and sources
handwritten in biro:

> No rhythm.
>
> Check *Angel Heart* Nightmare Tr. 1 5'50", Bendy voices etc
>
> 0:20:00 – 1:34:22
>
> Disorientation – tension to sting* on Brad's arm. Bourdon (v. light –
>
> gossamer). Bendy Voices from hell. Synclav Sting 1 + rototom PB
>
> effect: *Missa Creola* drum sample. V slow, languid.
>
> 1:11:12 start moving bass line (on door knock).
>
> *Angel* Bass Drums Boom Bah [bomba?]
>
>   ↓
>
> Con BD + Verdi BD
>
> *1:28:25 then fade to end.

In the multitrack notes for the cue, the column on the right-hand side contains
the remarks that:

> Tracks 1&3 are sinister atmos sounds in stereo. Track 2 is low end. Tracks
> 4&6 are the build up to the door opening and Brad's arm around Alex's neck.
> Track 5 is 'glass' melody.

The additional notes at the bottom of the page reinforce this by offering a more
sophisticated reading of the musical and affective content of the cue:

> This cue should seep in. We are aiming for a gossamer sinister atmosphere.
> The sounds on tracks 1, 2, 3 & 5 should hang like a mist until the door
> opens, and tracks 4 & 6 should grow until the sting hits. Depending on how
> much we need to shock the audience the level of the sting may be adjusted
> accordingly.

The final document in this chain of documentary materials relating to the recording is the score itself. A bound volume provided by Jones contains conductor (short) scores and full scores for all of the cues used in the film. A surprising amount of contextual detail is handwritten at the beginning of each cue as well as the expected technical data (video start and stop times, metronome rate, 'clicks in' and so on). In the case of 4M1, the following information is provided for this synthesizer-based cue:

> *Bourdon + light atmos, bendy voices, shards [?], saber (Hooverville atmos) + Missa Creole drum sample. Tension to sting on Brad's arm (PLI1) + rototom. Disorient#ation, loneliness. Move bass at 04:01:11:00. Sting 01:28:25 then fade. Eerie. 1' 14".*

In the Name of the Father

The rest of this chapter considers in more detail the film *In the Name of the Father*, directed by Jim Sheridan and first released in Ireland in December 1993, and examines how the working tapes and session recordings, score and data such as tracksheets, can support its analysis. *In the Name of the Father* is an account of Gerry Conlon (one of the so-called Guildford Four) and his father Patrick 'Giuseppe' Conlon, who were mistakenly arrested and imprisoned through an infamous miscarriage of justice by the British legal system. In Gerry Conlon's case, this was for his supposed involvement (along with Paul Hill, Patrick Armstrong and Carole Richardson) in the Provisional IRA's bombing of the Horse and Groom pub in Guildford in September 1974; his father and members of the Maguire family (and a family friend) were convicted of explosives offences. The convictions of the Guildford Four were overturned in 1989 and those of the Maguire Seven in 1991, although Giuseppe Conlon had died in 1980 while still in prison. Although marketed as a 'true story', a degree of artistic licence was employed, and some key facts were either ignored or glossed over. Despite this, it was a critical success and was shortlisted for seven Academy Awards in 1994.

There are six reels of tape with documentation related to *In the Name of the* Father in the Trevor Jones Archive, and these are labelled 1/7 to 7/7; tape 6 is apparently missing from the set, although it is not clear what was on it, given that tapes 5 and 7 seem to form a complete pair of music mix tapes (by and large, the final mixes that appear on the film). Tapes 3 and 4 are working tapes, tape 2 contains the remixes and the final credits alluded to by Jones and tape 1 has the album mix constructions. All of the cues recorded on the two-inch analogue tapes and the various dates on documentation are itemized in Table 1.1. The working tapes appear to have been recorded in the final few days of October 1993 and the main recordings mixed between the 9 and 17 November 1993. The album mix and the remixed cues including the end titles ('You Made Me the Thief of Your Heart') were recorded between 19 and 20 November 1993.

Table 1.1   Contents of the six tapes held in the Trevor Jones Archive of the University of Leeds

Tape	Date (side of Box)	Date (back of box)	Date (track sheets)	Contents
1/7	22/11/93	20/11/93	20/11/93	Album mix constructions. Three cues: 'Interrogation'. 'Walking the Circle', 'Passage of Time'
2/7 Music Cues	21/11/93	19/11/93	19/11/93	Music Cues Mixes: 9M1/3 sweetener; 1M1; 14M1 End Credits; 14M1 End Extended; 14M1 End Credits *
3/7 W1	None	27/10/93	No track sheets	Working Tape 1: 2M1 Ferry Farewell; 3M5 Gerry's Arrest; 4M1 Bomb Photo; 4M3 Interrogation; 5M1 'I'm Gonna Shoot Your Da'; 5M2 Da in Remand Prison; 5M3 Embrace in Remand Cell; 6M1 Motorcade; 7M1 '30 Years'; 7M2 Prison Arrival;
4/7 W2	None	29/10/93	No track sheets	Working Tape 2: 7M3 3 Minutes; 8M3 Promise Me; 8M4 Headbutt; 9M1/3 Confrontation; 10M1 Snow; 10M2 Film Show: 10M5 Torching; 10M6 Gerry Joins Campaign; 11M1 Hold My Hand; 11M2 Guiseppe [sic] Collapses; 13M1 Gerard; 13M2 Passage of Time; 14M1 Dismissed
5/7 Music cues	21/11/93	15/11/93	14–17/11/93	Music Cues Mixes Reel 2: 7M2; 8M3; 8M4; 9M1/3; 9M1; 9M1/3 for editing; 10M1; 10M2; 10M5; 10M6; 11M1; 11M2; 12M1; 13M1; 13M2
7/7	9/11/93	9/11/93	9–12/11/93 & 14–15/11/93	Music Cues Mixes Reel 1: 2M1; 3M5; 4M1; 4M3; 5M1; 5M2; 5M3 alt version; 5M3; 5M3; 6M1; 7M1; 2M1 remix.

The film elides conventional and compilation score by combining Jones's electronic and acoustic music, with the diegetic and non-diegetic use of popular songs; Table 1.2 lists both the popular music sources and cues specially composed for the film in sequence including several cues which were not eventually used. His original score for *In the Name of the Father* holds a very significant and prominent place in the film's narrative: it is often dark and disturbing, apparently including the musical language of Krzysztof Penderecki as one of its points of reference, a page of his composition *Threnody for the Victims of Hiroshima* being included in the full score along with four additional pages of aleatoric string notations. While the electronic writing perhaps suggests the Nono of *Ricorda cosa ti hanno fatto in Auschwitz*, the score also involves some very simple diatonic writing including a modal melody associated with the relationship between Gerry and his father which is first heard in cue 5M3 ('Gerry & Father Embrace') and gradually moves to the foreground from cue 10M1 ('Snow').

As well as transmitting the specific messages encoded within lyrics, musical structure and processes, and through its genre and instrumentation, popular music lets those with the relevant knowledge and experience (or to adopt Gino Stefani's term, competence[6]) to locate the film's narrative within relevant cultural times and spaces. As an example, satire is consciously inscribed on The Kinks' 1966 single 'Dedicated Follower of Fashion', the first two verses of which are heard non-diegetically as Gerry arrives back in Belfast on the proceeds of his break-in of the London prostitute's flat, dressed hippy-style in Afghan coat and John Lennon glasses to the amusement of troops and local children who mockingly bleat at him. In the context of the narrative, the upbeat mood and musical characteristics of the song – a vamping accompaniment, community sing-along quality and parodic upper-crust English accent – provide a moment of light relief that, by contrast, makes the emotional impact of his arrest soon after even more powerful. The allusions to the cultural geography of London and, in particular, Carnaby Street, offer a further semantic twist which is reinforced by the song lyrics' allusions to the foppish, but heroic, Scarlet Pimpernel ('They seek him here / they seek him there'); the famous references to the 'Carnabetian army' which appear later in the song, but not played in the film, neatly support Sheridan's reading (and Day-Lewis's performance) of Conlon as vain, foolish and easily led astray, but not an active Republican terrorist. When he sings the first line of the chorus of Gary Glitter's 'I'm the Leader of the Gang' to his sisters as he enters the family house in the Falls Road area of Belfast, this is a direct reference to a contemporary song (released in 1973) as well as taking on ironic significance given that 'his gang' will be deemed to be the Provisional IRA by the RUC.

---

6   Gino Stefani, 'A Theory of Musical Competence' [1987] in Allan F. Moore, *Critical Essays in Popular Musicology* (Aldershot, 2007), pp. 19–34.

Table 1.2   Musical cues by Trevor Jones listed in the score and source popular music used in the film *In the Name of the Father*.

Cue	Title	Duration of Jones's cues on source recordings	Orchestration of Jones's cues (from score)
1m1	'In the Name of the Father'; Bono; non-diegetic. On tapes but not score.		
Source	'Voodoo Child (slight return)'; Jimi Hendrix Experience; non-diegetic		
Source	'Like a Rolling Stone'; Bob Dylan; diegetic		
2M1	FERRY FAREWELL Not used in film	1'26"	Synthesized
Source	'Tiger Feet'; Mud; non-diegetic		
Source	'Billy Boola'; Bono, Gavin Friday; non-diegetic		
Source	'Dedicated Follower of Fashion'; The Kinks; non-diegetic		
Source	'Leader of the Gang'; Gary Glitter; diegetic (brief snatch sung by Gerry)		
3M5	GERRY'S ARREST	1'03"	3 alto flutes, 4 horns, 8 celli, 6 c'bass, synths, [wailing guitar]
4M1	BOMB PHOTOS	33"	3 alto flutes, 4 horns, 8 celli, 6 c'bass, congas, synths
Source	'Happy Birthday'; sung by police; diegetic		
4M3	GERRY'S INTERROGATION	4'36"	3 alto flutes, strings, synth
5M1	'I'm Gonna Shoot Your Da'	1'59"	4 horns, EWI, harp, strings, synth
5M2	DA IN PRISON	42"	Harp, strings, synth

Cue	Title	Duration of Jones's cues on source recordings	Orchestration of Jones's cues (from score)
5M3	GERRY & FATHER EMBRACE	38"	2 alto flutes, 3 horns, baritone sax, EWI, strings, piano, synth
6M1	MOTORCADE	1'09"	3 alto flutes, 4 horns, strings, synth, drums, [guitar]
7M1	30 YEARS	1'55"	Strings
7M2	PRISON ARRIVAL	43"	Contrabass clarinet in Bb, strings (12–10–8–8–6), EWI
Source	'Is this Love?'; Bob Marley; diegetic		
7M3	3 MINUTES Not used in film	3'10"	Bass clarinet, bassoon, baritone sax, 3 horns, harp, strings, synth
8M3	'Promise Me' (reference to 'You Made Me the Thief of Your Heart' not in score)	42"	Contrabass clarinet in Bb, strings, EWI
8M4	HEAD BUTT	44"	Cellos, basses, synth, [guitar]
9Ml /3	CONFRONTATION	2'31"	3 alto flutes, strings, synth, [guitar]
Source	'In the Name of the Blues'; Pete Cummins and John Fitzgibbons;		
10M1	SNOW	2'40"	Baritone sax, strings, harp, piano, EWI
10M2	FILM SHOW	1'08"	1 alto flute, 1 bass flute, 1 bass clarinet, 2 horns, strings, guitar
Source	'The Godfather'; Nino Rota		
10M5	TORCHING	2'35"	Contrabass clarinet in Bb, contrabassoon (optional), 4 horns (can be done with 2), baritone sax (optional), strings, synth, guitar

Cue	Title	Duration of Jones's cues on source recordings	Orchestration of Jones's cues (from score)
10M6	GERRY JOINS CAMPAIGN	1'57"	Baritone sax, strings, piano harp, synth
11M1	HOLD MY HAND Not used in film	57"	Strings, piano, synth
11M2	GUISEPPE [sic] COLLAPSES; No score; based on 'You Made Me the Thief of Your Heart'	55"	Strings (plus overdubbed violins and violas)
12M1	GUISEPPE'S [sic] DEAD 'In the name of the Father'	1'27"	No score
13M1	GERARD Not used in film	36"	Contrabass clarinet, 4 horns, strings (0–0–8–8–6)
	'Whiskey in the Jar'; Thin Lizzy; diegetic		
13M2	PASSAGE OF TIME	2'19"	3 alto flutes, contrabass clarinet, 4 horns, harp, strings, piano
14M1	DISMISSED	1'35"	Baritone sax, strings, piano, pipes
14M2	END CREDITS; 'You Made Me the Thief of Your Heart'; Sinéad O'Connor.	c4'00"	No score

Of the popular music cues specially written for the film, the two numbers that frame the narrative by accompanying its introduction and conclusion are perhaps the most significant and demand further discussion. 'In the Name of the Father' (Cue 1M1), composed by Irish musicians Paul David Hewson (Bono), Martin Fionan Hanvey (Gavin Friday) and Maurice Roycroft (Maurice Seezer), and performed by Bono and Gavin Friday, appears at the beginning of the film. While this has subsequently developed an autonomous musical identity outside the film, it is largely obedient to standard film compositional practices both in its establishment of mood and employment of signifying elements. It is organized in a kind of loose arch structure with introductory drums, a freely sung melody against a regular martial rhythm, a spoken text with dissonant interjections of a tritone in guitar, and an abbreviated reprise of the vocal melody and concluding drumbeat on fade-out.

Insistent and martial percussive rhythms (both the Lambeg drum and bodhrán, drums that represent the two traditions of Ireland) at the start of the song will become a key element of Jones's non-diegetic score. A vocal line with Mixolydian inflection that emerges and speaks of love (which we will later discover is Giuseppe's parental agapē) is almost like plainsong; it sits in a very different rhythmic, and, symbolically speaking, moral space to that of the drums – metrically free and floating above them. The hammered-out riff based on the pitches of an F♯ Dorian/Aeolian tetrachord (F♯–G♯–A–B) with lower subtonic (E) in a biting, largely dactylic, rhythm (F♯ A–G♯ B A–G♯ | A G♯–F♯ G♯–F♯ E) is first heard synchronized with the explosion in the Horse and Groom pub, and this gesture draws on an underlying double-tonic scheme that can be seen as a classic marker of both Ireland and Scotland (recalling, for example, the double-tonic of 'Brian Boru's March'). Its musical characteristics (reiterative rhythm, narrow pitch content) can be read as implying relentlessness, and, by association with the other musical characteristics, suggests intransigence. The religious insinuation of the film's title is reinforced by the invocatory quality of the performance and the spoken lines, at once incantation and poetic recitation: 'In the name of reason / In the name of hope / In the name of religion / In the name of dope'.

Of course, Bono is himself also part of the signifying system of the music and the film. Many viewers of the film will be aware of the band U2 and of their very successful protest song 'Sunday Bloody Sunday' from the album *War* released in February 1983, which looks back to the events of 'Bloody Sunday', 30 January 1972, when 13 people were shot dead by British troops in Derry. Equally, Bono's own 'mixed' religious affiliation – his mother was Protestant and his father Catholic, and he was brought up attending the Church of Ireland – places him in a rather special place in Irish society, both South and North.

There is only one further direct reference to the material from the song 'In the Name of the Father' in the rest of the score. This is in cue 9M1/3 'Confrontation', which is heard in the scene of the prison sit-in. Whereas in Jones's written score there is a reference to a semi-improvised lead guitar solo at the point where the riot squad enter to break up the protest, and this appears in the mock-ups on reel 4, in the session recordings the riff with its original bass line is heard at this juncture.

The final pair of cues cue of the score, 14M1 'Dismissed' and 14M2 'End Credits', begin at the point that the judge strikes down his gavel to dismiss the case, and they subsume the second song written by Bono, Friday and Seezer. The version on the second working tape (4/7) is fundamentally a mock-up of the cue as it appears in the score. Written in Bb minor and in 4/4, the score has three main elements: an ostinato based on the alternation of a thirdless B♭ and B♭⁷ sus 4 chords in the piano; a reiterated bodhrán rhythm that spans six beats (♫♫♫ ♫♫ ♫♫ ♫♫ | ♫♫♫ ♫♫♫) and the melody of 'You Made me the Thief of Your Heart' played on the uilleann pipe chanter (without drones or regulators).[7] One further element that is recorded on the working tapes, but does not appear at all in the score, is a repeated one-bar Dorian/ Aeolian figure played by violins in the style of a traditional Irish fiddle (Ex. 1).

---

7   According to the short score produced from the sequencer, the pipes were recorded on a D set, with the tape speed being set sufficiently fast to cause the guide track to play back a semitone higher than written. Subsequent replay of the tape at normal speed transposed the pitch down a semitone so that the melody appeared in B♭ minor.

Example 1.1   'Traditional' fiddle rhythm from cue 14M1 on working tape 4/7

The elements found in the mock-up are all present in the various versions of the final mixed cue, but the new and defining element is undoubtedly Sinéad O'Connor's voice, a remarkably impassioned performance, the intensity of which is clearly revealed by the unprocessed recording which forms track 5 of cue 14M1 'End Credits' on Tape 2. The pipe melody, piano and fiddle ostinati are still important parts of the fabric of the cue, but this is a more sophisticated arrangement than that found on the working tapes, and the Irish markers are even more prominent, the cue finishing with a traditional fiddler playing an energetic (and authentic-sounding) reel double-tracked across left and right speakers.

Although the underlying melody is found in the working tape for this cue it does not feature in the rest of the score or in any of the other cues in the working tapes. Rather, a simple diatonic melody whose basic configuration is E_4 | D_5 C_5 E_5 E_4 | G_4 is one of the key signifying elements – a musical figure that denotes Giuseppe's paternal love for Gerry (hereafter called the 'Guiseppe' motif). In arranging the music mixes, Jones took the opportunity to rework a number of earlier cues by introducing a melodic element from 'You Made me the Thief of Your Heart' (arguably a musical token for Gerry) and changing the role of the 'Giuseppe' motif in the process. Table 1.3 indicates the progress of the two motifs from score to final mixdown. In two cases, the cues which were scored and mocked up were not used in the film, and a third, 'Hold My Hand', was mixed but not dubbed. Given that the two ideas have melodic and harmonic configurations that permit them to readily substitute for each other, or even to be played in counterpoint (as in cue 8M3), this provided several advantages to the composer:

1. It allowed him to integrate more closely into the score the musical characteristics of the concluding song and generate a greater overall sense of coherence and consistency to the score.
2. It provided a means of both differentiating and connecting musically the two main characters of the film.
3. It offered a greater semantic potential, though the additional musical token.

Despite its composite sources, and considerable stylistic diversity, from avant-garde techniques to Gary Glitter, and Mud to Thin Lizzy, the music track for *In the Name of the Father* does sound remarkably well integrated. It is Jones's particular skill that he is able to compose music that is both unobtrusive (in that it rarely draws unnecessary attention to itself), highly integrated and effective in supporting the narrative while dovetailing with popular source cues. Access to primary materials, such as the sequencer short score, orchestral score, working tapes, session recordings and mix documentation, allows the scholar to comprehend more clearly the ways in which

Table 1.3 Use of the 'Giuseppe' and 'Thief of Your Heart' cues

Cue	Score	Working tapes	Mix tapes
2M1 'Ferry Farewell'	Not present	'Giuseppe' motif in guitar solo as father walks away	Cue not used in film
5M3 'Gerry and Father Embrace'	'Giuseppe' motif in EWI bars 5–11, C minor	As score	'Thief of Your Heart' motif, C minor
7M3 'Three Minutes'	'Giuseppe' motif in EWI from bar 17 *passim*, A minor	As score	Cue not used in film
8M3 'Promise me'	'Giuseppe' motif in EWI from bar 2, A minor	As score	'Giuseppe' and 'Thief of Your Heart' motifs played in counterpoint
10M1 'Snow'	'Giuseppe' in EWI from bar 8, A minor	As score	As score
10M6 'Gerry Joins Campaign'	'Giuseppe' in EWI from bar 8, A minor.	As score	Bars 9–16 'Thief of Your Heart', 'Giuseppe' on repeat (25–32)
11M1 'Hold My Hand'	'Giuseppe' in EWI from bar 2, EWI, A minor	As score	'Thief of Your Heart' from bar 2. Cue not used in film.
12M1 'Giuseppe's Dead'	No score	No mock-up	'Thief of Your Heart' motif against atmos tracks until near the end. Finishes with O'Connor singing 'Are You Lost?'

a composer such as Jones elaborates and develops his musical ideas in response to the film's narrative. It also demonstrates that the various musical materials form part of a process, that the written 'score' is but one stage within it, and that very many creative decisions take place during the final recording and mixdown of a film's soundtrack.

Music, Sound and the Moving Image: The Present and a Future?[1]

Anahid Kassabian

Music, sound and the moving image is without a doubt safely ensconced as both a field in musicology and as an interdisciplinary area in its own right. While there are many different ways to approach writing its history (tracing its roots in theatre and opera, studying early practices and their relationship to classical Hollywood scoring, a comparative study of how scoring traditions began and solidified internationally and so on), and while film music has been written and thought about since the earliest days of film, I would argue that the field as we know it actually begins to take shape with the publication of Claudia Gorbman's *Unheard Melodies* in 1987.[2] Following *Unheard Melodies* was a series of books throughout the 1990s, all of which came from film scholars.[3] As musicologists' interest in these works grew, and as musicology began to imagine including the study of film music, some scholars began to express their dissatisfaction with what they perceived as the musical imprecision, insensitivity or even incorrectness of these works. As a corrective to the – then and now – all-too-silent mainstream of film studies, these books were most welcome, but, it was whispered, they weren't always so good *musically*.

Of course, this may well be true. As someone who has studied piano, score-reading, harmony and composition, but has not a single degree in music, I am surely less attuned to musical detail than someone who has spent years as an analyst/theorist. (It is, however, also tempting to blame disagreements, which are not uncommon among analysts anyway, on inadequate education. One has only to attend a few conferences to hear the accusation.) But as more work came from

1   Some portions of this essay originally appeared in David Cooper, Christopher Fox and Ian Sapiro (eds), *CineMusic? Constructing the Film Score* (Newcastle, 2008).
2   Claudia Gorbman, *Unheard Melodies: Narrative Film Music* (Bloomington, IN, 1987).
3   Ibid.; Caryl Flinn, *Strains of Utopia: Gender, Nostalgia, and Hollywood Film Music* (Princeton, NJ, 1992); Kathryn Kalinak, *Settling the Score: Music and the Classical Hollywood Film* (Madison, WI, 1992); Royal S. Brown, *Overtones and Undertones: Reading Film Music* (Berkeley, CA, 1994); Jeff Smith, *The Sounds of Commerce: Marketing Popular Film Music* (New York, 1998).

scholars of music, it became clear that much of their work (although, of course, not all) has had a similar flaw. While deeply attentive to the music, the scholarship produced from within musicology – film scholars have said – has looked suspiciously like an analysis of a score and very little like a study of an audiovisual text.

I think both critiques, while perhaps a bit harsh, are not untrue.

We find ourselves, as a field, at an important juncture. On the one hand, film studies persist in a systemic lack of interest in sound and music, although the recent 'In Focus' section of *Cinema Journal*,[4] edited by Michele Hilmes, may be a welcome sign of a thaw. On the other hand, music, which as a discipline has welcomed film music studies in the past ten years (a mere century after the birth of film), has failed to integrate any serious study of the visual and narrative elements of film.

It is clear that all film music scholars should be serious students of both music *and* film. But we do not yet have ways of institutionalizing such study, and while taught MA programmes might well be a particularly good approach in both the UK and the US contexts (I don't know enough about others to comment), the few that have been on offer have not succeeded as one might have hoped. Nonetheless, my first point to any serious musicology student of film music is: study film. And vice versa. Audit classes, read introductory textbooks as well as serious scholarship, play – in every way possible – a serious game of catch-up in the other discipline. The following will not stand in for a solid grounding in both disciplines; however inconvenient that may seem, it is nonetheless absolutely clear to me that a reasonable command of both disciplines is a prerequisite to serious scholarship in this field.

It is possible, however, to describe certain basic or primary approaches. The first is to write a cue sheet, in as much detail as possible. A cue sheet is a spreadsheet with the following column headings (see Fig. 2.1).

Not everyone uses identical categories, but the fundamental idea is widely accepted in the field:

- *Time*: as specifically as possible, note the beginning and end of the cue
- *Music*: describe the cue, both aurally and affectively
- *Shot/Editing*: describe the visual components and how they match to musical events
- *Sound*: describe the other aural components, how they match to musical events, and how the soundtrack is mixed
- *Story*: note the place of the scene or sequence in the overall narrative of the film
- *Other Details*: note any relevant extrafilmic facts, such as the history of the song, or aspects of the actor's or musician's star-text that are relevant to understanding the scene
- *Significance*: connect the musical and other details to your reading of the film, or to other scenes you've already noted
- *Notes*: this is a space for anything else not covered by the above – while you may not have things to say here very often, it is useful in case you want

---

4   Michele Hilmes (ed.), 'In Focus', *Cinema Journal*, 48/1 (2008).

to remember a bit of technology or some other tidbit that doesn't belong elsewhere in the cue sheet.

SOURCE MUSIC	SCORE (by Jerry Goldsmith)		START TIME	END TIME	DIEGETIC / NON-DIEGETIC	NOTES
I "AC-CENT-TCHU-ATE THE POSITIVE"			00:00:13	00:02:40	ND	Complete under opening montage and v/o
II "OH, LOOK AT ME NOW"			00:04:40	00:06:10	AD	Playing in background at party
III "SILVER BELLS"			00:06:10	00:06:41	PD	Sung by Captain Smith
IV "SILENT NIGHT"			00:06:45	00:07:23	PD	Sung by drunken police
V "MELE KALIKIMAKA"			00:08:19	00:09:22	AD	On radio in liquor store
VI "THE CHRISTMAS BLUES"			00:11:32	00:11:45	AD	On radio/record player in apartment
(continues)			00:12:05	00:12:35	AD	On radio/record player in apartment
VII "JINGLE BELLS"			00:13:39	00:14:05	AD	Playing at police party (JG's arrangement?)
	Q1	Bloody Christmas	00:14:04	00:15:01	ND	. . . crossfades with previous cue
	Q2	(part 2)	00:15:08	00:15:40	ND	Violence motifs, abrupt end on photoflash
	Q3	Scene bridge	00:16:36	00:16:45	ND	V.short thematic pre-echo
VIII "LOOK FOR THE SILVER LINING"			00:21:44	00:23:30	AD	Background - playing in bar
IX "HIT THE ROAD TO DREAMLAND"			00:23:48	00:25:32	D to ND	Complete under narrative montage, begins on car radio. Lyrics provide ironic commentary: "Bye.Bye.Baby"
	Q4	Stensland's Last Day	00:27:32	00:28:10	ND	First appearance of trumpet theme
	Q5	Nite Owl Massacre	00:30:05	00:31:15	ND	First prominent appearance of the score, with suppression of dialogue and ambience
	Q6	Dramatic Motion 1	00:32:15	00:33:00	ND	Trumpet and piano 10ths in bass
	Q7	Dramatic Motion 2	00:35:48	00:36:31	ND	First appearance of 7/8 pattern - most 'complete' cue so far
	Q8	Q4 developed	00:45:42	00:46:26	ND	
	Q9	Arrest of the suspects	00:47:08	00:47:40	ND	Drums mirror movement and conflict
	Q10	'Whos' the Girl'	00:52:35	00:54:24	ND	Rewrite of Bloody Christmas - Bud White's 'impulsive violence' motif
	Q11	Q7 developed	00:58:04	00:58:58	ND	Fastest and most musically rounded cue to date
	Q12		00:59:18	00:59:46	ND	More percussive violence
X "WHEEL OF FORTUNE"			01:00:00	01:03:10	ND	Complete under montage showing development of each principal character
	Q13	Romantic theme	01:03:58	01:05:02	ND	First lyrical version of trumpet theme, VERY reminiscent of similar cue in Polanski's 'Chinatown' (also by JG). Was this on the 'temp track'?
XI "MAKING WHOOPEE"			01:06:00	01:08:30	PD	Gerry Mulligan 4tet at party!
XII "LADY IS A TRAMP"			01:08:31	01:09:36	PD	More Gerry Mulligan 4tet
XIII "POWDER YOUR FACE WITH SUNSHINE"			01:09:58	01:10:35	AD	Playing in bar
XIV "HOW IMPORTANT CAN IT BE"			01:10:54	01:11:32	AD	On radio/record player in apartment
	Q14	Inez' confession	01:11:50	01:11:32	ND	Slowed down trumpet theme
	Q15	Bud's story	01:13:47	01:14:15	ND	Very minimal and quiet cue supporting Bud's life story
	Q16	Scene bridge	01:16:26	01:16:54	ND	'Development' cue with trumpet matches the unfolding of clues
	Q17a	Rat' investigation	01:17:56	01:18:54	ND	Unsettling noises (late-20C 'modernist' language)
	Q17b	(part 2)	01:18:57	01:19:29	ND	Shock beginning, very low trumpets
	Q18	Slow unfolding	01:19:48	01:20:08	ND	Slow variation of the trumpet and piano bass ideas
	Q19	Slow unfolding 2	01:20:21	01:21:07	ND	Similar plus cluster chords & change of key
	Q20	Faster unfolding	01:22:55	01:23:43	ND	Similar but increasing pace and activity
XV "AT LAST"			01:23:45	01:25:25	AD	Playing in bar
	Q21		01:25:25	01:26:35	ND	Similar to Q14
XVI "LOOKING AT YOU"			01:27:03	01:27:52	AD	Playing in bar (quite loud!)
	Q22	Dramatic Gear-change	01:29:32	01:30:14	ND	Uses dramatic key change
XVII "BUT NOT FOR YOU"			01:30:14	01:32:43	AD	On record player in Lynn's apartment
	Q23	Rollo Tomasi sound	01:34:57	01:35:27	ND?	Strange synth sound - cued by Tomasi's name
	Q24	Rollo Tomasi repeat	01:36:19	01:36:48	ND?	ditto
	Q25		01:37:59	01:38:27	ND	Piano bass in tenths
	Q26	Exley framed	01:39:49	01:41:09	ND	Bud's violent impulse motif, gives way to strong lyrical extension of trumpet melody on horns
	Q27	Punch-up	01:43:12	01:44:22	ND	Bud's violence music
	Q28	Punch-up Part 2	01:44:30	01:44:41	ND	Ends on window smash
	Q29	Scene bridge	01:46:44	01:47:24	ND	Cut together of two cues
	Q30	Good Cop, Bad Cop	01:48:47	01:49:48	ND	More percussive violence, cries for help on horns
	Q31	Pas de Deux	01:50:04	01:50:37	ND	Mickey-mousing on stealthy entry to Patchett's house
	Q32	Urgent narrative bridge	01:51:10	01:52:58	ND	Long cue connects three scenes
	Q33	1st dénouement cue	01:53:30	01:55:56	ND	Complete 7/8 theme / Rollo Tomasi recall / dramatic set-up for shoot out - ends on first shot
	Q34	2nd dénouement cue	01:56:37	01:57:00	ND	Drum violence
	Q35	3rd dénouement cue	01:57:09	01:58:32	ND	Low drone anticipating more drum violence
	Q36	Final confrontation	01:59:12	02:01:20	ND	Rollo Tomasi sound / ends unobtrusively on shooting
	Q37	Valediction/Summation/Happy Ending	02:05:18	02:07:39	ND	Long piece, bringing together musically complete versions of all the principal themes

FEATURED SONGS

	Artist
"AC-CENT-TCHU-ATE THE POSITIVE"	Johnny Mercer
"OH, LOOK AT ME NOW"	Lee Wiley
"SILVER BELLS"	(performed by cast)
"SILENT NIGHT"	(performed by cast)
"MELE KALIKIMAKA"	Bing Crosby
"THE CHRISTMAS BLUES"	Dean Martin
"JINGLE BELLS"	unknown
"LOOK FOR THE SILVER LINING"	Chet Baker
"HIT THE ROAD TO DREAMLAND"	Betty Hutton
"WHEEL OF FORTUNE"	Kay Starr
"MAKING WHOOPEE"	Gerry Mulligan Quartet
"LADY IS A TRAMP"	Gerry Mulligan Quartet
"POWDER YOUR FACE WITH SUNSHINE"	Dean Martin
"HOW IMPORTANT CAN IT BE"	Joni Jones
"AT LAST"	Chet Baker
"LOOKING AT YOU"	Lee Wiley
"BUT NOT FOR YOU"	Jackie Gleason

Figure 2.1   L.A. Confidential complete music cues

I would go so far as to say that all good analyses are made possible by a well-prepared cue sheet. A cue sheet, however, is not only an important tool in its own right, but the starting-point for a number of methodologies. In a very broad stroke, scholarship on film music takes off from one of three perspectives – the composer's, the text's or the audience's. The first works, from Kurt London[5] and Leonid Sabaneev[6] through Adorno and Eisler,[7] were addressed to composers. What I mean here, though, is work like Miguel Mera's film-score guide to *The Ice Storm*,[8] which analyses the score from a compositional perspective. In terms of textual approaches, most of the major works by film scholars on music (for example, Gorbman, Kalinak, Flinn), especially in the 1980s, are grounded in film studies' main approaches which had their roots in literary studies. None of these perspectives is simple, and all approaches have strengths and weaknesses. It is not my intention to represent them here, but rather to point towards them, and to note that most scholarship in all three areas will begin with a cue sheet, even if the score is available. A cue sheet opens itself, in other words, to multiple methodologies.

My own approach has been to try to theorize listening, or to work from the position of the 'perceiver'. This is because my interest in film music, and in the study of culture more generally, has some roots in sociological or political concerns. That is to say, alongside a lifelong love of both music and film, I also think we must understand how we come to think, feel and respond the way we do to images, sounds and stories, because I think that has a direct and mutually causal relationship with how we see ourselves and what we think, feel and know about other people and the worlds around us. Leading on directly from this, then, my primary concern in studying film music is the relationship among perceivers and films.

As I argued in Chapter 2 of *Hearing Film*,[9] analyses of film music from the position of perceivers should spring from three basic questions:

1. How is the music's relationship to the narrative world of the film perceived?
2. How do we perceive the music's method within the scene?
3. What does the music evoke in or communicate to us?[10]

Each of these questions arises from a consideration of the relationships among a particular musical event in a film, each of the various threads of a filmic text and the theoretical perceiver(s), exactly as one does in creating a cue sheet. In that

---

5   Kurt London, *Film Music: A Summary of the Characteristic Features of its History, Aesthetics, Technique, and Possible Developments* (London, 1936).
6   Leonid Sabaneev, *Music for the Films* (New York, 1978).
7   Theodor W. Adorno and Hanns Eisler, *Composing for the Films* (London, 1994).
8   Miguel Mera, *Mychael Danna's The Ice Storm: A Film Score Guide* (Lanham, MD, 2007).
9   Anahid Kassabian, *Hearing Film: Tracking Identifications in Contemporary Hollywood Film Music* (New York, 2001).
10 Ibid., pp. 41–42.

chapter, I developed terminology that I still think works as a strong foundation for any analysis, so I will review it briefly here.

In answer to the first question, I argued that the traditional categories of diegetic and non-diegetic are inappropriate and should be abandoned immediately, for two reasons. First, as most writers on film music argue, there are frequently musical events in films that are not adequately described by either term.[11] Second, and at least as disturbingly, the notion of a 'diegesis' that may or may not include music suggests that music does not itself participate in the production of that diegesis. But how can something be defined in terms of that which it helps to define? Music certainly participates – quite strongly, I would argue – in creating the diegesis, 'the narratively implied spatiotemporal world of the film',[12] as Gorbman defines it. It cannot, therefore, be defined in terms of its relationship to the very world it helps create. I suggested, instead, that the language used by composers – dramatic scoring, source scoring and source music – offers a more expansive palette. In particular, it offers more room for further expansion, as in Elena Boschi's discussion of 'inner scoring'[13] in Ligabue's *Radiofreccia* (1998). By this beautifully descriptive term, she means one of the uses of music that Gorbman termed 'meta-diegetic' – that is, when we hear music that is coming from inside a character's thoughts. In the example that Boschi develops, the film's main character, Freccia, is accompanied by what seems to be dramatic scoring until, in a moment of desperation, he slams his hands over his ears and the music stops. There are undoubtedly countless other nuances of terminology yet to be developed, and a more open field of thought and vocabulary, which I believe the composers' vocabulary provides, will enable scholarship to move more quickly in these directions.

The second question, regarding the music's methods,[14] demands consideration of two continua, which I termed music history and attention. The first interrogates the relationship of any musical event to other musical events, and points along this continuum include: 'quotation', where a moment of music quotes another; 'allusion', where a quotation brings with it reference to another whole narrative; '*Leitmotiv*', a term from Wagner that is used, often quite loosely, to describe themes for characters or ideas;[15] and finally one-time music, which, while referring to

---

11   Gorbman chooses 'metadiegetic' (*Unheard Melodies*, pp. 22–23); Morris Holbrook in 'Ambi-Diegetic Music in Films as a Product Design and Placement Strategy: The Sweet Smell of Success', *Marketing Theory*, 4/3 (2004): 171–85 talks about 'ambi-diegetic' music; and Robynn Stilwell's piece, 'The Fantastical Gap Between Diegetic and Non-diegetic' in Daniel Goldmark, Lawrence Kramer and Richard Leppert (eds), *Beyond the Soundtrack* (Berkeley, CA, 2007) addresses these musical events.

12   'At this point, then, we may summarize and define 'diegesis' as being the '*narratively implied spatiotemporal world of the actions and characters*': Gorbman, *Unheard Melodies*, p. 21 (original emphasis).

13   Elena Boschi, '"Please, Give Me Second Grace": A Study of Five Songs in Wes Anderson's *The Royal Tenenbaums*', in Cooper, Fox and Sapiro, *CineMusic?*, pp. 97–110..

14   That is, how the music goes about accomplishing its purpose.

15   See, for a discussion of *Leitmotiv* in relation to film music, the opening section of James Buhler, Caryl Flinn and David Neumeyer (eds), *Music and Cinema* (Hanover,

musical codes generally, does not refer to any other specific musical event. Again, more points are almost certainly possible on this continuum, but these four offer a starting-point.

On the attention continuum, *Hearing Film* again posits four points: theme songs, sole-soundtrack music, music and sound without dialogue, and music beneath dialogue. The issue here is the relationship in the attentional field between this particular instance of music and other threads of the film, such as visual, sound and dialogue. While it is not easy to assign a cognitive or psychological measure of attention, it is nonetheless important to try to map the relative presence of music in the attentional field.[16] These possibilities, like those in the music history continuum, will already have been detailed on the cue sheet, so their study is more a matter of noticing salient relationships than finding them in the first place.

The third question is arguably the murkiest, the most challenging intellectually, and it has also been the focus of most film music scholarship, in one way or another. It is, of course, the question of meaning, and there are several different intellectual histories that converge here. On the one hand, we have the long-standing philosophical debates about musical meaning, which include classical treatises, papal encyclicals, eighteenth-century *Affektenlehre*, nineteenth-century writings on 'absolute music' and twentieth-century music semiotics. On the other hand, the introduction of literary theory into musicology brought with it a particular approach to the problem of meaning: beginning with semiotics (and, to a lesser extent, Russian formalism), moving into structuralist narratology, and then into psychoanalysis and post-structuralism, meaning was understood to be embedded in form, which opened new avenues for the study of musical meaning. Thus, the question of meaning in film music is a nexus point for several different, though related, intellectual and philosophical trajectories.

In *Hearing Film*, I argued that there are three kinds of meaning to be apprehended: identification, mood and commentary. These categories are not only not to be seen as exclusive, but must be considered as overlapping fields of activity. Music for identification can tell us everything from historical period and geographical location of the story or scene to all sorts of things – age, class, race, gender, sexuality, urban/rural – about individual characters. Mood music is simply that – cues that set the tone of a sequence, frequently informing us of how to feel before other aspects catch up to it with verbal and visual information. And commentary can be anything from the building of suspense that accompanies an otherwise innocent scene to

---

NH, 2000).

16   There are relatively few studies of attention in the contemporary study of culture; two important exceptions are Jonathan Crary's *Suspensions of Perception* (Cambridge, MA, 1999) and Jonathan Beller's *The Cinematic Mode of Production: Attention Economy and the Society of the Spectacle* ((Lebanon, NH, 2006). Questions of attention in music listening are addressed in Marta García Quiñones' 'Escucha Ambiental y Tradición Musical: Cuando las emisoras de música clásica programan para el oyente distraído', in Marta García Quiñones (ed.), *La música que no se escucha* (Barcelona, 2008), and Ola Stockfelt's 'Adequate Modes of Listening' in David Schwartz and Anahid Kassabian (eds), *Keeping Score* (Charlottesville, VA, 1997), pp. 129–46.

something more like *ostranenie* (the Russian formalist idea of defamiliarization) or *Vermfremdungseffekt* (Bertolt Brecht's idea, based on *ostranenie*, a distantiation or alienation effect). In this last usage, music discourages psychic identification with a scene or character, encouraging critical faculties to remain active.

When these various meaning formations of a cue overlap, very creative uses of music can arise. In *Hearing Film*, the example I used was the theme of *Jaws*, which, after its first appearance identifies the shark, its low-pitch ostinato signifying mood (threat/danger), and its appearance before the shark is visible, constituting commentary. Similarly, Boschi has argued that the use of Nick Drake's 'Fly' in *The Royal Tenenbaums* comments on Richie's state of mind, both lyrically and with reference to Drake's star-text, and creates a mood for his conversation with Margot.[17] And, for one last example, the sequence in *Bloodbath at the House of Death* (a spoof of horror films starring Vincent Price) in which a character walks down a hallway, the camera shooting over his shoulder, the solo cello increasing in volume, clearly signifying threat, until he reaches the end of the hallway, opens the door, and finds someone sitting on the toilet, trousers around his ankles, playing the cello. These complex and multivalent uses of music in films offer unusually wide ranges of possibilities for music in relation to other forms or aspects of a form.

With a carefully constructed cue sheet in hand, each of these questions should be reasonably easy to answer. The question then becomes what to make of it. Here, my approach always is to pinpoint music's distinctive contribution, which might be posed as follows:

- What do we hear that we don't see?
- What do we hear musically that we don't hear verbally?
- What do we hear musically *before* hearing it verbally or seeing it?

The meanings or ideas or emotions that music evokes or expresses in advance of, or exclusive to, other aspects often turns out to be very interesting indeed, in part because it may well be affecting perceivers' interpretations without consciously registering. The clearest example of this would be horror music, which is a very interesting topic indeed.[18] Horror films would be a great challenge without recourse to the musical tactics that build suspense and tension over the long sequences during which we, as audience members, know something is about to happen (even though most or all of the characters on screen don't), but not what or when. But more subtle uses can be found, too. *Dangerous Minds*, I suggested in *Hearing Film*, does something less predictable in the score (by Wendy and Lisa, formerly of Prince's orbit) than in the film, and it is certainly possible to interpret the score as an internal critique of the liberal-white-educator-saviour narrative that is the recognizable trajectory of the film.

17   Boschi, '"Please, Give Me Second Grace"'.
18   The edited collections from Mark Evans's series and from Routledge on horror film music.

In sum, then, a cue sheet makes possible interpretations of films that are subtle and supple and musically sensitive, and a series of well-executed cue sheets can lead to larger theoretical arguments about, for example, the relationship between specific film genres and specific musical strategies, or character types and musical genres, or orchestrations and affect.

But is a cue sheet a viable approach to the study of all relationships among music and moving image? While film music and sound are just barely taking their place in the academic canon of approved objects of study, film has already been supplanted, many would argue, by other forms as the dominant mediated narrative of everyday life in the West. Certainly television has occupied that place of honour, and it would not be difficult to contend that even television has been supplanted by the Web and videogames.

So what of the cue sheet in these media?

Well, the answer is not as simple as one might have hoped. In the case of television, which is by far the closest analogue to film, series demand an analysis that extends over multiple episodes, so the cue sheet remains pertinent, but multiplies even at first glance in number. Moreover, however, television studies since Raymond Williams's argument about 'flow' have recognized that the operative unit of television reception is not necessarily the single programme.[19] Programming happens in blocks, and it is advertised and written about in those terms. This is how television marketing is understood – a mode of thinking not similarly available to scholars. While compelling approaches to the study of flow are lacking, and while scholars still write about single programmes, or even single episodes of series, a clear and identifiable problem persists in thinking about music and television.

In 'Television Studies: Why the Silence?', Michele Hilmes has made this argument quite clearly. She suggests that we think of television in terms of its 'streaming seriality' and of its tendency to use sound 'to bridge the different textual levels and mark them within the diegesis', what she calls television's 'supertext'.[20] Clearly, the study of television music and sound presents problems not simply addressed by importing approaches from the study of film sound and music. Unfortunately, as Hilmes and others have argued, there is a dearth of scholarship in this area.

And that's only the beginning. The Web and videogames present a whole new order of problems. Almost all of film music scholarship is focused on the matching of visual and musical events. Meaning is produced – or, as I prefer, evoked – in that match. But neither music on websites nor videogame music can be organized by such events, because interactivity creates a situation wherein the control of the user is such that a change – of location, of activity and so forth – can happen at any time. This makes both matching and visual events associated with musical changes more or less impossible, unless, of course, one were prepared to tolerate

---

19   Raymond Williams, *Television: Technology and Cultural Form* (New York, 1975).
20   Hilmes, Michele, 'Television Sound: Why the Silence?' in Jay Beck and Tony Grajeda (eds), *Lowering the Boom: Critical Studies in Film Sound* (Champaign, IL, 2008).

musical 'jump cuts' – radical shifts from a prior unresolved musical field to a new, unrelated, unprepared one.

Music on websites and in video games, it seems to me, focuses on two of the categories I discussed above in relation to film music: identification and mood. Identification is a well-worn staple of film music, and discussions of these uses appear over and over again both in scholarship and in writings by, and interviews with, composers.

In July of 2007, the *New York Times* called to interview me for a piece about music on real estate developers' websites. Splashed on the front page of the section on 5 August 2007 was an article, 'Selling a Concept with a Song' by Stephanie Rosenbloom, about high-end condominium developers using music on their websites.[21] In preparation for our interview, I looked at and listened to lots of websites for high-end products such as condominiums, sports cars, designer clothing, jewellry and so on. To my surprise, most of these were silent.

Moreover, the ones that had music, like the ones Rosenbloom was interested in her article, were using music in highly predictable ways. Not only were they predictable, but they were very much like the videogames: they used classical music to signify elegance and class (Richard Meier's 'On Prospect Park'[22] has a minimalist piano piece, for example), smooth jazz to signify relaxation (the newly converted Plaza Hotel[23] has a jazz trio), world lounge and techno to signify downtown hipness (the Setai, New York,[24] bought tracks from the Buddha Bar CD series).

This is hardly surprising. Both composers and scholars – and producers of all kinds – know that music is a quick and effective shorthand to do the cultural work of communicating identity. And so both games and websites think of this as a possibility, and I think of it when I listen to them. (In fact, so did the article's author, Stephanie Rosenbloom. She heard most of the same things I did, which I take to indicate that our insights have been around long enough to have been made public, which seems to me to take somewhere from 10–20 years. That alone suggests it might be time for some new ones.)

The other major category of activity in film and television music has always been mood, and you hear this in the games and websites, too, but in a much more diffuse way. Because of the absence of synchronization, they can only communicate the most general and diffuse of moods, such as the relaxing 'vibe' of smooth jazz on the Plaza website. In games, one sometimes finds mood music in, for example, fight sequences. So while quest-based games more frequently use music to establish place and identity, as I discussed a minute ago, some hack 'n' slash games, such as *Devil May Cry*,[25] will have rock or dance music, such as darkwave, to accompany

21   Stephanie Rosenbloom, 'Selling a Concept With a Song', *New York Times*, Real Estate, 5 August 2007.
22   <http://onprospectpark.com/> (accessed 12 January 2008).
23   <http://www.theplazaresidences.com/index.php> (accessed 12 January 2008).
24   <http://setainy.com/> (accessed 12 January 2008).
25   *Devil May Cry* (Hideki Kamiya, 2001).

fight sequences. In mixed games, such as *Prince of Persia*,[26] music along those lines accompanies fight sequences, but not puzzle activities. What becomes clear, then, is the inversely proportional relationship between attention and synchronicity. When music is far forward in the attentional field, such as in websites, synchronicity is relatively minimal. When music is in the background, however, synchronicity helps to keep it that way, by practices such as 'sneaking', 'an industry term for beginning a musical cue at low volume usually under dialogue so that the spectator would be unaware of its presence'.[27] This is an area in music, sound and moving image studies begging to be studied.

This leads me to the question of areas of study. Music, sound and the moving image is a field with a very broad range of unexplored areas – it really is a paradise for postgraduates.

Before I offer an idea of a new theoretical direction, I want to reiterate a tentative list of topics I'd like to see studied. I first offered these at the Sound, Music and the Moving Image conference organized by the Institute for Musical Research in September 2007, and I was greatly heartened by the number of people who came up to me afterwards to tell me they were working on one or another of the things I mentioned. The list will quickly become dated, but it is important that we keep generating ideas of new areas into which the field should be pushed. Here's my current list:

1. Hollywood sound, and indeed, film sound in general, where Liz Weis's and John Belton's early and important anthology[28] was less generative than one might have hoped, although there are a few projects in the pipeline, including work by both Jay Beck and Tony Grajeda on point-of-audition and subjective sounds;[29]

2. Other national or regional cinemas, where the European Film Music collection edited by Miguel Mera and David Burnand[30] makes an important opening and where Phil Brophy's discussions of bodily sounds in sports and violent films[31] and sound design in anime[32] open whole new fields of inquiry; Mark Slobin's forthcoming collection on global film music will also add to this literature;

3. Non-Hollywood English language films, an area in which Annette Davison's book[33] stands alone, at least to my knowledge;

---

26   *Prince of Persia* (Jordan Mechner, 1989).
27   Kalinak, *Settling the Score*, p. 99.
28   Liz Weis and John Belton, *Film Sound: Theory and Practice* (New York, 1985).
29   Jay Beck and Tony Grajeda (eds), *Lowering the Boom: Critical Studies in Film Sound* (Champaign, 2008).
30   Miguel Mera and David Burnand (eds), *European Film Music* (Aldershot, 2006).
31   Philip Brophy, 'Body Mats and Super Slams: Sport, Sound and Violence', paper given at the Fourth Cinesonic International Conference on Film Scores and Sound Design (Melbourne, 2001).
32   Philip Brophy, *100 Anime* (London, 2006).
33   Annette Davison, Hollywood Theory, *Non-Hollywood Practice: Cinema Soundtracks in the*

4. Television music, where work by Norma Coates[34] and Murray Forman,[35] and the special issue of Popular Music edited by Keith Negus and John Street[36] are beginnings; questions to pursue would include the widespread use of popular music that has been commonplace at least since Dawson's Creek and many others;

5. Music video, which has generated a number of good books and articles but which has still not developed into a field with something between the most general theorizing and specific textual analyses of single videos;

6. Animation, which with the exception of Dan Goldmark's Tunes for 'Toons,[37] has seen startlingly little inquiry into films, including Disney, the brothers Quay, Wallace and Gromit, Jan Švankmajer, or television, including anime series, contemporary adult programming such as Adult Swim and so on;

7. Music in film and TV advertising, where I think Kaarina Kilpiö's work on ads from the 1950s to the 1970s shown in film theatres in Finland[38] is exemplary, and also the paper on TV ads by Barry Salmon[39] and the forthcoming collection edited by Nikolai Graakjaer and Christian Jantzen;[40]

8. TV sound, where the only work I know is by Norwegian scholar Arnt Maasø,[41] but there is indeed much to think about;

9. Experimental films, about which the artists themselves often express their thoughts on sound and music, but about which I know of no scholarly literature;

1980s and 1990s (Aldershot, 2004).

34 Norma Coates, 'Elvis from the Waist Up and Other Myths: 1950s Music Television and the Gendering of Rock Discourse', in Roger Beebe and Jason Middleton (eds), *Medium Cool: Music Videos from Soundies to Cellphones* (Durham, NC, 2007), pp. 226–51.

35 Murray Forman, 'Television before Television Genre: The Case of Popular Music', *Journal of Popular Film and Television*, 31 (Spring 2003): 5–17.

36 Keith Negus and John Street (eds), 'Music and Television', special issue of *Popular Music* 21/3 (2002).

37 Daniel Goldmark, *Tunes for 'Toons: Music and the Hollywood Cartoon* (Berkeley, CA, 2005).

38 Kaarina Kilpiö, 'The Use of Music in Early Finnish Cinema and TV Advertising' in Lotte Yssing Hansen and Flemming Hansen (eds), *Advertising Research in the Nordic Countries* (Copenhagen, 2001), pp. 68–76.

39 Barry Salmon, 'Music in Recent Car Advertisements on Television', paper given at the Twelfth Biennial IASPM International Conference (Montreal, 2003).

40 Nikolai Graakjaer and Christian Jantzen (eds), *Music in Advertising: Commercial Sounds in Media Communication and Other Settings* (Aalborg, 2009).

41 Arnt Maasø, 'Designing Sound and Silence', available online at: <http://www.nordicom.gu.se/common/publ_pdf/242_maaso_1.pdf> (accessed 2 October 2007).

10. Video art, an area with a very small, but growing, body of work led not least by my colleague's Holly Rogers' article[42] and book in progress;
11. Video games, another growing field, in which Karen Collins is one of the few experts – these studies should include the development of musical genres, of the relationships between musical practices and technological challenges and possibilities, and of expressly musical games;
12. Music on the Web – here I know of no scholarship whatsoever, and the questions and genres abound – Internet ads, viral videos, websites, porn sites, MMORPGs (Massively Multiplayer Online Role Playing Games) and other online game genres all present distinct challenges to prevailing scholarly models and tools;
13. Music in film and television documentaries – Alfred W. Cochran and Neil Lerner have each produced good work in this area, but it is crying out for sustained attention;
14. The various new forms being developed due to new technologies, from 'Misheard Lyrics' videos on YouTube (for example,. the one of Sean Paul's 'Temperature'[43] or the Moroccan videos that Tony Langlois discusses in Miguel Mera's forthcoming special issue of Music, Sound, and the Moving Image on adaptations,[44] in which artists use an astounding array of video clips to accompany their own works, to Shzr Ee Tan's paper on a podcast critical – in a very tongue-in-cheek, parodic way – of current politics in Singapore.[45]

All of these topics, and many others, should be generating many projects. We might think of music, sound, and moving image as an academic growth industry, not entirely in jest. I have always thought that this is one of the most important arenas of musical and media scholarship, on the one hand precisely because it has the least developed vocabulary, which makes it difficult for audiences to engage critically, and on the other hand because it teaches much – perhaps nearly all – about music and meaning to most listeners who grow up with films and television. It also invites connections to sound studies, an arena in which lots of very exciting scholarship is going on and which is, I would argue, another academic growth industry.

---

42   Holly Rogers, 'Acoustic Architecture: Music and Space in the Video Installations of Bill Viola', *Twentieth Century Music*, 2/2 (2005): 197–220.
43   <http://www.youtube.com/watch?v=nfXke_z6t3I>.
44   Tony Langlois, 'Pirates of the Mediterranean: Audiovisual Bricolage in Moroccan Music Video', in Miguel Mera (ed.), 'Prequels/Sequels/Translations/Re-Invention', special issue of *Music, Sound, and the Moving Image* (forthcoming).
45   Shzr Ee Tan, '"My Humping" the Prime Minister: Mash-up Podcast Politics in a Singaporean Context', paper presented at the Sound, Music and the Moving Image Conference, London, 2007).

But to return to the problem of new theoretical directions in this field, I'll begin from what might seem like an unlikely place. I've always thought that the critique of clichés in Adorno and Eisler's *Composing for the Films* was itself vulgar and wrong-headed, because it fails to understand the nature of signification. Music signifies precisely by using well-worn connections between musical materials and processes and non-musical ideas, just as language does. The connection between a sound and an idea is established through use over time, becoming a convention and ultimately a meaning. You can't abandon clichés, because they are precisely the tools of the compositional trade, at least in mainstream film production settings.

Remembering this gave me pause as I was thinking about the real estate websites. I know full well that what I'm saying runs the risk of being exactly the same thing I disagree with in Adorno and Eisler. But it seems to me – and I hope – that I'm thinking about the problem of clichés from a different direction. I'm not concerned that timbres or chord progressions mean particular things – that's not only quite useful, but also one of the fundamental strategies available to music and the moving image specifically, and to musical signification more generally. Rather, I'm concerned that the palette of ideas that people ask music to express is too limited.

There are two problems here, not one.

First, film music composers, and to a lesser extent theatre and opera composers before them, learned very early on that music could quickly and effectively communicate geography, history, class, race – all kinds of things we might call identity in a large way, or place in another generously conceived way. This means that for advertising especially, but for the games as well, communicating an identity or place is handy – it's well-prepared, easy to accomplish, and it can speak to either an audience's actual location, an aspirational one or a complete fantasy.

Second, I think we are at a challenging theoretical junction, created on the one hand by our overreliance on models from literary and cultural studies, and on the other by the centrality of place and identity in the study of culture generally. I'm always suspicious of arguments about the specificity of forms because they so often serve as excuses; nevertheless, I'm quite sure that the different relationships of sound and music to referentiality and representation mean not only that we need to develop our own theories about those things, but also that we need to imagine that things might be communicated aurally that are not communicated visually or verbally. Certainly in the growing arena of theories of affect, for instance, sound and music must have a particular place. I will return to affect below, because I think it may offer some interesting futures for us.

The prevalence of studies of identity across the disciplines is clear, and it has certainly left its mark on the study of sound and music in moving image media. *Hearing Film* was one of many works deeply marked by that tradition – I am by no means suggesting that it was unproductive or a dead-end. But it has in some ways become a path of least resistance, one well-worn way to think about the relationships of aural materials and visual images. As I argued earlier, identity/identification and mood are the two holdovers from film music practices into non-synchronous audiovisual forms like websites and especially videogames. These uses, combined with the challenge of non-synchronicity, open onto questions of affect in particular ways. As Patricia Clough writes in her introduction to *The Affective Turn*,[46] current scholarship treats

> ... *affectivity as a substrate of potential bodily responses, often autonomic responses, in excess of consciousness. For these scholars, affect refers generally to bodily capacities to affect and be affected or the augmentation or diminution of a body's capacity to act, to engage, and to connect, such that autoaffection is linked to the self-feeling of being alive – that is, aliveness or vitality.*[47]

This description resonated for me, from the moment I read it, with what music in general, and film music in particular, is routinely said to do. It draws on potential bodily responses, often autonomic, raising heart rate, tears and arousal of all kinds. This is what is generally called mood, although in the literature the term is far too broad to be useful. But the physiological responses we have to the musical processes that signify terror, for example, are preconscious, and if we could begin to understand these responses, we might be able to offer new strategies for website music and many other things.

Before readers assume that this might mean something that precedes the social, or that logically precedes consciousness, let me offer you Clough's next few lines.

> *Yet affect is not 'presocial,' as Massumi argues. There is a reflux back from conscious experience to affect, which is registered, however, as affect, such that 'past action and contexts are conserved and repeated, autonomically reactivated but not accomplished; begun but not completed.' Affect constitutes a nonlinear complexity out of which the narration of conscious states such as emotion are subtracted, but always with 'a never-to-be-conscious autonomic remainder'.*[48]

In other words, conscious experiences are banked in the body, accreting autonomic responses to them, so that in the future the response precedes conscious recognition of the stimulus. This is why my heart starts beating faster before I notice the rising rate and volume of the ostinato that warns me something is about to happen.

There is, of course, much, much more to say on the topic of affect, but I offer it here as a potential new approach. Here, then, we can see an approach to film music that sidesteps semiotic approaches to the question of music and meaning, moving instead towards a kind of embodied information storage and retrieval system that short-circuits, as it were, conscious or cognitive engagements. What I perceive consciously, first, is my body's responses, not the stimulus and its meaning. My point is simply this – our models for the study of audiovisual relationships and audiovisual media have relied on narration and narrativity on the one hand, and

---

46   Patricia Ticineto Clough, *The Affective Turn: Theorizing the Social* (Durham, NC, 2007).
47   Ibid., p. 2.
48   Ibid.

synchronization of sound and image on the other. If we begin to think about affect instead – provoked not least by the changes that videogames and websites make audible – new possibilities arise. This ability to produce affective responses, or affect itself, is one of music's singular strengths. Precisely because of its difficult relationship to referentiality and representation, music has always operated on the plane of affect. Thus while different forms of audiovisual media may require different methods of study – be they cue sheets, lists of songs across a programming block, or other as-yet-undeveloped tools – a consideration of affect may turn out to be a unifying approach across this widely disparate field of cultural activity. Our pounding heartbeats may yet lead us to new and fruitful theoretical approaches to the study of music, sound and the moving image.

Acknowledgement

My thanks to Maral Svendsen for generously sharing her wisdom on game music.

Films and Videogames

Bloodbath at the House of Death (1984) directed by Ray Cameron, music by Mark London and Mike Moran, Wildwood Productions.

Dangerous Minds (1995) directed by John N. Smith, music by Wendy and Lisa, Hollywood Pictures.

Devil May Cry (Hideki Kamiya, 2001).

Jaws (1975) directed by Steven Spielberg, music by John Williams, Universal Pictures.

Prince of Persia (Jordan Mechner, 1989).

Radiofreccia (1998) directed by Luciano Ligabue, music by Luciano Ligabue, Medusa.

The Royal Tenebaums (2001) directed by Wes Anderson, music by Mark Mothersbaugh, music supervisor Randall Poster, Touchstone Pictures.

Reinventing *Question Time*

Miguel Mera

Over the past 20 years the academic study of screen music has become an increasingly established field. Following the publication of Claudia Gorbman's groundbreaking *Unheard Melodies: Narrative Film Music* (1987) a substantial body of scholarship has emerged that explores music and the moving image using a variety of methodological approaches. The marked expansion of articles, books, anthologies and journals suggests that the study of screen music continues to move from the margins to the mainstream.[1] However, almost all extant work considers the role of music in *film*. Other media, such as television, are largely ignored despite clear cultural impact and ubiquity. Recent publications and work in progress suggest this is changing, but, for the moment, the study of television music remains something of a scholarly blind spot.[2]

The reasons for this *lacuna* are complex. A recurrent argument proposes that, in comparison to cinema which requires sustained and intense concentration, broadcast television is regulated by the limited attention span of the viewer. In the now classic work, *Visible Fictions* (1992), John Ellis explains that, when watching television, the spectator 'glances rather than gazes at the screen; attention is sporadic rather than sustained'.[3] He also outlines how broadcast TV 'offers a small image of low definition, to which sound is crucial in holding the spectator's attention'.[4] One could speculate that Ellis's perception of low-definition and smaller TV images will

---

1   For example, four new journals focusing on screen music and/or sound have appeared in recent years. These include in order of first appearance: *The Journal of Film Music* (International Film Music Society), *Music, Sound and the Moving Image* (University of Liverpool Press), *Music and the Moving Image* (University of Illinois Press) and *The Soundtrack* (Intellect).

2   Recent publications that challenge the undervaluing of television in screen music studies include Kevin Donnelly's *Film and Television Music: The Spectre of Sound* (London, 2008). Donnelly explores the role of music in television continuity segments as well as in television drama. One might also point to the current lack of work on videogames, music and sound in websites, or mobile media. A starting-point is Paul Hoffert's *Music for New Media* (Boston, MA, 2007).

3   John Ellis, *Visible Fictions* (London, 1992), p. 24.

4   Ibid.

be transformed in an era where widescreen TV and high definition broadcasting are becoming more prevalent, but his concept of sound as fundamental to the impact of television suggests its importance as a point of study. A similar idea is posited by Kevin Donnelly who observes that music in television is the 'prevailing agent of control',[5] and, because audiences often do something else while the television is on, '[w]e listen to television sometimes more than we watch it'.[6]

What these writers highlight, of course, is that television is principally a domestic medium, and it is this very domesticity that provides a unique perspective. Despite increased globalization, TV remains distinctly 'national' in the sense that British television represents a different domestic audience and sociocultural viewpoint than, for example, French television. As Ellis observes, 'Broadcast TV is the private life of a nation-state, defining the intimate and inconsequential sense of everyday life'.[7] Accordingly, television tends to adjust itself towards its audience in order to 'include the audience's own conception of themselves into the texture of its programmes'.[8] As a tool for social and cultural research, therefore, television provides extraordinary potential for understanding the role that music has in shaping its audience and how music is in turn is shaped by its audience.

However, one of the principal challenges in the study of television music is simply accessing materials for study. Although DVDs of some TV series are widely available, other source materials are not easy to locate. Individual broadcasters, such as the BBC, hold archives of their materials but these are not always readily available. Older programmes are especially hard to trace given that the use of videotape for archival purposes only began to gain momentum from the mid-1970s onwards, coupled with the notion that television might be more than an ephemeral medium with long-term value in terms of heritage and culture. Owing to the vast amount of content that is broadcast a policy of selective archiving is generally unavoidable.[9] Therefore, the study of a long-running television programme – as is my focus here – presents significant challenges in terms of access, even to the primary texts. Once physical materials have been accessed by the individual researcher, however, there still remains the problem of allowing others to hear and see it. For the purposes of this chapter, permission was requested to stream video examples via the Internet, but this was not granted: 'We are in a position at the moment where we cannot allow BBC identifiable footage to appear on websites.'[10] While the rights of copyright-holders must, of course, be protected, the development of the field is dependent on the ability to access materials in order to see and hear what scholars discuss. Distribution mechanisms and copyright law, to some extent, define the type of scholarship that takes place. As Katharine Ellis points out, 'musical research on

5   Donnelly, *The Spectre of Sound*, p. 111.
6   Ibid.
7   Ellis, *Visible Fictions*, p. 5
8   Ibid., p. 115.
9   See, for example, the BBC archive at: <http://www.bbc.co.uk/archive> (accessed June 2007).
10   E-mail from Christopher Gibson to author, BBC Motion Gallery, 2 June 2008.

the internet is straitjacketed by licensing anachronism, ill-defined and inadequate legal exemptions, and a species of risk-aversion that stems from fear – among researchers and publishers alike – of becoming a legal test case'.[11] However, we live in an increasingly digitally mediated world, and numerous digitization projects undertaken by broadcasters and other bodies are bringing about change that will eventually serve the field well in the future.[12]

This essay will examine the opening title music for the long-running British television debate programme *Question Time* which was first broadcast in 1979.[13] The *Question Time* theme music was originally composed by Stanley Myers (1930–93) and, to date, has been changed on four occasions.[14] However, instead of commissioning successive new themes, Myers's musical material has been used as the basis for 'reinvention'. In essence the same piece of music has survived since 1979, but has received differing interpretations and arrangements. If invention is the construction of that which has not existed before, the term 'reinvention' suggests recasting something familiar into a different – but equally original – form. Terms such as 'sequel', 'adaptation' or 'remake' do not seem appropriate, largely because of their association with film or literary theory, but also because they tend to focus on the idea of fixed texts at fixed points in history (for example, Hitchcock and Gus van Sant's versions of *Psycho* in 1960 and 1998 respectively). The danger in this approach, as Constantine Verevis has shown, is that most critical accounts highlight a one-way process, a movement 'from authenticity to imitation, from the superior self-identity of the original to the debased resemblance of the copy'.[15] But a long-running television programme – particularly one that receives a weekly broadcast, is concerned with topical issues and is constructed by its audience – is always in a state of reinvention, evolving through a feedback loop with the public. Value judgements about fidelity and/or originality in comparison to the source text would obscure understanding of what actually takes place when a work is changed, such as the social and cultural forces that shape the act of reinvention. The term 'reinvention', therefore, attempts to ascribe an appropriate level of importance to later text(s) which may well be just as creative and indeed 'original' as the

11   Katharine Ellis, 'Rocks and Hard Places', in Johanna Gibson (ed.), *Herchel Smith Intellectual Property Futures* (Cheltenham, forthcoming). Some issues in relation to publishing rights are also raised by Annette Davison in 'Copyright and Scholars' Rights', *Music, Sound, and the Moving Image*, 1/1 (2007): 9–14.

12   In the UK bodies such as the British Universities Film and Video Council (BUFVC) is a representative body which promotes the production, study and use of moving image, sound and related media in higher education and research.

13   The website for *Question Time* contains some details about its history and some classic editions can be streamed. See: <http://news.bbc.co.uk/1/hi/programmes/question_time/default.stm> (accessed June 2007).

14   Myers reveals his musical background in an interview on the CD *Stanley Myers: The Deer Hunter and Other Themes* (Milan 73138–35939–2). He began his musical career playing piano for cabaret shows, in bars, and as a rehearsal pianist. He is best known as a film composer for his work with Stephen Frears.

15   Constantine Verevis, *Film Remakes* (Edinburgh, 2006), p. 58.

primary text within their particular context. Furthermore, although we can select as an object of study any discrete moment in the history of *Question Time*, we must always understand this as part of a process of continuous evolution. Reinvention reflects a desire to reread or, as Leo Braudy observes, to 'believe in an explicit (and thematized) way that the past reading was wrong or outdated and that a new one must be done'.[16] In long-running television programmes, those moments when a new version must be done are like nodes reflecting the build-up of cultural, social, technological or political change.

Through an examination of the transformation of the *Question Time* theme this chapter will illustrate how the evolution of musical materials not only reflects societal change, but also parallels the shifting British political spectrum, from the right-wing Thatcherite government of the 1980s to the centre-left (New) Labour government of the late 1990s onwards. This evolution also highlights changing features of television scoring practice during the same period, including developments in music technology. Inevitably, there are issues of taste to consider, but, as Pierre Bourdieu has shown, taste is not pure or innocent.[17] Aesthetic choices are fundamental to the societal frameworks that encase them, including – I would argue – political frameworks. What this chapter hopes to show is that the study of television music raises new questions for screen music studies generally. These include the contrasts between ephemerality and longevity, the problem of sources, the social significance of music and moving image, and the interaction between music and political context.

Question Time: **The First Broadcast**

> *Hello, and here we are for the first of our weekly Question Times with an audience in a South London theatre which has been specially converted for television; that's to say the theatre has been specially converted not the audience, the audience are much the same people as they were when they came in. They are what's described in TV circles as 'real people' to distinguish them from people who work in television. We don't claim them to be a scientific cross-section of the British nation but they are a very good collection, a wide-ranging collection from a broad variety of groups, organizations and institutions, and to answer their topical questions I've got a pretty rich mixture of personalities here with me ...*[18]

16   Leo Braudy, 'Afterword: Rethinking Remakes', in Andrew Horton and Stuart Y. McDougal (eds), *Play it Again, Sam: Retakes on Remakes* (Berkeley, CA, 1998), p. 332.
17   Pierre Bourdieu, *Distinction: A Social Critique of the Judgement of Taste*, trans. Richard Nice (Cambridge, MA and London, 1984).
18   Robin Day's introduction to the first broadcast of *Question Time*, BBC 1, 25 September 1979.

So began Robin Day's introduction to the first broadcast of *Question Time* on 25 September 1979.[19] Although originally designed to fill a gap in the schedule, it has since become one of the most popular and enduring television programmes in the United Kingdom, offering the British public a unique opportunity to challenge leading decision-makers on contemporary issues. The format is simple and has remained unchanged since 1979. A panel consisting primarily of politicians, but which may also include newspaper editors, authors, religious leaders – anyone who is perceived to have an influence on the way nation and society is shaped – is asked questions by an audience representing a cross-section of British society. The panel is given no advance warning of the questions that will be put to them, but due to the topical nature of the programme a detailed knowledge of current affairs and of party policy (where relevant) is essential.[20] For the first broadcast the panel comprised Michael Foot (Deputy Leader of the Labour Party), Teddy Taylor (former Conservative Scottish Office minister), Edna O'Brien (novelist) and Derek Worlock (Archbishop of Liverpool).

Question Time generates the kind of debate that might take place in the House of Commons or the House of Lords, but the principal difference is that the public are central to the discussion and can directly hold their elected representatives to account. In his book *Radio, Television, and Modern Life*, Paddy Scannell recognizes a distinct form of connection in the talk show where the viewer is 'invited in' as a central aspect of its sociability.[21] The studio audience plays a vital role and is 'placed directly in the television studio as joint author of the text'.[22] Along with the presenter, the studio audience act as substitute for the absent or ghost audience who are at home and generate an experience of togetherness. In the case of *Question Time*, that studio audience literally acts as a microcosm of the nation, diverse in its

---

19   Robin Day (1923–2000) originally trained as a barrister, but after only a short period in practice he moved into journalism working initially for ITN and latterly for the BBC. In 1959 he stood as Liberal candidate for Hereford in the general election but failed to get into parliament. Alongside *Question Time* he also presented *Panorama*, and on radio was presenter *of The World at One*. He was widely regarded as one of Britain's finest political interviewers and was knighted in 1981. His autobiography is entitled *Day by Day: A Dose of My Own Hemlock* (London, 1975).

20   Conservative politician Boris Johnson (then the Shadow Minister for Higher Education but currently Mayor of London) seemed to be unaware of this in a broadcast on 8 July 2004 as he came unstuck while trying to bluff his way through a question about the government decision to admit Yusuf Al Qaradawi into the United Kingdom to speak on behalf of the Muslim Brotherhood. Johnson's lack of knowledge about the subject – he was unaware of his own party's stance and later admitted being too complacent to have read the newspapers before the broadcast – and his attempt to charm his way around a question about the incitement of racial hatred simply confirmed his reputation as a likeable buffoon.

21   Paddy Scannell, *Radio, Television and Modern Life* (Oxford, 1996), p. 28. See Chapter Two: 'Sociability'.

22   Sonia Livingstone and Peter Lunt, *Talk On Television: Audience Participation and Public Debate* (London, 1994), p. 36.

political views, gender, race, age and socioeconomic structure. It is unsurprising, therefore, that Robin Day's comments – as well as an extended camera pan of the entire auditorium – firmly establish the importance of the studio audience from the very outset. If it is true that a fundamental duty of citizenship within democracies is for individuals to form an opinion about public affairs and to express that opinion at the ballot box, televisation generally – and programmes such as *Question Time* specifically – make an important contribution to the democratic process. Furthermore, direct contact between decision-makers and 'real' people has contributed to the programme's lasting appeal.

Any UK citizen of voting age can apply to attend a broadcast, and all audience members are invited to submit potential questions.[23] The programme-makers select the shortlist of questions, depending on what they perceive to be of greatest national interest that particular week. The panellists' responses are interspersed with comments from the audience, and anybody who wishes to speak need only raise their hand in order to attract the attention of the chairperson. The programme is recorded live at around 20:30 GMT each Thursday and then broadcast at 22:35. The reason for not broadcasting live at 22:35 is 'to limit inconvenience to spectators and guests – enabling them to appear on the programme at locations across the country and still return to their homes at a reasonable hour – and therefore maximize the number of leading politicians and political commentators willing to take part'.[24] The recording is completed in a single take, precisely as if it were broadcast live, and any text messages sent in when the programme is broadcast are live responses to the guests' remarks. The discussion can vary from the intelligent and incisive to the frivolous and partisan. It may not quite accomplish the undistorted participatory communication between citizens that scholars such as Habermas believe to be the fundamental basis for a democracy,[25] but it is as free a debate as the mechanics of making a popular television programme will allow, and *Question Time* remains the only regular forum on UK television where senior politicians are challenged by ordinary members of the public, at times with extraordinary consequences.[26]

---

23 The one exception to the age limit is the annual *Schools Question Time* where pupils are nominated by schools around the country and those selected join the production team and help make a special edition of the programme. This is a good way of engaging Britain's youth in political debate.

24 <http://news.bbc.co.uk/1/hi/programmes/question_time/faqs/default.stm> (accessed June 2008).

25 German Political Philosopher Jürgen Habermas argued for public communication unfettered by institutional control. See *The Theory of Communicative Action. Vol. 2 Lifeworld and System: A Critique of Functionalist Reason*, trans. Thomas McCarthy (Cambridge, 1987); *The Structural Transformation of the Public Sphere: An Inquiry Into a Category of Bourgeois Society*, trans. Thomas Burger with the assistance of Frederick Lawrence (Cambridge, 1989).

26 For example, in an appearance in April 1983, Francis Pimm, then foreign secretary, stated that the Conservatives would not win the forthcoming general election by a landslide and that, in any case, landslide victories never produced effective government. His boss Margaret Thatcher disagreed and he was summarily sacked. Likewise, in 2001 First

This format seems perfectly natural to UK audiences today, but this was not the case in the late 1970s when politicians rarely engaged with the public in such a direct manner. In that same first broadcast, for example, the novelty and awkwardness is in constant display and delightfully illustrated as one audience member tries and fails to ask the final question of the evening.

Robin Day: *Well, we've got two or three minutes more on this enjoyable programme and I am going to call Mrs Dorothy Clark who has got, I think, a short question for us which will reveal what our guests are really like ... Mrs Dorothy Clark ... housewife ... are you there?*

Dorothy Clark: *Which question?*

Robin Day: *You had a short one I think about ... about the team ...*

Dorothy Clark: *About the beer?*

Audience laughter.

Robin Day: *About the what?*

Dorothy Clark: *(searching in handbag)... Oh, I'm doing the wrong thing, aren't I?*

Robin Day: *No, no, no, you're ... you just ask whatever you'd like to ask, but not a long political question.*

Dorothy Clark: *(searching through bits of paper and in realization) ... Oh!*

Robin Day: *You had one at the end, I think I remember, you had two or three ... I thought you wanted to ask one which ... how are you doing there?... what have you got in that handbag?*

Audience laughter.

Robin Day: *Well while you're waiting I'll tell you what it was, it was: what does the team like doing on a night out?*

Dorothy Clark: *Oh, what does the team like ...*

Robin Day: *Yes, we've got that.*

Minister of Scotland, Henry McLeish, resigned shortly after his appearance on *Question Time* after he was challenged about allegations that he sub-let part of his constituency office, which was funded by the taxpayer; the scandal became known as 'Officegate'.

With historical hindsight, presenter Robin Day's comment about 'this enjoyable programme' and the indication that the question will 'reveal what our guests are really like' seems naïve and patronizing. But, interestingly, Michael Foot finds this line of questioning uncomfortable: 'That's not going to be revealed on *this* kind of programme' (my italics). Foot's lack of comprehension about the relevance of his personal interests was not an uncharacteristic view for the time and represents a genuine concern about individual privacy versus public duty, as well as the value of serious political discussion as mediated through television. This same concern is reflected in the fact that it was not until 1989 that House of Commons debates were first televised in the United Kingdom.[27] Today, however, political life is constituted through its total immersion in a media-dominated world, and a contemporary, media-savvy audience is much better informed. In short, political debate has changed, the way politicians relate to the public and the media has changed, and – following that notion to its logical conclusion – the nature of democracy has changed. If, as Fiske and Hartley suggest, television is a social ritual in which 'our culture engages in order to communicate with its collective self',[28] then *Question Time* has consistently projected, represented and reflected an image of the British public back to itself.

Invention/Reinvention

It is interesting to note that musical reinventions of the *Question Time* theme have occurred principally at moments when a new prime minister takes office (see Fig. 3.1). The programme itself was created only months after Margaret Thatcher came to power and the music remained unchanged throughout the ten years in which she was prime minister, despite the fact the title graphics were revised on three occasions during this period.[29] The music was reinvented shortly after John Major and Tony Blair took office in 1989 and 1997 respectively. In 2006 – and with delicious irony – the music pre-empted Gordon Brown's premiership, which is something he had himself been doing for a number of years.[30]

---

27 It is interesting to note that Robin Day himself published a book advocating the televisation of parliamentary debate as early as 1964: *The Case for Televising Parliament* (London, 1964).

28 John Fiske and John Hartley, *Reading Television* (London, 2003), p. 64.

29 Although there is no evidence that the new government played any part in encouraging the birth of debate programmes such as *Question Time*, television coverage of the 1979 election campaign was particularly intense. All three major parties held daily press conferences and Thatcher worked especially hard to provide the media with photo opportunities. Curiously, however, she refused to appear on the programme *Weekend World* in a debate with Labour leader James Callaghan and Liberal leader David Steel. *Weekend World*, broadcast on ITV, ran from 1972 to 1988 and was presented by Brian Walden.

30 The origins of the tensions between Blair and Brown are neatly explored by James

The change that took place in 1994, however, seemed to coincide with the arrival of the new presenter, David Dimbleby. It has proved challenging to identify who arranged this version, but of all the reinventions this is by far the closest to Myers's original. In fact, apart from an additional introductory bar and a slightly tighter performance, the ensemble, instrumentation and orchestration are exactly the same as the original. In comparison to the other versions this is not so much a reinvention as a rerecording, reflecting a shift from analogue to digital recording technology from the late 1970s to the mid-1990s. The sound quality is punchier and the bass sound, in particular, is more heavily compressed. This return to the original version could also be understood as an attempt by the programme-makers to generate a link to between the new presenter David Dimbleby and the first presenter Robin Day. The gravitas that Day naturally commanded seemed to elude Peter Sissens's chairmanship in the early 1990s, and the appointment of David Dimbleby provided new energy in an attempt to reclaim the 'glory days' of the programme. Major reinventions – those that have incorporated new compositional elements or orchestrations – have occurred when there has been a change of government. The comparatively minor rerecording in 1994 therefore seems to reflect the arrival of the new presenter.

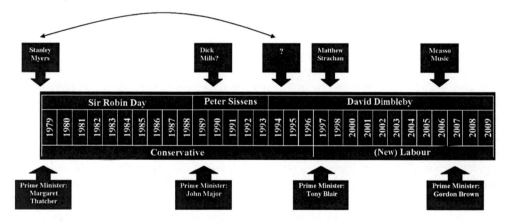

Figure 3.1 *Question Time*, Timeline, 1979–2009

It is important to understand the background to the creation of the original theme music. During the winter of 1978 the Labour government faced industrial disputes, escalating unemployment and deteriorating public services; it was dubbed the 'winter of discontent'. The Conservatives easily won the 1979 general

Naughtie in his book *The Rivals: The Intimate Story of a Political Marriage* (London, 2001). In October 2004 Blair announced that he would not lead the party into a fourth general election but would serve a full third term. Brown dropped any pretence of not wanting, or expecting, to move into the job and is widely believed to have pressured Blair to make an early departure.

election.[31] Britain had shown itself to be progressive by electing the first female prime minister of any Western nation and had given Margaret Thatcher a clear mandate to reform economic decline. On arrival at 10 Downing Street on 4 May, Thatcher famously paraphrased the prayer of St Francis of Assisi: 'Where there is despair may we bring hope.' The nation had emphatically requested a change, and it was with a sense of hopefulness that the new Conservative government took office. It is in this context that the birth of Question Time, only four months into the new Conservative government, should be understood. In a number of ways Myers's music reflects this hopefulness and optimism.

The dominant features of Myers score are a semi-quaver classical guitar pattern that generates momentum, and regular anacrusis and downbeat stabs that further contribute to the forward motion. The 'melodic' construction is modal with an avoidance of the raised 7th (G♯). The simple harmonic structure revolves around an A minor tonal centre, but 6th, major 7th and 9th chords add harmonic colour. Myers's interest in jazz and light music is also reflected in the instrumentation which includes piano, amplified double bass and drum kit (Ex. 3.1).

In 1978 Myers's music for the Vietnam War drama, The Deer Hunter (Cimino), brought him international recognition. The main theme 'Cavatina' had in fact been recorded by the classical guitarist John Williams long before. It first appeared in the film The Walking Stick (Till, 1970) and on the album Changes (1971).[32] In 1976 jazz singer Cleo Laine wrote lyrics for the theme and recorded the song 'He Was Beautiful', accompanied by John Williams. Following the release of The Deer Hunter in 1978 Williams's instrumental version of 'Cavatina' reached number 16 in the UK pop charts. The popularity of 'Cavatina' may have been an important factor in the decision to employ Myers as the composer for the Question Time theme; he may even have been encouraged to use the classical guitar as the centrepiece of the arrangement as a consequence. It is certainly a striking choice, quite unlike themes for other political programmes of the era. Indeed, the Question Time theme displays more than a passing resemblance to Isaac Albéniz's Asturias which was originally written for piano, but is better known in its arrangement for solo guitar. A number of features suggest – though not as strongly as might as full-blown temp-track – that Asturias was certainly an influence on Myers's thinking. In particular, comparisons could be drawn between the constant semiquaver movement over a pedal note, the modal melodic construction and the sudden fortissimo chord stabs that appear later in the piece (Ex. 3.2).[33]

---

31   The Conservatives won 339 seats compared to Labour's 269. The swing to the Conservatives of 5.2 per cent was the largest since 1945. Thatcher's win reflected the intense dissatisfaction with the Labour government as much as an endorsement of Conservative policies, but the desire for change was unequivocal.

32   Cube Records, producer: Stanley Myers (Fly/Fly 5, April 1971).

33   Myers had worked with John Williams on The Deerhunter and may well have been familiar with Williams's own recording of Asturias.

Example 3.1   Stanley Myers, *Question Time*, basic thematic material

Example 3.2   Isaac Albéniz, *Asturias*, opening, guitar transcription

An important sociocultural influence is the fact that international package tourism flourished in the 1970s and 1980s, when millions of middle-class Brits went in search of a fortnight's relaxation on beaches in Benidorm, the Costa del Sol or Mallorca and returned wearing a giant sombrero or carrying a stuffed donkey.[34] Spain was exotic, but not too exotic. As Karen O'Reilly has shown in her ethnographic study of communities living in the south of Spain, expatriates consistently emphasized the idea of 'continuity and change'.[35] They came on holiday, but stayed for the weather and the quality of life. It was just like home – not least because resorts were full of other Brits – but hotter. The use of the guitar in *Question Time* arguably taps into the particularly British obsession with Spain during this period. The popularity of recordings by John Williams and Julian Bream is part of the same cultural movement.

The *Question Time* theme also represents a more 'feminine' mode of scoring than other political programmes of the time such as *Panorama*, another long-running BBC current affairs programme first broadcast in 1953. *Panorama*'s thundering timpani, incisive brass and syncopated patterns epitomize – following Tagg's and Clarida's definitions – a masculine mode of scoring.[36] Myers's *Question Time* theme, then, sits somewhere in between stereotypical representations of masculine and feminine in television music, perhaps because the late 1970s and early 1980s witnessed the appearance of the masculinized woman, particularly in the workplace, where pronounced shoulder-pads and power dressing became commonplace. American television imports such as *Dallas* and *Dynasty* further emphasized this representation. Thatcher herself was mocked for being more masculine than her male cabinet colleagues. The extremely popular satirical puppet programme *Spitting Image*, for example, portrayed her as a fascist hermaphrodite: wearing power suits, using urinals and smoking cigars (see Fig. 3.2).

---

34 Roger Bray and Vladimir Raitz, *Flight to the Sun: The Story of the Holiday Revolution* (London, 2001).

35 Karen O'Reilly, *The British on the Costa del Sol: Transnational Identities and Local Communities* (London, 2000), p. 24.

36 Philip Tagg, 'An Anthropology of Stereotypes in TV Music?', *Swedish Musicological Journal* (1989): 19–42. Available at: <http://www.tagg.org/articles/xpdfs/tvanthro.pdf> (accessed June 2008); Philip Tagg and Bob Clarida, *Ten Little Title Tunes: Towards a Musicology of Mass Media* (New York and Montreal, 2003). This latter work is out of print but is available under a creative commons licence from: <http://www.mediamusicstudies. net/mmmsp/10Titles.html> (accessed June 2008).

Figure 3.2   Margaret Thatcher: the *Spitting Image* representation © Courtesy of Spitting Image Workshop, John Lawrence Jones

The most striking aspect of Myers's manuscript score is that there are significant differences between it and the recorded broadcast version. As far as can be ascertained, this is the only manuscript source in existence (Fig. 3.3).[37] The score is written in Myers's own hand and represents his orchestration, rather than that undertaken by an orchestrator from a sketch. Although they appear in the score, there is no string orchestra, bassoon, flute or harp countermelody, or cadential use of the horn in the broadcast version. The hi-hat plays a steady crotchet pattern and not the semiquaver pattern as it is notated. Furthermore, the entire B section of the ternary form score is not used for the broadcast version.[38] In short, Myers's broadcast music is a significantly pared-down version of the musical material contained within the score.

---

37   The MS is part of the Stanley Myers collection held at the Royal College of Music, London. The materials were donated to the institution by Nicholas Myers (Stanley's son) and consist of 18 A3 boxes of full scores for film and television. There are no parts. Scores are not normally held by television companies, so it is unlikely that further sources exist.

38   The B section appears on the second page of a three-page score and consists of 8 x 4/4 bars plus a 2/4 bar with a repeat.

Figure 3.3   *Question Time*, Stanley Myers, p. 1 of 3. Source: Stanley Myers Archive, Royal College of Music

There are a number of potential reasons for these differences. There is no date on the manuscript score so it is not clear when it was composed. It could be a draft version or might equally represent Myers original concept with budget restrictions or directorial influence resulting in the final pared-down version. Alternatively, the score may have been created for some other purpose, such as a soundtrack CD or for concert performance. Although Myers died in 1993, an album of his film and television music – including the music for *Question Time* – was posthumously released in 2001.[39] However, the arrangement on that CD does not bear a close relation to the manuscript score either. It is possible that Myers took the score into the studio and made alterations or recorded different versions during the session. In current industry practice composers produce extensive demos of their work on digital audio workstations, and the director can hear a detailed mock-up of a cue before a single note is recorded. This was not the case in the late 1970s when Myers's use of technology would have extended to a stopwatch, piano and pencil. The first time the director would have heard the music proper would have been in the recording session itself, leading to potentially greater variance from notated page to recorded artefact.[40] In any case, the manuscript score bears no close relation to any of the existing recorded versions, which raises challenging questions about the value and relevance of such source materials.

Reinvention: Rule Britannia?

It was not until 1990 that Myers's theme was first reinvented, a change that coincides with the arrival of the new prime minister, John Major. In 1989 he had inherited a deeply divided Conservative Party and was unable to prevent the rifts from tearing them apart. Major was mercilessly lampooned in the press, in particular by *Guardian* cartoonist Steve Bell who portrayed him wearing his underpants outside his trousers in an uptight and feeble imitation of superman (Fig. 3.4). Equally, on *Spitting Image*, Major's puppet was literally a grey man (in comparison to the other colourful puppets) who ate dinner with his wife in deathly silence, occasionally saying 'Nice peas, dear'.

---

39   Stanley Myers: *The Deer Hunter and Other Themes* (Milan, 73138-35939-2, 2001).

40   It has also been suggested that the score might have been written originally as a piece of library music which the *Question Time* producers asked Myers to rearrange for their purposes. However, it would seem to be an extraordinary coincidence for the composer to write a piece of library music that just happened to have the same title as a new television programme. This illustrates some of the potential challenges to dealing with source materials The minimal attempts at preservation of film music sources worldwide is a huge failing of the discipline. As Stephen H. Wright observes it may 'well be the largest obstacle to the widespread advancement of film music scholarship': H. Stephen Wright, 'The Materials of Film Music: Their Nature and Accessibility', in Clifford McCarty (ed.), *Film Music 1* (New York, 1989), p. 5

Figure 3.4   Three Cows on My Pants,[41] **Steve Bell, *Guardian*, 20 June 1996.
Reprinted by permission of Steve Bell**

The buttoned-up Britishness Major was perceived to represent was best exemplified by the phrase 'back to basics' which he coined in a speech in 1993 and which was an attempt to revitalize the government after the financial disaster of Black Wednesday.[42] 'Back to basics' was generally understood as a moral campaign

---

41   This is a parody of 'Three Lions' which was the official anthem of the England football team for the 1996 European Championships. The music was written by The Lightning Seeds and the lyrics were penned by comedians Frank Skinner and David Baddiel. The title of the song is derived from the English coat of arms. Steve Bell's reference to 'three cows' mocks Major's handling of the bovine spongiform encephalopathy (BSE) – more commonly known as mad cow disease – crisis. The epidemic was caused by feeding cows the remains of other cattle in the form of meat and bone meal. Nearly 4.5 million cattle were slaughtered in an attempt to eradicate the disease, and the European Commission banned unsafe British beef. In 1996 the link between BSE and variant CJD, the human form of the disease, was publicly acknowledged for the first time. Further cartoons of John Major drawn by Steve Bell can be seen at the British Cartoon Archive which is housed at the University of Kent.

42   Black Wednesday was the name given to 16 September 1992 when the Conservative government was forced to withdraw sterling from the European exchange rate mechanism as it was unable to keep the pound above its agreed lower limit following pressure from foreign exchange traders and speculators. Estimates of the loss to the British taxpayer vary between £3.3 billion and £27 billion.

emphasizing a romanticized, patriotic and innocent view of Britain of the 1950s. Ironically, the basics that most of the Conservative Party seemed to be getting back to involved illegal activities, sexual impropriety and abuses of power.[43] In addition, the party was in the throes of destroying itself over the United Kingdom's relationship with the European Union. It is in this context that the first major reinvention of the *Question Time* music is striking. The wholesome Elgarian musical gestures assert and emphasize a pompous, nationalist pride – a stiff upper lip combined with nostalgia for cucumber sandwiches and tea on the lawn with the vicar. The music represents an image of the nation that the government wished to portray but which increasingly clashed with reality.[44]

The Performing Rights Society records are somewhat unclear, but we can speculate that this reinvention was by BBC Radiophonic Workshop composer Dick Mills.[45] Although the same ♩ = 120 tempo as Myers's original it feels much slower. This is partly because the reinvention is more stately, ostentatious and 'Classical' in approach. The solo guitar has been replaced by piano and busy string countermelodies adorn the semiquaver pattern. In fact, so melodramatic are the countermelodies with constant running parallel 3rds and 6ths that they downgrade the centrality and importance of the semiquaver pattern. The arranger even makes slight alterations to the main theme in order to better accommodate this contrapuntal movement. The anacrusis upbeats have disappeared but are occasionally replaced by glissando flourishes. There is no regular drum pattern driving the arrangement forward. The result is a heavier sound, and the ostentatious music aims to generate an impression of rigorous substance and dramatic magnitude.

This sense of self-importance is also reflected in the revised graphics. Previously, images of the panel members were intercut with simple graphic designs based around the letter Q. In the reinvented version, however, icons representing the economy, justice and a map of the nation are used instead, each embedded within a tall-backed chair. The palm of a hand is used as the symbol for asking a question and acts as the centrepiece of the design. It is surely no coincidence that these graphics and the studio set match the green leather and brown wood panelling of

---

43   These included: Michael Mates's resignation as Northern Ireland Minister over his links with a fugitive tycoon; Tim Yeo's resignation after an extramarital affair resulted in him fathering a love-child with a Tory councillor; Stephen Milligan's death from an autoerotic asphyxiation accident; Neil Hamilton's acceptance of cash for questions; and Jonathan Aitken's procurement of prostitutes for businessmen, and his subsequent conviction and prison sentence for perjury and perverting the course of justice. Even the mild-mannered prime minister himself had an extramarital affair with his environment minister, Edwina Currie, although this was not revealed until after he had left office.

44   That approach is the sort of musical style that was parodied by programmes such as *Little Britain* only ten years later, which used a pompous, expansive theme to mock the idea of British identity as it is presented outwards to the rest of the world.

45   Because the programme's end credits during this period do not list either the composer or arranger, the Performing Rights Society, which collects royalties on behalf of composers, provides one way of identifying who composed a particular work.

the central chamber of the House of Commons. The studio is presented, therefore, as a space of vital national debate equal in importance to parliament.

Reinvention: Cool Britannia?

Tony Blair came to power on 2 May 1997 with a landslide victory. There was a sense of relief that 18 years of Conservative rule had come to an end, and something like a state of euphoria gripped the nation. Throughout the election campaign the D:Ream song 'Things Can Only Get Better' had been used as a New Labour anthem The country was desperate for a change, which Blair embodied. In the early hours of the morning after election day Blair exclaimed, 'A new dawn has broken, has it not?' and his messianic zeal seemed perfectly reasonable. On arrival at Downing Street massive crowds had gathered, and Blair was greeted like a rock star. He exuded optimism and possessed a natural ability to gauge the public mood. Indeed, this is arguably the principal feature of the Blair years. He understood the importance of the media and that controlling it was the key to political success. Blair appointed Alastair Campbell as his director of communications and strategy and he was given wide-ranging power to direct civil servants, even though he was unelected. The management of information and the attempt to provide positive exposure of the government's policies to key stakeholders became a central New Labour focus, and Campbell was frequently referred to by the pejorative term 'spin doctor'. Scholars such as Dominic Wring have referred to this political era as the 'public relations state'.[46] While evaluations of Blair as a parliamentarian differ, he is acknowledged to be a highly skilful media performer, appearing modern, charismatic, informal and articulate. Eric Louw explains that this kind of politician is, in fact, a function of the late 1990s media environment:

> To be pre-selected as a politician now required displaying an understanding of, and willingness to behave in accordance with, the requirements of hyped politics, and to stick to the script provided by impression managers. This has impacted on the political machine's staffing profile, so that it can be argued, televisualization impacts not only upon the hype dimension, but also upon the policy, dimension of the political process.[47]

Rather than the stately graphics of the 1990 version, the 1998 *Question Time* opening title sequence emphasizes action and energy. The focus is no longer on the panel members; instead, the public is centralized with animated faces and vigorous

---

46   Dominic Wring, 'The New Media and the Public Relations State' in Patrick Dunleavy, Richard Heffernan, Phillip Cowley and Colin Hay (eds), *Developments in British Politics 8*, (Basingstoke, 2006), pp. 231–50. See also Nicholas Jones, *Sultans of Spin: Media and the New Labour Government*. (London, 2000).

47   Eric Louw, *The Media and Political Process* (London, 2005), p. 34.

Figure 3.5   Blair with guitar, Frith Park Community College, 13 February 2003.
Reprinted by permission of the Press Association: EMP 1690863

hand gestures. Asking a question, it seems, involves confrontational gesticulation. Here is a population that is passionate and gets things done. The new version of the theme was reinvented by Matthew Strachan, who had previously composed the music for a number of television programmes including the global hit *Who Wants to be a Millionare?*. More than anything, the reinvented music seemed to capture New Labour's personification of a vibrant and energetic Britain. The most striking change is that the tempo is considerably faster at ♩ = 132 with a drum backbeat running throughout. In describing his modifications, Strachan explains: 'The most significant element would have been the electronic rhythm section which I think is what the producers wanted. Ironically, it's the aspect of the arrangement I don't like much.'[48] Strachan's comment suggests that he was pressured by the producers to add the percussive elements as a reflection of contemporary fashion in scoring practice. Furthermore, Strachan's interpretation is that this particular musical feature – in light of Blair's media charisma – was designed specifically to reflect the rise of New Labour. The instrumentation also includes distortion electric guitar, perhaps an allusion to the fact that, in his youth, Blair played guitar in the band Ugly Rumours. In the early phases of Blair's premiership, publicity opportunities

---

48   Matthew Strachan, e-mail to author, 26 March 2007.

highlighting these rock-star credentials were sought time and again (Fig. 3.5). Blair famously held a drinks reception on 30 July 1997 which later became known as the Cool Britannia party. Invited guests included an eclectic mix of pop and rock stars, actors, designers, contemporary artists and businesspeople, most of whom were Labour supporters. The enduring image, widely published in the press, was of the prime minister sipping champagne with anarchic Oasis front-man Noel Gallagher. Cool Britannia summed up a mood of optimism and a renewal of British pride and this is reflected in Strachan's reinvention.[49]

> *They wanted it to sound contemporary, which is the brief given by any TV producer! Essentially I provided a generic, piano-led, current affairs arrangement with a back beat. I think the desire to update the theme on the part of the producers certainly seems to chime with the ascension of New Labour.*[50]

Strachan explains that as part of the scoring process, 'I was given what I guessed was the original arrangement of the tune with the guitar at the centre. I elected to give the melody to piano though it is distinctly unpianistic'.[51] Strachan's reference to Myers's 'original' guitar version is not entirely accurate. In fact he was provided with the 1994 version, which is of unknown origin, although remarkably close to Myers's original. When each arranger is commissioned they receive a recording of the current theme tune from which they generate their own version. The result is rather like the playground game of Chinese whispers; the music mutates with each iteration reflecting the arranger's prioritized listening. Composers react locally rather than longitudinally. Strachan elected to give the main semiquaver melody to the piano yet seemed unaware, for example, that a version with piano as the lead instrument had been created in 1990. A historical perspective is not brought to the task; rather, a reflection of the cultural climate of the moment shapes the scoring process: 'I certainly had a sense of how to make it more in line with current affairs themes which were around at the time – mostly a matter of instrumentation.'[52] Instrumentation here refers as much to the means of production as the sounds sources that are used. Strachan's music is technologically mediated and generated in its entirety on his digital audio workstation. Both the software and hardware used and the collection of samples all define the sound-palette. Indeed, the soundworld – particularly the use of choral samples – bears comparison to that used in *Who Wants to be a Millionaire?* The sound is defined by the technology used and the resources available to the composer at particular points in history. Equally, the use of technology has the effect of dating the work: what seems cutting-edge one year is antiquated the following.

---

49 John Harris, *Britpop! Cool Britannia and the Spectacular Demise of English Rock* (London, 2004).
50 Strachan, e-mail to author, 26 March 2007.
51 Ibid.
52 Ibid.

Reinvention: Dour Britannia?

The most recent reinvention took place in 2006, prior to Gordon Brown's premiership in 2007. An important aspect of the working practice, in contrast to the examples explored thus far, is that the reinvention was undertaken by Mcasso Music Productions, a collective of composers who each produce an individual demo and then work together when the producers have identified the route they wish to pursue, rather like a graphic design company.[53] Mcasso state that they 'work individually and as a team, discussing each project together with the production department to provide clients with a diverse choice of tracks from which a master can be chosen'.[54] It is easy to see how this approach is appealing to television producers, providing them with a greater choice and potential flexibility. Composer Toby Jarvis explains how Mcasso came to be hired:

> Very simply, the Exec Producer of the programme is a friend of mine. They wanted to update the set, the titles and the graphics. I persuaded him to ask me to tender a new 'revamped' version of the music. Four of our composers would each supply a different demo/orchestration from which the client could pick their favourite, and then work up to a master.[55]

The collaborative approach employed by Mcasso challenges the common notion of the solitary *auteur* composer. As Vera John-Steiner observes, the twentieth century was moulded by the 'Western belief in individualism' but 'careful scrutiny of how knowledge is constructed and artistic forms are shaped reveals a different reality'.[56] This buried reality has been consistently undervalued in many disciplines, but particularly so in screen music studies. The concept of creation as a social, rather than individual, process is embedded in the collaborative nature of almost all screen production processes, yet composers have frequently been positioned as individuals with little or no reference to the industrial, political or creative processes that surround them during the making of a film or television programme.[57] This

---

53 The four composers who produced *Question Time* demos were Toby Jarvis, Stuart Hancock, Mike Connaris and Ben Foster. Mcasso Music Productions has since undergone a change in some of their personnel.
54 <http://www.mcasso.com> (accessed April 2007)
55 Toby Jarvis, e-mail to author, 4 April 2007.
56 Vera John-Steiner, *Creative Collaboration* (Oxford, 2000), p. 3.
57 The idea of the *auteur* director has been a consistent preoccupation in film studies since the 1970s. See John Caughie, *Theories of Authorship: A Reader* (London, 1981). Recent writing by Gorbman gives emphasis to *auteur*-ist approaches in film music studies. See Claudia Gorbman, 'Auteur Music' in Daniel Goldmark, Lawrence Kramer and Richard Leppert (eds), *Beyond the Soundtrack* (Berkeley, CA, 2007), pp. 149–62; Claudia Gorbman, 'Ears Wide Open: Kubrick's Music' in Robynn Stilwell and Phil Powrie (eds), *Changing Tunes: The Use of Pre-existing Music in Film* (Aldershot, 2006), pp. 3–18. Jason Toynbee refers to the idea of 'social authorship' throughout *Making Popular Music: Musicians, Creativity and Institutions* (London, 2000).

represents a failure to reflect how creativity interacts with political structures. Researchers often start from a position of supposed objectivity, justified by positivist attitudes and validated knowledge. When production processes are explored, however, different premises frequently present themselves. Radical misunderstandings or disagreements, naivety or prejudice on the part of those who control sight and script, as well as effective or ineffective communication patterns, may reveal more about the nature of screen music than we have been able to identify thus far. Consequently, Mcasso's approach not only highlights deficiencies in the field, but also challenges ideas about the development of musical materials in a collaborative context and how these might differ from more traditional practice. Jarvis explains the collective aesthetic approach to the task:

> *We were given the old title music and old graphic sequence. As everyone knows the music so well, we felt we couldn't rewrite it. Just give it a kick up the backside. It sounded very dated and limp. One of our demos had a violin playing the old piano line. They hated that! We tried to bring some contemporary sounds and beats to it. I wanted it to sound like it had been produced by a contemporary dance band, someone like Faithless.*[58]

It is interesting to note the recurrent focus on the outdated nature of the previous version. Jarvis talks about the 'old piano' line and explains that the collective were provided with the 'old title music and old graphic sequence' as a reference which needed a 'kick up the backside'.[59] The emphasis on the notion of the outmoded, archaic and obsolete seems to be the principal motivating factor in the compositional thought process: 'We wanted people to think how cool the new arrangement was.'[60] Just as with Matthew Strachan's version previously, the intention was to reflect contemporary tastes in the means of production, yet the source for comparison is always the current version not the original material or any of the other previous reinventions.

It is clear that Mcasso agreed ground rules before each composer developed their arrangement. Initially, the central semiquaver thematic material was transcribed: 'The only thing we notated down was the piano part.'[61] As the identifiable brand, Myers's theme was perceived to be fundamental although, interestingly, Jarvis notes that this was not a specific requirement of the production team: 'We were not asked to keep or ditch anything in particular.'[62] The importance of Myers's material seems to rest in the concept of familiarity because Mcasso did not want to 'scare

---

58   Jarvis, e-mail to author, 4 April 2007. Faithless is a British band most famous for the dance songs 'Insomnia' and 'God is a DJ'. Their music frequently blurs the boundaries between different genres, and elements of hip-hop, dance music and contemporary jazz can be heard on many of their records.
59   Jarvis, e-mail to author, 4 April 2007.
60   Ibid.
61   Ibid.
62   Ibid.

people off or alienate the existing audience'.[63] All the demos are at same tempo (♩= 132), in the same key, and have the exact same structure which consists of the full theme and cadential pattern which are then reduced in texture and repeated; finally, a slightly expanded version of the cadential pattern is used as a coda.

The preferred demo was by composer Ben Foster and although it is the dominant component in the final reinvention, elements from the other demos can also be heard. It has 'some great 909 snare fills, and trance like string runs, rushes and dance music references'.[64] Indeed, the most 'contemporary' feature of the final version is the use of sounds that are panned assertively across the stereo field and punctuate gestural phrase endings. The music represents work that is both individual and collective, and the use of technology allows for the detailed, creative interplay between the composers. Jarvis recalls that *Question Time* was 'the first title sequence I've recorded and mixed entirely in Logic'.[65] A digital audio workstation, such as Logic, is a complete project studio software environment for recording, creating, mixing and mastering music. As each composer in Mcasso works with the same software, set-up and resources it is easy to transfer files and musical ideas. While one composer may take the lead, others can pitch in as necessary, providing a fresh pair of ears while mixing, for example. The result is the democratization of the composition process as mediated through technology.

There are two central aspects to the final reinvention. First, the style is updated to sound more contemporary and that style is synonymous with the particular technological means of its production. Yet equally, rather than a development of the musical material, there is a greater emphasis on repetition within the new structure. The memorable cadential pattern is repeated three times and is used to punctuate various moments of structural importance in the presentation of the guests and the audience. The central section of the piece now serves to accompany short, snappy introductions to the guests from the presenter. In previous versions the guests were always introduced separately after the music had finished. Here, the revised structure generates a sense of urgency and immediacy; we are introduced to the protagonists in a tense political drama. In addition, Myers's original semiquaver pattern is often reduced to a simple oscillating minor third functioning like a 'till-ready' bar. The theme is more serious and weighty and, though full of contemporary features, does not have quite the 'pizzazz' of the previous version. It is not as radical. In relation to the current British government the reduction of the thematic material to minor thirds at various points and the recurrent repetition of the cadential mnemonic arguably suggest a form of efficient, no-nonsense politics. Though not as pompous as the 1990 reinvention, it is more solemn than the 1998 version.

At the time of writing it is impossible to predict whether Gordon Brown will continue with a modernizing agenda similar to that which marked Tony Blair's premiership before him. It is interesting to note, however, that press representations

---

63 Ibid.
64 Ibid.
65 Ibid.

of Brown have been consistently marked by attacks on his personality, focusing either on a lack of certainty in his decision-making or concentrating on his perceived sternness, ill-humour and gloominess. For example, the satirical animated television programme *Headcases* – in many ways the successor to *Spitting Image* – represents Brown as a modern-day version of Scrooge from Dickens's *A Christmas Carol* (Fig. 3.6). Instead of 'bah, humbug!' this may be the beginning of a political era that will be referred to a Dour Britannia.[66]

Figure 3.6   Gordon Brown as represented in *Headcases* (ITV) © Headcases/ ITV

Conclusions

While some scholars argue that programmes like *Question Time* do not represent true political activity, I would argue that they are in fact a vital part of how British democracy is articulated in the twenty-first century. *Question Time* is much more than a simple barometer of public opinion; it is a public sphere of discursive interaction that plays a large role in bridging the gap between our unrealized political ideals and our lived social relationships. It is surely no coincidence that reinventions to the *Question Time* theme have occurred, principally, at moments where there is a change of prime minister, where the renewal of leadership provides a clear focus for national concerns and future directions. Indeed, the most striking change to the theme music occurs as the government changes from Conservative to New Labour,

---

66   I am grateful to Tom Service for first suggesting the idea of Dour Britannia.

reflecting the euphoria that accompanied Tony Blair's initial arrival. I do not want to suggest solely that the music mirrors political transfer, but perhaps more contentiously that political change itself is a function of an evolving society that can be represented through its cultural outputs. The aesthetic choices composers and arrangers make are not divorced from the social climate that surrounds them. The musical reinventions are bound to erupt when social, political, cultural and technological fault lines collide. At the time of writing – some 30 years after the first broadcast – a number of transformations have been witnessed: a shift from the individual composer to the collective, from analogue to digital, from 'scored' to 'sequenced', and from the recording studio session to the project studio. In addition, the reinvented theme music has symbolized the changing British political spectrum as represented by its figureheads: Thatcher, Major, Blair and Brown. It is extraordinary that 30 seconds of music can act as a rich repository of meaning that reveals to its audience – the British nation – how it perceives itself.

Televised Live Performance, Looping Technology and the 'Nu Folk': KT Tunstall on *Later ... with Jools Holland*

John Richardson

Mediatized Live Performance and Narratives of Folk-Rock Authenticity

Authenticity in folk and rock genres has long been premised upon what some theorists have called 'the demonization of the visual':[1] by this I mean the idea that the serious business of folk/rock performance should be distinguished from those – commercially sullied – forms that depend on visual reinforcement in order to court a popular following.[2] But there are limits to the disdain of the ocular expressed by

---

[1] Christopher Martin, 'Traditional Criticism of Popular Music and the Making of a Lip-synching Scandal', *Popular Music and Society* 17/4 (1993): 63–81, at 67; Philip Auslander, *Liveness: Performance in a Mediatized Culture* (London, 2nd edn 2008), p. 91.

[2] I hold rock authenticity to be a transformation of folk authenticity, in line with the research since Simon Frith's article '"The Magic That Can Set You Free": The Ideology of Folk and the Myth of the Rock Community' in *Popular Music. Vol. 1: Folk or Popular? Distinctions, Influences, Continuities* (Cambridge, 1981), pp. 159–68. While folk advocated the effacement of the individual and a return to pre-industrial agrarian values, rock aesthetics saw the individual performer as a focus for self-identification in the context of mediatized, industrial society. See also Keir Keightley, 'Reconsidering Rock' in *The Cambridge Companion to Pop and Rock* (Cambridge, 2001), pp. 109–42. It is easy to agree with Theodore Gracyk's insistence, in *Rhythm and Noise: An Aesthetics of Rock* (Durham, NC and London, 1996), that authenticity 'is not on the wane in the rock community' (p. 222). However, his endorsement of Kurt Cobain as the epitome of the authentic rock performer brings into view the extent to which narratives of stardom (and in this case

rock critics. When it comes to authenticating musicianship, the question of liveness is frequently pushed to the fore, an aspect that is reinforced through the principle of 'seeing is believing'.[3] The role played by visual reinforcement is not, of course, new or exclusive to electronic and digital technologies. As long as music has been performed, it has had a corresponding visual component. Moreover, the advent of the recording age did not put an end to this state of affairs. Just how visually codified auditory experience has been throughout the twentieth century, a time when acousmatic listening[4] has prevailed, is apparent from research into consumption practices associated with gramophone records.[5] Furthermore, traces of visual experience are frequently retained in auditory forms including: the placement of musicians in the stereo or multichannel mix; the semiotic encoding of instruments to import spatial effects (horns for wide open space,; an acoustic guitar for intimacy); the spatial qualities of the acoustic environment (as determined by natural acoustics or simulated reverb, delay and compression); and other factors relating to the tactile and visual bases of auditory memory.[6] So, despite the impetus to bury the visual dimensions of auditory experience, whether in deference to rock ideology[7] or with a

---

    martyrdom) impinge upon perceptions of 'the music itself'. Above all, authenticity in rock and other genres is bound up with perceptions of creative agency and authorship, and how these are mediated in different musical and multimedia settings.

3   See Auslander, *Liveness*, p. 85. Whether a performer can 'cut it live' is a question frequently asked in rock criticism and is no longer easily answered. See Andrew Goodwin, 'Sample and Hold: Pop Music in the Digital Age of Reproduction' in Simon Frith and Andrew Goodwin (eds), *On Record: Rock, Pop and the Written Word* (London, 1990), pp. 258–73, at p. 268 for a consideration of how performers, including the Pet Shop Boys, have employed different tactics of legitimation by authenticating their performances more through their actions as *auteurs* rather than through conventional channels.

4   Electronically mediated listening in which the source of the sound is not visible.

5   See Dave Laing, 'A Voice without a Face: Popular Music and the Phonograph in the 1890s', *Popular Music* 10/1 (1991): 1–9 at 7–8; Jonathan Sterne, *The Audible Past: Cultural Origins of Sound Reproduction* (Durham, NC, 2003), pp. 215–33; and Andrew Goodwin, *Dancing in the Distraction Factory: Music, Television and Popular Culture* (London, 1993), p. 8.

6   For example, Auslander, *Liveness*, p. 85; Peter Doyle, *Echo & Reverb: Fabricating Space in Popular Music Recording, 1900–1960* (Middletown, CT, 2005); Evan Eisenberg, *The Recording Angel: Music, Records and Culture from Aristotle to Zappa* (New Haven, CT, 2005), p. 53; John Richardson, '"The Digital Won't Let Me Go": Constructions of the Virtual and the Real in Gorillaz' "Clint Eastwood"', *Journal of Popular Music Studies* 17/1 (2005): 1–29, at 15–17; Denis Smalley, 'Space-Form and the Acousmatic Image', *Organised Sound* 12/1 (April 2007): 35–58; Philip Tagg and Bob Clarida, *Ten Little Title Tunes: Towards a Musicology of Mass Media* (New York and Montreal, 2003), pp. 217–70.

7   Lawrence Grossberg, 'The Media Economy of Rock Culture: Cinema, Post-Modernity and Authenticity', in Simon Frith, Andrew Goodwin and Lawrence Grossberg (eds), *Sound & Vision: The Music Video Reader* (London, 1993), pp. 185–209, at pp. 204–205; Gracyk, *Rhythm and Noise*, pp. 75–79.

view to debunking bourgeois spectacle,[8] the visual has a tendency to resurface, much like the Freudian unconscious and with analogous affective implications. Contrary to the prevailing theoretical bias, this need not be understood to be an intrinsically bad thing. Like Kay Dickinson, I am distrustful of 'theoretical assumptions [concerning 'the political ordering of perception'] that tend only to recognize unitary, fenced in modalities'[9] – a theoretical line that stretches back at least as far as Eisenstein in audiovisual theory and Hanslick, in music theory, and which has been invoked in much of the subsequent twentieth-century writing.

The visual authentication of performers is inscribed in the format of BBC television's *Later ... with Jools Holland* (henceforth *Later*), a programme that continues the legacy of shows such as *The Old Grey Whistle Test* (1971–87) and *The Tube* (1982–87). In its advocacy of live performance, programming of this type has, for some time, stood in opposition to the widespread use of playback on *Top of the Pops* (1964–2006) as well as the prerecorded audiovisual 'distractions' of music video channels.[10] The role of Holland himself in the series is symptomatic; a virtuoso boogie-woogie and blues-style pianist, the compere of the show regularly proves his credentials as a live performer and thereby asserts his authority to front the show, in cameo appearances with top performers. Recently, the status of television programming that endorses live (rock) musicianship has nevertheless been eclipsed somewhat due to the popularity of the – highly commodified and tightly formatted – Idol franchise, as well as other 'reality' programming. The popularity of such shows could be attributed in part to their incursions into rock territory through an emphasis on live performance, just as rock values have been eroded at the other end of the spectrum through an increased willingness to flirt with visual spectacle among rock artists, from Pink Floyd to the Arctic Monkeys – albeit ironically in the case of the latter. And yet, these might be considered exceptions that continue to prove the rule; recognized pop acts known for their showmanship, including Robbie Williams and the Scissor Sisters, are still inclined to tone down their performances when appearing on *Later*, while rock acts have long been inclined to introduce an element of parody into their lip-synching and miming when appearing on *TOTP*.[11] Perhaps the truth of the matter is that greater pressures are being brought to bear on artists across the pop–rock divide to prove their mettle in the live arena, a matter that is certainly highlighted in KT Tunstall's debut appearance on *Later*.

---

8   Theodor W. Adorno, *Introduction to the Sociology of Music*, trans. E.B. Ashton (New York, 1976), pp. 81–84; also Guy Debord, *Society of the Spectacle* (London, 2004).

9   Kay Dickinson, 'Music Video and Synaesthesic Possibility' in Roger Beebe and Jason Middleton (eds), *Medium Cool: Music Videos from Soundies to Cellphones* (Durham, NC, 2007), pp. 13–29, at p. 15.

10   Cf. Goodwin, *Dancing in the Music Factory*.

11   For a comprehensive list of spoofing practices on (and of) TOTP, see the relevant Wikipedia site: <http://en.wikipedia.org/wiki/Top_of_the_Pops> (accessed 19 June 2008). The introduction of the *Later* spin-off show, *Later Live*, in 2008, could be understood as an attempt to reclaim the initiative from reality shows in live television programming.

Tunstall's metier is live performance, a point she has made relentlessly in interviews. And yet, as Theodore Gracyk has noted, the primary activity for many contemporary recording artists is not live performance but, rather, the labour undertaken in the studio beforehand.[12] Moreover there is often a sense of 'remediation' to stage performances of rock, which can easily be perceived as reworkings of recordings produced for consumption in different formats and media – such as CD, compressed audio (MP3, AAC) or music video.[13] What happens, one might ask, when the very act of remediation is spotlighted through the incorporation of multitrack recording techniques in live performance in a way that inscribes the musician's performativity? This question, I will argue, goes to the heart of Tunstall's breakthrough performance of 'Black Horse and the Cherry Tree' on *Later*, televised by the BBC on 22 October, 2004 (later released on the DVD, *Best of Later ... with Jools Holland: 2000–2006*). The choice of this performance is justified because it encapsulates, with uncommon lucidity, a cluster of issues that have come to a head in recent popular culture, relating to the changing nature of live television, the cultural meanings ascribed to repetitive music and the interface of digital technology with creativity in emerging audiovisual forms.

KT Tunstall and 'Black Horse and the Cherry Tree'

Tunstall appeared on *Later* only because of a last-minute cancellation by the rap artist Nas. Prior to this she was a virtually unknown aspiring 'nu-folk' performer performing in small venues to a scattering of enthusiasts. Some indication of the perceived strength of the *Later* performance can be surmised from the immediacy of its impact on her career. Tunstall surpassed established acts like The Cure and Jackson Browne in the popularity poll for the episode posted on the show's website, winning over half of the votes.[14] Her debut album, *Eye to the Telescope* (2004), was quickly released just over a month later with the newly popular 'Black Horse and the Cherry Tree' appended to it, whereafter it jumped to number 7 in the UK charts before peaking at number 3.[15] In the months that followed Tunstall was engaged for similar solo spots on the French live music programme, *Taratata* (on 12 May 2005)[16] and several North American talk shows, as well as headlining at Glastonbury. The pinnacle of exposure for Tunstall's music, if not the artist herself, came when *American Idol* contestant Katharine McPhee covered 'Black Horse' in

---

12   Gracyk, *Rhythm and Noise*, pp. 69–98.

13   Jay Bolter and Richard Grusin, 'Remediation', *Configurations* 3 (1996): 311–58 define 'remediation' as 'the representation of one medium in another' (p. 339). See also Auslander, *Liveness*, pp. 6–7.

14   Fiona Shepherd, 'Live and Proud', *The Scotsman*, 11 June 2005 at: <http://news.scotsman. com/kttunstall/Live--proud.2634231.jp> (accessed 19 June 2008).

15   Editorial, <http://acharts.us/album/14298> (accessed 20 June 2008).

16   See <http://video.mytaratata.com/search/?q=KT+Tunstall> (accessed 30 June 2008).

the final of the 2006 season, which resulted in a quantifiable peak in record sales.[17] This is ironic in light of Tunstall's scathing criticism of the show, which is consistent with outspoken comments on a range of issues, including the influence of the mass media, environmentalism and performers she does not wish to be compared to – including Dido and Katie Melua.[18] A conspicuous thread running though all this commentary is her stalwart commitment to the ethos of 'liveness' as it has been understood in folk-rock ideology.

Technology figured prominently in Tunstall's performances around this time. Prior to the *Later* appearance, she had completed a three-month solo tour of small venues where she beefed up her live sound using one of a new generation of digital looping pedals, the Akai E2 Headrush, which allows the simulation of multitracking studio techniques in 'real time'.[19] A further rationale for its inclusion in her live act was the simple fact that she could not afford a supporting band.[20] Several folk artists at the time were experimenting with looping technology, including Howie Day, David Ford and Foy Vance, and it is possible that Tunstall took inspiration from one or more of these musicians.[21] The fact that she refers to the Akai Headrush as 'Wee Bastard' opens up intriguing avenues for interpretative inquiry, along with the songwriter's self-description as 'a robbing gypsy bastard'.[22] Setting aside the

---

17   Chris Rolls, 'KT Tunstall: Slightly More Esoteric' at: <http://www.mp3.com/news/stories/10018.html> (accessed 19 June 2008).

18   'Tunstall apologies to Dido' at: <http://www.contactmusic.com/new/xmlfeed.nsf/mndwebpages/tunstall%20apologies%20to%20dido> (accessed 19 June 2008. Following unfavourable reactions to her comment, 'Dido can't fucking sing', Tunstall made the following retraction: 'I was slightly ashamed the other day, I responded in a very virile manner. It just sometimes gets very frustrating, particularly when it comes to playing live, because that is my domain. If there is one thing I can blow my own trumpet about it's that I can let rip at a live show'. See also the editorial, 'Tunstall Hates Melua Comparison'at: <http://www.contactmusic.com/news.nsf/article/tunstall%20hates%20melua%20comparison_1041625> (accessed 19 June 2008).

19   Chris Rolls, 'KT Tunstall: Slightly More Esoteric'. The Akai E2 Headrush, used by Tunstall in 'Black Horse' is one of a new generation of devices that features this functionality. The pedal is no longer in production and has been surpassed in its specifications by the Digitech Jamman and the Boss RC-20 Loop Station. Other songs performed by Tunstall with the pedal include The Jackson Five's classic hit 'I Want You Back', Tunstall's own 'Stoppin' the Love', Bob Dylan's 'Tangled Up in Blue' and Missy Elliot's 'Get Ur Freak On'.

20   Quoted in 'KT Tunstall: Refusing To Be "The Suicidal Girl With A Guitar"', *UltimateGuitar.com*, 6 November 2007 at: <http://www.ultimate-guitar.com/interviews/interviews/kt_tunstall_refusing_to_be_the_suicidal_girl_with_a_guitar.html> (accessed 23 June 2008).

21   Another artist to employ live looping on *Later* was the French singer Camille in the song 'Au Port', televised on 12 May 2006.

22   Sylvia Patterson, 'I'm a Robbing Gypsy Bastard' (KT Tunstall interview), *The Word* 37 (March 2006): 74–78, at 76 and 78. In a similar vein she describes herself in the same interview as 'a magpie' and one of a group of 'folk tart[s]' who use 'folk music as a bed – and then sleep[s] with other things' (ibid., p. 75).

potentially offensive stereotyping in this statement (which I do not underwrite), it is evident that Tunstall identifies with the pedal.[23] Herself an adopted child of mixed Scottish, Irish and Cantonese descent, through statements such as these she projects a road-hardened nomadic identity on to the mechanical apparatus that facilitates her performances, which in turn reflects back on to musical production. Of particular interest in this respect is contemplating how her use of digital looping technology and, more generally, her approach to songwriting might be informed by self-perceptions of this nature.

Tunstall's work is bound to other performers of her time, primarily though her interest in looping. Narrowing the focus further, it is easy to recognize an affinity with musicians associated with the label 'folktronica', a catch-all for all manner of artists who have combined mechanical dance beats with elements of acoustic rock or folk, such as Múm, David Gray, Tunng, The Books, Björk and the Blue Nile. Productive though the category may be, Tunstall's music is something of a square peg in relation to this round whole. Her reliance on traditional blues-based forms in tandem with the catchy guitar-pop side of her musical identity clearly set her apart from those working in more marginal aesthetic places. Her uses of looping in solo live performances produce similar sonic end-results, however, to those of some of her more experimental musical peers, and it is this aspect that I will focus on here.

Looping the Loop – Performing Control

Early shots of the *Later* performance capture the solitary figure of Tunstall stooping over the looping pedal while immersed in the labour of setting down the song's initial groove. Such a level of focused concentration is necessary as inaccuracies in timing can lead to a flawed underlying groove that will repeat embarrassingly throughout the duration of the song.[24] A distinctive feature of this performance is the attention the singer-songwriter pays to laying down a complex multipart groove. The ratio is somewhat different in other performances of 'Black Horse' in which Tunstall plays five verses. In the *Later* version there are only three; consequently, more than half of the song (bars 1–26 and 61–79 plus DVD timings can be extrapolated from Fig. 4.1) is taken up with the piecemeal construction, abrupt dissolution and reconstitution of the arrangement in audible processes that

---

23   In one interview, she comments, 'I have this theory that I can name and blame. ... Often, I press the wrong button to record stuff, and I just thought if I called it something derogatory that people would assume that it was because it was temperamental, not me': 'KT Tunstall: Refusing To Be "The Suicidal Girl With A Guitar"'.

24   In her performance of 'I Want You Back' on the French live music show *Taratata*, Tunstall was distracted by the audience clapping along with the beat and was forced to scrap her first attempt at setting up a groove.

resemble those found in musical minimalism.[25] In addition, a family resemblance to contemporaneous forms such as electronic dance music (EDM), remix practices and gaming music is likely to inform many listeners' experiences.[26]

Extraordinary about this mode of performance is the level of introversion required on the part of the performer. Consequently, the viewer becomes privy to processes of assembly that are usually conducted in private, rather than in the presence of a studio audience and television cameras. This aura of privacy is accentuated when a Steadicam-mounted camera encircles Tunstall, during the 'turnaround' chord sequence of the song's chorus, which engenders a tangible sense of intrusion. Only in those sections that are sung and where no new loops are introduced does the performer engage with the audience more directly, although even here she makes a conspicuous show of multitasking by stomping a tambourine with her left foot while her right remains free to control the looping pedal. Contrary to the received wisdom on looping and other repetitive practices, which portrays them as 'passive' and, when sampling is involved, 'parasitical', the evidence of this television footage points towards a heightening of agency through the performer's immersion in the act of composition, which is compounded by the fact that her role overlaps with that of the studio engineer. For this reason I consider the gerundive form 'looping' to be a more accurate descriptor of her activity than the noun 'loop'. The loop, in this instance, must be looped: the musical sample does not simply repeat; Tunstall must *repeat it*.[27] Further, the process of looping must be visually authenticated if agency is to be correctly assigned.

In the song's initial moments, Tunstall lays down a brisk 'um pa' beat with repeated soundboard hits on the acoustic guitar (bars 1–4). This pattern is quickly embellished with dampened rhythmic chopping, which establishes a skeletal groove for the verses (bars 5–8). The resulting pattern is recognizable as the 'hambone' (or Bo Diddley) rhythm, with its New Orleans-styled syncopations pulling against the first two beats prior to two emphatic unsyncopated accents.[28] An element of bluesy

25 John Richardson, *Singing Archaeology: Philip Glass's* Akhnaten (Hanover, NH, 1999); K. Robert Schwarz, 'Steve Reich: Music as a Gradual Process, Part 1'. *Perspectives of New Music* 19 (1981): 374–92; Dan Warburton, 'A Working Terminology for Minimal Music', *Intégral* 2 (1988): 135–59; Robert Fink, *Repeating Ourselves: American Minimalism as Cultural Practice* (Berkeley, CA, 2005).

26 Luis-Manuel Garcia, 'On and On: Repetition as Process and Pleasure in Electronic Dance Music', *Music Theory Online* 11/4 (2005), sections 1.1–7.4 at: <http://www.societymusictheory.org/mto/issues/mto.05.11.4/mto.05.11.4.garcia.html>; Stan Hawkins, 'Feel the Beat Come Down: House Music as Rhetoric' in Allan Moore (ed.), *Analyzing Popular Music* (Cambridge, 2003), pp. 80–102; Karen Collins, 'An Introduction to the Participatory and Non-linear Aspects of Video Games Audio' in John Richardson and Stan Hawkins (eds), *Essays on Sound and Vision* (Helsinki, 2007), pp. 263–98.

27 See Garcia, 'On and On', 3.9; also Christopher Small, *Musicking: The Meanings of Performing and Listening* (Hanover, NH, 1998).

28 On the history of the Bo Diddley beat, see Charles Keil and Steven Feld, *Music Grooves* (Chicago, 1994), pp. 104–106. It is possible to hear Tunstall's signifying on the beat as one in a line of 'mechanical participatory discrepancies' of the pattern that characterizes

soul enters the picture with the incremental addition of catchy woo-hoo accents, the 'hoos' falling on the downbeat – the 'woo' upbeat and the trailing melodic line spelling out the singer's blues credentials through vocal 'smears' on the third and seventh degrees. The first such loop, centred on the E minor tonic, is lent percussive edge by strident handclapping, a gesture designed to evince a response from the studio audience (bars 9–14). The second reinforces the first through harmonizing on the third (bars 15–17). With the song's basic groove in place, the accompaniment is filled out by the addition of live acoustic guitar. Some initial riffing high up the neck of the instrument precedes a dramatic downward slide in search of a resounding open-position E minor chord (bars 23–26). It is as if this chord cues the beginning of the performance proper, although the setting of the musical stage that has gone on beforehand is only nominally secondary to 'the song'.

David Brackett has addressed the sensory and symbolic significance of the open E chord in folk-rock styles in a probing discussion of Elvis Costello's 'It's Time'.[29] For Brackett, the use of the instrument's open strings in this chord and coincidences in its pitch organization with the overtone series are factors contributing to the unique power and resonance it is felt to have. In the context of folk-rock composition, he further argues that the 'sonic emblem' of the open E (in his discussion, E major) has mostly been exploited by singer-songwriters from the mid-1960s, the cultural affiliations evinced by this gesture effectively marking off such 'magic moments' from perceived African-American influences. In 'Black Horse' the articulation of this gesture, or something resembling it, is characteristically celebratory and resounding, an affective conditioning that the presence of the minor third does little to dispel. Undoubtedly, Tustall's jaunty oscillation between minor tonic and dominant seventh chords, both in resonant open-position voicings and striking up a spirited Bo Diddley beat, contributes to the euphoric charge of the song's opening dispatches (bars 27–30). The overriding affective message Brackett distils from earlier instances of the gesture is one of 'defiance, strength and resolution', often 'in the face of adversity, yearning [and] sneering',[30] a reading that resonates with Tunstall's performance.

An important difference between this usage and those covered in Brackett's discussion lies in the evocation of blues tradition through the use of the open G string (instead of the stopped G♯ of the major chord) in combination with the sung 'blues third'. If these techniques seem sufficient to indicate an overriding sense of 'African-American' parentage, a caveat or two should be noted. First, this is a minor blues, a form with a more flexible identity than its major counterpart due to its popularity in jazz. Second, while the song indisputably relies on blues-based (therefore African-American) expressive tropes, these come secondhand via the mediating hand of the British blues revival, as strains of Fleetwood Mac's 'Oh Well' and Led Zeppelin's 'Black Dog' are perceptibly woven into Tunstall's

---

the post-disco and boom box era.

29   David Brackett, 'Elvis Costello, The Empire of the E Chord, and a Magic Moment or Two', *Popular Music* 24/3 (2005): 357–67.

30   Ibid., p. 362.

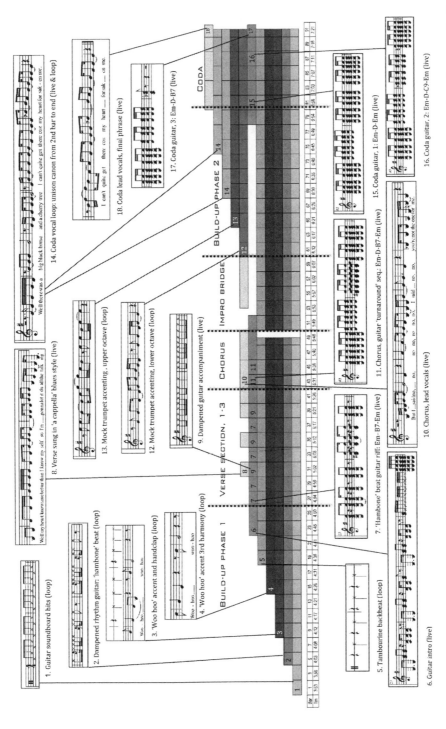

Figure 4.1 KT Tunstall's 'Black Horse and the Cherry Tree' on *Later … with Jools Holland*: transcription showing the organization of tracks and loops

call-and-response alternation of densely worded *a cappella* and instrumental phrases (bars 29–40).

Tunstall is an accomplished blues-rock vocalist, her gravely and improvisatory style ticking all the right boxes for the 'edgier' female performer working within these genres. Moreover, her ability to 'deliver the goods' by recording near-perfect overdubs in real time speaks to her professionalism and, at the same time, reinforces narratives of authenticity that have long been a part of blues-based and folk-rock idioms. What might seem tangential to these 'purely musical' considerations is the way these assumptions, as well as Tunstall's generic and geographical positioning, are reinscribed in the filming of the performance. Notably, the camera seems to dwell for an inordinate amount of time on veteran black soul singer Anita Baker's responses to Tunstall's blues-inflected vocals – a shot that coincides with the most impressive vocal layering in the song. As Goodwin has noted, the presence of black musicians or audiences was often used in early music videos to authenticate white performers.[31] On this evidence, the representation of black pleasure as a marker of authenticity is as potent a gesture as it was in the heady early days of music videos. Before rushing to judgement, though, it should be borne in mind that reaction shots such as this are integral to the format of *Later*, the appreciation of fellow musicians speaking above all to constructions of authenticity that purport to transcend divisions by race, gender or generation. The choice of reaction shots and how they coincide with the structures of the music does, however, underscore an aspect of aesthetic 'profiling' that is complicated in this context in a corresponding shot shown a moment later. Here indie-rock approbation is bestowed upon Tunstall by a group shot of the British guitar band Embrace, whose responses to the performance coincide with the dramatic second entry of the acoustic guitar, culminating on the resonant open E chord, with all of its 'invocations of bohemian discourses around alternative practices of accreditation'.[32] Thus, Tunstall's performance is authenticated visually on two fronts: in the approval she receives from a seasoned soul singer and in terms of the 'cool factor' garnered through association with members of the alt-rock establishment. This would mean very little were it not underscored by music that draws on codes established on both sides of the Atlantic and which is characterized by a fundamental duality (almost a schism) between the style of performance, which is 'traditional', and the way it is organized, which could be considered 'progressive' or 'experimental'.

The chorus (bars 43–49) is a timely reminder of Tustall's investment in the mainstream. It employs an energetic four-measure turnaround that might sound stereotyped in other circumstances. The i–♭VII–V7 sequence repeats several times before terminating on an accented ♭VI7 chord, a typical feature of minor blues. Insistent 'no, no, no' exhortations in the vocals add little in the way of narrative substance, serving primarily as a foil to the already established groove.

An emphasis on musical construction returns following an abrupt one-bar *tacet* in all the looped instruments, which above all evidences Tunstall's control over the

---

31   Goodwin, *Dancing in the Distraction Factory*, p. 116; also Auslander, *Liveness*, p. 113.
32   Brackett, 'Elvis Costello', p. 362.

technological parameters of her performance (see Fig. 4.1, bar 50). This dramatic solution is typical of loop-based forms, from electronic dance music to minimalism, and is a way of toying with listeners' expectations,[33] as is what follows – a second accumulation of instrumental capital culminating in the presence of no fewer than 11 simultaneous tracks (see Ex. 4.1). The accumulative process resumes with the recording of a two-part mock-trumpet fill, performed vocally in parallel octaves, thus reinforcing the kinetic impact of the rhythmic phrasing as well as defusing some of the seriousness of the performer's introspective actions (bars 61–68). The song's bravura move occurs shortly afterwards as Tunstall crafts one of the song's most memorable vocal lines into a four-bar loop ('Big black horse and a cherry tree / I can't quite get there coz my heart's forsaken me'), before superimposing over this a unison canon of the same phrase, offset by two bars (see Fig. 4.1, bars 65–76). This musical gesture, which would not be out of place in a Bach fugue or a process composition by Steve Reich, serves as further evidence of the performer's control over the performance situation, both in terms of her ability to 'cut it live' and to mix or 'DJ' it live. The impact of this sonic accumulation is strengthened by the dramatic reinstatement of the acoustic guitar in an elaboration of the earlier chord sequences that now incorporates the denser sonority of C9 (bars 87–91). Tunstall jams over this vocally for several cycles before dovetailing with the looped vocals in the very last phrase, which leads to a sudden cessation of all of the loops and the cheeky *a cappella* line 'my heart forsaken me' (see Ex. 4.1).

Notwithstanding the folk-revivalist aspects of Tunstall's performances and the cultural capital she procures through investment in this tradition, what is most remarkable about this mode of performance is the performer's ability to capture 'takes' from her own performances in real time and reorganize these into larger forms that resemble those found in differently accredited musical genres. Mark Spicer has illuminatingly researched the technological foundations to the proliferation of 'accumulative forms' in pop-rock styles, showing how changes in technologies, from the early days of multitrack recording in the 1960s to the use of sequencers and drum machines in the 1980s, channelled the compositional possibilities available to pop-rock musicians in hitherto unforeseen ways.[34] Significantly, the new tools permitted the same musician to lay down overdubs with a high degree of precision and reproducibility from one take to the next, opening up new expressive pathways that would mark the music as distinctive to its time. Similar forms had existed before, such as the characteristic 'terraced instrumentation' of much Baroque music or thematic techniques employed by North American composer Charles Ives, but not with the same combination of sounds and formal precision as would be afforded by the new technologies.[35]

This sense of the term 'accumulative form' is consistent with the nomenclature used in reference to early minimalist music. One of the founding figures of

---

33   See Hawkins, 'Feel the Beat Come Down', p. 91.

34   Mark Spicer, '(Ac)cumulative Form in Pop-Rock Music', *Twentieth-Century Music*,1/1 (2004): 29–64.

35   Ibid., p. 29.

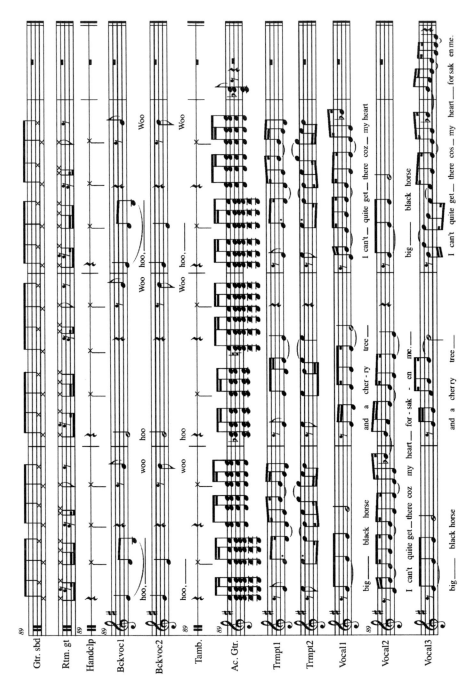

Example 4.1   Transcription of last four bars of the *Later* performance of 'Black Horse': in its final moments the song features as many as 11 overlaid tracks

minimalism, Terry Riley, described the technique of running tapes between two recorders in his early compositions, 'Mescalin Mix' (1960) and 'Music for the Gift' (1963), as 'accumulative technique' and 'time-lag accumulation'.[36] This approach, which characterizes Riley's work at the San Francisco Tape Music Centre in the early 1960s, would provide the inspiration for his early minimalist output constructed around repeated musical cells, including the seminal 'In C' (1964). Riley's looping techniques directly inspired Steve Reich to undertake similar tape-loop experiments in 'It's Gonna Rain' (1965) and 'Come Out' (1966), experiences with two out-of-sync tape recorders helping this composer to develop his trademark phase-shifting technique. Accumulative form aptly describes the processes at work in the two 'build-up' sections of 'Black Horse'. Nevertheless, I consider it unlikely that early minimalist experiments with analogue looping technology directly influenced Tunstall's approach.[37]

The interest of a growing number of folk artists in mechanized dance rhythms and looping practices indicates a possibly more productive line of inquiry, as do Tunstall's comments concerning the hybridized and stylistically 'promiscuous' foundations of her approach. Tunstall is no stranger to the attractions of the dance floor, as is perhaps best illustrated by her tendency to produce 'electrofolk' covers of disco and contemporary dance tracks in live performances, including the Jackson Five's 'I Want You Back', Chaka Khan's 'Ain't Nobody' and Missy Elliott's 'Get Ur Freak On'. It is instructive, therefore, to look towards writing on contemporary dance genres in order to learn more about the pleasurable foundations of her approach. Luis-Manuel Garcia's research on repetition in EDM offers a useful window onto the pleasurable foundations of looping in 'Black Horse'.[38] Drawing on the psychoanalysis of Karl Bühler, Garcia proposes a three-point model of repetition that counters the prevailing Freudian emphasis on regression and compulsion with the more positively coded categories of satiation pleasure, process pleasure, and the pleasure of creative mastery. Key to his analysis of EDM are the last two categories, process pleasure referring to an artist's immersion in the moment-by-moment constitution of the work in accumulative tasks, 'creative mastery' referring to the sense of accomplishment the accumulative technique engenders as expansive sonic edifices are compiled from humble material origins.

The distinctive process-based pleasures of loop-based forms are deftly realized in the accumulation of loops in the build-up sections of 'Black Horse', Tunstall's overlaying of parts defying expectations of what is possible for a 'folk singer', or

---

36   Quoted in Thom Holmes, *Electronic and Experimental Music: Technology, Music and Culture* (New York, 3rd edn 2008), p. 132.

37   The idea of indirect influence is plausible when one considers the number of popular artists who have drawn on the musical language of minimalism, including Mike Oldfield, Pete Townsend, Brian Eno, Suzanne Vega, David Bowie, and The Orb.

38   Garcia, 'On and On'. Unfortunately, the usefulness of Garcia's approach is limited by his dismissal of what he terms reflection theories, a factor that causes him to view sonic production in EDM looping practices in isolation from technologies in related artistic forms, not to mention the entirety of contemporary media culture.

anyone for that matter, in the context of live performance. Her repetitive but – in terms of the combinatory effect of the song's layers – constantly changing approach (even between performances, as Tunstall rarely configures her loops identically) redirects attention towards the sensory qualities of the sounds in a way that is equally true of minimalist music or EDM. At the same time, listeners' expectations are rewarded or confounded as the groove is pieced together bit by bit (the digital implications of this expression are intentional), eventually achieving an orchestral tapestry of textures – an electro-acoustic 'wall of sound' – that belies the modest instrumental means available to the performer.

'Suddenly I See': Exhibiting Mastery – Parodying Production

The idea of pleasure in creative mastery is also pertinent when it comes to evaluating Tunstall's live persona. Without question, what is at stake here is an exhibition of the performer's mastery over the performance situation in a way that challenges expectations. In the past, it might have sufficed for multi-instrumentalist 'authors' of popular music composition (from Mike Oldfield to Prince) to assemble the fruits of their creative labour in private by meticulously overdubbing parts in the studio, the concealment of these activities in the private sphere adding an aura of seriousness and mystery to the artist's achievements. Some musicians have adapted their studio overdubbing practices for 'live authentication' by moving between different instruments in rapid succession when performing on stage. Stevie Wonder is one such performer, an element of wonder in his musicianship being amplified by his visual impairment combined with the fact that he has to be guided around the stage. Roy Castle perhaps best exemplifies a vaudevillian strain within such practices in a performance for the 1970s television programme *Record Breakers*, in which the intrepid presenter played as many as 43 instruments within the span of a four-minute song. Tunstall is not averse to this brand of showmanship, as can be seen in her second *Later* performance, where she switches from electric guitar and vocals to drums in the final moments of 'Suddenly I See', a gesture that could be perceived as overdetermined and gimmicky in its insistence on telescoping the performer's agency. In the *Later* performance of 'Black Horse', Tunstall brings the folk concept of the one-(wo)man band to bear on this set of practices in such a way as to demystify prevailing assumptions about musical production and its economic foundations – the idea that overdubbing is a time-consuming, expensive and ultimately invisible process. Here she achieves comparable (if not perhaps as enduring) artistic end-results to those of some of her pop-rock composer/author precursors, in real time and with the sole assistance of her relatively inexpensive 'Wee Bastard' looping pedal.

I have noted above how 'Black Horse' bears a family resemblance to tape loop experiments conducted in San Francisco in the early 1960s. In terms of its theatrical slant, Tunstall's performance also coincides with the interest of Fluxus artists in performance, manifested above all in a refusal to separate private and public activities, as well as through the incorporation of technologies and the bodies operating them as constitutive of the aesthetic encounter.[39] Experimental music of all stripes is commonly thought to be exclusively about 'the music', a view that was not accepted by one of its leading exponents: 'Theatre is all around us', John Cage has commented, 'and it has always hung around music – if only you let you attention be "distracted" from the sounds'.[40] Visual 'distractions' in the performances of Fluxus composers Cage and Riley commonly included the technological means of musical (re)production, such as radios and tape machines, just as the visual identification of such means is integral to Tunstall's performance.

Tunstall undeniably possesses a keen sense of performative occasion, which may owe something to her training in Music and Drama at the University of London's Royal Holloway College. A question that might be asked is to what extent these priorities conflict with those raised above concerning the demonization (or suppression) of the visual as a linchpin of folk-rock credibility. There are intimations of this in *The Word* magazine's characterization of Tunstall as 'mainstream folk-rock pin-up',[41] her reduction to the status of glamour icon an ever-present danger for female artists in a marketplace dominated by traditional values. But it is a danger the performer apparently embraces, given the extravagant mode of self-presentation she has adopted at least since her third album, *Drastic Fantastic* (2007), the visual iconography of which gives a wide berth to traditional folk values; while the title of its immediate predecessor, *Acoustic Extravaganza* (2006), is oxymoronic to upholders of folk-rock semantics because of the obvious staginess of the concept 'extravaganza'.

Tunstall's conspicuous use of technology might be understood as an extension of her theatrical propensities. Electronic technology has, of course, long been a sticking-point for folk artists, at least since Dylan 'went electric' at the Newport Folk Festival of 1965. Like Dylan's electrification, looping in 'Black Horse' embodies, *while it signifies*, one of the dominant cultural forms of our age, an approach that is at odds with traditional folk aesthetics, which tends to idealize pre-industrial technologies. More pressingly, Tunstall's practices draw attention to themselves through an element of performativity that contaminates the audiovisual contract. As Robert Wechsler has noted, a big part of the attraction of technological media in live performance lies in the 'how'd-they-do-it?' factor, which causes spectators to focus attention on how the previously unseen (and unheard) was achieved, thereby pushing the media itself to the fore.[42] Auslander reiterates this point by arguing that

---

39 See Rose Lee Goldberg, *Performance Art: From Futurism to the Present* (London, 1988), pp. 123–38.

40 Michael Nyman, *Experimental Music: Cage and Beyond* (Cambridge, 2nd edn 1974), p. 22.

41 Joe Muggs, 'The Family That Plays Together', *The Word* 63 (May 2008): 50–51, at 50.

42 Robert Wechsler, 'Artistic Considerations in the Use of Motion-Tracking with Live Performers: A Practical Guide' in Susan Broadhurst and Josephine Machon (eds), *Performance and Technology: Practices of Virtual Embodiment and Interactivity* (Basingstoke, 2006), pp. 60–77.

the current fascination with technologically mediated spectacle and novelty derails artistic communication through a failure to attend either to expressive content or deconstructive intent.[43] Undoubtedly some spectators of the *Later* performance will privilege the novelty factor by concentrating on how the multitracking effect was achieved technically. It remains a matter of contention, though, to what degree this 'distracted' mode of apprehension can be thought to monopolize spectators' consciousness.

Arguably, what rises to the surface here is not the technological apparatus of the performance *as such* but Tunstall's mastery over it. In a sense, she becomes a present-day counterpart to the mythological figure of Echo, while going beyond the conventional passive role ascribed to this figure through the sheer force of her personality combined with her impressive 'remixing' abilities.[44] By this I mean that she takes existing musical elements that might be considered 'cheesy' or 'clichéd' in difference sonic contexts (a classic 'turnaround' chord sequence, a Bo Diddley rhythm, a half-remembered melody from Peter Green and so on.[45]), and incorporates them as building-blocks in musical processes that underwrite a different temporal logic than that which has prevailed in the dominant forms of Western music since the Renaissance.[46] Without wanting to downplay Tunstall's musical abilities, it is how she handles these 'raw materials' in her use of looping that allows her to make some of her most original and compelling artistic statements. Of course, this notion of 'originality' has undergone considerable revision since the dawn of the digital age. As Mark Katz suggests, sampling practices in the digital era are only coarsely described in terms of technological 'quotation'; sampling – and by implication, its temporal reproduction in looping – is, in his view, 'most fundamentally an art of *transformation*'.[47]

Tunstall's aesthetic of 'robbing' and 'stealing' is something she shares with countless current artists. This works well for her in the context of live performance, although questions have been raised about how convincing she is as a studio artist. Tunstall's LPs gravitate towards a reiteration of classical values, raising questions about how dependent her creative work is on visual authentication. In live performance, we have seen, she remediates existing forms and is therefore able to comment, on some level ironically, on the dominant cultural practices of our time.

---

43   Auslander, *Liveness*, p. 41. Marshall McLuhan made a similar point several decades earlier when stating that fascination with technological gadgetry could be regarded as an (alienated) extension of the human nervous system that leads irrevocably to experiences of 'numbness': *Understanding Media* (London and New York, 1964), pp. 95–121.

44   See Doyle, *Echo and Reverb*, p. 40.

45   Other 'derivative elements' include a name that resembles that of PJ Harvey and combinations of chord sequences and sounds on her latest album (*Drastic Fantastic*) that come conspicuously close to songs by David Gray and the Undertones.

46   See Philip Tagg, 'From Refrain to Rave: The Decline of Figure and the Rise of Ground', *Popular Music* 13/2 (1994): 209–22, at 219.

47   Mark Katz, *Capturing Sound: How Technology Has Changed Music* (Berkeley, CA, 2004), p. 156 (original emphasis).

Her recorded music has been perceived as doing nothing more than to reiterate the tried and trusted formulas of popular music – in other words, she is perceived as being *too transparent*. A contrast might be drawn between her recorded work and that of recording artists such as Gnarls Barkley, compromising the rapper/vocalist Cee-Lo Green (Thomas Callaway) and renowned multi-instrumentalist/producer Danger Mouse (Brian Burton). Positioned alongside musical arrangements whose technological estrangement points towards a twenty-first-century pop-remix aesthetic, Brown's traditional and frenzied soul-styled vocals are made to rebound in unexpected ways against listeners' expectations. The same might be said of media icon Amy Winehouse's collaborative work with producer Mark Ronson, this duo's lucrative retro-aesthetic to some degree reconditioning existing forms – albeit while reinforcing stereotypes and tropes of authenticity concerning the troubled pop diva.

A useful light is cast on Tunstall's looping practices by comparing them to those in experimental film. Jaimey Hamilton writes on how the phenomenal effects of repeated spectacle can affect our understanding of the mediated self.[48] For this writer, video loops in works by Bruce Nauman, Nam June Paik and Paul Pfeiffer, provide a continual oscillation that encourages the viewer to contemplate how similar images function at large in mediated society. In this way looped forms serve as eddies in the media flow of contemporary life, whose deleterious influence has been recognized in writing from Williams (1974) to Debord (2004).[49] By diverting attention temporarily away from ubiquitous narratives of progress and productivity, and the relentless flow of the media towards smaller units of encapsulated time that inhabit the media, Hamilton argues that looping practices can unleash considerable transformative potential.

Undoubtedly some of this potential is harnessed in Tunstall's *Later* performance, not every aspect of which is 'revisionist' or deserving of critical endorsement. Unquestionably, though, Tunstall's performance resonates with contemporary experience, offering a model of sorts for coming to terms with new technologies, of the struggle to assert agency in an increasingly prefigured world, and the ability to concentrate on the unfolding moment in unlikely material circumstances. Much could be said, of course, about how the format of (recorded) live television favours artists with Tunstall's theatrical leanings, and how the contradictions inherent in her approach are less flatteringly manifested in different formats and media. In this performance, though, she might be said to have succeeded in rewriting at least part of the script for her mythological precursor, Echo.

---

48 Jaimey Hamilton, 'The Way We Loop "Now": Eddying in the Flows of Media', *Invisible Culture: An Electronic Journal for Visual Culture* 8 (2004): 1–24.

49 Raymond Williams, *Television: Technology and Cultural Form* (London, 1974), pp. 77–120; Debord, *Society of the Spectacle*, pp. 86–92.

PART 2
Technology and Studio Production

Learning to Listen to Perfect Sound: Hi-fi Culture and Changes in Modes of Listening, 1950–80

Alf Björnberg

Introduction

One recurring strand in twentieth-century musical–cultural critique concerns the effects of the technicalization of music on listening behaviour, listener attitudes and modes of listening. Among the more well-known examples, Adorno's typology and critique of modes of listening may be mentioned.[1] His arguments, and those of other scholars in the same vein, have often been criticized for their strong normative aspect; however, such critique has tended to obscure some important insights into processes of change affecting music-listening as a result of technicalization and mediaization – the latter term referring to the processes whereby 'a form of music is changed in different ways and adapted to the media system'.[2] The insight that technologies of sound reproduction and media systems have deeply affected processes of production, distribution and reception of music since the late nineteenth century is, of course, not new. The last two decades have witnessed a growing body of literature dealing with the history of sound-reproduction technology not just from a technological perspective, but also from economic, social and cultural perspectives. It seems, however, that accounts of phenomenological aspects of the reception of mediaized music – how people have listened to recorded and broadcast music and conceptualized what they heard – are still somewhat underrepresented in this body of literature.

---

1   See, for example, Theodor W. Adorno, 'On the Fetish Character in Music and the Regression of Listening', *The Culture Industry: Selected Essays on Mass Culture* (London, 1991), pp. 26–52.

2   Dan Lundberg, Krister Malm and Owe Ronström, *Music, Media, Multiculture: Changing Musicscapes* (Stockholm, 2003), p. 68.

Arguably, these processes of change were particularly rapid in the decades around the mid-twentieth-century, due both to technological innovations in the field of sound reproduction, such as the tape recorder, the microgroove record, FM radio, transistor technology and the stereo record, as well as developments within amplifier and loudspeaker design and contemporaneous changes in musical style, music industry organization and the social organization of listening to music. Timothy Taylor has written of what he terms the 'technoscientific imaginary' of the post-war decades, and, in my material also, a strong valorization of technical progress per se appears to be prominently present, particularly in the 1950s and 1960s.[3] Thus, the purpose of this chapter is to study the interaction of technological innovation and modes of listening to music in post-Second World War society from the introduction of hi-fi around 1950 to the introduction of digital audio technology in the early 1980s. This interaction affects popular music as well as 'classical' art music, albeit in differential ways, and the chapter aims to demonstrate how the nature of the processes identified in the analysis varies according to musical genre.

Empirical data will be taken from Sweden, where the concept of high fidelity was introduced around 1954, and gathered from various sources – primarily periodicals in the fields of music and/or technology – displaying different strands of an evolving discourse around hi-fi, music and listening. The restriction to a Swedish context is mainly based on pragmatic considerations having to do with access to source material; however, to my knowledge, the developments identified in a Swedish context may well be fairly representative of general trends affecting large parts of the industrialized world during this period, although the details of these developments may vary from one country to another.

Listening, Truth to the Original and Transparency of the Medium

The relationship between changes in sound-reproduction technology and changes in listening behaviour is often conceptualized as a one-way process, with technological developments, as it were, 'producing' new ways of listening. However, Jonathan Sterne has argued that historically the evolvement of concentrated and directed modes of listening – what he terms 'audile technique' – preceded the development of sound-reproduction technology rather than the other way around. These listening modes were developed in conjunction with early-nineteenth-century technologies, such as the stethoscope and the telegraph, and then transferred to the realm of sound reproduction later in the century:

---

3   Timothy D. Taylor, *Strange Sounds: Music, Technology and Culture* (New York, 2001), pp. 43f.

*The techniques of listening that became widespread with the diffusion of the
telephone, the phonograph, and the radio early in the twentieth century were
themselves transposed and elaborated from techniques of listening developed
elsewhere in middle-class culture over the course of the nineteenth century.
… The growth of the early sound-reproduction technologies would be better
characterized as further disseminating previously localized practices than as
'revolutionizing' hearing as such.*[4]

Thus, these new listening techniques were originally mastered only by small
minorities of professional specialists – physicians and telegraph operators – and
their dissemination to wider strands of Western society occurred with the spread of
sound-reproduction technology – a technology which has most prominently been
used since the early twentieth century for the dissemination of music.

Sterne's analysis constitutes a useful corrective to the technological determinism
which often characterizes accounts of media history. At the same time, it also raises
further questions, such as the question of at what rate these practices disseminate
to different layers of society and at what point in time they may be characterized
as 'predominant' within a particular society as a whole. Further, a comparative
perspective appears useful for investigating the problem of the extent to which
the urban US middle-class practices analysed by Sterne are representative of
industrialized Western societies in general. Looking specifically at the situation
in Sweden, the general media-historical development throughout the twentieth
century seems to be rather typical of an industrialized Western country: phonograph
culture was introduced in the 1890s, public-service broadcasting started in the
mid-1920s, and the late 1920s witnessed a short-lived 'gramophone boom',
interrupted by the economic recession of the 1930s. Nevertheless, it seems that
important developments towards a widespread application of specific modes of
listening to mediaized music did not take place until the decades immediately
succeeding the end of the Second World War, in conjunction with the evolvement of
'hi-fi culture'. Although by 1950 gramophone technology was already more than a
half-century old, it could be argued that 'high fidelity' in important senses constituted
a 'new medium': the discourses evolving around it indicate that this technology
was accompanied by profound changes in listening techniques, an increasing
problematization of the act of listening to technologically reproduced music and
changes affecting the way in which relationships between live and reproduced
music – between 'original' and 'copy' – were perceived and construed.[5]

As indicated by the term 'high fidelity', central to these relationships is the
notion of 'fidelity', of 'truth to the original'. Sterne has positioned this notion within
a 'philosophy of mediation':

---

4   Jonathan Sterne, *The Audible Past: Cultural Origins of Sound Reproduction* (Durham, NC,
     2003), p. 90, p. 154.

5   Cf. the definition provided by Sterne: 'A medium is a recurring set of contingent social
     relations and social practices … the social basis that allows a set of technologies to stand
     out as a unified thing with clearly defined functions': ibid., p. 182.

> *Conventional accounts of sound fidelity often invite us to think of reproduced sound as a mediation of 'live' sounds, such as face-to-face speech or musical performance, either extending them or debasing them in the process. Within a philosophy of mediation, sound fidelity offers a kind of gold standard: it is the measure of sound-reproduction technologies' products against a fictitious external reality. From this perspective, the technology enabling the reproduction of sound thus mediates because it conditions the possibility of reproduction, but, ideally, it is supposed to be a 'vanishing' mediator – rendering the relation as transparent, as if it were not there.[6]*

As indicated in this quotation, truth to the original is often described in terms of a 'transparency' of the medium: when the medium is transparent, the technology of reproduction leaves no audible trace in the reproduced sound, rendering the reproduction phenomenologically equal to the 'natural' sound of live music. In Sterne's analysis, the simple notion of transparent mediation, of fidelity in the sense of perfect similarity to an original, unmediated sound, is problematized: 'fidelity' is also a matter of 'faith in the technology', a sort of contract between the listener and the technology, whereby the former invests a commitment towards the belief in the capacities of the latter to reproduce the original so faithfully that it could be mistaken for the original:

> *Sound fidelity is much more about faith in the social function and organization of machines than it is about the relation of a sound to its 'source'.[7]*

Sterne cites various testimonies to the perfection of early sound-reproduction technology – judgements which, from today's perspective, may appear rather incomprehensible – and his conclusion is that 'after 1878, every age has its own perfect fidelity'.[8] The criteria for fulfilling the ideal of transparency and fidelity are thus highly historically contingent and relative. Still – or rather, precisely because of this – the tropes of transparency, 'truth to life' and the interchangeability of reproduced music with unmediated music are persistently present in the discourses surrounding sound-reproduction technology throughout its entire history. This is also the case in the period covered in this study.

I have found it useful to utilize the trope of transparency also in a slightly different but related sense: in the practical everyday handling of music technology, it appears that this technology and the associated practices gradually assume a 'natural', unremarkable character as a 'transparent' element of normal, everyday social practice. As Friedrich Kittler has written, '[t]echnological media turn magic

---

6   Ibid., p. 218.
7   Ibid., p. 219. Also cf. Rudolph Lothar's 1924 essay on 'the capacity for illusion' necessary to allow a transparent mode of listening to reproduced sound, quoted in Friedrich A. Kittler, *Gramophone, Film, Typewriter* (Stanford, CA, 1999), pp. 45f.
8   Sterne, *The Audible Past*, p. 222.

into a daily routine'.[9] In interaction with other music-related practices, such transparentization processes may be expected to affect cultural conceptions of what constitutes and characterizes 'music' in general.

Swedish Hi-fi Culture in the 1950s–70s

The breakthrough of the concept of high fidelity in Sweden seems to have taken place rather suddenly in 1954, when several periodicals start referring to 'high fidelity' or 'hi-fi'. These are not the first instances of the use of this term in Swedish: the earliest example I have come across appears in a newspaper ad from 1943, advertising '"high-fidelity" radio'. The term does not seem to have had any wider currency before 1954 – for instance, it does not appear in a 1950 article on 'the gramophone revolution' of the microgroove vinyl record.[10] In 1954, however, references to high fidelity appear in several contexts. In a news item announcing the forming of the Swedish Long-Play Club in the spring of that year, it is mentioned that '[h]igh fidelity was one of the most often recurring words on the occasions when the club managed to meet during spring'.[11] Hi-fi is presented as a US innovation: it is mentioned that 'the Americans have launched a concept which they call High Fidelity'.[12] It is coupled with another media–technological innovation, the television, in an ironic comment on 'all the great hubbub surrounding television and the so-called Hi-Fi systems'.[13] A few years later the breakthrough is summed up in retrospective:

> High Fidelity is a relatively new concept for true-to-the-original sound reproduction, accomplished by means of special technical arrangements. Nevertheless, Hi-Fi has had an explosive development. In America, sales have increased nearly sevenfold from 1954 to 1957 inclusive.[14]

The hi-fi development in Sweden in the 1950s does not, however, seem to have been that 'explosive' in comparison with the situation in the USA.[15] On the basis of the evolvement of hi-fi discourse and its forums, the period dealt with here may

---

9   Kittler, *Gramophone*, pp. 35f.; also cf. Taylor, *Strange Sounds*, p. 206. For a discussion of transparency in connection with sound-on-sound recording see Alf Björnberg, 'Probing the Reception History of Recording Media: A Case Study', *Papers from CHARM Symposium 1*, 2005 at: <http://www.charm.rhul.ac.uk/content/events/s1Bjornberg.pdf> (accessed 1 October 2005.)

10   *Teknik för alla*, 19 (1950).

11   *Musikrevy*, 5 (1954).

12   *Estrad*, 11 (1954).

13   *Teknik för alla*, 24 (1954).

14   *Estrad*, 2 (1958).

15   On 1950s hi-fi culture in the US, see Keir Keightley, '"Turn it Down!" She Shrieked: Gender, Domestic Space, and High Fidelity, 1948–59', *Popular Music* 15/2 (1996): 149–77.

be divided into three distinct phases, roughly coinciding with the 1950s, 1960s and 1970s, respectively, and the first of these phases is one of a rather tentative build-up of a new technologically-based minority culture, albeit one with a prominent position within the 'technoscientific imaginary'.

There are no specialized periodicals dedicated to hi-fi or sound-reproduction technology in Sweden in the 1950s, but hi-fi is nevertheless discussed in several different contexts: the 'engineer' discourse of the general technological hobbyist, the 'classical connoisseur' discourse of the art-music listener and the 'fan' discourse of the jazz/popular-music listener. Each of these groups has at its disposal one or a couple of periodical publications, and although these target groups are – in all probability at least to a considerable extent – separate, the discourses represented in these periodicals are strikingly similar: in all these contexts, technological matters, as well as issues of musical aesthetics and modes of listening, are discussed.[16] Also, the hobbyist do-it-yourself ethos of early hi-fi culture, although most prominent in tech-hobby circles, is noticeable in all three contexts – for instance, when the art-music journal mentions 'the nice spare-time pursuit of building yourself a hi-fi amplifier from the rather splendid and not at all hard-to-grasp construction kits which exist'.[17]

The beginning of the second phase in the development of Swedish hi-fi culture, the 1960s, was marked by the emergence in 1960 of a specialized magazine in the field of hi-fi, *Musik och ljudteknik* ('Music and Sound Technology'). By this time Swedish hi-fi discourse was increasingly aimed at an 'audiophile' readership of hi-fi enthusiasts and experts. This was a rather specialized minority concern; the magazine was published jointly by the Swedish LP Club and the Swedish Magnetophone Club, which merged in 1964 to form *Ljudtekniska sällskapet* (The Society for Sound Technology), and it was thus a small speciality publication, emphasizing professional knowledge and authority.[18] Simultaneously, however, hi-fi formed the basis of a growing consumer culture, contrasting with, and gradually outstripping, the do-it-yourself ethos of the 1950s. A commercial hi-fi fair was arranged for the first time in Sweden in 1963 and thereafter recurred annually. In the audiophile magazine a certain frustration may be discerned over the perceived discrepancy between this expanding consumer culture and the lack of demand for the expertise which the magazine could provide:

---

16   These groups are represented in my material by the fortnightly magazine *Teknik för alla* ('Technics for All'), the eight-issues-a-year journal *Musikrevy* ('Music Revue') and the monthly magazine *Estrad* ('Bandstand'), respectively.

17   *Musikrevy*, 7 (1959).

18   The aims and activities of the Magnetophone Club appear to have been rather similar to those of its Dutch counterpart, the Dutch Society of Sound Hunters, of which a detailed account is presented in Karin Bijsterveld, '"What Do I Do with My Tape Recorder … ?": Sound Hunting and the Sounds of Everyday Dutch Life in the 1950s and 1960s', *Historical Journal of Film, Radio and Television* 24/4 (2004): 613–34.

The interest in 'High Fidelity' and sound technology is growing each year; a growing number of people are getting themselves better equipment. We believe that a large number of these would derive considerable benefit from The Society for Sound Technology – and not least Musik och ljudteknik![19]

Now, the basis for Musik och ljudteknik isn't very extensive ... The areas covered in these columns may be expected in a probably rather near future to interest far more people than is now the case.[20]

The 'near future' did not, however, bring an increase of this magazine's readership. Instead, the beginning of the third phase in Swedish hi-fi-culture history was marked by the launching, in 1970, of a commercial monthly magazine aimed both at a wider public of hi-fi consumers and at audiophile experts and entitled *Stereo-Hifi*.[21] In the first issues of the magazine, the view that the time was ripe for a publication of this kind was supported by arguments turning on the rapid increase in sales of audio equipment in the years around 1970:

Now the first speciality magazine for hi-fi is a fact. Hi-fi and stereo are becoming everyman's property and the sales increase is over 50 per cent per year. In 1969 we in Sweden bought approx. 100 million kronors' worth of sound gadgets, and interest seems to be steadily increasing.[22]

If the 1960s brought the major breakthrough for television and photography, one can with great certainty predict that the 1970s will be the decade of good sound.[23]

Stereo-Hifi remained the predominant periodical in the field throughout the 1970s, a decade characterized by a continuous expansion, technologically and economically, in the domain of sound reproduction.

In the following, I will analyse and discuss some important themes discernible in Swedish hi-fi discourse during the period under study. Some of these themes are present throughout the entire period, while others have a shorter currency. The aim of the analysis is to give a coherent picture of important changes in the way the relationships of music, technology and listening are conceptualized in the course of the evolvement of hi-fi culture.

---

19   *Musik och ljudteknik*, 1 (1965).
20   Ibid.
21   The name was changed in 1976 to *Hifi & musik*; the magazine is still published (2008).
22   *Stereo-Hifi*, 1 (1970).
23   *Stereo-Hifi*, 3 (1971).

The Ideal of Transparent Mediation

As already hinted at above, the 'philosophy of mediation' is prominently present in the discourse on sound-reproduction technology throughout the period studied here. At the time of the rather spectacular breakthrough of hi-fi in 1954, 'truth to life' – the Swedish equivalent literally translates into 'truth to nature' – is repeatedly invoked as a criterion and measure for the quality of sound-reproduction equipment:

> ... the highest possible truth to life in the recording and reproduction of music.[24]

> With a well-designed Hi-Fi system, reproduction becomes so perfectly lifelike that even the most sensitive musical ear is incapable of deciding whether a piece of music is played directly by an orchestra or played back by some electronic equipment.[25]

> Instrumental timbre is free, bright and transparent ... a naturalness in reproduction which produces a correct balance of sound ...[26]

> Hi-Fi, the perfect sound ...[27]

One recurrent rhetorical device used to emphasize the transparency of mediation is the trope of transport: the fidelity of sound reproduction is characterized as sufficient to give the listener an experience of being transported to the location of the musicians or vice versa:

> ... one can rejoice over the recording studio practically being moved into one's own room – so much the music comes alive ...[28]

> The reproduction of LP records is so lifelike that you have an illusion of the orchestra being in the same room.[29]

In 1958, with the advent of the stereo LP record, stereophonic sound reproduction enjoyed a major breakthrough similar to the one of hi-fi four years previously. Although prerecorded stereo tapes had been available on the Swedish market for a couple of years, tape-based stereo never became more than a very

---

24   *Estrad*, 11 (1954).
25   *Teknik för alla*, 3 (1955).
26   *Musikrevy*, 4 (1956).
27   *Teknik för alla*, 22 (1956).
28   *Estrad*, 3 (1955).
29   *Teknik för alla*, 8 (1956).

minor phenomenon due to the high prices of recorders and tapes.[30] Hi-fi and stereo were thus introduced on separate occasions but rather close in time, which renders a comparison of the statements articulated in the respective contexts instructive. To a considerable extent, at the broad-scale introduction of stereo in 1958, the same superlatives adduced over the previous years in connection with hi-fi are repeated once more. In particular, stereo provides an additional impetus to the trope of transport:

> *... a more correct and uncompromising sound reproduction ... possibilities to experience the acoustics of the concert hall and the atmosphere of the opera-house auditorium in a way which hasn't been possible before.*[31]

> *The illusion of being in the concert hall or at the jazz concert becomes perfect with the stereo record.*[32]

> *One is almost physically transported back to the original studio, concert hall or whatever room the sound has been recorded in.*[33]

It may be observed that some of these writers refer to the recording studio as the location of the 'original' sound. On the one hand, it may have been questionable how many contemporary readers would have any opinion of what the music would sound like in the recording studio; on the other hand, this may be taken as an indication of a growing awareness of the fact that a 'natural' concert situation would not necessarily be the obvious 'original' context for any recorded music.

After about 1960 the most panegyrical assessments of the transparency of mediation are gradually toned down. As already hinted at, however, appeals to the lifelikeness of reproduced sound continue to be present in hi-fi discourse throughout the period under study, although with an increasing number of qualifications and reservations. I will return below to later traces of the discourse of transparency.

Ear Training and Habituation

Although hi-fi sound is characterized as 'perfect' right from the introduction of the concept, there is also an awareness of the need for 'ear training' – that is, a purposeful training of the ability to listen to reproduced sound in order to develop sensitivity to distinctions in quality of sound and to the degree of fidelity to the original. Assertions to this effect appear already in the first phase of hi-fi culture and may be found throughout the period. This appears to be a characteristic

---

30   On the use of prerecorded stereo tapes see *Musikrevy*, 4 (1956); *Estrad*, 10 (1958).
31   *Musikrevy*, 7 (1959).
32   *Teknik för alla*, 18 (1958).
33   *Estrad*, 10 (1958).

clearly distinguishing hi-fi listening from earlier listening practices, judging from statements such as the following from the early 1950s – that is, from the pre-hi-fi period:

> Distortion in higher frequencies may come up to 10 per cent, but this can probably only be perceived by a small number of trained ears ...[34]

> When one listens to music it is rather difficult to determine how strong the distortion is, owing to the fact that one recognizes the character of the melody and follows it automatically.[35]

Advice from 'expert' writers in the 1950s often takes the form of rather patronizing normative views as to the 'proper' mode of listening to reproduced music. Statements of this kind may have a bearing on various aspects of the listening situation; some express opinions on the correct handling of sound reproduction technology:

> ... the frequency range is specified as 50–10,000 c/s. In order not to let this fine frequency graph be destroyed by persons who like so-called soft sound, the tone control has sensibly enough been eliminated.[36]

> It is impossible to believe beforehand that the difference can be so huge between different ways of reproducing sound. ... You will find that you hitherto have listened to mechanical music in a totally erroneous way ...[37]

> Train the ear correctly from the start![38]

> The most common by far is for people to listen 'darkly' ... Why not try to correct such an unsatisfactory state of things? ... try to handle the tone controls with discrimination ...[39]

Other statements concern the proper listening attitude which the authors consider necessary to do full justice to the music:

> Then you should relax, sit still and comfortably and listen relaxedly like at an ordinary concert. Concentration should be directed towards hearing stereo music as an artistic experience rather than exploring acoustic or technical

---

34   Review of a wire recorder in *Teknik för alla*, 3 (1950).
35   *Teknik för alla*, 4 (1951).
36   *Teknik för alla*, 19 (1952).
37   *Estrad*, 10 (1955).
38   *Estrad*, 1 (1957).
39   *Skivspegeln*, 9 (1959).

details. ... Stereo should be enjoyed in small doses and may give its owner good opportunities for putting together programmes for home concerts.[40]

The last quotation is rather representative of the attitude towards technologized listening in 1950s classical-music discourse, but similar attitudes may also be found in the expanding hi-fi consumer culture of the 1970s:

... in order for the musical experience not to become merely the sum of the details, an active effort by the listener is required. He [sic] should be interested and devoted, enter into moods and emotional trajectories, analyse logical connections if he likes to, make findings, observations and interpretations.[41]

The rapid pace at which the quality of sound-reproduction equipment was perceived to improve in the 1950s and 1960s might be expected to produce a rising level of expectations among listeners. Some statements indicating such increasing expectations may be found:

In this age of the grand loudspeaker sound, when we have become used to increasingly voluminous and timbrally qualified sounds, we have in some respects reached a kind of sound barrier, which cannot be stretched any further out of consideration for our own, the family's and the neighbours' auditory nerves.[42]

... the price has to be paid for the intensified musical contact. Sensitivity has increased, as well as the demands for perfection in the equipment. ... Hyper-sensitivity has engendered an entirely new basis for evaluation.[43]

However, there are also clear indications of tendencies towards habituation – that is, listeners having become used to a particular quality of sound, so that they do not necessarily accept technological improvements as such. As Sterne points out, 'listeners do not always or automatically understand improved technical specifications as resulting in "better" sound'.[44] In this situation, the expert writers in the periodicals often assume the role of advocates of progress, attempting to persuade the readership to endure the process of rehabituation necessary for the appreciation of new and, at least in technical terms, better equipment:

---

40   *Musikrevy*, 7 (1959).
41   *Stereo-Hifi*, 2 (1970).
42   *Musikrevy*, 7 (1959).
43   Ibid.
44   Sterne, *The Audible Past*, p. 277.

Maybe you yourself have difficulties perceiving any substantial difference, as new components are added one by one. This may be due to the critical faculty of the ear having become blunt and in need of a brushing-up.[45]

One so easily accustoms oneself to a piece of equipment, that a new acquisition often may give an impression of lesser quality.[46]

... don't count on being convinced of the advantages of the new reproduction after just one performance. One can have become so accustomed to coloured sunglasses that the colour range of the environment appears unnatural when one temporarily removes them.[47]

When your ears have accustomed themselves to the new sound, you cannot understand how you could content yourself with the old one.[48]

One attempted remedy for this unsatisfactory state of affairs was organized forms of listener training: in 1960, the Music-Historical Society in Stockholm started arranging 'gramophone concerts', and towards the end of the 1960s there are reports of hi-fi retailers arranging 'stereo-hi-fi concerts' for potential customers.[49] With the growth of hi-fi consumer culture, however, the value of technical specifications is gradually further relativized, as the scope for subjective evaluation of hi-fi equipment grows and genre-specific evaluation criteria are developed. I will return to these matters below.

Hi-fi, Domestic Space and Gender

A recurring theme in hi-fi discourse throughout the period under study concerns the problem of adapting increasingly bulky hi-fi equipment to existing standards of interior decoration and furnishing. 'Can one with reasonable demands for comfort place one's hi-fi system in the living room and also achieve a placing which does the audio capabilities of the equipment full justice?', a commentator asks rhetorically in 1959, and in 1970 another writer claims that '[t]he old radiogram was a piece of horror furniture but in its way more furnishing-friendly than most things on offer today'.[50] This is one of the realms where the gendered nature of hi-fi stands out most clearly. As William H. Kenney has demonstrated, early sound-reproduction

---

45   *Estrad*, 5 (1957).
46   *Teknik för alla*, 23 (1958).
47   *Skivspegeln*, 9 (1959).
48   *Estrad*, 5 (1959).
49   *Musik och ljudteknik*, 2 (1960); *Stereo-Hifi*, 1 (1971).
50   *Musikrevy*, 7 (1959); *Stereo-Hifi*, 3 (1970).

technology tended to be associated with a female rather than male sphere.[51] By the 1950s, however, hi-fi is a distinctly male domain. In his analysis of US hi-fi culture in the 1950s, Keir Keightley gives a picture of often strikingly antagonistic gender conflicts over domestic space associated with hi-fi.[52] In the Swedish context, this is contrasted by a considerably more low-key, although still clearly discernible, opposition between male-gendered hi-fi and female-gendered concerns for interior decoration:

> *The greatest resistance raised primarily by wives towards the acquisition of a system for high-quality sound reproduction is usually based on two recurrent arguments: 1) loudspeakers are ugly and too bulky for modern flats and 2) high-class loudspeakers are disproportionately expensive.*[53]

More extensive discussions of this problem are rare, however; rather, its existence is indicated by passing comments on the relation of loudspeaker placement to 'the mistress of the house' or references to 'housewife-friendly' mini-loudspeakers. However, advertisements tend to be rather more explicit than editorial material in relation to gender issues:

> *Make your wife happy with an extra loudspeaker in the kitchen and the rest of the family with a loudspeaker in the bedroom or some other space.*[54]

By the 1970s the growing consumer culture provides examples of some rather blatantly sexist attitudes in advertisements, such as loudspeakers advertised with a picture of a nude woman, accompanied by the caption 'The naked sweet sound'. In contrast, editorial material displays some tendencies towards a more conciliatory ambition to involve women, perceived as underrepresented in hi-fi culture, on an equal footing:

> *Why is the fair half of the population so rarely represented in the LTS [The Society for Sound Technology]? If we are writing too technically, ask Eve to take up her pen – that would be welcome!*[55]

In 1976 an editorial in *Stereo-Hifi* states that 'it is my experience that women often have a healthy and reality-based judgement when sound quality is concerned'.[56] This statement is not very representative, however; it is written by Kjell Stensson, the 'grand old man' of sound engineering in Sweden, one of the very few sound

---

51 William H. Kenney, *Recorded Music in American Life: The Phonograph and Popular Memory, 1890–1945* (New York, 1999), ch. 5.
52 Keightley, '"Turn it Down!"', pp. 149ff.; also cf. Taylor, *Strange Sounds*, pp. 78ff.
53 *Musik och ljudteknik*, 3 (1960).
54 Retailer advertisement in *Teknik för alla*, 26 (1957).
55 *Musik och ljudteknik*, 1 (1970).
56 *Stereo-Hifi*, 12 (1976).

engineers to have acquired the status of a public figure, and by this time someone with an exceptional licence for expressing controversial opinions.

The Privatization of Listening

Rather than emphasizing gender conflicts over the control of domestic space, discussions of the problems of hi-fi listening in a Swedish context tend to focus on the risk of 'disturbing the neighbours'. This is a reflection of typical housing conditions, since the majority of the population in the 1950s and 1960s lived in blocks of flats.

> ... one should preferably live without neighbours or have at one's disposal an environment of a tolerant and hardy kind in order to make the most of all the resources which exist.[57]

> It [a loudspeaker reviewed] can handle an output of six watts, which you seldom have the opportunity to use in a flat without the neighbours starting to take part in the concert with various poundings.[58]

One solution to this problem perceived to lie close at hand was listening through headphones:

> Headphone listening has a future before itself in our miserably soundproofed flats.[59]

> To achieve good dynamics one should also have a certain minimum of volume, but this is often not feasible due to protests from neighbours and one's own environment. One way out is then to use good headphones.[60]

The rather pragmatic attitude to the problem of the social maintenance of sound pollution expressed in these statements is given a further dimension in Evan Eisenberg's comment on headphone listening:

> ... living in the present is (contrary to vulgar opinion) nearly impossible in a modern city, which always hungers for the future and eats its past. One reason for the vogue of headphones among city dwellers is the sense they give that one has escaped the city's voracity, because one is inside the music.[61]

---

57   *Estrad*, 10 (1956).
58   *Estrad*, 5 (1959).
59   *Musik och ljudteknik*, 1 (1965).
60   *Musik och ljudteknik*, 4 (1970).
61   Evan Eisenberg, *The Recording Angel: The Experience of Music from Aristotle to Zappa*

In Eisenberg's account, this fits in with a wider argument about listening to technologically reproduced music as the 'ceremonies of a solitary', an inherently solipsistic activity carried out in isolation from the social environment.[62] This argument has been criticized by Kenney, who points to the social qualities historically characterizing much technologized music listening.[63] Sterne, on the other hand, emphasizes the role of the privatization of listening in the process of commodification of reproduced sound:

> The construct of a private, individual acoustic space is especially important för commodifying sound-reproduction technologies and sound itself since commodity exchange presupposes private property.[64]

Rather than committing oneself to one or the other of these positions, it appears reasonable to conclude that a number of social, economic and psychological factors have contributed to these processes of increased privatization of listening to reproduced sound. In the hi-fi period of rapid technological developments, technology is perceived not only to aggravate previously existing problems – potentially intensifying conflicts over volume levels – but also to enable new solutions to them. In my source material, discussions may be found of both the social and aesthetic consequences of headphone listening for the listening experience:

> Stereophony is the superior stimulant of the egoistic music lover. ... one can also lie in bed and listen to records, tapes and radio all night, if one so wishes, without disturbing the sleep of others.[65]

> The listener's concentration on the sound is deepened by the fact that external sources of disturbance are rendered relatively insignificant. The volume level and full dynamics do not trouble the surroundings, the listener is independent of time and space ...[66]

> One is forced [when listening through headphones] to listen to all passages in the music in a totally different manner.[67]

The curious choice of words in the last quotation may be taken as an indication of a certain ambivalence towards the aesthetic qualities of privatized listening: while

---

(Harmondsworth, 1987), pp. 44f.

62 Ibid., ch. 4.
63 Kenney, *Recorded Music*, p. 3f. On the differential effects of privatized listening for different genres of classical music, cf. Timothy Day, *A Century of Recorded Music: Listening to Musical History* (New Haven, CT, 2000), pp. 216ff.
64 Sterne, *The Audible Past*, p. 138.
65 *Musikrevy*, 7 (1959).
66 *Musik och ljudteknik*, 5 (1965).
67 *Stereo-Hifi*, 3 (1970).

enabling an intensified indulgence in recorded sound, it may also involve demands for a higher effort on the part of the listener. Some commentators – mainly those of an older generation – also express concerns about the loss of social contact brought about by technologized private listening:

> ... the radio and the gramophone to some extent shut the listeners out from the soil for emotion which is involved in listening together with many others and under the power of the personal charisma of those playing and singing.[68]

> Of course, for many people the experience itself, the presence, of a musical performance will continue to be an essential factor (jazz is a good example).[69]

> What a listening situation! It might well seem ideal. Maybe – maybe not. Still, we cannot disregard our need for the audience community and feeling of presence in the concert hall, can we?[70]

A quite different approach to the problem of disturbing the domestic environment is, of course, to make sound-reproduction equipment mobile. The striving for increased mobility is a recurrent aspect of the discourses on sound technology throughout the period studied. In 1950s hobby-engineer discourse this was manifested in a persistent do-it-yourself miniaturization fad, represented by, for instance, published instructions on how to build a radio receiver into a ballpoint pen or a man's hat.[71] By the 1970s the emphasis had switched to hi-fi stereo equipment for cars and boats – by 1976, Sweden was reported to have the world's highest per capita sales of car-stereo equipment[72] – and towards the end of the decade, a new phase in the mobility of sound was heralded in reviews of the Sony Walkman personal stereo, marketed in Sweden as the 'Freestyle'.

Aesthetics and Subjectivity

A concomitant of the privatization of listening is an increased emphasis on subjective experience and a widened range of listening modes considered legitimate, including those which focus on the sensual experience of sound. Despite the previously discussed efforts to school hi-fi users into active and concentrated 'structural' listeners, such listening modes seem to have been widely applied from the early days of hi-fi culture. Keightley has commented on the images presented in 1950s

---

68   *Skivspegeln*, 5 (1960).
69   *Musik och ljudteknik*, 3 (1965).
70   *Stereo-Hifi*, 2 (1970).
71   *Teknik för alla*, 24 (1954); *Teknik för alla*, 16 (1956).
72   *Stereo-Hifi*, 6–7 (1976).

US hi-fi discourse of the 'excessive' qualities of technologized sound, immersing and transporting the solitary listener, eyes closed, into realms of sonic indulgence, thus, according to Keightley, being precursory of aesthetic attitudes characteristic of 1960s psychedelia.[73] Similar images can also be found in the Swedish periodicals, in editorial material as well as in advertisements:

> *The first and lasting impression of High Fidelity is totally overwhelming – to the music enthusiast, High Fidelity is something invaluable.*[74]

> *One does not pass the threshold until one can without fear spread one's ears like radar aerials and absorb the cascades of sound in true sensual intoxication.*[75]

> *Never have you been surrounded by such a sea of sound – in stereo or mono! Never have you heard such reproduction – more faithful than from the finest hi-fi loudspeaker! Never have you been enclosed in such a world of music – disturbed by no one and disturbing no one!*[76]

By the 1970s a more mundane and lowbrow rhetoric has replaced the more lofty poetical effusions:

> *Of course we will deal with everything happening on the technological front, but we will also listen to nice sound and talk about what we think sounds nice.*[77]

> *... a sound consciousness is gradually evolving ... People want a nice sound ...*[78]

Even in these experienced times, however, unexpectedly strong listening experiences may trigger equally strong verbal reactions. In a remarkable reflection on first-time listening to quadraphonic sound, the writer displays a highly ambivalent attitude, indicating a fear of 'loss of self' in the face of sonic power:

> *I cannot remember that I've ever been so powerfully affected by music ... when exposing oneself or others to the intense bombardment which four-channel stereo may produce ... one should be aware of the fact that this may*

---

73 Keightley, '"Turn it Down!"', pp. 169ff.
74 *Estrad*, 2 (1958). Note the capitalization of 'High Fidelity', otherwise quite foreign to Swedish orthography.
75 *Musik och ljudteknik*, 2 (1960).
76 Headphone advertisement in *Musik och ljudteknik*, 5 (1960).
77 *Stereo-Hifi*, 1 (1970). The nuances of the Swedish adjective (*skönt*) are difficult to convey in translation; it has connotations of cosiness as well as of sexual pleasure.
78 *Stereo-Hifi*, 3 (1971).

*also involve a high strain, which calls for psychic balance in the receiver. ...
I was totally defenceless before the waves of music sweeping over me from all
directions.*[79]

Subjectivity is present in hi-fi discourse in yet another, and perhaps more
unexpected, way. Despite the emphasis on scientific objectivity and accuracy
inherent in the 'technoscientific imaginary', several writers in the mid-1950s were
already acknowledging the inability to judge the quality of equipment as perceived
by the listener solely on the basis of physical measurement data, particularly
regarding loudspeakers. This is a theme whose prominence increases over the
course of the investigation period:

*The fact is that the engineers' problems at present are situated on a quite
different level, namely the psychological one. Different ears and musical
views do not perceive music in the same way and a professional musician
doesn't regard music in the same way as a physicist.*[80]

*The weakest link in the reproduction of sound, next to the human ear [sic], is
the amplifier's loudspeaker system.*[81]

*... we neither can nor want to enter into more detailed assessments of
something as subjective as the merits of loudspeakers.*[82]

Here, only one's own taste can pass the final verdict![83]

... which type of loudspeaker one prefers is highly individual.[84]

*One should be aware of the fact that different persons perceive sound in
different ways, and it is not at all certain that what one thinks sounds best,
sounds as good to another one's ears. Here everyone has to listen himself [sic]
and decide what is best just for his ears.*[85]

Thus, hi-fi discourse contains a paradoxical ambiguity towards its own
foundation in scientific objectivity: as the experience and professionalization of
testing procedures of audio equipment increases, so does the uncertainty as to the
objective value of the results of such testing. In a 1980 article the value of testing
procedures in general is called into question:

---

79   *Stereo-Hifi*, 10 (1971).
80   *Teknik för alla*, 3 (1955).
81   *Teknik för alla*, 16 (1959).
82   *Musik och ljudteknik*, 3 (1965).
83   Comment on the testing of headphones in *Musik och ljudteknik*, 5 (1965).
84   *Stereo-Hifi*, 1 (1970).
85   *Stereo-Hifi*, 3 (1970).

> *... most tests of audio products carried out today are and remain very subjective, which is also indicated by the sometimes tremendous differences of opinion which may arise from different tests in different magazines of one and the same product.*[86]

Accordingly, by this time, notions of 'truth to nature' appear to have become considerably more complicated than a quarter of a century earlier. They are further complicated by questions of musical genre.

Differentiation of Genres: Concert Music versus Loudspeaker Music

The growing awareness of the significance of subjective judgement in the quality assessment of hi-fi equipment is connected to an evolving differentiation of sound ideals by musical genre – ideals which also imply a differential position on the question of the relationship of reproduced sound to an external 'original'. The earliest traces of this differentiation in my material appear in the mid-1950s in connection with discussions of the evolving genre of electro-acoustic music. This was characterized as 'loudspeaker music', as opposed to music performed live, and the arguments for its *raison d'être* were based on the contemporary technicalization and mediaization of music in general:

> *... as soon as one accepts the truism that 'music is meant to be heard', of course there is no earthly reason to distinguish the musical experiences in a concert hall and by a loudspeaker ...*[87]

> *... nowadays, we daily encounter most music by way of radio, film and gramophone records, without seeing a trace of any performer; and I don't know whether the knowledge of his [sic] existence matters much for the aesthetic experience.*[88]

The actual expression 'loudspeaker music' appears for the first time in my material in 1965. Interestingly enough, this is not in connection with electro-acoustic music; rather, the term is used as a designation for technologically-reproduced, 'non-live' music in general:

---

86   *Hifi & musik*, 5 (1980).
87   *Musikrevy*, 3 (1955).
88   *Musikrevy*, 2 (1958).

> *Loudspeaker music has come to the fore, primarily owing to Fylkingen's*
> *proposal of new forms of music distribution and concert activity, where they*
> *suggest State-produced 'records for the people', low-priced LPs ...*[89]

Although some spokespeople for electro-acoustic music were loquacious participants in public discussions on both music policy and music technology, in general the genre attracted little attention in hi-fi discourse. Instead, by the 1970s 'loudspeaker music' was taken to signify 'pop music', as opposed to 'serious music'.[90] This distinction often appeared in accounts of equipment tests – accounts which demonstrated an evolving understanding that these different genres required different sound characteristics for optimal reproduction:

> *The general impression is that the [stereo receiver] Beomaster 1200 is rather*
> *'pop-like' in its reproduction and that the unit doesn't provide the 'airiness'*
> *one generally desires when the large symphony orchestra strikes up.*[91]

> *A loudspeaker 'for pop music' (these actually exist) may not at all be suitable*
> *for the reproduction of serious music, due to the fact that the loudspeaker*
> *in question may have peaks, dales, distortion etc. lying in areas affected in*
> *various degrees by the spectral content of the sound.*[92]

> *... the loudness control ... is a control used by many when listening to pop*
> *music in order to achieve the rumbling bass.*[93]

> *... reproduction in the bass range was a bit uneven ... something which one*
> *heard most clearly when playing serious music, but which one hardly notices*
> *in pure loudspeaker music.*[94]

The distinction between pop, as 'youth music' and serious music was conceived of in generational terms. By this time it was becoming an accepted fact that a generation existed which had grown up with loudspeaker music:

> *Every day, we listen to loudspeaker sounds and there receive both important*
> *information and experiences of art. Thus a new generation of music listeners*

---

89 *Musik och ljudteknik*, 3 (1965). Fylkingen was founded in the 1930s as a society for chamber music; in the early 1950s, it switched its main focus to modernist avant-garde music, including electro-acoustic music.

90 The word 'pop' in Swedish in the 1960s was used as a generic term for music with lyrics in English influenced by US and British rock music. As rock music with Swedish lyrics gained wider circulation during the 1970s, the meaning of the terms 'rock' and 'pop' approached that of US/British usage.

91 *Stereo-Hifi*, 2 (1971).

92 *Stereo-Hifi*, 5 (1971).

93 *Stereo-Hifi*, 4 (1976).

94 Ibid.

has come into existence ... the loudspeaker generation. ... In the future we may consider it unnatural to listen to sounds coming directly from musical instruments. The natural and only right thing will then be loudspeaker sound.[95]

... for pop music, other criteria are valid than for other kinds of music. ... For example, most young people have never heard real natural music. They have grown up with so-called electrophonic loudspeaker music both at home and out at dance-venues. And in most cases, this music has been and is marred by rather large amounts of distortion of various kinds. That's why these people in most cases prefer some distortion in the sound ...[96]

As these last two quotations indicate, the assessments of this situation varied on a scale ranging from the celebratory to the intensely critical (note the contrasting of 'loudspeaker music' with 'real natural music'). However, the attitude represented in the first quotation appears to be something of an exception – it is taken from an interview with one of the pioneers of electro-acoustic music in Sweden, a man renowned for strong and controversial opinions; most commentators instead tend to the critical side. On closer analysis, the critique further appears to have two different, albeit related, dimensions: on the one hand, this is a musical–cultural critique of a music considered aesthetically inferior by many of these writers, on the other hand, the critique is directed at the 'unnatural' recording procedures utilized in the production of this music. This is particularly clear in the critique, recurrent throughout the 1970s, of the use of 'loudspeaker-music' procedures, such as multi-microphone recording and mixing, close-miking, compression and multitrack recording, in the recording of concert music:

... entertainment music is a kind of loudspeaker music or microphone music, requiring a wide range of technical equipment ... But one should not forget that we're talking here about a music whose artistic worth is rarely comparable to that with a serious bent. ... Whereas one tries within serious music to work with a minimum of microphones and make the most of the acoustics of the hall, when it comes to popular music one does just the opposite.[97]

... achieving concert hall acoustics at home is probably utopian – but subjecting classical music to techniques of signal manipulation created for economic reasons within pop and electrophony, that must be wrong.[98]

Today, the concept of 'commercial sound' is a sales argument also within serious music. Narrow dynamics in engraving and a compressed sound

---

95   *Stereo-Hifi*, 11 (1971).
96   *Hifi & musik*, 5 (1980).
97   *Stereo-Hifi*, 6 (1971).
98   *Musik och ljudteknik*, 1 (1975).

> produces records which sound good on most systems but lack space and depth. ... It has become so good, so good, too good. And bloody boring![99]

> ... when modern pop-production technique came to stay and became an important factor for the creation of a selling 'sound', in some quarters the use of a large number of microphones ... became frequent also for serious recordings. ... I feel that many modern productions of serious music have something synthetic and unnatural about them ... Technology is best when it is not conspicuous.[100]

The values at stake – cultural politics, musical aesthetics and ideologies of naturalness and authenticity – were aptly summed up in a review of Abba's album *Arrival* in 1976:

> *'Arrival' hardly contains one single human sound. Everything is 'sound' and effects. ... I imagine that this is computer music, programmed for and played by a computer. ... To me, this is a national anthem for a computer society ruled by technocrats.*[101]

The Transparency/Fidelity Ideal Revisited

As hinted at above, invocations of the ideals of 'truth to the original' and 'transparent mediation' continue to be an element of hi-fi discourse throughout the period studied here. Although by the 1970s unproblematical assertions of the complete interchangeability of original and recorded sound belong to the past, 'truth to life' was still a valid criterion of excellence in sound-reproduction equipment. This is indicated, for example, by the judgement of a pair of loudspeakers, used as a reference in a test, that they offer 'a reproduction which is manifestly true to life', or by the characterization of the sound of another loudspeaker as 'perceptibly "real"'.[102] In a 1973 article an account is given of how Leon Kuby, of the US audio-equipment manufacturer Harman Kardon, has presented the company's findings

---

99   *Stereo-Hifi*, 9 (1976). Note the critique of the 'larger-than-life' effect of the volume levels of hi-fi equipment already formulated in 1954, cited in Michael Chanan, *Repeated Takes: A Short History of Recording and Its Effects on Music* (London, 1995), p. 94.

100 *Hifi & musik*, 1 (1980). The Swedish equivalent of 'conspicuous' literally means 'falling into the eyes'; the writer here uses a pun on this, translatable as 'falling into the ears'. The Swedish original has the English word 'sound' in quotation marks; this has been used in Swedish since about 1970 in the context of descriptions of sound characteristics of popular music. For a brief historical account of the conceptualization of 'sound' in popular music contexts, cf. Paul Théberge, *Any Sound You Can Imagine: Making Music/ Consuming Technology* (Hanover, NH and London, 1997), pp. 190ff.

101 *Stereo-Hifi*, 12 (1976).

102 *Stereo-Hifi*, 5 (1971); *Stereo-Hifi*, 7–8 (1971).

concerning '*really* true-to-life sound reproduction'.[103] Two years later, one writer posits a 'higher fidelity' as a remedy for the perceived detriments of 'loudspeaker-music' production practices:

> By the use of [various technical means] one can today get far from the original sound. ... In this system, the producer assumes a central role when multi-channel recordings are to be mixed down into a finished product. It has even been suggested that this would be a new form of artistic creation, equal to that of the artists. ... It is understandable that enthusiasts in many countries rise and clamour for higher fidelity. They start reacting to the degenerate varieties of multi-microphone technique and the mediocre product standard of the record companies – even if lately![104]

At the same time, however, this fidelity has assumed an increasingly relativized character in several respects. To matters of individual taste in sound reproduction and genre-specific ideals of sound-reproduction aesthetics, already mentioned above, may be added, for instance, the valorization of earlier phases in the history of sound-reproduction technology and an explicit historicization of the frames of reference:

> ... take, for example, the needle scratch and 'canned sound' of the old 78s. That's not hi-fi, it is true, but it does contribute to the atmosphere one associates with, for example, Ernst Rolf and Enrico Caruso, with Fritz Kreisler and King Oliver, doesn't it?[105]

> ... if we cannot hear the differences today, we can be certain that many more will be able to hear them tomorrow when the programme material becomes so much better. ... As we all know, as soon as we humans get to experience and learn something new, our frames of reference are immediately changed, and then our standards are suddenly raised.[106]

To several writers, the logical conclusion of this state of affairs seems to be that perfect fidelity constitutes an ideal which certainly is asymptotically approachable but is ultimately unreachable and, moreover, in many contexts irrelevant:

> The experience of music – as it is perceived in the concert hall or the settings of the performance – cannot be replaced in its entirety by any hitherto known medium of reproduction. In other words, all reproduction of music is a substitute, which, it is true, may give various individuals a form of music

---

103 *Stereo-Hifi*, 9 (1973).
104 *Musik och ljudteknik*, 1 (1975).
105 *Stereo-Hifi*, 4 (1971). Ernst Rolf was a popular Swedish revue and gramophone artist in the 1910s–20s.
106 *Hifi & musik*, 5 (1980).

> *experience, but an experience conditional on the ability for and practice in listening to and assimilating reproduced music.*[107]

> *Today, when pure loudspeaker music is so predominant in record production, it may sometimes seem wrong to discuss what appears true to nature, since there is no natural reference in this context. As a result, one must instead resort to quality ratings such as good, impressive, etc.*[108]

> *When, a fair few years ago, people sat down trying to formulate a definition of high fidelity, serious music was taken as the point of departure. Hi-fi should refer to a reproduction showing a very high degree of accordance with a model, an original. ... Now, the hi-fi concept as a form of reproduction true to the original has probably almost had its day. Instead, one speaks of high-class reproduction, meaning that all forms of distortion are insignificant and various kinds of interference inaudible.*[109]

By the turn of the decade, a new phase in the history of sound-reproduction technology is heralded by the first articles on the soon-to-come digital audio technology. Just as, ten years previously, the 1970s were predicted to become 'the decade of good sound', it is now stated that the 1980s 'have every chance of elapsing in a spirit of euphony'.[110] However, at the same time as the superior technical characteristics of digital audio are extolled, the first critical accounts of the 'unnaturalness' of digital sound also appear, adding a further chapter to the continuing story of the complicated relationship of reproduced sound to 'reality'.[111]

Conclusion

To sum up, hi-fi discourse as it evolves in a Swedish context in the period 1950–80 seems to indicate that the emphasis on the transparency of the medium inherent in the hi-fi concept – 'fidelity to nature' – gradually assumes an increasingly problematical character. On the one hand, the processes of 'naturalization of the medium' which characterize the entire history of sound reproduction appear to continue, thus working towards increased transparency. On the other hand, the introduction of hi-fi is accompanied by an increased attention to nuances of transparency – that is, an increasing sensitivity to subtle differences in perceived

---

107 *Stereo-Hifi*, 5 (1971).
108 *Stereo-Hifi*, 4 (1976).
109 *Stereo-Hifi*, 9 (1976).
110 *Hifi & musik*, 1 (1980).
111 For example, in a news-item in *Hifi & musik*, 9 (1980), US psychologist John Diamond is cited on the topic of 'digital audio causing stress in humans'.

quality of sound reproduction. Thus, the increased transparency of the medium tends to promote a mode of listening reducing transparency.

During this period, transparentization affects not just the medium involved, but also the process of mediaization itself. In 1950 music performed live is the natural frame of reference for judging the quality of music reproduction; by 1980, this is no longer so. Although the discourse of 'truth to nature' is active throughout the period, there is an increasing acceptance of mediaized music, 'loudspeaker music', as a genre distinct from, but equal or maybe superior to, live music. In this process, different aesthetics applicable to different genres of loudspeaker music evolve, with the result that technologically reproduced music is not any longer necessarily measured against 'truth to the original' but, rather, against an 'autonomous' aesthetic ideal, particular to that music. Hi-fi discourse during the period 1950–80 thus traces, within the domain of music reception and music listening, the gradual emancipation of the recording as an independent entity – what Lee B. Brown has termed a 'work of phonography' – from any 'natural' sound extrinsic to the one reproduced by means of technology.[112]

---

112 Lee B. Brown, 'Documentation and Fabrication in Phonography', *Twentieth World Congress of Philosophy, Boston*, 1998 at: <http://www.bu.edu/wcp/Papers/Aest/AestBrow. htm> (accessed 13 July 2008.) Cf. Eisenberg, *The Recording Angel*, p. 110, on the quality criteria applicable when listening to 'pure phonography'.

Approaches to Analysing Recordings of Popular Music

Timothy Warner

The methods artists use (materials, tools, techniques, insights) have a profound, direct and instant influence on the nature of the work they produce.[1]

Nothing will come of nothing.[2]

Close analysis of popular music has come in for some criticism in recent years. As Allan Moore points out, 'The last two decades in particular have sown poststructuralist doubts deep within the close reading of music of all kinds, doubts which are directed not only at the authority of the composer but, perhaps even more strongly, at the identity, the coherence, the autonomy of the individual piece, work, song (however we choose to label it)'.[3] Such reservations have tended to undermine attempts to analyse popular music *recordings*, even before these truly achieved the status of 'text' by becoming the primary focus of analysis. This study seeks to revisit these issues: it aims to demonstrate the central position that recordings and modern music technology should hold in the study of popular music; provide an overview of existing approaches to the close analysis of popular music recordings; review the methodological issues raised; and posit a theoretical framework of creativity to support various approaches to analysing recordings of popular music.

There was popular music before recording was invented, and there are types of popular music that continue to thrive without being recorded, but for the past 70 years or so the sonic and musical characteristics of much popular music have been informed by the processes and technologies of audio recording. Similarly, most of the ways in which people interact and engage with popular music, as well as the diverse roles that popular music can play in societies, now explicitly depend on

---

1   David Hockney, *Secret Knowledge – Rediscovering the Lost Techniques of the Old Masters*, London, 2006), p. 51.
2   William Shakespeare, *King Lear*, act I, scene I.
3   Allan F. Moore (ed.), *Analyzing Popular Music* (Cambridge, 2003), p. 4.

recording technology – to put it simply, most people experience popular music most of the time by listening to *recorded* music:

> It is the technology of popular music production, specifically the technology of sound recording, that organizes our experience of popular music ... popular music is, at every critical juncture of its history, determined by the technology musicians use to realize their ideas.[4]

While it is evident that audio recording and related technologies play an important role in much popular music, there has been relatively little analytical work in this area – even from scholars such as Philip Tagg whose influential concepts and methods, although criticized for their 'alleged "scientism"',[5] remain relevant and pertinent to both popular musicology and this chapter. With regard to analysis, Tagg provides a useful focus when he raises the question '[W]hy and how does who communicate what to whom and with what effect?'[6] and points out that some areas covered have been tackled more extensively than others:

> Although we have considerable insight into socio-economic, subcultural, and psycho-social mechanisms influencing the 'emitter' (by means of biographies, etc.) and 'receiver' of certain types of popular music, we have very little explicit information about the nature of the 'channel', the music itself. We know little about its 'signifiers' and 'signified', about the relations the music establishes between emitter and receiver, about how a musical message actually relates to the set of affective and associative concepts presumably shared by emitter and receiver, and how it interacts with their respective cultural, social, and natural environments. In other words ... we could say that sociology answers the question 'who', 'to whom' and, with some help from psychology, 'with what effect' and possibly parts of 'why', but when it comes to the rest of the 'why' not to mention the questions 'what' and 'how', we are left in the lurch.[7]

Tagg's attempt to provide an insight into those issues of 'why', 'what' and 'how' is based on a 'hermeneutic-semiological' approach, derived from structural linguistics but which places the emphasis not so much on structure and syntax as on semantics – that is, the meanings (intentions and reactions) of the musical text – and pragmatics – that is, its function in a sociocultural context.[8] However, while Tagg's

---

4   Steve Jones, *Rock Formation: Music, Technology and Mass Communication* (London, 1992), p. 1.

5   Richard Middleton (ed.), *Reading Pop: Approaches to Textual Analysis in Popular Music* (Oxford, 2000), p. 23.

6   Philip Tagg, 'Analysing Popular Music: Theory, Method, and Practice', in Middleton, *Reading Pop*, pp. 71–103, at p. 74.

7   Ibid., p. 75.

8   Philip Tagg and Bob Clarida, *Ten Little Title Tunes: Towards a Musicology of Mass Media* (New York and Montreal, 2003).

demonstration is based on pieces of recorded music, which are acknowledged as such, the object of his analysis is primarily music per se, irrespective of the technologies that may have been called upon to realize it; furthermore, as should be evident from the above quotation, Tagg views popular music primarily as communication, rather than as art or even craft.

Similarly, Allan Moore in his chapter 'Elements of an Analytical Musicology of Rock' in *Rock: The Primary Text*[9] identifies and provides details of several distinct elements that he considers worthy of attention – 'rhythmic organization', 'harmonic patterns and formal structures', 'open-ended repetitive patterns' and so on – but, although the musical examples he provides are all taken from recordings, there is no suggestion that the technologies and the processes of recording may have had any significant impact on the final sonic artefact.[10] In a later book, *The Beatles: Sgt. Pepper's Lonely Hearts Club Band*, Moore initially asserts that 'the only thing we have approaching an authoritative score is ... the recording itself', yet the text that follows makes only a few, minor, passing references to the hugely significant role that recording studio technology played in the making of this seminal album.[11]

And there's the rub: if the recording can, in some respects, be considered as a medium, it is also much more than that. Even in the case of recordings of live performances, the recordings are often far from being transparent.[12]

---

9   Allan Moore, *Rock – The Primary Text: Developing a Musicology of Rock* (Buckingham, 1993), pp. 31–55.

10   In Chapter 4 of the same book, Moore introduces the concept of the 'sound-box', 'a "virtual textural space", envisaged as an empty cube of finite dimensions, changing with respect to real time (almost like an abstract, three-dimensional television screen)' (p. 106), where the vertical axis represents the register of each instrument or voice; the horizontal axis represents its left/right spatial position and the 'depth' axis represents its apparent proximity to the listener in relation to the other sounds. Although such a model does enable scrutiny of certain record production techniques used in popular music recordings, it fails to account for the conjunction of radically different spatial settings for individual instruments or voices within the same recording, which has been a characteristic of many popular music recordings since the 1980s.

11   Allan Moore, *The Beatles: Sgt. Pepper's Lonely Hearts Club Band* (Cambridge, 1997), p. x. Simon Frith confirms the importance of the album and the central role that technology played in its production when he writes: 'the emergence of rock as art was symbolized by the Beatles' self-conscious studio artifact, Sgt. Pepper's Lonely Hearts Club [Band]': quoted in James Lull, *Popular Music and Communication* (London, 1992), p. 62.

12   Hence Thin Lizzy's *Live and Dangerous* album, supposedly a recording made up entirely of live concert performances, actually involved considerable studio overdubbing after the event. Moreover, for most live popular music performances, there is the added complication of amplification, extensive signal processing and even the playback of prerecorded material (audio and MIDI). The volume levels (both relative and overall), the timbres and the numerous sonic enhancements that characterize any amplified popular music performance not only depend on a battery of modern audio technology, but also partially define the aural experience of the audience.

Of course, the level and variety of technological intervention, as well as the audible impact this may have on the final artefact, can vary considerably. For certain genres of popular music, most of the sounds, and the ways in which these are assembled and presented in time, as well as the methods employed to achieve structural cohesion, are produced and realized entirely through electronic manipulation (digital and analogue) rather than by musicians playing traditional, acoustically-based musical instruments. Indeed, several of the sounds that characterize popular music from the 1950s onwards are the result of the ever-increasing use of unnatural timbres derived from either electronic sources or electronic manipulation.[13] Even when sound and sound manipulation of this kind initially *seem* to have been kept to a minimum, the production process is likely to have called upon considerable use of such recording studio equipment. In fact, technological interventions occur at all levels: relative loudness is controlled by the amplifying circuitry of the mixer; dynamic range is modified and controlled through the use of compression; spatial positions are determined by panoramic potentiometer settings, microphone placements and the addition of either natural or artificially produced reverberation; timbres may be modified by resourceful equalization circuitry, special effects (chorus, flanging, phasing and so on) and a range of distortion processes; and 'performances' are revised through the use of overdubbing techniques and further modified by a range of editing practices.

The changes that all these technological processes bring about are considerable and can directly impact on every aspect of the listener's musical experience. Yet there are few psychoacoustic explanations or aesthetic conjectures forthcoming on why the extensive use of such technology is so prevalent on modern recordings of popular music. Hence, while it is generally acknowledged by the recording community that judicious use of audio compression and distortion, for example, enhance the impact of a popular music recording – they have been a fundamental part of modern record mastering for several years – the psychoacoustic or musical roles these play in a recording have yet to be thoroughly investigated. Indeed, dynamic compression is perhaps the least well explored or understood of all recording processes: while virtually every recording and broadcast that we hear has been compressed, often quite heavily, most listeners are not consciously aware of the impact this has on the resulting musical experience. This is perhaps because compression is not intended to change the timbre of part (or all) of a recording, but instead reduces its dynamic range, so that the overall level can then be raised, resulting in a more consistent, continuous and high level of loudness. And record producers, as well as record company executives, have long been aware that the more consistently loud a recording appears to be (in comparison to the recordings that precede and follow it), the more likely it is to impress the listener.

Similarly, the subtle kinds of audio distortion that sound engineers, and particularly mastering engineers, apply to popular music recordings give a brighter,

---

13 Consider the 'hollow', 'ghostly' and unnatural sound produced by applying 'slapback echo' to the lead vocal part, for example, that featured on many of the 'classic' rock and roll recordings of the 1950s and quickly came to aurally symbolize the genre.

more dangerous 'edge' or rawness to the sound that most listeners intuitively, even perhaps subconsciously, find both sonically exciting and particularly supportive of a certain kind of aesthetic found in much popular music.[14] Yet there are very few studies on the impact that a particular studio technique might have musically or how the listener might respond to it. Hence, while musicological approaches are able to demonstrate that a piece of music in a minor key will tend to be more harmonically and melodically unstable than a similar piece in a major key (due to the two possibilities for the sixth and seventh steps of the scale), there is no equivalent causal link with the many and much used studio techniques that are audible on recordings of popular music.

The view that audio technology simply seeks to literally 'record' the acoustic reality of traditional musical activity as transparently as possible is not only untenable, but also was hardly the case at the dawn of recorded music.[15] The levels of sonic manipulation of modern popular music recordings are not only very high, but also completely fly in the face of traditional musical activity. Virgil Moorefield points out that, for popular music in the last 50 years 'recording's metaphor has shifted from one of the "illusion of reality" (mimetic space) to the "reality of illusion" (a virtual world in which everything is possible)'.[16] In other words, all popular music recordings could be analysed as technologically determined artefacts, even though some might initially appear to be more the result of technological intervention and manipulation than others. For several genres of popular music, the level of intervention is explicit and immediately audible (as in the case of disco and most later forms of dance music, for example), for other genres (country and western, say) the levels of technological manipulation are often seemingly less apparent but in fact no less real. However, for most popular music analysts, the 'what' in Tagg's original question either focuses on traditional musical parameters – pitch, harmony and rhythm (as is the case with Moore, Covach, and others) – or the evocative (connotative) powers of these (Tagg), and tend to ignore the creative role that technology has played: as a result, technologically focused analyses remain extremely rare.

The reasons for this state of affairs are many and diverse. It is evident that some music commentators hold a fundamentally negative view of recording technology on ideological grounds. They feel that many musicians have become 'consumers of technology' and 'have witnessed the incursion of capitalist relations upon

---

14   And virtually every process and device from artificial reverberation and delay, which emulate and often distort acoustic phenomena, to sequencing and editing, which provide endless control of how each sound and gesture occurs in time, that are available in the modern popular music recording studio provide similar creative potential that is then realized on virtually all popular music recordings.

15   Even at the turn of the twentieth century, Stroh violins, brass instruments replacing lower strings and the success of specific vocal timbres that were more suited to the limitations of the acoustic recording process (for example, Caruso and Melba) were driven by musico-technological considerations.

16   Virgil Moorefield, *The Producer as Composer: Shaping the Sounds of Popular Music* (Cambridge, MA, 2005), p. xiii.

their creative practices at the most fundamental level';[17] or, rather more bluntly, that 'recording has always been a means of social control'.[18] Many musicians, on the other hand, have a deep-seated suspicion of modern music technology as they imagine that it both challenges and devalues the traditional performing and composing skills that they have spent years developing: for them, a successful popular music recording is often simply the result of studio trickery. Meanwhile, fans might be perplexed that in the high-profile world of commercial popular music, which places so much emphasis on celebrity, recording studio production teams seem happy to remain largely anonymous.[19] Similarly, most successful popular music recordings are the result of teamwork, and such collective creative practice tends to undermine the still somewhat prevalent romantic notion of the single, artistic genius. And, having produced a series of commercially successful recordings, the team might earn the label 'hit factory' and have their work dismissed as 'manufactured, production-line pop',[20] supporting the widespread belief that recording is a financially-driven industrial process, with only a secondary concern for art or craft and consequently involving little creativity.[21] A further possible reason why technologically-based analyses of popular music recordings are few and far between is that many commentators often lack expert technical knowledge and experience of recording studio practice: like any other creative process, a highly honed aural ability and rich musical imagination are required to successfully operate such equipment, and these are only acquired after much application.[22] And finally, by being somewhat unclear about popular music recording practice, commentators then fail to appreciate the high level of technological mediation that characterizes most popular music recordings. Consequently there is a general lack of appreciation of how *important* recording is, and this, in turn, accounts for why it is often neglected, at least from an analytical perspective, in popular music studies.

In fact, recording technology can have a direct and often profound impact even on the more traditionally analysed aspects of a recording. One might identify three distinct aural elements in any popular music recording: the realization of the

---

17   Paul Théberge, *Any Sound You Can Imagine: Making Music/Consuming Technology* (Hanover, NH and London, 1997), p. 255.
18   Jacques Attali, *Noise* (Minneapolis, 1985), p. 87.
19   There is also much ambiguity regarding the relative creative status of the producer in the recording process to consider. It is evident that while some producers stamp their creative authority on every recording they produce, others take a more supportive, facilitating role.
20   *Radio Times*, BBC4, 28 February 2008.
21   Related to this idea is the, often quite accurate, view that the named artist on a commercially successful popular music recording has, in reality, only made a relatively modest contribution to the production process, resulting in a spurious and undeserved artistic status.
22   Although the technology used to make artistically successful recordings of popular music is, in itself, neither particularly complicated nor demands a great deal of manual dexterity, a high level of musicality and creativity are prerequisites.

recording itself (that is, the artefact, as well as the processes and ways in which the various sonic elements have been manipulated and assembled); the performances of the singers and musicians; and the musical composition and/or arrangement. Yet these recording processes and manipulations can exert a considerable influence on the other elements of composition, arrangement and performance. Overdubbing can ensure a heightened and condensed level of performance; autotune and delicate editing procedures can enable increased accuracy of pitching and rhythm by the performers; and a range of signal processing devices can modify timbres either subtly or radically until the 'ideal' sound for the performer is achieved. In each case, the performance that took place in the studio will differ considerably from the 'performance' heard on the recording. Similarly, the composition that is taken into a studio at the beginning of the recording process will often undergo considerable modification as a result of the process itself. Indeed, many recordings of popular music are composed simply and directly through interaction with recording technology.

As mentioned above, while the degree of intervention might appear to vary there is no doubt that the use of technology in all recordings of popular music is both *creative* and *significant*. Yet the technologies and technologically-driven processes involved in the production of the very artefact that is most associated with, and has come to characterize, popular music – the cornerstone of the music industry – has, as yet, received scant attention from analysts of popular music. At the core of all these considerations is the issue of musical creativity and its relationship to the processes and artefacts of popular music production. And, for the purposes of this study, if such musical creativity is mediated by production processes, are these open to reflection and analysis?[23] The first stumbling-block is the material form and means that the analysis adopts to objectify the various elements of a recording; the second is the need to frame any analysis within a credible theoretical model of musical creativity itself.

'Hegel maintained that music was the first art to give us the sense of unification occurring in time rather than space',[24] yet demonstrating this sense of unification occurring in time through close analysis presents a considerable challenge: what approach will most adequately represent or highlight those sonic elements from an audio recording that are deemed worthy of attention? Traditional analyses of musical texts are usually presented in one of three basic formats – through the use of sound itself (that is, sonically), through language, or through visual representation

---

23   Some commentators have suggested that artefacts produced as a result of the technologically-driven activities associated with the modern recording studio are a distinct and separate form of sound-based art and consequently require a distinct and separate analytical approach – see Trevor Wishart, *On Sonic Art* (York, 1985) and Peter O'Hare, 'Approaching Sound: A Sonicological Examination of the Producer's Role in Popular Music', MPhil thesis (University of Glasgow 2008), for example. Yet such views implicitly tend to marginalize the central role that recordings play in contemporary musical life: recordings have changed forever our concept of what constitutes the art of music and cannot now be viewed as something separate from it.

24   Anthony Storr, *Music and the Mind* (London, 1997), p. 173.

– and each of these approaches may also be adopted for close analysis of popular music recordings.

Presenting an analysis of a recording in sound would appear to be the most appropriate approach, yet it is extremely rare. Hans Keller's 'Wordless Functional Analysis', devoted to classical rather than popular music, is one of the very few examples of this type of approach. Keller would write a series of analytical interludes, designed to be played between the movements of the work being considered, which would demonstrate in sound the underlying unity of themes in a work of apparently strongly contrasting musical ideas.[25] Although Keller's specific objective was to explore the melodic and motivic relationships in a particular piece of music, the basic principle of using sound to demonstrate musical analysis would also seem suitable for the scrutiny of popular music recordings. Yet, although the academic community has tended to avoid such an approach, practices by DJs, studio musicians and record producers, often involving the use of samples from a variety of recorded sources, can sometimes be seen to demonstrate musical relationships between and within recordings. For example, the DJ's seamless, but often quite lengthy, segue between two records may illustrate shared samples, timbres, tonalities, tempi or even melodic and harmonic patterns.[26] Similarly, popular music recordings based on the extensive use of a single, and often easily identified, sample from a pre-existing recording, as well as the processes of signifyin' and even remixing, can reveal significant commonalities on several levels. Finally, the mash-up – a new recording produced by combining two pre-existing, and often distinctly different, popular music recordings – directly demonstrates underlying musical relationships between two records, while also revealing some of the dramatic ways in which modern music technology is able to manipulate recorded sound.[27]

Turning to the use of language as a means of analytical elucidation, 'it is often said that "writing about music is like dancing about architecture", to which I would reply that dancing about architecture might be very illuminating if we all danced as much as we use language'.[28] Writing about popular music recordings is by far the most common form of scholarly discourse, and such texts often involve some elements of analysis. Yet using language to represent the sounds on popular music recordings inevitably raises issues of interpretation and description: one writer's 'dark and oppressive' reverberation setting might be 'warm and comforting' to another, for example.[29]

---

25 See Hans Keller, *Functional Analysis: The Unity of Contrasting Themes* (Vienna, 2001).

26 Such lengthy transitions are now also being accomplished with music videos.

27 It is perhaps significant that the phrase 'mash-up' is derived from web-based computer programming where data is combined from more than one source into a single integrated tool.

28 Robert Walser, 'Popular Music Analysis: Ten Apothegms and Four Instances' in Moore, *Analyzing Popular Music*, p. 22.

29 Writers who specifically address the ways in which modern studio technology has influenced popular music recordings include: Jones, *Rock Formation*; Jeremy J. Beadle, *Will Pop Eat Itself? Pop Music in the Soundbite Era* (London, 1993); Mark Cunningham,

Finally, rather than using sound itself or words to describe sound, some musical analyses have drawn upon a variety of kinds of visual representation as a means of demonstrating significant relationships within a recording of a piece of popular music. Until the invention of audio recording, music, like speech, was preserved in memory through a system of symbols: the musical score. The influential role that this notation system has played in Western art music is profound. Yet by representing the fleeting flow of a particular set of sounds organized in time as fixed signs on pages of paper, standard notation not only preserves musical invention, but also transposes it from the auditory to the visual sphere. As a set of reasonably precise instructions, the score enables musicians to re-create a piece of classical music as sound in time; it also allows analysts to *see* and ponder upon the individual elements that collectively make up that piece of classical music.[30]

However, while most classical music analysts focus on the score as the primary text, scores of popular music tend to be both rare and largely redundant, since the recording represents a far more complete and accurate 'record' of musical intention. Indeed, standard notation rarely figures as an important part of the popular music record production process, and when popular music is rendered as a score, usually in piano reduction, as is the case with sheet music, the results do not satisfactorily capture the musical and sonic subtleties of the recording. Hence analyses of popular music that rely exclusively on notation tend to impose a somewhat inaccurate perspective on their source material (the recording), while simultaneously ignoring the important, technologically-based processes that have brought it about.[31] Consequently, traditional, score-based methods of musical

---

Good Vibrations: A History of Record Production (Chessington, 1996); Théberge, *Any Sound You Can Imagine*; Albin J. Zak III, *The Poetics of Rock: Cutting Records, Making Tracks* (Berkeley, CA, 2001); Timothy Warner, *Pop Music: Technology and Creativity* (Aldershot, 2003); Mark Katz, *Capturing Sound: How Technology Has Changed Music* (Berkeley, 2005); and Moorefield, *The Producer as Composer*. A further strand of writing that can provide useful information regarding the production of popular music recordings may be found in a range of monthly music technology magazines, online articles and books, all of which tend to adopt a more populist and anecdotal approach. The latter include George Martin, *Summer of Love: The Making of Sgt Pepper* (London, 1995); Eric Olsen, Paul Verna and Carlo Wolff, *The Encyclopedia of Record Producers* (New York, 1999); Howard Massey, *Behind the Glass: Top Record Producers Tell How They Craft Their Hits* (San Francisco, CA, 2000); Kingsley Abbott, *The Beach Boys Pet Sounds: The Greatest Album of the Twentieth Century* (London, 2001); and Charles L. Granata, *I Just Wasn't Made for These Times: Brian Wilson and the Making of Pet Sounds* (London, 2003).

30   It is perhaps significant that traditional methods of musical analysis, by focusing on the score, tend to prioritize pitch over all other musical parameters, since this is the element that standard notation is able to depict most precisely.

31   As Robert Philip and Mark Katz demonstrate, several of the significant changes that have come about, even in the performance of classical music, in the past 100 years may be as a direct consequence of recording. See Robert Philip, *Performing Music in the Age of Recording* [New Haven, CT, 2004] and Katz, *Capturing Sound*.

analysis, when applied to recordings of popular music, often tend to be rather exclusive and limited in scope.[32]

More simply, a 'song's form could be easily diagrammed … which might give us a useful sense of its narrative progression, of how a listener experiences moving through time with the series of events it offers. … That this does not seem remarkable in itself should not distract us from realizing that it may be a crucial constituent of the song's coherent signification.'[33] Similarly, diagrams can be used to show how some aural aspect of a recording unfolds in time.[34]

As well as traditional notation and diagrams there are several other ways of representing sound visually that are available to support analyses of popular music recordings. One such is David Brackett's 'spectrum photos' of phrases sung by Hank Williams on his recording of 'Hey Good Lookin',[35] which do provide a rough indication of the frequency content of certain words, although the concrete analytical information derived from them is relatively modest. Also noteworthy is the development of the Sonic Visualiser by the Centre for the History and Analysis of Recorded Music (CHARM).[36] The Sonic Visualiser is a computer program that enables analysts to scrutinize the musical characteristics of recordings from a range of perspectives. CHARM's remit is largely based on the study of historic performance practice of classical music, as preserved on early recordings, but the Sonic Visualiser program could also be used to examine aspects of recordings of any genre of music, from any period.

With the development of digital audio workstations in recent years, the whole recording production process has become far more visually based.[37] Modern digital multitrack recording systems often include clear graphic representations of audio and MIDI data, providing precise details of the timbre, amplitude and timing for every element of the recording. These audio files may also preserve information of the production process – the order of recording the various elements, signal processor settings, details of the final mix, and so on – that could be extremely

---

32   See, for example, several of the chapters in John Covach and Graeme Boone (eds), *Understanding Rock: Essays in Musical Analysis* (Oxford, 1997).

33   Walser, 'Popular Music Analysis', p. 28.

34   See, for example, Warner, *Pop Music*, p. 134, which demonstrates the structural importance of the spatial parameter in a recording.

35   David Brackett, *Interpreting Popular Music* (Berkeley, CA, 2000), p. 93.

36   The Centre for the History and Analysis of Recorded Music (CHARM) was established in 2004 with a substantial grant from the Arts and Humanities Research Council in the UK. Based around a partnership of Royal Holloway (University of London), King's College (London) and the University of Sheffield, CHARM's 'aim is to promote the study of music as performance through a specific focus on recordings': <http://www.charm.rhul.ac.uk/index.html>.

37   'When we record music we see it on the screen': Nick McCarthy from Franz Ferdinand interviewed on *Front Row*, BBC Radio 4, 2 November 2007, 7.15pm).

valuable from an analytical perspective.[38] But, unfortunately, such files rarely come into the public domain.[39]

Yet depicting musical sound through static visual analogies, and particularly representing the temporal dimension spatially, cannot adequately demonstrate the vital characteristic of movement that is inherent in all music. Representing musical movement through the use of animated film would address this particular limitation, although such productions are beyond the scope of most musicologists.[40] Similarly, certain visual aspects of a popular music promotional video may provide insights into some of the musical characteristics of a popular music recording: as Björnberg points out, music videos can demonstrate 'a range of possible relationships between musical and visual structures'.[41] Moreover, music videos, which are designed to direct the listener to important aspects of the recording, can both represent musical movement visually and be scrutinized on a frame-by-frame basis. Hence the tempo of the editing, movement of the camera or the characters, lighting, setting, specific images or sequences and so on may be used to highlight important musical aspects of the recording and, as Walter Benjamin pointed out many years ago, a film 'lends itself more readily to analysis because it can be isolated more easily'.[42]

All these methods of representing musical sound are simply tools or techniques that have been developed to help musicologists explore and then communicate their interest in, or fascination for, a particular popular music recording. While they all tend to focus on the final recording as their starting-point, they ignore the recording process itself. The work that takes place in the recording studio –

---

38 With regard to pre-digital recordings of popular music, much useful information could be derived from multitrack tapes, track sheets, synthesizer patches, diagrams and data relating to the acoustic characteristics of the studio, signal processor settings, choice of microphones and photographs of their placements.

39 It is possible to find remix competitions on the Internet that make available some or all of the sound files of a recent popular music recording, but these are few and far between.

40 Some of the work of Canadian animator Norman McLaren and even sections of Disney's film *Fantasia* (1940) demonstrate a few of the possibilities that this approach might offer.

41 Alf Björnberg, 'Structural Relationships of Music and Images in Music Video', in Middleton, *Reading Pop*, pp. 359–60.

42 Walter Benjamin, 'The Work of Art in the Age of Mechanical Reproduction' [1936] in Francis Frascina and Jonathan Harris (eds), *Art in Modern Culture: An Anthology of Critical Texts* (London, 1992), pp. 297–307, at p. 303. Specific studio techniques may also be depicted in popular music videos. Take the video of Queen's 'Bohemian Rhapsody', for example, where the double- or triple-tracking of the vocal parts on the recording are shown as simultaneous multiple images of the singers' faces. Moreover, in the same video, a chord produced by the staggered entry of several vocal tracks on the 'o' of the word 'magnifico' is visualized by the image of the singer's face being multiplied across the screen in time with the entry of each new pitch on the recording. For a more detailed example of this approach see Tim Warner, 'Narrating Sound: The Pop Video in the Age of the Sampler' in Phil Powrie and Robynn J. Stilwell (eds), *Changing Tunes: The Use of Pre-existing Music in Film* (Aldershot, 2006).

the processes, both mental and physical, as well as the use of highly musically empowering technologies – will often play an important role in the musical character of the final recording. The last part of this chapter proposes a conceptual framework that would enable musicologists to explore the genesis of a recording as an intrinsic aspect of musical creativity.

Although musical creativity will often involve exploring a unique, and perhaps finally unknowable, series of sonic fascinations/obsessions from the imagination of one or several people and may well also include unfathomable leaps of synthesis, the processes and means by which these are realized in a popular music recording can be documented and explored with some level of certainty. The physical and mental processes that underpin the production of popular music recordings are complex, but four basic connected activities may be identified: conception; realization; perception; and contextualization (see Fig. 6.1). Crucially, these four are not to be seen as separate elements in a linear production process but rather as activities that occur concurrently, each informing, and often bringing about, modifications in the others.

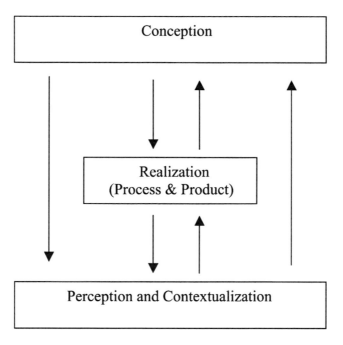

Figure 6.1   Genetic model of creativity

Conception represents the plans and ideas that are initially brought to the production process. These may be musical, organizational or technological, or a mixture of some or all of these. They may range from the highly defined to the extremely vague. They may also be the result of the work of one or more individuals.

Realization covers all the physical processes involved in creating the artefact, as well as the resulting product itself. Hence the initial ideas (musical, organizational and technological) represented by conception will have already undergone some kind of process of realization: they will have been played on an instrument, sung or recorded. The interactions between mental and physical processes – thought and expression – will bring about modifications in both; one will, to some extent, inform the other and vice versa.

Perception is the primary sensory response to the concepts being realized – in creative terms quite literally how they 'feel'. An initially intriguing or exciting idea will be repeated, explored and developed: this is a cyclic process involving modification of the evolving concepts, as well as their realization, that are continually being tested by perception. But, simultaneously, sensory perception will be tempered by the mental activity of contextualization – relating the concepts, their realization and how they are perceived to wider creative experience, which may be either real or imagined.

Turning specifically to the production of popular music recordings, the plans that are taken to the studio, often called 'preproduction', represent the initial ideas (conception). These will probably include musical ideas such as melodic and harmonic sequences, rhythmic patterns, arrangement, structure and tempo, as well as some kind of overall agreement by all parties involved in the production on the essential musical characteristics of the final recording. Preproduction may also include organizational plans: a schedule of how the recording will progress; deciding which musicians and operators of specific equipment will be required, and when; ensuring that the equipment required to make the recording is available at the right time and so on. Finally, technological issues will also be considered and these may include the use of specific devices (a synthesizer, the recording medium, a particular computer application and so on), or choice and placement of microphones with various kinds of signal processing for specific sounds, for example.

When the recording process is under way (realization) these initial plans will be implemented, but the people involved in the production are unlikely to simply follow them without thought. Instead, the plans are likely to be modified, refined and subject to further development during the processes of recording and mixing. Hence a musician or singer may struggle to successfully perform a particular part and this will have to be rewritten, or performed by someone else, to ensure a convincing performance; a device might provide a sonic element that had not been previously considered, or the recording that starts to emerge simply fails to satisfy, begins to sound stale and demands that the ideas are either radically reworked or the project is abandoned.

During the often lengthy and complex process of realization everyone involved in the production will be listening carefully, considering whether each sonic element complements and supports the overall character of the recording. For example, a lead vocal may take several hours or more to record, with the vocalist going over every phrase many times before a suitably convincing 'performance' is achieved. The decision as to what is convincing and what is not depends on perception and contextualization: every sonic element must be considered in terms of its immediate sonic characteristics – tuning, timing and timbre, for example – and also in terms of whether it fulfils more general stylistic expectations that relate directly to similar gestures heard on earlier successful popular music recordings.

Perception and contextualization not only play an important role in the creative process of popular music record production, but also inform the analytic listener's response to a particular recording and will account for their level of engagement, appreciation and methodological approach. Moreover, while a finished and released recording is sonically fixed – the sounds do not change – the ways in which these sounds are perceived and contextualized are far from static and may undergo considerable modification over time. As a result of these shifts in perception and contextualization, any interpretation of the musical concepts that underpin the recording may also alter, requiring different analytical approaches and demonstrating that all analysis is fundamentally interpretative, ideologically motivated and historically defined.

This basic genetic model of creativity (Fig. 6.1), designed to account for all kinds of artistic endeavours (production), might initially be regarded as presenting audio recordings simply as aesthetic objects and ignoring the many other ways in which they function. However, this model may prove rather more applicable than it first appears. Although it might seem to focus exclusively on the creative processes and technologies that define the essential sonic characteristics of the aesthetic object, the model could also underpin several other approaches. It could form part of an historical approach, demonstrating how audio technology has evolved and its subsequent impact on the creative process. It might be used as part of a didactic approach, elucidating both the processes and the ways through which sound can inform critical listening for the many aspiring studio musicians. It could underpin a study of the sociological make-up of any particular recording project, investigating the power structures of musical creativity. It might support the analysis of the psychological factors (both individual and collective) that bring about particular recordings. And, finally, it could be used to investigate the musical imagination of both the people who make recordings and those who appreciate them, both at the time of production and subsequently.

This chapter has made several suggestions in regard to approaches to analysing recordings of popular music. The primary contention is that virtually all popular music analyses will be directed at the recording, whether this is made explicit or not, and that audio recording, far from being a transparent medium, especially in the case of popular music, is symbiotically linked to (and influenced by) all the processes and devices that characterize the modern recording studio. Moreover, the musical composition and the 'performances' captured within a popular music recording will have been mediated by the technology and working practices of audio recording. Finally, a prerequisite for any close analysis of a popular music recording is some method of objectifying sound in time, either through sound itself, words, or visually with the use of diagrams, charts or moving images.

Returning to the 'what' part of Tagg's original question, it is evident that a single audio recording may be approached from many different angles: for Tagg it is an object of communication; for many musicians and music-lovers it is an aesthetic object; it is the result of a series of musically and technologically-based processes; it is the product of a unique set of working practices from a number of creative individuals; it can be an important element in defining the social characteristics of one or more subcultures; and, for some, it can come to represent an example of the fundamental socioeconomic forces that permeate, often subconsciously, the modern world.

The Art of Phonography:
Sound, Technology and Music[1]

Peter Wicke

More than any other form of musical practice, popular music is shaped in its development by sound recording (with its enormous possibilities for dissemination) and therefore by audio technology. For a good half-century, the involvement of this technology has meant that everything classified as 'popular music' has, for the most part, been *produced* music, not *performed* music and consequently music whose ultimate sonic form is achieved with the aid of technical equipment in a step-by-step studio process. Live music, then, imitates the sound produced previously in the studio by means of equipment-intensive reconstruction on stage. This state of affairs is something that tends to be considered only from the perspective of musical performance. The recording studio is normally understood as simply a new kind of place for music-making, a place where music-making has been extended by new possibilities, but has also been drawn into formerly unknown financial and technological dependencies.[2]

In the studio, it is not only music-making, but also the material in which this is executed, the sonic materiality of the music, that has been undergoing profound modification. By this is meant not merely the various technical interventions that may be made into the sound character, such as modifications of the frequency using an equalizer, manipulation of the structure of the produced sound by Aural Exciter, or the technical synthesis of sounds. What is meant, in a much more fundamental sense, is the way in which the physical parameters of sound are connected with

---

1   Translated from the German original by Derek B. Scott.
2   See B. Paul Clarke, '"A Magic Science": Rock Music as Recording Art', in Richard Middleton and David Horn (eds), *Popular Music. Vol. 3: Producers and Markets* (Cambridge, 1983), pp. 195–214, at p. 195ff; Michael Chanan, *Repeated Takes: A Short History of Recording and Its Effects on Music* (London, 1995); Paul Théberge, *Any Sound You Can Imagine: Making Music/Consuming Technology* (Hanover, NH and London, 1997); Mark Katz, *Capturing Sound: How Technology has Changed Music* (Berkeley, CA, 2004); and also, especially, Albin J. Zak III, *The Poetics of Rock: Cutting Tracks, Making Records* (Berkeley, CA, 2001) and Virgil Moorefield, *The Producer as Composer: Shaping the Sounds of Popular Music* (Cambridge, MA, 2005).

the aesthetic parameters of the music – in brief, the way sound is conceptualized as music-making material. In other words, the function of acoustic matter as sound in music is neither given nor certain, and music is in no way reducible to its character as sound. The physical acoustic matter does not function in the music simply as sound, as measurable sound pressure; rather, it is by being drawn via music-making into a culturally defined reference system (tone systems, aesthetic paradigms and so on), that it becomes aesthetically relevant and an ingredient of that which is understood in different cultures, each in a completely different way, as 'music'. That is the basis of the distinction in principle between sound in the physical–acoustic sense and sound as the material medium of music. So, despite the fact that it is possible to measure differences in the physical manifestation of a sound, a sound is perceived as the same sound at different spatial locations, even when it no longer exhibits the same acoustic conditions – in other words, despite the lack of an exact similarity of sonic structure. In the concert hall, we hear the same sound from whichever seat. This sound becomes a part of *music* only through a complex reference system that, in the context of a given culture, leads to certain acoustic events being interpreted as music.[3]

Hugo Riemann was already aware that the musical must be differentiated from the physical medium of audibility, when he formulated such ideas years ago in his ground-laying text *Ideen zu einer 'Lehre von den Tonvorstellungen'* (1914–15):

> [...] *that is to say, rather than being about the actual music that sounds, the alpha and omega of the art of sound are the relationships between the tones which live in the sound fantasy of the creative artist before being notated, and which, when performed, have their genesis again in the sound fantasy of the listener. The setting down of musical compositions in notation and the performance of the work are both only a means of transplanting musical experiences from the composer's fantasy into that of the musical listener.*[4]

Even today, often unconsciously, and especially in theoretical discourse about music that is informed by a rigid interpretation of the classical–romantic understanding of music, Riemann's idea that sound functions as a representation of tones (structure) has led to a musical absolute that cannot be analysed, although it is valid only in one culturally and historically limited case. And thus have been settled, without further question, the rules by which sound as sonic structure and sound as music are produced and perceived, while the technological mediation of sound production in the recording studio always held new possibilities.

---

3   In a markedly pioneering work, Stephen Feld has revealed this fundamental transformation process in the reconstruction of the music system of the Kaluli in Papua New Guinea. See *Sound and Sentiment: Birds, Weeping, Poetics, and Song in Kaluli Expression* (Philadelphia, PA, 1982).

4   Hugo Riemann, *Ideen zu einer 'Lehre von den Tonvorstellungen'* in *Jahrbuch der Musikbibliothek Peters* (Leipzig, 1914–15), pp. 1–26, at p. 2.

The special manner in which sound functions as a medium of music-making is based on cultural practice: in order to register and attribute correctly the sound experienced, it must be related each time to those who are making this music in the context of a given culture. This is the level of its 'cultural formatting', as it were – an analogy meant only as slightly metaphorical. In the same way as digital storage media needs to be formatted, sound has to be culturally formatted out of particular sonic concepts, in order to be able to record, or to 'store', that special form of human interaction that we call music. It is here that operators, technologies of articulation and their discourses, bound by this conceptual and processing parameter, come into play. The way in which sound is conceptualized, organized as music, or transformed into music, is always connected to the principal means of its generation and thus to whatever are the prevailing technologies of sound production. Clapping and vocal forms of sound production, which are found as the basis of music-making among almost all pre-industrial societies, create a musical universe quite distinct from that consisting of those mechanical sound machines that we conceptualize as musical instruments.

All this applies even more now that, as a consequence of creating sound in the recording studios' technically complex environment, music has undergone a much more profound transformation than anything music-making alone might have accomplished. When, first in the domain of rock music, the somewhat vague term 'sound' arose in the 1960s as an equivalent for style terms of earlier years, it was in reference to the sound image of produced music. This was not, however, the same conceptualizing of sound organization as a medium of music-making that had long been the case before. Whether recorded sound is considered as a technical image of acoustical reality, a representation or simulation or, instead, an acoustic structure that is ultimately an independently conceived artefact, has an effect not only on the sound patterns produced, but also on their sensual perception, which works as a pre-stored aesthetic process for recognizing what is music. It is not just a particular sound image, but also a particular concept of sound, that results from the creative handling of recording technology.

In recording studios, in recognition of the imperatives of this technology, it was necessary from the very start to restore the distinction between sound as the acoustic content actually heard and sound as the sensual medium of music-making, because the constraints of recording equipment meant that the culturally given correlation could no longer operate automatically. The restoration process that existed at the start of this development gave rise to a reconstruction process labelled 'high fidelity', which, in its final stage of development, became a process for organizing sound – the art of phonography.

Like mixing colours before actually beginning to paint, or selecting suitable material for a sculpture, sound design occurs in advance of music-making, creating the materials in which sound patterns are inscribed.[5] Even if both of these emerge

---

5   Bruce Swedien, currently one of most sought-after audio engineers, once explained:
     'I consider mics to be like paint brushes. They all do pretty much the same thing, but
     each has its own characteristics and best applications.' Quoted in Keith Hatschek, *The*

as one entity, independent professional functions have been developed during the process of the technical production of music. Identified with various roles – audio engineer, producer, musician – they have ensured that music-making has as much of an engineered, audio-technical quality as it has an artistic or, strictly speaking, musical dimension.[6] In the field of popular music, the audio-technical and the musical became so dependent on each other through the mass production of records that it is no longer possible to have an understanding of musical development without keeping both sides simultaneously in view. The history of music in the twentieth century was, indeed, written in equal measure by musicians and audio technicians.

That remark is not to be understood merely in the sense that songs first acquire their identity through studio recordings, but, rather, in the sense that they are already written with a mind to exploiting the enormously extended possibilities of the medium of sound that studio technology makes available (insofar as their character does not already spring from an interactive process involving the directly changed relationship with audio technology). Mike Stoller and Jerry Leiber, one of the most successful author-producer teams in the history of pop, not least because of their work for Elvis Presley, commented on this change tellingly with the statement, 'We didn't write songs, we wrote records'.[7]

Since music-making came into contact with audio technology in the closing years of the nineteenth century, it has been embedded in a process of technical sound-designs, in which the sonic materiality of the music connects, on a constantly expanding basis and ever more consciously and flexibly, with the particular system of cultural references from which the sound draws its musical–aesthetic relevance. Brian Eno explained this as follows:

> One of the interesting things about pop music is that you can quite often identify a record from a fifth of a second of it. You hear the briefest snatch of sound and know, 'Oh, that's "Good Vibrations"', or whatever. A fact of almost any successful pop record is that its sound is more of a characteristic

---

Golden Moment. Recording Secrets from the Pros (San Francisco, CA, 2005), p. 40.

6   That, in itself, is not so completely new, because instrument-makers also realize predetermined designs of sonorous material, something that is easy to perceive in the case of the legendary sound of the violins of the Italian master craftsman Antonio Stradivari (1644–1737) or the output of the Italian instrument maker Bartolomeo Cristofori (1655–1731) who presented the musical public with the fortepiano at the beginning of the eighteenth century – an instrument for which composers such as Carl Philip Emanual Bach, Josef Haydn, Wolfgang Amadeus Mozart and, not least, Ludwig van Beethoven developed a repertoire. However such immediate and direct effects on music remained the exception, on account of the sluggish development of instrument-making.

7   Quoted in Jan Pareles and Patricia Romanowski, *The Rolling Stone Encyclopedia of Rock & Roll*, (New York, 1983), p. 322.

than its melody or its chord structure or anything else. The sound is the thing that you recognize.[8]

The sound concepts that result from this fundamental combination of technology, sound and music are outlined, in what follows, at important stages in the development of music production technology: mechanical, electromechanical or electromagnetic sound recording, multitracking (overdubbing) and digital music production.

The Simulated Performance

The aim of recording, at the beginning of its development, was to offer within the four walls of the home, a listening experience of a live musical performance that created the illusion of being present at the actual event. At that time, nothing else was either conceivable or desirable, nor could it be achieved, given that the mechanical procedure allowed sound to be saved only to disc or cylinder. The recordings were considered an image not of the music, but of the sound events of its performance. Fred Gaisberg, who, from 1898, was in charge of the Gramophone Company that marketed Emile Berliner's patented records, and who has gone down in music history as the first producer, described his job in these words: 'We are out to make sound photographs of a performance.'[9]

The renowned 'tone tests', which the Edison Company between 1916 and 1925 used to prove the effectiveness of its phonographs among the competition, illustrate this concept of sound recording. By means of over 4000 such tests, Edison tried to convince the public that its phonographs were faithful to reality.[10] In 1916 an account of one of the first of these demonstrations in New York's Carnegie Hall appeared in the *New York Tribune*:

> *Startlingly novel even in this age of mechanical marvels was the concert that drew 2,500 persons to Carnegie Hall yesterday afternoon. Alone on the vast stage there stood a mahogany phonograph, apparently exactly like the tamed and domesticated variety that has become to be [sic] as much a part of the furniture of the ordinary drawing room as was the wheezy melodeon a generation ago. In the midst of the hushed silence a white-gloved man emerged from the mysterious region behind the draperies, solemnly placed a record in the gaping mouth of the machine, wound it up and vanished. Then*

---

8   Anthony Korner, 'Aurora musicalis' (An interview with Brian Eno), *Art Forum* 24/10 (1986): 76–79, at 76.

9   Quoted in Elisabeth Schwarzkopf, *On and Off the Record* (Boston, MA, 1992), p. 16; see also Frederick W. Gaisberg, *The Music Goes Round* (New York, 1942), p. 83ff.

10 See Emily A. Thompson, 'Machines, Music, and the Quest for Fidelity. Marketing and the Edison Phonograph in America, 1877–1925', *Musical Quarterly* 79 (1995): 131–71.

Mme. Rappold stepped forward, and leaning one arm affectionately on the phonograph began to sing an air from 'Tosca.' The phonograph also began to sing 'Vissi d' Arte, Vissi d'Amore' at the top of its mechanical lungs, with exactly the same accent and intonation, even stopping to take a breath in unison with the prima donna. Occasionally the singer would stop and the phonograph carried on the air alone. When the mechanical voice ended Mme. Rappold sang. The fascination for the audience lay in guessing whether Mme. Rappold or the phonograph was at work, or whether they were singing together.[11]

As sensational and valid demonstrations of that time, they had to guarantee that 'it was actually impossible to distinguish the singer's living voice from its re-creation in the instrument', as the *Boston Journal* commented after one such demonstration in the same year.[12] Today, this seems an even more amazing statement, because the sounds played back were still barely distinguishable from the noise of the medium. What is more, the frequency range lay between 250 and 2500 Hz and, therefore, covered only a fraction of the audible spectrum.

This insistence that the original and its technical reproduction were indistinguishable becomes comprehensible when one asks exactly what was being compared in these tests. It was certainly not sound quality in today's sense of the reproduction of timbre, because there was, at most, a mechanical correspondence. The playback was understood, rather, as a representation of the performance – as a sounding equivalent of the *activity* of music-making but not of its *results*. Even though the sounds of music-making were depicted in each case, if a precise comparison was made between such results and their technical reproduction there was barely any similarity to be found. Technical reproduction represented music-making as actions structured in time and, even then, only in the form that could be obtained via particular equipment. Sound quality per se is a secondary consideration in this regard; the function of recording was merely to outline the organized time structure of music-making and the sounds generated by that activity, relating one to the other.

The limits of audio technology in recording studios pushed to the forefront a concept of sound that dominated music production until the mid-twentieth century – one that focused on the dimension of its temporal unfolding (it would in fact be more precise to say production was *reduced* to that role). In view of the technical impossibility of portraying the acoustic reality of sonic events, audio technology shifted the aesthetic paradigm towards a studio-simulated interactivity of music-making intended to give listeners the illusion of its taking place in their own living rooms.

A vivid report of just these kinds of a-musical procedures in the mechanical recording of music is given by Joe Batten (1885–1955), originally a studio piano accompanist, whose later career included leading roles in different British record

---

11   'Edison Snares Soul of Music', *New York Tribune*, 29 April 1916, p. 3.
12   Quoted in Thompson, 'Machines, Music, and the Quest for Fidelity', p. 132.

companies. In his posthumously published memoirs of 1956 there is a description of his first recording session, completed as a 16-year-old in summer 1900 for the London Musiphone Company,[13] under the direction of a certain Dan Smoot.

> *Most of the space of the room ... was occupied by an improvised rostrum, five feet in height, upon which an upright grand piano had been hoisted to enable its sound board to be on a level with the recording horn. The back and front of the piano had been removed, so that the maximum of sound could be obtained, thus leaving only the action and sound board. ... I had to climb four high wooden steps to reach the piano, which brought my head to within a few inches of the ceiling. The singer, an arm resting on the piano, stood in front of a recording horn which measured five inches in diameter, in such a position that I could not see him. In this fantastic setting and throughout the sultry heat of the day A.H. Gee and Montague Borwell, baritone and tenor, alternated in singing, 'Come into the Garden, Maud', 'The Diver' and 'The Soldiers of the Queen'. Precariously perched on a stool on the rostrum, coat discarded, perspiring profusely, I hammered out the accompaniments. Dan Smoot had demanded of me to make the tone 'double forte', and double forte it was. From time to time the singers whispered appeals to 'keep it down'. If appalled myself at the din I was making, I did so, Dan Smoot would clamber up the rostrum with the agility of a monkey and fiercely command: 'Take no notice. Keep it loud. You're doing fine.' I could not judge. My brain, usually cool, detached and critical of what my hands were doing, was in a state of bewilderment, and I rattled off the accompaniments like an automaton.[14]*

In effect, it was not really a sound picture of a performance but, rather, a simulation of that performance in the temporal arrangement (*Zeitgestalt*) of sound. Since, in the early years, that could not be made available to the public without helpful information, until well into the 1910s an announcement was made at the beginnings of records, which served to introduce the imaginary performance on the virtual stage of the domestic gramophone or phonograph.[15]

When, in 1925, technical boundaries shifted substantially with the advent of Orthophonic Victrola electrical recordings (of Victor Records), recording technicians remained fully aware of the gap between the original sound and its technical reproduction. In the meantime, the function of recorded sound was to produce a mental image of a performance. In this, the quality of sound certainly

---

13   Originating in 1896 as the record label of Australian firm Craig Williamson Ltd; from 1906 taken over by the London-based Fonotopia Ltd, branded as *Odeon*.

14   Joe Batten, *The Joe Batten Book – Story of Sound Recordings* (London, 1956), p. 32.

15   See Tim Brooks, 'Columbia Records in the 1890s: Founding the Record Industry', *Association for Recorded Sound Collections* 10/1 (1978): 5–36, where the following example from a Columbia Records recording of the US Marine Band can be found: 'The following record taken for the Columbia Phonograph Company of Washington, D.C., entitled *The National Fencibles March*, as played by the United States Marine Band' (p. 15).

did not play a negligible role, but it remained a secondary consideration all the same. So it was that Bell Telephone Laboratories, in cooperation with Leopold Stokowski, conductor of the Philadelphia Orchestra, undertook the first systematic measurement of the frequency spectrum and dynamics of a symphony orchestra in 1930 and 1931. This led to more than the production of scientific data. After further developments in Bell Telephone Laboratories, Western Electric brought on to the market an electrical recording process with a frequency range from 50 to 6000 Hz and a dynamic range of several decibels. However, this merely allowed the recording and reproduction of a richer slice of the sound spectrum of a live orchestral performance. The director of research at Bell Laboratories, Harold D. Arnold, under whose direction the calculations had been made, summed it all up as follows:

> ... these facts are definite and conclusive as to the physical nature of the sounds present in orchestra music. They are not conclusive as to the aesthetic necessity of such wide ranges of either frequency or volume.[16]

Such a statement makes sense only with the imputation that the significant aesthetic parameters of music are not revealed in musical timbre, but in the temporal structure that acts as the common denominator of performed and recorded music. It is not the actual character of the sound image in terms of timbre and texture, but rather the act of its formal presentation in music-making (hence, the performance) that is considered to be the crucial aesthetic dimension of musical sound (in contrast to its fully revealed physical acoustic condition). Until the introduction of electrical recording, this was linked to considerable interference in the hiring of musicians and in arranging music, and this did not cease where classical repertoire was involved. It was usually accepted without complaint and did not hamper the rapid distribution of records.[17]

---

16   Quoted in Robert McGinn, 'Stokowski and the Bell Telephone Laboratories: Collaboration in the Development of High-Fidelity Sound Reproduction', *Technology and Culture* 24/1 (1983): 38–75, at 48.
17   It elicited a complaint from the Berlin musicologist and journalist Max Chop (1862–1929), who wrote for the *Photographische Zeitschrift Plattenrezensionen* that appeared in Berlin from 1900 on, about the mutilation of recorded works by inappropriate interventions, although he always considered such adaptations legitimate for the purpose of recording. In an essay of 1909, in which he took stock of these developments, he commented cautiously: 'Vor allem habe ich an der orchestralen Fassung und Bearbeitung manches auszusetzen. Man sollte da jede Willkür im Ersatz meiden und nach Möglichkeit das Original berücksichtigen, soweit dies eben die Eigenart der Membran zulässt. Dass die Bässe und Violoncelle [*sic!*] vor der Hand auszuschalten und durch tiefe Holz- und Blechbläser zu ersetzen sind, ist dura necessitas, die der Schmiegsamkeit der Linien manches nimmt, aber schließlich das ganze Klangbild nicht zu sehr verändert. Der willkürliche Austausch von hohen Streichern gegen hohe Blasinstrumente (Flöten, Klarinetten, Trompeten) ist entschieden zu mißbilligen. Die Geiger, wenn sie nur in gehöriger Zahl besetzt sind und mit ihrem Klange Holz oder Blech aufwiegen, müßten

The priority of temporal organization in relation to other sound parameters justifies, as it were, the secondary position of the aesthetic response. Performance is a prerequisite for music recorded (better, *produced*) in the studio. The performance, in reality, has to precede the studio simulation; so, the sound image needs to be established as that which constitutes the music-making before it can act as advocate for the representation of that music-making in recorded form. That does not mean it was mandatory for recorded pieces of music to be always well known and popular, although this was regularly the case for commercial reasons. It means only that the sound of recorded music had to be locatable in the world of musical performance. Sonic simulation had to be recognizable as a depiction of something that went beyond what was actually heard. A performance consisted of something played and, therefore, of something that had been played earlier. Musical demands are satisfied by focusing on performers' interpretations, and, since the music acts as a common reference point for these sonic structures, it acquires an abstract identity, such as 'song' or 'work'.

Thus, the concept of sound prevailing in recording studios became quite separate from the sound of the music played there, and modifications to improve the technology initially amounted to nothing: the recording remained uniquely tied to the temporal arrangement of sound and, therefore, to the simulation of performance. When, at the beginning of the 1930s, the credo of the industry became 'high fidelity', this particular aspect was raised to the level of a major advertising campaign. In 1936 R.C.A. Victor was boasting that its discs were 'the most faithful reproduction of actual performance that has been developed'.[18] Conditions for recording live performances in studios now became more similar, but many musicians had difficulty accommodating themselves to the absence of the public and the lack of a stimulus from a specific social context.[19]

Because of technological imperatives, the concept of sound that was valid in recording studios was one that responded directly to music–making, for the only kind of music found there related, more or less deliberately, to the existing paradigms. In his published autobiography of 1942, Gaisberg remarked that only music that supplied the best results on disc was selected for recording: 'At first we had to choose our "titles" so as to obtain the most brilliant results without revealing the defects of the machine'.[20] It was hardly surprising that musical forms like jazz, Tin Pan Alley or different types of dance music, whose development was most directly linked to recording in those years, was focused similarly on the temporal

---

unter allen Umständen beibehalten werden': Max Chop, 'Ergänzungsfragen für die Sprechmaschinen-Literatur', *Phonographische Zeitschrift* 10/4 (1909): 75–78, at. 76.

18 Quoted in Alexander Boyden Magoun, 'Shaping the Sound of Music: The Evolution of the Phonograph Record, 1877-1950', PhD diss. (University of Maryland, College Park, 2000), p. 187.

19 See in this connection the very informative interviews with musicians in John Harvith and Susan Edwards Harvith, *Edison, Musicians, and the Phonograph: A Century in Retrospect* (New York, 1987).

20 Gaisberg, *The Music Goes Round*, p. 83.

organization of sound and, thus, on the metric–rhythmic side of music-making. Above all else, however, simulated performances and their different musical interpretations now began to find themselves in competition across all areas of recorded music, a process that, once printed advice notes appeared, led to much deliberation about the recorded creative output of composers and songwriters.

The Simulated Space

For a long time, the idea of a record demonstrating 'fidelity to the original', understood as meaning as faithful an image of the performance as possible, remained the credo of sound recording.[21] Only with the arrival of magnetic tape in music production at the end of the 1940s did it begin to undergo modification.[22] In 1948 Capitol Records in Los Angeles, at the time one of the leading popular music labels in the USA, became the first company to convert all production to tape, replacing the former practice of cutting the recording directly on to a master disc. The near-unlimited scope for repetition, as well as the possibility of splicing together the most successful passages from different recordings, meant, primarily, that production costs could be lowered for the first time. Even then, it was not long before a concern arose about the finished products leaving the studios: *de facto* assemblages of tapes constructed from several takes. Owing to the fragility and detail of the master tapes, a special 'production master' was always made for cutting discs and archiving the recording (since splices disintegrate with frequent play and long storage). This process cannot be reconstructed, because the splicing cannot be retraced. According to reports, however, it was already common, shortly after the introduction of magnetic tape to music production, to piece together a three-minute popular song from at least three or four takes. Walter Afanasieff, who, with his work for Mariah Carey and Céline Dion, enjoys a pre-eminent profile among present-day producers, offers the following explanation:

> When you are doing a recording, it needs to be done so that everyone appreciates it – it's the best that it could be, it's the absolute finest that we can achieve in the studio given the money spent, the people hired, the technology afforded. ... A lot of people don't have the ability; but they are great artists, great performers, great talented people, and not everything they do in one take in the studio is what should be on their record. There have to be multiple takes, everyone does it. I don't care if you're Tony Bennett or Mariah Carey

---

21   For more detail, see Lars Nyre, *Fidelity Matters. Sound Media and Realism in the 20th Century* (Bergen, 2003).

22   On the development of sound tape and its role in music production, see John T. Mullin, 'Creating the Craft of Tape Recording', *High Fidelity* (1976): 62–67, as well as David L. Morton, *Sound Recording: The Life Story of a Technology* (Baltimore, MD, 2006).

or Celine Dion, Whitney Houston, Aretha Franklin – everybody has multiple takes. Frank Sinatra used to do three takes.[23]

In this way, music was not only removed from its previously inescapable real-time reference, but, through the technology of electromagnetic recording and through the transformation and storage of an electrical equivalent of the soundwave, sound also acquired a form of existence in which it could be processed and arranged in a manner that went far beyond the possibilities of mechanical sound production by musical instruments.[24] This process would prove to hold consequences just as serious for music as did, centuries before, the introduction of notation, which presented the sound patterns of music in graphic form. It now made available direct access to the physical materiality of sound. With the introduction of electric recording and the technology to write to magnetic tape, the signal into which sound was transformed was no longer a mere transitory stage in the recording process, but something saved as an independent collection of acoustic matter.[25] This new configuration formed the prerequisite for enabling sound, as a medium of music-making, to be extended to another dimension, one previously outside of sound organization but now in the centre of its design – the dimension of space.

The space in which music resonates has always significantly affected the perception of music. It is evident in the shape of church buildings, whose layout is designed to create an overwhelming acoustic space, or in the acoustically informed architecture of nineteenth-century concert halls that optimized the aesthetic experience of musical sound.[26] Yet that remained a feature external to the music itself. With electromagnetic sound storage, however, it became possible to inscribe this dimension in the very medium of sound and, combined with echo and reverb, to fix it there as a design feature. The recording as a simulated performance now turned into a simulated performance with a given spatial character and, soon after, a simulated performance in a simulated space. This was enabled by the sensitivity of microphones, increasing rapidly with the transition to electric recording. The microphones were able to pick up not only the direct sound from instruments, but

---

23   Quoted in David John Farinella, *Producing Hit Records. Secrets from the Studio,* (New York, 2006), p. 136f.

24   One of the first to understand and make use of the artistic possibilities was Pierre Henry, who, after the new edition of the *Messe Pour Le Temps Present* (Philips, France, 1997), was rescued from the periphery of French *musique concrète* and rediscovered as the grandfather of techno. See also Michel Chion, *Pierre Henry* (Paris, 2003).

25   Paul D. Green describes this as follows: 'A new and understudied means of music making has emerged within and among the world's musical cultures. It is driven not so much by the vibration of membranes, chords, hard surfaces, or molecules of air but rather primarily by the manipulation of electrical impulses': Paul D. Greene and Thomas Porcello (eds), *Wired for Sound: Engineering and Technologies in Sonic Cultures,* (Middletown, CT, 2005), p. 1.

26   One of the few works to pursue this unusual secondary aspect for understanding music history is Emily A. Thompson, *The Soundscape of Modernity. Architectural Acoustics and the Culture of Listening in America, 1900–1933* (Cambridge, MA, 2002).

also the reflected sound in the performance space. Admittedly, this was initially considered an undesirable feature of recording technology, because it was seen as an interference that could not be calculated, or as an unwanted reinforcement of individual frequencies. The recording studio was, therefore, covered with sound-absorbing material and transformed as far as possible into a non-sound-reflecting space (*anechoic*), in order to eliminate its own sound character from the recording. Only as the microphone acquired ever more externally formed qualities of recording behaviour,[27] and multichannel recording using several microphones linked to one output had arrived on the scene, was it possible to introduce, in a controlled manner, the difficult-to-calculate reflected sound in recordings. From now on, recordings acquired a particular sound from the character of the space in which they were made. These spaces were promoted as part of the brands of the various studios. Producer and audio engineer Tony Visconti – associated with Procol Harum and Joe Cocker, as well as David Bowie and a number of the most important representatives of the post-punk era, such as Iggy Pop and Adam Ant – once commented apropos of this: 'It's not so much the instrument; the room is very much part of the sound.'[28]

Sound design, with regard to the formation of spatial aspects, became an ever more important constituent of recorded music, and now, as a self-standing aesthetic–creative component of produced music, it occupied ground apart from the conventional music-making of voices and instruments. Even if the competence needed to deal with it usually lay in the hands of audio engineers, it was not long before composers, like the author-producer teams emerging in the 1950s (Leiber–Stoller, Holland–Dozier–Holland and so on) or musicians themselves (for instance, Brian Eno, Peter Gabriel, David Byrne and Steve Albini) cared actively about this side of their art.[29]

---

27 The first microphones to pick up sound from a certain direction only (unidirectional in distinction to omnidirectional) had already come into use in radio broadcasts as speaker microphones from the 1930s on (Harry F. Olson's series of Ribbon Microphones developed for RCA), but were not used in music production until their improvement in the 1940s (Sure Unidyne from 1941 and Neuman U-47 from 1947). See John Borwick, *Microphones: Technology and Technique* (London, 1990).

28 Quoted in Howard Massey, *Behind the Glass. Top Record Producers Tell How They Craft Their Hits* (San Francisco, CA, 2000), p. 145.

29 Of outstanding importance in this connection is the swing guitarist Les Paul (Lester Polfus), who not only finds a place in history through having designed the legendary 'Gibson Les Paul' guitar, but also with his sound-on-sound method became one of the first musicians to be involved with the development of new recording procedures. The development of the eight-track machine, which had then become the studio standard, can also be traced back to a suggestion of his. The prototype, baptized 'Octopus' by Les Paul, was built for him under the designation Ampex A 300-8 1956 by the Ampex Electric and Manufacturing Company. See Les Paul, 'Multitracking: It Wasn't Always This Easy …, in George Petersen (ed.), *Modular Digital Multitracks* (Emeryville, CA, 1997), pp. 1–7, as well as Mark Cunningham, *Good Vibrations: A History of Record Production* (London, 1998).

As long as the processing of electronic sound was in its infancy, the ambient sound of the recording venue, its response behaviour, its reflective conditions and the absorbent properties of the materials used in the room all played a crucial role, since subsequent corrections to the spatial character of the recorded sound were next to impossible. Converted spaces in churches, with non-linear response behaviour, supplied the best sound characteristics, and featured prominently in the activities of the legendary recording studios. Columbia Records' studio in New York, in which music history was made between 1946 and 1983, was located in a former Greek Orthodox wooden church on 30th Street, on Manhattan's East Side. In those years, Frank Sinatra and Billie Holiday, then Bob Dylan and Simon and Garfunkel, and later Miles Davis and Bruce Springsteen were among those of reputation and status to be recorded in that 30-metre-high space with its wooden walls and floors – the former nave. Malcolm Addey, who was active as an audio engineer from 1958 to 1968 and later ran a renowned remastering studio in New York, recollected:

> It took EMI engineers years of studious nipping-and-tucking to finally arrive at the desired echo balance and tonality that you hear on those Beatles records. To tell you the truth, we were really after Columbia's sound – at one point we even went over to the 30th Street Studio to find out what they did to make those records sound so special. And actually, we got pretty close to it.[30]

Other major studios were (and still are) accommodated in former churches. Former auditoriums also enjoyed great popularity, since they were normally already built to provide the best acoustic conditions possible. At the beginning of the 1950s Capitol Records' studio in Los Angeles became famous for its transparent sound – crystal clear in the heights, full and rich in the depths. It was a converted theatre that had served as a broadcasting studio before being taken over by Capitol in 1948 and went on to serve as the recording studio in the newly established Capitol Tower from the mid-1950s until the label disappeared. Bing Crosby, Frank Sinatra and Nat King Cole made a number of their most important records here.[31]

Once the spatial dimension had become a constituent of the sound concept of recorded music, the next step was to simulate sound characteristics from various spaces, in order to extend the organizational possibilities of this dimension beyond the current practice of using different recording studios for different musical purposes. Acoustic echo chambers – often in curious form – marked the first step towards simulated space. Here, the effect is created separately from the music, through the parallel transfer of the recording into an especially rich, reverberant space, which is then mixed with the sound as desired. Toilets, stairwells, vaults and cellars were often used. Because of the flexibility they offered to sound organization,

---

30   Quoted in David Simons, *Studio Stories* (San Francisco, CA, 2004), p. 31.
31   An instructive overview of the most important studios and their recording spaces can be found in Jim Cogan and William Clark, *Temples of Sound: Inside the Great Recording Studio* (San Francisco, CA, 2003).

they were soon being applied as the regular space acoustic of a particular studio.[32] For instance, the echo chambers at Gold Star Studios in Los Angeles became world-famous for Phil Spector's 'wall of sound', and from 1950–84 were home to a host of major stars (among them, Brian Wilson and the Beach Boys, Herb Alpert, Bob Dylan, John Lennon, Art Garfunkel and Leonard Cohen), which put them among the most sought-after music studios for over three decades.[33]

Bill Putnam, who not only operated one of the first independent studios in music history, but also, with his company Universal Audio, was one of the pre-eminent names in the development of top-class audio technology, used opera house toilets as an echo chamber at the Universal Studio in Chicago that served as his home base.[34] Among other things, an unmistakable character was given to VeeJay, Mercury and Chess Records from the sessions that took place there with Dinah Washington, Muddy Waters, Willie Dixon, Bo Diddley, Little Walter and Chuck Berry. Columbia, which maintained a second studio complex on New York's Seventh Avenue (it had already functioned as a station of the Columbia broadcasting system in the 1930s), used the building's ten-floor stairwell as an incomparably variable echo chamber. Phil Ramone, who took over the studio from Columbia in 1977, produced some of his most successful work there up to the mid-1990s, for (among others) Ray Charles, Gloria Estefan, Billy Joel, Elton John, Madonna, Paul McCartney, George Michael and Sinéad O'Connor. Despite the fact that similar technical solutions for this purpose were available in analogue and, later, digital form, he continued to use the stairway as an echo chamber, even if this meant, in practice, that it could only be operated at night, when no public traffic impaired the recordings. Atlantic Records' studio, too, had a famous echo chamber at its disposal. It was built in 1959 by Tom Dowd, who was active from 1954 as a leading recording engineer for Atlantic, and who made a multiplicity of influential recordings here with the Clovers, Ruth Brown, Joe Turner, Clyde McPhatter, LaVern Baker, the Drifters, Ray Charles and others. In so doing, he created pop history like no other producer.[35]

---

32   John Palladino, who was responsible for the technical side of productions for Capitol Records from 1948–61, later revealed: 'The whole secret of Capitol 's sound, and something that was given a great deal of attention, was the use of acoustic echo chambers.' Quoted in Cogan and Clark, *Temples of Sound*, p. 18.

33   They had been built after plans by David S. Gold, one of the founders and owner of the studios, who was also responsible for their technical design. They consisted of two complementarily arranged trapezoidal spaces on a 6 × 6 metre large surface in the cellar of the house. With their special wall geometry and their use of insulating material of a substance that was never precisely known, they were considered absolutely perfect.

34   See Robert Pruter, *Doowop: The Chicago Scene* (Urbana, IL, 1996), p. 16f.

35   Tom Dowd described it in the following words: 'I bought lots of boxes of leftover tiles from local hardware stores because I only wanted fractured pieces. We intentionally had the most non-symmetrical room in the city! We did everything the total opposite to what a carpenter or mason would do. We made that room so screwed up that the only thing level was the floor, and the ceiling and four walls had nothing in common with symmetry whatsoever! When we put the tiles on, we did it in such an erratic fashion that no two pieces looked the same. I mean, it was a nightmare of a room, aesthetically;

Even if sound coloured by the complex reflective conditions that occur within a real space was thought irreplaceable, tape was already being used, shortly after its introduction, to simulate spatial resonance. Tape delay – the use of running time differences between the record and playback heads for reverb and echo effects[36] – was heard for the first time in Les Paul's 'How High the Moon' of 1951, recorded with Mary Ford (Capitol Records, USA). Later, Sam Phillips made it a hallmark of his Sun Records in Memphis in the form of slap-back echo, which, if nothing else, gave its inimitable character to his early recordings of Elvis Presley, since a not insignificant part of their effect depends on it.[37] Phillips later explained that, given the constraints of his studio which was converted from his former shop for fan heaters, the idea of space simulation was a primary motive for the development of slap-back echo:

Any time that you can do a thing where you have an automatic natural blend, it is absolutely much better. It keeps it out of the pure mechanical world, and now that's what we're getting into. After I discovered my slapback echo I found usually that it gave a type of liveness that was very difficult [to capture]. I never went for [it myself, but] back then people wanted a fairly dead studio, and I wanted to keep it as live as I could and still be able to handle it in there and be able to let each of the members of the band work.[38]

Since then, simulated space has become a normal part of the sound concept of recorded music.[39] It is also found in music practice and, most of all, began to play a role in arrangement, something now laid out increasingly in line with realizable spatial effects. In this connection, Allan Moore speaks aptly of 'virtual-textural'

---

but it was a nice echo chamber.' Quoted in Cunningham, *Good Vibrations*, p. 49.

36   If the signal at the tape machine's playback head is returned to the record head, then before the sonic event is recorded an echo-like repetition takes place because of a time misalignment that corresponds to the length of tape between the record head and playback head. The principle is also the basis of the tape-looping echo devices, which were used frequently in the 1960s and 1970s, with the difference that, here, the distance between record and playback head can be variably adjusted.

37   You can hear this, however, only on the 1954 Sun Records originals, because all later releases, even those early Sun productions briefly rereleased after Presley's transfer to RCA Victor in 1956, are remastered. The Memphis Recording Service Ltd, a British enterprise without connection to Sun Records or the Sun Studio Museum in Memphis, which possesses some of the original matrices of Presley's Sun recordings, released a limited number of pressings of the original matrix of 'That's Alright Mama' in 2004 to celebrate the fiftieth anniversary of Presley's first studio session, and on these the effect is present.

38   Quoted in Cogan and Clark, *Temples of Sound*, p. 90.

39   Peter Doyle provides an instructive outline not only of recording technology, but also of technological issues in the organization of musical space, in *Echo and Reverb: Fabricating Space in Popular Music Recording, 1900–1960* (Middletown, CT, 2005).

space.[40] From here, it was only a small step to its being no longer a matter of real types of space but, rather, of an acoustic architecture created in the studio that had nothing to do with the actual performance conditions of music. The prerequisite for this possibility was the ability to break down the sound structure into its constituent parts during recording – multitracking technique.

Emancipated Sound

Since the 1930s several microphones had been used in the recording of swing big bands, in order to distinguish the sounds made by soloists from the rest of the band. The mixers essential for this had been available even in the early 1930s, having been developed for the production of film soundtracks.[41] However, in the production of music, and in contrast to the mixing of language, noise and music in film, the bringing together of several signals proved to be a far from unproblematic process. Since, unlike acoustic waves, electrical waves are two-dimensional, the production of a composite signal from several audio signals with overlapping frequency ranges, as happens with musical ensembles, is highly susceptible to interference – loss or reinforcement of individual frequencies due to the overlap of their wave forms – and this brings with it audible, and mostly unwanted, sound effects. Multichannel recording was established properly at the end of the 1940s, only after the introduction of magnetic tape into music production. The uncomplicated way in which a tape recording allows repeated hearings enabled miking to be corrected and, if necessary, filtering of the captured audio signals to suppress problematic frequency ranges and obtain the best results. But multitracking opened new perspectives again on sound organization and technical sound design by making possible the separate, but synchronous, recording of different audio signals and their subsequent treatment, permitting them to be merged at one remove from the recording process.[42] An individual sound concept could now be implemented that carried the audible imprint of the audio engineers and producers involved.

Moreover, it was not just music-making that was emancipated in this context; sound design, too, had finally achieved its own value outside of the performance paradigm. While, in acoustic reality, sound cannot be separated from the spatial and temporal conditions in which it occurs, multitracking now permitted sound

---

40   Allan Moore, *Rock: the Primary Text. Developing a Musicology of Rock* (Aldershot, 2nd edn, 2001), p. 125.

41   The first models built from 1931 on by Western Electric in the USA had four, with an on/off switch providing inputs for the connection of microphones that were regulated by an assigned rotary potentiometer leading to an output. By the mid-1940s these had become eight inputs, while the big Hollywood studios, which often had equipment made after their own specification, were already using consoles with ten or 12 inputs.

42   See William Moylan, *Understanding and Crafting the Mix: The Art of Recording* (Amsterdam, 2007).

concepts that were completely liberated from actual spatio-temporal conditions. The recording, then, is neither a copy nor a simulation of acoustic reality but, rather, a new form of sonic reality.[43] Out of sound design comes a relatively autonomous constituent of production about which decisions need to be made, such as which sound concept should be treated as fundamental to the recording. Brian Eno, who claimed tape was his most important musical instrument, explained the way this development runs its course in a lecture held in New York, 1979, entitled 'The Studio as Compositional Tool':

> *I often start working with no starting point ... You're working directly with sound, and there's no transmission loss between you and the sound – you handle it. It puts the composer in the identical position of the painter – he's working directly with a material, working directly onto a substance, and he always retains the options to chop and change, to paint a bit out, add a piece, etc.*[44]

In phonographic art, which music production had now become, artistic inspiration and technical know-how grew inseparably together. Music production now creates 'phonographic artworks' and no longer simply songs. The recording itself has become the normative musical paradigm.[45]

At the beginning of the 1950s two- and three-track machines were already found in studios, but at first they allowed only the simultaneous recording of tracks. Thus, soloist and instrumental accompaniment, or various instrumental ensembles, could be recorded separately from each other, but nothing else was possible except the readjustment of volume before they were transferred simultaneously to the full-track tape.[46] Multitrack machines that allowed multiple recording, a thorough multitrack technique, appeared in studios in 1955, after the US manufacturer Ampex had made it possible for the record heads to be switched on or off during playback (SelSync), so that the misalignment between the two, and its inevitable time-lag, was removed. This meant that multilayered recording became possible, and the recording of one track during the simultaneous playback of existing tracks opened the gates to almost boundless experimentation with sound design. At the beginning of the 1960s there were already 12 channels at the producer's disposal,

---

43　Paul Théberge has described this as a transition from a form of sonic representation that documents a pre-existing event in the studio, to a form of the sonic representation that constructs such an event. See Paul Théberge, 'The "Sound" of Music: Technological Rationalization and the Production of Popular Music', *New Formations* 8 (1989): 99–111.

44　Brian Eno, 'Pro Session: The Studio as Compositional Tool', *Down Beat* 50 (1983): 65–67, at 67.

45　See also, in this connection, Theodore Gracyk, *Rhythm and Noise: An Aesthetics of Rock* (Durham, NC, 1996).

46　See John T. Mullin, 'Magnetic Recording for Original Recordings', *Journal of the Audio Engineering Society* 25/10–11 (1977): 696–701, at 699f.

although four-track technology remained the standard, especially since it was only in the 1960s that pop music production changed over to stereo.

Norman Petty's recordings of Buddy Holly, beginning in 1956, are among the first in which sound design has freed itself completely from performance models (and performance practice). Petty did not even have a multitrack machine available at his mini-studio in Clovis, New Mexico. He recorded in mono, and copied that, together with other recordings, on to a second machine.[47] This is how, for instance, a sound concept that departed from acoustic reality is realized in Buddy Holly's 'Words of Love'.[48] The overdubbing effects, here – the doubling of Buddy Holly's voice – are already much more than a technical gimmick. Vocal interaction with the technical trace of his own voice does not simply allow the singer to be doubly audible. Rather, the doubled voice becomes a demonstration of the technical ability to record sounds from resonating bodies separately and then combine them on one track. Thereby, the voice becomes a technological construct, a synthesis of human generation and machine mutation. The pop star's 'natural' voice may, indeed, be capable of forming unusual sounds, but an unprocessed and unamplified voice does not 'sound' correctly in the context of this medium and needs to be presented to the senses via technology. Without the microphone and amplifier, such voices do not exist; they are disembodied through technical production, set loose from their origins in the larynx and lodged, in their special sound quality, somewhere between the human and the machine. The star singer supplies only the raw material. The microphone becomes the instrument of the bodiless sound of the media age.

In another respect, too, the Norman Petty productions are decidedly pioneering works of those years. They combine two diverging spatial perspectives in their sound design.[49] This would scarcely have been accepted by the public as long as musical developments were dominated by live performance, but that changed fundamentally with the triumphant advance of the rock 'n' roll single. Thus, the

---

47   In so doing, Petty referenced the sound-on-sound method of Les Paul, who had already practiced the technique of multi-layered recording via copy-transfer in the 1940s, and achieved spectacular results that were well in advance of his time. Joe Mauldin, from 1957 bassist in Buddy Holly's backing group the Crickets and, from 1963 an audio-engineer in the Gold Star Studios, Los Angeles, where he was involved as a second engineer in Phil Spector's trailblazing productions, recollected: 'Petty was among the new breed of technicians who took the rock 'n' roll sound to new heights, using Les Paul's overdubbing principles, even though he was yet to invest in a multitrack recorder. Norman's mainstay tape machine was a mean momma Ampex 600 portable which allowed him to remove it from the studio and take anywhere he wanted. But he also had an Ampex 327 mono machine on which he would make duplicate copies. He recorded us in mono and would use the two machines, playing back on to one the music he had just recorded while recording a new part along with it'. Quoted in Cunningham, *Good Vibrations*, p. 48.

48   Coral Records, USA, 1957.

49   Albin Zak has noted in his, in this regard, groundbreaking study *The Poetics of Rock*, the various juxtapositions of spatial perspective in Norman Petty's Buddy Holly productions; see p. 81ff.

rhythmic–harmonic contribution of percussion and bass to 'Words of Love' is recorded in a pronouncedly 'dry' manner, Petty having made use of a cardboard box instead of a snare drum to provide a 'dry' background to Buddy Holly's reverberant guitar and voice.[50] The snare drum had proved unsuitable because it did not stand out sufficiently from the guitar line, or work effectively at a correspondingly high recording level; it was also too resonant in a dry acoustic. The reverberation on voice and guitar was recorded in the building's toilet, which had been converted into an echo chamber. These sounds could not possibly occur together simultaneously in a real place, any more than Buddy Holly could really sing a duet with himself. However, with the separation of sound from its location in time and space – developed to perfection a little later by Phil Spector – and, with it, the detachment of the parameters of performance, the sensual value of sound in itself moves into the foreground. Therein lies a major reason for the fascination these recordings are still able to exercise a half-century after their initial appearance. With their minimal arrangements – at most, a singer, guitar, drum kit and bass – they still, in one way, captured an ideal of recorded music but, in another, had already moved light years away from it.

The sound concepts that formed the basis for recordings that enabled audio engineers to rise to unexpected prominence,[51] gradually led to the dismantling of sonic material into the single constituents of its wave form, based on its signal and electromagnetic storage, in order to reassemble it independently of the laws of acoustics. Reference, for example, may be made to the prolonged audible decay of the final chord of The Beatles' album *Sgt. Pepper's Lonely Hearts Club Band* (1967).[52] It is raised above the audibility threshold for more than a minute by use of a compressor.[53]

---

50 See John Goldrosen, *The Buddy Holly Story* (New York 1979), p. 85ff.

51 Since 1959 the National Academy of Recording Arts and Sciences (NARAS) in Los Angeles awards a Grammy for the Best Engineered Album. The first, in 1959, went to Ted Keep, the joint founder of Liberty Records, who, as sound engineer for 'The Chipmunk Song' (Liberty Records, USA, 1958), had realized a multilayered recording of David Seville's voice with different tape speeds to create the sound of the Chipmunks. The first non-American to receive such a Grammy was the British tone engineer Geoff Emerick in 1968, for the sound design of The Beatles' album *Sgt. Pepper*.

52 Parlophone, GB, 1967.

53 On the technical production details, see Geoff Emerick, *Here, There and Everywhere: My Life Recording the Music of The Beatles* (New York, 2006), p. 132ff; also Kevin Ryan and Brian Kehew, *Recording The Beatles: The Studio Equipment and Techniques Used to Create Their Classic Albums* (Houston, TX, 2006).

Simulated Sound

With the digitization of the medium of sound, a further crucial step in this process took place. In its binary representation, sound has freed itself entirely from the modalities of its production. It is now subjected to calculated real-time simulation, in which the simulation process and repeated hearings attained via the digitized number values of the D/A (digital/analogue) transducer mean that differences between the physical, mechanical and electronic signal-based forms of sound production not only become insignificant, but also start to disappear. The rhythm samples and sound patterns of techno or hip-hop tracks can be machine-generated or created by hand using a MIDI keyboard. There may be a mixture of both: for instance, a continuous loop can be made from either a played or sampled musical figure. It is no longer possible to be confident about identifying the mode of sound production – conventional instruments, technical effects, audio manipulation and transformation, synthesis – on the basis of the final sound. With this development, sound underwent wide-ranging de-referencing of its elements. It was once the symbolic medium *par excellence* – each sound heard referred to a significant kind of vector that was always more or less unique to the spatio-temporal mode of its creation or production and was, therefore, firmly connected to a dimension of meaning that made it comprehensible. In digitized form it broke away completely from this, free of former links, of origins, of tracks and, furthermore, free of the meanings relating to space. Digitized sound represents, then, nothing more than binary numbers, even if they gain value and acoustic reality from the sampling of natural sounds. At this point, sound began to be perceived on its own terms, and the link between material, medium and acoustic perception was broken forever. Digital technology was already found in recording studios of the 1970s, although digital productions were released in analogue form on vinyl before the development of the CD. Ry Cooder's *Bop Till You Drop*[54], produced by Lee Herschberg using a digital recorder of the American 3M company, is acclaimed as the first wholly digital album.[55] Among earlier attempts were those made, with an eye on the classical audiophile market, by Decca and the Japanese audio technology manufacturer Denon, but they failed to win general acceptance. It was only at the end of the 1980s that digital technology began to be used as more than a mere aid to production – such as when mixing recordings. With its falling costs, it became an alternative means of commercial music production in various dance and club-based subcultures, which is where its sonic possibilities were discovered. Of great importance, here, are the techno pioneers of Detroit, such as Kevin Saunderson, Juan Atkins and Derrick May. The tracks they created on their computer screens and released under various pseudonyms (Rhythim Is Rhythim, Reese & Santonio, Cybotron and so on) laid the basis of a sound concept that relied on the computer

---

54   Warner Bros. Records, USA, 1979
55   See '1978 3M Digital Audio Mastering System', *Mix Magazine*, 1 September 2007, p. 112.

simulation of sonic events and, by so doing, lost the causal connections common to other kinds of sound production.

The uncomplicated manner in which sound was previously be heard as signs of emotion, expression, subjectivity, inwardness or as a symbolic representation of narrative meaning has its parallel now in the matter-of-fact way in which sound is taken as a medium whose origin (whether played, technically manipulated or technically generated) is insignificant: sense and meaning are now a consequence of links and transformations that are, as it were, slotted into the overall pattern of sound. 'Access', understood according to database principles (a universe that is relatively and abstractly addressable), and 'linking', the connection of elements to networks without touching on their identity, are the technical codes of a form of sound production that side-steps the term 'music' and, instead, leads to 'techno' – an emblematic designation for the technology of sound production.[56] A central feature, here, is machine-generated repetition – loops, or synth lines that replace quasi-narrative musical sequences. The consequence is a far-ranging erosion of sound's references to external sonic events, and this increasing abstraction, in a very basic way, affects the two parameters within which, until then, every type of music had been audibly anchored: the parameters of time and space.

Even in its technological transformation, sound is always heard as originating from a particular place, one that refers back to the act of music-making. Whatever meaning music is able to create, carry, or communicate always has a great deal to do with the place in which it emerges. Music is never heard as an abstraction. This did not really change when, through saving and transmitting media such as records and radio, the technical possibility existed for misaligning the space–time continuum. The space–time parameters from which the sound medium's context-setting matrix was drawn remained a fixed point for the way the music was heard, even if these parameters took on an increasingly virtual character in the studio. The evocative quality and apparent immediacy of music relate to the fact that sound is inseparably marked with the signature of its time and place of origin, even if these are suspended in the process of developing and assembling configurations of sound in the studio. The transmission of time and space that now became possible through media technology was not enough to undermine the authenticity of place. It need only be remembered that America, enjoying mythological status as a musical place of origin, was home not only to a huge quantity of pop music, but also, for a long time, most other varieties of music. In the digital universe of real-time audio simulation, however, only the place of hearing is real and authentic. It is there, only, that the simulation (the D/A transformation) takes place.

The same applies, also, to the second fundamental parameter of sound. Sound patterns are time patterns, and they are this because, up to this point, each audio production technique was always bound to the time sequence of the sound-producing process. Playing an instrument or singing always happened in the studio in unity and in synchronization with the unfolding of the audio production.

---

56   See David Battino and Kelli Richards, *The Art of Digital Music* (San Francisco, CA, 2005).

In digital real-time simulation of sound, this time pattern is no longer embedded in the running time of its production but, rather, is set in any way that is desired in an apparatus-specific configuration. Thus, the time parameter is moved from the process of production to the place of hearing. Sound abandons spatio-temporal anchorage, in the abstract sense of the word. As a pure state of perception, which it now is, it offers far more possibilities than the new dimensions and horizons for music-making that began to open up a broad front in the 1990s. All in all, its cultural 'reformatting' changed the cultural practices tied to music profoundly.

And so, at this provisional end of the triadic development of sound, technology and music, there exists a literally boundless reservoir of sound concepts ranging from the link with performance to the computerized simulation of sound. They may have taken a long time to become available, but they now offer inexhaustible design possibilities for new musical perspectives – and it should be borne in mind that the new dimensions presented by digitally propagated forms of music were never foreseen in the past.

PART 3
Gender and Sexuality

Genre, Subjectivity and Back-up Singing in Rock Music

Susan Fast

Something is slightly wrong with this scenario: bluegrass artist Alison Krauss steps up to the microphone to sing her *a cappella* version of the hymn 'Down In the River to Pray' and, behind her, a trio of back-up singers provide soothing harmonies, at first simply vocalizing warm 'ooohs' and eventually joining in with the words. The back-up vocalists are men, and the man standing in the middle of the group is rock singer Robert Plant. His characteristic wail has been reduced to a near whisper, and except for the occasional moment of timbral recognition, his voice blends seamlessly with the others. Sonically, he has become like so many back-up singers – anonymous – but, visually, blending is impossible. His imposing physicality (he crouches between the two men in order to match their lesser height), long blonde curls, leather pants, celebrity status and (generically specific) musical history create a kind of fission that jars.[1]

Even for those who know that Plant's musical tastes run deep and wide (let alone for those who might only know him as the front man of Led Zeppelin), this is a peculiar moment. Not only is Plant a celebrity, which draws attention to him in a way unsuitable for the role of back-up singer, but generic conventions that govern back-up singing in his home genre of hard rock (some would say metal, or proto-metal), dictate that he is decidedly out of place. Men rarely sing back-up in rock unless they are members of the band, who also play instruments. In subgenres of rock where back-up singing by session singers is normative (as in Southern rock, for example), those singers are mainly women. Because rock music is still made largely by men, we rarely see men backing women singers in rock; in fact, even the few rock singers there are employ women back-up singers, so strong is this convention. Further, lead singers in rock music, like Plant (who certainly helped define the role), work hard to develop a vocal and performance persona that is aggressive, loud (aurally and visually), strong, flamboyant and distinctive, characteristics that work in tandem with others to construct masculinity in ways particular to the genre.

---

1   This is a description of the Plant/Krauss performance at the Molson Amphitheatre in Toronto, 14 July 2008, which I attended.

Being in the background and blending with others is anathema to this construction. As one reviewer of the Plant/Krauss show commented, 'When you've seen Plant crowding a mike with two other guys ... you glimpse a streak of humility not often seen before'.[2]

In the context of bluegrass or country music, male back-up singers, whether in support of male or female lead singers, are not all that unusual; this performance makes perfect sense in the context of Alison Krauss's generic home, and had the three back-up singers not included Plant, it would probably not be worthy of much comment. But we are so used to the conventional ways in which lead and back-up singers are deployed in different genres of popular music that, even though Plant does a commendable job, both live and on the record he and Krauss made last year, *Raising Sand*, the reviewer quoted above has difficulty conceding his success:

> The show's most striking limitation was that Plant is a lead singer through and through. His one major effort at singing a sustained harmony part ... was overbold and a bit precarious. It was much easier for Krauss to harmonize with him, and she did the job so well that at times she might have been a hired backup singer.[3]

Krauss has an equally powerful and distinctive voice; I would argue that the idea that she makes a better back-up singer has less to do with how the pair sound singing together than the generic, and gendered, conventions surrounding back-up singing in rock music.

Back-up Singing and Genre

The ways in which identity is constituted through, or in relation to, back-up singers has been little examined, although they are a ubiquitous presence in most popular music genres. They are one of those musical 'conventions', as Susan McClary calls them, that are so common as to be rendered invisible, 'a procedure that has ossified into a formula that needs no further explanation ... [that] appear[s] to have transcended signification'.[4] But, as McClary further offers, it is precisely in such conventions that important ideological work is carried out, and this is why they are worthy of our analytical attention. '[W]hether noticed or not, they are the assumptions that allow cultural activities to "make sense." Indeed, they

2   Robert Everett-Green, 'Familiar Tunes, Surprising Angles', review of Robert Plant and Alison Krauss at the Molson Amphitheatre, Toronto, 14 July 2008, *The Globe and Mail*, Wednesday 16 July 2008 At: <http://www.theglobeandmail.com/servlet/story/RTGAM.20080716.wplant16/BNStory/Entertainment/home> (accessed 17 July 2008).
3   Ibid.
4   Susan McClary, *Conventional Wisdom: The Content of Music Form* (Berkeley, CA, 2000), pp. 2–3.

succeed best when least apparent, least deliberate, most automatic.'[5] The focus of this chapter is to begin to plot out how the convention of back-up singing in one particular genre, rock music, might be analysed and how this analysis might bring us closer to understanding constructions of subjectivity in this genre.

Since I am casting my analysis in terms of genre (that is, back-up singing as a generic convention in rock music), I will begin with some general comments concerning genre and popular music and how back-up singing can productively be thought of in generic terms.[6] As Robert Walser has written, '[n]owhere are genre boundaries more fluid than in popular music'.[7] The idea of neatly defining what constitutes the genre of 'rock music' is not only futile, given the great diversity within this category and the ways in which elements are constantly shifting, but mistaken. Genres are socially situated and contingent; they exist only within the context of human interaction, not as fixed and culturally transcendent categories. Fans, musicians and those in the music industry all have particular stakes in creating, maintaining, nuancing or thwarting popular music genres.[8] Nevertheless, 'musical structures and experiences are intelligible only with respect to these historically developing discursive systems'.[9] When we hear the term 'rock music' we have expectations that are either fulfilled by an individual song (for example) or frustrated by it; indeed, it is generally only when our expectations are frustrated that generic conventions are brought into consciousness. Genre offers a means through which we can '[place] the meaning of an individual song [or performance, artist and so on] within a larger field of meaning', enabling us to make sense of a musical experience or understand why we chose to engage in that experience in the first place.[10] As Fabian Holt puts it, 'the concept of music is bound up with

---

5   Ibid. The whole of McClary's book is devoted to an exploration of such conventions in a range of music from different historical periods and genres. As McClary herself notes, her definition of 'convention' resonates with what 'Raymond Williams calls "structures of feeling", Frederic Jameson "the political unconscious", Roland Barthes "mythologies", Thomas Kuhn "paradigms", Kaja Silverman "dominant fictions", or Ross Chambers simply the "social contracts" that establish the conditions for the production and reception of artworks (p. 5).

6   The term 'genre' is used loosely in music studies. It is often used interchangeably with 'style' to '[erect] categorical distinctions, of identifying similarity between different pieces (songs, objects, performances ...).' For an exploration of these two terms see Allan Moore, 'Categorical Conventions in Music Discourse: Style and Genre', *Music and Letters* 82/3 (2001): 432–42, at 432.

7   Robert Walser, *Running With the Devil: Power, Gender and Madness in Heavy Metal Music* (Hanover, NH, 1993), p. 27. Walser's discussion of genre in music (pp. 27–34) is an important contribution to the subject and is relevant well beyond the specific genre with which he is concerned.

8   For a study of how genre works within the music industry, see Keith Negus, *Music Genres and Corporate Cultures* (London, 1999). For a broader study that engages in ethnography as well as musical analysis see Fabian Holt, *Genre in Popular Music* (Chicago, 2007).

9   Walser, *Running with the Devil*, p. 27.

10   David Brackett, '(In Search Of) Musical Meaning: Genres, Categories and Crossover'

categorical [genre] difference. There is no such thing as "general music," only particular musics'.[11]

Since back-up singing is ubiquitous in popular music, why think of it as a specific generic marker in rock music? Back-up singing functions in ways particular to this genre; '[generic] conventions and expectations are established through acts of repetition',[12] and we see, in example after example of rock music, back-up singing being utilized in ways that come to signify meaning, socially and musically, in the same or similar ways. This does not mean that back-up singing is always used in rock, or even in particular subgenres of rock, nor that it is always used in the same way. But there is enough consistency to identify a pattern, and that pattern is socially significant.

Despite a few exceptions, rock is still the music of white, straight men, especially certain subgenres such as metal, the blues-inspired rock of, say, the Rolling Stones, or the 'art' or 'progressive' rock of bands such as Pink Floyd. Certainly, women, people of colour, and gays and lesbians participate in the production of rock music, but they are either considered exceptional or are marginalized in the discourse.[13] The generic markers of this kind of rock music – use of technology (including varying degrees of instrumental virtuosity, especially with respect to the electric guitar), loudness, aggressive modes of bodily display – have been mobilized to construct white masculinity in a particular way.[14] Back-up singing in rock music participates in this construction; in fact it often strengthens prevailing ideas of heteronormativity and whiteness, but also brings the important contribution of women into the discussion.

Insiders and Outsiders

While my search for articles related to back-up singing in scholarly sources proved almost futile,[15] journalistic literature and the Internet yielded sparse, but interesting

---

in David Hesmondhalgh and Keith Negus (eds), *Popular Music Studies* (London, 2002), p. 66.

11 Holt, *Genre in Popular Music*, p. 2.

12 Ibid., p. 3.

13 For a discussion of women's marginalization in rock music discourse see Susan Fast, '"Girls! Rock Your Boys": The Continuing (Non)History of Women in Rock Music' in Annette Kreutziger-Herr and Katrin Losleben (eds), *History/Herstory: Alternative Musikgeschichten*. (Köln, 2008).

14 For further discussion of rock, metal and masculinity see: Deena Weinstein, *Heavy Metal: A Cultural Sociology* (New York, 1991); Walser *Running With the Devil*; and Susan Fast, *In the Houses of the Holy: Led Zeppelin and the Power of Rock Music* (New York, 2001).

15 The invisibility of this convention is so profound that I know of only two scholars, Jacqueline Warwick and Annie Randall, who have given it serious attention, and that very recently (at the time of writing). See Jacqueline Warwick, '"And the Colored Girls Sing": Backup Singers and the Case of the Blossoms' in Steven Baur, Raymond Knapp

results. The *Wikipedia* article on 'Backing Vocalist',[16] problematic in many respects, plays directly into an important genre-defining issue: if backing vocalists are used in rock music, are they band members or instrumentalists playing with a lead singer – that is, 'insiders' to the group – or are they session musicians who are external to the group, 'outsiders?' The author of the article makes the assumption, uncritically, that backing vocalists are always insiders and this is because the repertory of music discussed is rock of a particular kind: Red Hot Chili Peppers, Green Day, Linkin Park, Aerosmith and AC/DC are some of the bands mentioned. In rock bands such as these, the group is conceived of as a self-contained fraternity. Backing vocals by members of the band serve to strengthen the fraternal bond, not only lending the lead singer support but also demonstrating the unity of purpose among band members.[17] As Robert Walser writes, '[t]hese additional voices serve to enlarge the statements of the solo vocalist, enacting the approval or participation of the larger social world, or at least a segment of it', and he gives, as an example, the way in which the band joins in on the chorus of the Van Halen song 'Runnin' With the Devil', where 'these chorus vocals virtually demand that the listener feel included'.[18] Back-up singers, in general, might represent the 'larger social world' and they certainly often urge the listener to participate, but if they are members of the band, the larger social world they are enacting is quite specific. It is the world of the band, or of a larger brotherhood (which does not mean that women cannot participate – it is precisely the image of hegemonic power produced in this musical configuration that can make it attractive to those outside of it[19]); this is particularly true when we *watch* these bands perform (as opposed to listening to recordings) and where we *see* band members other than the lead vocalist step up to the mike to

---

and Jacqueline Warwick (eds), *Musicological Identities: Essays in Honor of Susan McClary* (Aldershot, 2008), pp. 63–77, which includes information gleaned from an interview with Fanita James; and Annie Randall, 'Migrations of Soul' in *Dusty! Queen of the (Post) Mods* (New York, 2008), which includes an assessment of the influence of backing singer Madeleine Bell on Dusty Springfield's musical style and, by extension, the influence of other black American back-up singers on the white pop of the 1960s. My thanks to Professor Randall for sharing this chapter with me prior to its publication. In addition to its absence from scholarly journal articles, back-up singing is not given any mention in *Grove Music Online* or any encyclopedias of popular music.

16 'Backing Vocalist' *Wikipedia*, at: <http://en.wikipedia.org/wiki/Backing_vocalist> (accessed 11 July 2008).

17 Jacqueline Warwick writes that girl back-up singers in girl group music of the 1960s serve a similar function, although with vastly different gendered associations: '[b]ackup singers [in girl group music] conjure a sisterhood, lending their voices to strengthen the statements of an individual vocalist' and 'most Girl Group songs are best understood as representing a single – if often conflicted – subjectivity, wherein the interplay between lead singer and backing singers performs the struggle between different points of view that accompanies any individual's choice-making': Jacqueline Warwick, *Girl Groups, Girl Culture, Popular Music and Identity in the 1960s* (New York, 2007), pp. 48 and 115.

18 Walser, *Running With the Devil*, pp. 45–46.

19 For more on how women participate in hard rock and metal see Susan Fast, *In the Houses of the Holy*.

join in singing at certain points. Unlike the often anonymous backing vocalist who is an outsider, we know who these men are, what their other function(s) in the band are and what their relationship to the lead singer is. Further, when band members sing back-up, they do this in addition to their role as instrumentalists, which is perceived as their more primary and 'serious' function in the group. Back-up singing is an additional responsibility, which makes it seem less weighty, requiring less skill than their role as instrumentalists.

It is crucially important to note the distinction between those rock groups that do allow outsiders in as backing vocalists and those that do not. The subgenres of hard rock and metal are least likely to allow outsiders in; they are most concerned with establishing a kind of closed society in which the fraternal bonds between band members are firmly established and maintained. Elsewhere I have written that Led Zeppelin was a quintessential example of the closed society, almost never inviting outsiders of any kind, instrumental or vocal, to perform on their records and, with one or two exceptions in their 11-year career, never including another musician on stage with them.[20] In fact Led Zeppelin almost never used back-up vocals at all, and this is not uncommon in hard rock and metal.

So, if backing vocals are rarely or never found in some of this music, what social message is being sent? It lends to the idea of the lead singer as all-powerful, invincible and self-reliant. Brian Johnson's robust vocal on AC/DC's 'Back in Black' offers a good example. Even though the rhetoric of the chorus cries out for reinforcement, Johnson powers his way through largely unaided (his voice is multitracked, or band members join in, barely audible, on the last line of the chorus; the final time we hear the chorus, backing vocalists chime in, repeating the line 'I'm back' but they do not sing *with* Johnson). This underscores Johnson's insuperable control of the music and the power of his instrument, and adds to our understanding of the dominant construction of masculinity in this genre. Further, those instrumentalists who do not participate in the singing of back-up vocals in these rock groups remain more mysterious than those who do, and this contributes to myth-building, which is important to some rock bands (it certainly was to Led Zeppelin); but not singing back-up, or having instrumentalists do it as a secondary function or throwaway task, could also be viewed in gendered terms – that is, that singing, unless it is the kind of powerful singing associated with lead singers, is effeminate and is often dismissed as requiring little skill, or at least less skill than playing an instrument.

'Outsiders', or session back-up singers, pierce the membrane of the rock band unit, weakening the idea of fraternity and altering the idea of community significantly; Walser's idea that the 'larger social world' is referenced through back-up singing works better here, because this larger world is suddenly allowed into the fraternity. And it is not only other white men who are allowed in, but, in fact, mostly women.[21] Often, these women are either African-American, or white, but

---

20 Ibid., pp. 74–75.
21 Male back-up vocalists in rock music exist, but are quite rare. An example is session musician Bernard Fowler, who has long sung back-up with the Rolling Stones. Luther Vandross sang back-up for David Bowie (along with several African-American women)

sonically marked as black. This racialized and gendered sound is not specific to rock music; as an industry representative expressed it 30 years ago, 'the style [of back-up singing] today is the black sound. ...The influence of three-voice black female trios is pervasive.'[22] Jacqueline Warwick argues that this influence probably originates with the Blossoms, whose backing vocals graced innumerable recordings in the 1960s.[23] Annie Randall also points out that the use of black women gospel singers in the musical *Black Nativity* in 1961 was crucial in establishing these voices and this particular musical style (gospel) as a significant presence in popular music; she cites the scholar Charles I. Nero as arguing that this musical 'signaled the advent of a *new type of singing voice* for the Broadway stage: the female gospel-trained voice' that became a primary musical marker of black authenticity and, according to Hughes's conception, positioned gospel-voiced women as the 'carriers of black communal values'.[24] This is certainly significant to the use of this voice in rock music, a point I will discuss in more detail below.

Structure(s) and Function(s), Musical and Social

Contrary to the *Wikipedia* article on back-up singers, the British-based website *Vocalist* approaches the subject from the perspective of the singer who is an 'outsider', offering lessons and advice for aspiring professional session singers.[25] The distinction is made between 'the band member who sings a bit' and the 'dedicated session singer' employed by 'major touring artists and recordings studios. The definition of back-up singing is given as consisting of 'anything from repeating a word, passage or chorus of the song to providing a continuing harmony in time with the lead vocalist'.

Both the distinction between session singers and band members singing back-up and the definition of back-up singing provided in this article are useful. The professional session singer 'can vocally reproduce what they hear to create a harmony vocal line without requiring written sheet music or direction from the songwriter or producer', they must be able to 'learn songs quickly' and, preferably

during his 'white soul' period of the 1970s (specifically, on the album *Young Americans*). In both these cases, the men are African-American; see below for analysis of the racial significance of this. Probably the most famous example of reversal of the trio of women backing singers is Gladys Knight and the Pips – three men who back a woman lead singer – but this falls outside the genre of rock music.

22   Quoted in Don Heckman, 'The Backup Singers: High Reward for a Privileged Few', *High Fidelity and Musical America* 28 (1978): 120–22.
23   Warwick, '"And the Colored Girls Sing"'.
24   Randall, 'Migrations of Soul'.
25   <http://www.vocalist.org.uk/index.html> (accessed 14 July 2008). The specific article on back-up singing, from which I have taken quotes, appears at <http://www.vocalist.org.uk/backing_vocalist.html>. Backing vocalist Kim Chandler reinforces much of what is said on this website in 'Backing Up', *The Singer* (2004): 21–22.

be able to sight-read. Unlike the band member who sings back-up, the session singer is technically skilled and versatile.[26] Singing, not instrument-playing, is their primary area of musical expertise, and often when back-up singers are used in rock their voices outshine those of the band members, even the lead singers (see below for more on this point). On one hand, back-up singers are meant to 'blend' well and are not supposed to overpower a lead singer or sound distinctive; but timbral contrast and vocal power and control are often precisely the functions that back-up singers have in rock; they are meant to reference a social world different from that of the band members and, for this, we must be able to hear their otherness. In particular, it is often crucial that the black gospel sound come through and, of course, that we recognize the voices as women's voices.

Why is this important? Barbara Bradby has written about the presence of women singers on dance records of the early 1990s, noting that most of the time these singers' voices are contrasted with that of a male rapper and that, on the one hand, this gendered division of vocal labour perpetuates stereotypical gender roles because rap is more closely linked to speech and language and hence to technology, while song is more tied to melody than to verbal messages and is therefore construed as more emotive.[27] On the other hand, Bradby notes that the kind of female voice most often used in these recordings is that 'of black women soul singers ... [who] evoke strength, maturity, deep emotions–typical "maternal" qualities. ... They also give voice to a female sexuality that is not confined within [especially white] notions of "romance".'[28] Adam Krims has also noted the increasing use of women's voices used to sing the choruses in harder styles of male rap music, stating that '[t]he popularity of such choruses is all the more remarkable when one recalls how just a few short years [ago], singing, not to mention a substantial female presence of any sort, had been the mark of "softer" styles. That mark, of course, had served to threaten the masculine-identified reality rap authenticity.'[29] The same could probably be said for the exclusion of women back-up singers from some styles of rock music – that is, that it disrupts constructions of masculinity.[30]

For the remainder of this chapter I wish to build on these discussions by addressing three specific instances of back-up singing in rock music: the Black Crowes' 'Remedy', the Rolling Stones' 'Gimme Shelter' and the use of back-up singers over the course of an entire album, Pink Floyd's *Dark Side of the Moon*. I want to examine particular pieces of music in order to address exactly where and how back-up singers are used within a particular song or album because knowing

---

26   For further discussion of the training and versatility of session backup singers see Warwick, '"And the Colored Girls Sing"'.

27   Barbara Bradby, 'Sampling Sexuality: Gender, Technology and the Body in Dance Music', *Popular Music* 12/2 (1993): 166–67.

28   Ibid., pp. 172–73.

29   Adam Krims, *Rap Music and the Poetics of Identity* (Cambridge, 2000), pp. 85–86.

30   Robert Walser has discussed exscription as one way in which metal artists deal with women in lyrics and videos, but not including them as back-up singers is another means through which women are exscripted from this music. See Walser, *Running With the Devil*, pp. 114–15.

these details allows us to understand how social issues are developed in this kind of musical narrative. I have chosen these examples fairly randomly as starting-points for research into this subject, although I have been intrigued by the gender and racial politics of 'Gimme Shelter' and *Dark Side* for years. The three examples use back-up singing in distinctive ways, but each example also conforms to conventional practices.

The Black Crowes, 'Remedy'

The Crowes' 'Remedy' is an example of a song that employs a group of backing vocalists during the chorus only, one of the most prominent ways in which back-up singers are used not only in rock music, but also in a variety of popular music styles. In this role, back-up singers sing the same music and lyrics repeatedly, which restricts their creativity and independence – this is a non-developing part of the song – and also links them to the song as commodity, since the chorus normally provides the hook, the most memorable part, and also the part intended to sell it. But this is also precisely why the chorus is an incredibly important feature. This most memorable part of the form usually represents a moment of repose – of coming back to something familiar, comforting, something that is 'known' by the listener. Technically, the women are there to reinforce the importance of the chorus, to underline the hook, making it fatter by adding more voices and making it distinct from the verse by changing the vocal timbre. But adding voices at the chorus also links this familiar, comfortable moment in the song with the notion of community (as Walser suggests happens in the Van Halen song). In fact, the very anonymity of 'outsider' backing vocalists strongly suggests the idea of listeners joining in, since their anonymity ties them much less to celebrity and more to the 'everyday' than a lead singer whose identity is known. This anonymity is also problematic – in terms of class, as well as gender and race – since the back-up singer's vocal labour makes a substantial material contribution to the song, even though they are often given little or no recognition or credit for this.[31] This occurs, for example, in the Crowes' 'Remedy', where the women backing vocalists are credited in the liner notes as 'Barbara and Taj', whereas the other musician who contributed to the album, but who is not part of the band, the (male) conga player, is listed with both first and last name. This way of representing the women back-up singers not only keeps them anonymous, but also suggests that they are not professionals – perhaps friends or girlfriends – of guys in the band.

In 'Remedy' the general ideas that I have just laid out about the use of backing vocalists in the chorus of a song are all operative. But meaning is also generated through the particular kinds of voices that are heard: these are sonically marked

---

31   See Warwick, '"And the Colored Girls Sing"' for a discussion of anonymity with respect to the Blossoms, and her book *Girl Groups, Girl Culture* for the an analysis of the importance of vocal labour in girl group music.

as black women's voices. I say 'sonically marked' because I do not know whether these women are black or not, only that they sound black. Although it might seem as though this puts us into dangerous essentialist territory, Warwick's interview with Blossoms' singer Fanita James makes it clear that back-up singers not only understand and discuss the different ways of sounding 'black' and 'white', but, regardless of their ethnicity, are also often required to shift how they sound along racial lines when they are used on recordings, where they are not seen.[32] As back-up singer Kim Chandler points out, this changes in live performance, where 'height, build, color, gender and age, more often than not play a large part in determining which singers get booked for a particular gig'.[33] On 'Remedy' the voices are stylistically aligned with blues/gospel/R&B, and some of what Bradby suggests about the gospel/R&B-inflected singing style of women singers on dance records applies here. The melody is pitched in a moderately low range, which makes the voices sound warm, relaxed and comforting – no straining. The vibrato adds to the warmth and also helps mark the style (as does the hint of a southern accent). The melodic line is rhythmically straight, creating very little physical tension and reinforcing the relaxed quality. The only tension in the melody comes from a blue note that is sung on the strong beats of the bar, creating a seductive pull into the back-up singers' music. They begin each line singing in harmony, but sing in unison on the word 'remedy', giving them a small amount of individuality from one another that, in the end, collapses into sameness. Compare this to what Chris Robinson, the lead singer of the band, does vocally: even though the verses are relatively structured and he adheres to a set melody most of the time, he has a high degree of autonomy in the choruses and in the improvisatory section after the guitar solo. After each line of the chorus is sung by the women alone, he reiterates it, or part of it, improvising a new melody, new rhythms and new timbres, secure in the knowledge that they are there to carry the melody while he plays with it. When he threatens to lose the words – and melody, for that matter – altogether during his improvisation after the guitar solo, dissolving into a scream, the backing singers begin to be heard far back in the mix, under him, anchoring him, gradually coming more up front, but never completely to the fore; they could never be construed as taking over the vocal, but they do sweep in to save him.

The women's voices in this song do provide some sense of community for Robinson – they affirm the lyrical message – but because they are women's voices, we must also hear them in other ways (in other words, why not just have the guys in the band sing back-up, or why not other men, white or black?) We could hear the voices as maternal, as Bradby suggests they sometimes are, or surely in the traditional female role – there to support the man who is experimenting, taking risks out in the world. In fact, if we listen carefully to that section after the guitar solo, it is not only Robinson who takes off, but all the other men in the band as well. The women are the only ones who don't improvise; they anchor all of the male band members. But attractive as this interpretation is, it is a bit too simple because,

---

32   Warwick, '"And the Colored Girls Sing"', p. 66.
33   Chandler, 'Backing Up', p. 28.

even though the women are confined to repeating the same three lines of lyric over and over while Robinson carries the much wider verbal message in the verses, it can also be argued that they are the ones with a coherent verbal message while Robinson, towards the end of the song certainly loses or relinquishes language when, presumably, he is overcome with emotion. Here, the women singers hang on to verbal skills, to technology, to rationality, while Robinson gives them up.

The women's voices are also a kind of ear candy. They are sensual, seductive, and because they are sonically marked as black, while the band members are white, we might also hear them playing into white male fantasies of black female sexuality, while at the same time reaffirming hegemonic power structures – keeping these women in their place. But they are most certainly also there to authenticate the performance of blues-based music by white performers, and so the question becomes how? I'd like to explore this further by turning to my second example.

The Rolling Stones, 'Gimme Shelter'

In the Stones' 'Gimme Shelter', a single backing voice is used. Merry Clayton's strong, virtuosic voice is contrasted with Jagger's, whose technical abilities, by contrast, are quite limited. Here, the woman is not part of a group identity that is confined by, and subservient to, a powerful male leader; her individual subjectivity is foregrounded in this song through her singularity and her greater, if still limited, musical freedom.

Stylistically, Clayton again invokes the black gospel/R&B tradition. In fact, Clayton is African-American and had impressive R&B credentials – as a member of Ray Charles's Raelettes, for one thing – prior to singing for the Stones.[34] Her immense vocal power and virtuosity are pressed into the service of a kind of catharsis of which Jagger is incapable. Difference between the two vocalists is marked so emphatically in this song that one has to wonder: why relinquish such vocal power to the black woman Other? Why highlight the lead singer's limited vocal abilities by juxtaposing them with such a powerful, controlled voice? Musically, it might have been strategic because these voices are difficult to compare: choosing a black woman to contrast with the white man's voice almost makes comparison irrelevant. Had a black male gospel voice or, better, another, more virtuosic white blues-based male rocker's voice been set against Jagger's, the temptation to make a comparison would be greater. In contrast, choosing difference guarantees that the comparison will be minimal, assuring that the lead singer retains power, control and respect as a vocalist.

But there are other very good historical reasons for relegating the cathartic moments of the song or album to a woman and especially to a black woman. Consider how this works in 'Gimme Shelter'. Like so many other songs in which

---

34   Biographical information can be found on Clayton's website: <http://www.soulwalking. co.uk/Merry%20Clayton.html> (accessed 11 August 2008).

a back-up singer is used, Clayton joins the lead vocalist for the chorus. But after the first verse, she also joins Jagger for the second half of each line of subsequent verses and is also featured in a brief solo, so her presence in this song is substantial. Clayton's role is certainly to provide the voice of cathartic emotional release: every time she sings, she belts full out and high in her range. As one commentator writing about 'Gimme Shelter' has stated, Merry Clayton's voice is there 'to add a crucial layer of warmth and power',[35] which the men's voices apparently are incapable of providing (and which is somehow, at least by the quoted writer, deemed important to the song). But this is an issue not only of gender, but also of race: it is common in white culture to assign the ability to emote to blacks. Choosing singers that come from the musically cathartic tradition of black gospel singing reinforces this stereotype. To relinquish the most intensely emotive moment – one of daring vocal extreme and licence, of catharsis, a moment that can transport the performer and the listener – to the black woman Other speaks to what bell hooks states is the white person's belief in that Other's

> ... capacity to be more alive, as holding the secret that will allow those who venture and dare to break with the cultural anhedonia – the insensitivity to pleasure, the incapacity for experiencing happiness – and experience sensual and spiritual renewal.[36]

But there is something else at work here in terms of race (as there is in the Crowes example, where a similar black vocal tradition is drawn upon), and that is whether the black musician might be heard as an 'original' voice. Does it set into relief the white simulation of black musics on which the Stones' career has certainly been built? Does it serve to authenticate the efforts of the white blues musicians to appropriate these musics?

What I have been calling cathartic moments in this song can also be viewed as musically transgressive, or excessive. The first notable thing about Clayton's performance is that she exceeds the range of all other instruments and Jagger's voice (she sings an octave above him), as well as the murky, dark texture of much of the song. Her voice escapes that texture, rising above it. Clayton also quickly transgresses the formal arrangement established at the opening of the song, where we think that the lead singer will sing the verses and be joined by the backing singer on the choruses. This norm is already broken in the second verse when Clayton sings the second half of each line with Jagger. She also adds a descending vocal melisma at the end of each chorus, which Jagger does not sing. After the guitar solo, Clayton has a gripping solo in which she sings the music of the chorus, but with new lyrics, thereby breaking out of the confines of repeating the words

---

35   Steve Appleford, *The Rolling Stones: It's Only Rock 'n' Roll: The Stories Behind Every Song* (London, 1997), p. 87.

36   bell hooks, 'Eating the Other: Desire and Resistance' in Meenakshi Gigi Durham and Douglas M. Kellner (eds), *Media and Cultural Studies: Key Works* (New York, 2001), pp. 424–38, at p. 428.

of the chorus. While the lyrics of this song have, up to this point, articulated some general angst about the horrors of war (it was written as the war in Vietnam was escalating), the specific, most brutal violations – rape and murder – are left to Clayton to articulate alone. Her voice is more upfront in the mix during this section and more reverb is thrown on to it, making it even more powerful than previously. Further, she repeats the lyrics three times, instead of the normal two times that had been established previously for the chorus. This formal 'norm' is transgressed again at the end of the song, and this time Jagger joins in the transgression; but by this point the mould has already been broken.

Clayton's prominent role in this song and the ways in which she is allowed to break out of the constricted form could certainly be celebrated. As Mary Douglas has written in her book' *Purity and Danger*, with regard to patterns (which we could equate with musical form), 'though we seek to create order, we do not simply condemn disorder. We recognize that it is destructive to existing patterns; also that it has potentiality. It symbolises both danger and power.' It is in moments of mental disorder, she argues, that the most powerful ideas can come forth.[37] But we must also remember that at least since the nineteenth century in the West, musical transgression or excess by women has been associated with madness and sexual deviance, as Susan McClary has pointed out.[38] While this mapping of musical excess on to madwomen is clear in opera – the kind of music McClary discusses – through the libretto, in a song like 'Gimme Shelter' there is a lot of ambivalence. Can Clayton be considered a madwoman, breaking out of the formal constraints of the song, ranting about rape and murder? Has she been assigned this role because of her gender and her race, so that this excessive emotional outpouring and the articulation of an intense cultural burden in the song is possible without sullying Jagger – keeping him at a safe distance from it?

Or can it be argued that Clayton's powerful presence in this song – her distinctively black, female presence – offers Jagger, the imitator of black music, an encounter with this Other that might allow him to experience hooks' concept of renewal more intensely. Does the *physical* presence of the Other, as opposed to simply imitating the Other's style, bring that experience closer, making possible the desired transformation that hooks speaks of? Does it make it easier to 'become the Other', as hooks believes the objective to be?[39] Or (and?) does the presence of the Other – the originating voice – have the effect of pointing to the synthetic character of the white musician's performance?[40] These ideas can be further pursued by turning to the use of back-up singers over the course of an entire album that has a coherent lyrical narrative.

---

37   Mary Douglas, *Purity and Danger: An Analysis of the Concepts of Pollution and Taboo* (London, 1966), p. 94.

38   Susan McClary, 'Excess and Frame: The Musical Representation of Madwomen' in *Feminine Endings: Music, Gender, and Sexuality* (Minneapolis, 1991; rev. edn 2002), pp. 80–111.

39   hooks, 'Eating the Other', p. 427.

40   My thanks to Phil Auslander for suggesting this point.

Pink Floyd, *Dark Side of the Moon*

In the video documentary *Classic Albums: Dark Side of the Moon*,[41] the camera pans across the original recording log and under the title of the song, 'Time', is scrawled 'girls', indicating the first entrance of the quartet of back-up singers. They are also referred to as 'girls' in this documentary by engineer Alan Parsons. In fact, 'the girls' are veteran back-up singer Doris Troy, Barry St. John, Leslie Duncan and Liza Strike. They provide the chorus of backing vocals on the songs 'Time', 'Us and Them', 'Brain Damage' and 'Eclipse'. These voices do not sound remotely girl-like – they are mature and have been delegated serious semiotic functions on the album – yet the use of the term 'girl' (which, as Jacqueline Warwick notes, has traditionally been one of 'condescension and belittlement'[42]) perpetuates the idea of back-up singers as, obviously, female, youthful and insubstantial.

Dark Side of the Moon, the quintessential rock concept album of the 1970s, explores weighty existential themes about the alienated self, ambition, power, mental illness, ageing, political conflict and spirituality. These ideas are expressed by male singers, band members David Gilmour, Richard Wright and Roger Waters. When a harmony line is added, it is either double-tracked by the lead singer (in 'Time' Gilmour's voice is double-tracked), or sung by another band member (Richard Wright sings harmony against Gilmour in 'Us and Them'). Philosophy, on this record, belongs to men. Even the famous talking voices, who express a folksy kind of philosophy, are all male, except for one instance in which a woman's voice says 'he was cruisin' for a bruisin'' – hardly comparable to some of the more deeply philosophical sentiments expressed by the male voices ('I am not afraid of dying', or 'I've always been mad … like most of us').

'The girls' and vocalist Clare Torry, who sings 'The Great Gig in the Sky', do not sing words: they vocalize. It is not their verbal ideas that are significant, not a logocentric view of the world that they offer. The first time we hear a woman's voice on this record is during the opening 'overture', ('Speak to Me') which brings together excerpts of the non-musical sounds heard throughout the album (cash register, talking voices, running feet and so on). This montage of sound ends with a fragment of Clare Torry's gospel vocal from 'The Great Gig in the Sky', and the way it is used here suggests the idea of birth. Taken out of the context of the rest of her performance in 'Great Gig', this excerpt sounds like a tortured scream arising out of pain, not like singing at all. The scream ends the overture and ushers in the band; Torry, standing in for woman, gives birth to the album and the narrative. This interpretation is clichéd, of course, until one considers the moment more deeply. Torry's scream moves us away from the mundane sounds of everyday life into the powerful world of organized musical sound. It frames music as emanating from the feminine, and, in this case, metaphorically from the female body, which is related to the long-held idea in Western culture of music as feminine, generally, and more

---

41 *Classic Albums: Dark Side of the Moon* (London: Eaglerock Entertainment, 2003).
42 Warwick, *Girl Groups, Girl Culture*, p. 3.

specifically feminine because of its association with the body vis-à-vis dance.[43] Like Merry Clayton's vocal in 'Gimme Shelter', the scream also offers one of the most emotionally charged moments of the album and foreshadows that this terrain will belong to women, not men. But Torry's scream can also be read as giving voice to the narrative of the album, the point of origin for the philosophical musings that follow; this interpretation obviously gives the moment considerable importance.

Torry improvised her powerful vocal on 'The Great Gig in the Sky' over the existing keyboard track; her only direction from the band was to think of 'death' and 'horror' in shaping the melody.[44] She was paid £30 for the session, but in 2005 she won a lawsuit claiming that she should receive songwriting royalties for 'Great Gig' and it is now credited both to her and Richard Wright instead of Wright alone.[45] During the recording process, this song was called 'Religion', and Torry's vocals bespeak a particular kind of religious experience: the catharsis associated with the black church. Torry is not black (a fan on one forum I consulted was incredulous to learn this: 'Man, all these years later & I find out she's white? I always pictured a '70s Nina Simone'),[46] but her vocals on this track certainly reference black gospel; indeed, in an interview she was asked whether she had other singers in mind as models when she was recording, since to the interviewer's ears she sounds 'quite black; quite gospelly'.[47]

'Religion', then, is construed in a particular way on this album, as feminized and African-American. It is linked with the irrational (no words) and the hyperemotional. Since it is this same gospel-inflected, if less emotionally charged, style of singing that we hear from 'the girls' in other places on the album, we might understand it to be referencing the idea of religion/spirituality there as well, undergirding the lead singers' philosophical ruminations and, at times, sense of hopelessness, about the safe haven of religious community. They offer comfort in an otherwise harsh world. This occurs most profoundly in 'Eclipse', where one of the girls' voices breaks out of the backing chorus towards the end of the piece, repeating a couple of text fragments (not complete ideas) in gospel improvisatory style; again, the intense, emotional, spiritual experience is relinquished to a black woman, while the men sing the same melody over and over, never breaking out of its narrow confines. This reverses the more 'normal' function of the background singer and also the more typical experience described in my analysis of 'Remedy', where it is the women who are confined and the male singer who improvises. Here, however, we understand these women's improvisations as providing the emotional

---

43   See McClary, *Feminine Endings*, pp. 17–18.

44   *Classic Albums*, interview with Rick Wright.

45   'Pink Floyd: Pink Floyd Singer Wins Settlement from Band', *ContactMusic.com* 13 April 2005, <http://www.contactmusic.com/new/xmlfeed.nsf/mndwebpages/pink%20floyd%20singer%20wins%20settlement%20from%20band> (accessed 19 July 2008).

46   <http://www.tdpri.com/forum/bad-dog-cafe/31706-not-another-pink-floyd-lawsuit.html> (accessed 19 July 2008).

47   The interview can be found at: <http://www.brain-damage.co.uk/other-related-interviews/clare-torry-october-2005-brain-damage-excl.html> (accessed 19 July 2008).

content – the warmth, comfort, and catharsis – that the men never achieve. This is especially true on *Dark Side of the Moon*, where throughout nearly the entire album the men's singing is emotionally contained, soft and dulled of expression ('Money' is the exception, and there what is expressed is cynicism and possibly some anger). Women fall into their traditional role of providing a kind of maternal comfort on this album. But what is different here is that the black gospel style is also linked specifically to the idea of religion, whereas in much popular music it has been removed from this context. It is difficult to imagine any other musical reference to Christianity as being acceptable or appropriate within a rock context, but referencing this religious tradition through black gospel *is* appropriate here, because it is linked to the oppressed Other and to a musical tradition that provided the backbone for rock.

The quartet of 'girls' is used on the B sections of 'Time', 'Us and Them' and 'Brain Damage' (these sections are chorus-like, but have different words each time they appear, so do not function as 'real' choruses; interestingly, all three songs have a similar formal structure), as well as 'Eclipse', filling out the texture with a warm, rich sound. In 'Time' and 'Us and Them', the B section momentarily tonicizes the submediant, changing the prevailing modal quality, from minor to major for 'Time' and the opposite for 'Us and Them'. This harmonic shift coincides with a textural shift that moves from soft and introspective, to louder, fuller and more 'public'. The emotional pitch of these sections, as well as that of 'Brain Damage' (which moves to the subdominant for the B section), is more intense than what has preceded it; it is an outpouring, musically and emotionally, and the women's voices are there in order to bring the loner, the philosopher, into a more social realm. Again, in the context of this mostly bleak album, women provide warmth and a link to the social, reinforcing the role that women generally play within culture. That this is couched in terms of black women's voices that are clearly drawing on gospel as their primary musical source links the whole idea of redemption (again, within the context of this album), both social and spiritual, to an African-American Other; it does not come out of white culture. hooks' idea that the black Other is thought to offer spiritual renewal to whites seems operative here.

*****

'The lot of the backup singer', as one blogger put it, 'is a sad one. … They add incalculable flavor to countless albums and mask the technical deficiencies of those for whom they work.'[48] Yet, they toil in anonymity and rarely step out front to have their own careers as lead singers (Sheryl Crow being an exception). Sadder still, perhaps, is that we erase them from the discourse about songs and their musical operations and cultural meanings. We expect them to be there, we may sing along with them, but we rarely stop to reflect on what roles they might be playing

---

48   Larry Grogan, 'Merry Clayton – Gimme Shelter', Funky16Corners, 31 August 2005, at: <http://funky16corners.blogspot.com/2005/08/merry-clayton-gimme-shelter.html> (accessed 19 July 2008).

depending on the context in which we hear them. We understand, unconsciously, that back-up singers are, by and large, women, without articulating how this reinforces the role of women as 'supporters' within culture generally; and we do not consider, how, in the context of different musical genres, these women function differently, how – especially for white rockers – their black, female sound generates particular social meanings. These meanings may be of considerable importance in terms of reinforcing normative gendered and racialized representations, but they may also signal ways in which the back-up singer contributes significantly to a song's or album's narrative (as in the case of *Dark Side of the Moon*), where the voices are responsible for substantial elements of the narrative, however stereotyped. In rock music, it is an important way in which women are there – at all.

Acknowledgement

I wish to thank the Social Sciences and Humanities Research Council of Canada for funding this work and my research assistants Sean Luyk and Lane Osborne.

Notes on
Musical Camp

Freya Jarman-Ivens

Many things in the world have not been named, and many things, even if they
have been named, have never been described. One of these is the sensibility –
unmistakably modern, a variant of sophistication but hardly identical with it – that
goes by the cult name of 'camp'.

Thus begins Susan Sontag in her famous – infamous, perhaps – 'Notes on
"Camp"'.[1] Sontag's 'Notes' are a crucial reference point in discussions about camp,
and yet, since its publication in 1964, one site of camp remains unnamed, or (if
named) significantly underdescribed. The ways in which music might be camp is
something has received very little attention in comparison to camp in visual and
written cultures. Yet, there are camp associations with certain pieces of music, and
I would argue that there is even camp to be found in musical objects: numbers
from musicals and films ('Big Spender' or 'Don't Rain On My Parade'), lounge
tunes ('Perhaps, Perhaps, Perhaps' or 'Mambo Italiano'), torch songs ('You Don't
Have To Say You Love Me') or classic disco hits ('Tragedy' or 'I Am What I Am').
With musical material abounding, it is surprising that so little has been written
about camp and music. Sontag offers a small selection of musical examples and
indicates that classical works may also offer up camp elements: opera and ballet,
citing Bellini operas and *Swan Lake* specifically, and with the caveat 'the operas
of Strauss but not Wagner'; 'much of Mozart'; and yé-yé.[2] Yet Sontag's notes are
more about aesthetics than examples, and her examples are mostly drawn from
visual or written arts. Certainly, she doesn't explore specific musical qualities – that
is beyond the scope of the essay – but, reading through 'Notes', one does get the
sense that she's naming and describing camp at least as much *through the act of
finding examples* as she is seeking the *qualities of camp* per se. Nonetheless she does,
over the course of 'Notes', set out some terms and ideas that are useful at least in

---

1   Susan Sontag, 'Notes on Camp' [1964] in Fabio Cleto (ed.), *Camp: Queer Aesthetics and
     the Performing Subject: A Reader* (Edinburgh, 1999), pp. 53–65.
2   A female-dominated style of popular music that emerged from France and French-
     speaking Canada in the 1960s.

starting to talk about camp, and that might be transferable to music. There is also a handful of articles about camp and popular music[3] and a book on the campness of MGM musicals,[4] but such texts are often only nominally 'about' music, as they tend to focus on videos or other visual elements that exist alongside the musical. Kay Dickinson makes some interesting observations about camp and voice in particular relation to the vocoder,[5] but there is clearly much more work on camp to be done from a committed musicological perspective.

This chapter will start by outlining the key debates in response to camp, the most significant of which are the relationships among camp, homosexuality, and queerness, and the extent to which camp can operate politically. The substance of the chapter will then be concerned with ways of thinking about camp in relation to music, to equip readers with a foundation for undertaking effective camp readings of musical texts. As with all things camp, there are several disparate strands to be pulled together, and there is a central relationship between text (object) and context (reading) that will be opened up here. Consequently, my musical analyses will consider extramusical and paramusical factors[6] and the ways in which camp may be read in musical texts. At the same time, I will argue that there are specific musical gestures with which listeners can identify in camp ways, or use to explain the presence of camp, and that even if these are not inherently camp, they may invite a camp interpretation of the text by a performer or a camp reading by a listener. Musical examples will be drawn from a range of genres, to be explored in terms of musical content and cultural contexts, and juxtaposed with each other. Furthermore, they will be set in terms of wider discourses about music and musical value. The aim is not only to identify whether there are musical and performance gestures relevant to what camp might be in music, but also to draw out the most significant issues in any discussion thereof.

---

3   See, for example, Thomas Geyrhalter, 'Effeminacy, Camp and Sexual Subversion in Rock: The Cure and Suede', *Popular Music* 15/2 (1996): 217–24. See also Gillian Rodger, 'Drag, Camp and Gender Subversion in the Music and Videos of Annie Lennox', *Popular Music* 23/1 (2004): 17–29.

4   Steven Cohan, *Incongruous Entertainment: Camp, Cultural Value, and the MGM Musical* (Durham, NC, 2005).

5   Kay Dickinson, '"Believe"? Vocoders, Digitalised Female Identity and Camp', *Popular Music* 20/3 (2001): 333–47.

6   A neologism used by Tagg meaning 'alongside or concurrent with the music'. Tagg explains that he uses this term as distinct from the word 'extramusical' because 'the latter means outside the music and because it is both practically and conceptually problematic to view, say, a pop song's lyrics or an underscore's visual counterpart as 'outside' rather than 'alongside' the music in conjunction with which they occur'. See Philip Tagg, 'Introductory Notes to the Semiotics of Music', Version 3 (July 1999), p. 29 n. 50, at: <http://tagg.org/xpdfs/semiotug.pdf> (accessed 18 June 2008).

Sontag's Configuration of Camp

As problematic as Sontag's 'Notes' may be – and I will consider the problems along the way – her description of this 'sensibility' is an important starting-point in the present discussion, because her key points about camp have been taken up and used and/or critiqued in most subsequent formulations. To start with, then, let us review the key terms used by Sontag, with a view to understanding the extent of their validity and how they might apply to a musical context.

Style, Aesthetics, and Value

The first set of ideas to be dealt with is that pertaining to the aesthetics of camp and the relation of those aesthetics to various systems of value. Sontag's emphasis from the beginning of 'Notes' is on camp as a sensibility concerned with image – style. It is, she writes, a 'victory of "style" over "content"', or 'a vision of the world in terms of style'. Specifically, it is a style that is extravagant and tends towards the glamorous. Indeed, there is a sense that this may be excessive – a value judgement itself, but one that speaks of a distinct element of exaggeration or gaudiness, or (in slightly less ideologically-laden terms) theatricality. This excess, as Sontag sees it, is certainly an issue of value, and she writes: 'Camp is art that ... cannot be taken altogether seriously because it is "too much".' The implications for value are certainly contentious and not agreed on by other writers on camp, but the principles here are generally agreed. Moe Meyer asserts that camp is a kind of parody[7] and implies a sense of performativity and an emphasis on signifying practices over signified content. As David Bergman summarizes, 'everyone agrees that camp is a style ... that favors "exaggeration," "artifice," and "extremity"'.[8]

The significant issue arising when considering music in these terms is that of precisely what constitutes 'style' and also 'content'. The notion that style and content are too intimately related to be separated is one that has strong roots in the literary theory of the 1970s and 1980s, although, in musical terms, similar issues can also easily be traced back to the tangled nineteenth-century debates over 'absolute' music and the extent to which music can ever 'mean' something outside of 'itself'. What, then, is the nature of the musical object, which would have style on the one hand and content on the other? Is the content of music not only manifested through its style? Or can we, for instance, propose melody and harmony as content, and arrangement or orchestration as style? The question of meaning in music is amplified by its essential status as non-representational. It is easy enough to identify words in songs as meaning-making, but when comparing a melody with, say, a still-life painting it is easy to understand the latter as inherently more representational

---

7   Moe Meyer, 'Introduction: Reclaiming the Discourse of Camp' in Moe Meyer (ed.), *The Politics and Poetics of Camp* (London, 1994), pp. 1–22, at p. 9.

8   David Bergman, 'Introduction' in David Bergman (ed.), *Camp Grounds: Style and Homosexuality* (Amherst, MA, 1993), pp. 3–16, at p. 5.

than the former. This is not to say, however, that music lacks meaning. Musical gestures have, of course, become coded and their codes are reinscribed and redefined over the course of recurrent usage. Thus, combinations of instruments, turns of melodic phrase, intervals, chord progressions and more have associations that are formed intertextually by a network of musical events, each contributing to an overall sense of what a given musical moment 'means'. But to identify music as meaning-laden is not to make progress with the complex relationship between style and content in music. Indeed, the complexity of that relationship in all art forms presents a significant and fundamental challenge to Sontag's assertion that camp is more about style than content. Nonetheless, as I will go on to argue, once we accept that music is meaning-making despite its non-representationality, we can certainly trace the presence in musical texts of 'extravagance', 'theatricality' and so on.

Such aesthetic qualities inevitably have implications for perceptions of value in musical objects, and I have already noted that Sontag's identification of camp as 'extravagant' or 'gaudy' implies a negative value judgement. Indeed, these value judgements are linked with gendered discourses in ways that are worth exploring briefly here. There are genres and artists/composers who are more frequently written about in music scholarship than others, and these same objects of musical study frequently enjoy a higher status in popular discourse about music. In relation particularly to popular music, Anahid Kassabian explains: 'It is relatively easy to assign cultural value to rock and other sub- and countercultural musics ... because their value derives directly from the degree of opposition to high culture.'[9] I would go on to say that a broader sense of oppositionality – opposition to a perceived 'mainstream' (of which high culture may be a part) is the most useful governing theme when it comes to the relationship between cultural value (in scholarship and popular discourse) and musics. In fact, it is a *fantasy* of oppositionality, although there is insufficient space to explore the fantastic qualities fully here. In short, several complex value systems that have sedimented over long historical periods are competing for primacy, fighting for dominance in a battle that simply cannot be won, because of the latent tensions and contradictions in and between the value systems. These questions of value intersect with equally complex and competing questions to do with class, race, gender, sexuality and so on. There is a complicated relationship between musical text and cultural or academic value that, again, there isn't space for here. But ultimately, those musics and musical textual features that I will come to identify as related to camp broadly parallel those that are considered 'unworthy' in academic and popular discourse.

Meaning and Political Work

Sontag goes on to suggest that the lack of significant and meaningful content in camp means that it is a style devoid of political potential. This may well be the most

9   Anahid Kassabian, 'Popular' in Bruce Horner and Thomas Swiss (eds), *Key Terms in Popular Music and Culture* (Oxford, 1999), pp. 113–23, at p. 119.

contentious point of her 'Notes', as her emphasis on camp's frivolity over morality positions it in opposition to satire, and by extension as precisely not a form of critique. Although some post-'Notes' work, such as Pamela Robertson's *Guilty Pleasures*, has taken frivolity to be the point of camp and has viewed it as necessarily anti-critical,[10] most post-'Notes' work on camp agrees that it is a political phenomenon. Moe Meyer asserts this clearly, describing it as a '*queer* cultural critique' and stating explicitly that 'Camp is political'.[11] Similarly, David Bergman adopts a term of Judith Butler's to imply camp as a 'strategy of subversive repetition';[12] Pamela Robertson describes camp as 'a political tool';[13] and Andrew Ross argues that the theatricality of gender roles in camp in particular asks us to question the presumed stability and naturalness of those roles.[14] As I have noted, some of the specifics of camp are argued over, but certain features are agreed consistently as being symptomatic (although not necessarily determinants) of camp: flamboyance and extravagance; excess and exaggeration; artifice and parody. Moreover, its relation to popular culture is itself extravagant, exaggerated and, on some level, parodic. Sontag's assertion of the depoliticized (or possibly entirely apolitical) nature of camp is, of course, contentious because of the implications for cultural value. Conversely, I would argue that it is in camp's relation with popular culture that it is at its cleverest, as it infiltrates popular culture posing as valueless, while presenting a parodic challenge to presumed norms of gender/sex relations in particular.

Queer

Such a challenge leads in turn to the question of the queer status of camp. On the one hand, as we have seen, Meyer describes it specifically as a '*queer* cultural critique'. At the same time, Sontag draws (quite blindly on some occasions) on examples from gay male history: Samuel Barber's opera *Vanessa*; Tchaikovsky's *Swan Lake*; Oscar Wilde's epigrams (indeed, she dedicates the 'Notes' to Wilde.) She also makes connections between male homosexuality and camp aesthetics that are certainly of their time in their primitiveness: 'The Camp insistence on not being "serious," on playing, also connects with the homosexual's desire to remain youthful.' On the other hand, she undermines the exclusive gay male ownership of camp, suggesting that 'if homosexuals hadn't more or less invented Camp, someone else would'.[15] Yet these last sentences have elided homosexuality with queerness in a way that is misleading. In its broadest sense, the term 'queer' can incorporate a wide range of

---

10   Pamela Robertson, *Guilty Pleasures: Feminist Camp from Mae West to Madonna* (London, 1996), p. 1.
11   Meyer, 'Introduction', p. 1 (emphasis added).
12   Bergman, 'Introduction', p. 12.
13   Robertson, *Guilty Pleasures*, p. 6.
14   Andrew Ross, 'Uses of Camp' in Bergman, *Camp Grounds*, pp. 54–77, at p. 72. See also Robertson, *Guilty Pleasures*, p. 6.
15   Sontag, 'Notes', p. 64.

sexual practices and fetishes that may not be related at all to homosexuality. But the sense in which I want to use the term here, and the sense in which I understand it primarily being used in relation to camp, is summarized by Annamarie Jagose:

> Broadly speaking, queer describes those gestures or analytical models which dramatise incoherencies in the allegedly stable relations between chromosomal sex, gender and sexual desire. Resisting that model of stability – which claims heterosexuality as its origin, when it is more properly its effect – queer focuses on mismatches between sex, gender and desire. Institutionally, queer has been associated most prominently with lesbian and gay subjects, but its analytic framework also includes such topics as cross-dressing, hermaphroditism, gender ambiguity and gender-corrective surgery.[16]

Oxymoronically, Jagose's choice of the word 'mismatch' does rather imply that the 'relations' of which she speaks are in fact stable, but the emphasis in her point is clearly intended to be their merely *alleged* stability – that is to say, 'queer' is not the *deconstruction* of those relations (since they are only ever precarious at best), but those gestures which *dramatize incoherencies* in an already tenuous set of links are what bring the precarious nature of the relations to the foreground. In fact, homosexuality argues for its own set of normalized gender and sex relations, where the queer is committed to the disruption of those relations. And, I would argue, such a disruption emerges in part in camp's parodic response to popular culture.

Here, it is also worth thinking briefly about the relationship between camp and kitsch as two very closely related, but subtly distinct, ideas, and this is where things start to get particularly messy. One common articulation of kitsch is that it lacks the intentionality that camp enjoys. That is to say, both are 'off', 'wrong' or 'awful', but camp enjoys and glorifies its own awfulness whereas kitsch doesn't recognize it. This might in turn be related to the question of time, age and detachment that comes through in Sontag's writing. She asserts that a sense of detachment from an object is part of its camp status and associates this with an ageing process: 'It's not a love of the old as such. It's ... that the process of aging or deterioration provides the necessary detachment. ... What was banal can, with the passage of time, become fantastic.'[17] Thus, certain images or objects that seem camp now may well have been taken as kitsch on their first outings in the world. However, we must also take into consideration the commonly formulated distinction between high camp and low camp, and thus turn momentarily to Christopher Isherwood and his formulation of camp in the novel *The World in the Evening*. Isherwood describes low camp as an 'utterly debased form' and gives the example of 'a swishy little boy with peroxided hair, dressed in a picture hat and feather boa, pretending to be Marlene Dietrich'; meanwhile, high camp – which, Isherwood suggests, can spill

---

16   Annamarie Jagose, 'An Extract from "Queer Theory"', *Australian Humanities Review* 4 (December 1996). Available at <http://www.australianhumanitiesreview.org/archive/Issue-Dec-1996/jagose.html> (accessed 23 August 2008).

17   Sontag, 'Notes', p. 60.

over from gay culture into straight culture – is a case of 'expressing what's basically serious to you in terms of fun and artifice and elegance'.[18] Sontag, on the other hand, distinguishes between 'naïve' or 'pure' camp, which is unintentional, and 'deliberate' camp, which she describes as 'usually less satisfying'. This is one of several points at which I am not convinced Sontag is really thinking clearly about the questions at hand. If we are to agree with her that the operas of Strauss are camp, but not those of Wagner, we must at the same time acknowledge the very apparent (and, I would argue, intentional) sense of playfulness at work in Strauss and absent from Wagner. By Sontag's own definitions, Wagner's operas are more likely to be pure camp than Strauss's, given how very, very seriously they take themselves, and how very much 'too much' (in a sense) they end up.

Camp in Music

Since we are getting closer to questions about the musical text, let us now take the plunge into the murky waters and explore some very specific musical examples. The first example I would like to take – Tchaikovsky's Piano Concerto No. 1 in B flat minor (op. 23, 1875) – is not obviously nameable as 'popular music', but I want to consider a performance of it that sits very clearly within popular culture. Specifically, I will compare two performances of the first movement, focusing on the first couple of minutes, as a way of exploring the relationship between text and performance, the position of camp in relation to popular culture and the importance of detachment in the enactment of camp. The piece is everything one might hope for from a Romantic piano concerto: big, bold, chords and arpeggios using the full stretch of the keyboard; a large orchestra dominated in the first instance by the brass; and later, lush, thick, string-centred textures. In short, it is a piece characterized by a certain excess. It was used in the soundtrack of the 1941 film *The Great Lie* (dir. Goulding), starring Mary Astor, Bette Davis and George Brent, and so, on that basis as well as the textual one, it could be associated with camp. Indeed, Ivan Raykoff has written on the so-called 1940s concerto film, of which *The Great Lie* is but one (the Warsaw Concerto from *Dangerous Moonlight* [dir. Hurst, 1941] is another, and Rachmaninov's Second Piano Concerto in *Brief Encounter* [dir. Lean, 1945] is a third). Raykoff specifically states that 'the 1940s "concerto film" is typically classified as melodrama', a term that we can certainly associate with camp, but let us see what different pianists make of it in performance.[19]

The two performances I am considering here are one by Vladimir Horowitz in 1943 and one by Liberace on *The Liberace Show* in 1969.[20] Classical cover versions,

---

18 Christopher Isherwood, *The World in the Evening* (New York, 1954), p. 110.
19 Ivan Raykoff, 'Concerto con amore', *ECHO* 2/1 (2000): para. 44. Available at <http://www.echo.ucla.edu/Volume2-Issue1/raykoff/raykoff-article.html> (accessed 28 August 2008).
20 One big problem in writing about recordings and performances, rather than scores,

as we might term them, operate on slightly different terms from cover versions in the popular music arena, not least because the prescriptive text absolutely cannot be changed. Replace a piano with an acoustic guitar, by all means, when covering an Elton John song, for instance, but absolutely do not decide to put a Mozart oboe line on a harmonica! Nevertheless, several miles of interpretive possibility remain in the space between the printed score – however directive it may initially seem – and the performed sound. In any case, it is my contention that one of these recordings is significantly more camp than the other one, and that leads me to suggest that Tchaikovsky's text may be kitsch, but that it is the performance that makes it camp. For its part, *Wikipedia* notes that Horowitz was 'sometimes criticized for being overly mannered and showy',[21] something we might take as an indicator of camp. And yet, it will doubtless be no surprise that I consider Liberace's to be the more camp of the two performances. However, I must be clear that I am not basing this interpretation on any visual aspect. Rather, I am proposing that there are identifiable musical moments, found in his interpretive decisions, which invite a camp understanding of his performance.

First, the attack on the opening chords (see Ex. 9.1) differs noticeably between the two performances. It is possible to hear Liberace's hands bouncing off the keyboard from one chord to the next, while Horowitz's seem to hold on to the chords a little before moving. The earlier performance has a sense of austerity in this respect, whereas the later one is 'skippier', more playful and frivolous.

Example 9.1   Opening piano chords: Tchaikovsky's Piano Concerto No. 1 in B flat minor (measures 8–11)

Then, in the piano's first statement of the theme (Ex. 9.2), Liberace draws out the semiquavers in bar 27, invoking the true sense of the word 'pathetic', whereas Horowitz punctuates them very properly and carefully. Immediately after this, at bar 31, the same happens with a related set of triplets (Ex. 9.3), and these two moments provide the first hint of the musical melodrama about to ensue at Liberace's hands.

---

is the challenge of providing soundclips to accompany the analysis, and restrictive copyright legislation is frustrating to this writer. I therefore direct the reader to two URLs, since YouTube thankfully provides at least a partial solution. It is my hope that these URLs will remain available long enough to be useful: Horowitz: <http://www.youtube.com/watch?v=c4Zc8SonNBQ>. Liberace: <http://www.youtube.com/watch?v=GVuxReEE1Ic>.

21   <http://en.wikipedia.org/wiki/Vladimir_Horowitz> (accessed 2 September 2008).

Next, at the accelerando at bar 32, Horowitz builds the tempo gradually, carefully again, subtly and non-uniformly. In contrast, Liberace launches straight into a much increased tempo in what can only be described as a crude interpretation.

Example 9.2   **Statement of theme: Tchaikovsky's Piano Concerto No. 1 in B flat minor (measures 25–28)**

Example 9.3   **Triplets and accelerando: Tchaikovsky's Piano Concerto No. 1 in B flat minor (measures 30–32)**

After the accelerando comes the piano's first truly solo moment: here, a four-note motif, with accents on each note, gives way to rapid (in 14ths no less), rising diminished seventh arpeggios, played in intervals of sixths by the two hands (Ex. 9.4). Liberace holds each accented note dramatically longer than Horowitz: it may be just a little too long – a little 'too much' – to be taken entirely seriously. His is an exaggerated tension and an exaggerated display of release. Horowitz, by contrast, can hardly be accused of overworking that tension and release: rather, we would be inclined so say that he works *with* it, being audibly lighter on the diminished sevenths and using the four-note descending motif to move forward rather than hold back. Finally, throughout the performance, there is a much less subtle gradation of dynamics in Liberace's performance than in Horowitz's, again pointing to a sense of exaggeration.

Example 9.4   **Four-note motif and rising diminished sevenths: Tchaikovsky's Piano Concerto No. 1 in B flat minor (measures 40–44)**

What this comparative analysis reveals, then, is that the display and flamboyance are certainly present in the text, but they are drawn out beyond the serious and foregrounded by Liberace in his performance. In fact, what characterizes each of the moments I have identified are the particular attacks and decays on relevant notes. The 'bounce' in Liberace's opening chords is a sharper attack; the intense stress on the four-note motif is a longer decay. So we have tension and release, and attack and decay as part of their production. I would argue that this kind of tension and release is generating here a profoundly bodily response, conditional as that may be on the careful, consistent and not-altogether-conscious training of our ears to understand Western harmonic patterns. Anahid Kassabian has written on the idea of hearing as a contact sense,[22] of sound as producing physical responses in

22   Anahid Kassabian, *The Soundtracks of Our Lives: Ubiquitous Musics and Distributed*

various ways, and David Huron, in *Sweet Anticipation*, has written on the processes of expectation in music (and, indeed, expectation more generally) and how their relation to neurobiological processes. Huron writes:

> ... the ability to anticipate future events is important for survival. Minds are 'wired' for expectation. Neuroscientists have identified several brain structures that appear to be essential for prediction and anticipation. These include the substantia nigra, the ventral tegmental area, the anterior cingulated cortex, and the lateral prefrontal cortical areas. Most people will regard such biological facts as uninteresting details. For most of us, the more compelling details pertain to the subjective experience. From a phenomenological perspective, the most interesting property of expectation is the feeling that can be evoked.[23]

Huron turns throughout the book to specific musical examples and their complex productions of expectation in the listener, relating all the examples to different kinds of expectation and 'expectation-related emotions',[24] such as surprise. It is equally my contention that the production of anticipation is a physical response to the sound. Moreover, I want to propose that the exaggerated production of anticipation, as brought about by Liberace, might intensify that sense of physicality to the music, and this is a place where camp is surely invited in. We can, for instance, tentatively propose some binarisms connecting seriousness and the intellectual on the one hand, and flamboyant exaggeration and the bodily on the other. Yet Kassabian has also written – admittedly briefly – on attack and decay, claiming them as places where questions of narrativity might be rethought. In work on techno music in film soundtracks, she writes of notes and tracks that lack noticeable attack or decay, being instead 'all middle', and lacking the (narrative) trajectory of regular notes.[25] Here, by contrast, I am talking about very sharp attacks or extended decays. However, if we follow Kassabian and others in thinking of narrativity in gendered and sex(ualiz)ed terms, the question of camp in relation to these notes becomes very pertinent. Indeed, in her work on hearing as a contact sense noted above, she also ends with the question of narrativity. This leads me to think that, in these musical moments I have been identifying, narrativity would be a very relevant idea to pursue, and that perhaps this is also one area in which some kind of political work is being done. In fact, it opens up an interesting internal tension, since a great deal of work on narrativity – famously including Susan McClary's *Feminine*

Subjectivities (Los Angeles, CA, forthcoming).

23 David Huron, *Sweet Anticipation: Music and the Psychology of Expectation* (Cambridge, MA, 2006), p. 7.

24 Ibid., p. 18.

25 Anahid Kassabian, 'The Sound of a New Film Form' in Ian Inglis (ed.), *Popular Music and Film* (London, 2003), pp. 91–101, at p. 98.

Endings[26] – has proposed it as 'structurally masculine'.[27] Such a structuration is eloquently invoked as a metaphor by Robert Scholes, quoted by both McClary and Theresa de Lauretis when talking of narrative:

> ... the archetype of all fiction is the sexual act. In saying this I do not mean merely to remind the reader of the connection between all art and the erotic in human nature. Nor do I intend simply to suggest an analogy between fiction and sex. For what connects fiction – and music – with sex is the fundamental orgiastic rhythm of tumescence and detumescence, of tension and resolution, of intensification to the point of climax and consummation. In the sophisticated forms of fiction, as in the sophisticated practice of sex, much of the art consists of delaying climax within the framework of desire in order to prolong the pleasurable act itself. When we look at fiction with respect to its form alone, we see a pattern of events designed to move toward climax and resolution, balanced by a counter-pattern of events designed to delay this very climax and resolution.[28]

Kassabian argues that techno music counters such traditionally phallic narrative trajectories through its characteristic 'all middle' qualities, produced both by the ways in which techno music ends (without climax) in the films she examines and by the subdual of obvious attacks and decays. By extension, we might propose that the attacks and decays of Liberace's performance conversely exaggerate the structural masculinity of the narrative – something that, on the surface, would not seem to accord with notions about camp. Yet Kassabian is careful to note that the act of opposing 'phallic directionality' does not make techno necessarily feminine.[29] Similarly, it is my contention that the exaggerated sense of this 'phallic directionality' found in Liberace does not make his performance normatively masculine in its narrativity. Quite the contrary: I would argue that the exaggeration enacts a sense of performativity in relation to that phallic masculinity and that such playfulness with gendered codes is precisely at the heart of camp.

Life is a Cabaret

And so I turn now to my next example, one that very obviously produces tension and release, achieving it partly through the careful use of attack and decay: Liza Minnelli's famous performance of 'Auf wiedersehen mein Herr' in *Cabaret* (dir. Fosse, 1972). As Minnelli crosses the stage to take her position on a chair, the band plays her in with a simple tonic-dominant oscillation. But already, a certain

---

26 Susan McClary, *Feminine Endings: Music, Gender, and Sexuality* (Minneapolis, 1991).
27 Kassabian, 'The Sound of a New Film Form'.
28 Scholes quoted in McClary, *Feminine Endings*, p. 126.
29 Kassabian, 'The Sound of a New Film Form', p. 98.

tension is established: because the song is in a minor key, the dominant tension present is greater than it would be with a major tonic. It is a very simple thing to say that tonic-dominant tension is greater with a minor tonic, but the simplicity of the statement does not detract from the tension in the music. Alone, of course, this fact does not produce camp, but the establishment of tension by whatever means is, I propose, one necessary part of its production. At the same time, the out-of-tune instruments put the listener immediately on edge, the timbre enhancing the tension of the text. (Here, we might also invoke what Sontag concludes is 'The ultimate Camp statement: it's good because it's awful'.[30]) To talk in terms of tension and resolution is not only to use the language of music analysis, but also perhaps to imply the language of physics, albeit that 'resolution' is there termed 'equilibrium'. And thinking in terms of physics yields other terminology relevant to the present discussion, while also allowing it to be nuanced somewhat, as both momentum and potential energy in the music are carefully manipulated throughout this performance of 'Auf wiedersehen', and while 'potential energy' in musical terms could also be described as tension, to do so could easily confuse matters.

Introducing Minnelli's opening lines, the band once again oscillates between tonic and dominant, but here – the real start of the song – the tension is held, leaving a dominant chord unresolved for a second before Minnelli sings. In the three first lines, Minnelli utters her lines with pitches that imply a speech-like manner, and the vocal lines are balanced by the piano's antiphonal interjections. Thus, the intimate vocality and lack of instrumental support produce a sense of anticipation while the piano's responses imply mild surprise. The future of the song is uncertain, and the sense of expectation is high. A brief respite of predictability is offered in the ensuing lines ('So I do / what I do / When I'm through / then I'm through / And I'm through') before a pregnant pause before the resolution (in musical and other senses) at 'Toodle-oo'. Then, leading into the first verses, the tempo slows, and Minnelli drags out each word: 'Bye ... bye ... mein'. Momentum builds up gradually through verse one (to 'you're better off without me mein Herr'), but more instrumentally than vocally, as Minnelli tends obviously to draw each word out against the accompaniment and places her words just behind the beat.

The momentum achieved through the second verse is suddenly removed at the return to the opening material, providing a brief surprise appeased by the familiarity of the material. The build-up to the next verse is an exaggerated form of what has already taken place, with the listener's sense of anticipation enhanced by the piano tremolo throughout, where previously there had been minimal instrumental accompaniment to Minnelli's singing. Then, the lines 'But I do / what I can / Inch by inch / Step by step / Mile by mile / Man by man' are drawn out into an overstated passion where the earlier iteration ('when I'm through ...') is dismissed. That earlier moment is itself campily flippant and frivolous, but this later one enacts the great exaggeration of camp. At the next 'Bye bye mein ...', the words are more drawn out than their earlier counterparts, enhancing the sense of expectation. At the same time, a rhythmic shift is put in place, as a cymbal hit sharply punctuates

---

30   Sontag, 'Notes', p. 65

the words over the continuing tremolo. These percussive interjections foreshadow an offbeat pulse in the following verse – drawn attention to by finger-clicks from Minnelli and the dancers – whereas the first verse had emphasized the downbeats. The slow pace of this offbeat pulse generates a sense of potential energy in the music – a potential that eventually gives way to a kinetic return to the downbeat emphasis. Repeatedly, the momentum increases, with the song racing towards its end through two rising modulations that add to the effect. It is in these last lines that we get the clearest sense yet of Minnelli's manipulation of attack and decay in her vocal delivery. At her last delivery of 'though I used to care / I need the open air', she builds the syllables 'used' and 'op-' through a gradual attack into a rapid decay, the effect being accentuated by the silences and punctuations of the band, such that the accompaniment works with the voice to amplify the flamboyance of this vocal mannerism. Yet throughout the song, Minnelli manipulates attack and decay, using them exaggeratedly to effect a kind of 'punch' in the voice that counters her belting voice.

Text and Context

What we find clearly in both Minnelli's and Liberace's performances is a sense of exaggeration, flamboyance and playfulness, achieved in part through an overworked system of tension and release. Yet they both also raise the final issue central to any discussion of camp: the question of the relationship between text and context. That is, to what extent do we read these performances as camp because of the contexts in which they exist? Liberace, after all, adorns himself, his piano and his stage with all the hallmarks of camp at the same time as his musical interpretation might be read as such. And, in turn, do we read those hallmarks as camp now because of our detachment from them, because of their being *démodé*, to use Sontag's word? A final brief example serves to illustrate the issues for consideration here, and that is the song 'Don't Rain On My Parade'. Most famously associated with Barbra Streisand's performance in *Funny Girl* (dir. Wyler, 1968), I want to take three other performances: Judy Garland and Liza Minnelli (1964); Charlotte Church (2001); and Linda Eder (2003).[31] Based on my analyses thus far, I feel justified in proposing that this song is readable as camp today. However, a number of questions arise. Was it camp in 1964, in that different musical environment? Is it more camp now because we're 44 years on? Is it camp because of the iconic status of Garland (and indeed Minnelli) in gay history? To what extent can we separate those questions out? Comparing the Minnelli's 1964 performance with that of Charlotte Church in 2001 reveals that there is something in the performance – something beyond the prescription of the text and yet not beyond the text itself – that might be

---

31   Again, YouTube will aid the investigative reader: Garland and Minnelli: <http://www.youtube.com/watch?v=C3czjFAM9RQ>. Church: <http://www.youtube.com/watch?v=OuvGYuS34CY>. Eder: <http://www.youtube.com/watch?v=I_6n3drbhV0>.

identifiable as camp, as the older recording is clearly more camp than this young singer's formulaic and emotionally flat performance. Much, I would argue, is to be explained by Garland's and Minnelli's uses of the voice, comparable in many ways to Minnelli's in 'Auf Wiedersehen mein Herr', with a short, sharp, spitting delivery juxtaposed with portamento-and vibrato-laden belting voices. Comparing it, on the other hand, with the performance by Linda Eder demonstrates that it is not only a temporal separation that yields camp in the performance, as there are places in Eder's rendition that may be even more camp than Garland's and Minnelli's. Take, for instance, Eder's articulation of the lines 'I'll march my band out / I'll beat my drum' nearly two minutes into the performance. Here, Eder draws out individual words in an overstated belting voice in a way that enhances both anticipation on the part of the listener and the vocal flamboyance of the performer. This contrasts with an acute version of a punchy delivery – for example, during the lines 'But whether I'm a rose of sheer perfection / A freckly on the nose of life's complexion'. Hence the contrast is exaggerated by the fact that each end of the vocal spectrum is taken to extremes. And intriguingly, both Eder's rendition and the Garland/ Minnelli performance are arguably subtly more camp than Barbra Streisand's in *Funny Girl*, which draws attention more to the defiance and hopes of her character at this point in the film's narrative.

So, in 'Don't Rain On My Parade', as with the other examples considered in this chapter, there are textual, contextual and performance elements that must be taken into consideration when identifying the thread of camp in the fabric of the music. The clear separation of such elements is, of course, not entirely possible, but I hope I have demonstrated that, with detailed performance analysis and a sound theoretical foundation, highlighting camp in music is not impossible either.

Who Are You?
Research Strategies of the
Unruly Feminine

Sheila Whiteley

My fascination with gendered identity – what is a man (Mick Jagger, Jimi Hendrix, Ziggy Stardust, Eminem, Morrissey?), what is a woman (Marianne Faithfull, Siouxie Sioux, Madonna, Skin, k.d. lang?) that blend of the real and the unreal that constitutes both the 'imagined' character and the performativity of gender (are they the same?) – has dominated much of my academic life. As Judith Butler observes, 'for a woman to identify as a woman is a culturally enforced effect'.[1] Moreover, the feminine is never constant. It shifts with the cultural norms surrounding sexuality, sometimes bounded by, sometimes transcending, both class and ethnicity. Becoming gendered involves impersonating an ideal, an archetype that nobody actually inhabits, so raising the question, 'Who are you?'.

What I didn't know when I first started researching and writing on popular music and gender was how to unpack this tantalizing question. What I did know was that I was not unique, that others before me had tried to fathom out that elusive essence that situates women as other. Maybe it was their smaller brains – and hence the justification of both their hysterical nature and the impossibility of their intellectual worth that stamped their femininity and accounted for their unnaturalness, their mannishness, when pursuing suffrage or, indeed, an academic or musical career. Then again, sometimes that mannishness comes in useful – not least when it comes to taking on 'men's work' in times of war before returning to that ideal home and the appropriate role of a 1950s 'new' woman. But is this freedom, or 'is it more a question of how to work the trap that one is inevitably in'?[2] As Butler states, 'gender can't be taken on as a kind of consumerism; it cannot be treated deliberately, as if it's an object of choice'. Being gendered is itself a restriction, and gender roles are constrained and 'constructed by the repetition of often oppressive and painful

---

1   Liz Kotz, 'The Body You Want: Liz Kotz Interviews Judith Butler', *Artforum* 31/3 (1992): 82–89, at 84.
2   Ibid.

gender norms'.[3] If this is true for women in general, what about women musicians, and how do I, as a researcher, avoid simple description and tackle, instead, the issues surrounding being a woman in a man's world? How do I unpack gender and what analytical strategies are there to help understand femininity within the gendered constraints of popular music?

What I have learned, from my forays into sexuality and gender in *Sexing the Groove*, through *Women and Popular Music* to *Too Much Too Young* and *Queering the Popular Pitch* is that you cannot simply impose an interpretation on a song or an album. Nor do I believe that it is appropriate to take one analytical approach – whether this is poststructuralism or postmodernism – and apply it across the spectrum of gender analysis. The ironic stance of postmodernism, for example, cannot account for the struggles of such artists as Janis Joplin or Joni Mitchell and their individual tussles with popular music's patriarchal structure during the 1960s and early 1970s. It is also apparent that while the former expressed her feelings largely through cover versions, the latter wrote both the words and the music as a personal testimony to her life experiences at the time. The question thus arises as to how we, the listener, interpret their work and why it is that lyric analysis is lacking that crucial ingredient when exploring meanings. For musicologists, both popular and traditional, the answer is simple. Lyrics are not poems and, as such, it is the way in which the words combine with the music (harmony, rhythm, arrangement and vocal gesture) that both impacts on and informs the melodic nuance and hence the meaning of the words. A suspension imparts an unresolved tension to the phrase 'I love you', as Joni Mitchell was only too aware.

But does 'meaning' only exist in an analysis of the musical text? Clearly, this is a crucial ingredient, but it is also evident that meaning is situated both socially and historically, that it works through 'dialogue – echoes, traces, contrasts, responses – both with previous discursive moments and, at the same time, with addressees real or imagined'.[4] The ideal of being together at Christmas, for example, is given a particular focus by Joni Mitchell in her 1971 album, *Blue*. Prefaced by songs which highlight homesickness ('California', 'This Flight Tonight'), 'River' constructs an introspective vision of the tensions inherent in the romantic ideology surrounding the Christmas season. Opening with a moody and resolutely minor 'Jingle Bells', the 'out–of–tuneness' of the piano introduction provides a musical metaphor for not belonging within the context of Christmas, a time when the awareness of being alone is particularly acute: 'cutting down trees', 'putting up reindeer', 'singing songs of joy and peace'. The mood of nostalgia, of looking back over the past, is highlighted by an all-pervading sense of absence – of snow, of money and of her lover. The bleakness of the narrative is underpinned by the repetitiveness of the vocal line to create a musical alignment between the 'what he did for me' and the 'why' of loss. The introspection of the lyrics, the underlying pain, is thus heightened by the formal tensions of the music. The narrative of loss is rooted in

---

3   Ibid.
4   Richard Middleton (ed.), *Reading Pop: Approaches to Textual Analysis in Popular Music* (Oxford, 2000), p. 13.

repetition, creating a musical metaphor for the introspection accompanying a failed romance, ('He tried hard to help me ... he loved me so naughty)'; the need to escape ('I would teach my feet to fly') by upward melodic movement and chord colouring; the desolation inherent in being alone, by the lack of harmonic resolution in the final chorus ('I wish I had a river I could skate away on') and the reprise of 'Jingle Bells', twisted harmonically as a musical metaphor for self-reproach ('I made my baby cry'). But there is no going back, and the next song, 'A case of you' creates a mood of even deeper introspection and aloneness: 'I could drink a case of you, darling, and I would still be on my feet'.[5]

The biographical detail in *Blue* provides a context for analysis, framing Mitchell's experiences, what she learned, who she met, where she went. She is the theme and is placed at the centre of her story: travelling through Europe, earning her own living, homesick for California, reflecting on the 'acid, booze, and ass, needles, guns and grass' ('Blue') of the late 1960s. Personal experience is thus contextualized by an evolving history that relates to contemporary culture (political, social, ideological and musical) while weaving a semic thread which opens up a subjective vision of possibilities: the sonic space that makes the listener want to listen. It is here that the concept of dialogic exchange provides a particular insight into intertextuality and how meaning in popular music is produced at many different levels. As Richard Middleton explains, 'a textual analysis of lyrics and musical style provides one important methodological trajectory, but meaning is also produced through dialogue within the textures, voices and structures; between producers and addressees; between discourses, musical and other'.[6]

The 'other' is significant. Popular musicology goes beyond the more obvious concern with form, structure, harmony, melody, the voicings within the arrangement, the singing style. It is also concerned with image, the visual gesture, with sexuality and gender and, significantly, the ideological interests that support dominant interpretations. As Middleton perceptively notes:

> ... it is apparent that how one "tells" the story is crucial to its interpretation. In effect, the story told is one among many, and while musical analysis and research into historical and cultural data remain important, meaning is always at issue. There is no one scientifically "true" account of the music, but rather a sense of collective complicity: is this story plausible, is my interpretation plausible?[7]

Queering, for example, has challenged cultural and social norms, subverting the gendered heterosexual bias in popular music by invoking a different way of listening, a queer sensibility. The emphasis on 'throwing into question old labels and their meanings so as to reassociate music with lived experience and the broader

---

5   Sheila Whiteley (ed.), *Christmas: Ideology and Popular Culture* (Edinburgh, 2008), pp. 106–107.

6   Middleton, *Reading Pop*, p. 13.

7   Ibid., p. 14.

patterns of discourse and culture that music both mirrors and actively produces' remains important.[8] It involves different interpretational strategies which question inherited conventions, which explore musical constructions of gender and sexuality[9] and, hence, the relationship between music and queerness – itself a problematic concept. As Richard Dyer points out, 'there is no pure expression of queeritude, uncontaminated by an equally unalloyed straightness surrounding it. [Rather, queer] works with and within the wider culture, of which [it] is an ineluctable part.'[10] Queer and straight are thus neither exclusive nor equal categories; both are in part structured out of the other. What is significant to an understanding of queer is the felt or perceived difference and how this relates to (musical) language (expression, emphasis and tone), what is glimpsed, what is sensed in performance. Once framed, once recognized as queer, the artist/performance can then be identified as expressing particular perspectives and sensibilities which resonate with lesbian/gay culture.[11] By merging social relations with musical discourses it is thus possible to trace the transforming significance of popular music and how both hetero-normativity and resistant queer sexualities are constructed and situated in historical time. In doing so, it becomes apparent that popular music has played a significant, if often ambiguous role, in the shaping of identity and self-consciousness. For example, Dusty Springfield:

> ... *created a decidedly queer persona, while achieving popular success in a trendy milieu in which lesbianism, lacking the criminal status and thus the glamour of male homosexuality, remained invisible and unfashionable. Utilizing the tactics of camp, she adopted more visible (and modish) marginalised identities by becoming a gay man in drag (or conversely a female female impersonator) visually and a black woman vocally. In this manner she pushed accepted notions of femininity to absurd extremes.*[12]

---

8   Philip Brett, Elizabeth Wood and Gary C. Thomas (eds), *Queering the Pitch. The New Gay and Lesbian Musicology* (New York, 1994), pp. viii–ix.

9   The continuing significance of a theorist such as Susan McClary lies in her questioning approach towards the gendered codes inherent in femininity – the need to confront existing theoretical explanations, to ask why certain framings of the feminine have historical currency and how and why these impact on musical meaning. As she observes in *Feminine Endings: Music, Gender, and Sexuality* (Minneapolis, 1991), p. 25: 'music is not a universal language – it changes over time and geographical locality' and is 'always dependent on the conferring of social meaning' :– a tacit reminder that researchers cannot rely on existing explanations but must continuously engage with the politics and ideology surrounding contemporary culture.

10   Richard Dyer, *The Culture of Queers* (London, 2002), p. 9.

11   Richard Dyer provides a fuller discussion of 'the culture of queers' from which these thoughts are drawn. See ibid., pp. 8–10.

12   Patricia J. Smith, 'You Don't Have to Say You Love Me': The Camp Masquerades of Dusty Springfield' in *The Queer Sixties* (London, 1999), p. xviii.

As Patricia Juliana Smith writes, such artists 'evoke a response of affection identification, and admiration from a devoted queer or audience [due to the] presence in each of characteristics that were, in their time, implicitly or explicitly contrary to societal or cultural ideals and sexual mores in a manner resonant with queer sensibility'.[13] Her observation can be usefully applied to k.d. lang's album, *Absolute Torch and Twang*, where 'irony, wit, and [the] artifice of camp work to reveal the constructedness of the conventions of straight sex and gender systems'.[14] In particular, the stylistic conventions of country in such songs as 'Three Days' and 'Big Big Love' (covers of songs 'belonging' to men) are compromised by a tongue-in-cheek play on double-entendre, which is given particular emphasis by lang's flamboyant performance style, so 'inviting dyke-oriented readings'. As Mockus wittily observes, 'for lang, to restore, or uncloset, the "real humor or twang" of country music is to engage with a camp musical strategy',[15] which recognizes 'the disciplinary production of gender and the challenges to this that performance makes through, for example, masquerade and/or irony'.[16] The mid-West home-centred connotations of 'gals' ('Big Boned Gals'), for example, and the male sexual imagery associated with a 'big big love' which is 'growin'', 'showin'', is undercut by a daring premise of queer affection and desire. In effect, 'conventional *musical* signs – standard form, regular harmony and predictable rhythms – [are juxtaposed] with a wonderfully mischievous vocal performance, so enacting a radical and dykish twist in *gender* signs'.[17]

Lang's queering of the traditional codes of country (not least its strict presentation of gender and sexuality[18]) provides a particular insight into the way in which music is open to different interpretations that work to free the queer imaginary, so contributing to a more thoughtful understanding of identity, of 'who I am', and hence the quality and meaning of relationships. This is also evidenced in Jason Lee Oakes's discussion of performative gender play in 'Queering the Witch: Stevie Nicks and the Forging of Femininity at the Night of a Thousand Stevies',[19] an event that was celebrated in New York for some 13 years. As the sign at the entrance of Jackie 60 claimed, this is 'a club for dominant women, poets, gay men and

---

13   Ibid., p. xv.
14   Martha Mockus, 'Queer Thoughts on Country Music and k.d. lang' in Brett, Wood and Thomas, *Queering the Pitch*, pp. 257–74, at p. 265.
15   Ibid.
16   Judith Butler, 'Performative Acts and Gender Constitution: An Essay in Phenomenology and Feminist Theory' in Sue-Ellen Case (ed.), *Performing Feminisms: Feminist Critical Theory and Theatre* (Baltimore, MD, 1990), pp. 66–67.
17   Mockus, 'Queer Thoughts on Country Music', p. 263 (original emphasis).
18   As Mockus notes, the butch-femme aesthetic in country music was probably first set in motion by Dolly Parton, whose self-consciously excessive femininity can be read as a humorous critique of gender stereotyping. Needless to say, Parton also enjoys a huge lesbian and gay audience. Mockus, 'Queer Thoughts on Country Music', p. 270.
19   Jason Lee Oakes, 'Queering the Witch: Stevie Nicks and the Forging of Femininity at the Night of a Thousand Stevies' in Sheila Whiteley and Jennifer Rycenga, *Queering the Popular Pitch*, (London, 2006), pp. 41–54.

lesbians, freethinking heterosexuals, transvestites and transsexuals, fetish dressers, bisexuals and those who love them', and the annual Night of a Thousand Stevies (NOTS) welcomed a serial procession of Nicks impersonators, performing a single song, well into the early hours. As Oakes argues, this event attempted to reconcile femininity and feminism – so accounting for Stevie Nicks's contradictory reception. While her 'witchiness and hyperfemininity may confirm gender stereotypes for more conservative listeners, from another perspective she serves as a model of female – and more specifically, feminine – empowerment'.[20] Nicks's polysemous perversity thus provided impersonators with an opportunity to confirm their transgressive desires through multiple readings of her image and queer 'hearings' of her music.[21]

Oakes's discussion of 'Rhiannon' is particularly interesting in that he turns to musical analysis for the unique insights it provides, more specifically its feminine-associated traits:

> *The entire song, except for a brief bridge section, is based around a circular chordal movement that alternates between A minor and F major, meaning that it's difficult to find an unambiguous cadence point … Meanwhile the lead guitar and vocal outline the main melody, but in a heterophonic relationship where they seem to chase each other up and down the circuitous melody – moving repeatedly up and down the same trajectory – and never matching up in perfect unison … The vocal melody of Rhiannon is filled with a constant stream of nonchord tones including suspensions, anticipations, passing tones, and neighbouring tones. These melodies are not provided with a sense of resolution, as they never conclude on the root of the chord, thus giving the impression of an unsettled Nicks/Rhiannon who is unwilling to be pinned down, tonally, melodically, or otherwise … Much like the Stevie 'Twirl' and the feminine associated tambourine, Nicks's vibrato and her melodies work in perpetual motion around a seemingly fixed point of arrival that is never reached.*

> *These musical and kinaesthetic qualities – whether labelled as circuitous, oblique, mutable, undifferentiated, oceanic, and so forth – are typically gendered as feminine [and it is] the non-teleological 'feminine' quality of Nicks's music [that] is open to widely varying interpretations.*[22]

As Oakes explains, for some listeners the music comes across as 'flaky' and 'indecisive', so connoting the negative stereotypes of femininity, while others may hear her 'musical indeterminacy as a form of resistance'.[23] In association with the gendered subject-matter of many of her songs, and the prominence of gender and

---

20   Ibid., p. 52.
21   Ibid.
22   Ibid., pp. 50–51.
23   Ibid.

sexuality in the discourses surrounding Nicks, there is a space for potential queer hearings of her music.[24]

While readers are urged to read Oakes's full analysis of 'Rhiannon', his conclusion that femininity can be engaged as a construct to be applied strategically and that music provides 'a pathway for queering sexual and gender boundaries'[25] draws attention to the importance of theorists who have provided particular insights into the construction of the feminine. As Judith Butler explains, 'genders can be neither true nor false, but are only produced as the truth effects of a discourse of primary and stable identity'.[26] They require the repetition of a set of acts and the reiteration of signifiers, and while masculinity is commonly situated as the norm – as natural, original and absolute – femininity is understood as both performative and constructed, emanating from the idea of what 'femininity' is not in relation to masculinity and so operating as a binary opposition – a construction that dates back to Aristotle and his identification of woman as an incomplete man. As such, 'the concept of identity' and its relationship to gender are tenuous: 'all gender formations are results of careful and sustained practice and are thus not simply *formations*, but "*per*-form-ations".'[27]

Butler's emphasis on the performative and the construction of femininity has been significant for the analysis of popular music texts and, as Judith Halberstam observes, the power of her work 'lies in her ability to show how much has been excluded, rejected, abjected in the formation of human continuity and what toll those exclusions take upon particular subjects'.[28] Not least, 'hegemonic gender formations enforce especially effectively the criteria to which the subject must conform if s/he desires the attendant privileges of a hegemonic gender identity',[29] an observation that is pertinent to Oakes's framing of the witch as an index of societal attitudes towards femininity, whereby 'markers of witchiness paint a picture of femininity unbounded, rooted largely in a fear of female sexuality that overflows strict boundaries'.[30] Returning to Stevie Nicks, it is thus possible, as Oakes suggests, to interpret her performance of 'Rhiannon' as an expression of disruption which invades and reverses the pejorative associations of femininity by transforming the negative (hysterical, seductive and capricious) into the positive (sensitive, sensuous and adaptable),[31] so providing a particular insight into the way in which the myths surrounding femininity can be reclaimed musically as a basis for female empowerment. Nicks as Rhiannon/witch becomes 'the enchantress',

---

24   Ibid.
25   Ibid.
26   Judith Butler, *Gender Trouble: Feminism and the Subversion of Identity* (London: Routledge, 1999; orig. pub. 1990), p. 174.
27   Ian Biddle and Freya Jarman-Ivens, 'Introduction', in Freya Jarman-Ivens (ed.), *Oh Boy! Masculinities and Popular Music* (New York, 2007), p. 5.
28   Judith Halberstam, 'What's That Smell? Queer Temporalities and Subcultural Lives' in Whiteley and Rycenga, *Queering the Popular Pitch*, pp. 3–26, at p. 4.
29   Biddle and Jarman-Ivens, 'Introduction', p. 5.
30   Oakes, 'Queering the Witch', p. 52.
31   Ibid.

'the goddess', an archetypal image of femininity that embodies both mysticism and strength.

The relationship between feminine archetypes and composition/performance is important in providing a cipher of provisional identities. As Sheila Rowbotham observes:

> *The writing of our history is not just an individual venture but a continuing social communication. Our history strengthens us in the present by connecting us with the lives of countless women. Threads and strands of long-lost experience weave into the present. In rediscovering the dimensions of female existence lost in the tangled half-memories of myth and dream, we are uncovering and articulating what it is to be a woman in a world defined by man.*[32]

This sense of a social communication between past and present – 'the unwritten history of mankind from time unrecorded'[33] – has particular relevance to women whose assertion of the self has been bounded by the confines of patriarchal definition. By associating with the inner world of dreams, myth and legend, different combinations of the feminine emerge, other forms of consciousness, so creating alternative definitions of femininity which resist and confront women's gendered subjectivity. 'All the most powerful ideas in history go back to archetypes'[34] and consciousness, as Jung observed, 'does not create itself – it wells up from unknown depths'.[35]

While Jung was first and foremost an empiricist and practising psychologist, his fascination with primordial images and the fundamental tensions between consciousness and the unconscious opens out the discourses surrounding femininity by relating the psyche to the collective unconscious. As he writes in *Archetypes and the Collective Unconscious*, 'It is quite impossible to conceive how "experience" in the widest sense, or, for that matter, anything psychic, could originate exclusively in the outside world. The psyche is part of the innermost mystery of life, and it has its own peculiar structure and form like every other organisation.'[36] As such, the ego, or conscious mind, while 'ostensibly the thing we know most about' is nevertheless 'full of unfathomable obscurities'. Defined as 'a relatively constant personification of the unconscious itself, or the Schopenhauerian mirror in which the unconscious [which includes both memories that can be easily brought to mind and those which are suppressed] become aware of its own face',[37] the nature and activity of

---

32   Sheila Rowbotham, 'Dreams and Dilemma',in Sara Maitland (ed.), *Women Fly When Men Aren't Watching* (London, 1993), p. 86.

33   Carl Jung, 65.280, in *Psychological Reflections: An Anthology of his Writings 1905–1961*, ed. Jolande Jacobi (London, 1971), p. 27.

34   Ibid., p. 39.

35   Ibid., p. 22.

36   Ibid., p. 3.

37   Ibid., p. 9.

the psyche also relates to the collective unconscious, which influences emotions, behaviour and, significantly, creativity. As a form of 'psychic inheritance', it relates to spiritual experience and mysticism and to their parallels in dreams, myths, fairytales and legends, so engaging with both fantasy and the imagination: 'Every psychic process is an image and an "imagining," otherwise no consciousness could exist and the occurrence would lack phenomenality. Imagination itself is a psychic process, for which reason it is completely irrelevant whether the enlightenment be called "real" or "imaginary".'[38] As such, there is comparability with dialogic exchange and its relationship to meaning, the 'echoes, traces, contrasts, responses – both with discursive moments and, at the same time, with addressees real or imagined'.[39]

The dynamics of the psyche are governed both by opposition and equivalence – good : bad : equal – and, as such, it is interesting to return once again to the example of the witch as embodying the perverse sexuality of women, so marking her as contrary to patriarchal definitions of femininity as submissive, receptive and nurturing. As Tori Amos observes, 'Behind the Christian love-your-neighbour-as-yourself facade, there was another story. There was not a lot of compassion there if you had been deemed a sinner.'[40] By working with archetypes, there is thus the opportunity to connect with a feminine that transcends written history, 'to walk into a violated space and sing it from that space without wavering',[41] as exemplified in 'Waking the Witch' from Kate Bush's album *Hounds of Love* (1985). Prefaced by 'Under Ice', trying to 'get out of the cold water', the focus on alienation and being estranged is resurrected in a chilling track which explores the fate of a young woman condemned as 'guilty, guilty, guilty' through fractured electronic sounds which evoke the horror of exorcism and torture: 'Help this blackbird, there's a stone around my leg'. As Sara Maitland explains, for women 'freedom consists of voices that have been broken and blood that has been shed. Freedom tastes of pain ... There is no objectivity ... there is only the vision of possibility',[42] a psychic imagining which, for Jung, is expressed through fantasy, 'the creative activity from which the answers to all answerable questions come; it is the mother of possibilities, where, like all psychological opposites, the inner and outer worlds are joined together in living union'.[43]

The relationship between fact and fantasy (the actuality of subordination and the imaginary of the narrative) thus provides an important insight into the historical construction of femininity. The association of hysteria, dementia and neurosis with the 'unnatural' emotional extremes of women's sexuality, for example, resonates with the Gothic imagination in Emily Brontë's novel *Wuthering Heights* (1847) which situates the love of Catherine and Heathcliff within the untamed wildness

---

38   Ibid., p. 10.
39   Middleton, *Reading Pop*, p. 13.
40   Tori Amos and Ann Powers, *Tori Amos, Piece by Piece* (London, 2005), p. 37.
41   Ibid., p. 11.
42   Maitland, *Women Fly*, p. 85.
43   Jung, 69: 78, in *Psychological Reflections*, p. 9.

of the moors where 'visions rise and change that kill me with desire'.[44] The obsessiveness of erotic longing and loss, the wuthering (literally, howling) heights of passion which consume Brontë's star-crossed heroine provides another insight into a dialogical exchange between addressees real and imagined, so reflecting Rowbotham's conceptualization of history as a continuing social communication that connects past and present. Catherine's obsession resonates with the nineteenth century's perception of the hysteric as mentally insane and, as such, comparable to an irresponsible child, and it is this sense of childlikeness that informs Kate Bush's vocal characterization of Cathy in her 1978 promo single 'Wuthering Heights', so creating an intertextuality that is marked by nineteenth-century Romanticism, by Brontë (as omniscient author), and Catherine (as both fictional heroine and Heathcliff's anima – his soul and his life [45]). For Bush, Cathy's unresolved passion for Heathcliff (the sense of being torn between love and hate for her 'one dream', her 'only master') is underpinned by a mood of dramatic longing. Her eerily-pitched vocal, like the repetitiveness of the piano accompaniment, constantly turns in on itself to mirror the obsessive eroticism of desire. It is both wispy and wraithlike in its high register, pleading and childlike in its cry to be recognized ('Heathcliff, it's me, I'm Cathy, I've come home') but there is no cadential resolution, and the plea 'let me grab your soul away' is characterized by a repetitive sinuous motif which conjures up the spectral vision of the child Catherine appearing at the window of her old chamber at Wuthering Heights, begging to be allowed in. The portrayal of a love that can only be reconciled in death (when the two spirits can roam the moors together) relates Cathy's unnatural/supernatural desire to the Gothic vision of nature as wild and untamed. Her soul is in torment, consumed by a love which continues beyond death, and the sensual longing expressed in the chorus rises and falls like the wind with subtle shifts in the metre (see Ex. 10.1).

While Cathy's death draws on the traditional concept of the woman who is punished for her sexuality, her untamed nature, 'Wuthering Heights' also draws on the mythological in Heathcliff's embodiment of the beast, the major mythic figure of masculine potency. He is both Eros and the source of Cathy's fantasy fixation. In traditional fairytales she would nurture and tame him, but, for both Brontë and Bush, Catherine/Cathy personifies the feminine erotic: Beauty stands in need of her Beast rather than vice versa and is forever condemned to 'roam in the night'. Her need of him is part of her own carnal nature; she has chosen the beast because his

---

44   Emily Brontë, 'The Prison' (1846).

45   The animus is the archetype that completes women and represents the male-defined qualities of reflection, deliberation and self-knowledge. The anima represents the female traits that a man's persona lacks – generally the ability to form relationships and be related – and it is female. The relationship of the anima/animus to the individual is always emotional and has its own dynamic, because, as archetypes, the anima and animus are impersonal forces. The animus of a woman and the anima of a man take the form of a 'soul-image' in the personal unconscious; this soul-image may be transferred to a real person who naturally becomes the object of intense feeling, which may be passionate love or passionate hate. See: <http://academic.brooklyn.cuny.edu/english/melani/novel_19c/wuthering/psych.html>.

Example 10.1   Kate Bush, 'Wuthering Heights'

animal nature excites her and gives her desires licence, so invoking the darker side of women's fantasy lives.[46] As Jung notes, 'It is a great mistake to treat an archetype as if it were a mere name, word, or concept. It is far more than that: it is a piece of life, an image connected with the living individual by a bridge of emotion',[47] which Ian McEwan terms 'the unruly unconscious'.[48] For such artists as Kate Bush and Tori Amos, who acknowledge the importance of Jungian psychology and iconography in their exploration of femininities, archetypes provide a way of addressing both the specific subjugation and revitalization of women's experience by drawing on the tensions between representation and its relationship to history, ideology and culture, marginalization, and its impact on cultural self-expression. As Tori Amos explains:

> *As a songwriter, if you're honest, you begin to find the qualities you scorn within yourself. When you are able to crawl inside and stop judging for one second and just find that place within where you could do that thing that horrifies you most – you need to find the incest victim in you, the perpetrator of incest in you, the killer and the killed: you need to find all those places. You*

---

46   In the collective unconscious, the shadow is absolute evil. In the personal unconscious, the shadow consists of those desires, feelings and so on. which are unacceptable, perhaps for emotional or for moral reasons. The shadow is generally equated with the dark side of human nature. For a full discussion of *Wuthering Heights* and Jungian psychology, see <http://academic.brooklyn.cuny.edu/english/melani/novel_19c/wuthering/psych.html> (accessed 2 February 2008).

47   Jung, 8: 96, in *Psychological Reflections*, p. 43.

48   McEwan characterizes the unruly unconscious as the 'celebration of sexuality in both its joyous and darkest manifestations'; see the back cover of Angela Carter, *The Bloody Chamber* (London, 1979).

have go get the ego out of it to do this exercise, because if you don't it will make you very, very uncomfortable.[49]

... When you are working with archetypes you are connecting with an essence much older than yourself.[50]

While it is tempting to revisit my earlier discussions of Tori Amos in *Women and Popular Music* and *Too Much Too Young*, her 2005 album, *The Beekeeper*, has a particular intrigue which resonates with my experience of being stalked and the mystery surrounding the Rosicrucian text 'dat rosa mel apibus' and its mysterious appendage 'mundus anus'.[51] The bee (apis) is feminine in Latin and it is this interpretation of the bee as a feminine principle that informs Amos's album. As she says, 'this feminine association of bees was known and honoured in ancient times: priestesses of the goddess Artemis were called *melissae*,[52] and Demeter was called "the pure mother bee"'.[53] The relationship between bees, the garden and the hive is integral to the six interrelated segments of the album, which Amos likens to the structure of hexagonal cells that make up the beehive, and to the six days that it took God to create the world, so linking biblical and feminine mythologies. The Garden of Eden, the Garden of Original Sin, metamorphoses into the Garden of Sin-Suality, symbolized by a six-sided hexagram made from two interconnected shapes, the feminine V of the chalice and the masculine Λ of the blade, signifying the intimate union of opposites. The six sonic gardens that comprise the hexagram of the Garden of Sin-suality are grouped under feminine-associated themes (desert garden, rock garden, roses and thorns, the greenhouse, the orchard, elixirs and herbs),[54] where different archetypes relate to different queen bees drawn from a diffuse mythology which relates not simply to the biblical text (Mary Magdelene,

---

49   Amos and Powers, *Tori Amos*, p. 10.
50   Ibid., p. 80.
51   Sheila Whiteley, *Mindgames* (Lulu.com, 2008).
52   As Derek Scott notes, in spite of book 4 of Virgil's *Georgics*, I think *calle melissae* must be *kalle melissai* in ancient Greek rather than Latin, meaning beautiful bees. Kallos (beauty) is usually a noun rather than an adjective, but I suspect it's a variant from some ancient text. Melissa is a bee, of course. The legend is that a nymph of that name helped Zeus when his father, Cronos, was out to kill him. As a consequence, Cronos turned her into a worm, but when Zeus got power he turned her into a bee.
53   Amos and Powers, *Tori Amos*, p. 79.
54   A concept confused by the order of the printed lyrics on the CD booklet, which are contained within their own individual hexagonal shapes, reminding the listener that the songs are both independent and connected to each other, that the bee can fly anywhere and that cross-pollination is integral to the cycle of life. This sense of moving into different gardens, different spaces is also present in the sequence of songs on the CD, which again follow a different order so informing the concept of the beekeeper who precipitates 'a myriad of other related concepts that all deal with the male and the female, the union, birth and death, and the art of relationships stripped to its foundation ... relationships healthy and unhealthy': Amos and Powers, *Tori Amos*, p. 130.

for example, in 'Marys of the Sea') but also to Freya (the Nordic goddess of youth and beauty, in 'Sleeps with Butterflies'), Daphne du Maurier's Rebecca (in 'Jamaica Inn') and the enigmatic woman with a parasol from Seurat's painting, 'La Grande Jatte' ('Parasol'). The intertextuality is also marked by Sylvia Plath's poem, 'The Beekeeper's Daughter', and a subtext which recontextualizes musical fragments from, for example, Amos's first album, *Little Earthquakes* ('China'/'Goodbye Pisces') so reconciling the experience of broken relationships within a more assured and nuanced interpretation.

It is not surprising, then, that the album would also provide a space to revisit the personal trauma of miscarriage earlier explored in 'Spark' (*From the Choirgirl Hotel*, 1998) where the lines 'She's convinced she could hold back a glacier / But she couldn't keep Baby alive' resonate with the self-reproach of loss. The experience of pregnancy in 'The Beekeeper' is thus informed by a nervous anxiety that this time all will be well. This tension between despair, hope and reassurance is opened out by a vocal characterization which contrasts two melodic motifs. The narrow vocal range of the verse, which draws on the association between nature ('It is time for the geese to head south'), life and death ('I have come with my mustard seed / I cannot accept that she will be taken from me'), is coloured by ornamentation, melisma, passing notes and neighbouring notes which enhance the folk-like quality of the narrative. The fall and rise of the vocal line (Gb–Eb / Db–Eb) follows the inflection of the words so effecting an expansion and contraction of the melodic motif (the flexible rhythms providing a contemplative space where, for example, syllables can be stretched to effect a mood of melancholic yearning) while being contained within the same introverted trajectory (Ex. 10.2).

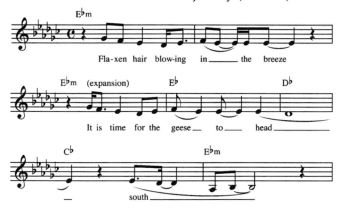

Example 10.2   Tori Amos, 'The Beekeeper' (1)

The narrow vocal range of the motif and the lack of cadential resolution creates an introspective mood which is heightened by a dramatic leap to Bb in the final phrase of the verse, where the fear of losing my 'mustard seed', 'my queen' breaks through the narrow confines of the motif before subsiding to the Bb below middle C in a vocal gesture of resignation. In contrast, the voice of the beekeeper is given a purity of tone and a sensuous motif which shifts upwards into Amos's higher vocal register to effect a mood of transcendence (Ex. 10.3). She is there 'to illuminate, to inform, to recognize the interlocking importance of all the players in the cycle of life'.[55]

Example 10.3   Tori Amos 'The Beekeeper' (2)

While Amos's voice defines the shape of the melody and time signature, the sounds of the two B3 Hammond Organs provide another layer of meaning. Amos had called her first Hammond 'Big Momma', and its soulful sound and melodic configurations symbolize the feminine. The bass pedal on the second Hammond organ is played by Jon Evans and the interaction of the two B3 players – one female, the other male – relates to Amos's musical conceptualization of the hive as embodying fertility and regeneration, and to her own fear of losing her child. In the verse, the darkness of the bass pedal penetrates the shimmering tones of the melodic line, creating a tonal conflict in the dissonant harmonies that underpin the mood of hope/despair. The dense texture of the verse also contributes towards a feeling of being in a shadowland, a mood which lightens in the chorus which is dominated by the feminine of Amos's soulful accompaniment. While the changing mood of the accompaniment is governed by stepped dynamics (the dense texture of the verse – the light texture of the chorus), the constant dynamic of Mark Chamberlain's electronic drum pattern, which runs throughout the song, creates a tattoo-like pattern evocative of the 'tap dancers', the returning bees whose dance at the edge of the hive communicates guidance and a sense of direction.

The relationship between the musical arrangement, the inner space of the imagination and the outer space of the lyrics is thus integral to the shaping of the song's theme of maternal loss, and Amos emphasizes the importance of drawing on feminine archetypes in her compositional process. Her identification with Demeter, the Greek goddess of agriculture and fertility, whose grief is so great at the sudden loss of her daughter, Persephone, that it plunges the entire earth into barrenness

---

55   *The Beekeeper*, DVD.

relates to her own sense of loss, 'I didn't want it to happen to me and of course it didn't happen just once – it happened three times.'[56] Unlike *From the Choirgirl Hotel*, however, where 'Playboy Mommy' situates the trauma of miscarriage as rejection), Amos's quest involves supplication ('Anything but this. Can you use me instead?') As guardian of the hive, the Beekeeper has power over life and death. This time, it seems, she is just 'passing her by', and as the rising chromatic harmonies ('[she] will a-wake') and teasing phrases ('somewhere, tomorrow, somewhere') finally resolve, there is a fleeting promise of hope (Ex. 10.4).

Example 10.4   Tori Amos, 'The Beekeeper' (3)

Postscript: Women Writing Women

As the reader will have noticed, my analytical approach has been underpinned by Middleton's discussion of dialogics, which has provided a framework for the issues to be addressed while prompting me to explore how 'meaning' can be inscribed within the shifting formulations of femininity. As such, my quest has involved research into history, literature, biography, queering, archetypes and Jungian psychology, a trajectory which has been shaped by my choice of women singer-songwriters, and informed by an engagement with academics who have brought cultural theory and a feminist critique into popular music studies. While this has provided insights into the relationship between femininity and popular music, as Middleton observes, 'meaning is always at issue' and the challenge of identifying ways in which a feminist critique impacts on musical codes is problematic. For researchers, the need to engage with previous analytical strategies is balanced by the urge to originate ideas that evidence both scholarship and critical thinking. There is, then, a sense of looking backwards while moving forwards, of finding

---

56   Amos and Powers, *Tori Amos*, p. 150.

new interpretational strategies which challenge received meanings, of being aware of the ways in which gender and sexuality inflect meaning, and this, surely, is the continuing challenge for popular musicologists.

'I'm a Man':
Masculinities in Popular Music

Jason Lee Oakes

What does it mean to be a man, and what does it mean to be masculine? Are these questions one and the same? And how can popular music help to answer them?

Taking the last question first, in almost every instance, popular music is continually and compulsively bound up with the interrogation of gender. Entire genres are named for gender- and/or sexuality-based identities – for example, girl groups, boy bands, riot grrrls, cock rock, womyn's music, queercore and genres cultures[1] operate in a network of gendered codes and institutions.[2] Thus, if one wants to explore the associations, ideologies and behavioural norms that circulate around masculinity, popular music is a good place to start.

In this chapter I will consider three different approaches taken to masculinity in popular music cultures: first, 'masculinity as essence' – defined through binary distinctions; second, 'masculinity in crisis' – threatened through multiple contradictions; and, third, 'masculinity without men' – displaced through the abject sublime. To illustrate each of these three models, I will focus on three songs in turn – Bo Diddley's 'I'm A Man', Pulp's 'I'm A Man', and PJ Harvey's 'Man-Size' – relating each to research on popular music.

In songs with titles such as 'I'm A Man' and 'Man-Size', it is implicitly acknowledged that gender is not a given essence. These seemingly self-evident statements are not self-evident at all when gender must be deliberately asserted. In *Gender Trouble*, Judith Butler uses a song to illustrate this very point – Aretha Franklin's '(You Make Me Feel Like) A Natural Woman'.[3] Despite the obvious effort in *performing* gender – 'feeling like a woman' is not taken as a given but takes effort – Franklin's womanhood is presented as 'natural' nonetheless. This apparent contradiction is managed through reference to other mutually constitutive binaries. First, the song assumes a naturalized binary relationship, where one's gender is

---

1   Fabian Holt, *Genre in Popular Music* (Chicago, 2007).
2   Of course, dominant genderings of musical genres are routinely subverted by musicians and audiences, and they change over time and across different settings.
3   The song was co-written by Carole King and Gerry Goffin.

established through the 'invocation of the defining Other'.[4] It takes *you* to make *me* feel like a natural woman. Second, in assuming a 'stable and oppositional heterosexuality',[5] the sexual desire experienced on either side of the gender divide is mutual and mutually constituting (sexuality is likewise assumed to operate along a strict homo/hetero binary divide). The dependency of the masculine/feminine binary on heterosexuality goes some way towards explaining why an artist such as Eminem 'uses homophobic language to critique gender behaviour, not sexual orientation',[6] where '*sexual* deviation is merely a metaphor – albeit the most inflammatory – for sex-gender deviation'.[7]

In its binary construction, essentialized gender is produced as much from without as from within – defined not only by what the subject is, but also by what they are not (for example, a man is *not* a woman, a masculine subject is *not* homosexual). Masculinity is 'in effect, defined as not-femininity … [where] masculinity is the unmarked term, the place of symbolic authority'.[8] With masculinity as the default and dominant subject position, the key question becomes: how is femininity different? In what ways does femininity not 'measure up' to masculinity? In *Feminine Endings* (1991), Susan McClary notoriously exposed the means through which femininity has been musically marked off as different and inferior (for example, the 'feminine' cadences which give the book its name). Masculinity is musically encoded as well, but so pervasively as to be taken for granted,[9] resulting in the concealed masculinist perspective that McClary observes in Western art-music.

---

4   Judith Butler, *Gender Trouble: Feminism and the Subversion of Identity* (New York, 1990), p. 22.

5   Ibid.

6   Vincent Stephens, 'Pop Goes the Rapper: A Close Reading of Eminem's Genderphobia', *Popular Music* 24/1 (2005): 21–36, at 21. Despite his frequent use of the term 'faggot', Eminem defended himself against charges of homophobia by claiming that '[t]he term "faggot" doesn't necessarily mean a gay person' and 'faggot is like taking away your manhood – you're a sissy, you're a coward … It doesn't necessarily mean you're being a gay person' (quoted at ibid., p. 26). According to Stephens, such attitudes are more accurately labeled as 'genderphobia' than 'homophobia'.

7   Mark Simpson, *Male Impersonators: Men Performing Masculinity* (London, 1994), p. 2.

8   R.W. Connell, 'The Sociology of Masculinity' in Stephen M. Whitehead and Frank J. Barrett (eds), *The Masculinities Reader* (Cambridge, 2001), pp. 30–50, at p. 33.

9   Susan McClary, *Feminine Endings: Music, Gender, and Sexuality* (Minneapolis, 1991). See also Charles Ford, 'On Music and Masculinity' in Derek B. Scott (ed.), *Music, Culture, and Society: A Reader* (Oxford, 2000), pp. 77–82. When gender is made explicit in the Western art music tradition, it has typically been in dealing with the 'character' of women, such as in Mozart's *Così Fan Tutte*, or in marking off a particular performance setting or instrument as feminine. In respect to both, Ruth Solie has demonstrated how the parlour piano, popularized during the eighteenth century, was considered the province of young women and served to 'produce women who [were] correctly *gendered* according to the needs of the society in which they were destined to take their places'. Ruth Soli, 'Gender, Genre, and the Parlor Piano', *The Wordsworth Circle* 25 (1994): 53–56, at 56.

Bo Diddley's 'I'm a Man': Masculinity in Essence

Beethoven may have extolled the 'Brotherhood of Man' in his Ninth Symphony, but 'man' was a stand-in for 'humanity'.[10] Bo Diddley – one of the primary architects of rock 'n' roll – had something very different in mind on 'I'm A Man' (1955). Released as the flip-side to the tremolo-heavy, syncopated 'Bo Diddley', 'I'm A Man' comes across as more musically 'direct'. Throughout the song, vocal lines alternate with a blues-derived four-note riff played on piano and harmonica, accompanied only by a dotted-rhythm snare drum and maraca. The lyrics open with a declaration of underage sexual prowess ('at the age of five / had something in my pocket / kept a lot of folks alive'). Now that he's 21, the narrator promises 'baby, we can have a lot of fun'. Thus 'man' is counterposed not so much to 'woman' here, but more so to 'boy'. The refrain, set against unchanged accompaniment, declares simply 'I'm a mannnnn ... I spell M-A-N'. Following a brief section of textless moans in unison with bent notes on the harmonica, Diddley continues to boast of his lovemaking ability and stamina. A harmonica break revolves around a two-note trill embellished by few quick blues-scale licks. Two more verses and refrains follow, and the song fades out.

In 'I'm A Man', masculinity is unmistakably aligned with heterosexuality, sexual potency, mastery and control ('The line I shoot / Will never miss'). However, these qualities are not expounded upon at great length in the lyrics. As long as women are present so that Bo Diddley can demonstrate these qualities, he need offer no other explanation or justification of his masculinity. It just *is*. He is a M-A-N. This inevitability is underlined by the insistent repetition and seeming effortlessness of the groove. The musicians don't modulate through the standard blues progression but instead repeat the riff *ad nauseam*. Of course the song is not as 'simple' as it may sound; there are subtle rhythmic and timbral inflections throughout, and no one could ever hope to sound exactly like Bo Diddley. However, the song does give a carefully constructed *impression* of ease, tapping into a mythic black masculine potency that stretches back to the dozens and forward to rock 'n' roll and hip hop. This 'hard' masculinity is not 'hard' in the other sense of the word, but is linked to notions of natural ease and authenticity. In a *Rolling Stone* feature on musical icons and their influences, Iggy Pop (no slouch in the masculinity department) expresses his admiration for Bo Diddley in just these terms:

> Bo Diddley's music is enormous ... it has the sultry, sexual power of Africa.
> There's all sorts of mystery in that sound ... he played really simple things
> but with incredible authority ... he really controls the guitar ... and his voice

---

10   What's more, according to R.W. Connell, '[In Europe] before the eighteenth century ... women were certainly regarded as different from men, but different in the sense of being incomplete or inferior examples of the same character. Women and men were not seen as bearers of qualitatively different characters; this conception accompanied the bourgeois ideology of 'separate spheres' in the nineteenth century'. Connell, 'The Sociology of Masculinity', p. 30.

is so damn loud. It's just a huge voice ... he was a bull; he had a bullish quality.[11]

Thus, Bo Diddley's masculinity (in the eyes of Iggy Pop and, one assumes, other musical inheritors and fans) is rooted in constructions of race; in notions of 'natural' ease; in images of size, control and power; and in how all three are believed to interrelate. As in Aretha Franklin's performance, this natural status is reciprocally defined, but Bo Diddley takes on the active rather than the passive/receptive role in this interaction.

This is all a long way from commonly circulated depictions of femininity, especially 'white' femininities. In contrast to men, it is widely acknowledged that women have to work for their femininity, whether in respect to their physical appearance or domestic duties. For instance, in Peggy Lee's recording of 'I'm A Woman' (1963), an answer song of sorts to 'I'm A Man', being a woman requires washing socks, ironing, cooking, shopping, cleaning the house, attending to children, applying make-up, going out dancing, stretching the family budget, nursing her man back to health and pleasing him sexually. The song was written by two men (Jerry Leiber and Mike Stoller) as an obvious parody – a parody that effectively captures the absurd expectations placed upon women, and acknowledges the pleasure taken in their obvious effort. This effort is also encoded in musical terms. While it cops the trademark riff of 'I'm A Man', the Lee recording is highly arranged and doesn't sound at all 'improvisatory'. It includes a small brass section and features a contrasting B section in the chorus. Lee's vocal performance is marked as virtuosic as she squeezes a seemingly impossible number of syllables into a limited space, aurally reflecting the harried superwoman theme of the lyrics.[12]

Lyrically and musically, Peggy Lee is placed in the 'marked-off' category. Likewise, the feminine subject has traditionally been Othered in both meanings of the word: functioning as the masculine subject's '*other* half', and as the expelled *other* who is cast out of masculine homosocial environments (defining them as such through her absence). Rather than being an immutable universal, it has been noted that this model of gender relations is a historical development that 'accompanied the bourgeois ideology of "separate spheres" in the nineteenth century'.[13] In an article entitled 'The Gendered Carnival of Pop', Diane Railton

---

11   Iggy Pop, 'The Immortals – The Greatest Artists of All Time: 20) Bo Diddley', *Rolling Stone* 946 (15 April 2004).

12   The parodic origin of the song is rarely referenced. In the many cover versions and variations that have followed – with the exception of Maria Muldaur's Bo-Diddley-beat-inflected hit version – the absurdity of the super-woman is usually exchanged for fawning (self-) admiration. This shift was first effected in the popular Enjoli perfume commercials of the 1970s, with altered lyrics such as 'I can bring home the bacon / and fry it up in pan'. In the commercials the woman's ability to 'do it all' seems to be taken as a point of pseudo-feminist pride.

13   Connell, 'The Sociology of Masculinity', p. 30. In addition to the link above between gender and race, here we have an explicit link between social class and gender. In fact, gender is considered by many to be the master trope that serves as a model, and works

compares the development of separate spheres in early modern bourgeois culture to the development of separate spheres in popular music beginning in the late 1960s. As with male-dominated eighteenth- and nineteenth-century coffee houses, salons and spas that 'facilitated bourgeois hegemony in both politics and arts … rock culture served as the starting point for the hegemony within popular music discourse of particular ways of understanding and appreciating music'.[14] Likewise, the dominance of the rock aesthetic (repositioned as 'artistic expression' versus 'mass culture') was established in large part by linking it with masculinity and with homosocial settings. It has since come to be a truism that rock is deliberately produced as 'masculine'[15] – 'in terms of band membership and production, lyrical content, and political agenda'[16] – especially the 'hard' rock genre such as heavy metal, punk rock and their various substyles and offshoots, such as grunge.

In rock and in other masculinist popular music cultures, women are both desired as the sexual Other, and reviled as the Other who threatens the homosocial sphere of the musician and the 'serious' music fan (with notable exceptions, of course). This otherness is reinforced in the gendering of non-rock 'pop music' as feminine.[17] It has come to be the case that almost any artist or genre culture that desires legitimizing authenticity in the global music marketplace is at pains to clearly distinguish themselves from 'market-driven', 'calculated' pop music. In hip hop, for example, 'selling out is … associated with being soft, as opposed to hard.

---

to structure, other binary identity formations: including race (black versus white) and class (high versus low). Given the strong link between popular music and gender, it shouldn't be surprising that associated practices and ideologies are routinely (but with much variation) broken down according to binary distinctions – for example, authenticity versus sell-out, cover versus original, sample versus source, verse versus chorus, duple versus triple, major versus minor – thus providing a powerful field for articulating binary social systems such as masculine versus feminine.

14   Diane Railton, 'The Gendered Carnival of Pop', *Popular Music* 20/3 (2001): 321–31, at 321–22.
15   Mary Ann Clawson, 'Masculinity and Skill Acquisition in the Adolescent Rock Band', *Popular Music* 18/1 (1999): 99–114; Sara Cohen, 'Men Making A Scene: Rock Music and the Production of Gender' in Sheila Whiteley (ed.), *Sexing the Groove: Popular Music and Gender* (London, 1997), pp. 17–36; Simon Frith and Angela McRobbie, 'Rock and Sexuality' [1978] in Simon Frith and Andrew Goodwin (eds), *On Record: Rock, Pop, and the Written Word* (London, 1990), pp. 371–89; Marion Leonard, *Gender in the Music Industry: Rock, Discourse and Girl Power* (Aldershot, 2007), pp. 1–41; Simon Reynolds and Joy Press, *The Sex Revolts: Gender, Rebellion, and Rock 'n' Roll* (Cambridge, MA., 1995).
16   Railton, 'The Gendered Carnival of Pop', p. 322.
17   In the case of pop music, Railton draws a parallel between pop and the carnival of the late modern era. Carnival was a time of transgression where 'sex and the body were central [and] status was undermined' (ibid., p. 327). With its own forms of carnivalesque display, in pop music the bodies of performers and dancers are vitally important, much more so than in rock (the bourgeois public sphere values 'masculine' rationality and technology over the body), and genre and audience distinctions are not as carefully policed.

Within the context of hip hop, these oppositional terms are very clearly gender-specific, with soft representing feminine attributes and hard representing masculine attributes'[18] such as 'staying true to yourself', and adherence to 'the underground', 'the street' and 'the old school'.

This binary gendering of popular music genres reaches into every aspect of their associated cultures: from musical instruments to musical pedagogy, from performance conventions to audience conventions, from practices of consumption to clichés of music criticism, from recording technology to record consumption and radio formats. For instance, the electric guitar, with its strong association with rock music, has been gendered masculine in most quarters. This has strongly impacted on how the instrument is taught and learned, how it is played and heard, and how it is experienced in performance and on record.[19] When it comes to consumption and fandom, even the simple act of shopping for music carries gendered implications. Nick Hornby lampooned (and paid tribute to) the masculine space of the 'connoisseurist', independent record store in his hit novel *High Fidelity* (1995). Making note of this and other representations, Will Straw notes that 'record collecting, within Anglo-American cultures at least, is among the most predictably male-dominated of music-related practices'.[20] Furthermore, with the rise of electronic music and hip hop, the record-collector mindset has had a far-reaching effect on musical practices and sounds that have come to dominate more and more of the popular music landscape.[21]

Despite the 'natural' status it is accorded, maintaining the binary model takes work. For instance, Will Straw notes that archivist-minded record collecting stands 'in an uncertain relationship to masculinity'[22] portrayed alternately as a public display of mastery or as a private refuge from sociability/sexuality; as rooted in objective, rational ordering or betraying irrational obsession; as demonstrating that knowledge is power or a compensation for lack of power. How, then, are the many loose strands and contradictions around masculinity stitched together into a coherent whole? In an ethnographic study on masculinity in an Indonesian pop song, Henry Spiller demonstrates how Sundanese dance events naturalize and thus obscure these contradictions:

---

18   Kembrew McLeod, 'Authenticity within Hip-Hop and Other Cultures Threatened With Assimilation', *Journal of Communication* 49/4 (1999): 134–50, at 142.

19   Steve Waksman, 'Every Inch Of My Love: Led Zeppelin and the Problem of Cock Rock', *Journal of Popular Music Studies* 8 (1996): 4–25; Mavis Bayton, 'Women and the Electric Guitar', in Whiteley, *Sexing the Groove*, pp. 37–49.

20   Will Straw, 'Sizing up Record Collections: Gender and Connoisseurship in Rock Music Culture' in Whiteley, *Sexing the Groove*, pp. 3–16, at p. 4.

21   Straw argues that there has been a 'successful adaptation of rock music's masculinist impulses to an era of sampling or niche market obscurantism', (ibid., p. 15), and consequently, newly assimilated female rock musicians have discovered 'the lines of exclusion are now elsewhere. They emerge when the music is over, and the boys in the band go back to discussing their record collections' (ibid.).

22   Ibid., p. 5.

The complex system of contradictions, double standards, and desires that constitute gender ideology is reproduced ... by aestheticizing the contradictions, these performances smooth over the inconsistencies and make them appear natural – even beautiful.[23]

This statement also applies to many other settings and genres, where male and female are made coherent as opposing poles by aestheticizing and naturalizing the contradictions inherent in each. Given that much popular music is described and discussed almost entirely in aesthetic terms – in terms of what is 'good' versus 'bad', or what is 'beautiful' versus 'ugly' – it follows (non-intuitively) that popular music is deeply imbricated in negotiating and naturalizing cultural contradictions.

Traditionally, whatever the stated ideal or the chosen style, aesthetics has tended to be male-dominated field. In comparison to music-making itself, taste-making roles in popular music are closely aligned with male homosocial worlds. Aesthetic gatekeepers are concentrated in social settings and in professional occupations that are notoriously male-dominated – for example, record collectors, record producers,[24] and music critics and journalists.[25] This goes a long way towards explaining how masculinity has retained a surprising degree of power and coherency in many domains of popular music, as well as the vehemence with which homosexuality is often discouraged and disparaged (given the potentially flimsy line between the homosocial and the homoerotic).

Pulp's 'I'm a Man': Masculinity in Crisis

With its strong melodic hooks, lush production, sensual vocal style, and ear-candy arrangement, Pulp's 'I'm A Man' is an aesthetically 'beautiful' song about the contradictions of masculinity. Released on the album *This Is Hardcore* (1998), the song is consistent with the album's 'uncomfortable mixture of complicity

---

23   Henry Spiller, 'Negotiating Masculinity in an Indonesian Pop Song: Doel Sumbang's "Ronggeng"' in Freya Jarman-Ivens (ed.), *Oh Boy! Masculinities and Popular Music* (London, 2007), pp. 39–58, at p. 42.

24   Evan Eisenberg, *The Recording Angel: Explorations in Phonography* (New York, 1987); Joseph Glenn Schloss, *Making Beats: The Art of Sample-Based Hip-Hop* (Middletown, CT, 2004), pp. 57–61.

25   Helen Davies, 'All Rock and Roll is Homosocial: The Representation of Women in the British Rock Music Press', *Popular Music* 20/3 (2001): 301–19; Brenda Johnson-Grau, 'Sweet Nothings: Presentation of Women Musicians in Pop Journalism' in Steve Jones (ed.), *Pop Music and the Press* (Philadelphia, 2002), pp. 202–18; Kembrew McLeod, 'Between Rock and a Hard Place: Gender and Rock Criticism' in Steve Jones, *Pop Music and the Press* (Philadelphia, 2002), pp. 93–113; Anna Feigenbaum, '"Some Guy Designed This Room I'm Standing In": Marking Gender in Press Coverage of Ani DiFranco', *Popular Music* 24/1 (2005): 37–56.

[with] … and critique'[26] of masculine subjectivity. In a musical and lyrical analysis, Eric Clarke and Nicola Dibben focus on the title song which is 'concerned with a man's experience of a complex mixture of sexual fantasy and reality',[27] and which is accompanied by music that is likewise rooted in ambiguity. The overall effect is to alternately engage and alienate the listener through shifting array of juxtaposed stylistic references, production techniques, formal structures and generic allusions.[28] Outside of the title song, masculinity is the common link on the album in songs that deal with atypical pop-song subjects such as pornography, fatherhood, marriage and divorce, and ageing ('teach you stuff although he's looking rough'), all of which are faced with ambivalence and uncertainty.

Despite the self-assurance of the title 'I'm A Man' – a declarative phrase that never appears in the song itself – the narrator admits in the first verse to 'wonder[ing] what it takes to be a man'. He goes on to link being a man with learning to 'drink … smoke, and … tell a dirty joke', driving a car that can 'get up to a hundred and ten', and being 'a beauty' vain enough to 'hold [his] stomach in'. In contrast to Bo Diddley's all-conquering 'natural' man, observable effort goes into projecting masculinity – propped up by manly pursuits, possessions, and physical appearance. Masculinity is not defined against the feminine Other; in fact there is no mention of women at all, whereas the work that goes into masculinity appears to be isolating and alienating. In his fast car, the narrator complains 'you've nowhere to go but you'll go there again'. This alienation is subtly reinforced in the shift from a first- to a second-person address beginning in the first chorus. Speaking to a hypothetical 'you', one could take away the impression that the narrator has stepped out of his skin and is observing himself at a distance.

This theme of multiplicity and contradiction is reinforced throughout the song. In the verses, Cocker sings from a resonant and deep chest tone. The half-sung, half-spoken delivery places an emphasis on consonants and aspirated syllables. The style is strongly reminiscent of French singer-songwriter Serge Gainsbourg, a widely noted influence. Considered an icon of Gallic masculinity – debauched, dispassionate, gangly, iconoclastic and apparently irresistible – Gainsbourg was famously fond of smoking, drinking and dirty jokes.[29] Also in Gainsbourgesque fashion, the underlying music is vaguely funky and attenuated, slowly building in intensity over the course of the verse. In the choruses Cocker's vocal delivery

---

26   Eric F. Clarke and Nicola Dibben, 'Sex, Pulp and Critique', *Popular Music* 19/2 (2000): 231–41, at 238.
27   Ibid., p. 232.
28   Ibid., pp. 234–39.
29   For instance, Serge Gainsbourg recorded an entire album on the theme of *merde* and flatulence, and once told Whitney Houston he wanted to 'fuck her' on live television; see Sylvie Simmons, *Serge Gainsbourg: A Fistful of Gitanes* (Cambridge, 2002). Previous to *This Is Hardcore*, Cocker used the 'Serge voice' mostly in textual settings of sly, erotic seduction. Cocker has performed an outright homage to Gainsbourg on a tribute album – covering 'Je suis venu te dire que je m'en vais' ('I Have Come to Tell You I'm Going') on *Monsieur Gainsbourg: Revisited* (2006) – and also recorded a song with Serge's daughter Charlotte Gainsbourg, included as a bonus track on Air's *Pocket Symphony* (2007).

shifts to a high-pitched, expressive style that recalls David Bowie more than Serge Gainsbourg, and emphasizes open vowels through extended duration and dynamic accent. The song breaks into a soaring wall-of-sound instrumentation – stomping piano/keyboard chords, sustained and distorted rhythm guitar, and wailing, wah-wah slide guitar reminiscent of Mick Ronson's guitar work – unmistakably glam in texture and timbre. The stylistic dissonance between verse and chorus is compounded in the dissonance between text and music – the most doubtful, tortured lyrics are set against the most triumphant, resounding music. Lyrically, the narrator goes positively existential, demanding to know 'just why we're alive' and concluding that one becomes a man by simply 'hang[ing] around too long' and by closing oneself off emotionally: 'Nothing ever makes no difference to a man.'

The sonic references to glam, and more specifically to Bowie, are further highlighted in the overall form – restrained verse followed by explosive chorus – and in the syncretic stylistic fusion of blues metal and music hall melodic balladry.[30] These musical allusions evoke the illusory nature of gender when one considers glam rock's gender politics. According to Philip Auslander, glam rock broke with prevalent notions of authenticity in countercultural rock, by adopting an explicitly performative and theatrical stance. With the star's subjectivity shifting from 'inhabiting an identity' to 'playing a role',[31] a major strategy (perhaps *the* major strategy) for communicating the shift lay in foregrounding the performativity of gender. Indeed, it was the gender-bending aspects of Bowie's 'transvestite alien(ated)' character Ziggy Stardust that attracted the most commentary.[32]

In 'I'm A Man', masculinity is presented as a performance, and Cocker has a bad case of performance anxiety. The trappings of masculinity have lost their potency for both the narrator and their intended recipients: '[you] show them what you've got though they've seen everything.' Defined not as some interior essence, masculinity is instead linked with objects and activities that can be learned or bought. The linkage of masculinity with the market is made explicit in the first line of the song, with the subject watching 'advertising sliding past [his] eyes' as unreal as 'cartoons from other's people's lives'. These lines perhaps respond to the past decades' intensified marketing of masculinity (with men more frequently presented as 'pinups') and the increased number and variety of products aimed at

---

30   Barney Hoskyns, *Glam! Bowie, Bolan and the Glitter Rock Revolution* (New York, 1998), p. 32. In my mind, the structure and vocal contrast correspond to David Bowie's 'Starman' which features a similarly (and literally) alienated subject and a melodic leap in the chorus as the voice moves from the first to the second syllabus of 'star-man'.

31   Philip Auslander, *Performing Glam Rock: Gender and Theatricality in Popular Music* (Ann Arbor, MI, 2006), p. 25.

32   The character of Ziggy Stardust, as well as Bowie's other fictionalized personas, ably captures the key contradictions in which masculinity is trapped: on one hand, the artistic mindset, the work ethic and the behind-the-scene stamp of the *auteur* that leads to a creation such as Ziggy Stardust; and, on the other, the apparently natural, effortless and emotionally inexpressive qualities that are likewise associated with masculinity (and anathema to a creation such as Ziggy). Both of these are centered on the key masculine trait of *control*, but control exercised in two very different manners.

men (including traditionally feminine items such as beauty products). Whatever Cocker's intentions, he taps into anxieties that have been widely noted and brought together under the label 'crisis in masculinity'. At the centre of this crisis is a shift in gendered consumerism, leading to entirely new labels such as the 'metrosexual' – a moniker that links anxieties stemming from perceived contradictions between (and within) gender, sexuality, class and consumer practices.

This crisis in masculinity thus shares something in common with the more generalized crisis of identity associated with 'postmodernism' or 'the cultural logic of late capitalism'.[33] According to early theorizers such as Jean-François Lyotard,[34] grand narratives have given way to contingency; single frameworks have been disunified and decentred, and gender is among these decentred perspectives/narratives: 'Lyotard unapologetically takes gender to be one of the most important philosophical problems of the twentieth century.'[35] On the other hand, the multiplicity and contradiction of postmodernism is not an entirely new invention; Marx observed that contradiction is central to the capitalist mode of production. Along these lines, some argue that 'the postmodern condition' is in fact nothing new (perhaps, at most, a symptom of late modernity) and likewise that 'masculinity, however defined, is, like capitalism, *always* in crisis'.[36] While it is beyond the scope of this chapter to pursue this debate further, one important point to take away is that contradiction – and the reflexive examination of contradictions – can sometimes lead to a paradoxical consolidation of power. Terry Eagleton has noted that, just as 'history' and 'totality' have been declared dead, capitalism has moved into its most totalizing phase.[37] Ironically, it seems, a stated 'state of crisis' can be a means of survival and even of consolidation. Likewise, 'masculinity in crisis' has led to a reflexive examination of said masculinity, often followed by a reassertion of masculinity (whether rooted in a newly emergent or a residual and conservative approach to gender). One can easily observe this reassertion of masculinity in various social and political settings and in popular music as well. In the past several decades, despite being challenged in turn by feminism, the gay rights movement and metrosexual consumerism, masculinity seems more relevant than ever – as evidenced by new genres, songs and discourses that (however

---

33 Fredric Jameson, *Postmodernism, or, the Cultural Logic of Late Capitalism* (Durham, NC, 1991).

34 Jean-François Lyotard, The Postmodern Condition: A Report on Knowledge [1979], trans. Geoff Bennington and Brian Massumi (Minneapolis, 1984).

35 Margaret Grebowicz, 'Introduction: After Lyotard' in Margaret Grebowicz (ed.), *Gender: After Lyotard* (Albany, NY, 2007), pp. 1–12, at p. 1.

36 Abigail Solomon-Godeau, 'Male Trouble' in Maurice Berger, Brian Wallis and Simon Watson (eds), *Constructing Masculinity* (New York, 1995), pp. 69–76, at p. 70 (original emphasis). Some might argue that these are largely one and the same crisis, as the male subject position is still normative within such theorizations. Furthermore, both of these crises might be viewed as responses to the threatened decentering of the white, male, middle-class subject – dressed up in linguistically-arresting labels such as 'postmodernism' and a 'crisis in masculinity'.

37 Terry Eagleton, *The Illusions of Postmodernism* (Oxford, 1996).

contradictory) seem more explicitly concerned than ever with masculinity and its meaning(s).

As concisely summarized by Mark Simpson, beginning in the 1980s there was 'a "crisis of masculinity", brought about, it was said, by the advances of feminism and the gay movement allied to the economic upheavals of post-Fordism, the switch from "male" heavy industries to "female" service industries'.[38] As a response, this same period saw the birth of the 'men's movement', but this movement-of-sorts was just as contradictory as masculinity itself:

> *Some men's groups, for example, developed alongside feminism and in support of it ... Other men's groups developed out of men's frustration with what they say as anti-male prejudice in society ... For others again dissatisfaction with the roles allocated them in society was the impetus to gather together and explore unconventional options.*[39]

Robert Bly, in his highly influential and much pilloried *Iron John*, portrays men as victims of both 'hard' manhood (which demands they be self-sacrificing and inexpressive) and post-feminist 'soft' manhood (where sensitive men lose touch with the Wild Hairy Man inside). Again, the 'feminizing' of culture is linked both to feminism and consumerism. In addition to the women's movement (which Bly praises overall, despite some deleterious effects on men), the corporate world is also held to task for its role in 'produc[ing] the sanitized, hairless, shallow man'.[40]

In the men's movement, and in the crisis discourse more generally, men are viewed as victims of the contradictory roles and expectations that they are expected to fulfil. For instance, Roger Horrocks argues that 'masculinity in crisis' can be 'expressed as a simple paradox':

> *Patriarchal masculinity cripples men. Manhood as we know it in our society requires such self-destructive identity, a deeply masochistic self-denial, a shrinkage of the self, a turning away from whole areas of life, that the man who obeys the demands of masculinity has become only half-human.*[41]

In other words, masculine power brings powerlessness. Modern psychoanalysis is no more kind to masculinity, seeing as men are doomed to not 'measure up' to

---

38   Simpson, *Male Impersonators*, p. 1.
39   Anne Cranny-Francis *et al.*, *Gender Studies: Terms and Debates* (New York, 2003), p. 79.
40   Robert Bly, *Iron John: A Book About Men* [1990] (New York, 1992), p. 6. Channelling both Joseph Campbell and Camille Paglia, Bly advocates the revival of 'myths, stories, and songs that embody distinctively male values' (p. 15), together with the revival of male initiation rites (resulting in many a drum circle) to heal the damaged masculinity of the modern day.
41   Roger Horrocks, *Masculinity in Crisis: Myths, Fantasies and Realities* (New York, 1994), p. 25.

the phallus – the towering symbol of male, patriarchal power. Rachel Adams and David Savran summarize the psychoanalytic perspective:

> The Lacanian phallus is not an organ but a sign, a privileged symbol of patriarchal power and authority that becomes associated with the penis, but cannot be that with which it is associated ... the phallus is a source of considerable anxiety. Following Freud, Lacanian psychoanalysis proposes that because no subject can actually possess the phallus, both men and women suffer the mark of castration, albeit in different ways.[42]

The penis in relation to the phallus is like a 'copy with no original', to borrow the striking phrase Judith Butler has used to describe gender. The phallus has no substantial reality; its domain is the imaginary and the symbolic and it is all the more powerful, and powerless for it.

I would submit here that this phallic formation has particular significance for music in the age of sound recording and mass mediation. In 1936 Walter Benjamin famously observed that 'that which withers in the age of mechanical production is the aura of the work of art',[43] indicating that there is no longer perceived to be a hierarchical relationship between a singular artistic creation and copies made of the artwork. He goes on to outline both the anxieties and potential realized when mass reproduction 'substitutes a plurality of copies for a unique existence'.[44] The similarity of Butler's and Benjamin's formations are striking – whether in regard to art in the age of mechanical reproduction or gender in the age of reproductive technologies, the very notion of a 'copy' is contradictory if one lacks a singular ideal or object to be copied. In popular musics where new sound technologies are constantly being introduced – from the microphone to multitrack recording, from analogue sound synthesis to digital sound sampling – the discourses around these technologies situate them ambiguously between their alienating, distancing effects and the degree of intimacy and control they offer musicians and listeners. Thus, a fixation on 'authenticity' – how it is defined, how it is expressed, and how it is framed in terms of control gained or lost – is a near-constant in various popular musical worlds.[45] The most undermining insult directed at popular musicians is being labelled a 'sell-out' or 'poseur'. To be labelled as such is to lose masculine authority and authorship. Authenticity, defined variously across various genres, is consistently aligned with corresponding notions of gendered authenticity that revolve around masculinity. Similar themes of power, control and anxiety are

---

42 Rachel Adams and David Savran, 'Introduction', in *The Masculinity Studies Reader* (Oxford, 2002), pp. 1–8, at p. 11.

43 Walter Benjamin, 'The Work of Art in the Age of Mechanical Reproduction' in *Illuminations* [1936], trans. Hannah Arendt, ed. Harry Zohn (New York, 1968), pp. 217–51, at p. 221.

44 Ibid.

45 Simon Frith, 'Art versus Technology: The Strange Case of Popular Music', *Media, Culture & Society* 8/3 (1986): 263–79.

brought to the fore, reinforced by the stereotypical alliance of masculinity and technology. Thus, the *contradictions* around notions of 'authenticity' in popular music (that is, copies with no original) are crystallized in the gendered discourse of popular musics, with masculinity especially prone to the back-and-forth highlighting/sublimation of contradiction.

With remarkable consistency, the central theme in writings on masculinity and popular music has been masculinity's inconsistency – that is,. the *contradictions* that are highlighted or sublimated within various popular music cultures. A number of commentators have used popular music to demonstrate that the instability of masculine is nothing terribly new, existing long before the 'crisis of masculinity' discourse of the 1980s and 1990s. For instance, Richard Mook appraises the nostalgic reconstruction of imagined Victorian masculinity in barbershop quartet singing during the 1920s and 1930s,[46] and Roger Gilbert argues for a reappraisal of Frank Sinatra's recordings of the 1950s, arguing that his music from this period 'became the classic embodiment of fifties culture not because he represented an idealized male image ... but because ... he fully articulated its contradictions, anxieties, and ambivalences'.[47] At the same time, other writers have intimated that the current crisis is unique and unprecedented. Either way, many other studies of masculinity centred on individual performers have taken contradiction as their key concept.[48]

---

46 Richard Mook, 'White Masculinity in Barbershop Quartet Singing', *Journal of the Society for American Music* 1/4 (2007): 453–83.

47 Roger Gilbert, 'The Swinger and the Loser: Sinatra, Masculinity, and Fifties Culture' in Leonard Mustazza (ed), *Frank Sinatra and Popular Culture: Essays on an American Icon* (Westport, CT, 1998), pp. 38–49, at p. 40.

48 These include Elvis Presley: see Marjorie Garber, *Vested Interests: Cross-Dressing and Cultural Anxiety* (New York, 1997), pp. 363–74; Erika Doss, *Elvis Culture: Fans, Faith, and Image* (Lawrence, 1999), pp. 116–61; Mark Duffett, 'Caught in a Trap? Beyond Pop Theory's "Butch" Construction of Male Elvis Fans', *Popular Music* 20/3 (2001): 395–408; Freya Jarman-Ivens, '"Don't Cry, Daddy": The Degeneration of Elvis Presley's Musical Masculinity' in Jarman-Ivens, *Oh Boy!*, pp. 161–80;, Al Jolson and John Lennon: see Richard Middleton, 'Mum's the Word: Men's Singing and Maternal Law', in Jarman-Ivens, *Oh Boy!*, pp. 103–24); Roy Orbison: see Peter Lehman, *Roy Orbison: The Invention of an Alternative Rock Masculinity* (Philadelphia, 2003); Mick Jagger: see Sheila Whiteley, 'Little Red Rooster v. The Honky Tonk Woman: Mick Jagger, Sexuality, Style and Image' in Whiteley, *Sexing the Groove*, pp. 67–99; Bruce Springsteen: see Gareth Palmer, 'Bruce Springsteen and Masculinity' in Whiteley, *Sexing the Groove*, pp. 100–17; Pink Floyd: see Matthew Bannister, 'Dark Side of the Men: Pink Floyd, Classic Rock and White Masculinities' in Russell Reising (ed.), *'Speak To Me': The Legacy of Pink Floyd's The Dark Side of the Moon* (Aldershot, 2005) pp. 43–55; the Velvet Underground: see Jeremy Gilbert, 'White Light/White Heat: *Jouissance* Beyond Gender in the Velvet Underground' in Andrew Blake (ed.), *Living Through Pop* (New York, 1999), pp. 31–48, at pp. 41–45; Freddie Mercury and Justin Hawkins: see Sheila Whiteley, 'Which Freddie? Constructions of Masculinity in Freddie Mercury and Justin Hawkins' in Jarman-Ivens (ed.), *Oh Boy!*, pp. 21–37; Morrissey: Mark Simpson, *Saint Morrissey: A Portrait of This Charming Man by an Alarming Fan* (New York, 2005), pp. 105–42;, Pet Shop Boys: see Stan Hawkins, 'The Pet Shop Boys: Musicology, Masculinity and Banality' in Whiteley,

Also, genres and scenes have been examined from the standpoint of contradictory masculinity. Authors often address these masculinities as they are discursively and actively linked to other categorical distinctions ranging from race and class to religious, regional, political or ideological distinctions.[49]

Among these various artists and genres, the proliferation of approaches to, and associations made with, masculinity has led to a pluralizing of the term.[50] This is part of a broader trend in gender studies where references to 'masculinities'

Sexing the Groove, pp. 118–34; Fred E. Maus, 'Glamour and Evasion: The Fabulous Ambivalence of the Pet Shop Boys', *Popular Music* 20/3 (2001): 379–93; Ian Balfour, 'Queer Theory: Notes on the Pet Shop Boys' in Roger Beebe, Denise Fulbrook and Ben Saunders (eds), *Rock Over the Edge: Transformations in Popular Music Culture* (Durham, NC, 2002), pp. 357–70; Jeff Buckley: see Shana Goldin-Perschbacher, '"Not With You But Of You": "Unbearable Intimacy" and Jeff Buckley's Transgendered Vocality' in Jarman-Ivens, *Oh Boy!*, pp. 213–33; Tupac Shakur: see Michael Eric Dyson, *Holler If You Hear Me: Searching For Tupac Shakur* (New York, 2001), pp. 141–74; and Justin Timberlake: see Stan Hawkins, '[Un]*Justified*: Gestures of Straight-Talk in Justin Timberlake's Songs' in Jarman-Ivens, *Oh Boy!*, pp. 197–212..

49   These include the black masculinities of hip hop; see Joan Morgan, *When Chickenheads Come Home To Roost: My Life As A Hip-Hop Feminist* (New York, 19990, pp. 49–81; Imani Perry, *Prophets of the Hood: Politics and Poetics in Hip Hop* (Durham, NC, 2004), pp. 117–54; Freya Jarman-Ivens, 'Queer(ing) Masculinities in Heterosexist Rap Music' in Sheila Whiteley and Jennifer Rycenga (eds), *Queering the Popular Pitch* (London, 2006), pp. 199–219;, and gangsta rap: see Todd Boyd, *Am I Black Enough For You? Popular Culture From the 'Hood and Beyond* (Bloomington, 1997), pp. 60–81; Eithne Quinn, *Nuthin' But A 'G' Thang: The Culture and Commerce of Gangsta Rap* (New York, 2005), pp. 92–115; the white masculinities of indie rock: see Matthew Bannister, '"Loaded": Indie Guitar Rock, Canonism, White Masculinities', *Popular Music* 25/1 (2006): 77–95; the working-class masculinities of heavy metal: see Robert Walser, *Running With the Devil: Power, Gender, and Madness in Heavy Metal Music* (Hanover, NH, 1993), pp. 108–36; and country music: see Aaron A. Fox, *Real Country: Music and Language in Working-Class Culture* (Durham, NC, 2004), pp. 249–71; the rural 'outback' masculinities of Australian pop: see Greg Young, '"So Slide Over Here": The Aesthetics of Masculinity in Late Twentieth-Century Australian Pop Music', *Popular Music* 23/2 (2004): 173–93; the politically-militant masculinities of straight-edge punk: see Ross Haenfler, *Straight Edge: Clean-Living Youth, Hardcore Punk, and Social Change* (New Brunswick, NJ, 2006), pp. 102–31; the gay masculinities of disco: see Peter Shapiro, *Turn the Beat Around: The Secret History of Disco* (London, 2005), pp. 57–88; and house music: see Stephen Amico, '"I Want Muscles": House Music, Homosexuality and Masculine Signification', *Popular Music* 20/3 (2001): 359–78; the suburban masculinities of emo: see (Andy Greenwald, *Nothing Feels Good: Punk Rock, Teenagers, and Emo* (New York, 2003), pp. 133–39; Sarah F. Williams, '"A Walking Open Wound": Emo Rock and the "Crisis" of Masculinity in America' in Jarman-Ivens, *Oh Boy*, pp. 145–60; the Islamic masculinities of raï: see Marc Schade-Poulsen, *Men and Popular Music in Algeria: The Social Significance of Raï* (Austin, TX, 1999); and the postmodern masculinities of Japanese pop: see Fabienne Darling-Wolf, 'SMAP, Sex, and Masculinity: Constructing the Perfect Female Fantasy in Japanese Popular Music', *Popular Music and Society* 27/3 (2004): 357–70.

50   R.W. Connell, *Masculinities* (Berkeley, CA, 1995).

have become the norm. While this splintering of masculinity is often linked to the 'crisis' discourse, Richard Middleton argues that this plurality can just as easily serve to stabilize masculinity 'because normative (male) masculinity can appear as such only through its positioning within a broader, highly variable range of masculinities'.[51] This point is in keeping with the 'crisis' discourse and much of the men's movement, which highlights the inconsistencies of masculinity in an effort to resolidify the masculine subject position. It is notable, then, that critiques of 'contradictory masculinity' can easily serve directly opposed aims, either seeking to save masculinity or to further dissect it.

PJ Harvey's 'Man-Size': Masculinity without Men

Among the non-normative masculinities referenced by Middleton is 'female masculinity', a term popularized by queer theorist Judith Halberstam. 'Butch' women and 'tomboys' are, she argues 'far from being an imitation of maleness ... female masculinity actually affords us a glimpse of how masculinity is constructed as masculinity ... masculinity becomes legible as masculinity where and when it leaves the white male middle-class body'.[52] Halberstram counters the common perception, in both hetero- and homo-normative cultures, that female masculinity is a 'pathological sign of misidentification and maladjustment ... situated [in homo-normative cultures] as the place where patriarchy goes to work on the female psyche and reproduces misogyny within femaleness'.[53] Instead, she finds female masculinities to be just as unsettled and contradictory as masculinity itself, where they may sometimes 'coincide with the excesses of male supremacy' and, in other instances, 'codify a unique form of social rebellion'.

In popular music, researchers have examined numerous female masculinities in practice, often perched between reinforcing and subverting familiar gendered subject positions.[54] One frequent case study has been the band PJ Harvey, led by

---

51   Middleton, 'Mum's the Word', p. 104.
52   Judith Halberstam, 'An Introduction to Female Masculinity: Masculinity Without Men' [1998] in *The Masculinity Studies Reader* (Oxford, 2002), pp. 355–74, at pp. 355–56.
53   Ibid., p. 360.
54   See, for instance, Philip Auslander, 'I Wanna Be Your Man: Suzi Quatro's Musical Androgyny', *Popular Music* 23/1 (2004): 1–16; Bayton, 'Women and the Electric Guitar'; Francesca Brittan, 'Women Who "Do Elvis": Authenticity, Masculinity, and Masquerade', *Journal of Popular Music Studies* 18/2 (2006): 167–90; Barbara Ehrenreich, *et al.*, 'Beatlemania: Girls Just Want to Have Fun' in Lisa A. Lewis (ed.), *The Adoring Audience: Fan Culture and Popular Media* (London, 1992), pp. 84–106; Judith Halberstam, 'Queer Voices and Musical Genders' in Jarman-Ivens, *Oh Boy*, pp. 183–95; Caroline O'Meara, 'The Raincoats: Breaking Down Punk Rock's Masculinities', *Popular Music* 22/3 (2003): 299–313; Jason Lee Oakes, 'The Filth and the Fury: An Essay on Punk Rock Heavy Metal Karaoke', *Current Musicology* 85 (2008): 73–112; Jennie Ruby, 'Women's "Cock Rock" Goes Mainstream', *Off Our Backs* 35/7–8 (2005): 42–44; and Sue Wise,

Polly Jean Harvey.[55] In the song 'Man-Size' – included on the 1993 album *Rid of Me* – Harvey addresses what it takes to be a man from a first-person perspective, but from a significantly different perspective than either Bo Diddley or Pulp. As Judith A. Peraino points out in her analysis of the song, 'to be "man-sized"… is not the same thing as being "a man"'.[56] The narrator of the song 'want[s] to fit' and to 'let it all hang out', expressing anxiety at how (s)he will 'measure' up to the expected dimensions of the phallus both literally and figuratively. As if to underscore this anxiety and the contradictions that underlie it, 'Man-Size' appears twice on the album *Rid of Me* in two radically different versions.

In the first version of the song – titled 'Man-Size Sextet' after the chamber music ensemble accompaniment – panicked-sounding strings provide an uneasy avant-garde/modernist sonic backdrop for Polly Jean Harvey's voice. The song opens with Harvey's assurance that she is 'man-sized', immediately juxtaposed with the horrific image of being 'skinned alive'. Sung in a strangulated voice, Harvey outlines the various accoutrements of her masculine self-image: 'leather boots', 'iron knickers' and a 'girl [who's] a wow'. Despite there being 'no need to shout', she seeks assurance: 'Can you hear / can you hear me now?' In the first chorus the sextet players shift to *collegno* articulations as Harvey repeats, 'I'm man-sized'. The claim is somewhat belied by her hesitant singing and the attenuated dynamics of the strings.

The second verse shifts to a heterogeneous backing of pizzicato strings, percussive effects and whining high harmonics. The breakdown of unified timbre is reflected rhythmically, as the individual players sound disjointed and out of sync, skittering under the surface of Harvey's voice like audible goose bumps. With her 'voice [left] in an unmetrical musical void',[57] Harvey nonetheless claims the objectivizing masculine authority to 'measure time' and 'measure height' – although in a note of doubt, even her masculine 'birthright' must be 'calculate(d)'. In the lead-up to the second and concluding chorus, layer upon layer of polyrhythm and dissonance builds to a climax in a fury of shrill cries. The musical texture of the climax strongly resembles Bernard Herrmann's famous 'shower scene' motif that accompanies the murder of Marion Crane in Alfred Hitchcock's *Psycho*.[58] Harvey moves into

---

'Sexing Elvis' [1984] in Simon Frith and Andrew Goodwin (eds), *On Record: Rock, Pop, and the Written Word* (London, 1990), pp. 390–98.

55   Raised in rural south-west England, Harvey describes her childhood self as a tomboy: 'I used to pee backwards, all the classic symptoms … I was devastated when I started growing breasts': quoted in Reynolds and Press, *The Sex Revolts*, p. 242. Having confronted her dis-ease over femininity in song (for example, 'Dress', 'I Think I'm A Mother', 'When Under Ether'), Harvey hardly appears any more comfortable with masculinity (for example, 'Me-Jane', 'Working for the Man' and 'Man-Size').

56   Judith Peraino, 'PJ Harvey's "Man-Size Sextet" and the Inaccessible, Inescapable Gender', *Women & Music* 2 (1998): 47–63, at 54.

57   Ibid., p. 60.

58   This similarity struck me upon first listen, and it has been widely noted elsewhere (ibid.). I would guess that the same association is made by many listeners, given the overall familiarity of the Herrmann theme and the many pop culture references that are

a higher register and repeats 'man-size' eight times; her wavering voice gives the impression of pleading, reinforced by the stabbing strings. Bending the last syllable of 'man-size', first down and then up, further evoking uncertainty, especially in the ascending tones of a question. Finally, in a brief coda Harvey's voice is stripped bare. She returns to a more comfortable register and sings *a cappella* 'Silence my lady head / Get girl out of my head', followed by a final image of dousing the lady head in gasoline and setting it on fire.

Four tracks later, the same lyrics (under the title 'Man-Size') are accompanied by a rock ensemble of heavily distorted guitar, bass and drums.[59] Together, they pound out riffs in a style that, by rock standards, would be considered more 'masculine' than the previous version. This time around, Harvey's voice is less uncertain and more aggressive; perhaps she has convinced herself of being man-sized by this point in the album.[60] However, there is still ample evidence of anxiety. The primary riff, introduced by Harvey's solo guitar, is played in an 11-beat cycle (3+3+3+2) which gives the riff a stuttering, uncertain quality. Harvey enters on vocals at the same time as a single snare drum plays duple pattern against the triple-time of the guitar line, contributing further to the nervous, lurching quality of the asymmetrical meter. As the song continues to build, each sonic layer adds a new degree of rhythmic ambiguity, creating an 'anti-groove' as described by Judith Peraino.[61] The disorienting/intoxicating push and pull of overlapping rhythmic frameworks is a strategy Harvey uses elsewhere, often coinciding with lyrics that deal explicitly with gender and its discontents – see, for instance, Mark Mazullo's analysis of 'Dress' and 'Hair' on PJ Harvey's debut album.[62] Notably, the second iteration of 'Man-Size' is followed by a song called 'Dry' with the refrain 'You leave me dry'. One can only guess that the efforts and assurances of 'Man-Size' have failed, even in the masculinist rock setting.[63]

While the gendered critique of 'Man-Size' may be similar to Pulp's 'I'm A Man' in some respect – that is, masculinity portrayed as ambivalent and contradictory – the perspective of the Pulp song is, by comparison, coherent and easy-to-read,

---

made to it.

59   The trio of Polly Jean Harvey, Steve Vaughan and Robert Ellis were the members of the *band* PJ Harvey on the first two albums, a naming practice that further confused stable distinctions of identity.

60   In the interim, and in the first single take from the album ('50 Ft. Queenie'), Harvey brags of being 'a big queen' who is 'king of the world', inflating the size of her phallus to 20, 30, 40 inches and finally 'you come on measure me / I'm fifty inches long!'

61   Peraino, 'PJ Harvey's "Man-Size Sextet"', pp. 54–57.

62   Mark Mazullo, 'Revisiting the Wreck: PJ Harvey's *Dry* and the Drowned Virgin-Whore', *Popular Music* 20/3 (October 2001): 431–47, at 442–44.

63   In their two versions of 'Man-Size' on *Rid of Me*, PJ Harvey subverts both the conventions of cock rock and of twentieth-century elite atonal art music equally. While the latter is 'perhaps a less famously macho musical idiom, [it is] nonetheless imbued with the masculine aesthetics of rugged individualism and rational evolution': Peraino, 'PJ Harvey's "Man-Size Sextet"', p. 62. Each genre is both lovingly recreated, and at the same time submitted to grotesque caricature.

whereas Harvey is notorious for *her own ambiguity*. As Mark Mazullo puts it, many of Harvey's songs combine 'a self-consciously byzantine act of storytelling and a pointed commentary', conflating 'myth and the thing itself'.[64] It is thus left largely up to the listener to figure out what exactly she is trying to say, or if she intends a single, coherent 'point of view' at all. This 'slipperiness as an artist' has 'frustrated [some] critics' and listeners, while attracting just as many others.[65]

Central to this ambiguity is a paradoxical attraction to dis-ease and discomfort, where dis-ease is metaphorically linked to disease – that is, a poor state of mental or bodily health. In 'Man-Size', masculinity is audibly 'sick' – both sick in terms of perversity and sick in terms of weakness and decline. In Harvey's work, sickness is a consistent motif. Images of bodily violence and degradation appear throughout her songs and on her album sleeves. With the body 'almost invariably a source of discomfort and conflict in her songs', one finds a pervasive 'eroticization of disgust [with] embarrassment and the blush as a kind of rapture'.[66] What is the supposed appeal found in this abject state of being, and why might PJ Harvey and their audience find pleasure in displeasure?

The answer may have something to do with what Aaron Fox calls the 'abject sublime'. Whether experienced in music that is paradoxically 'so bad that it's good', or in songs that delight in disgust, or even in self-destructive behaviours often associated with popular music-making (for example, drinking, smoking, slam dancing) Fox observes that 'it is in this apparent contradiction, this alchemical transformation of the hated, killing object in the object of intense desire, that the sublime also resides, as Julia Kristeva also famously proposed'.[67] Julia Kristeva directly links the simultaneous attraction/revulsion of the abject sublime to the bodily 'collapse of the border between inside and outside',[68] 'the in-between, the ambiguous, the composite … [that] disturbs identity, systems, order'.[69] Furthermore, Kristeva observes that this abjection is commonly gendered as feminine,[70] linked with stereotypical depictions of the feminine subject as impure, unstable, irrational, unfathomable and always subject to change.

---

64   Mazullo, 'Revisiting the Wreck', p. 433.

65   Ibid.

66   Reynolds and Press, *The Sex Revolts*, p. 338. Simon Reynolds and Joy Press go on to quote Harvey, where she admits: 'I have a complex about my body … I like to turn it on myself and make myself feel more ridiculous as a way of dealing with it ... I like to humiliate myself and make the listener feel uncomfortable. [Combining the two] would be the ideal package' (p. 338).

67   Aaron A. Fox, 'White Trash Alchemies of the Abject Sublime: Country as "Bad" Music' in Christopher J. Washburne and Maiken Derno (eds), *Bad Music: The Music We Love To Hate* (New York, 2004), pp. 39–61, at p. 55.

68   Julia Kristeva, *Powers of Horror: An Essay on Abjection* [1980], trans. Leon S. Roudiez (New York, 1982), p. 53.

69   Ibid., p. 4.

70   Ibid., pp. 157–73.

In performing songs that 'foreground the untidiness of gender and sexuality',[71] PJ Harvey evokes abjection in both the literal and metaphorical sense – a physical messiness that makes a mess of surfaces, subverting clear and 'clean' boundaries such as that between masculine and feminine. While abject grotesqueries have traditionally been linked to the female body, Harvey turns the tables by submitting the masculine and feminine alike to the same messy treatment. Where more conventional critiques of masculinity point up contradictions in a highly rationalized manner, this can have the effect of reinforcing gendered dichotomies as much as breaking them down (in other words there are still coherent *opposites* to be contrasted such as 'reality versus fantasy'). These critiques may also unconsciously reinforce gender binaries such as the rational masculine versus the feminine irrational. Rather than taking refuge in clear-cut contradictions, Polly Jean Harvey produces music that is just as 'troubled' as the 'gender trouble' she often takes as her subject. By transforming gender into a kind of freak show, 'abject masculinities' are paraded before our eyes and ears, and masculinity is revolting in both senses of the word.

Conclusion

The three songs analysed above draw on established images and associations made with masculinity, but also draw on musical reference points and other sonic markers (for example, the voice) to express notions of gender with greater clarity than words alone could ever provide. While some popular music cultures can tell us much about residual masculinities and those who wish to preserve them, others anticipate emergent masculinities before they cross over to wider acceptance, providing a valuable indicator of what may be considered normative in the future. Thus, it would be to the great advantage of all gender researchers and theorists to familiarize themselves with the ever-developing literature on popular music and masculinity.

---

71   Mazullo, 'Revisiting the Wreck', p. 432.

PART 4
Identity and Ethnicity

The Woven World:
Unravelling the Mainstream
and the Alternative in
Greek Popular Music

Kevin Dawe

If you enter the woven world
you won't easily find a way out
and without Ariadne's clue
you'll be trapped forever in the labyrinth[1]

In studying the role of music in the tightly woven world of Greek culture and society, Ariadne's clue is as relevant today as it was millennia ago. Travellers to the musical labyrinth discover new dimensions of time and space, forever shaped and censored by the musical Minotaur. In this world of underground passages and dead-ends, a clear identification of 'the problem' is demanded of the intrepid researcher. The threads of theory and method that bind the research project must be tightly woven together, for it is crucial that such a guide holds firm for the journey in, as well as the journey out of, the musical labyrinth.

This chapter provides a modest introduction to the rich sonic and cultural landscape of Greek popular music. As an ethnomusicologist who has studied both regional traditional music and popular music in Greece, I note some of the ways in which my own home discipline has contributed to the formation of popular musicology's global turn. I note ethnomusicologists' well-established and ongoing engagement with the 'broadly popular' and the 'technologically popular',[2] popular

---

1   Kristi Stassinopoulou, 'woven world' from *Ifantokosmos* (Thesis SA, Greece, TH008, 1997).
2   Mark Slobin, 'Ethnomusicology' in *Continuum Encyclopaedia of Popular Music. Vol. 1: Media, Industry, Society* (London, 2003), pp. 72–74, at p. 73.

music being one among many types of music studied by ethnomusicologists, in contradistinction to the terrain usually covered by the popular musicologist. Not that the popular musicologist works within a monoculture. Indeed, my own case study shows how two Greek musicians take inspiration from electronica, psychedelic rock and ambient music – genres which are now well established in a Greek context. My case study also points to some of the ways in which these musicians attempt to put a local stamp upon their music.

The work of Athens-based singer-lyricist Kristi Stassinopoulou (who represented Greece in the Eurovision Song Contest in 1983) and composer/multi-instrumentalist Stathis Kalyviotis provides the basis of my case study. The band works under the name of its lead singer, Kristi Stassinopoulou. They describe their music as 'alternative' (*kati allo*) to the 'mainstream' (*epikatrousa tasi*) of Greek popular music (both older *laiko* and modern *laika*). Their work has even reached the top of the World Music charts, where 'World Music' is known as *ethnike mousike* in Greece. A short extract from their web pages, might usefully set the scene for later discussion: Kristi Stassinopoulou's long-time collaborator, the late Thaleia Iakovidou, notes:

> *Her [Kristi Stassinopoulou's] albums have been gathering enthusiastic reviews all around the globe (fRoots, New York Herald Tribune, Global Village, Jazz Times, El Pais, Billboard, Time Out and many more), while she has been compared at times to Hedningarna, Steeleye Span, Patti Smith, Grace Slick, or Björk.*[3]

Elsewhere, I have written briefly about Kristi Stassinopoulou and about some of the many other, largely unstudied, musicians making popular music in Greece during the last decades of the twentieth century and into the twenty-first century.[4] Such a multifaceted world is often eclipsed by *rebetiko* music and its academic study (now known as rebetology),[5] and the 'mainstream': *bouzouki*-based popular music

---

3   At: <http://www.krististassinopoulou.com>.

4   Kevin Dawe, 'Between East and West: Contemporary Grooves in Greek Popular Music (*c.*1990–2000)' in Goffredo Plastino (ed.), *Mediterranean Mosaic: Popular Music and Global Sounds in the Mediterranean Area* (New York, 2003), pp. 221–40; and 'Regional Voices in a National Soundscape: Balkan Music and Dance in Greece' in D. Buchanan (ed.), *Balkan Popular Culture and the Ottoman Ecumene: Music, Image, and Regional Political Discourse(s)* (Lanham, MD, 2007). See also Ioannis Polychronakis, 'Anna Vissi: The Greek "Madonna"?', paper from the Conference 'Inter: A European Cultural Studies Conference in Sweden', Advanced Cultural Studies Institute of Sweden, 2007, at: <http://www.ep.liu.se/ecp/025/>; and Jane Cowan, 'Greece' in *The Garland Encyclopedia of World Music. Vol. 8: Europe*, ed. Timothy Rice, Christopher Goertzen and James Porter (New York, 1998), pp. 1007–28.

5   The work of Risto Pekka Pennanen and Dafni Tragaki provides usefully contrasting perspectives on *rebetiko* music. Pennanen undertakes a detailed analysis of musical structures in 'The Development of Chordal Harmony in Greek Rebetika and Laika Music, 1930s–1960s', *British Journal of Ethnomusicology* 6 (1997): 65–116, and in *Westernisation and Modernisation in Greek Popular Music* (Tampere, 1999). Tragaki provides rich cultural

with roots in the 1950s and 1960s (*laiko*), and Anglo-American pop, rock and dance music as it features and is appropriated into the Greek soundscape (*laika*).

Popular Musicology and Ethnomusicology

Taking its shape and substance from a range of theoretical and methodological perspectives, how useful are the ideas contained within the field of popular musicology when applied to music made popular in local contexts around the world? Clearly, the scope and prospectus of popular musicology, as well as some of its core theory and method, have felt the influence of ethnomusicology (and vice versa). It might be said that popular musicology and ethnomusicology have danced the *syrtaki* and the *lambada* together in an increasingly critical analysis of popular music from around the world.

Mark Slobin notes that ethnomusicologists have been largely responsible for importing local models of popular music culture from across the world into the study of popular music (a field developed, but not exclusively, by North American and North European scholars).[6] However, Slobin makes the input of ethnomusicology clear:

> ... *ethnomusicologists have continued to study 'what's popular' − meaning not only what's currently fashionable, or produced by the recording industry cartel, but also what people most commonly or passionately choose as the basis for dancing, listening, identifying with and remembering. This analytical attitude can be subdivided into headings: What is broadly popular among given genders, social formations, locations, and so on.*[7]

Slobin makes the case that ethnomusicologists have tended to deal with issues that extend the study of popular music beyond issues of commodification: working with musical systems based on heritage and affinity and studying musical forms that move freely between cities and rural areas. Moreover, ethnomusicological studies have revealed that 'issues of popular taste spill beyond issues of mediaization'.[8] He notes also the movement from ethnographic 'fieldwork on person to person transmission to mediated forms of performing and perceiving' in the 1980s.[9]

---

historical and ethnographic insights in *Rebetiko Worlds: Ethnomusicology and Ethnography in the City* (Newcastle, 2007).

6   Slobin, 'Ethnomusicology'.

7   Ibid., p. 73.

8   Ibid.

9   Ibid. See also Christopher Waterman, *Jùjú: A Social History and Ethnography of an African Popular Music* (Chicago, 1990); Louise Meintjes, *Sound of Africa! Making Music Zulu in a South African Studio* (Durham, NC, 2003); and Paul Greene and Thomas Porcello (eds), *Wired for Sound: Engineering and Technologies in Sonic Cultures* (Middletown, CT, 2005).

The 'impact' of rock, pop, blues, jazz and European classical music, which are now truly global in their reach, was noted by ethnomusicologist Bruno Nettl in a seminal 1985 publication.[10] New forms of popular music have sprung up across the world as globally mobile music was combined with local approaches to musical performance. Moreover, reggae and salsa, for example, have proven to be just as mobile as rock and jazz, and genres such as flamenco and klezmer have not only taken root widely in diasporic communities, but have also been taken up by musical groups in contexts that have no origins in, or indeed few ties to, Spanish or Jewish culture. Local appropriations of rock, pop and jazz have created a profusion of hybrid musical genres across the globe, and ethnomusicologists and others can now be quite specific about genre and stylistic influences.[11] For example, it is clear that electronica, psychedelic rock and ambient music have been influential in the music of Kristi Stassinopoulou.

It was surely Peter Manuel's *Popular Music of the Non-Western World* (1988)[12] that helped stimulate the interest of a generation of ethnomusicologists in the major syncretic forms of popular music around the world (from Afrobeat to zouk). Manuel's useful survey of popular genres demonstrates that ethnomusicologists had been engaging with the study of popular music well beyond North American and North European shores for some time. Furthermore, in almost every issue of *Popular Music* since 1981 there has been an increasing number of case studies of popular music genres from outside of Europe and North America (sometimes with themed issues: Africa, Latin America, the Middle East).

Popular musicology has tended to concentrate on the analysis of Anglo-American popular music: a focus which, by very definition (popular 'musicology'), leads one to expect a study of the *music itself*. Clearly, this is not always the case, and an important distinction must now be made (as such a definition does little justice to developments in musicology either). A broader concept of music-making and how music makes meaning is now demanded. Moreover, the more inclusive analytical approach, coming under the rather unwieldy heading of 'popular music studies', is also completely necessary. Yet 'musicology' has also been through a series of transformations as the 'new musicology' of the late 1980s – for example, incorporating studies of gender and sexuality, power and control, and the critical analysis of composer biographies. It has also become clear that any analysis of commercial recordings that is, music made for the purpose of profit, whether by Elgar or the Sex Pistols – must include notes on the recording process, production

---

10   See Bruno Nettl, *The Western Impact on World Music: Change, Adaptation, and Survival* (New York, 1985).

11   See George Lipsitz, *Dangerous Crossroads: Popular Music, Postmodernism and the Poetics of Place* (New York, 1994); Timothy Taylor, *Global Pop: World Music, World Markets* (New York, 1997); and the more recent survey by Arthur Bernstein, Naoki Sekine and Dick Weissman, *The Global Music Industry: Three Perspectives* (New York, 2007), which provides for greater contextualization.

12   Peter Manuel, *Popular Music of the Non-Western World: An Introductory Survey* (Oxford, 1988).

values, sleeve design and details of all those involved (including producers and engineers). Moreover, live recordings (incorporating stage performance and audience participation) as well as the use of multimedia, music video, MTV and film, might all come under the rubric of popular musicology. Thus, a broad range of scholars now grapple with the music of popular culture.

Music of all types can be found on the Internet, even if only in fragmented form and detached from the context from which it takes its meaning. It is likely that even the most obscure music will have some reference made to it on the Internet, and this likelihood increases if the subject of study is music made for commercial use or public consumption. The Internet is now part of the 'field' in ethnomusicology, as much as the technologically popular media (broadsheets, radio, recording studios, records, CDs, MTV) has always provided for the basis for a popular musicology. A deep immersion in the field must now be accompanied by a study of artists' web pages, blogs, CD iconography, and reviews in the popular press. In this informational labyrinth, the question arises: where is the artistic work located? But there is also a serious epistemological problem: is one dealing with informational surfaces, fragments and discontinuities? Or is the information before one's very eyes and ears part of the living world of the performer/performance itself and therefore a meaningful, insight-giving, part of the local research problem?

The Problem of Meaning

The ethnomusicological approach tries to ensure a rigorous, balanced and critical assessment in a study of the ways in which popular music is made (wherever that may be) and is made to convey meaning (as the creative expression of culture-bearers). Crucially, when defining the music they are studying as 'popular' music, ethnomusicologists take their lead from the terms used by musicians and others in the myriad local contexts of its production and consumption, as well as applying common sense. Yet, perhaps not surprisingly, each and every musical genre or style deemed 'popular' reveals a complexity of interpretations and specific meanings associated with it in a local context – whatever meaning it may take on elsewhere. Other music is no less complicated but is, perhaps, less open to interpretation, often held in place as part of sacred or secular rituals and celebrations, with smaller audiences, and not commercially available. We must also study how the Vietnamese or the Brazilians view the music of Björk or Muse or Neil Diamond or Nina Simone.

In rethinking popular musicology, one must surely prioritize a study of the ways in which music is made meaningful within a particular locality. Martin Stokes argues that the 'strongest grounds for a convergence of ethnomusicological and music theoretical interest', for instance, is music's 'semiotic multiplicity'[13] which

---

13   Martin Stokes, 'Talk and Text: Popular Music and Ethnomusicology' in Allan F. Moore (ed.), *Analyzing Popular Music* (Cambridge, 2003), pp. 218–39, at p. 239.

can only be understood through a deep immersion and prolonged study of music in its cultural setting. Must we do this for each and every popular music genre or style that we find on our travels? As an ethnomusicologist, I would argue, yes.

The ways in which the constituent elements of the *lyra* music of Crete, for example, come together in the context of a local and diasporic recording and cultural/media industry has exercised me for some time.[14] In the context of that particular musical labyrinth, it was crucial to address 'the notes' as much as the 'social significance of music as culture'.[15] For the very structures of *lyra* music (an upright bowed lute accompanied by one or two plucked lutes) can be said to be engendered, its sound politically charged, imagery nostalgic, the lyrics of songs and other poetic forms empowering and so on. And there are several interpretations of what this local music should now be about, from that of the observer with a casual interest to the aficionado who sees *lyra* music as a part of the Cretan republican movement. Furthermore, the ways in which local gender ideals help to shape *lyra* music performance call for a highly detailed and prolonged analysis of local values and beliefs. Such values and beliefs find their way into the production aesthetic and promotional culture of the local recording industry (run by Cretans). *Lyra* music is at once a site of an idealized continuity with the past and a site of contest in the present. It has many subtly different interpretations, on and off the record. Many younger Cretans will listen to Björk and Muse, while being able to dance to the sound of the *lyra* at highly ritualized wedding celebrations.

Referring specifically to the study of Turkish popular music, Stokes makes the comment that '[t]he attempt to grasp Arabesk 'as music' is clearly vital and the republican commentators, who have repeatedly tried to understand Arabesk as a kind of social 'text', have missed the crucial point that animates Arabesk socially and politically: it is music, mediated through social space in ways which are specific to an extremely popular mass-mediated music'.[16] Grounded in an ethnographic fieldwork methodology, what can ethnomusicology offer to the study of popular music in this case? Surprisingly, Stokes notes from his fieldwork on Turkish popular music that '[e]hnography ... entirely removes the possibility of searching for an authentic, transparent "native model". If anything, it provides exactly the opposite: instances of musical production in which different modes of knowing music compete, and only occasionally connect, with one another.'[17] These comments have a certain gravitas in the context of my own case study as presented here: the artists consider themselves as part of the 'underground' music scene in Greece. Their model of 'authenticity' claims to be at odds with the 'mainstream'. In this context there are several 'native models' (part of one bigger model) which may or may not be entirely 'native'. Such models give voice to a range of possible interpretations,

---

14   See Kevin Dawe, *Music and Musicians in Crete: Performance and Ethnography in a Mediterranean Island Society* (Lanham, MD, 2007).
15   After Stokes, 'Talk and Text'.
16   Ibid., p. 239.
17   Ibid.

all plausible, and revealing the local musical, political and economic context and climate in which the music is made.

Whereas the mainstream sticks to well-established formulaic models, or unashamedly combines local sounds with a limited range of pop and rock styles, the underground music scene makes the claim to authenticity. In my case study, aspects of electronica, psychedelic rock and ambient music take on new meaning as they provide an alternative means of 'authentication' in a Greek context. These genres are combined with local textures and timbres arising out of the use of instruments such as bagpipes, *sazi* (long-necked Turkish lute), *lyre* (upright bowed fiddle, in this case, from Crete) and *ney* (end-blown Turko-Arab flute) with distorted electric guitars, loops, samples and synthesizer padding. The resulting mix, the fusion of timbres and textures, thoroughly localizes globally mobile forms (subgenres) as part of local scenes. But this music is as much an interpretation of the local past as of the global present. Meanwhile, the subject-matter of songs draws on local subjects: images of escape from the city, the petit bourgeoisie, commerce and tourism. A sense of loss is evoked, a loss of innocence, and a claim that a simple life is better, preferable to the demoralizing, often-brash, crass commercialism of the pop music industry: remaining true to oneself, island-hopping with a sleeping bag on one's back, a guitar and a notebook represent the Bohemian libertine. Of course, the artists can only claim to have set themselves adrift from the mainstream in terms of the processes that contribute to the production and consumption of their music. And, in this respect, it is crucial to consider both 'talk and text'.[18]

The Woven World

Greece presents a challenging context in which to examine popular music. It is a country once central to the European constitution (in every sense of the word) but now somewhat peripheral to the centres and seats of power of Fortress Europe. However, although it has a well-established music industry, that industry is further supported by its connections to the multinationals – for example, EMI-Greece or EMI-Music Box International-Aerakis Records (Crete). With the help of non-Greece-based companies, such as the Greek-owned Trehantiri record shop in London, it manages to disseminate its products to a target audience of Greek-speakers across the diaspora. Back in Greece, these wider corporate connections not only help to sustain and perpetuate commercial recordings in Greece (the Minos Matsas company being a leader in this respect), but also meet the desire or need for wider commercial success beyond the limited population of Greece and, in some cases, even beyond its diaspora to non-Greek-speakers.

Drawing on a wide range of sources over a number of years, it has become clear to me that popular musicians in Greece see themselves and their music as somehow 'between East and West', 'a farrago', with influences from both Asia and Africa, yet

---

18   After Stokes, 'Talk and Text'.

rooted in the musical cultures of the Balkans and the Eastern Mediterranean.[19] Any popular musicology of Greece must carefully identify and assess the historical and social forces that have affected the course and development of popular music. As noted earlier, an investigation into the musical roots of Greek popular music is flourishing with respect to the study of *rebetiko*. There is little written about the life and work of popular musicians in Greece today.

Also as previously noted, younger generations of Greek musicians are combining genres such as electronica, psychedelic rock and ambient music with regional Greek sounds from Byzantine chant to regional songs. I managed to make contact via e-mail with two such musicians – Kristi Stassinopoulou and Stathis Kalyviotis in the hope that I might be able to strike up a discussion with them. This was something of a novelty for me: contact in cyberspace would have been out of the question with most of the musicians I have interviewed in the past. However, conducting interviews and documenting how locals talk and write about music are very much central to my work as an ethnomusicologist. After an initial enquiry via their promoters' e-mails, I was put in touch with Kristi and Stathis, who promptly responded to my questions, as noted below.

Q. If I was to choose one song from Echotropia[20] and one song from The Secrets of the Rocks[21] that really sum up your work, which songs would you want me to write about and why?

> **Kristi and Stathis:** *It is really difficult to us to choose just one song which is summing up our work. Since they are our own songs, we cannot ourselves clearly distinguish which one of them might be 'characteristic' of our style.*
>
> *The fusion of the musical elements is totally spontaneous when we write our songs. We play with sounds, with instruments, with voices, with words etc., trying to create an atmosphere, to narrate what we want and there comes out either a totally acoustic song or a totally electronic one, either a rootsy feeling or a simple western tune. They are all ours and we cannot say which one of them is more characteristic …*
>
> *The Greek peninsula is a crossroads of three continents, situated in the far south-eastern edge of Europe, right above Africa and right next to Asia. Our music is influenced by all the different kinds of music that could be heard by someone with open ears here, all these last decades.*

---

19   See Dawe, 'Between East and West', and 'Regional Voices in a National Soundscape'.

20   *Echotropia* (Lyra – Musurgia Graeca, Greece, ML4942, 1999; Tinder Records, USA 2001; MCD, Brazil, 2001). No. 6 World Music Charts Europe, May 2000. Three months in top 20 World Music Charts Europe. See: <http://www.weltmusik.de/charts/wmce200005.htm>.

21   *The Secrets of the Rocks* (Hyke Records/Wrasse Records: WRASS103, 2002; Wrasse Records, GB, 2003; Tinder Records, USA, 2003; Resistencia, Spain).

Q. *How should an academic interested in popular music approach your music? What would you expect me to look for and write about? What do you think I should be looking at?*

> **Kristi:** *Our music and albums cannot be considered Greek mainstream popular music. Here in Greece we are mostly known and respected by the audience who mainly praise the innovative air of our albums and our alternative way of working in the Greek music scene. Stathis is writing the music and I am writing the lyrics, usually simultaneously and then both together we make the production of the album.*

> **Stathis:** *We are trying not to sound predictable 'Greek' or 'ethnic'. We admire the truth of traditional music which has no need of interviews, public relations, managers, labels etc. But we cannot be, or pretend to be, traditional musicians since first of all, we have not grown up in the countryside. We are grown up in Athens, a big city which has many unique things and many things in common with other cities. And we are lucky enough to live in a peaceful era when —among many other things – hundreds of different music styles, old and new, are easy to discover, to explore and to enjoy. Our music, like any music made with truth, love and respect, is the sound reflection of our mind, soul and the things that surround us.*

> **Kristi:** *Byzantine music and traditional songs/music mainly from the rural areas of Greece have always been an inspiration to us. We use some very old traditional instruments, like the Greek gaida [bagpipes] that was forgotten and now 'revived', the Cretan lyre, the laouto [long-necked lute], the daouli [drum], etc. Some of our songs are based on Greek traditional dancing rhythms.*

> *Very often we feel that the repetitive motives that create that trance dance feeling in Greek traditional music sound a lot like electronic dance music and that it's interesting to mix them. Stathis likes to work on the sampler and the computer as a musician, creating his own sounds and loops and never using preset things. Sounds from nature, samples of machines or boats or goat bells or human voices are often used in these loops.*

The Secrets of the Rocks

The images on the cover and in the liner notes, the lyrics, a traditional island song (from Amorgos), the instruments and also the ambient sounds make it clear that this is an album about islands – to be precise, the Aegean islands. As Kristi notes:

> *The lyrics in The Secrets of the Rocks were all written by the sea, living freely in remote beaches of the Aegean Sea and listening to the sounds of nature*

> *around and socializing and playing music with the other people staying in the nearby beaches. It's praise to this kind of living, which is getting lost.*

It is also important to note that the liner notes are in Greek and English and thus open to interpretation by a wider audience. Greek reviewer Nondas Kitsos is able to add some insider knowledge regarding the themes on the album in his *RootsWorld* review. In his opinion:

> *The Secrets of the Rocks establishes Stassinopoulou as the High Priestess and Patron Saint of the venerated tradition of island-hopping, Athens style. This is the process in which, during each summer, all Athenians leave their city to the tourists (mostly over the weekend) and go to sunbathe, swim and sun-worship on one of the hundreds of Aegean islands. There are distinct subgroups and Kristi has aligned herself with the most hardcore of those, the one which is a direct descendent of the Sixties and early Seventies, the 'me, my pals, my tent and an empty beach' clan. She is so cool that she even keeps secret the names of three of the beaches that inspired her record to protect them from the unwanted.*[22]

BBC reviewer, Fiona Talkington, on the other hand, gives a general sense of what she thinks the album is about:

> *Don't get me wrong, this is one of the strongest world music albums around, and if I simply describe it as an album inspired by the sounds of the Greek islands and the ocean, infused with a mixture of traditional instruments (saz, bagpipes, flutes and accordion), with beats and electronica (oh, and waves crashing against the shore), please don't run a mile! Maybe it's because I've just done four summer festivals in a row and I can only hear music while sitting on the grass underneath blue skies that I think this is the perfect outdoor CD.*[23]

The back cover features a dedication, presumably by Kristi and Stathis:

> *To those who have spent summers and more, but are eventually losing places like [list of beaches] and all the rest of the beaches we didn't get to know before they became 'civilized'.*

With these comments in mind, a glance down the list of song titles immediately highlights the overall concept or subject-matter of the album, revealing a narrative tread that relates to island-based encounters:

---

22   Nondas Kitsos, '*Secrets of the Rocks*: RootsWorld Review, at: <http://www.kristi stassinopoulou.com/?show=reviews&rId=5&lan=1>.
23   Fiona Talkington, '*The Secrets of the Rocks*: BBC Review', at: http://www.kristi stassinopoulou.com/?show=reviews&rId=4&lan=1>

Ta mistiká ton Vrákon – The Secrets of the Rocks (06:11)
Kímata – Waves (04:25)
Amoryianó mou pérama – Amorgos Passage (04:58)
Apagorevtikó – Strong Winds Blockade (04:58)
Klíno ta mátia – Close My Eyes (04:57)
Kókkines ohkiés – Red Adders (03:03)
Dínes – Whirlpools (04:03)
Ta nisiá – The Islands (05:17)
StoPatithráki – A Rock Ledge on the Sea (03:00)
E Míres – The Fates (03:47)
E méres pernáne – The Days Go By (04:05)
Calima – Calima [east wind] (04:47)
Fengári kalokairinó – Summer Moon (05:10)

Clearly, a close look at least one of the songs is needed. The reader will find below a brief analysis of track 2, 'Waves'.

Waves

Features of an island landscape emerge as the songs progress. The terrain is known well to island-hoppers like Kristi and Stathis who have spent many summers on the beaches of the Aegean islands. The striking imagery of the lyrics of 'Waves' reveals how the island-hopper goes back to nature:

Káto apó to fos ton asterión	*under the starlight*
Áplosa to sleeping bag mou	*rolled my sleeping bag*
páno sto Vasíleo ton nerón	*on the water kingdom*
Eki ksáplosa	*there, I laid down*
To móno pou kreázesai te níhta	*the only thing you need at night*
Ene énas vrákos platís	*is a wide rock*
Ke mia pétra maksilári	*and a stone for a pillow*

The lyrics on this track mention the sea, waves, rocks, seagulls, the horizon, stars, local trees, herbs, goats, reptiles and a monastery, providing a real sense of seascape, landscape, warmth and atmosphere. This is a sensual world, reminding one of long hot summer days filled with the scent of herbs and the taste of salt on one's lips. To anyone who has ever been to the Aegean islands, the sights and sounds begin to return. But this is a world that, perhaps understandably, the island-hoppers are reluctant to want to share with too many people, content to reveal, as it were, the 'secrets of the rocks' on record only. However, Kristi and Stathis helped me to reveal some of the secrets of the music, as noted below.

Some Structural Landmarks

'Waves' mode: B♭ C D♭ E F G A♭ B♭

Introduction

- Synthesizer: held note, oscillating B♭ (with glissandi to and from the fifth above).
- Improvisation on *ney* (end-blown Turko-Arab flute): introduces mode and mood, and 'gives the feel of the wind'.[24] The *'ney'* is made from 'the broken parts of a push broom' and its solo 'could mostly be called a *scaros*, which means an improvisation usually with a wind instrument playing on a more rural, pentatonic traditional scale'.[25] The *ney* is accompanied by constant and less regular percussive sounds: 'In this song you can hear the crackle of an old wooden door of a very old, remote, tiny church situated on a steep mountain slope on top of the Aegean sea on the island of Sikinos. Then the bells of this same church can be heard. Stathis recorded these on the spot while we were wondering across the island's small pathways.'[26]
- Spoken lyrics.

Section One

- Short solo *sazi* section introduces main melodic material: basic figure of F G A♭ G F E F played with open drone strings.
- Vocalist imitates and extends this material in the melody.
- Strong and constant 4/4 rhythmic pattern held by kit drums (emphasis on beats 2 and 4). The *defi* (hand-held frame drum) provides for syncopation across kit drum pattern).

Section Two

- Key melodic phrase carried by vocalist based on: D natural, C, B♭..
- Singer's voice is processed, 'like saying your news to a friend on the telephone'.[27]
- *Ney* fill–ins.
- Spoken line.
- In a similar fashion, the sections repeat one more time.

---

24   Kristi Stassinopoulou and Stathis Kalyviotis, correspondence.
25   Ibid.
26   Ibid.
27   Ibid.

Some Final Comments

I feature two reviews below that provide some useful descriptors of the sounds of not only *The Secrets of the Rocks*, but also of the sound of Kristi's and Stathis's work overall. I find these interpretations insightful, but not least for the forum of critical debate that they must be seen to precipitate. Nondas Kitsos notes again in his *RootsWorld* review:

> As it is always the case with her [Kristi], it is the arrangements and the wide use of samples that creates a soundscape that is distinctly Greek, a record that has as many links with the psychedelic Anglo-Saxon Sixties and Seventies as with the Mediterranean musical traditions. ... It is also a great idea, as those two musical languages (Greek tradition and psychedelia) go very well together.[28]

Kitsos considers the music to be 'distinctly Greek', as marked out by its combination of psychedelic and 'Mediterranean' music which, in his opinion, 'go very well together'. In *fRoots*, magazine editor Ian Anderson might seem to concur with Kitsos as he takes up the theme of the 'underground' and the 'Greekness' of Kristi's and Stathis's music. In a review of *Taxidoskopio*[29] Anderson notes:

> Kristi and partner Stathis have long had a world vision in their music, which has kept them somewhat underground in Greece as their international appeal has grown ... more distinctly Greek – a strange, other-worldly Greekness, for sure, but a 21st century Greekness that's modern within its own culture, out there, ahead and rooted rather than just banging off some local language version of what the globalised industry dictates. No predictable Greek rock, Europop or hip-hop here then.[30]

These interpretations are quite consistent. The claims and qualifiers for 'distinctiveness', 'Greekness' but also 'underground' and 'alternative' begin to stack up. It is clear that the artists and their critics see this music as still rooted in Greek cultural space: Greeks making popular culture using both the apparatus of the global music industry in a 'distinctly Greek' way, and not 'just banging off what the globalised industry dictates'. This is, of course, but one form of consensus that I have gained from a small sample of reviews loaded up on to the artists' website.

---

28   Nondas Kitsos, '*Secrets of the Rocks*: RootsWorld Review, at: <http://www.kristi stassinopoulou.com/?show=reviews&rId=5&lan=1>.

29   *Taxidoscopio*, Resistencia, Spain (November 2006, for Spain and Portugal), Heaven and Earth, Germany (January 2007, for Germany, Austria and the UK) [HE18/RESCD201], King Records, Japan (August 2007, for Japan, Taiwan, Hong Kong, S.Korea), Prostasis Records, Greece (November 2007).

30   Ian Anderson, '*Taxidoskopio*: fRoots review', at: http://www.krististassinopoulou.com/? show=reviews&rId=35&lan=1.

It is clear, though, that the views put forward touch upon crucial issues of Greek identity: how do Greeks see themselves and how do others see them? No wonder, then, that the ethnomusicologist must now respond to the technologically popular when it touches on such deep-seated issues relating to ethnicity and identity, and their negotiation and construction in a transnational musical context.

Kristi and Stathis, brought up in cosmopolitan Athens, have a different audience in mind: high in the world music charts their music appeals to island-hoppers everywhere. As young Athenians with a particular background and upbringing, their orientation towards the *ethnos* is subtly different to Greeks elsewhere. Moreover, their music does not claim anchorage in one particular place, and they say that they are not trying to be 'Greek' or 'ethnic'. But their use of the Greek language immediately pulls them back into port. *The Secrets of the Rocks* is a highly evocative and nostalgic piece of work, celebrating an alternative life in a particular setting: the Aegean islands. As the musicians return again and again to their summer lives on the Aegean islands, so too do they sample music from beyond Greek shores (or, at least, music that has drifted in from elsewhere before being washed ashore and pulled up the beach).

More than one alternative comes into view through their music: alternative lives in Greece (Athenians, islanders), an alternative life on the islands, the possibility of going to ground/underground, and a vision of the musical alternative (as played out in myriad musical contexts throughout the world). Here, it is psychedelic rock as opposed to boy bands, but psychedelic rock as defined, appreciated and appropriated locally, for instance, standing in marked contrast to *bouzouki*-driven ballads. Also noteworthy is the use of Middle Eastern instruments that not only cross political borders and add interesting timbres and textures, but also risk misinterpretation as exotica in the setting of popular music and world music.

Kristi and Stathis admire 'the truth' of traditional music; their use of bagpipes and the Cretan *lyre* is a reference to that belief, to 'traditional' music which they see as 'truthful' and to a vision of music which they also see as 'truthful'. This also affects their approach to the use of technology – no 'presets', just samples of the 'sounds of nature'. Here is an alternative to alternatives found elsewhere, a world without presets, where loops are ultimately man-made, as if they were alternative technology. The best of the old world meets the best of the new? The best hope for a New Age in which technology (*technología*) is the vessel (*skáfos*) of the libertine (*éklitos*)?

These elements of a broad, but localized, ideology interrelate (their relationship fostered) in intriguing, but also creative, ways – arguably, in 'distinctly Greek' ways. Greeks and others may have either marked or subtly different notions of 'Greekness', alternativeness and authenticity, but popular musicology's global turn and the turn to popular musicology in ethnomusicology have the potential to reveal much of the complex, polysemic and tightly woven worlds of popular music that surround us all.

Acknowledgements

I wish to thank Kristi Stassinopoulou and Stathis Kalyviotis for their helpful correspondence in matters pertaining to this chapter.

Dayton Street Funk: The Layering of Multiple Identities[1]

Portia K. Maultsby

Funk is a Black thing. There is a need to express yourself as an African American. You need to be your own person.
Danny Webster, guitarist and vocalist for Slave

This chapter, based on a case study of Dayton Street Funk, employs ethnographic methods combined with the analysis of library and archival sources, recordings and other artefacts to explore the construction of identities in black popular music. Of central focus are the ways in which identities – manifested in the sonic, lyrical and visual dimensions of musical performance – juxtapose and superimpose markers of a region, city and local African-American communities. The emergence of funk parallels the transition of American society from the era of sanctioned racial segregation known as Jim Crow (1890s–1960s) to the 1970 decade of 'integration' and 'affirmative action'. It also parallels the shift from an industrial to a technological and service-oriented society. Both of these developments helped shape and define the multiple layers of identity associated with funk during its nearly two decades of popularity.

My initial research on Dayton Street Funk was conducted in conjunction with the development of a museum exhibition, 'Something in the Water: The Sweet

1   This chapter draws and revises some material from another by the author, 'Funk Music: An Expression of Black Life in Dayton, Ohio and the American Metropolis' in Hans Krabbendam, Marja Roholl and Tity de Vries (eds), *The American Metropolis: Image and Inspiration* (Amsterdam, 2001), pp. 198–213. The initial field research for this essay was conducted in 1997; this was later combined with library and archival research while a Fellow at the Center for Advanced Study in the Behavioral Sciences, (1999–2000) Stanford, California and on sabbatical (2004–2005). This essay is based primarily on extensive interviews with musicians and members of the Dayton community and in-depth analyses of sound recordings, photographs and album jackets. I am grateful for the financial support by the Andrew W. Mellon Foundation and the College of Arts and Sciences, Indiana University, Bloomington.

Sound of Dayton Street Funk' for the National Afro-American Museum and Cultural Center (Wilberforce, Ohio) whose objective was to bring greater public and scholarly awareness to this tradition. The approach to this project involved searching for artefacts and memorabilia (musical manuscripts, original recordings, videos of performances, instruments, photographs, album jackets, costumes, posters, promotional materials and so on) conducting interviews and locating archival and library materials.[2] The interviews conducted with musicians, high-school music teachers, club and retail record store proprietors, radio disc jockeys, parents, local historians, sociologists and politicians provided a context for interpreting the environment and circumstances that fostered musical creativity throughout Dayton's African-American community. These interviews were used in conjunction with local histories of Dayton's African-American community, memoirs written by those involved in the funk scene, articles from national and local newspapers as well as music trade publications, analyses of recordings and musical transcriptions/manuscripts, album jackets, photographs and other memorabilia and artefacts mentioned earlier.

The interpretation of data included the perspectives of musicians and others intimately involved in the creation and popularization of Dayton Street Funk. This collaborative or 'double-lens' approach, which former museum curator Rowena Stewart terms 'people-oriented' (versus 'object-oriented'), combines research methods employed by curators of African-American museums with those of ethnomusicologists. Stewart has suggested a five-step approach for collecting and presenting African-American documents, one component of which involves the curator enlisting the artefact holders or 'keepers of the tradition' in the initial interpretation of the objects, photographs or documents.[3] Similarly, in the field of ethnomusicology (and other disciplines), participants (musicians and members of the community) contribute to the interpretation of musical traditions through feedback interviews. This technique involves eliciting comments about a musical performance from the original participants in an attempt to reconstruct its meaning.[4] Current technological media developments in the field of ethnomusicology enable researchers to record and annotate digital video in the field. While viewing the

---

2   The museum's curator Michael Sampson and I served as co-curators for this exhibition. Michael was responsible for collecting and labelling objects for display. My charge was to conduct research for developing a historical and sociocultural history of Dayton Street Funk and to identify characteristic musical features as well as the innovations of the artists.

3   For a discussion and critique of this approach see Rowena Stewart, 'Bringing Private Black Histories to the Public' in Janet W. Solinger (ed.), *Museums and Universities: New Paths for Continuing Education* (New York, 1990); Edmund B. Gaither, '"Hey! That's Mine": Thoughts on Pluralism and American Museums' in Ivan Karp, Christine Mullen Kreamer and Steven D. Lavine (eds), *The Politics of Public Culture: Museums and Communities* (Washington, DC, 1992), pp. 56–64.

4   Ruth Stone and Verlon Stone, 'Event, Feedback, and Analysis: Research Media in the Study of Music Events', *Ethnomusicology* 25/2 (1981): 215–25.

event, participants' comments can be documented using an annotator's program, which allows for a written dialogue about the event.[5]

My approach to this study also considers the social and historical context for the development of funk. Funk, an urban form of dance music, is a by-product of post-World War II industrial cities, the Vietnam War and the 1960s Black Power movement. When millions of African-Americans migrated from the rural South to industrial centres during and after the Second World War, they anticipated new opportunities for a better life. Even though they fared better in cities by earning higher wages, economic and social challenges prevailed. Discriminatory practices restricted their employment to unskilled, dirty and low-paying menial jobs. Segregated policies in housing and the use of public facilities confined their mobility to designated areas within cities.[6] Beginning in the mid-1940s, black Americans openly protested these and other forms of racial inequalities by organizing grassroots demonstrations and boycotts. Such activities, in conjunction with lawsuits filed by the National Association for the Advancement of Colored People (NAACP), contributed to the rise to the modern civil rights and Black Power movements and led to modest improvements over the following two decades.[7]

The passage of the 1960s Great Society legislation and the establishment of Affirmation Action programmes in the 1970s raised expectations among African-Americans of racial equality and economic and political empowerment. The emergence of funk as the most popular form of urban black musical expression

---

5   The Ethnomusicology Video for Instruction and Analysis Digital Archive project is an effort to establish a digital archive of ethnomusicological video for use by scholars and instructors. In addition to digitally preserving valuable ethnographic field videos of musical events, EVIA allows the original researcher to annotate their own footage, providing users with detailed explanations of the participants' activities and extensive contextual data. For more information about the project, see the EVIA website at: <http://www.indiana.edu/~eviada/>.

6   For a discussion of these issues, see Steven F. Lawson, *Running for Freedom: Civil Rights and Black Politics in America since 1941*, (New York, 2nd edn 1977); Harold X. Connolly, *A Ghetto Grows in Brooklyn* (New York, 1977); Nicholas Lemann, *The Promised Land: The Great Black Migration and How It Changed America* (New York, 1991), pp. 61–107; Thomas J. Sugrue, *The Origins of the Urban Crisis: Race and Inequality in Postwar Detroit* (Princeton, NJ, 1996), pp. 92–123; Joe William Trotter, Jr and Eric Ledell Smith (eds), *African Americans in Pennsylvania: Shifting Historical Perspectives* (University Park, PA, 1998); Michael B. Katz (ed.), *The 'Underclass Debate': Views from History* (Princeton, NJ, 1993); Robin D.G. Kelley, 'The Black Poor and the Politics of Opposition in a New South City' in Katz, *The 'Underclass' Debate*, pp. 293–333.

7   For accounts of these activities, see: Matthew J. Countryman, *Up South: Civil Rights and Black Power in Philadelphia* (Philadelphia, PA, 2006); Marable Manning, *Race, Reform, and Rebellion: The Second Black Reconstruction in America, 1945–1990*, (Jackson, rev. 2nd edn 1991), pp. 40–85; Robert Brisbane, *Black Activism; Racial Revolution in the United States, 1954–1970* (Valley Forge, PA, 1974); John P. Roche, *The Quest for the Dream: The Development of Civil Rights in Human Relations in Modern America* (New York, 1963); Joe William Trotter, Jr, *River Jordan: African American Urban Life in the Ohio Valley* (Lexington, KY, 1998), pp. 149–50.

in the 1970s paralleled a paradoxical era of social unrest and ubiquitous optimism that prevailed among black Americans. As a musical style, funk communicated a revolutionary spirit, an urban attitude of defiance, and black solidarity associated with the late 1960s and early1970s. Its pioneers and popularizers were from San Francisco, Los Angeles, Chicago, New York City, Brooklyn, Jersey City, Detroit, Minneapolis, Cleveland, Cincinnati, Dayton, Louisville, Atlanta, New Orleans, and Memphis. Funk is urban at its core, blending industrial-based and technological sounds with song lyrics about black urban life, the universe and the tenets of Black Power. As such, funk is a contemporary 'expression of social change, cultural liberation, and musical experimentation that revealed the resilience and creativity of African Americans under changing social [and economic] conditions'.[8]

Although funk scenes existed in urban centres throughout the United States, I focus on Dayton as a case study to explore issues of identity for various reasons: first, Dayton, a small industrial Midwestern city without the presence of a record label, became a major centre for the production of funk music; second, 14 of the city's funk bands secured recording contracts with major labels;[9] third, between 1968 and 1999, 13 of these groups collectively produced 143 songs that landed on *Billboard's* R&B/soul music charts – the most songs charted by funk groups of any one city;[10] and, fourth, each of these bands, as well as those without recording contracts but with local followings, evolved their own signature sound and unique persona. Despite these developments and with few exceptions,[11] Dayton Street Funk has not been the topic of comprehensive study by scholars, which has contributed to its omission from many major annals on American popular music.

Building Communities: Dayton and the Black Migration

Dayton Street Funk is rooted in the social and cultural history of this city – a history shaped by the migration of thousands of southern rural African-Americans during the two decades that followed the Second World War. These former sharecroppers,

---

8   Portia K. Maultsby, 'Funk' in Ellen Koskoff (ed.), *The Garland Encyclopedia of World Music. Vol. 3: The United States and Canada* (New York, 2001), p. 680.

9   These groups are: the Ohio Players (Westbound/Mercury), Roger (Warner/Reprise), Zapp (Warner/Reprise), Lakeside (Solor), Steve Arrington/Steve Arrington and The Hall of Fame (Atlantic), Slave (Cotillion/Atlantic), Heatwave (Epic), Sun (Liberty/ Capital) , Dayton (Capitol), Shadow (Elektra), Faze-O (S.H.E./Atlantic), New Horizons (Columbia), Junie (Westbound/Columbia/Island), and Platypus (Casablanca).

10   For the charting of these groups, see Joel Whitburn, *Joel Whitburn's Top R & B Billboard Singles 1942–2004*, (Menomonee Falls, Wisconsin, 2004).

11   The first study of the funk that devotes attention to the Dayton groups is Rickey Vincent, *Funk: The Music, the People, and the Rhythm of the One* (New York, 1996). Twelve years later, and expanding on Maultsby's study, 'Funk Music', published in 2001, Scot Brown published the first essay devoted to Dayton Funk, 'A Land of Funk: Dayton, Ohio' in Tony Bolden (ed.), *The Funk Era and Beyond* (New York, 2008), pp. 73–88.

tenant farmers and domestics, among others, settled in Dayton and other northern cities anticipating high-paying factory and government jobs, seeking better educational opportunities and escaping the racial inequalities sanctioned by Jim Crow laws.[12] Although life in these cities had certain economic benefits, it also presented numerous challenges, many of which stemmed from discriminatory practices in the workplace, poor working conditions, limited educational opportunities and restrictive housing covenants. These conditions, coupled with the segregated structure of cities, shaped community-building among African-Americans, which I will explore to establish the environment from which Dayton Street Funk emerges.

The growth of an African-American community in Dayton, Ohio, follows the trajectory of events associated with Second World War migration and the reconfiguration of the labour force in industrial cities. According to historian Joe William Trotter, Jr:

> The percentage of blacks living in the North and West rose from 23 percent in 1940 to 40 percent in 1960 and 47 percent in 1970. Despite the persistence of racial discrimination, Northern blacks increased their foothold in industrial jobs, gained access to new business and professional opportunities and took influential positions in urban politics.[13]

Dayton became the 'promised land' for many disenfranchised African-Americans from Alabama, Georgia, Mississippi, Louisiana, Tennessee and Kentucky. African-Americans from all educational backgrounds found Dayton to be an attractive option. Between 1941 and 1960 the city's black population increased from 20 229 out of a total population of 210 718 (representing 9.6 per cent) to 57 189 out of a total population of 262 332 (representing 21.8 per cent).[14] Discriminatory hiring practices, however, restricted the employment of blacks to low-paying menial jobs such as janitors, dishwashers and domestics. Black professionals, many of whom graduated from colleges in the area,[15] also faced discrimination in employment. Although Dayton's economic infrastructure required both a blue-collar and professional workforce, black professionals were denied jobs commensurate with their education.[16] As noted by sociologist Bart Landry, mainstream society

---

12 The major employers in Dayton were Wright-Patterson Air Force Base, McCall's Publishing Company, General Motors, Delco, Inland, Frigidaire, GH&R Foundry, Dayton Tire and Rubber, National Cash Register, the Duriron Company, and Reynolds and Reynolds.

13 Joe William Trotter, Jr, 'Blacks in the Urban North' in Katz, The 'Underclass' Debate, pp. 55–81, at p. 80.

14 Margaret Peters, Dayton's African American Heritage (Virginia Beach, VA, 1995), p. 85.

15 Most were graduates of the two historically black universities, Wilberforce University and Central State University, located about 30 miles from Dayton. A smaller percentage came from white universities located in or near Dayton, including the University of Dayton, Wright State University, Antioch College and Ohio State University.

16 Lloyd E. Lewis, Jr, interview with author, Dayton, Ohio, 19 August 1997; Margaret

'continued to oppose entry into areas involving service to whites and competition with whites'. Therefore, employment opportunities for black college graduates were limited to occupations that 'directly served the needs of the black population' such as the ministry, social work and the teaching profession.[17]

In addition to restrictive employment opportunities, Dayton's black residents also faced discriminatory housing practices. The shortage of homes in Dayton, restrictive covenants, agreements among real-estate agents and biased bank lending practices resulted in the concentration of African-Americans on the city's Westside where their population increased from 84 per cent in 1940 to 95 per cent in 1960.[18] In protest against racial discrimination in the mid-1950s, local civil rights activist W.S. McIntosh organized demonstrations against the city government, banks and stores.[19] These activities, in conjunction with the lawsuits filed by the NAACP mentioned earlier, eventually led to new employment opportunities for African-Americans of various educational backgrounds. The rapidly changing job market produced conditions for black workers to advance into high-paying union jobs on assembly lines as skilled labourers, craftsmen and foremen, and to obtain work as clerical and government postal employees.[20] Using census data that covered the period from 1941 to 1960, Margaret Peters discovered:

> The top five categories for the 14,271 employed 'non-white' males were 3,578 operatives (skilled laborers, as in a factory), 2,452 laborers, 2,442 service workers (except domestics), 1,935 craftsmen and foremen, and 1,135 clerical workers. The top five categories for the 9,724 females were 2,660 service workers, 2,502 private household workers, 769 operatives, and 624 professional and technical workers.[21]

In essence, less than half of the black workers were in labour/service jobs.

As African-Americans increasingly moved out of the domestic and general labour sectors and into the industrial and professional sectors, many factory

---

Peters, interview with author, Dayton, Ohio, 18 August 1997; Charles Spencer, interview with Stephanie Shonekan, Dayton, Ohio, 24 July 1998; James Caldwell, interview with Stephanie Shonekan, Dayton, Ohio, 24 July 1998.

17 Bart Landry, *The New Black Middle Class* (Berkeley, CA, 1987), pp. 2, 56–57.

18 Peters, *Dayton's African American Heritage*, pp. 144–45; Peters, interview, 18 August 1977; Richard C. Dixon, interview with author, Dayton, Ohio, 18 August 1997; John VanZant, interview with Stephanie Shonekan. Dayton, Ohio, 13 March 1998. For similar practices in other cities see Lemann, *The Promised Land*; Sugrue, *The Origins of Urban Crisis*; Trotter Jr and Smith, *African Americans in Pennsylvania*; Katz, *The 'Underclass' Debate*; Connolly, *A Ghetto Grows in Brooklyn*; and Kelley, 'The Black Poor'.

19 Peters, *Dayton's African American Heritage*, p. 94; Peters, interview, 18 August 1997.

20 Dixon, interview, 18 August 1997; VanZant, interview, 13 March 1998. For similar trends in other cities see:Lemann, *The Promised Land*; Sugrue, *The Origins of the Urban Crisis*; Trotter Jr and Smith, *African Americans in Pennsylvania*; Katz, *The 'Underclass' Debate*; Brisbane, *Black Activism*; and Lawson, *Running for Freedom*.

21 Peters, *Dayton's African American Heritage*, p. 108.

workers earned salaries equivalent to black professionals. At the same time, college graduates, such as engineers and scientists, found employment in private industries and government facilities. The ongoing infusion of college graduates into a thriving working-class black community provided what former State Representative and local businessman Lloyd Lewis, Jr called a 'mix of education, professionals and money'.[22] This transformation of Dayton's black occupational and economic structures led to the blurring of boundaries between the black middle and working classes due to their similar incomes and access to material goods.

Many of Dayton's black professionals, working-class members and entrepreneurs lived in the same neighbourhoods, attended the same churches and belonged to the same fraternal, service and social organizations where they frequently intermingled. Although an attitude of elitism existed among some professionals, the polarization between these groups appears to have been less pronounced than it was in large urban cities with long-standing and well-established black middle and elite classes such as Chicago, Atlanta and Washington, DC.[23] As a collective, the working class, professionals and entrepreneurs contributed to the economic growth, as well as the social and cultural life, of West Dayton. The establishment of a vibrant black business and entertainment district brought black people together from all social classes and professions, creating an environment that produced many of the country's finest musicians and a unique Midwestern funk style known as Dayton Street Funk.

Although Dayton's funk groups appealed primarily to the poor and working classes in the South and Midwest, they also had fans among black college students[24] and professionals in cities across the country. The sound of Dayton Street Funk embodies the sensibilities and the aesthetic and musical values shared by black people of these social classes, and the messages spoke to their daily realities. For example, the Ohio Players' bluesy sound ('Far East Mississippi' [1976]) and the lead singer's southern drawl are in line with the sensibilities of the poor and working classes, while the disco-jazz flavoured and synthesized sound of Dayton ('The Sound of Music' [1984]) is associated more with those of black professionals of the social-middle class. Crossing and appealing to all social classes are the

22 L. Lewis Jr, interview, 19 August 1997; also Charles Lewis, interview with author, Dayton, Ohio, 18 August 1997; Peters, interview, 18 August 1997; Charlie White, interview with author, Dayton, Ohio, 19 August 1997; Ricky Smith, interview with author, Dayton, Ohio, 18 August 1997.

23 White, interview, 19 August 1997. For a general discussion of social classes in African-American communities, see Landry, *The New Black Middle Class*; Lawrence Otis Graham, *Our Kind of People: Inside America's Black Upper Class* (New York, 1999); Edward Franklin Frazier, *The Black Bourgeoisie* (New York, 1962); Nathan Hare, *The Black Anglo-Saxons* (New York, 1965); David J. Dent, *In Search of Black America: Discovering The African-American Dream* (New York, 2000); and Richard B. Freeman, *The Black Elite* (New York, 1976).

24 Many black college students were from working-class black families. Those attending predominately white institutions, for the most part, represented the first generation of families to attend college.

electronic-derived soul-blues-funk vocal and instrumental sounds of Roger and Zapp ('More Bounce to the Ounce' [1980]).

West Dayton: A Blend of Southern and Midwestern Traditions

The steady influx of African-Americans from the Deep South continually rejuvenated the southernness of West Dayton. While the sounds of folk spirituals, gospel music and lined-hymns reverberated off the walls of their churches and into the broader culture of West Dayton, so did the sounds of the blues and R&B from the juke joints or clubs. When new people came to Dayton, 'they brought with them their own ideas from a musical standpoint. They brought different rhythms [and melodies] and incorporated them into existing situations.'[25] Although black professionals often expressed a preference for arranged spirituals, hymns, anthems, Western European classical traditions and jazz, this musical divide became less significant when the community intermingled across social classes. Former mayor Richard Dixon explained that, because of circumstances in West Dayton and the isolation of its African-American community, 'we were forced to create our own social activities and we always did that through music and dance'.[26] West Dayton's entertainment district of approximately 15 clubs and performance venues attracted people from all socioeconomic classes – the skilled and unskilled labourers, professionals, liberal church-going folk, street hustlers, players, pimps and prostitutes[27] – who dressed in the latest fashions and drove the newest cars to project a street image popularized by the Hollywood film *Shaft* (1971). This movie portrayed John Shaft, the main character, as a lady's man who wore colourful suits and shoes, gold accessories, large hats with feathers and large tie sticks, and drove an Eldorado with custom lights on the front. Following the release of this film, flashy clothes and cars became associated with a 'hip' lifestyle in African-American urban communities throughout the country.

The Ohio Players, Dayton's first funk band, adopted this uniquely urban persona as manifested in the group's name, stage costumes and imagery on their album jackets.[28] While some jackets portrayed the group as 'players', others exploited sexual images of women. Dressed in tuxedoes, furs, hats, diamond rings and

---

25   Spencer, interview, 24 July 1998.
26   Dixon, interview, 19 August 1997.
27   Marshall Jones, interview with author, Dayton, Ohio, 19 August 1991. Jones identified 'players' as men who held full-time jobs, bought nice cars, dressed well, and frequented clubs to 'play with the ladies' but later married and had families. In contrast, he contended that pimps' involvement with women constituted a business enterprise.
28   Greg Webster, interview with Stephanie Shonekan, Dayton, Ohio, 12 March 1998. Webster explained that the term 'players' conveyed the group as God's gift to women.

other fashionable 'street' attire, the Ohio Players attracted female consumers who comprised 85 per cent of their fans. To increase the market share of male consumers, they created a new image exclusively for this group. The Players' first album to make a national impact, titled *Pain* (1971), showcased a skimpily dressed black bald woman holding a whip. The albums that followed, including *Skin Tight* (1974), *Fire* (1974), *Honey* (1975), *Contradiction* (1976), *Angel* (1977), and *Mr. Mean* (1977), also featured scantily dressed and nude women. The success of this marketing strategy conceived by the Ohio Players revolutionized the way record companies packaged and mass marketed black music.[29]

In live performances, the Ohio Players replicated aspects of Dayton street life on stage. These concerts constituted elaborate theatrical productions that featured light shows, sound-effects and stage props as described by Keith Harrison:

> *The Players was the first group to use lasers. People never knew that. They had mirrors set up and used laser lights way back then and before productions became a big thing. The Players painted all their equipment white, which brought another brightness to the stage. They started adding the siren to 'Fire'. On 'Skin Tight', Marshall came out and blew a tuba. They were adding other things to try to make to make their stage production a little bigger because Earth, Wind, and Fire was their biggest competitor when it came to stage production.[30]*

Through these shows, the Ohio Players established new trends in live productions of black popular music and they advanced the level of musical creativity to new heights, competing with funk groups such as Earth Wind and Fire, Kool and the Gang, and Parliament-Funkadelic from Chicago, Jersey City and Detroit, respectively.

Dayton's street life became a resource for musical creativity. The culture, behaviour, vernacular language and activities of the black poor and working classes provided the Ohio Players with content and vocabulary for song titles and lyrics. The hit song 'Skin Tight' (1974), for example, describes the movements of women attired in clothing that reveals the curvature of the body, whereas 'Jive Turkey' (1974) speaks of deceitful women. Relating to a different group of consumers, 'Streakin' Cheek to Cheek' (1974) recounts the adventures of students who streak on college campuses. Other songs such as 'Fire' (1974), 'FOPP' (1975), 'Honey' (1975), 'Sweet Sticky Thing' (1975), and 'Angel' (1977), extol sexual pleasures using double entendre or coded language.[31]

Although the Ohio Players came from working-class backgrounds and had a large following among this group, their music also appealed to black professionals. Bridging cultural differences between the two groups, the Players economized the use of words and evolved a musical style marked by the values of both social

---

29   James 'Diamond' Williams, interview with author, Dayton, Ohio, 19 August 1997.
30   Keith Harrison, interview, Dayton, Ohio, 19 August 1997.
31   Ibid.

classes. According to bass player Marshall Jones, they employed as few 'words as possible to make a point because we weren't playing for an educated class. But at the same time, we recognized that educated people were there.' Although Marshall contended that their musical style 'wasn't just all funky or all real smooth and glossy', it represented a blues–jazz–funk hybrid as illustrated in 'Pain' (1971), 'Skin Tight' (1974) and 'There it Is' (nd).[32] By fusing elements from these traditions with the sounds of street life, Dayton Street Funk reflected the musical traditions, aesthetic values and cultural sensibilities of both the black working and social-middle class.

In earlier decades various black musical traditions had been the focal point of West Dayton's social and cultural life. In the 1940s and 1950s the theatres and clubs featured jazz greats such as Cab Calloway, Count Basie, Ella Fitzgerald and Billy Eckstine. In the 1950s and 1960s blues and R&B artists, including Little Richard, Jimmy Reed, Big Maybelle and Fats Domino, as well as soul-music artists, frequently performed in Dayton. Moreover, the city developed and showcased its local musicians, many of whom joined the bands of Jimmie Lunceford, Lionel Hampton, Duke Ellington, Count Basie, Dizzy Gillespie and Ray Charles. Several local bands also travelled with, or backed up, national R&B acts that came to the city such as James Brown, Wilson Pickett, The O'Jays and Motown's artists.[33]

Rooted in southern vernacular traditions, members of the Ohio Players first played in blues and jazz bands and served as studio musicians under the name of the Untouchables for R&B singers Jackie Wilson and the Falcons. Reorganizing as the Ohio Players in 1965, the group evolved a unique instrumental sound defined by a rhythmic 'groove' that interlocked a syncopated bass guitar and drum pattern over which a 'riffing' horn and a pulsating rhythm section provided layers of different rhythmic structures. The rhythmic patterns and bodily movements of dancers in clubs inspired Marshall Jones's bass lines: 'I'd always find somebody on the dance floor and I would watch how they moved. I would watch them flowing with the hips and then move. And I would get in sync with that pattern.'[34] Examples of this pattern are heard in 'Fire' (1974), 'Who'd She Coo?' (1976), and 'O-H-I-O' (1977). Roger and Larry Troutman, protégés of the Ohio Players, also recognized the importance of deriving rhythmic patterns from the moves of dancers: 'A lot of times, we'll watch people in discotheques and say now, we need to make a song to make people dance. And we'd make comments to each other as we watch people moving in discos. That's how "Dance Floor" came about.'[35] These forms of musical and social interactions with black people kept the Players, Roger and other funk groups in touch with the pulse and changing dance trends in African-American communities.

---

32   Marshall Jones, interview, 19 August 1991.
33   Ibid.; VanZant, interview, 13 March 1988; L. Lewis Jr, interview, 19 August 1997; Ralf McGinnis, interview with author, Dayton, Ohio, 18 August 1997.
34   Marshall Jones, interview, 19 August 1991.
35   Roger Troutman and Larry Troutman, interview with Karen Shearer Productions, Los Angeles, California, 8 August 1982.

As the Ohio Players evolved the street funk sound in West Dayton, Charlie White, a local teenager in the 1960s, observed that they provided entertainment for the community:

> Groups of bands were everywhere, on corners. I remember the Ohio Players practicing every Saturday outside of this garage on Western Avenue. Kids from that neighborhood and every other neighborhood would come and it was almost like a talent show going on right there. They had the electricity hooked up for their instruments and someone provided them with long extension cords to practice. And adults would stop what they were doing and come over and listen.[36]

These weekend activities soon became commonplace in every Westside neighbourhood and led to the formation of approximately 20 teenage bands whose members later came under the mentorship of the Ohio Players. According to Roger Troutman:

> All of the groups that came from this area bounced off the Ohio Players. When the Ohio Players reached their success, they reached into each local group in Dayton, Ohio and picked out one or two members to play with them. When they left the Ohio Players, they went back to their friends and formed their own groups. I think that's why so many [successful] groups came from Dayton – the impact that they [the Ohio Players] had on young talent.[37]

The empowered and cohesive middle-class communities supported the musical ambitions of Dayton's youth by purchasing and renting instruments, sound systems and vans; providing rehearsal space in their homes, garages and clubs; and serving as managers, chaperones and costume designers. Participating in music school programmes and performing in talent shows, clubs and venues throughout the community prepared these bands to open shows for, and back up, nationally renowned singers, and to perform in the surrounding areas of Kentucky, Indiana, and Virginia while in high school.[38]

---

36   White, interview, 19 August 1997.
37   Roger Troutman, interview with Karen Shearer Productions, Los Angeles, California, 4 August 1983.
38   Harrison, interview, 19 August 1997; Verneda Sandridge, interview with Stephanie Shonekan, Dayton, Ohio, 12 March 1998; White, interview, 19 August 1997; Caldwell, interview, 24 July 1998; McGinnis, interview, 18 August 1997.

Dayton Street Funk in the Context of Economic and Social Change

In the mid-1970s the first of these Dayton funk bands secured recording contracts with major record labels in New York City and Los Angeles.[39] Their first charted songs appeared during the changing economic and social conditions of the 1973–75 recession. Historian Joe Trotter observed:

> The growing exodus of industrial jobs from the central cities signaled a new phase in black urban life; it cut them off from employment opportunities and facilitated the expansion of what we now call the urban underclass. One result was increasing frustration and anger.[40]

This phase of industrialization coincided with the government's policy of fiscal conservatism and society's retreat from the 1960s equal rights legislation. Collectively, these developments brought about a changing mood in African-American communities. The optimism that once prevailed in the middle class transformed into feelings of ambivalence, and the unemployed expressed their disillusionment at the system that had failed them.[41] Black professionals in suburban and metropolitan areas, who earlier had moved out of African-American communities, often retreated from their integrated neighbourhoods and work environments into black city neighbourhoods. Intermingling and re-establishing social ties with the black poor and working classes in clubs and other social settings, the black poor/working classes and the middle classes 'temporarily liberated themselves from the restrictions and frustrating encounters in mainstream society. Funk music prevailed in these social settings, and party-funk reigned supreme.'[42]

Party-funk encouraged black people to 'hang loose' and 'boogie' on the dance floor. Building on the foundation established by the Ohio Players, the second wave of Dayton musicians produced a party-funk style that Norman Beavers of Lakeside described as 'a form of escapism from social problems'. To help black people 'forget about the bad times', Lakeside recreated past eras of adventure. Drawing from childhood fantasies, they wrote songs and created personas around historical characters such as Robin Hood on *Shot of Love* (1978), Arabian knights on *Your Wish*

---

39 'Sound of Dayton: 9 Local Bands Gain Success by Recording', *Dayton Daily News* (16 March 1980): 1-D.

40 Trotter Jr, 'Blacks in the Urban North', p. 80.

41 William Moore Jr and Lonnie H. Wagstaff, *Black Educators in White Colleges* (San Francisco, CA, 1974); George Davis and Glegg Watson, *Black Life in Corporate America: Swimming in the Main Stream* (Garden City, NY, 1982); Gerald R. Gill, *Meanness Mania: The Changed Mood* (Washington, DC, 1980); Manning, *Race, Reform and Rebellion*, pp. 61–113; Brisbane, *Black Activism*; Sidney Fine, *Violence in the Modern City: Race Relations, Cavanagh Administration, and the Detroit Race Riots of 1967* (Ann Arbor, MI, 1989).

42 Maultsby, 'Funk', p. 683.

is My Command (1982), cowboys on Rough Riders (1979), pirates on Fantastic Voyage (1980), and FBI agents on Untouchables (1983). In live performances they brought life to these characters.[43]

Imaginary people and places served multiple functions for African-Americans. They provided social spaces for black people to exercise cultural autonomy, to redefine their world and to temporarily escape the hardships and frustrations of daily life. The Detroit 'funkateer' George Clinton, the mastermind of the P-funk (pure funk) concept, was the first to introduce fictionalized black characters to signify a new black world order. The manifestation of this concept in the spectacular theatrical productions of Clinton's groups – Parliament, Funkadelic, Parlet, Brides of Funkenstein, and Bootsy's Rubber Band – advanced live performances of funk to another level.

P-Funk: The Construction of a Chocolate City

P-funk is defined by a philosophy, attitude, culture and musical style. 'Grounded in the ideology of Black Power, P-funk advocated self-liberation from the social and cultural restrictions of society by creating new social spaces for African Americans to redefine themselves and celebrate their blackness.'[44] In a National Public Radio profile of George Clinton, producer Steve Rowland contended that various socioeconomic classes of African-Americans embraced P-funk because '[i]t appealed to the heads and to the hard core, to the intellectual and to the street'.[45] Using advanced technologies, Clinton created and staged elaborate funk-operas about black people from a black perspective. These stories centred on black mythical and science-fiction heroes and villains and, according to Clinton, 'place[d] blacks in places where you don't conceive of them being'.[46] For example, the production of the P-funk Earth Tour, based on the concept of the Mothership Connection (1975) by Parliament, placed the original funkateers on an imaginary planet.

Clinton, as Dr Funkenstein, and his crew returned to earth to bring back the funk – the aesthetic values, traditions and spiritual force that underlay black cultural expression. During the ship's landing, a battery of synthesizers produced an array of sound effects accentuated by spectacular and colourful flashing lights, lasers, smoke machines and other props. After landing, dressed in unconventional and space-fashioned costumes, the group performed a medley of songs, such as

---

43 Lakeside, interview with Karen Shearer Productions, Los Angeles, California, 28 January 1982.

44 Maultsby, 'Funk', p. 683.

45 Steve Rowland, 'Live Commentary on "Profile of George Clinton, the Master of Funk"', Weekend Edition, National Public Radio, 6 February 1994.

46 George Clinton, interview with author, Bloomington, Indiana, 5 March 1995. As a resident of Washington, DC, Newark, New Jersey and Detroit, he had a unique perspective on life in the black metropolis.

'P. Funk (Wants to Get Funked Up)', 'Mothership Connection (Star Child)', 'Unfunky UFO', 'Supergroovalisticprosifunkstication', and 'Night of the Thumpasorus Peoples', which employed a range of black musical traditions. In subsequent recordings and tours, Clinton fully developed the funk-opera concept, constructing stories around the imaginary characters of 'Sir Nose D'Voidoffunk', 'Mr Wiggles', 'Rumpofsteelskin', and 'Gloryhallastupid'[47] in *Clones of Dr. Funkenstein* (1976), *Funkentelkechy vs. the Placebo Syndrome* (1977), *Motor Booty Affair* (1978), and *Gloryhallastupid* (1979).

The influence of Clinton's P-Funk production concepts, especially his use of technology, was evident in the live performances of Sun, a group from Dayton that struggled to established musical direction. Influenced by the films *Close Encounters* (1977) and *Star Wars* (1977), Sun dressed in costumes that symbolized the universe and they created synthesized out-of-space sound effects in songs such as 'Sun Is Here' (1978) and 'Radiation Level' (1979). Their shows, however, were far less elaborate than Clinton's productions. Nevertheless, Sun's employment of technology reflected changing trends in American popular music that, in the 1980s, had an impact on the Dayton Street Funk tradition.

The 1980s Techno-Funk: Black Culture and American Popular Music

In the 1980s, and at a time when all inner-city communities were in chaos, funk music evolved in many new directions. The second recession (1980–82), ongoing fiscal and social conservatism, President Ronald Reagan's gradual dismantling of Affirmative Action programmes and the cumulative impact of deindustrialization, thrust poor and working-class blacks into severe poverty. Abandoned factories, boarded buildings, dilapidated houses, the homeless, and drug addicts were common sights of community devastation.[48] Within this context, party-funk became 'a way of sustaining the everyday rituals of black folks. It ... comforts a wounded folk.'[49]

Party-funk echoed the sounds of the American metropolis during the 1980s Advances in musical technology, the emergence of disco as a distinct techno-pop style in the late 1970s and the pressure put on black groups by record labels to produce a slicker and homogenized sound for mass marketing propelled changes

---

47 Photos of these characters and scenes from the P-Funk Earth Tour are included in Diem Jones, *#1 Bimini Road: Authentic P-Funk Insights* (Oakland, CA, 1996). For more detailed information on P-funk and other funk groups, see Vincent, *Funk*, pp. 231–64.

48 Landry, *The New Black Middle Class*, pp. 196–233; Manning, *Race, Reform, and Rebellion*, pp. 191–213; Sugrue, *The Origins of Urban Crisis*, pp. 259–71.

49 Cornell West, Radio interview on 'Profile of George Clinton, the Master of Funk', *Weekend Edition* (National Public Radio, 6 February 1994).

in this tradition. The new musical technologies first popularized in disco influenced the reconfiguration and shifts in the musical directions of many funk bands. By the late 1970s, according to Marshall Jones of the Ohio Players, 'computers had started coming into the industry and the beat was more infectious because computers can do things rhythmically that musicians actually can't do'.[50] To remain competitive against the popularity of disco, many funk bands replaced bass and horn players with synthesizers and incorporated disco elements into their music.

In making these changes, some groups experienced difficulty in redefining their musical direction. The group Dayton, for example, reached its maturity in the transitional period between disco and funk. Trumpet and keyboard player Chris Jones recalled: 'There wasn't a whole lot of deep funk with Dayton.'[51] Dayton's use of advanced technology resulted in a more sophisticated and disco-oriented sound with less obvious funk roots. Similar to Heatwave's 'Boogie Nights' (1977) and 'The Groove Line' (1978), Dayton's sound was a funk-disco-jazz hybrid ('I Got My Eye on You' [1980] and 'The Sound of Music' [1983]) that reflected the musical values of the metropolis. Their biggest hit, 'Hot Fun in the Summertime' (1982), however, was a funk-disco remake of a song by Sly and the Family Stone. In contrast to Dayton, Steve Arrington (former member of Slave) successfully incorporated synthesizers and disco elements, including the disco-beat in his Dayton funk style. A drummer turned vocalist, Arrington cleverly used technology to add new textures and a different type of rhythmic complexity to the Dayton funk sound in 'Nobody Can Be You' (1983) and 'Dancin' in the Key of Life' (1985).

Funk groups from other cities also faced the dilemma of adjusting to changing trends in popular music, including the Memphis-based group Con Funk Shun. Con Funk Shun's first charted singles in the Top 10, 'Ffun' (1977) and 'Shake and Dance with Me' (1978), employed the traditional funk style that featured a prominent horn section and a heavy rhythmic foundation. A year later, and with the release of 'Chase Me' from the album *Candy* (1979), the group began moving away from the traditional funk sound. According to vocalist and synthesizer player Felton Pilate, 'Disco was really happening and we tried to fuse funk and disco [on 'Candy']. Another song 'Let Me Put Love on Your Mind' was experimental – rock guitar solos over a ballad kind of feeling.'[52] In 1980 Con Funk Shun experimented with 'pop' elements as noted in the promotional materials released by Mercury/PolyGram Records:

> 'Too Tight', the first single from Con Funk Shun's newest album Touch marks a departure from their traditional funk trademark, and may have the distinction of helping to create a new musical category – 'pop-funk'.

---

50   Marshall Jones, interview, 19 August 1997.
51   Chris Jones, interview with author, Dayton, Ohio, 18 August 1997.
52   Felton Pilate, interview with Karen Shearer Productions, Los Angeles, California, 7 June 1985.

'Too Tight' peaked at no. 8 on Billboard's Rhythm and Blues charts. Two years later, Con Funk Shun recorded many songs without a horn section, replacing it with synthesizers. Pilate explained: 'Most of the hits that are out now are just not saturated with horns anymore. I try to be a competitive writer and if I'm going to try to be commercial, then I got to pay attention to what's really happening'.[53]

By 1984 Con Funk Shun had moved even further in the 'pop' direction as described in the promotional materials that accompanied the release of *Fever* (1984):

> *Since singing with Mercury in 1976 and releasing their debut LP, Con Funk Shun...the band became known for their horn-driven funk sound, but recently they've played down that element somewhat, while still remaining decidedly funky. On the new LP, only one song features brass. 'We've used more synthesizers instead' explained vocalist Felton Pilate 'This way the LP sounds more pop, which is what we want.'*

Although Con Funk Shun employed different concepts on each album in response to new trends and technologies in popular music, another Memphis group adapted to these changes without compromising the essence of their funk style. The Bar-Kays maintained a successful career that spanned over three decades by staying in touch with the changing trends in the black community, especially among its youth. Lead singer Larry Dodson explained the role of this group in inspiring musical creativity:

> *We try to grow with each album. We always try to reach and touch the younger people. We can stay ahead of the masses by listening to the younger people. They are the best judges that we have of our music.[54]*

The Bar-Kays integrated technology and pop elements into their sound in a way that reflected the musical tastes and dance trends of black youth. Without diluting their southern party-funk style, marked by an intense and punctuating horn section and heavy rhythmic foundation, they produced many hits throughout the disco era. While keeping abreast of new trends in popular music and acknowledging that 'synthesizers have taken over', the group used 'horns as though they were an electronic instrument like synthesizers and mixed them in'.[55] Rather than eliminating horns, the Bar-Kays used them in a different way – one that blended in acoustic sounds of the South with the technological sounds of the metropolis. This successful mix of regional traditions is heard in 'Move Your Boogie Body' (1979),

---

53 Ibid.
54 Larry Dodson, interview with Karen Shearer Productions, Los Angeles, California, 17 July 1984.
55 Harvey Henderson, interview with Karen Shearer Productions, Los Angeles, California, 17 July 1984.

'Hit and Run' (1981), 'Do It (Let Me See You Shake)' (1982), and 'Freakshow on the Dance Floor' (1984).

Roger and Zapp (two groups comprised of overlapping family musicians) were among the most innovative funk groups in the 1980s. Employing advanced technology to modernize the Dayton Street Funk sound, they produced heavy dance rhythms combined with distorted and varied vocal and instrumental timbres. Roger Troutman experimented with the talk box (also known as the voice box) to 'find new ways to express words in music' as illustrated in 'More Bounce to the Ounce' (1980), 'I Heard It through the Grapevine' (1981), and 'Dance Floor' (1982).[56]

As George Clinton had done a decade earlier, Roger and Zapp used technology in ways that emphasized those aesthetic qualities associated with the black working class. Clinton, who built on the tradition of Sly and the Family Stone, the architects of funk, cleverly used synthesizers as an extension of both the voice and electric instruments, and to vary textures, timbres and moods of songs. Clinton and Stone also juxtaposed and blended a range of southern vernacular and urban musical genres, drawing from Negro spirituals, classical music,[57] blues and R&B to produce new interpretations of these musical genres in the funk tradition.[58]

Sly Stone and George Clinton also restored the blues as a major ingredient in contemporary black popular music. Clinton recognized the significance of this tradition in urban expressions when he described the rock style of Jimi Hendrix as 'loud blues': 'That's when I realized it was psychedelic. It was basic loud blues and a good show, good showmen. All the blues guys could play behind their head and in their teeth.'[59] While Hendrix became known as a blues-rock icon, Sly and the Family Stone from San Francisco developed a funk style that borrowed technology from rock such as the wah-wah pedal, fuzz box, echo chamber and vocal distorter. Sly Stone also incorporated the blues-rock guitar style with jazz flavourings to create a unique style that some critics labelled psychedelic-funk. George Clinton built on this tradition with his P-Funk All Stars, featuring blues-rock guitarists and positioning the guitar at the centre of musical activity. The younger black guitarists from Slave, Cameo, Con Funk Shun, as well as Rick James, adopted the blues-rock style and the showmanship of blues performers popularized by Jimi Hendrix. In essence, Stone and Clinton situated black popular music in vernacular traditions, thus exposing the blues roots of urban black musical expression and the blues roots of rock. The aesthetic of the blues appealed to the black poor and working classes

---

56 Roger Troutman, interview, 4 August 1983.

57 In Parliament's 'Mothership Connection (Star Child)', Clinton borrows the phrase 'swing down, sweet chariot/stop and let me ride' from the Negro spiritual 'Swing Low Sweet Chariot'. Clinton fuses elements from classical music in a Broadway-styled song 'Let Me Be' from *Chocolate City* by Parliament.

58 Maultsby, 'Funk', p. 684; and Portia K. Maultsby, 'Funk', in Mellonee V. Burnim and Portia K. Maultsby (eds), *African American Music: An Introduction* (New York, 2006), pp. 305–306.

59 Clinton, interview, 5 March 1995.

who identified with this sound in funk as well as the song lyrics based on their daily experiences.

Many funk musicians grew up in black poor and working-class communities with whom they maintained social ties after becoming successful musicians. Mark Adams of Slave acknowledged the importance of these ties for bands seeking to create music that mirrored the experiences of these groups:

> We knew certain things are going to happen because we never lose contact with our outside friends or just people in general. We hangout and talk to people. We study people ... we watch people and we just absorb what people are into, what people don't like, what makes a person sad, what makes a person happy. ... And that's how we come up with our music, our songs, our show. We base everything on that concept.[60]

Taking this same approach to musical creativity, the Bar-Kays wrote 'Shine' (1978) to take 'some of the pressure off people. It was designed to give people hope and help'.[61] Similarly, Roger wrote for Zapp 'I Can Make You Dance' (1983) so people 'could forget about their problems by just dancing'. Roger explains that the phrase 'so ruff, so tuff out here' in 'So Ruff, So Tuff' (1981) references 'the economy, the taxes, the phone bills, the whole bit'.[62]

The success of funk groups was also predicated on their ability to communicate messages using the vernacular language of the poor and working-class communities. Since black vernacular expressions and other cultural practices changed over time, musicians could miss cues if they remained outside the community loop for an extended period. James Alexander, the leader and bass player of the Bar-Kays, attributed the group's success for over three decades to keeping abreast of cultural change:

> We want to keep our black following. A big part in remaining popular is being able to change. People change and music changes and if you don't keep in constant communication and contact with the people that buy your records, they will leave you. They will change, they will have a different language and they will use another set of words that always mean the opposite....If you're not here hanging and dealing with your audience, then you will lose them.[63]

Phrases and words such as 'It's All the Way Live' (1978) and 'Outrageous' (1984) by Lakeside, 'Fresh' by Kool and the Gang' (1984), 'Word Up' (1986) by Cameo, 'Hit and Run' (1981) by Slave, and 'Jive Turkey' (1974) and 'Skin Tight' (1974) by the

---

60 Slave, interview with Karen Shearer Productions, Los Angeles, California, 21 October 1981. Interactions with the black community inspired the hit songs 'Slide' (1977) and 'The Party Song' (1977).
61 Dodson, interview, 17 July 1984.
62 Ibid.
63 James Alexander, interview with author. Los Angeles, California, 13 March 1983.

Ohio Players, illustrate how funk musicians incorporated black slang of the poor and working classes into the funk tradition.

Although vernacular expressions dominate in party-funk tradition, they are found in lyrics discussing social and political commentary,[64] romance[65] and general life experiences. The lyrics of funk musicians also reflected changing conditions in African-American inner-city communities. When the traditional economic resources and recreational programmes were no longer available, especially for youth, drugs infiltrated and became commonplace in urban communities in the 1970s. Robin Kelley noted that 'massive joblessness contributed to the expansion of the underground economy, and young people, not surprisingly, are among its biggest employees'.[66] Many funk and other musicians used and wrote about drugs. This theme, often masked through the use of double entendre, is found in the 'Mothership Connection' (1975) by Parliament, 'Riding High' by the Dayton group Faze-O (1977), and 'Mary Jane' (1978) by Rick James.

In contrast, Earth, Wind and Fire from Chicago promoted universal messages of love and world peace that are best illustrated on the album *That's Way of The World* (1975). Maurice White, the group's leader and primary songwriter who described himself as a spiritual and philosophical person, wrote the title song 'with so much desire for balance in the world … for peace and harmony and love. … It was written with the desire for establishing awareness of self and awareness of your fellow man and the awareness of the world around.'[67] A few years earlier, Sly Stone and his interracial group promoted an end to racial injustices through universal love and harmony in 'Everyday People' (1969) and 'Stand!' (1969).

In the 1980s songs with a different universal message brought people of different races and background together around a common cause – to celebrate! The song 'Celebration' (1980) by Kool and the Gang was based on the concept of 'people getting away from the day to day things and having a party, living their life'. Ronald Bell believed that this song crossed racial, class, social and generational boundaries because 'the timing was right, the mood of the country, whether it was the return of the [Iran-Contra] hostages, the Super Bowl games – everything was a celebration'.[68] Since all people celebrate various events, 'Celebration' quickly became a favourite among many people throughout the country, as illustrated by its wide use in television and radio commercials.

---

64 These songs include: Sly Stone, 'Everyday People' (1969), 'Stand' (1969), 'Don't Call Me Nigga, Whitey' (1969); Kool and the Gang, 'Who's Gonna Take the Weight' (1970); War, 'Slipping into Darkness' (1971) and 'The World is a Ghetto' (1972); and Ohio Players, 'Far East Mississippi' (1976).

65 All funk groups recorded ballads or love songs that were called funk ballads because of their underlying funk rhythms.

66 Robin D.G. Kelley, *Yo' Mama's DisFunktional!: Fighting the Cultural Wars in Urban America* (Boston, 1977), p. 47.

67 Maurice White, Interview with Karen Shearer Productions, Los Angeles, California, 10 February 1983.

68 Robert 'Kool' Bell, interview with Karen Shearer Productions, Los Angeles, California, 20 October 1983.

Social trends in popular culture also inspired other songs of universal appeal. The song 'Ladies Night' (1979) by Kool and the Gang, for example, referenced a marketing strategy of discotheques that admitted women without admission on a designated weeknight. Songwriter Robert 'Kool' Bell explained the source for the lyrics of this song: 'I was hanging out in New York City and I noticed in a few clubs on Wednesday nights were "Ladies Night". And I said, hey, that could be a good concept for an album and a song. We all got together and we came up with "Ladies Night".'[69] Many clubs throughout the country hosted a 'Ladies Night', and 'Ladies Night' became the theme song used to promote this event.

Although funk music originated in working-class communities, in the 1980s its audiences grew beyond these areas through the popularity of disco music. Just as funk musicians incorporated disco elements in their music, many disco artists added funk to their disco sound. Artists such as Silver Convention, Chic, A Taste of Honey, Cheryl Lynn and Sister Sledge among others, further spread funk into the mainstream by borrowing the rhythms and musical stylings from this tradition in the creation of a disco-funk hybrid style.

Regardless of these and other musical borrowings, funk retained its regional identities through various stages of musical change. Dayton's Street Funk groups, for example, can be identified by certain markers that define their roots in the Midwest, Ohio, and Dayton, which are manifested in group names, their constructed images and song lyrics. In the name Ohio Players, 'Ohio' references the state of Ohio and 'Players' references the people associated with West Dayton's street life and night life. Similarly, the group Dayton signifies the city of Dayton, as well as the cultural values of college graduates who comprised a component of the black middle class. First known as the Imperials in high school, Shawn Sandridge, the group's leader adopted a conservative, professional image in contrast to the players' persona of the Ohio Players. Shawn's mother selected and coordinated the costumes for the Imperials, who performed in and around the surrounding states:

> I didn't want them going out with outrageous outfits. I kept them in shirts, ties, and suits and things like that, except if it were casual, we would have shirts with their names on it, different colors, still very conservative. And they didn't seem to mind. They got a lot of compliments, especially [from] the older people ... 'cause they liked the way they dressed.[70]

Shawn retained this conservative persona when he founded Dayton.

Lakeside also embodied local markers of the city, adopting their name from a local amusement park and entertainment venue complex called the Lakeside Palladian. This entertainment venue featured performances by national black artists and Dayton's funk bands.[71] The amusement park housed many of the characters

---

69   Kool and The Gang, interview with Karen Shearer Productions, Los Angeles, California, 29 September 1981.
70   Sandridge, interview, 12 March 1998.
71   Ibid.; L. Lewis Jr, interview, 19 August 1997.

from which Lakeside drew themes for song lyrics and constructed various stage personas. Moreover, the rides from this park provided a source for metaphors in songs like 'Love Rollercoaster' (1975) and 'Merry Go Round' (1977) by the Ohio Players. Lastly, many of the songs recorded by the Dayton funk groups represents the traditions, lifestyles and heterophonic voices of West Dayton's diverse, yet cohesive, black community.

Although regional and local markers distinguished funk groups from one another, these groups also shared many common lyric themes, images and practices that had social and cultural meaning among black people across regional and class boundaries. Regardless of region and community of residence, the social and economic policies of the 1970s and 1980s had some form of negative impact on the lives of African-Americans. The recessions and budget cuts, the elimination of social and recreational programmes, the militarization of urban life, and the physical deterioration of inner cities resulted in experiences and responses shared by residents of these communities. Resistance to, and changes in, Affirmative Action programmes also generated a common set of responses among many members of the black middle and elite classes. Changing social and economic policies, as well as musical innovation, underlie the success of funk musicians across regional and class boundaries, as illustrated in the popularity of the P-Funk tours and described by Rickey Vincent:

> The thematic content of the music and art created by the P-Funk mob has reached people far and wide. What Clinton and his funky tribe did was to create an alternate world view, complete with the creation [of] myths, funky super-heroes, and a framework for black fantasy and spiritual cultivation that could withstand the pressure of living in a white world. By reaching audiences on their terms, Clinton and his band created a center from which urban blacks could interpret conscious and unconscious reality, and operate as if they were already free. The impact of this body of work lives on today.[72]

The music, lyrics and images of Dayton's Street Funk groups impacted on African-Americans in similar ways and they continue to take on new life in American popular culture through funk tours, television programmes, media advertising and funk samples used in hip-hop music.[73]

---

72   Vincent, *Funk*, p. 263.
73   The Ohio's Players' 'Funky Worm' (1972) and Zapp/Roger's 'More Bounce to the Ounce' (1980) are among the songs most sampled by hip-hop groups.

Interviews

Recordings of the following interviews have been deposited at the Indiana University, Archives of African American Music and Culture as part of the Portia Maultsby, Dayton Funk and Karen Shearer collections.

Alexander, James, Personal interview. Los Angeles, CA. 13 March 1983.

Bell, Robert 'Kool'. Interview with Karen Shearer Productions. Los Angeles, CA. 20 October 1983.

Caldwell, James. Interview with Stephanie Shonekan. Dayton, OH. 24 July 1998.

Carter, Iula Carter. Interview with Stephanie Shonekan. Dayton, OH. 11 March 1998.

Clinton, George. Personal interview. Bloomington, IN. 5 March 1995.

Dixon, Richard L. Personal interview. Dayton, OH. 19 August 1997.

Dodson, Larry. Interview with Karen Shearer Productions. Los Angeles, CA. 17 July 1984.

Harrison, Keith. Personal interview. Dayton, OH. 19 August 1997.

Henderson, Harvey. Interview with Karen Shearer Productions. Los Angeles, CA. 17 July 1984.

Jones, Chris. Personal interview. Dayton, OH. 18 August 1997.

Jones, Marshall. Personal interview. Dayton, OH. 19 August 1997.

Kool and The Gang. Interview with Karen Shearer Productions. Los Angeles, California. 29 September 1981.

Lakeside. Interview with Karen Shearer Productions. Los Angeles, CA. 28 January 1982.

Lewis, Charles. Personal interview. Dayton, OH. 18 August 1997.

Lewis Jr, Lloyd E. Personal interview. Dayton, OH. 19 August 1997

Locket, Thomas. Personal interview. Dayton, OH. 18 August 1997.

McCloud, Harry. Personal interview. Dayton, OH. 1 July 1997.

McGinnis, Ralph. Personal interview. Dayton, OH. 18 August 1997.

Peters, Margaret. Personal interview. Dayton, OH. 18 August 1997

Pilate, Felton. Interview with Karen Shearer Productions. Los Angeles, CA. 7 June 1985.

Pilate, Felton. Personal interview. Dayton, OH. 18 August 1997.

Sampson, Carol. Telephone interview. 14 June 1998.

Sandridge, Verneda. Interview with Stephanie Shonekan. Dayton, OH. 24 July 1998.

Slave. Interview with Karen Shearer Productions. Los Angeles, CA. 21 October 1981.

Smith, Ricky. Personal Interview. Dayton, OH. 18 August 1997.

Spencer, Charles. Interview with Stephanie Shonekan. Dayton, OH. 24 July 1998.

Troutman, Roger. Interview with Karen Shearer Productions. Los Angeles, CA. 4 August 1983.

Troutman, Roger and Troutman, Larry. Interview with Karen Shearer Productions. Los Angeles, CA. 8 August 1982.

Troutman, Terry. Personal interview. Dayton, OH. 19 August 1997.

VanZant, John. Interview with Stephanie Shonekan. Dayton, OH. 13 March 1998.

Webster, Danny. Personal interview. Dayton, OH. 18 August 1997.

Webster, Greg. Interview with Stephanie Shonekan. Dayton, OH. 12 March 1998.

West, Cornell, Radio interview on 'Profile of George Clinton, the Master of Funk', *Weekend Edition* (National Public Radio, 6 February 1994).

White, Maurice. Interview with Karen Shearer Productions. Los Angeles, CA. 10 February 1983.

White, Charlie. Personal interview. Dayton, OH. 19 August 1997.

Wilder, Johnny. Telephone interview. 19 August 1997.

Williams, James 'Diamond'. Personal interview. Dayton, OH. 19 August 1997.

Williams, Walt. Telephone interview. 15 June 1998.

Discography

Arrington, Steve, 'Nobody Can Be You', *Steve Arrington's Hall of Fame, Vol. 1* (Atlantic 7800491, 1983)

Bar-Kays, 'Do It (Let Me See You Shake)', *Propositions* (Mercury SRM-1-4065, 1982).

——, 'Freakshow on the Dance Floor', *Dangerous* (Mercury 818478-1, 1984).

——, 'Hit and Run', *Nightcruising* (Mercury SRM-1-4028, 1981).

——, 'Move Your Boogie Body', *Injoy* (Mercury SRM-1-3781, 1979).

——, 'Shine', *Light of Life* (Mercury SRM-1-3732, 1978).

Con Funk Shun, 'Ffun', *Secrets* (Mercury SRM-1-1180, 1977).

——, 'Let Me Put Love on Your Mind', *Candy* (Mercury, 1979).

——, 'Shake and Dance with Me', *Loveshine* (Mercury SRM-1-3725, 1978).

——, 'Too Tight', *Touch* (Mercury SRM-1-4002, 1981).

Dayton, 'Dancin' in the Key of Life', 1985.

——, 'Hot fun in the Summertime', *Hot Fun* (Liberty LT-51126, 1982).

——, 'I Got My Eye on You', *Dayton* (Liberty LT-1025, 1980).

——, 'The Sound of Music', *Feel the Music* (Capitol ST-12297, 1983).

Heatwave, 'Boogie Nights', *Too Hot to Handle* (Epic EK-34761, 1977).

——, 'The Groove Line', *Central Heating* (Epic JE-35260, 1978).

Kool and the Gang, 'Celebration', *Celebrate!* (De Lite DSR 9518, 1980).

——, 'Fresh', *Emergency* (De Lite 422 943-1 M-1, 1984).

——, 'Ladies Night', *Ladies Night* (De Lite DSR-9513, 1979).

——, 'Who's Gonna Take the Weight?', *Live at the Sex Machine* (De Lite DE-2008, 1970).

Lakeside, 'Outrageous', *Outrageous* (Solar 60355-1, 1984).

Ohio Players, 'Angel', *Angel* (Mercury SRM-1-3701, 1977).

——, 'Far East Mississippi', *Contradiction* (Mercury SRM-1-1088, 1976).

——, 'Fire', *Fire* (Mercury SRM-1-1013, 1974).

——, 'FOPP', *Honey* (Mercury SRM-1-1038, 1975).

——, 'Funky Worm', *Pleasure* (Westbound W-220, 1972).

——, 'Honey', *Honey* (Mercury SRM-1-1038, 1975).

——, 'Jive Turkey', *Skin Tight* (Mercury SRM-1-705, 1974).

——, 'Love Rollercoaster', *Honey* (Mercury SRM-1-1038, 1975).

——, 'Merry-Go-Round', *Angel* (Mercury SRM-1-3701, 1977).

——, 'O-H-I-O', *Angel* (Mercury SRM-1-3701, 1977).

——, 'Pain', *Pain* (Westbound WB 2015, 1971).

——, 'Skin Tight', *Skin Tight* (Mercury SRM-1-705, 1974).

——, 'Streaking Cheek to Cheek', *Skin Tight* (Mercury SRM-1-705, 1974).

——, 'Sweet Sticky Thing', *Honey* (Mercury SRM-1-1038, 1975).

——, 'There It Is', (nd). *Ohio Players: Funk on Fire* (Mercury 314 528 102-2)

——, 'Who'd She Coo?', *Contradiction* (Mercury SRM-1-1088, 1976).

Parliament, 'Let Me Be', *Chocolate City* (Casablanca NBP-7014, 1975).

——, 'Mothership Connection (Star Child)', *Mothership Connection* (Casablanca NBLP 7022, 1976).

——, 'Night of the Thumpasorus Peoples', *Mothership Connection* (Casablanca NBLP 7022, 1976).

——, 'P-Funk (Wants to Get Funked Up)', *Mothership Connection* (Casablanca NBLP 7022, 1976).

——, 'Supergroovalisticprosifunkstication', *Mothership Connection* (Casablanca NBLP 7022, 1976).

——, 'Unfunky UFO', *Mothership Connection* (Casablanca 7 NBLP 022, 1976).

Roger, 'I Heard It through the Grapevine', *The Many Facets of Roger* (Warner Bros. BSK-3594, 1981).

——, 'So Ruff, So Tuff', *The Many Facets of Roger* (Warner Bros. BSK-3594, 1981).

Slave, 'The Party Song', *The Hardness of the World* (Cotillion SD 5201, 1977).

——, 'Slide', *Slave* (Cotillion SD 5200, 1977).

Sly and the Family Stone, 'Don't Call Me Nigga, Whitey', *Stand!* (Epic BN 26456, 1969).

——, 'Everyday People', *Stand!* (Epic BN 26456, 1969).

——, 'Stand!', *Stand!* (Epic BN 26456, 1969).

Sun, 'Radiation Level', *Destination: Sun* (Capitol ST-11941, 1979).

——, 'Sun Is Here', *Sunburn* (Capitol ST-11723, 1978).

War, 'Slippin' into Darkness', *All Day Music* (United Artists UAS-5546, 1971). [remove g from slipping]

——, 'The World Is a Ghetto', *The World Is a Ghetto* (United Artists UAS-5654, 1972).

Zapp, 'Dance Floor', *Zapp II* (Warner Bros. 1-23583, 1982).

——, 'I Can Make You Dance', *Zapp III* (Warner Bros. 1-23875, 1983).

——, 'More Bounce to the Ounce', *Zapp* (Warner Bros. BSK 3463, 1980).

Black, White and Brown
on the Dance Floor:
The New Meanings of Panjabiyat
in the Twenty-first Century

Anjali Gera Roy

The relationship between music, ethnicity and identity is nowhere as apparent as in popular and academic discussions of Bhangra including those in anthropology, sociology and studies of culture, religion, music and dance, in addition to the print and electronic media. Bhangra scholarship examines it largely in relation to the identity politics of South Asian diasporic formations in Britain, Canada and North America in which Bhangra becomes the site for the production and contestation of hybrid, in-between diasporic identities by second- and third-generation youth of Indian/South Asian origin. Even though the euphoric declarations of 'the Asian youth finding their voice' of the late 1980s and early 1990s[1] gradually gave way to wry cynicism in the unpacking of the new politics of ethnicity and identity in subsequent examinations of South Asian youth subcultures,[2] Bhangra continues to be theorized through an ethnic lens even in more recent studies.[3] With its heavy

---

1   Sabita Banerji, 'From Ghazals to Bhangra in Great Britain', *Popular Music* 7/2 (1981): 207–14; Sabita Banerji and Gerd Baumann, 'Bhangra 1984–8: Fusion and Professionalization in a Genre of South Asian Dance Music' in Paul Oliver (ed.), *Black Music in Britain: Essays on the Afro-Asian Contribution to Popular Music* (Milton Keynes, 1990), 137–53; Marie Gillespie, *Television, Ethnicity, and Cultural Change* (London, 1995).
2   Sanjay Sharma, John Hutnyk, and Ashwani Sharma (eds), *Disorienting Rhythms: The Politics of the New Asian Dance Music* (London, 1996); Bennett, Andy, 'Bhangra in Newcastle: Music, Ethnic Identity and the Role of Local Knowledge', *Innovation: The European Journal of the Social Sciences* 10/1 (1997): 107–16.
3   R.K. Dudrah, 'Drum N Dhol: British Bhangra Music and Diasporic South Asian Identity Formation', *European Journal of Cultural Studies* 5/3 (2002): 363–83; Tony Ballantyne, *Between Colonialism and Diaspora: Sikh Cultural Formations in an Imperial World* (Durham, NC, 2006).

investment in the politics of race, ethnicity, language, gender, caste, region and religion, it is not surprising that aesthetic or musical analysis of Bhangra texts has been marginalized to ideological considerations or the focus on uses and gratifications that is found in media and cultural studies. In this chapter I wish to investigate the production of Bhangra with the objective of examining the consolidation of ethnic identity in multicultural nations and societies in the wake of globalization and to focus on the benefits and dangers of the return of ethnicity in the identity discourses in the global village. The rhetoric of cultural difference in multiculturalism is seen as emerging from, and replicating, the older politics of race, colour, caste and religion in addition to building a new politics of ethnicity in which a mobilization of ethnicities fills us with multicultural hope but also makes us uncomfortable as participants in a neo-orientalizing world.

Bhangra scholars have highlighted the connection between the Bhangra revival of the mid-1980s and the construction of a distinctive South Asian identity, viewing it largely as a 'response to the pressure to perform a coherent, stable and essential ethnic identity in the face of white racism'.[4] At the same time, they have raised concerns about the valorization of the 'authentic ethnic' within flows of global capital[5] and the appropriation of ethnic difference as exotica by white mainstream performers thereby normalizing the resistance of South Asian subcultures while relegating serious concerns about racism, violence and exploitation in the lived experience of South Asian ethnicities to the background.[6] Early celebrations of Bhangra hailing it as the ethnocultural signifier of South Asian identity have come in for a lot of criticism, particularly from younger South Asian scholars, on account of their reductionism which repeats the anthropological project of essentializing South Asian others by subsuming differences of language, region, ethnicity, religion, gender, class and ethnicity under a single category.[7] These scholars, while acknowledging Bhangra's role in consolidating South Asian identities in the face of white racism, have underlined the need for sensitivity to particular differences within South Asian groups that forge 'a strategic retreat to more defensive identities ... in response to the experience of cultural racism'.[8] Warning against reproducing

---

4   Raiford Guins and Omayra Zaragoza Cruz, *Popular Culture: A Reader* (London, 2005), p. 298. From Dick Hebdige's classic statement about Bhangra breaking up an 'imaginary Britishness' to Timothy Taylor's statement about its being 'the first music in this community to help promote and solidify a unified Anglo-Asian identity', Bhangra has been viewed as critical to 'Anglo-Asian self-fashioning'.

5   Ashwani Sharma, 'Sounds Oriental: The (Im)possibility of Theorising Asian Musical Cultures' in Sharma, Hutnyk and Sharma, *Disorienting Rhythms*, pp. 1–11.

6   John Hutnyk, *Critique of Exotica: Music, Politics and the Culture Industry* (London, 2000); Virinder S. Kalra and John Hutnyk, 'Visibility, Appropriation and Resistance', Seminar 503 (2001). Available at: <http://www.india-seminar.com> (accessed 11 August 2008).

7   Sanjay Sharma, 'Noisy Asians or "Asian Noise"?' in Sharma, Hutnyk and Sharma, *Disorienting Rhythms*, pp. 32–57; Hutnyk, *Critique of Exotica*; Dudrah, 'Drum N Dhol'.

8   Stuart Hall, 'New Ethnicities' in A. Rattansi and J. Donald (eds), *Race, Culture and Difference* (London, 1992), pp. 252–59, at p. 308. As Kuljit Bhamra, one of the earliest producers of Bhangra, put it, 'There is really a need to stay together and be amongst

ethnographic essentialisms, they have drawn attention to the constructedness of identities produced in relation to Bhangra, illustrating Judith Butler's notion of performance and identity both literally and metaphorically.[9]

Bhangra's performance of diasporic youth and Panjabi ethnic identity must be examined in the context of the implication of cultural practices including dance, music, film, theatre and so on in the struggle for representation. The early responses in the UK to Bhangra that it is 'South Asian youth finding their voice' is predicated on the power of representation and the exclusion of South Asian groups from the space of representation. Commentators on Bhangra, focusing on the sense of being '(dis)located within a scopic economy of black and white', despite half a century of immigration, ascribe Bhangra's emergence to the erasure of South Asians in the British cultural space.[10] Invited to enter the sphere of production due to the shortage of human resources after the Second World War, South Asian migrants in the UK either remained silent or were misrepresented in high and popular national media. However, as the British nation was divided between the opposition of black against white, brownness could be articulated only in an idiom of blackness. Shut out from the exclusionary space of whiteness, Asians began by identifying with black culture and blackness, as is evident in this oft-quoted statement of Cobra's lead singer:

> *I can remember going to college discos a long time ago, when all you heard was Reggae, Reggae, Reggae. Asians were lost, they weren't accepted by whites so they drifted into the black culture, dressing like blacks, talking like them and listening to reggae. But now Bhangra has given them 'their' music and made them feel that they do have an identity. No matter if they are Gujratis, Punjabis or whatever, – Bhangra is Asian music for Asians.*[11]

Bally Sagoo, whose remixes of traditional Bhangra were instrumental in ushering the Bhangra revolution in Britain along with the Bhangra reggae fusions of Apache Indian, agreed:

> *Indian music was Indian music. So I just left that side of things and I moved into the Western side of things and I was getting into English and American music … I was a typical example of someone who didn't know what Asian people were about. I was too much into the Western society business. My friends were mainly black and I didn't have many Asian mates because of, talking fifteen years ago you know, we didn't have funky Asian music. Then*

---

your own owing to racism, and bhangra music has provided(for) that need'. Bhamra quoted in Gerd Baumann, *Contesting Culture: Discourses of Identity in Multi-Ethnic London* (Cambridge, 1996), p. 91.

9   Gayatri Gopinath, 'Bombay, U.K., Yuba City: Bhangra Music and the Engendering of Diaspora,' *Diaspora* 4/3 (Winter 1995): 303–21.

10   Guins and Cruz, *Popular Culture*, p. 299.

11   Lead Singer of Cobra quoted in Baumann, *Contesting Culture*, p. 156.

all of a sudden things just changed. I just got so much into it and my mates were like 'my god Bally Sagoo's doing Indian music'.[12]

However, Sagoo believed that the new music which 'incorporates black music, Indian music, all kinds of flavours' produced an inclusive black, rather than an occluding Panjabi or South Asian ,discourse of identity.[13] The reinvention of Bhangra in Britain in the mid-1980 occurred through this strategic alliance between black and brown that created a new musical genre of 'Punjabi-South Asian origins fused with Western/black dances musics'.[14] The words of Apache Indian, who is hailed as the first cross-over South Asian artist, sum up the spirit of British Bhangra:

My music is a reflection of all the influences that I grew up with. I mix the Indian sound and language from home with the reggae music on the street.[15]

A new metropolitan Bhangra, produced by 'processing traditional dhol and drum beats and Punjabi folk melodies with synthesizers and samplers, with a heavier bass line and mixed with Western pop and black dance rhythms' was first heard in the UK, although Bhangra had been around as long as the immigrants from Panjab.[16] Sagoo's famous recipe for Bhangra originally given to *Time* magazine: 'A bit of tablas and a bit of the Indian sound, but ring on the bass lines, the funky drum (dhol) beat and the James Brown samples' made it a global phenomenon in the next two decades.[17]

However,in the 1980s Bhangra attracted media attention, largely in connection with the afternoon raves or day-jams organized by enterprising DJs and event managers for second-generation South Asian immigrants to circumvent nighttime curfews and parental surveillance. Bobby Friction's experience is representative of those who frequented these parties:

I turned 15 in 1986and I'd go from school to the first Daytimers, at the Empire, Leicester Square, in the afternoons. The girls went into McDonalds' toilets to change and put on their make-up. There was nothing outside our front doors then for young Punjabis and British Asians; it was like being Azerbaijani in

---

12   Shireen Housee and Mukhtar Dar, 'Remixing Identities: "Off" the Turntable' in Sharma, Hutynk and Sharma, *Disorienting Rhythms*, pp. 81–104.

13   'Bally Sagoo', *Wikipedia: The Free Encyclopedia* at: <http://en.wikipedia.org/wiki/Bally_Sagoo> (accessed 11 August 2008).

14   Sharma, 'Noisy Asians or "Asian Noise"?'

15   Apache Indian, 'Music has no Colour, no Barriers', *The Rediff Chat*, 1 August 2001 at:<http://www.rediff.com. E:\Books\Bhangra\Bhangra\Artist A–Z\Apache indian\rediff_com.Chat\Transcript\ApacheIndian.htm> (accessed 11 August 2008).

16   Ashwani Sharma 'South Asian Diaspora Music in Britain', *South Asian Diaspora Literature and Art Archive*, at: <http://www.salidaa.org.uk/salidaa/docrep/docs/sectionIntro/music/docm_render.html?dr_page_number=1> (accessed 11 August 2008).

17   Bally Sagoo, interviewed by Housee and Dar in 'Remixing Identities'.

London today. We had a chance to go to a nightclub in the West End during the daytime – white and black kids couldn't do that![18]

Media focus on repressive South Asian family structures and teenage truancy marginalized the arrival of this new genre of British popular music which acquired a global following over the next decade. Moreover, the repressive South Asian family subplot not only fascinated journalists and mediapeople, but also intrigued serious music scholars such as Sabita Banerji and Gerd Baumann.[19] Nevertheless, it was Banerji and Baumann who announced the arrival of a new trend in music and must be hailed as the historians of a new musical revolution. Gerd Baumann in his *Contesting Culture: Discourses of Identity in Multi-Ethnic London*, which begins forearmed against the pitfalls of ethnographic reductionism of the kind that arranges groups and cultures in polarized binaries of Asian and British, displays an uncommon sensitivity to contingency and context while practising 'ethnography' on his unsuspecting Southall subjects.[20] In contrast to Baumann's dispassionate ethnographic tone, Marie Gillespie's enthusiastic welcome of the new sonic experiment – 'neither *gori* (white) nor *kala* (black): it has made British Asian youth both audible and visible for the first time on the British musical scene' – was eminently quotable, despite its incorrectly conjugated Hindi words, and became the definitive statement on Bhangra as the voice of the South Asian youth that would be singled out for its paternalistic ethnocentricism in the years to come.[21] But Gillespie's conclusions about the link between Bhangra and identity, based on her limited fieldwork in Southall, are corroborated by the public statements of Bhangra producers and consumers.[22] The mission of the oldest Bhangra groups, such as Heera, Apna Sangeet and Alaap, as articulated by its lead singer Channi Singh, appears to have succeeded over the years:

---

18   Quoted in Sue Steward, 'Bhangra Spreads Its Empire', *Observer Music Monthly*, 14 October 2007 at: <http://www.guardian.co.uk/music/2007/oct/14/urban>> (accessed 11 August 2008).

19   Sabita Banerji and Gerd Baumann, 'Bhangra 1984–8: Fusion and Professionalization in a Genre of South Asian Dance Music' in Paul Oliver (ed.), *Black Music in Britain: Essays on the Afro-Asian Contribution to Popular Music* (Milton Keynes, 1990), pp. 137–53.

20   Baumann, *Contesting Culture*. Yet these well-intentioned efforts to bring these efforts to public attention by sociologists and cultural anthropologists are underscored by ethnographic paternalism of the benign variety. As a former immigrant, Baumann empathizes with the South Asian immigrants whose lives he documents but is at the same time distanced by his white, male, middle-class location.

21   Gillespie, *Television, Ethnicity, and Cultural Change*, p. 46.

22   As Kuljit Bhamra put it: 'I think people maybe felt the need to identify themselves, and in order to do that a medium was needed, and that medium is bhangra. There is always this roots feeling and people will always want to know where they came from: we are a different colour, we are from a different country, so where do we fit in?' Quoted in Gopinath, *Popular Culture*, n.p.

> We noticed that young Punjabis in London knew little about their own
> culture and language and were steeped in the English disco scene. We started
> our Bhangra songs to bring them back into their own culture. But for the
> music to appeal to them, we had to add the Western touch with a drum beat
> and synthesizers.[23]

Even after two decades, clichéd admissions of identification with Bhangra – 'It's my roots' – confirm DJ Ritu's announcement 'Bhangra was roots. Bhangra reaffirmed cultural identity – positively' in her entry on Bhangra in *World Music: The Rough Guide*.[24] From New Delhi to New York, the claim to Bhangra as origin is repeated almost tautologically by Bhangra producers and consumers.

Although class is an important variable in these musical collaborations, British cultural studies and sociology tend to single out the 'working-class' solidarity angle to the exclusion of several other sources of British Asian musical production. In contrast to the class focus of Asian music studies and the race orientation of black cultural studies, an important factor that producers do not fail to mention remains neglected in locating the sources of Bhangra – namely, ethnicity. Although this aspect began to receive greater attention after the publication of Gillespie's book, a fundamental confusion persists in its articulation at times to a specifically Punjabi and at others to a generalized South Asian identity. Bhangra's producers continue to be predominantly first- or second-generation immigrants of Panjabi origin who often collaborate with white or black musicians. Bhangra lyrics are almost always in Punjabi although their subject-matter varies. 'It's more accurate to say it's Punjabi music than Indian, because Punjabi is India and Pakistan,' DJ Rekha clarifies.[25] Similarly, in a recent feature article, Sue Steward emphasizes its Panjabi provenance: 'Bhangra is part of every Punjabi Briton's life, regardless of whether they arrived in the 1960s wave which established the UK's largest community, in Birmingham, or in drifts from post-Amin Uganda, or – like Bobby Friction and most bhangra artists – were British born.'[26] This is in sharp contrast to the sociological and ethnographic analysis of the late 1980s and early 1990s that focused exclusively on isolating Bhangra's distinctive Asianness from the rhetoric of blackness. In viewing Bhangra as a signifier of South Asian cultural identity, it was often forgotten that the memory of Panjabi harvest music and dance is not shared across other South Asian ethnicities that converge on Bhangra in places of migration in the UK, Australia, Canada and the US. As Baumann learnt from his Southall respondents, it would be

---

23 Channi Singh, *Guardian*, 'Weekend', 13 March 1993, p. 32.
24 DJ Ritu, 'Bhangra/Asian Beat: One-way Ticket to British Asia' in Simon Broughton, Mark Ellingham and Richard Trillo (eds), *World Music: The Rough Guide Volume 1* (1999) at: <http://www.ulme-mini-verlag.de/CR.HTM> (accessed 11 August 2008).
25 Quoted in Alona Wartofsky, '"What's Shakin"? Bhangra. Big Time. Take Traditional Punjabi Music, Add Drum Machines – and Hip-Hop to It', Special to *The Washington Post*, 13 May 2001 at: <http://www.washingtonpost.com/ac2/wp-dyn?pagename=article &node=&contentId=A14732-2001May11> (accessed 11 August 2008).
26 Steward, 'Bhangra Spreads Its Empire'.

erroneous to assume the existence of a unified South Asian community based on young people's identification with Bhangra as those young people would belong to multiple communities, depending on the context.

Panjabi beats and rhythms – the essence of Bhangra – are deeply entrenched in the Panjabi home culture and gurdwara community centre of the Bhangra producers.[27] 'How much of the gurdwara does one have', is how DJ Rekha of Basement Bhangra fame distinguishes between different categories of second- and third-generation migrants – a fact overlooked in the homogenized South Asian youth category of sociology and cultural studies.[28] Although the transition from the spiritual to the secular is difficult to make and the gurdwara *sewadharis* would be loath to associate themselves with 'ungodly' youth cultural settings, Bhangra producers, if not consumers, do have a lot of the gurdwara in them, whether they flaunt it or react to it. Gurdwaras have done more to preserve Panjabi language, script and culture in the Panjabi diaspora than any other secular institution. It is not uncommon to find Sikh youth accompanying parents to the gurdwara and conforming to Sikh codes of behaviour and conduct. It is the remarkable cultural retention in Sikh homes reinforced by the gurdwara space that accounts for the Sikh youth's rootedness in Panjabi language and culture which puts them at an advantage compared to other diasporic South Asian ethnicities.

'Having the gurdwara in one' can denote a musical lineage through inheriting the musical talent of a *raagi* father or a *sabad* singer mother in the gurdwara or a social association through Sunday visits to reaffirm Sikh spiritual and community values. Beginning with the British Asian Bhangra pioneer Apache Indian who acknowledged the contribution of his mother who sang *kirtans* in the gurdwara, the majority of Bhangra producers confess to having the gurdwara in them. Sukhbir, a Dubai-based Sikh from Kenya was introduced to music by his father, a *gyani* at the gurdwara in Nairobi. Montreal-born Rup Magon, a practising Sikh, admits that his first experience of music was in the gurdwara and that he picked up the tabla by listening to professional *ragis* and accompanied his mother when she sang there.[29] Not to speak of the 'Crown Prince of Bhangra' Jazzy B from Nawanshair who was recently accorded the rare privilege of recording hymns in praise of the Sikh guru. Even 'bad boys' and 'bad girls' on the Bhangra beat would be cautious about denying the gurdwara in their childhood. Gurdwaras in the UK, US, Canada, Australia and every place of Sikh settlement have served to play more than a spiritual role in the lives of the Sikh community. In neigbourhoods where South Asian community

---

27 Gudwara is a Sikh place of worship.
28 DJ Rehka, personal communication, 2008.
29 Rup Magon, personal communication, 2007. 'I was heavily influenced by the Gurdwaras. I started off doing lots of Kirtan (still do actually) and playing tabla at the Gurdwara,' Rup Magon stated. So did Sukhbir: 'My father has been a priest in the Sikh community. I was trained in the classical tradition of music and used to accompany my father at the *Shabad-Keertan* in the *Gurdwara* on harmonium and tabla. I grew up in a Gurdwara and that's where my music took a start'. Quoted by Syeda Farida, 'Pioneer in Bhangra Pop', *The Hindu*, Metro Plus Hyderabad, 18 June 2002.

spaces are scarce, the gurdwara space might even invade consciousness which it is least expected to. Nasreen, a twice migrant Dawoodi Ismaili from Kutch in Toronto,[30] admitted to childhood memories of participating in gurdwara cultural activities in Edmonton along with her Sikh friends and even participating in the street parades on Sikh festivals.[31] She believed that the increasing Islamic codes imposed on her as she entered her teens, the *hijab* as she called it, forbade her from mixing with Hindu or Sikh friends, and cut her off from her early induction into the gurdwara space.

But Bhangra's signification extends further than British Panjabis or Canadian Sikhs to other non-Panjabi ethnicities – Indian as well as South Asian – who would have few opportunities to participate in the secular spiritual space of the Sikh community. Sikh majoritarian status in the South Asian diaspora and the older history of migration might be offered as a facile explanation for the identification of non-Panjabi youth with Bhangra, but claims are made on Bhangra by all South Asian groups irrespective of nationality, language, caste, class or religion. The mixed ethnicities converging on Bhangra may be illustrated through the Bhangra performance by BILZ, a Canadian Bhangra band that had crossed over in 2007 with its 'Two-Step Bhangra' as a grand finale to the annual South Asian festival 'Masala! Masti! Mehndi!' in Toronto. As the BILZ (short for Brothers-in-law) signed autographs for their adoring fans, conversations with the fans revealed that Bhangra's constituency included South Asian youth of all colours, castes, religions, nations, classes and ethnicity and that its Panjabi lyrics posed no barriers to its multi-ethnic, multicultural admirers.[32] The BILZ, Canada's first Bhangra band to have hit the mainstream, is of Bangladeshi origin, but the singers could produce Panjabi beats without speaking the language.

Bhangra's elevation to the status of the ethnocultural signifier of South Asian identity in the British media thus complicates issues of ethnicity, culture and identity. While engaging Bhangra's ethnic location, it must be kept in mind that the second generation is too distant from the rustic *panjabiyat* of their parents to be able to identify with pure Panjabi sounds, but reproduces a form of ethnic identity through a selective appropriation of *panjabiyat*. South Asian ethnicities' identification with Bhangra as 'roots' occurs due to its deterritorialization, even though the inspiration for the music produced was the records and cassettes brought back by Panjabi migrants from visits home, Panjabi family and community functions, and the musical contribution of the gurdwara. Panjabi lyrical content is integrated in their compositions as a celebration of ethnic origins rather than a serious involvement

---

30   The term 'twice migrant' is used by Parminder Bhachu in *East African Sikh Settlers in Britain* (London, 1985). It refers to someone who migrated to Africa from India and then to different parts of the world after being driven out of Africa.

31   Interviewed by Anjali Gera Roy, Toronto, 17 July 2007.

32   Intrigued by the darker colouring and smaller build of the brothers-in-law in comparison with Bhangra's Panjabi practitioners, my tentative introduction was cut short by the BILZ's Bengali conversation starter, *'aapni Bangali na ki'* ('You must be Bengali!'): personal communication Toronto, July 2007.

with issues and concerns in the homeland. Most Bhangra producers and consumers make a point of saying that they would find it hard to identify completely with the *pendu* or rustic music that their parents brought from their visits home or enjoyed listening to because it represented a culture of which they had no or little experience. This alienation from originary cultures dilutes *panjabiyat* in Bhangra is diluted and points to a token allegiance to origins. Through the essentialization of *panjabiyat* as rustic exotica, Bhangra in the diaspora crosses over to non-Panjabi South Asian ethnicities to whom generalized, rather than particularized, Asian sounds signify home. With their Panjabi content diminished to 'roots', non-Panjabi ethnicities can participate in a process of identification with Asian roots while dis-identifying with its specific Panjabi location. At the same time, it allows an abstraction of *panjabiyat* that might be mobilized in the consolidation of Panjabi identity globally.

To grasp the identification of Bengali, Tamilian, Gujarati and Pakistani youth with Panjabi dance and music, one needs to understand the complex ways in ethnicity is asserted. The contextual and contingent nature of ethnicity comes into force in Bhangra's acquisition of the status of the signifier of South Asian ethnocultural identity. Cross-community identification with Bhangra in South Asian youth subcultures should not blind one to the fact that youth might in fact owe allegiances to ethnic communities that might differ from, or even be hostile to, the originary ethnic location of Bhangra music. Because of these cross-identifications Bhangra may be appropriated in the performance of multiple identity narratives ranging from the exclusionary Sikh identity discourse to the inclusive youth subcultural discourse.

Theorists of globalization have rectified the view of globalization as homogenization by calling attention to the countertrend towards the multiplication and intensification of boundaries through which increasing unification of the globe is balanced by fragmentation and, ironically, by a greater recognition of difference.[33] The other trajectory of globalization might be elucidated as the alternation of translocal with vernacular movements, large-scale migrations to the Euro-American centre that brings the Other into the midst of the Euro-American self, the transnationalization of production and relocation of Euro-American cosmopolitans in new localities in the global South, the rise of neo-fundamentalisms and so on., Through the twin metaphors in its title, Benjamin Barber's book *McWorld versus Jihad*, in particular, captured the centripetal and centrifugal movements within globalization – one leading to a greater integration of the world into global capitalism and the other to the consolidation of ethnic, cultural and religious boundaries.[34] Barber's book seemed to corroborate Samuel Huntington's thesis in *The Clash of Civilizations* about the imminent division of the

---

33   Mike Featherstone, *Global Culture: Nationalism, Globalization and Modernity* (London, 1994); Fredric Jameson, 'Notes on Globalization as a Philosophical Issue' in Fredric Jameson and Masao Miyoshi (eds), *The Cultures of Globalization* (Durham, NC, 1996), pp. 54–77.

34   Benjamin R. Barber, *Jihad vs McWorld: How Globalism and Tribalism Are Reshaping the World* (New York, 1995).

world along cultural lines and the wars in the future being about ethnicity and culture.[35] While Bhangra studies have made extremely valuable contributions to the understanding of South Asian subcultures and identities as well as to the South Asian discourse on the limits of visibility and multiculturalism, they have largely embedded it in the politics of nation-states in the context of multiculturalism. It was Gillespie who addressed a transnational, even global, return of tribes – ethnic, sectarian, racial, caste – in the era of globalization. While observing the new trend for ethnic chic that opened up a space for Bhangra, other studies of Bhangra did not touch upon worldwide phenomenon of ethnic returns in depth. The new fad for ethnicity that Sharma observed in Britain appears to be ruling not only global cities like London and New York, but also local software capitals like Bangalore and small towns in *sada Panjab* (our Panjab), connected to the global city through networks of migration and capital.

Jonathan Friedman attributes the rise in ethnicity to the threat to the nation-state from within and without. Observing an ethnification of the nation-state via three separate processes of fragmentation – indigenization, regionalization and ethnification of migrants and nationals – he argues that the ethnification surrounding the nation runs parallel to the ethnification of the nation-state itself. Calling this ethnification a form of a 'declining hegemonic order in the global system', Friedman sees, in lieu of a declining modernism, a return to roots, to fixed identification.[36] Ethnification permits Friedman to discuss two dissimilar forms of identifications – regional subnational and the new immigrants – in the same breath. The identity narratives produced in relation to Bhangra may be found to display shades of both regional subnational and new immigration. The revival of Bhangra against the backdrop of the celebration of hybrid, in-between, cosmopolitan identity discourses associated with the various 'posts' – that is, postmodernism, postcolonialism, postnationalism – immediately implicates the Bhangra text in critiques of essentialist narratives of the self and community, as well as in a retrogressive return to Sikh religious identity. Ethnicity causes the divergent discourses of diasporic hybridity and regionalism within the nation to converge, and in this convergence representation through cultural texts such as Bhangra acquires strategic importance. Ethnic difference engages in both locations with dominants of race, class, gender, religion, location, caste and so on. If Bhangra becomes the site of resistance to white, male, middle-class hegemony in the diaspora, it must engage with the domination of Hindi, Hindu and brahminism within the nation. 'Ethnicity is in', as Ashwani Sharma has proclaimed, not only in cosmopolitan Europe and America but also within India as the master-narrative of

---

35 Samuel Huntington, *The Clash of Civilizations and the Remaking of World Order* (New York, 1996).

36 Jonathan Friedman, 'Global Crises, the Struggle for Cultural Identity and Intellectual Porkbarrelling: Cosmopolitans versus Locals, Ethnics and National in an Era of De-hegemonisation' in Pnina Webner and Tariq Modood (eds), *Debating Cultural Hybridity: Multi-cultural Identities and the Politics of Anti-Racism* (London, 2000), pp. 70–89, at p. 71.

the nation-state is threatened from within and without through globalization and the rise of subregionalism.[37] Although Bhangra in India is not as unambiguously implicated in the fad for ethnicity as it is in the diaspora, ethnicity remains the primary source of its appeal. Through its implication in the opposed discourses of hybrid cosmopolitanism and regional subnationalism, Bhangra complicates the meaning of ethnicity as it is appropriated in the production of hybrid migrant identities in the diaspora and rooted regional identities in the homeland.

While Bhangra's centrality to a transnational diasporic politics of representation cannot be underestimated, diasporic producers, consumers and scholars of Bhangra, in appropriating Bhangra as a diasporic representational form for 'new ethnicities' in the diaspora, display an ignorance of its intersection with a regional politics of representation on the subcontinent signalled through a simultaneous Bhangra revival. It must be noted that the British reinvention of Bhangra in the mid-1980s coincided with the revalorization of Panjabi 'materialism' within the Indian nation. In a move similar to the engagement with ethnic stereotyping and 'Othering' in the diasporas, Bhangra's mainstreaming in the Indian popular musical space through Gurdas Mann in the early 1980s and Daler Mehndi in the early 1990s demonstrates the symbolic capital of popular culture in the politics of representation. A positive narrative of Panjabi corporeality that demystifies popular representations of Panjabis and *panjabiyat* in the Indian media has been visible since the mid-1980s and this has culminated in the valorization of *panjabiyat* as the source of authenticity at the end of the millennium, with popular cinema, television and advertising competing with one another in the production of a positive Panjabi ethnic identity. Since Daler Mehndi became the first regional star to challenge the Hindi film-dominated music industry, the stock of Panjabi music rose to the extent that Bollywood cinema co-opted Bhangra into its song and dance grammar, transforming Bhangra into national popular music.

Similarly, the celebratory narratives of Bhangra within and outside the nation overlook a transnational discourse of Sikh identity, an exclusionary identity discourse that signals the intensification of boundaries and primordial returns that counter the homogenizing thrust of globalization. As the demand for a separate Sikh nation has always been couched as a linguistic demand in subcontinental politics before and after partition, the discourse of global *panjabiyat* is deeply imbricated with a transnational consolidation of Sikh ethnic identity. In contrast to the visible politics of race, class and ethnicity, the politics of religious identity works in a more clandestine manner in which Bhangra producers and consumers might become willingly or unwittingly implicated. The 'gurdwara in them' often implicates Sikh Bhangra practitioners in a transnational consolidation of *sikhi* or Sikh identity camouflaged as *panjabiyat* as articulated below by Jazzy B:

> *Bhangra pop is both a service to Punjabiyat as well as business to me – I earn my bread and butter from pop so its [sic] my business but at the same time*

---

37   Sharma, 'Sounds Oriental'.

293

it's a service to Punjabiyat since its [sic] only because of Punjabi songs that youngsters abroad are connected to Punjab.[38]

A discussion thread on a Sikh site, *The Langar Hall*, asks the important question: 'Is bhangra tying together generations of Sikh Punjabis from Indian Punjab, or is it tying together ALL Punjabis?' The responses to the thread posted by the group confirm the leader's perception that 'oftentimes our Sikh and Punjabi identities are at odds with one another, and other times they are so intertwined that it is hard to untangle the cultural from the religious'.[39] Other discussions, however, tend to veer towards a separatist Sikh identity discourse that lends itself to a transnational mobilization of the demand for a separate Sikh nation, Khalistan.

Tony Ballantyne, in his book *Between Colonialism and Diaspora: Sikh Cultural Formations in an Imperial World*, argues that Bhangra 'cannot be identified as a strictly "Sikh tradition" because it emerged out of a broadly peasant, but more specifically Jat Punjabi performative tradition that was pancommunal'.[40] He also shows that a close examination of popular forms such as Bhangra can 'open up questions about the systematization and performance of identities, the circulation of cultural forms, and the relationship between technologies, economic structures and social formations'.[41] Ballantyne traces the history of Bhangra from a localized peasant form to its appropriation 'in the growing equation of bhangra with "Panjabiyat" after Partition'[42] and the regional government's attempt to construct a coherent state culture that transcended the deep divisions that were laid bare after partition. Ballantyne's point that Bhangra's transformation into the icon of Panjab and *Panjabiyat* was carefully cultivated by the state government provides a glimpse into the politics whereby cultural forms can acquire iconic value and identities are constantly produced. Ballantyne's work is particularly significant as it links post-independent provincial identity and a distinctively regional culture to their innovative and challenging reworking in Great Britain.[43]

For someone observing the musical production of Panjabi and South Asian diasporic youth from the outside, it is difficult to imagine their psychological and emotional investment in musical sounds, particularly of the kitschy commercial variety, until they are familiarized with the sociopolitical contexts from which the music has emerged. The relationship of South Asian youth dancing the Bhangra to issues and concerns about identity, belonging and culture may be understood with respect to the social experience of majoritarian dominance and the exclusion of

---

38   Quoted in Harneet Singh, 'All Jazzed up!', *The Times of India*, 22 November 2002 at: <http://timesofindia.indiatimes.com/articleshow/29091271.cms> (accessed 11 August 2008).

39   Camille, 'Bhangra is our Common Link?', *The Langar Hall » Blog Archive*, 1 February 2008 – 08:40 at: <http://thelangarhall.com/archives/111> (accessed 11 August 2008).

40   Ballantyne, *Between Colonialism and Diaspora*, p. 124.

41   Ibid.

42   Ibid., p. 125.

43   Ibid., p. 130.

minorities within and outside the nation, and to the complex relationship between performance and identity. Young South Asians in different Western locations often speak of sharing the experience of being made to feel different in school, of shuttling between an Asian/Indian home space and an alienating one, and of having to make the painful journey from denial, rejection and acceptance of ethnic difference. To a generation negotiating the conflicting demands of the two worlds it inhabits, a new genre of music expressing a diasporic South Asian sensibility – whatever its ethnic content specificity – offers a means of relocating itself in the South Asian space of the home and the community, as well as realigning its relationship with the mainstream.

Bhangra, which has attracted media and academic attention as a new genre, signifies to its users more than aesthetic or cultural form. According to Bhagwant Sagoo, a broadcaster and producer of the Asian Network at BBC Three Counties Radio (UK), '[f]or a generation of British Asians, Bhangra music is their music. They eat, sleep and play Bhangra and the beat of the dhol (drum) is the beat of a Punjabi identity surfacing to reclaim its heritage in an adopted nation.'[44] To South Asian youth in other diasporic spaces as well, Bhangra signals a distinctive South Asian material and cultural space within the new multicultural nation-state. When Bally Sagoo voiced his dream of a future in which South Asian youth would be able to blast Bhangra from their cars instead of listening to it with their windows shut, he was echoing the sentiments of the majority of South Asian diaspora youth.

A decade later, Alona Wartofsky's report from Washington made Sagoo's wish appear almost prophetic:

> *A while back, Jerard Duncan was filling his car at a Brooklyn gas station when he heard what sounded like a strange kind of hip-hop. The percussion was unfamiliar, and the rapping was not in English. He asked the Indian kids in the next car what this music was, and they told him: bhangra.*[45]

Even as community worker Pardeep Nagra held forth on the identity politics of playing Bhangra on one's car stereo in downtown Toronto in 2007, a right hard-won for the youth after decades, if not centuries, of struggle, a sports car packed with turbaned and clean-shaven Sikhs booming Bhangra raced past. The simple thumbs-up sign exchanged between Nagra and the youth, the sartorial statement they all made by wearing the turban even after several instances of mistaken identity after 9/11, demonstrated the power of symbolic acts in making claims to nationality, citizenship and belonging.[46] While baffled parents fail to connect entertainment with politics, to the youth dressed in ethnic clothing, dancing to ethnic music is a serious business, consolidating their claim to British, American or Canadian

---

44   Bhagwant Sagoo, 'Bhangra: The Best Asian Beats from the Streets, at: <http://www.unionsquaremusic.co.uk/titlev4.php?ALBUM_ID=351&LABEL_ID=2> (accessed 17 April 2009).
45   Wartofsky, '"What's Shakin'?"'.
46   Pardeep Nagra, personal communication, 2007.

citizenship without having to compromise their ethnic identity. Sue Steward witnessed the relationship between performance and identity at the London Flavas stage, where the Sony-award-winning BBC Radio 1 DJ, Bobby Friction, and his DJ partner, Nihal, were 'geeing up the crowd as if working a wedding party':

> I'm locked in with a group of 19- and 20-somethings from Southall and east London. The parents are 'over there'. When Birmingham's superstar bhangra singer, Sukshinder Shinda, now in his mid-forties, fills the air with the sharp, thunderous rhythms from two dhol drums (the instrument synonymous with bhangra) and his cinematically heroic voice, the cheers are deafening. When he bursts into 'Par Linghade', an old Punjabi folk tune given the bhangra treatment, the girls squeal. Nineteen-year-old Sheena from Chiswick, whispers: 'This has been around for years – it's the Indian version of the Romeo and Juliet story, and we all love it.' Their male friends, in turbans and baseball hats, fling up their arms and sway like dazed cobras, and everyone sings along.[47]

Alona Wartofsky observed a similar phenomenon in DJ Rekha's Basement Bhangra in New York city:

> Early during 'Basement Bhangra,' when Rekha opens with sets of hip-hop and reggae dancehall, the floor belongs to young women and couples who dance enthusiastically but demurely. But once she starts spinning the percussive bhangra beats, most women are relegated to the edges of the club, and both the dance floor and the elevated stage become the province of men. Their heads bob from side to side. They lift their shoulders up and down, with one arm raised. A raised hand reaches up and forward, twisting as if screwing in an imaginary overhead light bulb. The other hand may be cupping an ear or clutching one's heart, suggesting that the dancers are hearing and feeling the music.[48]

Anjali Gera Roy was witness to the performance of *panjabiyat* in the Indian software capital of Bangalore by youth of all complexions when Bally Sagoo had arrived to ring in the new millennium:

> The Punjabi munda from Birmingham transforms into a star as he changes into a shiny T-Shirt and creates pure magic through sheer technology on the console. Punjabi poses no barrier to Bangalore mini-skirted and blue-jeaned teens as they simulate Punjabi dance steps in the banquet hall of Taj Residency to gud nalon ishq mitha. K3 G is still fresh in the memory to forget to make the bangles tinkle to the beat of lai ja lai ja. When Bally attempts a new mix of Shava Shava, even uncleji and auntieji descend on the jam-packed

---

47 Steward, 'Bhangra Spreads Its Empire', n.p.
48 Wartofsky, '"What's Shakin'?"'.

floor egging on toddlers and infants. On this occasion, mesmerized by Bally the star and a neo-ethnographer, I forgot to check what language the teenagers spoke at home and where was their 'native place'. But the visual image they projected was that of the hip metropolitan youth who had been chosen to be present on the big evening.[49]

Another performative space, hidden from media and anthropological gaze, may be located in real Bhangra performances at Panjabi family weddings and community functions, which also reappear on the Web. Dudrah demonstrates how the performance of dance can be simultaneously used to consolidate caste and religious boundaries as testified by one of her respondents, Manjit:

In some of the songs you get the higher castes chatted about, especially the jat. It's as if the jats only listen to Bhangra or live in the Punjab. It can kind of isolate the other castes. Don't get me wrong, I mean for a lot of young people caste doesn't really matter, but now and then you still get some people, young and old, who are into caste and shit and when those kind of songs are played it can be ammunition for them.[50]

The recent brouhaha over the hip-hop veteran Snoop Dogg's wearing a Sikh outfit in a Bollywood song 'Singh is Kking' in a film of the same name demonstrates that Bhangra space can include as well as exclude.

In addition to its musical or aesthetic content, the symbolic act of performing ethnic difference through dancing Bhangra reinforces the relationship between ritual performance and *communitas* as outlined in the work of Victor Turner, Richard Schechner and others.[51] Borrowing van Gennep's idea of the liminal and the liminoid, Turner revealed that it is not just liminal activities that affirm community values and structures; activities that would be considered subversive or liminoid also play an important role in performing *communitas*.[52] Bhangra offers scope for the performance of both – the liminal in Panjabi family settings where it is made to produce *panjabiyat* and the liminoid in the subversive play of youth subcultural spaces in which the playful engagement with tradition can, in fact, be respectful and perform a form of *communitas* different from that produced through the liminal. The dance floor on which youthful bodies congregate becomes the space for the play of the liminoid where South Asian youth articulate through bodily signifiers and movements resistance to both the non-dominant parental culture that prohibits social dancing and mixing as well as to the dominant white culture from which they are excluded. Dancing the Bhangra becomes a public declaration

49   Anjali Gera Roy, 'Who is Dancing to the Bhangra?', *Phalanx: A Quarterly Journal for Continuing Debate* 1 (2006), at:. <http://www.phalanx.in/pages/article_i001_dancing_bhangra.html> (accessed 11 August 2008).
50   Dudrah, 'Drum N Dhol'.
51   In Marvin Carlson, *Performance: A Critical Introduction* (New York, 2004).
52   Ibid.

of the rejection of exclusionary white spaces of consumption from which South Asian immigrants have been traditionally excluded despite their induction in the economy of production. Malkit Singh's simple lyrics *'aj bhangra paun noon ji karda'* ('Today I feel like dancing to bhangra / Today I'm not going to sing the white man's disco') acquire cult status for Bhangra's consumers because they articulate their deepest sentiments. Performing ethnic movements to the beats of Asian music becomes a symbolic rejection of the white popular cultural space, closed to South Asian musical production and consumption, as well as an identification of a specifically South Asian cultural space within mainstream popular culture. Shouting, screaming, throwing challenges and behaving 'South Asian' becomes a reaffirmation of a disclaimed South Asian or Panjabi cultural identity.

Figure 14.1   Birmingham-based singer, Malkit Singh

However, the dance floor is also a space in which parental taboos with respect to mixing must be flouted. In communities where cross-mixing across linguistic, religious or even caste groups is strictly forbidden, the free mingling of brown, black and white bodies on the dance floor constitutes a form of resistance to essentialist narratives of identity based on class, caste, religion, nation, gender, language and ethnicity carried across from the homeland to the diaspora. The dance floor on which bodies of all shapes, colours, gender, ethnicity and nations collide and converse presents a correlative of musical mixing that together articulate an ethic of hybridity. By dancing the Bhangra not the way it is danced at home, but by adding to it reggae, dancehall, hip-hop and even rap moves and mixing pure Panjabi with multiple linguistic and sonic traditions, South Asian youth forge a new diasporic identity in opposition to essentialist Asianness or whiteness.

On the subcontinent, Bhangra's return was triggered by, and triggered, the desire of the Indian citizen-subject to interrogate the discourses of social and political control through which the 'spiritual' Indian subject was produced. The Bhangra body, representing the body in pleasure, is that of the Other that the self has repressed in order to produce the disciplined body of the ascetic. Challenging the ethic that demands that the body be disciplined to attain its ultimate goal of salvation, the body of the leaping, bounding, rioting Other teases the self to investigate those disciplinary discourses through which the ideal subject of Indian modernity came to be constructed. The return of Bhangra and its penetration into the national mainstream signals the return of the repressed Other, whose body had been subjected to brahminical discipline. Its celebration of the materiality of the body as beautiful, excessive or ugly marks an eruption of the body on the Indian popular cultural space in which the Panjabi body becomes the object of the nation's desire. The Bhangra body becomes a crucial site of the struggle for control over the meanings and pleasures of the body.

Bhangra studies in Britain have devoted a considerable space to the emergence of Asian Kool and Bhangra's role in changing the stereotyped representation of Asians in the British perception. Ashwani Sharma, Rupa Huq and others have examined the reasons for the reversal of the stereotyped representation of Asians in the British imagination through the emergence of a new fashionable, fun-loving Asian that has made the Asian 'Kool'.[53] Sharma and Huq have pointed out Bhangra's contribution to the reversal of the stereotype of the Asian as industrious, studious and spiritual in Britain through its appropriation of features of black culture that are perceived as 'Kool'. Bhangra's arrival on the Indian popular cultural scene has similarly altered the stereotype of the Panjabi in the national imagination through the emergence of Panjabi 'Kool'. Panjabi Kool is produced essentially by responding to the materialism ascribed to Panjabi ethnicities through returning it to its etymological meaning and reconnecting it with the geocentricity of the harvest rite. Materialism, redefined as earth-centricity, is juxtaposed against the spiritualist interpretation of Indian traditions. Black Kool – the key ingredient in the shaping

---

53   Sharma, Hutnyk and Sharma, *Disorienting Rhythms*; Rupa Huq, *Beyond Subculture: Pop, Youth and Identity in a Postcolonial World* (London, 2006).

of Asian Kool in Britain – and Panjabi Kool appear to have many things in common. The Panjabi self is associated with vitality and raw energy that is attributed to black cultures in white societies in the Indian mind. An identical desire to appropriate these qualities of vigour, energy and spontaneity attributed to the Other – black or Panjabi– might also be discerned in the revalorization of Panjabi music and dance in India.

Bhangra's performance of ethnic identity – Panjabi, Indian, South Asian, brown, or black – must be framed against the postmodern conceptualization of both identity and ethnicity as in-process, contingent and constructed. Hall's essay 'New Ethnicities' is perhaps the most lucid and succinct elucidation of the construction and play of black cultural identities in the postcolonial context. Bhangra constructs a politics 'which works with and through difference, which is able to build those forms of solidarity and identification which make common struggle and resistance possible without suppressing the real heterogeneity of interests and identities'.[54] While Hall constantly warns that blackness, and thereby all essential categories, are politically and culturally constructed categories, identity narratives converging on Bhangra – irrespective of the politics of representation it is appropriated in – often run the risk of giving in to the same fixities that they set out to dismantle. But questionings of the self as reflected in the following blog underline the fact that *panjabiyat* will continue to be produced in different ways in different places:

> *Has our sense of who is Punjabi shifted with the shifting borders of our parents' homelands, or are subsequent generations building a community identity, again, in the diaspora? Or, because of our relatively large numbers in California, our lack of non-religious community spaces (i.e., the gurdwara is, for many, the only site of community gathering), are we simply given more of an opportunity to remain in our own enclaves?*[55]

---

54 Hall, 'New Ethnicities', p. 92.
55 Camille, 'Bhangra is our Common Link?', n.p.

PART 5
Performance and Gesture

Musical Persona: The Physical Performance of Popular Music[1]

Philip Auslander

The visual aspects of musical performance, by which I mean its physical and gestural dimensions, have not received the attention due them. Even scholars who are sympathetic to the idea that physical performance, not just the production of sound, is important to music tend to treat it as something apart from the music itself. Alan Durant, for example, argues on the one hand, 'to take as music in all instances only what is heard is to abstract … an acoustic dimension of practices always and only realizable within definitions and limits of a given scenario' while also saying, on the other, that 'the physical dimensions of music in performance' only contextualize or position the sound.[2] Nicholas Cook argues that Jimi Hendrix's performances can be seen as 'instance[s] of multimedia' because 'while his physical motions were inevitably linked to the music … they went far beyond it. They became an independent dimension of variance. …'[3] Both authors thus imply that the physical aspects of musical performance should be seen as separate from, supplementary to, or providing context for the auditory aspects, not as an integral part of the production of music.

Although I do not intend to pursue this direction here, I will note, by way of a rejoinder, that a substantial amount of research in experimental psychology focusing on musical perception has come to very different conclusions regarding the relationship between the visual and the auditory aspects of performance. Scholars in this field have shown that the visual dimensions of musical performance convey musical information and shape the audience's perception of the musical event. The musical information imparted by the visual aspects of performance is both formal (that is, related to the perception of characteristics such as dissonance, phrasing and intervals) and affective (that is, related to the performer's interpretive intentions

---

1   Parts of this chapter are redacted from Philip Auslander, 'Musical Personae', *The Drama Review* 50/1 (2006): 100–119 and 'Performance Analysis and Popular Music: A Manifesto', *Contemporary Theatre Review* 14/1 (2004): 1–13.
2   Maultsby, 'Funk', p. 683.
3   Nicholas Cook, *Analysing Musical Multimedia* (Oxford, 1998), p. 263.

and the emotions he or she wishes to convey through the music). A report on one series of such experiments concludes:

> *To a surprising extent, facial expression and other bodily movements affect music experience at a perceptual level and an emotional level. Different facial expressions can cause the same musical events to sound more or less dissonant, the same melodic interval to sound larger or smaller, and the same music to sound more or less joyful. In short, listeners integrate visual with aural aspects of performance to form an integrated audio-visual mental representation of music, and this representation is not entirely predictable from the aural input alone.*[4]

This work provides an important empirical grounding for seeing physical performance as an essential part of the production of music. My own approach is social and cultural in emphasis, and is informed by the disciplinary contexts of theatre and performance studies. In a remarkable essay published in 1943, D.C. Somervell, assessing the situation of musical performance in a world increasingly dominated by radio, sought to grasp just what the visual aspects of performance bring to the experience of music. He anticipated the psychologists' findings by declaring that visual information causes the auditor to hear musical sound differently. In the portion of the essay whose implications I wish to pursue, however, Somervell discusses the significance of the use of sheet music in performance:

> *Why do chamber music players retain their often quite unnecessary copies? It is not wholly satisfactory to say that they need the music in order to cooperate with each other. The answer probably is a matter of visual effect. The very name, chamber music, implies a certain intimacy and informality. The audience has the privilege of hearing them, but they are not addressing it: they are playing for their own and each other's satisfaction. ... [W]hy must the orchestra have music? An experienced orchestra can hardly need the music of Beethoven's Fifth Symphony. ... The answer is, of course, that the members of the orchestra are not 'performers' in the sense in which we have used the term. They have sunk their personalities and become a single instrument, and the 'performer' is the conductor.*[5]

As Somervell suggests, the visual aspects of musical performance are not merely functional and do not convey only formal information. Musicians do not only play music; they also play roles. Somervell describes musical performance in terms of an impression the performers seek to create on the audience – an impression

---

4   William Forde Thompson, Phil Graham and Frank A. Russo, 'Seeing Music Performance: Visual Influences on Perception and Experience', *Semiotica* 156/1–4 (2005): 203–27, at 220.

5   D.C. Somervell, 'The Visual Element in Music', *Music & Letters* 24/1 (1943): 42–47, at 47.

of who they are, their relationship to the music, the nature of the interrelations among themselves, and the kind of interaction they are offering to the audience. Such impressions are created both aurally and visually and imply a social narrative. They are also relative to genre: the same musician who disappears behind the music stand as the member of an orchestra plays a role that depends on visible insularity when performing with a chamber group. It is these roles, and the means musicians use to perform them in popular music, that I wish to explore here.

Person, Persona, Character

We may not usually think of musical performance, apart from opera and musical theatre, as entailing role-playing in the conventional dramatic sense. Nevertheless, we must be suspicious of any supposition that musicians are simply 'being themselves' on stage. Simon Frith helpfully identifies three different strata in pop singers' performances, all of which may be present simultaneously. He proposes that we hear pop singers as 'personally expressive' – that is, as singing in their own persons, from their own experience. But two other layers are imposed on that one because popular musicians are 'involved in a process of *double enactment*: they enact both a star personality (their image) and a song personality, the role that each lyric requires, and the pop star's art is to keep both acts in play at once'.[6] I shall both systematize and expand on Frith's account. From this point on, I will refer to the three layers of performance he identifies as the *real person* (the performer as human being), the *performance persona* (the performer as social being) and the *character* (Frith's song personality).

All three layers may be active simultaneously in a given musical performance. For example, when Kelly Clarkson, the winner of the 2002 *American Idol* television singing competition, sang a duet on television with country star Reba McIntyre, they performed a song in which they played the roles of women competing for the affection of the same man. In addition to these characters, however, they also portrayed musical personae of the experienced veteran singer and her young acolyte (and perhaps future competitor); these personae were delineated through the same performance as the characters in the song but were independent of those characters – the singers could have performed their personae regardless of what song they chose. The presence of the performers as real people was implied through Clarkson's televised announcement that she had always idolized McIntyre and had therefore chosen her as her duet partner when she was in the position to do so by virtue of having won the competition. Whether true or not, this appeal to personal experience was layered into the performance alongside the two women's performance personae as seasoned trouper and young up-and-comer and their

---

6   Simon Frith, *Performing Rites: On the Value of Popular Music* (Cambridge, MA, 1996), pp. 186, 212 (original emphasis).

characters as romantic rivals; all three levels of personification framed the audience's perception and interpretation of the music.

Although popular music fans frequently think – or would like to think – otherwise, the real person is the dimension of performance to which the audience has the least access, since the audience generally infers what performers are like as real people from their performance personae and the characters they portray. Public appearances off-stage do not give reliable access to the performer as a real person, since it is quite likely that interviews and even casual public appearances are manifestations of the performer's persona. Whereas a performer may take on different characters, even in the course of a single performance, the persona remains consistent (at least with respect to context) and is the point of identification between performers and their audiences. For these reasons, *persona* is the most important of the three roles musicians play.

Lorraine Daston and H. Otto Sibum usefully define *persona*, glossing Marcel Mauss:

> *Intermediate between the individual biography and the social institution lies the persona: a cultural identity that simultaneously shapes the individual in body and mind and creates a collective with a shared and recognizable physiognomy. The bases for personae are diverse: a social role (e.g. the mother), a profession (the physician), an anti-profession (the flâneur), a calling (the priest). ... Personae are creatures of historical circumstance; they emerge and disappear within specific contexts. A nascent persona indicates the creation of a new kind of individual, whose distinctive traits mark a recognized social species.*[7]

It is important to emphasize the social, collective and historical nature of personae: although individuals construct personae, they do so in ways that are recognizable in relation to conventions external to themselves. Musical personae are based in social perceptions of the musician as the follower of a profession or calling, but also on other grounds, such as the social roles of venerated mentor and young acolyte performed by McIntyre and Clarkson respectively. I trust it is clear that a given musician may perform multiple personae in different contexts, just as Clarkson performs the subordinate role when singing with McIntyre, but not when performing solo.

There are several sets of constraints on the construction of musical performance personae, the most immediate of which are genre constraints. This much is obvious: rock musicians simply do not look and act like classical musicians who, in turn, do not look and act like jazz musicians and so on. Even within genres there are distinctions: psychedelic rockers do not look and act like glam rockers who do not look and act like punk rockers and so on. New genres involve the development of new personae. The ease with which these facts can be stated belies their importance

---

7   Lorraine Daston and H. Otto Sibum, 'Introduction: Scientific Personae and Their Histories', *Science in Context* 16/1–2 (2003): 2–3.

within musical cultures: musical genres and subgenres define the most basic and important sets of conventions and expectations within which musicians and their audiences function. Genres can and do overlap, and musicians can draw on genres other than their own in their performances (rocker Mick Jagger, for instance, is said to have derived much of his movement style from Tina Turner, a soul music artist[8]). Genre conventions also change over time and never have the force of absolute dicta, although they are crucially important to performers in constructing their performance personae and to audiences in interpreting and responding to them.

Another, broader, set of constraints on persona are the sociocultural conventions of the societies in which they appear – conventions that popular music both reflects and contests. The gender ambiguities of glam rockers' personae, for example, challenged the gender norms of American and European societies in the early 1970s. The performance of glam was a safe cultural space in which to experiment with versions of masculinity that clearly flouted those norms. Glam rock was, in this respect, a liminal phenomenon in Victor Turner's sense of that term, a performance practice through which alternative realities could be enacted and tested.[9] Inasmuch as glam rock was almost completely dominated by men and took the performance of masculinity as its terrain, however, it was also entirely in line with the conventions of rock as a traditionally male-dominated cultural form that evolved from male-dominated cultural and social contexts. Popular music is not entirely constrained by dominant ideologies, but neither is it entirely free of their influence.

A very brief example, which I can only sketch here but have elaborated elsewhere,[10] will suggest how these frames and signifiers interrelate in a single performance. In a 1973 television performance of her hit song 'Can the Can', Suzi Quatro presented her persona as a black leather-clad, tough rocker woman – a persona that intentionally challenged both social conventions of femininity and the more vulnerable or ethereal feminine images created by earlier women rock musicians, even such powerful performers as Janis Joplin and Grace Slick. (This persona, which Quatro developed with her British management team, was quite different from her first performance persona in the mid-1960s as a mini-skirted, braless member of an all-girl Detroit-based bar band called Suzi Soul and the Pleasure Seekers.)

Like her costume, Quatro's voice, an aggressive scream, was not stereotypically feminine. Unlike most female rock performers of the time, Quatro was an instrumentalist as well as a singer – she played bass guitar with all the showy panache of a lead guitarist, wearing the instrument low, down around her hips in a masculine position and sometimes holding it away from herself to showcase her

---

8   Sheila Whiteley, 'Little Red Rooster v. The Honky Tonk Woman: Mick Jagger, Sexuality, Style and Image' in Sheila Whiteley (ed.), *Sexing the Groove: Popular Music and Gender* (London, 1997), pp. 67–99, at pp. 76, 97.

9   Victor Turner, *From Ritual to Theatre: The Human Seriousness of Play* (New York, 1982), p. 85.

10   Philip Auslander, *Performing Glam Rock: Gender and Theatricality in Popular Music* (Ann Arbor, MI, 2006), pp. 193–226.

playing. Her movements were not dance movements but the characteristic bob and stomp associated with male rock musicians. Her facial expressions communicated the pleasure that musicians take in the urgency and hard work of playing rock – they were the expressions of her rocker persona, not of the character evoked in the song. Although the fast tempo and boogie rhythm of 'Can the Can' was consistent with her masculine rocker persona, the character depicted in the song placed Quatro in a more conventional role for a female pop artist, since the protagonist is advising an implicitly female listener – albeit in very aggressive terms – to safeguard her male love interest against the blandishments of other women.

This fragment of analysis suggests that Quatro's performance can be read in relation to two sets of conventions for female comportment – social conventions and those of her musical genre – and that the performance persona she created through such means as costume, movement, facial expression and the on-stage manipulation of a musical instrument can be defined explicitly as an entity distinct from the characters she portrayed in the song's narrative. Although Quatro's persona was decidedly more aggressive than the norms for feminine behaviour of her time, the inversion of gender roles it implied was consistent with the gender play that is a defining characteristic of the glam rock genre frame. The tension between the social and musical unconventionality of her persona and the conventional views expressed by the character she portrayed reflects the complexity of performances carried out within multiple frames.

Popular musicians do not perform their personae exclusively in live and recorded performances; they also perform them through the visual images used in the packaging of recordings, publicity materials, interviews and press coverage, toys and collectibles, and other venues and media, including music video. The ability to perform the persona across a multitude of platforms has become particularly important now that the traditional profit centre of the music industry, the sound recording, is becoming increasingly less viable. It is generally the case, of course, that performers are not the sole authors of the personae they perform in these many contexts: producers, managers, agents, publicists and the entire machinery of the music industry collaborate with artists, and sometimes coerce them, in the construction and performance of their personae. It does not follow from this for me, as it does for some commentators, that these aspects of pop music performance have everything to do with marketing and commodification and nothing to do with artistry and musical aesthetics. Although the commodity critique of popular music is important, it implicitly de-emphasizes the importance of attending to the details of particular performances since all popular musical personae and performances are equivalent commodities. Part of the audience's pleasure in pop music comes from experiencing and consuming the personae of favourite artists in all their many forms, and this experience is inseparable from the experience of the music itself and of the artists as musicians.

I will qualify this developing schema for popular music performance by indicating that character is an optional element that comes in primarily when the musician is a singer performing a song that defines a character textually. In other cases, the performance may be perceived as a direct performance of persona unmediated by character. This is particularly true for non-singing musicians who do not develop characters through voice and lyrics, but whose personae may play roles in other kinds of staged narratives. Jazz musicians, for example, often have very distinctive personae as instrumentalists and bandleaders, expressed not only in the way they play, but also in their appearance, the way they move, the way they address the audience and the way they deal with their fellow musicians.

During a visit to New York City jazz clubs in 2001, I saw performances by two tenor saxophonists and bandleaders a musical generation apart: Pharaoh Sanders, a veteran of the jazz experimentalism of the 1960s and Joe Lovano, who came to prominence in the late 1980s. Sanders, dressed in a light-coloured Nehru suit, presented himself as a beatific elder statesman who drifted in and out of the performance, seemingly picking up its flow when the mood seemed right. At the end of the set, he invited the audience to participate in a sing-along on a spiritual theme; holding out the microphone for responses, he seemed completely unfazed when no one in the audience replied – he was absorbed in the moment and nothing else mattered. Lovano, like the rest of his group, dressed in a jacket and tie, conversed and joked with his band mates and the audience, establishing a generally upbeat, informal atmosphere that was quite different from the reverential tone of Sanders' performance and that also belied the rigours of the hard bop Lovano and his band were playing. Lovano also seemed to be more a working member of an ensemble than the relatively aloof Sanders, who remained to the side or off-stage during substantial portions of the set. The personae these musicians performed may have some relationship to their off-stage personalities and values; audiences may in fact be eager to believe that they do. But this does not mean, once again, that Sanders and Lovano were simply 'being themselves' on stage. Other jazz musicians, notably the members of the Art Ensemble of Chicago and Sun Ra's Arkestra, have performed obviously constructed and artificial personae to demonstrate that jazz performance personae need not be identical with the musicians' identities as human beings.

Persona as Social Front: Setting, Appearance and Manner

Because I am treating the musical persona as a species of self-presentation, I turn now to Erving Goffman's *The Presentation of Self in Everyday Life* for a taxonomy of the means performers use to define and project personae. Goffman calls the means a performer uses to foster an impression the 'front', which consists of 'expressive equipment of a standard kind intentionally or unwittingly employed by the individual during his performance'.[11] (It is worth emphasizing that performance, in Goffman's sense, may be undertaken either consciously or unconsciously. When asked to describe blues guitarist B.B. King's gestures in a video recording, a musicologist responded, 'I don't know where it comes from, but as a guitarist you just do it. Jimi Hendrix, Eric Clapton, all these guys, they bend notes and

---

11   Erving Goffman, *The Presentation of Self in Everyday Life* (New York, 1959), p. 22.

they lean back. It's a physical thing'.[12] That a guitarist does this because it is what guitarists have always done, and gives no conscious thought to the impression she thus creates, does not negate the fact that the physical routine functions as expressive equipment and contributes willy-nilly to the impression she makes on the audience.) Goffman divides front into two aspects: 'setting' (the physical context of the performance) and 'personal front' in which are included the performer's '"appearance" and "manner"'.[13] The 'front' is a point at which performances intersect with larger social contexts and conventions, as all aspects of a front must be legible to a specific audience.

Settings contribute to the impressions created by musical performances by drawing upon existing cultural connotations. The Rose Theater, for example, part of the Frederick P. Rose Hall, is a new complex built to house the Jazz at Lincoln Center programme in New York City. Opened in 2004, it is described in publicity materials on the programme's website both as part of 'the first facility ever created specifically for jazz' and as a 'symphony in the round'.[14] Both this description and the design of the theatre, whose layout recalls that of a symphony hall, suggest the venue is intended to attach the cultural prestige of the symphony orchestra (and perhaps its access to wealth and power) to jazz, as is its Lincoln Center affiliation. The theatre itself, as a piece of expressive equipment, thus communicates to the audience that it is to understand and respond to jazz as 'America's classical music', not as a form of popular music, an implicitly less 'serious' and more 'vulgar' category.[15] The performance space thus provides a definition of the musical and cultural situation.

Individual musicians can use the cultural associations of a particular venue or kind of venue to assert their personae, either by invoking them or subverting them. Cellist Matt Haimovitz, for example, supported his persona as a youthful, experimental, somewhat iconoclastic classical musician by doing on his 2002 tour 'what no classical musician of his stature had done in living memory, navigating the country not by way of its acoustically precise concert halls but instead by its coffeehouses and clubrooms. Most radical was his performance at CBGB's, the

---

12   Quoted in Thompson, Graham and Russo, 'Seeing Music Performance', p. 209.

13   Goffman, *The Presentation of Self*, pp. 22–24.

14   Jazz at Lincoln Center, 'The Architecture', <http://www.jalc.org/fprh/architecture.html> (accessed 23 September 2005).

15   The phrase 'America's classical music' is not used in the Jazz at Lincoln Center materials, but it is one way in which jazz is often described by its advocates. See, for example, the website of the American Jazz Museum in Kansas City (<http://www.americanjazzmuseum.com>). The Rose Theater institutionalizes both an analogy between jazz and classical music and the practice of staging jazz concerts at halls devoted to classical music that began in the 1930s with Benny Goodman's Carnegie Hall concerts (of course, Goodman also performed classical music on occasion) and continued in the 1940s with Norman Grantz's Jazz at the Philharmonic series. Since the 1960s it has been fairly common for regional classical music venues in the United States to programme at least some jazz artists, often those like Dave Brubeck whose music has affinities with classical or contemporary 'serious' music.

legendary punk room in Manhattan'.[16] If the Rose Theater seems intended to frame jazz as classical music, Haimovitz seemed to frame classical music as popular music through his choice of venues. Whereas Haimovitz depended on the existing cultural connotations of CBGB's for his performance of persona, I recall, by contrast, the Preservation Hall Jazz Band of New Orleans encouraging the patrons of Boston's staid classical music venues to dance in the aisles, thus subverting the performance space's usual cultural significance and transforming it into a setting appropriate to their performance.

In his description of personal front, Goffman includes both 'relatively fixed' signs, like those denoting race and sex, and 'relatively mobile' signs 'such as facial expression'.[17] Although I shall focus here primarily on the more mobile signs, fixed signs are clearly of critical importance, given the way so many musical genres are stratified in relation to social identities (for example, the problematic status of white jazz musicians, black classical musicians, female conductors, women in rock and jazz, among others). Goffman proposes that routines tend to draw on an existing vocabulary of personal fronts with established social meanings; the rather quaint examples he provides are of chimney sweeps and perfume clerks who 'wear white lab coats ... to provide the client with an understanding that delicate tasks performed by these persons will be performed in what has become a standardized, clinical, confidential manner'.[18] The white lab coat garnered such meanings in its primary scientific and medical uses – meanings that are then generalized to the other contexts in which it appears. In the 1950s male jazz musicians (both black and white) frequently opted for Ivy League-style suits as their stage wear (Miles Davis was one of the more prominent musicians to dress this way). This fashion, exemplified by Brooks Brothers, carried with it culturally encoded connotations of conservative sophistication as well as upward mobility.[19] Jazz musicians thus presented themselves not as members of a disreputable subculture, as they were often thought to be, but as respectable, middle-class men (regardless of what their actual class status may have been).[20] In this case, the existing connotations of the Brooks Brothers suit were generalized to a specific musical persona when adopted as part of the front.

Some genres of popular music clearly permit more individual variation of personal front than others. Doo-wop groups of the 1950s usually dressed in identical suits, a practice that persisted in rock and pop music throughout the 1960s.

---

16 Daniel Oppenheimer, 'Gladiator: Matt Haimovitz Fights the War on Terror with an Unlikely Weapon', *Valley Advocate*, 25 March 2004. Available at: <http://www.valley advocate.com/gbase/Arts/content.html?oid=oid:59415> (accessed 10 January 2005).

17 Goffman, *The Presentation of Self*, p. 24.

18 Ibid., p. 26.

19 Paul Gorman, *The Look: Adventures in Pop and Rock Fashion* (London, 2001), p. 29.

20 It may or may not be coincidental that modern jazz musicians started dressing in this very respectable way just around the time that American sociologists began to characterize their professional milieu as a deviant subculture. See, for example, Howard Becker's classic ethnographic study, 'The Professional Dance Musician and his Audience', *American Journal of Sociology* 57/2 (1951): 146–54.

Psychedelic rock musicians of the mid- to late 1960s had a much broader range of possibilities available to them, but their choices were governed nevertheless by a basic definition of the social situation. If one of the reasons for the sartorial choices of doo-wop groups was to identify the singers clearly as entertainers and thus to distinguish them from their audiences, psychedelic rock musicians sought, for ideological reasons, to convey the opposite impression. By wearing clothing that partook of the same fashions as their audiences, and presenting themselves in a way that seemed to allow for dialogue between performers and audience, they presented themselves as continuous with their audience and implied that, in principle (if not in fact), any member of the audience could become a musician.

The vocabulary Goffman uses to describe 'manner' as an aspect of personal front might be taken to suggest that he has in mind something like personality: he contrasts 'a haughty, aggressive manner' with a 'meek, apologetic manner'. But Goffman's formal definition indicates that manner is not an expression of the performer's personality but, rather, a set of 'stimuli which function at the time to warn us of the interaction role the performer expects to play in the oncoming situation'.[21] In other words, the performer's manner is specific to a particular, situated performance of persona rather than an expression of an ongoing set of personality traits.

One key aspect of jazz musicians' manner are the means they use to distinguish moments in their performances meant to be perceived as improvisational from moments when they are playing composed music. I will briefly analyse a portion of a specific performance of 'So What' by Miles Davis, with John Coltrane in his group, from a CBS television programme entitled *The Sound of Miles Davis* that was aired in April 1959.[22] The musicians in this clip distinguish improvisation from composition in several ways. For example, Davis underlines the transition from playing the theme to improvising a solo by lowering his trumpet, then bringing it back up to his lips, moistening them and checking his mouthpiece. Apart from this one instance, he never moves the instrument away from his lips, even between phrases when he might have time to do so. Moving the trumpet down, and then back up, clearly reads as a way of segmenting the performance, of emphasizing the transition from playing composed music to improvising.

When playing the theme, Davis looks off to his right, as if he does not need to give this task his full attention. When he solos, however, he gazes ahead and somewhat downward, his eyes either closed or fixed in a stare that is not focused on anything, suggesting concentration and inward attention. He leans backward, arching his back and bending his knees in the pose that became an iconic sign for Miles Davis as seen, for example, in the cover image for the 1970 album *A Tribute to*

---

21   Goffman, *The Presentation of Self*, p. 24.
22   The line-up for this performance included: Miles Davis (trumpet); John Coltrane (tenor sax); Wynton Kelly (piano); Paul Chambers (bass); Jimmy Cobb (drums); and members of the Gil Evans Orchestra, including Frank Rehak, Jimmy Cleveland and Bill Elton (trombones).

Jack Johnson. Both his facial expressions and physical demeanour thus differentiate playing composed passages from improvising.

When Davis is finished, he steps aside, allowing Coltrane to take his place on stage. This suggests that stage position contributes to the impression of improvisation. The actions of other musicians also reinforce the status of the soloist as improviser. Before Coltrane steps forward, he respectfully focuses his attention on Davis, though not necessarily by looking at him. Coltrane's head and body movements, even his turning away from Davis, denote that he is giving Davis's solo his full, appreciative attention by following its unfolding. When soloing, Coltrane behaves very similarly to Davis. Although he mostly keeps his eyes closed in an expression of deep concentration, he too arches his back away from the microphone as he plays in a conventional gesture similar to the one guitarists make when bending notes, as mentioned earlier. As he completes his solo, he bends forward, as if bowing, and starts to move backward, out of the soloist's space, thus relinquishing that status and passing it on to the pianist. It is worth mentioning that, when performing with his own groups around the same time, Coltrane would often stand completely still when playing the theme, with only his shoulders rising and falling in time with his breaths. When improvising, however, he became much more animated, bending backward and far forward, his facial expressions depicting profound effort and immersion in the moment.

The area of the stage where the musicians stand when not playing is a region of the kind Goffman calls 'backstage', even though it is in full view.[23] The behaviour of the musicians in this area is noteworthy, since it combines the respectful attention to the soloist apparently expected of a musician waiting to play with such seemingly opposite behaviours as smoking and chatting. This combination of engagement and detachment may be at least somewhat specific to the subgenre of jazz being played, since 'cool' jazz musicians were sometimes thought to be 'emotionally detached from their creation' while simultaneously recognized as virtuosic.[24] The behaviours I have described are both individuated and conventional. They mark certain passages of music as improvised and thus communicate to both musicians and audience that those passages should be heard differently from those marked as composed.

Conclusion

I have outlined a schema for understanding popular music performance in terms of frames and signifieds. The frames are the most important contexts to be borne in mind: the general context of sociocultural norms and conventions within which performed musical behaviour must be understood and the more immediately

23   Goffman, *The Presentation of Self*, p. 11.
24   Mark C. Gridley, 'Cool Jazz', *Grove Music Online*, at: <http://www.grovemusic.com/shared/views/article.html?section=jazz.100900> (accessed 15 March 2008).

framing context of musical genre conventions that govern the expectations of audience and performer and the ways they communicate with one another. The performer combines three signifieds: the real person, the performance persona and the character. I present these entities in what I take to be the order of their development. The process begins with a real person who has some desire to perform as a popular musician; this may include the desire to participate in a certain musical genre or the desire to express certain aesthetic or sociopolitical ideas through popular music. In order to enter into the musical arena, the person must develop an appropriate performance persona.

This persona, which is usually based on existing models and conventions and may reflect the influence of such music industry types as managers or producers, becomes the basis for subsequent performances. The performer may use all of the available means to define and perform this persona, including movement, dance, costume, make-up, facial expression and gesture (including the manipulation of musical instruments). I have borrowed Goffman's vocabulary of front, which consists of setting, appearance and manner, to categorize these means. In some performances, the persona enacts a third entity, a character portrayed in the text of a song. This character may be the implied narrator of the song or a subject described in the song; it is also possible for the performer to embody more than one of the characters in a particular song. While the performer embodies different characters for each song, the performance persona remains constant, at least within a specific performance context. As I noted earlier, not all musical performances involve character – a singer or instrumentalist may well perform a persona without portraying other characters, and performed narratives may be constructed directly around personae rather than characters.

I place the performance persona at the centre of the schema outlined here and nominate it as the single most important aspect of the performer's part in that process. The persona is of key importance because it is the signified to which the audience has the most direct and sustained access not only through audio recordings, videos and live performances, but also through the various other circumstances an media in which popular musicians present themselves publicly. The persona is therefore the signified that mediates between the other two: the audience gains access to both the performer as a real person and the characters the performer portrays through his or her elaboration of a persona.

Audiences for popular music do not receive the performers' representations passively, but respond to them actively. Audiences, too, take on personae. Conventions for audience behaviour, like those of musical performance itself, are genre-specific (sometimes even performer-specific – think of the Deadheads or Jimmy Buffett's Parrothead fans). The audience responds to the performers, and this feedback is crucial to the cultures of popular music. In live performances, audiences may respond directly to performers in ways that are not limited to applause and cheering, but may include singing along, direct address to the performers, choice of costume and make-up, dancing and so on. Outside the context of live performance, audience response comes in a wide variety of forms, including such physical responses as dancing and playing air guitar, collecting audio and video recordings, participating in fan clubs and online chatrooms, and incorporating the music into everyday life. Audiences avail themselves of most of the same means of expression as popular musicians themselves in their responses to them, including playing music. Perhaps the ultimate response to popular music performance is when a young person aspires to become a musician herself and to join the performers she has seen on-stage.

Vocal Performance and the Projection of Emotional Authenticity

Nicola Dibben

Performing Identities

When he opened his mouth, out flew his soul – and beautifully rasping roars of love, life and loss.[1]

One of the most important elements of pop music culture is the star, and one of the predominant ways in which vocal performances of contemporary popular music are understood is in terms of the communication of authentic emotion through that star. Belief in a singer's authenticity reflects one of the most prevalent ideologies of music creation and reception and of the person in contemporary society – the idea that people have an inner, private core. Public interest in the private lives of stars reveals a desire to go beyond the image of the star and to the reality of a star's private self: the mediated personas of stars are so ubiquitous, with their images circulating in the public domain and their private lives the subject of gossipy journalism, that it can feel as though we know them intimately. The fascination with stars in general is at least partly attributable to the way in which they enact for us ways of making sense of the experience of being a person.[2]

But what or who is a singer communicating? Simon Frith summarizes the play of identities in pop performance as follows:

> First, [pop singers] are involved in a process of double enactment: they enact both a star personality (their image) and a song personality, the role that each lyric requires, and the pop star's art is to keep both acts in play at once ... the performer is thus the singer and not-the-singer simultaneously. ...

1   Billboard poster for the LaMontagne album and tour, *Trouble*, London 2006.
2   Richard Dyer, *Heavenly Bodies: Film Stars and Society* (London, 1987), p. 17.

> *The second complication in the pop singer's enactment of the pop star is that she ... is also the site of desire – as a body, and as a person. ... In performance, then, in the playing of the various song parts, instead of 'forgetting who they are', singers are continuously registering their presence.*[3]

The star-image referred to by Frith is the amalgam of all the information and products pertaining to that star, including their music and other artistic products released in their name, as well as publicity material, interviews, public appearances and media coverage.[4] The star-image is central to the effective workings of the publicity machine within the music industry since it provides a single-author image around which products and publicity can cohere. However, this also means that there is a potential for dissociation between the star-image, which is never completely owned or managed by the star or their management, and the 'real' person.

One task for popular music research is to determine *how* performance communicates these various identities and to what extent the way pop sounds is congruent with, and perhaps shaped by, its social and economic context. Previous research has focused on the musical constituents of authenticity, its economic ramifications, and lyrical and analytical analyses of the subjectivities afforded by pop.[5] Rather than reiterate these theories, this chapter investigates the role of two relatively neglected attributes of pop: first, the virtual sound world of the recording (and amplified sound) and its role in creating what can be heard as psychologically revealing, intimate musical expression, and, second, the role of body movement in communicating performing identities. The reason for focusing on these two modes of expression is that they are important factors in the expression of authentic emotion: technological changes in music production and reception personalizes the relationship between artist and public, and prioritizes the personal and individual.[6] This, together with the direct address of the audience, constructs pop performances as personal expressions for private consumption, even when it is a collective experience, as in live performance.

---

3   Simon Frith, *Performing Rites: Evaluating Popular Music* (Cambridge, MA and London, 1996), p. 212.

4   Dyer, *Heavenly Bodies*.

5   For an example of musicological analysis of authenticity see Allan Moore, 'Authenticity as Authentication', *Popular Music* 21/2 (2002): 209–23; for discussion of the economic implications of the ideology of authenticity see Lee Marshall, *Bootlegging: Romanticism and Copyright in the Music Industry* (London, 2005); for an analysis of emotional authenticity conveyed in pop recordings see Nicola Dibben, 'Subjectivity and the Construction of Emotion in the Music of Björk', *Music Analysis* 25/1–2 (2006): 171–97.

6   P. David Marshall, *Celebrity and Power: Fame in Contemporary Culture* (Minneapolis, MN, 1997).

Performing Intimacy: Virtual Space in Recordings

The history of recording contains within it a chronicle of virtual space, some varieties of which may only ever have existed on the recording and could never be realized through other means. Researchers are beginning to explore the history of these practices and the sound worlds they create,[7] but for the purposes of this chapter there are three main points to be made. First, electrical amplification and recording allow forms of vocal expression which are intimate. The introduction of the microphone in the 1930s enabled the voice to be amplified above other sound sources and gave rise to vocal styles which were softer and more intimate than had previously been possible with the same size ensembles and venues. Second, this change in production coincided with changes in consumption: it was now possible to listen to music in the comfort and intimacy of one's own home.[8] Third, the normative arrangement of vocals within the mix placed the voice centrally, and louder than other sounds, creating what Tagg calls the 'monocentric mix':

> *This not only implies that the singer is, as usual, the central 'reference point' of the piece but also that she has had her mouth placed nearer the listener's ear, not only by proximity to the recording mike, but also by the relative volume accorded to the main vocal channel(s) in the final mix. This technique creates an actual or imagined distance between two persons (the singer and the listener) which is that of an intimate and confidential monologue (of potential dialogue).*[9]

The effect of the voice at the front of the mix is a prioritization of attention on the artist and his/her identity, and that of the character performed by the artist.[10] Running parallel with this mode of reception is a compositional ideology in which singers understand themselves to be expressing things about or from their own experience. These factors mean that the idea of emotional authenticity held by artists, engineers and audiences alike is manifested in the sound of recordings. In contemporary popular music recording techniques, such as reverb, delays, filters and overdubbing, help 'stage' voices, which are, as Serge Lacasse terms it, the

---

7   For work on the history of the virtual sound space of recording see: Peter Doyle, *Echo and Reverb: Fabricating Space in Popular Music Recording, 1900–1960*, (Middletown, CT, 2005); Serge Lacasse, '"Listen to My Voice": The Evocative Power of Vocal Staging in Recorded Rock Music and other Forms of Vocal Expression', PhD diss. (University of Liverpool, 2000), at: <http://www.mus.ulaval.ca/lacasse/texts/THESIS.pdf> (accessed 28 May 2008); Allan F. Moore and Ruth Dockwray, 'The Establishment of the Virtual Performance Space in Rock', *Twentieth Century Music* (forthcoming).

8   Richard Middleton, *Studying Popular Music*, (Milton Keynes, 1990), p. 85.

9   Philip Tagg, *Fernando the Flute* (Liverpool, 1991), p. 60.

10   In the natural world, humans show an orienting response to sound events – that is, they turn the body and head centrally towards the sound source thereby placing it in the centre of the perceptual field. Placement of the voice centrally within a stereophonic mix therefore affords attentional focus on the voice.

'aural index' of the singer's persona and represented emotions.[11] However, whereas Lacasse reveals the narrative meanings staging gives rise to, it is possible to use this approach to investigate the creation of intimacy between singer and audience.

The production of an intimate sound in a recording has a psychoacoustical basis in the amount of reflected sound and the relative loudness of sounds within the mix. First, in the real world (as opposed to the virtual world of recordings) the amount of reverb (reflected sound in which there is no discontinuous repeat of the original sound) differs according to the proximity of a sound source to reflective surfaces: the closer a sound source to reflective surfaces, the more continuous the reverb will sound; the further away a sound source from the reflective surface, the greater delay there will be between original and reflection, and the reflected sound will be heard as an echo rather than as reverberation. The amount of sound coming direct from the sound source relative to reflected sound also differs according to the position of the listener in relation to the source of the sound: when the listener is close to the sound source he or she will hear a larger proportion of direct sound than reflected sound. Thus, sounds recorded close to a microphone contain more of the recorded signal direct from the source and less reflected sound (reverb), suggesting that the listener is in close proximity to the sound source. Second, in the real world the relative amplitude of sounds specifies their proximity to the listener: hence, sounds which are louder in the mix in a recording tend to be heard as being nearer the listener than sounds which are quieter. Thus, manipulation of these elements in the recording and production process can specify varieties of physical space (size and type), the position of the sound source within that space and the proximity of the sound source to the listener. These in turn influence the emotional character of a recording, because they specify a location and physical relationship between listener and sound source.

The production norm for amplification and recording of pop singers has two important effects: it creates intimacy between listener and singer, and communicates the 'inner' thoughts of the song character and/or performer.[12] This convention is so normative that it is only when it is deliberately highlighted or disrupted during performance that we become aware of its presence at all. For example, in Björk's track 'There's More to Life than This' (1993) there is a sudden change of virtual space from the normative acoustic space of a dance track to the inside of toilets in a club: this sudden relocation, announced by the banging of a door, the change in the prominence of the 'dance track' sounds in relation to Björk's voice and the heightened intimacy of Björk's whisper, brings the disorienting realization that what had been experienced as a performance by Björk was in fact a performance within

---

11   Serge Lacasse, 'Persona, Emotions and Technology: The Phonographic Staging of the Popular Music Voice', CHARM Symposium 2: Towards a Musicology of Production (part of The Art of Record Production conference), 17–18 September 2005 (London, 2005). Available at: <http://www.charm.rhul.ac.uk/content/events/s2Lacasse.pdf> (accessed 28 May 2008). See also Lacasse, '"Listen to My Voice"'.

12   A detailed analysis of aural intimacy manifested in a pop track can be found in Nicola Dibben, *Björk* (London, forthcoming).

which she, too, was the audience, and the 'real' song (the expression of her thoughts and experiences for the listener) begins only with the move into the more intimate space of the toilets. The aural intimacy which is normative to pop production and performance is significant because it contributes to, and is produced by, the star system, within which the private life of a celebrity is an important part of their public persona, communicated by press coverage and prominent entertainment values in newspaper journalism.[13]

Performing Bodies: Body Movement and Gesture in Pop Performance

The example of the sudden perceived spatial and relational relocation in Björk's track 'There's More to Life than This' highlights the second part of this consideration of pop performance: if pop is understood to be communicating authentic emotion in an intimate relationship with the listener, then whose emotions are these, and to what extent is intimacy maintained in live performance, where 'private' emotions are performed to a mass audience?

Approaches to popular performance have studied the development of popular performing style in rock, viewing it as the result of confluence between black performance style and the need to express the individuality of the performer.[14] Analyses have also focused on the performance of gender and sexual identities, and the role of performance as 'seduction'.[15] Here, my focus is on the performance of star persona, song personality and the notion that there might be a 'real' person 'behind' the star image. One empirical approach to this topic is to study body movement in musical performance. Social psychological theory has posited the existence of a repertoire of body gestures and facial expressions, which are an important source

---

13   DeCordova traces the association between stars and interest in their private lives to the emergence of the film-star system in America in the twentieth century: the increase in information about film stars' lives outside the roles they played in films occurred because only by knowing something about the 'private' lives of stars could the star persona exist separate from the different roles the star played in film. See Richard DeCordova, *Picture Personalities: The Emergence of the Star System in America* (Chicago, 1991). In cinema, the star persona was supported by material aspects of production, just as in pop music different technological factors facilitated emergence of the star-image: whereas in cinema film close-up camera shots allow a close view of the actor's face and draws the spectator's attention to the actors' looks rather than their role, the microphone creates intimacy between listener and musician.

14   P. David Marshall argues that the transitional figure in the development of the contemporary performing style was Johnnie Ray. See Marshall, *Celebrity and Power*.

15   Simon Frith *Performing Rites*; Sheila Whiteley, 'Little Red Rooster v. The Honky Tonk Woman: Mick Jagger, Sexuality, Style and Image' in Sheila Whiteley (ed.), *Sexing the Groove: Popular Music and Gender* (London, 1997), pp. 67–99.

of non-verbal communication and form part of the production and structuring of expression. Musical performers make movements superfluous to those required for the execution of musical sound, just as speakers make movement 'unnecessary' to speech production. Gesture in performance also shares similarities with the kinds of movements that accompany speech, particularly for singers who are also engaged in vocal performance and who may have no instrument to 'get in the way' of gestures.[16]

Jane Davidson's analyses of performances by British pop stars Robbie Williams, Annie Lennox of the Eurythmics and the Irish band The Corrs, analyse the performers' and audiences' gestures in terms of movement types, in order to show how particular gestures communicate ideas about the shaping of musical structure and expression, allow coordination between performers on stage and create varieties of interaction with the audience.[17] She also uses her analyses to provide evidence of the distinction drawn by Simon Frith and others between the performer as narrator and performer as star: she uses her analysis of body movements to show how musical performance can both communicate a star persona with its associated showmanship and entertainment value (through what she terms 'display' movements) and reveal states which appear to be more intimate, personal and communicative of the 'ordinary' person (through the category of 'adaptor' movements – small movements of which one is often unaware, such as tossing the hair or scratching the face). For example, she argues that Williams's own statements in interviews about his experience of flicking between a 'stage

---

16   There is currently no agreed framework for analysing body movements, so applications to music have tended to adopt different models of non-verbal communication. However, Jane Davidson has analysed performances by classical and pop singers using a classificatory scheme proposed by P. Ekman and W.V. Friesen, 'The repertoire of nonverbal behaviour: categories, origins, usage and coding', *Semiotica* 1 (1969): 49–98; and Martin Clayton has analysed Raga performance using a later classificatory scheme for speech-related hand gestures proposed by Bernard Rimé and Loris Schiaratura in 'Gesture and Speech' in Robert S. Feldman and Bernard Rimé (eds), *Fundamentals of Nonverbal Behaviour* (Cambridge, 1991), pp. 239–81. Adopting a model from speech may inadvertently mask types of behaviour particular to musical performance. Therefore one of the priorities for research into body movement in pop performance is to critically assess the application of models from speech and gesture to music. For example, gestures which accompany the ideational flow of speech have been interpreted in musical contexts as indicating a performer's understanding of the flow of musical structure, but empirical evidence is relatively scarce.

17   Jane W. Davidson, 'The Role of the Body in the Production and Perception of Solo Vocal Performance: A Case Study of Annie Lennox', *Musicae Scientiae* 5/2 (2001): 235–56; Jane W. Davidson, '"She's the One": Multiple Functions of Body Movement in a Stage Performance by Robbie Williams' in Anthony Gritten and Elaine King (eds), *Music and Gesture* (Aldershot, 2006), pp. 208–25; Kaori Kurosawa and Jane W. Davidson, 'Nonverbal Behaviours in Popular Music Performance: A Case Study of the Corrs', *Musicae Scientiae* 9 (2005): 111–37.

persona' and 'intimate, shy self' is manifested in performance in the kinds of body movements he makes.[18]

Davidson's argument that body movements can reveal something of the 'inner' emotional state of a performer depends on an interpretation of 'adaptor' movements as 'emotional leakage'.[19] There is general agreement that adaptors satisfy physical or emotional needs, and, because the person making such movements is often unaware of them, they have been interpreted as revealing otherwise hidden emotional states and attitudes. An alternative interpretation is that self-adaptors are a form of attentional self-regulation which emerge when a speaker undergoes interference with attention or disorganized thought; in other words, self-adaptors allow speakers to maintain their performance when potentially distracted.[20] In either case viewers use the information from adaptors gestures to make judgements about the emotional and physical state of the speaker and therefore offer a means of investigating non-verbal communication of performer identity.

In order to examine how star image and song character are kept in play during a performance, and the extent to which these express authentic emotion, I present two analyses. The classificatory scheme adopted here is derived from Rimé and Schiaratura[21] since this is equally adapted to textless music as well as music with lyrics, and allows classification of movement types at a greater level of detail than the competing model from Ekman and Friesen used by Jane Davidson.[22] I adopt three additional categories to provide a more complete analysis of the performance situation: Martin Clayton's categories of 'physical movements necessary to sound production' and 'manipulation of the body and immediate physical environment' (which encompasses 'adaptors')[23] and Jane Davidson's notion of 'display' gestures. The method involves repeated viewing of the performances, transcription of musical and visual features, and thematic categorization of movements based on the classification system in Table 16.1. The analyses explore the extent to which this

---

18   Davidson, '"She's the One"', p. 213.
19   'Adaptors' have been classified by Ekman and Friesen into three types: self-adaptors, in which one part of the body manipulates another, such as rubbing the nose, biting the lip or holding the forehead; object-adaptors, in which an external object is repeatedly manipulated or brought into contact with the body but not to perform a task, such as twirling a pencil, scratching an ear with a pen, or repeatedly adjusting cutlery on a table; and alter-adaptor, in which movements are in relation to, or making contact with, another person, such as restless movements of the legs, or movements towards or away from another person.
20   Evidence that body-focused movements are a form of attention regulation comes from studies by Freedman in the late 1970s. Cited in Jinni Harrigan, 'Proxemics, Kinesics and Gaze' in Jinni Harrigan, Robert Rosenthal and Klaus R. Scherer (eds), *The New Handbook of Methods in Nonverbal Behaviour* (New York, 2005), pp. 137–98.
21   Rimé and Schiaratura, 'Gesture and Speech'.
22   Ekman and Freisen 'The Repertoire of Nonverbal Behaviour'.
23   Martin Clayton 'Communication in Raga Performance' in Dorothy Miell, Raymond MacDonald and David J. Hargreaves (eds), *Musical Communication* (New York, 2005), pp. 361–81.

theory of body movement and gesture can shed light on the performance of song and star identities.

Table 16.1   Classificatory system of body movement in musical performance Jarvis Cocker: Performing the Star Persona

Gesture category	Gesture subcategory
Gestures referring to the ideational process	Non-depictive gestures/ speech-marking / music-marking (pulse, cadence, structure, tapping/ nodding in time)
	Depictive gestures: ideographs which track the speaker's thought process or musical flow
Gestures referring to the object of speech (depictive):	Iconic
	Pantomimic/mimetic
Gestures referring to the object of speech (evocative)	Deictic (pointing)
	Symbolic/emblems
Physical movements necessary to sound production	
Manipulation of the body and immediate physical environment	Includes 'adaptors'
Display	Iincluding dance movements and therefore similar to music-markers

The song 'Common People' by English band Pulp uses a standard rock structure and arrangement: it is tonal, in 4/4 time and has a verse/chorus structure with an instrumental section and coda. The song's lyrics tell a first-person narrative reporting the meeting between the character sung by Jarvis and a fellow college student from a rich background who attempts to experience the life of the 'common people' with whom the singer and audience are identified.[24] The tone is scathing, mocking but also self-righteous as the rich girl's attempts to be 'common' are sent up, and the 'common people' are celebrated. The song was an anthem of the Britpop music scene in England in the 1990s.

Comparison of body movement in a pop promo video and a live performance of the same song allows an investigation of the performed identities and of the extent to which these differ in different contexts of production and consumption.

---

24   The biographical salience of the song would not have been lost on its audience who would have been aware of Jarvis Cocker's own background as a student of St Martin's College of Art in London.

Two performances of 'Common People' are analysed here: the music video (dir. Pedro Romhanyi, 1995) intended for domestic consumption, and a recording of a live performance (Brixton Academy, London, 1996), which I treat here as a window on to the live performance rather than studying the video recording as a text. The pop promo is made for television viewing and therefore includes close-ups of the performers' facial expressions, whereas the film of the live performance is constrained by the limitations of what can be captured in live performance and cut to film. The video, made to promote the single and album, is shorter in duration at 4:09 minutes compared to 9:19 minutes of the live performance, which includes two extra verses and an extended coda.

The music video keeps in play two identities: the first-person narrator song character and Jarvis Cocker's star persona. One of the primary means by which the video does this is through a literal presentation of the two performers; we see two Jarvis Cocker's – the star, who is featured performing with the band on stage as if at a glitzy, retro, 1980s club, and a second Jarvis who acts as narrator (see Fig. 16.1). A second means by which these two identities are kept in play is through the use of stylized and slick body movements. The majority of body movements and gestures used by Cocker are gestures referring to the object of the lyrics (either by depicting or evoking the referent) (Table 16.2).

Table 16.2   Movement types in 'Common People' (Pulp, 1995)

Gesture	Video – 1995		Live – 1996	
	Frequency	%	Frequency	%
Non-depictive gestures/speech-marking	12	23	12	13
Depictive gestures: ideographs which track the speaker's thought process or musical flow	0	0	4	4
Iconic	3	6	14	15
Pantomimic/mimetic	11	21	6	7
Deictic (pointing)	6	12	21	23
Symbolic/emblems	10	19	11	12
Manipulation of the body and immediate physical environment (includes 'adaptors')	2	4	3	3
Display/dance	8	15	21	23

The use of depictive gestures in particular is much higher than for other performers. Pantomimic gestures occur frequently: for example, on the lyrics 'Smoke some fags, and play some pool / Pretend you never went to school' (third verse), Cocker first sweeps his hand from his mouth as if discarding a cigarette, then swipes his hand at hip level as if miming the action of a pool cue, then wags his finger in the emblem of refusal on the word 'never'. Gestures representing the object iconically, a second type of depictive gesture, are also common: for example, Cocker's circling of his eye on the final word of 'That's where I caught her eye' is both deictic, and pictographic; it provides a visual emphasis which supports the rhyme between 'I' and 'eye' and exaggerates the different meanings of the two words. Other examples of iconic gestures are placing his hands with palms together at the side of his head to indicate lying down, placing a hand above his eyes to symbolize 'looking', and putting his hand to his forehead to indicate 'thinking'. Gestures which evoke the object of the lyrics are also frequent. Cocker uses symbolic gestures, such as shaking his head or wagging his finger to indicate the negative, and pointing, a gesture which appears here when Cocker, the first-person narrator of the song points to himself on 'I' and to the viewer ('you'). One of the few self-adaptors is Cocker's picking of his fingers as the rich girl lip-synchs to his singing voice, suggesting a nonchalant attitude towards her (Fig. 16.1). Unlike most adaptors, this gesture is performed self-consciously, in a deliberate enactment of the first-person narrative. The high frequency of gestures depicting or evoking the lyrics gives the performance a knowing quality as it plays out the dual identities of Jarvis Cocker as star and Cocker as song character. It is these kinds of possibilities in video performance which lead Simon Frith to comment that 'music videos are less interesting as mini-films, as visual narratives, than as ideal types of performance ...'.[25]

Figure 16.1 The two Jarvis Cockers and the rich girl in the music video 'Common People' (1995) Reproduced under license from Universal Island Records Limited

---

25   Frith, *Performing Rites*, p. 224.

In this example the authenticity of the star image resides in the knowingness of this dual performance, and in the enactment of the star image through display movements. An extreme example is the large jump and flailing limb movements which occur at climactic structural moments, such as the end of the chorus into the third verse, the end of the third verse into the chorus and at the end of the coda. These moments of display are in complete contrast to the expressionless, lethargic dancing of the 'clubbers' and serve to highlight Cocker's presence as star performer, both within the diegesis of the video and in the real world. Cocker's performance of his body as the site for audience desire can be attributed to these moments of display – for example, the jump and large limb movements coinciding with the 'bolt-of-electricity' musical effect display an energy, fluency and (apparent) spontaneity at odds with the stylized and knowing gestures accompanying his lyrics. It is as though these display gestures arise from, and are part of, the musical sound and its non-verbal communication, unlike the other gestures which are tied to verbalized meanings. Indeed, it is possible to see Cocker's movements as taking on the expressivity of the music, perhaps even giving rise to it, in an erotic enactment of power.[26]

Compare this video performance with the live performance of the same song from a year later. The two performances share many similarities in the use of types of gesture at certain locations, although the exact gesture used and its size differ between performances. Gestures referring to the object of the lyrics occur in the same locations, but are sometimes different: for example, the self-reference in the first verse ('That's where I caught her eye') is indicated by a finger pointing to the head in the video, but in live performance is a larger gesture in which the back of the hand is drawn across the face. There are also many more 'display' movements in the live performance, as Cocker acts out his star image and interacts with the audience. Both performances attempt to draw the audience into the first-person narrative through direct address. In both cases Cocker approaches the audience and whispers asides, inviting closeness and intimacy between performer and audience, or implicating the audience, but in the live performance Cocker points at the audience many more times, replacing the role of his gaze into the camera in the video performance with deictic gestures. These whispers and approaches to

---

26 This is a different explanation of music's association with sex than offered elsewhere. Simon Frith, in *Performing Rites*, argues that music's association with sex is sociological rather than musicological: he argues that we hear rock as sexual due to the cultural ideology that African-derived musics (such as rock) are more 'natural' and therefore more directly in touch with the body (p. 127), and that rhythm is sexual because it provides an easy way for the unskilled to enter into the music, and experience the body and experience a sense of presence in time (p. 144). Frith suggests that the listening fantasy 'is that we control the music (the sexual exchange) when, in fact, the performer does' (p. 215). I suggest that part of the erotic power of popular music performance comes from participating in the musical unfolding which is perceived as though it is controlled by, or emanating from, the performer and is thereby experienced as power and control enacted by the performer on the listener. Which of these interpretations is true can perhaps only be decided by empirical research into experience of pop.

the audience allow the fake promise of private intimacy, which, as Frith remarks, is a listening fantasy in which we believe the offer to 'know' the star could be made 'just for us' – even if the 'us' in the context of public performance is experienced as a collective. The effect is simultaneously a self-conscious enactment of the song personality (the narrator) and the star image, as entertainer and site of desire.

Amy Winehouse: Performing the Private for Public Consumption

The example above illustrates a performance style in which the elision between star persona and song character is knowingly enacted. Furthermore, it is possible to understand the performance as revealing something of the person behind the persona – in this case, a person dealing with a self-perceived mismatch between rock star persona and self-identity as a lanky, geeky, working-class lad from Sheffield (the self-conscious enactment of the star persona allows Cocker to be the song character, the site of audience desire and 'ordinary' person). However, there are other cases where the enactment of star persona and song character become indistinguishable and in which the public performance of the 'private' life of the star arguably becomes exploitative. A recent example of perceived identity between star image and song character is English singer-songwriter Amy Winehouse, whose rise to fame in 2006 was accompanied by notoriety for her misuse of alcohol and drugs, self-harm, a tempestuous relationship with her husband and legal difficulties. Public and critical reception of her music draws on an ideology in which great artistry is perceived as arising from pain and tragedy, and in which, as Sheila Whiteley observes, death is seen as the 'ultimate form of excess'[27]: for example, one journalist remarked that if Winehouse's real-life situation improved, her music might suffer.[28] The critically acclaimed song 'Rehab' from her second album *Back to Black* (2006), written by Winehouse and produced by Mark Ronson, epitomizes the entanglement of Winehouse's personal and public lives.[29] Public reception and Winehouse's statements about the track make a direct association between her biography and the lyrics and video of the single, which recount her record company's wish that she attend drug rehabilitation, her father's opinion, her

---

27 Sheila Whiteley, 'The Killing Fields of Popular Music' in Sue Holmes and Sean Redmond (eds), *Framing Celebrity: New Directions in Celebrity Culture* (New York, 2006), pp. 329–42.

28 Joan Anderman, 'Of Course She Should Go to Rehab: But Like the Troubled Talents Who Came Before Her, Amy Winehouse Made her Pain Part of her Artistry', *Boston Globe*, 16 December 2007.

29 'Rehab' won numerous awards, including the Ivor Novello Award for Best Contemporary Song in 2007 and three Grammy Awards in 2008: Record of the Year, Song of the Year and Best Female Pop Vocal Performance.

brief visit to a clinic, explanation of her state, and diagnosis, and refusal to attend rehabilitation ('They tried to make me go to rehab, I said "no, no, no"'):

> I was having a particularly nasty time with things and just drinking and drinking. My management decided to stop buying for me and said they were taking me to rehab. I asked my dad if he thought I needed to go. He said: 'No but I should give it a try.' So I did, for just 15 minutes. I went in said 'hello' and explained that I drink because I am in love and have f***ed up the relationship. Then I walked out.[30]

The song and early performances can be understood as a transformation of personal suffering into public performance, and display the control and musical skill necessary to such artistry. However, during 2008 Winehouse's performances became increasingly chaotic, as the impact of her widely publicized drug and alcohol addictions affected her musical abilities. Amid media speculation as to whether she would be able to perform, she came out of rehabilitation in June 2008 to do two televised performances in England (a concert in honour of Nelson Mandela's 90th birthday in Hyde Park, London, and Glastonbury Festival), the first of which I analyse here.

'Rehab' consists of repeated chorus and verses, with a Motown-inspired instrumental ensemble and harmonic structure. Winehouse's rather shambolic performance is evident from the opening of the song as she first struggles with the microphone stand and then misses an entry as a member of stage crew adjusts it for her. By the end of the first chorus she has settled in to the performance, but the performance lacks polish: lyrics become slurred at the end of second verse, and the vocal improvisation and ornamentation at the end of the second chorus lacks melodic fluency and intonational accuracy.

Winehouse uses a very limited range of movement types, with few directed at communicating the ideas in the song: there are no gestures depicting or evoking the object of lyrics, or engaging with the audience, or referring to the underlying logic of the lyrics. The majority of movements are what might loosely be described as dance movements – a form of display which is normative for female pop performers. These movements are extremely restricted compared to those of her male backing singers, and physically constrained by her tight clothing and high-heeled shoes: her legs remain close together, and her steps are very small, demarcating a small personal space on-stage. Many of her display movements draw attention to her body as the site of desire: for example, the hip bounces and shifts in weight draw attention to her crotch and bottom, her arms raised to her chest with elbows out draw attention to her breasts, and her dancing posture of chest out, bottom out and head tilted slightly back and up are sexually inviting. To some extent, these movements can be understood as non-depictive gestures marking musical processes and structures, and therefore communicating her

---

30   Amy Winehouse cited in Jacqui Swift, 'Wine, Woman and Song', *Sun*, 27 October 2006.

understanding of musical structure. For example, many of her dance movements mark different levels of musical pulse: her posture in the first verse is with hands on hips and small circular movements of her hips, in time with the pulse of the song; in the second chorus she introduces a small bouncing movement with the hips at the level of the quaver beat; and in the second verse this shifting of weight switches to the crotchet level. Similarly, arm movements occasionally demarcate phrase structure. For example, in the first verse she raises her arms slowly above her head then lowers them again during the phrase 'I didn't get a lot in class / But I know we don't come in a shot glass'. In the corresponding position within the second verse she raises her arms again ('I'm gonna, I'm gonna lose my baby'), but this time the gesture turns into a clichéd dance movement of alternate arms raised and dropped every minim beat, as though the arm movement has lost its original purpose half way through.

One type of movement in particular becomes increasingly extreme during the performance – she holds on to the bottom of her dress and raises it to reveal her thighs and crotch.[31] This action first appears in the first verse and gradually becomes more frequent and exaggerated until the final verse when it becomes uncomfortably exposing. Holding on to the bottom of her skirt and raising it is a self-adaptor gesture: the action does not illustrate lyrics or music, and the skirt is already very short so raising it further seems superfluous to any need for display. These movements reveal the workings of a private 'inner' self as opposed to an enacted song character. Other elements of the performance also enact Winehouse's private life for public consumption: the lyrics to her songs and her comments about their biographical relevance in performance, her dedication of her songs in performance to her jailed husband, and the wearing of his name as a hair ornament hold up her performance as a display of her troubled private life. In this context, the 'emotional leakage' or loss of attention indicated by her adaptor gestures can be read as evidence of the disturbed mental state of Winehouse the star, rather than a song character she is playing.

Consequences of the Ideology of Authentic Emotional Expression

This chapter has focused on two relatively neglected aspects of popular music with the aim of furthering understanding of the way in which pop performances offer identities for audiences to respond to and the kind of engagement afforded. It explored the correlation between the 'closeness' characterizing celebrity culture and aural closeness afforded by amplified sound and recordings. It also showed how the virtual space of recorded performances contributes to expression of intimacy

---

31   See the clip at: <http://www.youtube.com/watch?v=F4CPgcfO79Y> from 2 minutes 45 seconds into her performance.

and investigated the role of body movement in keeping in play the dual identities of star persona and song character in performance.

One aspect highlighted here has been the uneasy balance between musicians' desire to express themselves and the danger that it can entail public exposure and prurient interest. Pop musicians work within a compositional aesthetic of self-expression in which their musical output is received as though it is the expression of biographical events and reveals the inner life of the performer. However, when things go wrong, whether caused by celebrity status (what Sheila Whiteley has termed 'famed damage'[32]) or writ large by it, the recorded sound of authentic emotional intimacy has social and cultural ramifications. The normative staging of pop voices provides aural intimacy with the star and therefore contributes to the notion of access to a 'real' person behind the star-image. This desire for access to the person behind the persona manifests in media pressure on celebrities to give ever more personal information in interviews and to access the personal lives of stars and their families, and is implicated in the extreme reactions and obsessions exhibited by some fans.

Interviews with star performers reveal an awareness of the problems wrought by the idea of authenticity and the cultural construction of their work as emotional expression. In a documentary interview, Björk observed of her own motivations to make music:

> ... *what drives you, is you want to give something of you. And I guess with people who have similar job as I have [sic] it gets misunderstood . .... And so you kind of get confused and start giving things that maybe nobody wants, or the media will ask you for things that is nobody's business. And then you stop giving what you wanted to give in the first place. But there is still .... a part of me that has hope and wants to give and communicate something that is quite private, but it has nothing to do with my everyday life still. It is still this bubble, this kind of fantasy fairytale bubble.*[33]

What this quotation reveals for me is the entanglement of two things. On the one hand, it highlights the motivation an artist might have to express herself through music, which can be seen as produced by a cultural system within which music is a means for self-expression. On the other hand, it embodies an ideology of psychological intimacy and access to the star, caused by the way in which artistic expression is co-opted by the culture industry.

Different artists have different ways of dealing with this situation. In the case of Jarvis Cocker, for instance, a distance is created between inner, private person

---

32 Sheila Whiteley, 'The Killing Fields of Popular Music', p. 330. Whiteley's claim that 'it is the intimacies of an individual's personal life that exerts such a fatal fascination' (p. 329) implies that some of the psychological breakdowns and deaths of star musicians can be attributed to their celebrity status.

33 Björk in *Björk: Miniscule*, dir. Ragnheidur Gestsdóttir (Wellhardt/One Little Indian, 2001).

and audience through a knowing enactment of star persona and song character in performance. A second type of response to the focus on a star persona is to diminish the salience of the star image by choosing not to present onself as the musical and visual focus. For example, although Icelandic alternative rock band Sigur Rós has a singer (Jonsi Birgisson), the music and visual aspects of performance minimize his position as attentional focus. Their tracks mix instrumental and vocal lines such that they are at an equal dynamic level and their music lacks easily decipherable lyrics, such that the voice becomes just another instrument. The aural equality between voice and ensemble is manifested visually in the on-stage relationship between singer and band: on-stage lighting is usually extremely low, with spotlights used only occasionally. This performance strategy is also carried through to the band's publicity material: the cover art and music videos rarely feature members of the band, and for a long time the band avoided interviews:

> ... we want people to hear the music. They won't hear the music if they read an article about us or look at our photo. It was never a plan to be this mystery band or anything – we just want people to hear the music rather than looking at our faces.[34]

Sigur Rós present one strategy by which to minimize focus on the star persona of the individual artist and the celebrity culture that accompanies it, although as they operate within the music industry and the habitual reception practices of audiences, it is impossible to avoid entirely.

This chapter demonstrates that if we are to understand why popular music is the way it is, then we need to pay attention to both its material characteristics and their relationship to the social and economic circumstances of production and consumption. I have highlighted two areas deserving of more attention and the techniques that exist for their analysis. However, these techniques need to be developed further; there is much more potential to use analyses of body movements to further understanding of communication in performance and to employ new methods for the analysis of sound recordings to explore the different varieties of virtual sound world embodied in recorded sound. Analysing the body movements in performance can help us understand how identities are maintained and communicated through performance, how body movement contributes to the entertainment value of performance and how performers manage the distance between performer and audience. How and to what extent performance contributes to perceptions of authentic emotion is an important component in understanding one of the most prevalent reception ideologies of contemporary pop.

---

34   Sigur Rós interviewed in James Keast, 'Exclaim: Sigur Rós – 20,000 Icelanders Can't be Wrong', cited in *Eighteen Seconds Before Sunrise*, at: <www.sigur-ros.co.uk/media/articles/exclaim0.php> (accessed 22 May 2008).

Discography

Amy Winehouse, 'Rehab', *Back to Black* (CD, Island, 2006).

Amy Winehouse, 'Rehab', *46664 Concert: Honouring Nelson Mandela at 90*, 27 June 2008, <http://www.46664.com/354/> (accessed 20 August 2008).

Björk 'There's More to Life than This', *Debut* (CD, One Little Indian, 1993).

Björk: Miniscule, dir. Ragnheidur Gestsdóttir (DVD, Wellhardt/One Little Indian, 2001).

Pulp, 'Common People', dir. Pedro Romhanyi 1995, *Pulp Hits* (DVD, Island, 2002).

Pulp, 'Common People', *Ultimate Live: F.E.E.L.I.N.G.C.A.L.L.E.D.L.I.V.E.* (DVD, Island, 2005).

'Chelsea Rodgers' was a Model – Vocality in Prince of the Twenty-first Century

Stan Hawkins

Introduction

If there is a vocal style to define all pop styles it is Prince's. 'Come on,' he instructs his model. 'Go ahead, teach me! Go ahead Chelsea.' Released worldwide in August 2007, 'Chelsea Rodgers', the second single from *Planet Earth*, Prince's twenty-sixth studio album, is neatly sandwiched between ten tracks.[1] Raunchy in its feel, this disco-funk track displays all the musical playfulness that harks back to earlier triumphs, like 'Musicology', 'Black Sweat' and 'Housequake'. Thirty years into his career I wonder if there is that much in this track we have not heard before? Frankly, no. But, one thing is for sure – there are few musicians who manage to tug at the groove in the way he does, and that's what I set out to explore.

This chapter is admittedly an exercise in taste, wading right into one's own aesthetic preferences. For evaluating any recording has to do with empathy and affinity, and, most of all, with what one feels for a singer in a given context. A prime factor accounting for personal taste in music, I want to argue, lies in the singer's presence in the mix. So how does hearing a pop voice link style to function? And, in what ways might we go about interpreting vocal performance? Pop music, in the main, is mediated vocally, entailing vocal strategies and performance tricks. This is why taking a look at a stripped-down disco track seems a good place to start working out vocal performance and all its peculiarities.

Based on a number of findings, my musicological interpretation of this song impinges on the music analytical. Yet, the music analytical terrain is fiddly, and, as Prince's 'produced identity' demonstrates, there are a multitude of pervasive details that define his audio image. For instance, his articulation of register, range, pitch inflections, resonance, rhythmic articulations, spoken fills, pitch control and

---

1   'Chelsea Rodgers' from *Planet Earth* (NPG/Sony BMG, 2007).

melodic angularity certainly shape the aesthetics of the song. At the same time, there is the matter of sonic treatment – the mastering of the mix and the utilization of production techniques, such as compression, expansion and limiting. Further, the employment of clarity or fuzz, single precision, double precision or floating points in the digital processing of a vocal line and the high use of frequency response to simulate vocal depth all display the intricacies of the recorded pop voice. So, any number of musical details may verify an artist's vocal style, and implicit in the process of identification, through attentive listening, is the task of trawling through a range of musical events.[2]

Vocal Coordinates: Dialogue and Performance

Conceived for repeated listening, the pop song is often crammed with details. Take Prince's productions as a case in point. Invariably, they involve meticulous attention to compositional features, which become a dominant stylistic trait. The recording of 'Chelsea Rodgers' is no exception, with a range of devices that are discernible in the levels of polyphonic mobility, phrasing and tessitura. In no uncertain terms, the vocals on this track are about a felt *presence* in all sorts of guises. And as well as sung phrases, many other vocal sounds fall outside the realm of singing – grunting, groaning, wailing, talking, shrieking and shouting – and form part of the pleasure in experiencing this song.

One feature I am keen to address is the chemistry between Prince and singer, Shelby Johnson. It is as if every vocal sound is measured by the close rapport of these singers, who willingly take on girl/boy roles. Via tessitura (I am referring to the technical idiosyncrasies of the voice in terms of muscular control and exertion, inflections and the rise and fall of pitches), their voices are distinguished by their genders. And, as the song's narrative unfolds, curiosity is aroused as to who Chelsea Rodgers is and what role she plays in Prince's life.[3] How, then, does Prince fashion an act that becomes so tantalizing and flirtatious? And why does he target the female model?

---

2   For an in-depth discussion of structural listening and the potential sloppiness of music analysis, see Fred Maus, 'The Disciplined Subject of Musical Analysis' in A. Dell'Antonio (ed.), *Beyond Structural Listening: Postmodern Modes of Hearing* (Berkeley, CA, 2004), pp. 13–43.

3   On the main online fan community for Prince (<http://prince.org/>) considerable speculation as to the identity of Chelsea Rodgers followed the release of the song and video. One fan reckoned that she was purely a Prince creation (with his second name spelt with a 'd'), and most certainly not a model, while another revealed that Chelsea was indeed a clothes model, but now just designed clothes. It was also disclosed that Chelsea was not only wearing T-shirts with his name on them, but also promoting his new fragrance, 3121. See also 'What's Up With all the Chelsea Rodgers Adulation?' at: <http://www.housequake.com/showthread.php?s=&threadid=88982>,and the model's own website, at: <http://www.chelsearodgers.com/>.

Let us start with the idea of vocal polyphony in the pop recording. As well as multilayering through track placement, this is shaped by subtle fluctuations in register, rhythmic detail and editing. Predominantly, it is the angular shapes of melodies that convey a high dose of musical activity that ultimately teases out the narrative. Indeed, the alternating levels of polyphonic density affect the presence of the vocals in the audio image and cement the relationship between Prince and Johnson. One might say that the symbiosis between Prince, Johnson and his entourage of brilliant musicians has the effect of bringing to life the plight of supermodel, Chelsea Rodgers. As I read it, the relationship between Prince and Johnson in the performance of this song helps position *his* desire. This point I will dwell on later. Meanwhile, the interaction between both singers is impassioned and responsorial, as illustrated in Table 17.1, during the first chorus and verse (0:36–1:21). Worth observing are the levels of repartee between Prince and Johnson, which, free-flowing, help Prince to negotiate a variety of positions. By mounting the groove, which is grounded by the repetitive details of the bass, kit, guitar, brass and synthesizer parts, both singers have ample opportunity to generate their parts. And, articulated and organized in terms of phrasing, their phrases of varying lengths traverse the song, providing lively interjections and quasi-conversational responses.

The content and form in the first chorus and verse (0:36–1:17 – see Table 17.1) prompts a consideration of a number of features that relate to vocal polyphony. Not only do dynamics play a major role in the interaction of the voices, but register and breath also control and shape the polyphonic contours. With singing we know that breathing involves the technical exertion of the voice and a resulting tone that is unique to an individual. Prince's style of singing is predicated upon stark variations in breath control induced by the contractions of his vocal muscles and diaphragm. Notably in this first part of the track, both singers deliver their phrases with a relaxed, open-throated voice that is resonant and rich. Only occasionally is there any sense of straining. And when this does occur, the voice is used percussively, melismatically or in a screeching falsetto. Contrasting vocal registers are positioned in the middle of their 'natural' range, with Prince's voice generally lower than Johnson's. Also, the vocal idioms employed encapsulate an African-American musical heritage, as evident in the stylistic referents of funk, soul and disco, not least through exclamations, such as 'ow', 'mm', 'uh', 'ehhhh', 'a-ha', which are more nasalized than the sung phrases. Intermittent nasality found in these utterances is bound up in a mannered attitude. All through the track his enunciation of consonants is clipped and precise; he accents key words in the lyrics through a range of sharp, percussive and vocal timbres. Vocally, Prince approaches melodic phrasing through the technical demands of pitch inflection, intervallic rises and falls, rapid tempo changes and utterances that create tension and release. Furthermore, the timbral contrasts between Prince and Johnson vividly demonstrate the extent to which their vocal rapport functions.

Table 17.1   'Chelsea Rodgers': vocal interchange in the first chorus/verse

Phrases/Lyrics/Duration	Prince	Johnson
Chelsea Rodgers was a model (0:36–39)	X	X
Thought she really rocked the road (0:39–42)	X	X
yes she did (0:42–43)		X
Kept her tears up in a bottle (0:43–47)	X	X
Poured them out to save her soul (0:47–51)	X	X
Soul, soul (0:51)		X
Ask her what she liked the most (0:51–53)	X	X
She said (0:54)		**X**
she liked to talk to Jimi's ghost (0:55–58)	X	X
Ow! (0:58)		**X**
Fantasy, her friends boast (0:59–1:02)	X	X
This girl is fly (1:02)	**X**	
Chelsea's fly, like coast to coast (1:03–1:05)	X	X
Mmmm (1:06)		**X**
Hollywood or Times Square (1:06–1.09)	X	X
Uh, eh (1:10)	**X**	
If the party's fly, my girl is there (1:11–1:13)	X	X
yes she is (1:14)	**X**	
Purple's on and bounce in her hair (1:15–1:17)	X	X
21st Century hippy, Chelsea don't care (1:18–1:21)	X	X

All this returns us to the matter of vocal presence in the mix, which connotes something physiological and mediated, especially in relation to gendered constructions. Producer-performer, and very much in charge, Prince's identity comes across as 'master supreme' and surfaces as a norm, albeit often in the form of quirky representations of masculinity and a send-up of phallocentricity.[4] What I

---

4   In an earlier study I have entered into a lengthy discussion of the gendered implications of Prince's production and relationship with women. See Stan Hawkins, 'Subversive Musical Pleasures in "The Artist (Again) Known as Prince"' in *Settling the Pop Score: Pop Texts and Identity Politics* (Aldershot, 2002), pp. 159–200. For another study, which

Table 17.2   'Chelsea Rodgers': formal structure and events chart

Duration	Sections	Bars	Vocal input type	Musical events
0:00–0:35	Introduction	18 (4+6+4+4)	Spoken/sung Compressed, echo on some words, non-reverb	Prince and Johnson's voices introduced in call 'n response in tandem with the bass line; synth gliss, guitar riff, hi-hat splashes and main chord sequence established (Bb–Cm–Fm)
0:35–0:51	Chorus	8 (4+4)	Sung Medium reverb; vocals chorused Overdubbing	Main chorus melody introduced, heavily punctuated by brass licks (four even eight notes followed by stab on final offbeat of bar)
0:51–1:22	Verse	16 (8+8)	Sung; foregrounded Reverb; mixed to the fore	First half played with simple backing; in the second half the intensity is increased by the brass and keyboards entering the mix
1:22–1:37	Chorus	8 (4+4)	Sung	Chorus melody returns with very clipped brass and guitar stabs contrasting against the vocal flow; soft keyboards in the background give a sense of vocal sustain
1:37–2:09	Verse	16 (8+8)	Sung/spoken/ rapped	Embellishment of melody in a manner that becomes more fragmented and clipped; much emphasis on the lyrics, as vocals are pushed to the fore of the mix
2:09–2:23	Chorus	8 (4+4)	Sung	Elated delivery of chorus melody; synth glissandi; elaborate bass fills
2:23–2:47	Bridge	12 (4+4+4)	Scatting	Loud brass riffs take over with vocal grunts and shouts
2:47–3:18	Verse	16 (8+8)	Sung/rapped/ shouted	Build-up in intensity as the brass licks and guitar riffs are levelled up to the vocals dynamics; much activity in the mix due to panning, compression and high levels of dubbing

Duration	Sections	Bars	Vocal input type	Musical events
3:18–3:48	Chorus	16 (4+4+4+4)	Sung	Extended chorus signifies an arrival point; the rhythmic energy is heightened by the introduction of sharp, treble, hand-claps on all the offbeats (2 and 4); high dose of overdubbing on Prince's and Johnson's vocals; bass line becomes more ornamented, producing a greater sense of bounce in its movement
3:48–4:36	Break	24 (8+8+8)	Scat and response	Saxophone solo (8 bars), trombone solo (8 bars), trumpet solo (8 bars); vocal responses in the overlay to the solos
4:36–4:58	'Fake' ending!	12 (4+4+4)	Scat, wails, yells Prince falsetto 'peak'	Drums + synth gliss (4 bars), added guitar riff (4 bars), added vocal scat ending on 'Chel' (last beat of 3rd bar) and a scratch on an anticipated 3rd beat in final bar (4th bar)
4:58–5:06	Final Bridge	4	No vocals	Guitar riff solo – embellished and angular, doubled in octaves, panned
5:06–5:41	Chorus + coda	16 (4+4+4+4)	Sung	Vocals, brass, bass and guitars mixed at the same level; the song ends with a brass stab on off beat.

am suggesting by this is that contemplating gendered performance is paramount to any musicological consideration of the voice, for it arouses and assuages pleasures that denote the peculiarity of 'musical attitude'. After all, attitude confers symbolic power, and in Prince's case it incorporates elements of opportunity that are legitimated in a context that matters to the fan – one might say that his well-worn funk clichés are all about attitude in action!

Swirls around the Groove

Vocality in 'Chelsea Rodgers' is very much bound up in the groove. Circular in its rhythmic propensity, the groove is driven by the most energized bass line imaginable (see Ex. 17.1). The funk referent of the bass is located in the melodic and rhythmic content, and more: in fact, the angularity of this slap bass and its timbral content becomes a prime indicator of attitude. As I read it, everything stems from this – the pulse, the instrumental interjections, the kit figure and the vocal retort. Beginning with the few bars of kit that introduce the jerky bass line, the groove-line asserts the song's stylistic mission. So catchy is the bass line that it is able to sustain a simple harmonic structure throughout, iv–v–i (B♭m–Cm–Fm).[5] Modal in feel (F dorian), the harmonic fabric is escorted by the fabulous bass line (Ex. 17.1) that steers the groove with great panache.[6]

Example 17.1   Bass riff in 'Chelsea Rodgers'[7]

Of the many appealing features of the groove is its seamlessness. What I mean by this is that the groove functions as a harmonic continuum that is injected by musical ideas that randomly enter and exit the mix (Table 17.2). For the moment, though, I want to dwell a little longer on the implications of the groove in the vocal performance.

theorizes Prince's masculinity, see Robert Walser, 'Prince as Queer Poststructuralist', *Popular Music and Society* 18/2 (1994): 79–89.

5   Of course, these three chords are extended, voiced and altered throughout the song in interesting ways, which also helps maintain a high degree of harmonic interest.

6   Musicologically, I have made a similar argument in an earlier analysis of a Prince song where the harmony is grounded around one pitch, C, with an extraordinary richness in harmonic detail. See Stan Hawkins, 'Prince: Harmonic Analysis of "Anna Stesia"', *Popular Music* 11/3 (1992): 325–36.

7   Thanks to Per Elias Drabløs and Eirik Askeroi for their assistance in the transcriptions, and acknowledgments to colleagues Mats Johannson, Eystein Sandvik and Oss Skårberg for helping me to hear this song in different ways.

Kit, bass and guitar riff are chief components in most groove-lines over which there is a stacking up of other vocal and instrumental parts.[8] Dominating the groove in 'Chelsea Rodgers', the bass figure (Ex. 17.1) is irresistibly playful and cheeky. Syncopated, buoyant and not least raunchy, it tugs away at the metrical divisions, defining the richness of rhythmic and textural overlay. Indeed, the groove's constituents are dependent on the occurrence of numerous structures: rhythmic patterns in the kit part, intervallic leaps in the bass line, backing guitar, brass licks and so on. As I have already intimated, the stacking up of layers in Prince's music includes the many levels of vocal display. Take the strong contrasts in the vocal 'feel' from verse to chorus to break passages, which constitute key elements in the arrangement. As well as dynamic changes, fussy editing and cunning devices shape the vocal timbral flavour, framing the aesthetics of the song.

More details can be taken up with regard to the groove: what is the regulatory energy of the groove and, in terms of its function, how does it reinforce vocal and instrumental response? Certainly, the groove enlivens vocal tessitura by inducing movement in the body. In general terms, patterns of rhythmic organization in this groove result in emotive responses as Prince and Johnson exchange melodic lines (Table 17.1). Set against the discipline of the straight four on the beat kick drum, punctuated by snare, hi-hats and later on hand-claps, the vocals are ordered in ways that feel chilled and relaxed., The groove consistently has a direct bearing on the singers' response to the lyrics. Much of this is down to the production. Commanding his band and co-singer to 'follow' him, Prince leads them to the two climactic points in the song (3:48–4:36 and 5:06–5:41). Not only is there call and response between him and Johnson, but also the instrumentalists; the solos feel improvised and act as an invitation for everyone to participate. In particular, the treatment of the vocals in the recording – the overdubs, multitracking, use of effects, unison and chorusing –create the impression of a large carnivalesque occasion centred around Prince, who controls everyone's performance. Ultimately, the style of the song, a highly polished and flashy affair, is determined by the performance *as* production. Crafted around brass licks on extended and altered jazz chords, the flashiness is unmistakably tinged with references to Earth, Wind and Fire – which brings us back to the question of strategy and what might lie behind an arrangement.

Generalizing Strategies: Open and Filled Spaces

Effortlessly, vocal parts can shift the mood of a song. This aspect of an arrangement is critical in denoting stylistic signification. Let me explain. The timbral and

---

8   Richard Middleton argues that the disco groove is characterized by a 'heavy, regular beat' supported by a backbeat snare drum and sixteenth note 'cymbal chatter' (p. 110). See Middleton, 'Popular Music Analysis and Musicology: Bridging the Gap' in Richard Middleton (ed.), *Reading Pop: Approaches to Textual Analysis in Popular Music* (Oxford, 2000), pp. 104–21.

textural overlay of vocalization in 'Chelsea Rodgers' provides precisely the kind of subtle variations that become the hallmark of a disco-funk track. As I have been suggesting, the produced voice adds a vital dimension to the performance, and Prince's meticulous ear for detail is discernible through the minute edits of every vocal utterance. Indeed, his vocal skills create the illusion of a live performance through heavily processed effects. Yet, this is all down to the virtuosic recording production. In an arrangement that is slick, every musical event is eased into the groove with the utmost precision. Above all. the responsorial utterances that support the diva's part express the values of control and submission, whereby the latter is executed through a sense of resignation. Taking over from the female, dialogically, Prince's approach is alluring as he deploys a different timbre through a fuller-throat voice. The vocal dubbing used especially empowers him as he juxtaposes *his* voices over another, heightening the sense of play in the performance. A fitting example of this is in the second part of the final verse on the lines 'No cut diamonds, and designer shoes (Uh, no-no!) / 'Cause she's too original from her head down to her feet' (1:53–2:00). In such instances, dubbing heightens the chorus effect as Prince's voice, close-miked and superbly magnified, is panned back and forth from left to right in the mix, with ever so slight touches of delay. Notably, the singing style employed in this passage is near-spoken through a nonchalant, boasting, rap style that Prince employs to dub one set of voices at a higher register. Routinely, such recitative lines provide relief from the sung lines and come across as very camp. At the same time, another vocal detail is discernible in the overemphasis of sibilance – the 'sss' sound on 'diamonds', 'designer shoes' and 'she' demonstrates this, while the 's' in 'Chelsea' stands out as one of the main sibilant moments in the entire track.

Master of intrigue, and, in effect, slave to none, Prince navigates a rich tapestry of vocality in order to mediate his complex identity. In the passage referred to above, the difference between the dynamic levels on the various vocal tracks highlight Prince's subjectivity while simultaneously extracting the meaning of the lyrics. Substantial use of dynamics are prevalent in the moment when the brass takes over (2:31–2:46), where his and Johnson's vocals are set far back in the mix, at a *pp* level. In the audio image at this point, it is as if they are surveying the musical terrain, while urging the brass on with 'ah, come on'. Vociferations of this kind focus the attention on the brass lick motif, providing necessary respite from the vocal timbres. Given the lengthy duration of this track (5:41), it is such techniques that make the song endurable.

Consistently, Prince and Johnson embellish melodic material in ways that underlie the funk-disco style of the track. By means of rapid appoggiaturas, vibrato on long notes and other forms of inflection, they elaborate on the melodies in subtle ways. Quite predictably, the levels of vocal elaboration in the final chorus become dense, with a sense of resolution that comes over as submission, where all performers gain equal status in the mix. Such a build-up in intensity helps fashion the vocal lines as we move towards the final jam section. This climactic arrival point (4:35) follows on from a virtuoso solo passage, starting with the groove stripped down to just the kit, with a gurgly synth glissando. Sixteen bars of playing around ensue – vocal scatting, guitar riffs, synth sounds – before the bass part and brass licks return. Compositionally, this marks the point where everything blends into a purple sweat for one last time in a fervent funk-based jam session.

From this we can begin to see that the ways in which the vocal parts work in 'Chelsea Rodgers' are instructive. One might concede that the intensity of vocal activity is reinforced by the variable techniques of phrasing that stage the narrative. Put another way, vocal choreography is modelled by the intricate identity traits of each performer and made tangible by the connotations of their performance style. While Prince's performance tends towards funk, Johnson's is more soul and disco in flavour. Hence, their vocal dialogue generates a level of musical interest through the elaboration and interpolation of their phrases. In other words, the charge of the dialogue between both singers betrays their stylistic identities, with Prince reshaping every vocal fragment in a far more improvised (read: domineering) way than Johnson. During the course of the song it is the general tendency towards call and response that results in a particular African-American aesthetic. Such eloquence in singing practice is contingent on the symbiosis between the symbolic and the real. And it is in this space that Prince reveres the woman as Other, whose very presence spells out his desire for the gorgeous Chelsea Rodgers. Yet, as Lacan has taught us, the mastery of any voice over another, while mobilizing desire, is never determinable in any absolute manner, for, in order to convince, the performing subject has to engage the listener. In other words, musical performativity confirms the sonic means of delivering an act, telling us a story about the social and cultural location of the artist.

'I dunno – ah-huh' – And not a Hair out of Place

How, then, does the recorded voice connote things? What is the effect of an airbrushed recording, in which the performance come across 'without a hair out of place'? Musical figurations, fussy edits and production tricks certainly snapshot the body as the product of a controlled, calculated agency. In pondering over Prince's agency, I want to further consider the link between the signifiers that account for vocal identification. Effectively, his personalized style stretches well beyond the designated role of heteronormativity by conflating the category of black male: he loves women like he loves himself, and his persona is enshrined in the *materiality of jouissance*. Let us say that Prince's biography, his cultural presence and his invasive musicalized energy, negotiates a traversing of desire – a desire of and *for* the Other. Moreover, it is as if there is a secret longing for the voice of Johnson, the product of the Other which he can never attain.[9] After all, the voice in the mix has to be activated – from the pop artist, to the boyfriend, to the girlfriend, to the

---

9   I am indebted to Sarah Niblock for this valid point. See her psychoanalytical study of Prince – 'Prince: Negotiating the Meanings of Femininity in the Mid-1980s', PhD diss. (Middlesex University, 2005).

lover, to the Other. What I mean by this is that Prince's voice connotes a slippery construction of masculinity, sexuality and race that is mediated by an agency that is omnipresent.[10]

In itself the Princian voice is a symbol of desirousness; it is a signifier of indelible desire. As primary signifier, the voice sacrifices itself to the onlooker, seeking to win over recognition and affection the more it replicates itself. It thus symbolizes a site for experiencing a subject-position through which the emotional life of the artist singing can be imagined and refashioned. Rob Bowman, in his reference to rap artists, insists that the 'refashioning of older material as new composition' re-encodes music with new meaning.[11] And, during this process, performance style redefines sonic material in ways that (re)confirm a sense of identity on the part of the listener and the performer.

But Prince's presence in the mix is also illusionary. For his presence is not necessarily created immediately upon listening, but rather post the event. And it is from this position that his vocalized subjectivity leaves us in doubt as to who he is, or what indeed he might be up to. This would explain why repeated listenings are constitutive of subjectivity, whose fleeting existence is contingent on the memories of gestures, actions, whims, clichés and idioms that occur musically. Idealized, glossy and smartly edited, Prince's voice elicits desire through the gymnastics of musical virtuosity. Virtuosity, in his case, is a configuration of ideas that establishes selfhood. For desire is the agent of the pop artist, achieving its presence through the signifier of musical style. But, how?

As intimated earlier in this chapter, 'Chelsea Rodgers' is an appropriation of styles by which subjectivity is refashioned along the lines of nostalgia. Relevant to this is the idea of style as a fluid entity that evolves over time, where personalized expression affirms its subjective status by always being open to something else. By this I mean that transformation or development does not necessarily imply a loss of meaning. Rather, it suggests that the staging of the voice entails processes of negotiation that acquire authenticity over time. Given this, what are the interpretive strategies required to pin down a style – an impudent disco-funk style?

The context of 'Chelsea Rodgers', after all, is the catwalk. Its promotional video comprises footage of the band's appearance at London Fashion Week, premiered on 28 October 2007. All along, Prince's conception of fashion breeds new musical directions. This is verified by the 'jam' aspect of the track, which suggests an array of musical attributes that are consistent with his experimental approach. The convergence of musical styles in the 1970s resulted in a fragmentation of the popular music field that had an unprecedented effect on black musicians, who felt united through the vociferous expression of a musical heritage. The later years of

---

10 See also Nina Sun Eidsheim, 'Voice as a Technology of Selfhood: Towards an Analysis of Racialized Timbre and Vocal Performance', PhD diss. (University of California, San Diego, 2008).

11 Rob Bowman, 'The Determining Role of Performance in the Articulation of Meaning: The Case of "Try a Little Tenderness"' in Allan F. Moore (ed.), *Analyzing Popular Music* (Cambridge, 2003), p. 129.

this decade then witnessed a broadening out of funk into a genre that consisted of many stylistic trends that formed its vocabulary. In 1978 Prince's career launch would serve as a propulsive force for extending funk, R&B and soul into disco. Plus, the strong African-American inflection of disco has always been a studio-based medium, the outgrowth of ideas by producers, studio musicians and engineers. The point here is that Prince's style, as a recorded form, coincided with a range of technological developments, such as automated consoles, 24-track desks, MIDI and a new generation of commercial synthesizers. Moreover, the way his voice was recorded in the late 1970s navigated an intriguing pathway into the twenty-first century. Strongly influenced by the productions of Giorgo Moroder, Pete Bellote and Quincy Jones, and their innovative ways of treating the voice in the mix, Prince's pop productions would accommodate new, exciting musical structures (formal, melodic, harmonic, rhythmic) that were inflated and seemed larger than real life. Because disco was never meant to be performed live, it became liberated from the traditions of sonic realism (perfected by imaginative producers such as George Martin). All along, Prince would know that the test of a good disco track lies in the recorded 'diva' voice, which distinguished this style from funk where the male voice is usually dominant. Prince's ability to assimilate disco into funk lies in the realm of his production work. That is, his productions confirm the construction of his own subjectivity or, better, his ego, which is choreographed through the mix.

In reproducing the subject, 'Chelsea Rodgers' addresses aspects of masculinity that are conditional on the female's presence. Particularly powerful in her top range Johnson's voice shapes an aesthetic that is an important indicator of what Prince is about. Right from the outset of this track the sensuality of her vocals blend with Prince's to deliver the song's narrative (see Table 17.1). For Prince, the conversation style of African-American music is critically important as he searches for his voice alongside that of others. Things really come to a head in the final jam session (4:36–4:58 – see Table 17.1), during the 'fake ending' (where there is a sense the song is grinding to a halt), as Prince competes with his female counterpart in aiming for the highest pitch in the form of a screech. Notably, in the first part of this passage he responds with words and phrases, such as 'dance' and 'check that body move', 'make that body work', 'shake it like a juicy juice' as the energy builds up to a peak. At 4:36 the material is suddenly reduced to a bland four-on-the floor drum riff that is joined a little later by the guitar riff to usher in the wailing of the soul diva at 4: 46. Entering with falsetto (4:53 – Ex. 17.2), on a strained high E♭ yowl (E♭^{1}), sustained and nasal, Prince, without any warning, leaps to C♭, a minor 6th up, before descending in fourths and fifths to a C natural.

Example 17.2   'Chel' – horn – scratch!

In this phrase, the initial slide up to E♭ suggests an ever so mischievous hint at the most famous disco hit ever from 1975 – Donna Summer's 'Love to Love You Baby'.[12] Summer, the first 'lady of disco', who unleashed all her sexual yearning in 23 simulated orgasms, would start her famous refrain with a similar glide up to C^1, a minor 3rd lower than Prince's, holding it for the same duration – four bars. It is difficult to say how intentional this moment might be in 'Chelsea Rodgers', but, in my reading, it stands as a confirmation of a stylistic code that acts as a mirror in the advent of disco. As Richard Middleton puts it, disco might have marked a moment 'when "slaves" … Woman, Black, Low, the "living dead" rising from the grave of history were summoned to the dance floor and took it over'.[13] With more than just a subtle touch of parody, this referent directs us to the final downward arpeggio, with an offbeat vocal stab on 'Chel' and a cheeky offbeat gated scratch that substitutes for the second syllable (Ex. 17.2). Despite this crude 'masculine ending', the material struggles with closure. Why? Compositional devices such as these are not uncommon in Prince's vocabulary, often pre-empting a climax that, unlike Donna Summer's, never quite 'comes' – a musical *coitus reservatus* that lures the receiver into submission. Musical exhortations of this kind call to attention Prince's obsession with small musical gestures that are manipulated to surprise and titillate. I read this moment as an affirmation of bliss – its aesthetic only made meaningful in the context of the fantasy of a live performance.

In moments such as these, we are reminded that Prince's vocal signature in 2007 showed little sign of dwindling. His ability to flesh out his voices forms part of a strategy of seduction, something smarmy yet charming, queer and extraordinary. Flirting is integral to Prince's vocality and performance act – I am referring to a quality of sound that stems from the warmth of the body and promises an intimacy that engages our desire. Hence, the challenge is to work out what Prince is saying and to fathom out who *he* is when singing about Chelsea Rodgers.

Consider alone the transgressional qualities of his many voices. This idea is useful for pursuing the transient dimension of his stylistic image. In many of Prince's tracks, nuances in the manipulation of the artist's identity occur during a relatively short space of time, and 'Chelsea Rodgers' is no exception. Notwithstanding the duet work with Johnson, there are many moments where Prince seems over-preoccupied with himself. Self-obsession is articulated by vivid contrasts in timbre, register, rhythmic emphasis and vocal edits that suggest he is intent on wallowing in the sound of his own voice. Of course, the glamour of the recorded voice is dependent on the idealized image of the artist himself. Yet, the recorded voice depends on an absence from the 'real' in order to allow for complex constellations of imagined desire on the part of the receiver. Invariably, Prince's vocality symbolizes excess,

---

12   For an analysis of this song, Summer's performance and a thorough discussion of its disco aesthetic, see Robert Davis, 'Who Got Da Funk? An Etymophony of Funk Music from the 1950s to 1979', PhD diss. (Université de Montréal, 2005).

13   Richard Middleton, '"Last Night a DJ Saved My Life": Avians, Cyborgs and Siren Bodies in the Era of Phonographic Technology', *Radical Musicology* 1 (2006), para. 15, at: http://www.radical-musicology.org.uk/2006/Middleton.htm.

which has far-reaching implications. His powerful agency, his mastery, his active positioning is about erotic self-identification – a controlling force that extrapolates the strength of his presence in the mix. And, all along, he knows that the fan knows that these are the traits that many disavow.[14]

Conclusion

In this chapter I have considered the role of the voice in a pop song and its active involvement in the construction of identities. Granted, listening experiences are always personal, placing the interpreter in an active and imaginative role. This is why interpreting a song is an intimate activity and only a start at understanding some of the details that go into convincing us of a musical performance. Beyond describing the musical features of a song, though, is the task of evaluation as both part of a narrative and the fantasy of an imagined response. Central to Prince's vocal performance is a knowing problematization of male subjectivity that appears in a multitude of ambiguous ways. For one thing, he breaks with the traditional conceptions of gender binarisms, revolutionizing the way we hear and perceive masculinity. All this he achieves through the playfulness of stylistic appropriation. Prince's voice, then, constitutes a style in itself – a stylized way of making oneself heard. Finally, if I were to qualify the vocality of his act I might be tempted to point out the appeal of a masculinity that is built on intrigue. For, aesthetically, Prince's subjectivity is furnished by vocal excess and subterfuge. It is, as evident in 'Chelsea Rodgers', his most endearing virtue.

---

14   I have theorized at length the role of empathy in pop songs and how the contract between an artist and fan is based on notions of exclusivity. See Hawkins, *Settling the Pop Score*, Chapter 3.

Singing Style and White Masculinity

Jacqueline Warwick

In 1998 the Hal Leonard publication of *The Beatles: The Complete Scores* conferred legitimacy on the compositions of four untrained musicians, suggesting that The Beatles' work is worthy of serious analytical attention. At over 1000 pages, the tome presents painstaking transcriptions of everything the Fab Four recorded, meticulously documenting the sounds resulting from specific guitar strings and drumhead tunings. Merely holding the weighty book makes it obvious that it is a scholarly resource rather than a songbook for performers to play from. The transcription of each song resembles an orchestral score in its scope, and the book's publication conferred grandeur and gravitas on the work of The Beatles and – by extension – on popular music in general.

And yet, while song transcriptions provide information on the Beatles' rhythmic and instrumental work, with special notation symbols designed to indicate variations of timbre, phrasing and articulation in every instrumental line, the vocal parts are not subject to technical scrutiny at all. Indeed, the song lyrics and voice melody lines resemble those found in functional sheet music sold for amateur performance; clearly, the vocal particularities of John, Paul, George and Ringo were deemed insignificant in comparison to their important achievements as instrumentalists.

Until quite recently this indifference to voice and vocality has been pervasive in the scholarship on popular music, and indeed in rock's fan cultures.[1] The careful

---

[1] For recent work exploring the meanings of singing, see, among others: Gage Averill, *Four Parts, No Waiting: A Social History of American Barbershop Harmony* (New York, 2003); Shana Goldin-Perschbacher, '"Not with You but of You": "Unbearable Intimacy" and Jeff Buckley's Transgendered Vocality' in Freya Jarman-Ivens (ed.), *Oh Boy! Masculinities and Popular Music* (New York, 2007), pp. 213–34; John Potter, *Vocal Authority: Singing Style and Ideology* (Cambridge, 1998); Laurie Stras, 'Voice of the Beehive: Vocal Technique at the Turn of the 60s' in Laurie Stras (ed.), *She's so Fine: Whiteness, Femininity, Adolescence and Class in 1960s Music* (Farnham, forthcoming); and my own *Girl Groups, Girl Culture: Popular Music and Identity in the 1960s* (New York, 2007); and '"And the Colored Girls Sing": Backup Singers and the Case of the Blossoms' in Steven Baur, Raymond Knapp and Jacqueline Warwick (eds), *Musicological Identities: Essays in Honor of Susan McClary*

documentation of The Beatles' instrumental work showed the high level of skill and musicianship of the legendary group, and *The Beatles: The Complete Scores* did much to demonstrate the worthiness of popular music to a scholarly community largely invested in the virtuosity, complexity and originality of European concert music. Nevertheless, an effort to identify these values and achievements within certain styles of popular music (say, the work of Jimi Hendrix) has often led to the dismissal, and even denigration, of styles that operate according to different aesthetics (say, the work of the Monkees). Most crucially for my purposes here, an emphasis on instrumental techniques overlooks the highly individual voices that, for many listeners, are the most important features of their favourite songs.

Whereas in the context of most formal study of singing the goal is to attain a prescribed and uniformly beautiful sound, many popular music singing styles are valued for their idiosyncrasies, and the most distinctive, unusual voices are often prized for the way they seem to represent a singer's unique personality and lived experience. Within a rock ideology that values sincerity, spontaneity and directness, the sound of a formally trained singer can be heard with suspicion, suggesting a self-consciousness and forethought that are at odds with simply singing from the heart. And yet, the craft of performing well is crucial to success as a rock singer, even when the tedium of study and rehearsal is kept carefully hidden by a conceit that the singer's voice 'just comes out that way'. This need for mystique veiling the work involved in rock singing is dramatized in a scene in the 2001 film *Rock Star*, starring Mark Wahlberg as the singer for a humble tribute band, who is suddenly catapulted to stardom as new lead singer for his favourite group. Asked to account for his singing prowess at a press conference, Wahlberg's character obligingly begins to describe his training in high school and community choirs, when one of his new bandmates cuts him off, assuring reporters instead that his vocal power is derived from frequent oral sex with women.

What can scrutiny of singing reveal about rock culture? In this chapter I will explore some possible rewards of analysing vocal style in popular music. Shedding light on the artistry of singing may draw attention to an aspect of rock culture that most fans would prefer to take at face value, as natural, individual and unconnected to social trends or ideology, so while I'm at it I might just as well tackle that other elephant in the room – the subject position of straight, white masculinity, which continues, in dominant discourse, to be considered neutral, natural and 'just normal', despite the growing importance of work critically analysing whiteness, masculinity and other forms of privilege.[2] As David Wellman has written about men in US culture,

> *Until recently, the categories 'white' and 'male' were taken for granted. Being white and being male was being 'normal'. The taken-for-granted world of white, male Americans, then, was their normalcy, not their whiteness or their*

(Aldershot, 2008), pp. 63–76.

2   See, among others, Mike Hill (ed.), *Whiteness: A Critical Reader* (New York, 1997); George Lipsitz, *The Possessive Investment in Whiteness: How White People Profit from Identity Politics* [1999] (Philadelphia, rev. edn 2006).

gender. As a result, the privileges that came with whiteness and masculinity were experienced as 'normal', not advantages.[3]

I acknowledge that my focus on this dominant version of manhood could be seen to bolster its value, as Bryce Traister has suggested.[4] In fact, it is precisely the taken-for-granted normalcy of white, American masculinity that I wish to analyse here through my study of voice types for rock singers, and I hope that other essays in this collection, read in dialogue with mine, will lead to a nuanced understanding of this and other subject positions.

Within the context of rock culture, masculinity is an issue of central importance. The African-American bluesmen of the late nineteenth and early twentieth centuries, who came to have such an influence on ensuing generations of (primarily white) rockers, were at pains to demonstrate their manliness – indeed, their humanity – to a racist social order. Future rock gods, such as Eric Clapton, were inspired by the notion of 'one man and his guitar against the world', and their constructions of white, adult masculinity in turn inspired later generations of rockers. The history of rock can, in interesting ways, be understood as a history of masculinities and of whiteness.[5] In what follows, then, I'll examine three of the prevalent singing styles associated with young white men (as distinct from boys) in rock genres of recent decades, and I'll consider how these vocal styles portray specific versions of manhood. In so doing, I hope to point to some of the ways in which white masculinity is constructed through popular music and to suggest what the study of singing style can reveal to us about the codes and conventions of manhood.

Chad Kroeger and the Voice of Meat-and-Potatoes Rock

The enormous success of Alberta's Nickelback in the first decade of this century is matched perhaps only by the sizeable backlash against the band; for every published

---

3   David Wellman, 'Minstrel Shows, Affirmative Action Talk, and Angry White Men: Marking Racial Otherness in the 1990s' in Ruth Frankenberg (ed.), *Displacing Whiteness: Essays in Social and Cultural Criticism* (Durham, NC, 1997), pp. 311–32, at p. 321.

4   Bryce Traister, 'Academic Viagra: The Rise of American Masculinity Studies', *American Quarterly* 52/2 (2000): 274–304.

5   The crude history of blues-influenced rock I present here is necessarily partial and simplistic; for more sophisticated thinking about masculinity and guitar-based rock culture, see Robert Walser, *Running with the Devil: Power, Gender and Madness in Heavy Metal Music* (Hanover, NH, 1994); Steve Waksman, *Instruments of Desire: The Electric Guitar and the Shaping of Musical Experience* (Cambridge, MA, 1999); Susan Fast, *In the Houses of the Holy: Led Zeppelin and the Power of Rock Music* (Oxford, 2001); Matthew Bannister, *White Boys, White Noise: Masculinities and 1980s Indie Guitar Rock* (Aldershot, 2006); Glenn Pillsbury, *Damage Incorporated: Metallica and the Production of Musical Identity* (New York, 2006); and Chris McDonald, *Rush, Rock Music and the Middle Class: Dreaming in Middletown* (Bloomington, IN, forthcoming).

article and fan site celebrating their music, it seems, there is one denouncing them as sell-outs and *poseurs*. For the scholar of rock ideology, Nickelback and the discourses surrounding them are endlessly fascinating. Central to all commentary on the band, whether from adherents or detractors, is an emphasis on the vocal work of lead singer and principal songwriter Chad Kroeger, whose coarse, gritty baritone seems the perfect medium for his brooding, angst-ridden lyrics.

Nickelback formed in the late 1990s, adhering artistically to the musical style of grunge bands such as Pearl Jam (whose producer eventually worked with Nickelback), Alice in Chains, Soundgarden and the iconic Nirvana. An early Nickelback hit such as 'Leader of Men' (2000) demonstrates all the hallmarks of the grunge aesthetic: a long, brooding verse with tense, harmonically static and percussive guitar work, vocal lines low in the singer's register, and quiet drumming; and then a sudden and dramatic shift to a chorus featuring a soaring vocal in a higher tessitura, and greater volume, intensity and melodic and harmonic development in the instrumentation. As in other Nickelback songs, Kroeger's rough singing evokes the stance of a tortured outsider baring his innermost feelings, in keeping with the vocal style of mid-90s grunge forbears Kurt Cobain (of Nirvana) or Eddie Vedder (of Pearl Jam).

Yet Nickelback's staggering commercial success – at the time of writing, they have just signed a three-album, three-tour deal with promoters Live Nation worth an estimated US\$ 50–70 million[6] – is at odds with the ideology of grunge as an oppositional, anti-commercial music. Purists are horrified at grouping the band, and Kroeger in particular, alongside such worthies as Vedder and Cobain (although, to be sure, these men achieved immense commercial success themselves). Thus, Kroeger's choked, emotive growl is derided by critics as 'singing with a hernia'[7] and singing 'while suffering from chronic constipation'[8] and even as 'the sound of hell opening up',[9] while fans celebrate its sincerity, sexiness and raw passion.

Moreover, the gulf separating Nickelback fans from detractors is casually gendered in this online response to a news story about the band: 'Meh, these guys are awful. But the girlies seem to like them …'[10] As any connoisseur of rock culture knows, the teenage girl is the most contemptible fan of all, and the mere suggestion that a band is popular with 'the girlies' may suffice to conjure the whiff of artistic failure. Freya Jarman-Ivens notes that '… supposedly "masculine" genres such as rock musics are culturally privileged as "authentic" and "meaningful," in contrast to so-called feminine genres such as "teen-pop," which is widely perceived to be

---

6   No author cited, 'Nickelback Signs 3-album Deal with Live Nation', at: <http://www.cbc.ca/arts/music/story/2008/07/08/nickelback-deal.html> (accessed 8 July 2008).

7   Stephen Thomas Erlewine, '*All The Right Reasons*', at: <http://www.allmusic.com> (accessed 9 July 2008).

8   John Murphy, 'Nickelback: *All the Right Reasons*', at: <http://www.musicomh.com/albums/nickelback-2_1005.htm> (accessed 9 July 2008).

9   Peter Robinson, 'The Next Worst Thing', *Guardian*, 9 February 2008. Available at: <http://www.guardian.co.uk/theguide/music/story/0,,2253822,00.html> (accessed 9 July 2008).

10   Mister E, at: <http://www.cbc.ca/arts/music/story/2008/07/08/nickelback-deal.html#articlecomments> (accessed 9 July 2008).

devoid of significant meaning',[11] and the scorn heaped upon music that appeals to huge, presumed female, audiences demonstrates Andreas Huyssen's famous argument about the perceived femininity of mass culture.[12] It is intriguing to encounter this strategy in connection to Nickelback, because my perusal of fan sites and my reading of my own students' papers suggests that the band actually has a very healthy following among young white men, particularly in the armed forces. For the commenter cited above, disdain for Nickelback's music may have led to the assumption that only 'girlies' could possibly like them, in a neat grouping of two mutually reinforcing negatives.

Derided by grunge fans as copycats who appeal to teenage girls, it is hardly surprising that Nickelback seeks to distance itself from the grunge genre, as Kroeger declares: 'People have always tried to label us … Oh, it's alternative. No, it's post-grunge. What the hell is it? I'll tell you what it is. We are a meat-and-potatoes rock band.'[13] Indeed, the 'meat and potatoes' moniker is attached to Nickelback in countless reviews and press releases, and evidently is meant to signal the band's status as ordinary, hardworking and unconcerned with artistic posturing. The male, adult and heterosexual status of this ostensibly neutral position become clear in country star Alan Jackson's 2000 song, 'Meat and Potatoes Man', with its beer-drinking, football-watching and poodle-despising narrator. With their invocations of meat and potatoes, then, both Jackson and the members of Nickelback claim the position of the unvarnished 'regular guy' that corresponds with conceptions of white, heterosexual masculinity as normal and unmarked.

If we are to accept Nickelback as an unpretentious, crowd-pleasing, middle-of-the-road rock band, in the tradition of fellow Western Canadians The Guess Who and Bachman Turner Overdrive, then it seems reasonable to understand their sound as emblematic of normative, white, adult masculinity at the turn of the century. Kroeger's deep, throaty growl can be heard as the voice of the American everyman to whom beer, trucks and spectator sports are advertised, the blue-collar suburbanite whose pedestrian tastes inspire such contempt in rock critics, but whose consumer habits nevertheless dictate the direction of mainstream popular culture. Kroeger's low vocal melodies are somewhat unusual in rock music, as most male singers tend to work in the tenor tessitura, often exploiting the audible strain of singing uncomfortably high in order to signify powerful emotion (Robert Plant, for instance). In Kroeger's case, his baritone rumble connects him simultaneously to the few other rockers who sing in his range (notably, Eddie Vedder of Pearl Jam and

---

11 Freya Jarman-Ivens, 'Oh Boy! Making Masculinity in Popular Music' in Jarman-Ivens, *Oh Boy!*, pp. 1–20, at p. 3.

12 Andreas Huyssen, 'Mass Culture as Woman: Modernism's Other' in *After the Great Divide: Modernism, Mass Culture, Postmodernism* (Bloomington, IN, 1986), pp. 44–62.

13 Heath McCoy, 'Critics Be Damned, Nickelback Rawks', *Calgary Herald*, 15 November 2003, ES.01.F; cited in Leanne Fetterley, 'Hey, Hey, I Wanna be a Rock Star: Nickelback, Sincerity and Authenticity', paper presented at the annual meeting of IASPM-Canada, 2008, at Brock University. My thanks to Leanne for graciously making her paper available to me prior to publication.

Scott Stapp of Creed) and also to conventions holding that a deep voice is a manly voice. Kroeger's singing is thus distinctive and highly recognizable to his fans, and his sound also appeals to them as ordinary, unaffected and genuinely manly.

A concern with masculinity is apparent in many Nickelback songs, and many of them express ambivalence towards traditional male roles; 2001's 'Too Bad' reproaches Chad Kroeger's father for abandoning his family early on, and in 2002's 'Never Again', a little boy tries to protect his mother from a violent, abusive father.[14] In both these cases, the boy's pain and powerlessness are recounted in Kroeger's gritty baritone, and the voice's rough edges support the listener's sense of a hurt child who has become a strong, albeit bitter, man. As harrowing as the songs' narratives are, the fact that they are being told as first-person accounts by an adult proves that these experiences are survivable, and the songs celebrate the endurance of the kind of man who can survive. What is more, it is surely significant that the boy in 'Never Again' is injured in coming to his mother's defence; this reinforces conventions of male strength which insist that a 'real' man does not object to his own pain and suffering, but rather is called to act only on behalf of those weaker than himself.[15]

Kroeger's preoccupation with the meaning of being a man is nowhere more evident than in his 'Hero', a song recorded for the soundtrack of the 2002 summer blockbuster film *Spiderman*, based on the comic-book series. The song is not by Nickelback; it is a duet between Kroeger and the improbably named Josey Scott (front-man of rap-metal band Saliva), backed by other well-known instrumentalists. Stylistically, 'Hero' is a power ballad: the sounds of distorted guitar power chords low in their range dominate; a faintly-heard violin and the ballad-styled 6/8 metre confer a sense of nostalgia and longing; and the anthemic chorus allows the voices to soar with lyrics about the need for ordinary men to become heroes. The song superbly serves the function of the power ballad in the late 1990s, as described by Ann Powers:

> ... the power ballad has spoken for the masculine heart of hard rock, uniting artists and fans in mutual catharsis ... Arena rockers [in the 1970s] gave their male working-class fans a way to believe in themselves when others degraded them; today's alternative rockers [in the 1990s] express the doubts of young middle-class men about the power they inherit. Like the weeping patriarchs of the Christian group Promise Keepers, they consider getting in touch with one's feelings the ultimate heroic act.[16]

---

14   In interviews, Kroeger is careful to insist that 'Never Again' is not an autobiographical song.

15   See, among others, Raewyn W. Connell, *Masculinities* (Berkeley, CA, 1995); William Pollack, *Real Boys: Rescuing Our Sons from the Myths of Boyhood* (New York, 1999); Dan Kindlon and Michael Thompson, *Raising Cain: Protecting the Emotional Life of Boys* (New York, 2000); and Michael Kimmel, *Manhood in America: A Cultural History* (Oxford, 2005).

16   Ann Powers, 'The Male Rock Anthem: Going all to Pieces', *The New York Times*,

Most importantly, the vocal lines of Kroeger and Scott harmonize in thirds whose sweetness is kept in check by both singers' raspy, full-throated timbres, with Scott's Tennessee twang and more flexible voice winding itself around Kroeger's staunch grit.

Although Powers does not identify the power ballad as an explicitly white genre, all of the songs she identifies as exemplars are performed by white artists with predominantly white fan bases. I want to focus in particular on the gravelly vocal timbre as signifier of earnestness that connects Aerosmith's 'Dream On' and Lynyrd Skynyrd's 'Free Bird' to Kroeger's and Scott's 'Hero'. These singers participate in a convention established by the likes of Robert Plant, Bruce Springsteen and Roger Daltrey, whose coarse, raspy voices are understood to speak the inarticulate anguish of the proudly uncouth and embattled working-class white man.

Not without irony, I note that the earliest recordings documenting this vocal style were made in the 1930s by African-American bluesmen such as Blind Willie Johnson and Robert Johnson; the Johnsons' choked, aching voices were emulated by white British blues and rock singers in the 1960s. Later, this vocal technique was imitated by rock singers following the examples of Led Zeppelin and The Who and was understood by fans to demonstrate authenticity, grit and the personal experience of having been marginalized – the style reached its apogee in the tortured howl of Kurt Cobain. In the twenty-first century, as Leanne Fetterley observes, the value of this vocal style as a signifier of rock authenticity has perhaps finally been exhausted: '… this coarse vocal timbre effectively "signaled" sincerity and authenticity for grunge pioneers like Cobain, Pearl Jam's Eddie Vedder, and others, [but] Kroeger's similar vocal delivery can only be understood as an imitation; thus, it "signals" that he is playing a part – one that is inauthentic and insincere.'[17]

How, then, might a young white man today signal his sincerity through singing style? If the strained, throaty rasp of Kroeger and his peers, Chris Daughtry or Bo Bice (both former contestants on the television programme, *American Idol*) is now considered a charade of rock authenticity – perhaps even a self-serving appropriation of historically black singing styles – then musicians seeking to be sincere must steer clear of this kind of vocality. Many of these will choose an aesthetic that aligns more closely with nineteenth-century effete English poets than with 1930s Delta bluesmen; since at least the 1960s, the swaggering, rough-voiced machismo of rock singing has always been balanced by the limpid voices of singer-songwriters.

---

1 February 1998. Available at: <http://query.nytimes.com/gst/fullpage.html?res=9E07E4 D8173AF932A35751C0A96E958260&sec=&spon=&pagewanted=print> (accessed 15 July 2008).

17   Fetterley, 'Hey, Hey, I Wanna be a Rock Star'.

Singer-Songwriters as Modern-Day *Flâneurs*

I use 'singer-songwriter' to designate music characterized by confessional, poetic lyrics that are often sad, present a sense of intimacy and involve performers and listeners primarily from white middle-class backgrounds and of university age. The rugged version of manhood presented by the voices of Chad Kroeger and his ilk may be unattractive to young men in this group, who seek instead bookish, sensitive models. For the purposes of this discussion, I am avoiding distinguishing between solo performers and bands, because I want to insist that the centrality and particularity of the voice is a unifying feature – Sufjan Stevens and the Arcade Fire can thus be grouped together.

Indeed, the example of Arcade Fire helps me underscore my point: as much as members insist that they are a band and work collaboratively, vocalist Win Butler is invariably identified as the leader and spokesman for the group. To someone interested in the politics of the division of labour, this focus on Butler, a refugee from the privileged milieu of New England prep schools, becomes even more intriguing when we note that band member Régine Chassagne, the daughter of Haitian immigrants (and also Butler's wife), had studied voice at McGill University and was performing as a jazz singer in Montréal when she met Butler. He, by contrast, styled himself at the time as a guitarist who also played piano, yet it is his voice, not hers, that is at the centre of the Arcade Fire's sound.

It is clear that a new kind of singer-songwriter has achieved mainstream success in the past decade or so, following in the wake of artists like the late Jeff Buckley and including figures such as Sufjan Stevens, Damien Rice and women like Leslie Feist and Regina Spektor. The influential singer-songwriters of the 1960s and 1970s (James Taylor, Neil Young *et al.*) tended to promote the importance of the song ahead of the singer, generally accompanying their own singing with non-virtuosic playing of acoustic guitar or piano to avoid overshadowing the message conveyed through the lyrics. Supported by stripped-down production values, this style conjured a sense of a lone individual whose personal, artistic musings just happened to be caught on tape, giving the listener a peek into someone else's private feelings and also inviting the possibility of reproducing the songs. Many of these songs – 'Blowing in the Wind', 'You've got a Friend', 'The Circle Game' – became staples of campfire sing-alongs, as fans were not so awestruck by the musical performances that they could not attempt making them their own.

It is more difficult to imagine work by Devendra Banhart or Sufjan Stevens featuring in campfire sing-alongs. In distinction to the aesthetics of earlier singer-songwriters, the current style often involves much larger instrumental and creative forces: orchestral music, horn sections and pipe organ are heard alongside punk-influenced guitar and drum kit as often as acoustic guitar, and some artists explore odd metres and challenging rhyme schemes. But the voice, sibilant and whisper-light in juxtaposition to grand and often gorgeous instrumentation, seems most crucial. Consider the contrasts and continuities between James Taylor in his 1971 recording of 'You've Got a Friend' and Sufjan Stevens in 2005's 'Chicago': in both cases, we hear a thin tenor voice singing in a light, detached manner with close miking that permits a sense of physical closeness between singer and listener, but the ambitious orchestral and choral forces accompanying Stevens dispel any illusion that we are sitting next to him on the sofa. The intimacy created in 1970s recordings produced by figures such as Lou Adler, Peter Asher and sound engineer Henry Lewy favoured clarity and warmth, and Lou Adler described his Grammy-winning work on Carole King's 1971 *Tapestry* as striving to create the sense of being in the room with her at the piano.[18] This conceit is not possible with the broader instrumentation used by Stevens, even when the vocal tracks seem to be as close, or even closer at times. The intimacy constructed here, then, is of a different sort, involving an almost Spectoresque dramatic range alongside the clarity.

Stevens's imaginative combining of such disparate sounds as banjo, orchestral woodwinds, distorted electric guitar and children's choirs, is creative and sophisticated, partly influenced by his training in orchestral music (Stevens spent a year studying oboe performance at the prestigious Interlochen Arts Academy).[19] His arrangements, along with the work of Devendra Banhart, Leslie Feist, Regina Spektor and other new singer-songwriters, also owe an artistic debt to the work of Donovan, who juxtaposed similar sounds on his 1966 album *Sunshine Superman*. Brian Wilson, whose musical journey has ranged from clean-cut teen Beach Boy to mad recluse and musical alchemist, is another muse and model to a new generation of white, indie rock musicians – even Wilson's sweet, high tenor voice is uncannily emulated in the 2000s by young singer-songwriter Panda Bear. Similarly, other white artists in the late 1990s and the early twenty-first century study the output of such wan 1960s figures as Gram Parsons and Nick Drake with as avid an ear for imitation as Keith Richards and Mick Jagger ever brought to Muddy Waters. This interest in the gentle, melancholy anti-heroes of rock's golden age may perhaps be understood as an effort to counter the menacing versions of black manhood demonstrated in rap and hip hop, as Sasha Frere-Jones has suggested in a controversial article.[20] It is surely also important to acknowledge the class implications of some indie rockers' disavowal of heavy bass lines and powerful grooves:

> It's a cliché to picture indie musicians and fans as well-off 'hipsters' busily gentrifying neighborhoods ... this is the music of young 'knowledge workers' in training, and that has sonic consequences: Rather than body-centered, it is bookish and nerdy ... it shows off its chops via its range of allusions and high concepts with the kind of fluency both postmodern pop culture and higher education teach its listeners to admire. (Many rap MCs juggle symbologies just as deftly, but it's seldom their main point.) This doesn't make coffeehouse-

18   Cited in Reebee Garofalo, *Rockin' Out! Popular Music in the USA* (Boston, MA, 1997), p. 268.

19   Nic Harcourt, 'One Man Band', *Smithsonian Magazine*, October 2007, at: <http://www.smithsonianmag.com/arts-culture/10036476.html> (accessed 31 July 2008).

20   Sasha Frere-Jones, 'A Paler Shade of White', *The New Yorker*, 22 October 2007, at: <http://www.newyorker.com/arts/critics/musical/2007/10/22/071022crmu_music_frerejones?currentPage=1> (accessed 18 July 2008).

indie shallow, but it can result in something more akin to the 1960s folk revival, with fretful collegiate intellectuals in a Cuban Missile Crisis mood, seeking purity and depth in antiquarian music and escapist spirituality.[21]

If these musicians and their fans reject the Nickelback style as crude and vulgar, and demur from hip hop in order to avoid the taint of appropriation and racism, then the arty, contemplative work of 1960s singer-songwriters might indeed appear an attractive model.

Jeff Buckley emerges as an important link between artists of the 1960s and the 2000s, although his style differs significantly from that of either his father Tim Buckley or Sufjan Stevens. Fans of his work are drawn above all to his singing, which Daphne Brooks has described as 'a controlled spectacle of artfully losing control with the voice'.[22] In a discussion of Buckley's deliberate, embodied fragility, Shana Goldin-Perschbacher has noted that, in recording 'Mojo Pin' (1994), one of his best-known songs, Buckley refused 'de-essing' – the conventional cleaning up of tongue and mouth sounds – in order to convey intimacy and vulnerability.[23] The recent success of artists like Stevens or Damien Rice suggests that this vocal style has become increasingly influential in the decade since Buckley's death in 1997. It is worth noting that the album *Grace* (on which 'Mojo Pin' appears) was not very successful when it was released in 1994, at the height of the grunge craze, but its popularity has increased steadily and it achieved gold status in 2002.

How can we interpret the contemporary appeal of this kind of vocal identity for young white men from middle-class backgrounds? The attraction seems to revolve around the willingness to expose frailty – both emotional, in the content of songs, and physical, in the emphasis on the delicate, embodied voice – while at the same time demonstrating detachment and serenity. Taken together with inventive, large-scale musical backdrops, the singer seems almost a dispassionate, self-aware observer of events happening at some distance, like Charles Baudelaire's *flâneurs*. Baudelaire identified a specific kind of bourgeois Parisian in the mid-nineteenth century, who strolled the city streets, observing and analysing the complexities of modern life but shying away from the dangers of involvement.[24] The *flâneur* exists in an interior and exterior space simultaneously, occupying the landscape of his mind and the physical landscape of the city as he wanders, and I suggest that the juxtaposition of wide-open and intimate space conjured in these recordings mirrors this experience.

In some cases, the feelings and events described in the song are in striking contrast to the cosy, confessional delivery, and this disjuncture seems intended to rivet the listener's attention. In Sufjan Stevens's 2005 song about notorious serial killer John Wayne Gacy, his tenor voice breathes gently into the microphone accounts of Gacy's

---

21   Carl Wilson, 'The Trouble with Indie Rock', in *Slate.com*, at: <http://www.slate.com/id/2176187> (accessed 21 July 2008).
22   Daphne Brooks, *Grace* (New York, 2005), p. 92.
23   Goldin-Perschbacher, 'Not with You but of You', p. 217.
24   Charles Baudelaire, *The Painter of Modern Life* [1863] (New York, 1964).

seduction and murder of young boys, concluding numbly that 'And in my best behaviour / I am really just like him / Look beneath the floorboards / For the secrets I have hid'.[25] Here, the soft voice and simple acoustic guitar accompaniment invite the listener to share Stevens's horrified fascination with Gacy's gruesome crimes, and to hear the singer's confession of his own dark impulses and ugly secrets.

We can, I think, understand this newly popular singer-songwriter style as a kind of sonic *flâneur*-ism, and artists like Stevens as twenty-first-century versions of Baudelaire's concept. Given the male privilege that is a prerequisite to being a *flâneur*, could we extend it to include female singer-songwriters like Leslie Feist, whose work demonstrates a comparable aesthetic of interiority/exteriority? Feist describes her own thin, expressionless singing style with her own invented term, 'jhai': 'if a song is really sad ... it's a bit melodramatic to sing it in musical theatre style, really broken-hearted sad ... it's more interesting to perform that sad song with no expression ... it leaves room for people to relate more.'[26]

It is attractive to connect this to the notion of the *flâneur*, but we must also acknowledge the ways in which Feist's account of her style coincides with many repressive conventions of white, middle-class femininity. She is deliberately performing in a way intended to erase her own presence as much as possible in order to enable her audience to project their own, more important, emotions on her work. Western culture abounds with versions of blank female forms that the listener/viewer/reader fills up with meanings and makes his own – indeed, this seems to be the preferred model of femininity for many artists, as numerous theorists have argued.[27] Further, the story of how Feist's distinctive singing style developed can almost serve as a cautionary tale for loud-mouthed women; she fronted a punk band and sustained vocal damage from her forceful, aggressive screaming. Her only way forward as a singer was to back away and adopt a light, whispering, ladylike technique, and her new voice led her to international acclaim.

When a man uses a similar vocal technique, it signals an alternative masculinity – an anti-heroism that rejects the swagger most closely associated with blue-collar bravado. This aesthetic of a distinctive, vulnerable voice floating against instrumental backdrops that range dramatically serves, perhaps, to reassure and comfort, and to provide a sense of intimacy and human connection in ways that more robust, assured singing cannot. Whereas the earnest performances of singers like Chad Kroeger seem forced, listeners can believe in the sincerity and humanity of singers whose voices are flawed and vulnerable; this might explain why Win Butler's anguished, uncertain voice is better suited to the work of Arcade Fire than that of trained singer Régine Chassagne.

What is more, the new pairing of close-miked voices with large-scale instrumentation has to be understood in the context of contemporary listening

---

25   Sufjan Stevens, 'John Wayne Gacy Jr.', *Illinois* (Asthmatic Kitty, 2005).
26   Cited at: <http://www.el-oso.net/blog/archives/2005/08/11/feist/11> (accessed 26 May 2008).
27   See, among many others, John Berger, *Ways of Seeing* (London, 1972); and Laura Mulvey, *Visual and Other Pleasures* (Bloomington, IN, 1989).

practices. Walter Benjamin described the *flâneur's* 'incomparable privilege of being himself and someone else as he sees fit. Like a roving soul in search of a body, he enters another person whenever he wishes.'[28] Whereas in the pre-headphone days the simple, direct aesthetic of singer-songwriters mirrored the experience of listening to a record in a peaceful, domestic space, the disjuncture between sweeping orchestral forces and the sounds of breath, tongue and teeth of today's singer-songwriters is nowadays not as outlandish as it might have seemed in the 1970s. This aesthetic matches the experiences of listening to whispering voices that burrow into our ears as we go about alone in the big noisy world. Modern-day *flâneurs* who watch and blog from the safety of their isolated privacies have, perhaps, a need for quirky, frail voices to anchor them and provide evidence of humanity. This delicate singing style suggests a refusal of privilege and a distaste for the melodramatic vocal strength conventionally presented in arena rock's early 1980s' heyday, by the likes of superstars Foreigner or Journey.

Power and Power Ballads: The Strange Journey of Journey

The smooth, powerful tenor voice became a crucial feature of rock anthems in the early 1980s, heard in such iconic songs as REO Speedwagon's 'Can't Fight This Feeling' or Foreigner's 'I Want to Know What Love Is' (both released in 1984). Singers of this type may usefully be considered alongside legendary tenors such as John McCormack or Mario Lanza, who enjoyed mass popularity (but less critical praise) for their sentimental, dramatic singing of opera arias and popular songs alike. In the 1970s and 1980s the bombast of arena rock was particularly compelling to young white men on the fringes of respectable youth culture, as Ann Powers notes:

> *The prevailing stereotype of the arena rocker depicted a party animal, occupying the lowest rung on the ladder of American pop culture. Even other rock fans saw them as pot-smoking dropouts who had betrayed rock's countercultural potential. Power ballads offered these so-called losers a vision of honor and strength ... [the] songs employed the rhetoric of comic books and fantasy novels: low culture insisting on its right to mimic high art. A hamburger flipper still living with Mom could imagine himself a warrior in their midst.*[29]

Powers's hamburger flipper could take defiant pride in being part of the enormous, fist-pumping and lighter-waving fan base of bands such as Journey.

---

28 Walter Benjamin, 'Charles Baudelaire', cited at: <http://www.thelemming.com/lemming/dissertation-web/home/flaneur.html> (accessed 21 July 2008).

29 Powers, 'The Male Rock Anthem'.

This archetypal arena rock band formed in the late 1970s and has undergone several changes in its members, enjoying its greatest renown and commercial success in the early 1980s with Steve Perry as lead singer and front-man. In terms of range, timbre, flexibility and stamina, Perry's voice is consistent with the style of other power balladeers such as Kevin Cronin (REO Speedwagon), Dennis DeYoung (Styx) and Brad Delp (Boston). The technical skill and strength of Perry's warm, vibrant tenor voice are undeniable, and while his quasi-operatic histrionics are risible to some, his work has been perceived as genuinely moving and soulful to his fans. Songs such as 'Don't Stop Believin'' (1981), 'Open Arms' (1982), 'Separate Ways' (1983), and his solo hit 'Oh Sherrie' (1984) were Top Ten hits and still are inspirational touchstones for countless listeners.

'Don't Stop Believin'' is undoubtedly the band's signature tune, and its message of optimism and endurance is masterfully conveyed; it opens with the sound of lone piano treated with a great deal of echo, suggestive of a church setting, and virtuosic guitar work and splashy drumming are tastefully restrained up to the climactic move to the hook and title lyrics, suspensefully delayed until the end of the song. Soaring over it all is the vibrant, fluid voice of Steve Perry, creating a uniformly relaxed, but powerful sound on melismatic passages and long-held high notes (B and C above middle C), with lyrics about lonely people keeping the faith.

Perry's career as front-man of the band bears comparison with the experiences of mainly female singers in the big band era; he was at once resented and appreciated for his ability to connect with fans and give the band its commercial appeal. Perry joined the group at the insistence of their manager after they had already released three modestly successful albums of mainly instrumental, improvised jazz/rock, because it was felt that putting a singer in front of the band, rather than having one of the instrumentalists double as singer, would broaden Journey's horizons. Unfortunately, as Robert Walser observes in his study of heavy metal in the mid-1980s, 'Spectacles are problematic in the context of a patriarchal order that is invested in the stability of signs and that seeks to maintain women in the position of objects of the gaze',[30] and the notion of a front-man who does nothing but sing was resisted by the original members of Journey. Perry reports that 'they didn't want to make it with a lead singer – they wanted to make it *without* one'.[31]

Nevertheless, Perry's showmanship and vocal virtuosity, famously modelled after African-American gospel and soul icon Sam Cooke (whose influence is heard most clearly in Journey's 1978 'Lovin', Touchin', Squeezin'') enabled him to leave his construction job and propel the band to international success. However, the demanding performance schedule that was manageable for his bandmates as the band's fame grew was in conflict with the care needed to keep him in good voice. While guitarist Neal Schon could play night after night and replace instruments as easily as he damaged them, Perry's increasingly fretful concern with vocal

---

30   Walser, *Running with the Devil*, p. 108.
31   Alex Pappademas, 'He Didn't Stop Believin'', *GQ Magazine*, June 2008, at: <http://men. style.com/gq/features/full?id=content_6818&pageNum=11> (accessed 30 July 2008).

health became frustrating.[32] Tensions between Perry and the instrumentalists eventually led to his exit from the group in 1987, and then again in 1998 after a 1995 reconciliation – during these decades, other members of the group also came and went, with only group founder Neal Schon remaining constant.[33]

In the minds of millions of fans, however, Steve Perry remains the voice, and thus the soul, of Journey, and the 2007 addition of Arnel Pineda as lead singer of the group has generated considerable discussion of vocal sincerity and rock authenticity in mainstream popular culture. In the midst of trendy nostalgia for 1980s' music, Journey's 'Don't Stop Believin'' anthem was used in June 2007 for the final moments of the critically acclaimed television series *The Sopranos*. Although Journey had hired Steve Augeri and later Jeff Scott Soto as lead singers after Perry's final exit, they had no vocalist in 2007 and were thus not in position to capitalize on the wave of interest that resulted from this high-profile use of their song. Unwilling to let this opportunity pass by, band founder Neal Schon spent hours online looking at YouTube clips of Journey tribute singers, and ultimately came across some footage of Pineda performing with his band The Zoo in an upscale Manila nightclub. After a successful audition in Los Angeles, Pineda went into the studio as the new lead singer of Journey to record a new album, 2008's *Revelation*.

The introduction of a Filipino singer, some 20 years younger than his new bandmates and fresh from earning his living through the painstaking imitation of singers like Perry for the amusement of tourists, provoked outrage among some of Journey's loyal fans. Members of the band, on the other hand, were pleasantly surprised to experience a dramatic spike in popularity with young Asians, and keyboardist Jonathan Cain has remarked that 'I kind of like the whole idea of having a singer like him. It's exotic'.[34] The anti-Pineda faction was often scathing in its disgust for this pretender to the throne, some denouncing him with racist language and all insisting on the singularity of Perry's soulful voice and the impossibility of a mere karaoke singer replicating it.

These responses to the addition of Pineda all demonstrate incredulity that the masterful, distinctive singing of Steve Perry could be produced by someone so utterly different from him. And yet the resemblance is uncanny, as Neal Schon observed while shopping online for a new vocalist. What is more, perusal of more of Pineda's performances with his Manila band The Zoo suggests that he

---

32 Alex Pappademas, 'Foolish, Foolish Throat: A Q&A with Steve Perry', Men.Style.com, 29 May 2008, at: <http://men.style.com/gq/blogs/gqeditors/2008/05/foolish-foolish.html> (accessed 29 July 2008).

33 The disputes and tensions among members of Journey make it impossible to write a succinct, neutral account of how and why – even when – Perry actually left the band. Although his official departure was occasioned by his bandmates' impatience while he delayed getting hip replacement surgery after an injury in 1996, there are clearly many other factors at play, and in my account I have highlighted the ambivalent relationship Journey had with the very notion of a lead singer.

34 Cited in Paul Liberatore, 'An Incredible Journey for Band's New Frontman', *Marin Independent Journal*, 27 December 2007, at: <http://www.marinij.com//ci_7826224?IADID=Search-www.marinij.com-www.marinij.com> (accessed 30 July 2008).

could also do credible impersonations of Robert Plant, Kurt Cobain, Sting and Bryan Adams.[35] This shape-shifting flies in the face of assumptions about rock authenticity, particularly the cherished notion of the untutored rock voice that signifies the individual travails of the singer. Steve Perry's Portuguese heritage and his careful efforts to mimic his idol Sam Cooke, a singer trained in black gospel singing and who suffered the hardships of living in the racist 1950s, are overlooked by listeners disgusted that a Filipino would presume to emulate the voice of a true-blue, working-class, white American.

This irony becomes delicious when the details of Pineda's biography are taken into account. On a television interview in the summer of 2008, Pineda, in halting English, described his life as the child of garment workers in Manila, whose gift for music was revealed early and led to endless singing competitions. After the death of his mother from cancer, the 13-year-old Pineda lived on the streets, sleeping in parks and often literally singing for his supper. His skill at mimicking famous rock voices eventually led to a steady job fronting The Zoo, a band that performed careful versions of popular rock songs in an upscale nightclub, and ultimately to his fateful discovery by Neal Schon.[36] In another interview, Pineda defends his years of singing cover versions by gesturing to the context of rock'n'roll in the Philippines:

> *While the U.S. occupation shaped Filipino musical culture during the late nineteenth and early twentieth centuries, the Philippines truly became a cover-band nation in the '60s, when the islands served as a way station for troops en route to or from the Vietnam War and every nightclub needed bands who could entertain American servicemen with Top 40 rock 'n' roll. To this day, Pineda says, 'if you only play original songs, [audiences in the Philippines] will not appreciate you 100 percent. They want to hear you singing other bands' songs that made it to number one. Like Beatles, Led Zeppelin, Journey'.[37]*

The impersonation of other rock singers, so looked down upon in rock culture in the United States, is thus explained as a strategy that actually proves authenticity and value in the former American colony. Pineda's ability to listen closely and imitate accurately the voices he heard, perfecting timbre, phrasing, accent and inflection, are not prized in a US rock culture that values spontaneity and individualism, but these skills are central to the tradition of karaoke that originated in Japan in the 1970s. Christine Yano explains that an ideology of *kata*, the repeating of patterned forms, is important to Japanese cultural practices such as flower-arranging, martial arts and karaoke: '*Kata* becomes a distillation not merely of an individual way of doing things but of a historic panoply of teachers present and past, embedding the

---

35 A collection of Pineda's early work can be seen at: <http://www.youtube.com/profile_videos?user=ndgomez777&p=r> (accessed 31 July 2008).

36 Interview on *CBS News Sunday Morning*, 1 June 2008.

37 Pappademas, 'He Didn't Stop Believin''.

doing and the doer in a thick diachronic text.'[38] Pineda's demonstrated familiarity with the techniques of classic rock singing established him as a rock expert in the Philippines, worthy of ascending to the position of rock star.

Judith Halberstam and Eve Kosofsky Sedgwick have argued that heterosexual and masculine identities can exist only in contrast to versions of identity that are *not* straight, *not* 'manly', and that these other models are thus crucial for the continued readability of dominant versions.[39] Perhaps the existence of a singer like Pineda, who fluidly switches between his Steve Perry voice and his Kurt Cobain voice, is needed by some fans to bolster their belief in the genuineness of both Perry and Cobain, the simulacrum that proves the existence of the original.[40] But in his influential work *Culture and Imperialism*, Edward Said asked: 'Who in India or Algeria today can confidently separate out the British or French component of the past from present actualities, and who in Britain or France can draw a clear circle around British London or French Paris that would exclude the impact of India and Algeria upon these two imperial cities?'[41] I might ask: who could confidently identify the aspect of white men's rock singing that is neither copied nor copiable, and who could point to aspects of white male identity that bear no traces of influence from other cultural sources?

The ease with which Pineda assumes different vocal masks of rock authenticity creates anxiety for rock fans and also threatens many taken-for-granted beliefs in masculinity as innate, genuine and immutable. Heard in another way, though, Pineda's chameleon vocals can provide liberating, exciting possibilities for all types of singer. Indeed, all the singers I have discussed here can be identified as skilled performers of specific versions of male identity, providing models of manhood for listeners in turn to emulate. If every one of them is a carefully honed construction – an actor playing a role tutored by extensive listening and imitation of others – then the rigid boundaries of rock authenticity, and of manhood, become less constricting.

---

38 Christine Yano, 'The Floating World of Karaoke in Japan', *Popular Music and Society* 20/2 (1996): 1–18, at 3.

39 Judith Halberstam, *Female Masculinity* (Durham, NC, 1998); and Eve Kosofsky Sedgwick, *Epistemology of the Closet* (Berkeley, CA, 1990).

40 Jean Baudrillard, 'The Precession of Simulacra' in *Simulacra and Simulation* (Ann Arbor, MI, 1995), pp. 1–42.

41 Edward Said, *Culture and Imperialism* (New York, 1993), p. 15.

Talking Music, Making Music: A Comparison between Rap and Techno[1]

Antoine Hennion

It's listeners who make music ...[2]

This contribution, being work in progress, gathers together in an open fashion a body of reflections from a seminar given over to a comparison between rap and techno, and I begin with a brief reconsideration of common assumptions. The seminar was given with the object of studying listening, beginning with a series of juxtaposed experiments.[3] The starting idea was simple: to regard music as being of an uncertain affect that depends on what its listener makes of it and not as being an experience that is merely received. The word 'experiment' can, indeed, create confusion. It does not mean that we subjected guinea-pigs to regulated tests, in order to measure the best possible listener reactions to a given object,[4] although it

---

1   Translated from the French original by Derek B. Scott.
2   To paraphrase Marcel Duchamp's famous 'Ce sont les regardeurs qui font les tableaux' ('It's the viewers who make paintings').
3   I am only the compiler of this chapter; it would be more correct to speak of the collective work of participants of the CSI-School of Mines/CNRS seminar, 'Aimer la musique. Musicologie du goût, sociologie de la musique, histoire de l'amateur', which I directed with J.-M. Fauquet. See Antoine Hennion, 'L'Ecoute à la question', *Revue de musicologie* 88/1 (2002): 95–149. I thank, in particular, Morgan Jouvenet for the part on rap. An early French version of the present text appeared as 'Musiques, présentez-vous!', *French Cultural Studies* 16/2 (2005): 121–34.
4   It is not a question, either, of revealing that the social determinations of people's tastes are personal and subjective, in accordance with the familiar critical posture of the sociologist (Pierre Bourdieu, *Distinction: A Social Critique of the Judgment of Taste* [London, 1984]), nor of imagining a wild typology of listeners born of our own aesthetic conceptions, following the example of what Theodor Adorno does with as little scruple as talent ('Types d'attitude musicale', *Introduction à la sociologie de la musique* [Genève,

would, of course, be one way of showing what music is. Rather, moving in exactly the opposite direction, we have tried to make listeners the experts on their own listening, so that they can teach us what musical experience is for them.

The musical object is not already present, ready to undergo the various listenings directed towards it that, in turn, we would then be able to measure. Even its immediacy is in question. Analysing the musical moment is not a matter of measuring the way we hear various sounds. This would postulate music as already present, when the question is what makes it appear as such. It is not simply a matter of putting a CD in a CD player, and suddenly *there* is the music That is why the listener's cooperation in defining what happens is needed.

In the first instance, one of our objectives is to benefit from the immense know-how that the listener deploys in seeking out preferences, managing pleasure, evaluating, testing, making an immediate judgement or delaying diagnoses. We wanted, with the listener's help, to test certain methods of accounting for all this. However, beyond this insider shrewdness, listeners have created a framework for their listening, having built their aural competencies over a long period of time. Ways of listening have a history as much at the personal as at the collective level (it is always necessary to think of listening as a plurality). They are not reducible to the vibration of a tympanum: they have been constructed through the invention of formats and repertoires, systems and arrangements, all of which have been passionately debated by fans of various types of music.

We also wanted the listener – a participant little considered in musicology – to be given back a place in musical analyses. To the extent that, historically, the author-producer came to occupy the centre ground of artistic creativity, studies of classical music became enthusiastically aligned in conformity with literary production. Instead of treating music as a complete object, they reduced it to the score alone; thus it became at one and the same time an effect of, and the driving force behind, the new subjugation of music to graphic reason.[5] In passing, these studies had rid themselves of the listener, who was now handed over to the psychologist or acoustician. Some musicological work has certainly begun to take the listener back into account,[6] but it would still be going too far to speak of the listener's uninterrupted presence in musical analyses.[7]

1994], pp. 7–25).

5   J. Goody, *La raison graphique: La domestication de la pensée sauvage* (Paris, 1979). For a musicological critique of the privilege accorded to the score, see Joseph Kerman, *Contemplating Music: Challenges to Musicology* (Cambridge, MA, 1985); on the particular difficulties of the scholarly analysis of popular music, see Richard Middleton, *Studying Popular Music* (Milton Keynes, 1990).

6   Mary Sue Morrow, *Concert Life in Haydn's Vienna: Aspects of a Developing Musical and Social Institution* (Stuyvesant, NY, 1989); James H. Johnson, *Listening in Paris: A Cultural History* (Berkeley, CA, 1995); and William Weber, 'Did People Listen in the 18th Century?', *Early Music* (November 1997): 678–91.

7   As is the case with Tia DeNora's approach: "Music as a Technology of the Self", *Poetics* 26 (1999): 1–26; and *Music in Everyday Life* (Cambridge, 2000).

Listening is not, as many musicologists appear to believe, a means of accessing music by the back door. It is both an activity and a presence. The listener who participates in the production of the music he listens to can be compared with the image of the reader depicted by Proust[8] – a listener (reader) who is also an actor of the music (of the literature), made up of a sum of attitudes that are not outside the music, but *within* it. And this return of the listener calls forth much else besides: music emerges only in a local context, through different places and means of listening; it presupposes bodily drives and is made in different ways; it relies on the existence of a collective. It is not a question of the autonomy of music and of shaping an equally autonomous musical subject to be taken, in turn, as an analytic object cut off from its historic production; no, the listener is also an effect of reception, in the same way as is the music.[9]

Rap and Techno: Music Already Inundated with Discourse

Starting from the foregoing assumptions, what experiments should be devised for these new kinds of music? Indeed, they pose a particular problem. There are already a great number of social discourses firmly attached to them – youth, revolt, immigration, violence, festivals, drugs and so on. Instead of criticizing and reformulating this critical commentary in our account, we tried to show the way in which rap and techno could present 'themselves'. Rather than pretending to determine the meaning and the contents of the music in line with such and such a discipline, it was more a practical matter of seeing how various elements combine and co-construct *themselves* – the discursive and the gestural, the somatic and the musical, the scenic and the ideological (particularly according to issues recurrently raised by rap and techno, such as gender, violence, the media) – and how these elements 'make' rap or techno. In this way, we were merely extending the seminar's general methodology: each meeting was to begin with situations where the music is played, heard, interpreted and commented on. This would enable us to study the way in which the pairing 'music-fan' is animated through the critical activity of 'listeners' themselves, when, starting from past experience that is not shared equally, they discussed between themselves, compared, reconsidered their first impressions, returned to other experiences, relativized the conditions of the present listening, corrected previous opinions and so on.

---

8   In Marcel Proust, 'Sur la lecture' ('On Reading'), Preface to *Sésame et les Lys* (*Sesame and Lilies*) by John Ruskin, trans. Marcel Proust (Paris, 1987).

9   On reading, which occupies in relation to the book a position very analogous to that of listening to music, we have been inspired by numerous arguments in the work of Roger Chartier, *Lecture et lecteurs dans la France d'Ancien Régime* (Paris, 1987) and his edited anthology *Pratiques de la lecture* (Paris, 1993); see also Hennion, 'L'Ecoute à la question', and Antoine Hennion, 'Listen!', *Music and Arts in Action* 1/1 (2008): 39–45. Also available at: <http://musicandartsinaction.net/index.php/maia/article/view/listen>.

This time, the idea behind the experiment was to reap benefit from the ambivalent relations between rap and techno, from their proximity and opposition, and to organize a comparative demonstration: to present these musics, to put them to the listening test, to show their way of functioning, what they hold of interest, the debates that they arouse. And this was not done from the 'outside', with recourse to musical and social characteristics aimed at objectifying them (such as musicological descriptions, origins and history, social background, media reports and current success), but, in conformity with the seminar's ground rules – namely, on the basis of how they are listened to and how they are presented by fans – in order to try to understand how and for whom rap and techno 'make music'.

One argument maintains that there is an important and arbitrary distance between the musical elements of rap or techno and the social meanings and practices that are grafted on to these musical genres. Another runs contrary to this, claiming that the former is strongly determined by the latter. Only experiment can cast light on the respective merits of these positions, or perhaps reveal a variety of situations and evolutions. This prompted the idea that we ought to look at both the music that is made and the music that is spoken about: sounds and contexts. By controlling the conditions of the experiment, the registers that are mobilized to present the interest shown in a particular form of a music are left open, and no attempt is made to solve *a priori* the question of the existence and solidity of the relationship between one and the other. Another way of describing our aims is: to evaluate simultaneously, in reciprocal fashion, music and the criteria of its perception; to resist choosing between music and words, and, instead, to let the musical and social characters of rap and techno emerge together; to discover what the relevant features of these genres are for their followers, to feel what it is they hold; to perceive more easily how they lend themselves to the construction of differences and formulation of judgements; and, more generally, to understand how they attach their publics to themselves. Lastly, there is an intention to examine the more or less necessary connections that these genres establish between the musical products themselves and the comments to which they give rise.

The meeting takes place in a room of the Bibliothèque Nationale de France, equipped with a comprehensive sound system, and a technician also present. The two members of the seminar who have volunteered to present 'their' music are both free to conceive and organize their presentations how they wish, and make full use of their access to this equipment. Members of the seminar gather their friends to act as a public, and there are about 30 people in the room. We first approach rap, then techno, and we then link them together afterwards in a general debate about what has taken place.

Rap: Music or Revolt?

Within the framework given, Pierre, who has put together a presentation on rap (or *of* rap), chooses to offer his contribution to the sociology of musical genres by exploring how playing and listening to musical excerpts might change the character of an academic argument: what is it that listening alone is able to render comprehensible?

> *I should like it to be the music that makes us speak rather than the reverse (the sociologist would usually wish to say something concerning the music). I hope that the pieces I've chosen will make the audience react, while I will arrange the recorded titles a bit like a DJ, in accordance with his own reactions ...*

The idea is to approach as closely as possible the ordinary, commonplace conditions of listening – leaving aside the oddity of this room as an environment for rap. To be strictly accurate, therefore, it is not about putting on a show: there are no vinyl records, sampler, computer or microphone, only simple CDs and cassettes, the most common supports of rap appreciation (along with radio broadcasts, some of which Pierre has recorded on cassette). Pierre specifies, finally, that he is a researcher, and that the problem is not whether or not he is huge fan of rap: 'I am not trying to convince anyone of the "quality" of the music ...'

The first song, 'Touche pas à ma musique' ('Don't Touch My Music'), speaks about the relationship between words, music and origins – 'ma clique' (my crew [gang]) – and of the relationships of the rapper with the media and the public; it highlights the difficulty of not privileging voice and text in the analysis of this production. Pierre points out that fans act similarly; they read the lyrics in the booklet, and the dedications and 'messages to Allah', before listening to the CD they have just bought. The photographs, the garish logos and graphics also influence their listening. The listener would also do well not to disregard the device of self-presentation with which the singers unceasingly make play: scenes of studio activity and the rapper's lifestyle, obsession with realities, constant references to social background and continual demands that listeners 'open their eyes' to the world. Another characteristic of rap is to play with this intricate web of enunciations and reminders of the context of these enunciations on the disc itself: the presence of intros, outros and other interludes which are inserted among the pieces, made up of played scenes, studio out-takes, telephone conversations; these are all means of ensuring the rapper reappears in the context of his production and are often present also, as Pierre says, 'to reinforce a social layer'. Rap is not detached from the rapper; the production forms part of the product. In a symmetrical way, among fans, the same applies to 'promo' clips, which are always accompanied with abundant notes: they reforge the link between the music, the rapper and the social message of rap. The common practice of fans never ceases to show that they themselves privilege these aspects, and they associate them, above all, as values that have come out of what they consider rap. A rapper like MC Solaar, for example, is criticized for the distance he has moved from his social origins, rather than for his music; he is regarded as having become too integrated.

Pierre tries to choose titles from a great variety of styles to counter the current gibe, 'rap, it's always the same': 'We Tryin' to Stay Alive' by Wyclef Jean, an American rapper labelled more 'commercial', a production starting out with a well-known 'sample' of the Bee Gees; Wu Tang Clan, a celebrated New York group with a dark and tortured sound; an excerpt from two contrasting albums by Stomy Bugsy; and two deliberately very different songs from an album by NTM,[10] 'La Fièvre' and 'Paris sous les bombes'). The audience comments most of all, in rather crude terms, on the moods that the pieces unleash: harder or more festive, darker or more dancing ... The rhythm and tempo sometimes seem more stereotyped, sometimes more unusual or studied. Lastly, the manner of declamation, the accents and use of the voice take us back to what seems to be the most salient element of the genre, speech-song.

In the discussion, which opens up little by little, participants suggest that the rather stable character of the musical background, once the piece begins, invites few remarks, whereas the words call automatically for social commentary. The same goes for rapping: to what extent is it really possible to vary it? Is this not typically the *trick*, the key feature whose success certainly gave rap its strong image, but also brings the danger, as with punk or pure and hard rockabilly, that such an over-rigid process can be captive to a binary choice: either you obey it (although it is very determining and constraining) and you rap, or you free yourself of it, you twist it, you shift, but almost immediately you do so, you are no longer rapping.

From here, questions slip inexorably towards two topics, despite the efforts of Pierre, who tries to retain everyone's focus on the precise sound aspects of the songs: on one side, the mode of production and the rappers' social context and, on the other, the content of the words and, more particularly, their social import. The problem, also, is that the object leaves us no choice. The desire to determine it externally, outside its own criteria, does not lead to the revelation of a level that is usually invisible or latent. It just misses the specific space where arrangements, variations and relevant connections come together – that space to which we are sent back constantly when following up the sayings and doings of actors and musicians as much as consumers or commentators. Consequently, Pierre is led to explain the way in which rappers work, the origin of the 'samples' and, more generally, the relations that allow the social milieu of rap to function, the DJ market, the origins of the movement in the United States and in France. But he is reticent: all this can be found in the literature that has multiplied on the subject of rap.[11] The debate becomes animated around the greater or lesser degrees of 'gangsterism' found in this milieu and the type of relations that reign there: clans, mafia-like godfathers, influence and threats, machismo, the rule of money and of bragging. How much of

---

10   'Nique ta mère' ('Fuck your mother'), one of the first famous rap groups in France.
11   Among the best-informed French texts are the following, rather arbitrarily selected from a now abundant field: George Lapassade and Philippe Rousselot, *Le Rap ou la fureur de dire* (Paris, 1990); S.B.G. Desse, *Freestyle* (Paris, 1993); Hugues Bazin, *La Culture hip hop* (Paris, 1995); O. Cachin, *L'Offensive rap* (Paris, 1996); José-Louis Bocquet and Philippe Pierre-Adolphe, *Rap ta France* (Paris, 1997); Manuel Boucher, *Rap expression des lascars: significations et enjeux du rap dans la société française* (Paris, 1998); Christian Béthune, *Le Rap: une esthétique hors la loi* (Paris, 1999); E. Grynzpan, *Bruyante Techno* (Nantes, 1999); S.H. Fernando Jr., *The New Beats: Culture, musique et attitudes du hip hop* (Paris, 2000); and 'Territoires du hip hop', *Art Press*, Hors Série (December 2000).

this is real or simply myth-making – in a symbolic inversion of the dominant order, as sociologists might say? What are the practical consequences, in everyday reality, of this aggressive behaviour, even if it is in large part provocation and ostentation?

The room reacts in particular to the violence, racism or sexism of certain words, comparing these features with those of earlier movements such as rock 'n' roll or punk, while trying to decide if they are irony or provocation, and insisting that these are not simply the same things in all cases. Several speakers consider, for example, that the use of Nazi insignia by punks, or the satanic imagery of hard rock, is more a means of displaying excess and dramatizing their gestures of provocation, whereas the macho violence of rappers seems closer to the reality of their practices. But the positions are not distinctly taken: there is a feeling that it is difficult, where this topic is concerned, not to fall into well-worn debates of this kind, so everyone maintains a highly questioning stance.

This method is no less effective for that. It allows two current questions, often hostile to the genre, to be stated and discussed together: does rap reflect (at best) or reinforce (at worst) youth violence? Is it not, at the same time, a commercial and mediatized music, completely integrated, so that its provocative character, far from constituting a revolt and a challenge to 'society', helps it, above all else, to *sell* (a question posed in similar terms in connection with the Rolling Stones in the early days of rock 'n' roll)? Moving in another direction, a condescending complacency is identified and criticized, one that would excuse rap of any moral or political responsibility in the name of the social and ethnic origins of its actors: one cannot, without going to extremes, use this as an excuse for regarding an insulting and aggressive vocabulary as merely a matter of choice of style, something neutral or unimportant on the political, human or moral level, and without effect on individuals or communities.

Techno: Grasping the Sound

Paul, in presenting techno, takes a resolutely different approach. For him, showing is doing. He arrives with two friends, one of whom is a DJ, and all their hardware, in particular their metal bags filled with vinyl discs. In front of the two turntables, installed with the help of the technician, they provide a brief history of the origins and the various types of techno. The room quickly stifles its questions about the reality of events or filiations, the alternatives to this account, its mythological character, its grey areas: we understand that there will be no chatting about these. That is not what it is about. This 'history' is that of a young collectivity rewriting itself in real time. It furnishes techno with some worthy ancestors such as Pierre Henry, Tangerine Dream and Kraftwerk and, if this mythology is extended, Schaeffer, Russolo, Stockhausen. It retraces techno's origins to key moments and founding places, already so familiar: Jamaicans in New York, garages in New Jersey, English dance clubs, the French disco DJs who preceded them. It is myth in the strong sense, a performative history: a genre is created in front of us through the story it tells of itself.

In the same way, the succinct presentation of the principles of production and the hardware required ('kick', beat boxes, samplers, MIDI sequencer), followed by a classification of the types of techno presented by their English names and their tempo ('bpm' or beats per minute), leaves us with the impression of a catalogue. Can a genre be adequately defined with reference only to a certain number of beats per minute? From trance, at between 125 and 140 bpm, and tribal techno, one goes up and up, passing by 'acid core' in the neighbourhood of 150–160, then 'gabber' and hard-techno, until we reach 'hard core' at 180–250, but which, we are told proudly, can go up to 300 bpm. We assume that it is not a matter of analysis but, rather, a verbal characterization, and it will be more a question of measuring its appropriateness and effectiveness than engaging in discussion. In fact, it is an introduction to this world – a guide to places and a lexicon of the names of the various components of these subgenres. This brief account leads on to a rapid characterization of 'hard core', the genre that Paul and his associate are now going to illustrate.

They play several discs, as for a mini-set, and show us the principal forms of DJ intervention, how vinyl discs are chosen, the use of headphones and techniques for handling decks in order to superimpose and connect discs, and how they conceive their temporal mode of working as being similar to 'telling a story'.[12] They call some people to the front to have a go at handling the consoles and at coordinating their movements so as to mix sounds and alter speeds ('mixes' and 'scratches'). They discuss with us the tricky moments that the DJ encounters and whether or not these mistakes – blank spaces, ruptures, feelings of missed transitions, an overall mood that is awkward to assess – are perceived by those in the know, or by us.

The opposing strategies adopted by Pierre and Paul are seen in every detail of their two demonstrations: Pierre's warning not to take him for a rapper is answered by Paul's personal image, his shaven head and posture indicating clearly: 'I am one of them!' The analytical effort of the first is answered by the hip vocabulary of the second, which for the uninitiated resembles a code. The effort to objectify and set apart is countered by teaching by example – 'see it and do it yourself' – and the imitative seduction that witnessing a passionate interest arouses. Pierre even started debates he wanted to avoid – but these verbal skids clearly revealed rap's constitutional character. Paul creates the desire on our part (at least temporarily) to share in and to live the object that his presence and gestures conjure up before us and among us – at the same time as he forces us to delay any effort to analyse what comes out of this.

And, indeed, as soon as Paul and his friend go into action, the nature of the scene changes. They have invested a great deal of themselves in the meeting and have thought meticulously about their discs. They put body and soul into it. The very institutional character of the place acts as a challenge to these underground musicians, who are excited with the idea of dynamiting the interior of such a temple (and, perhaps, the normal procedure of the seminar, too), in 'making the BNF collapse under the kilowatts' (even if, as a concession to our eardrums, they officiate with a tenth of the power of some sound systems). The effect is powerful,

---

12   Morgan Jouvenet, '"Emportés par le mix": les DJ et le travail de l'émotion', *Terrain* 37 (September 2001): 45–60.

and several among us comment on it in various ways: the issue is no longer that of wondering whether or not this music is liked, which would be too much the question of an outsider, but of seeing it actually being made, feeling those moments that are more or less successful, following the variations, recognizing the variables on which the DJ works, the more or less reverberant or dry timbres, the density of texture, the continuity of sound, its ruptures and restitutions, the more or less intense or relaxed moments and so on.

It is an important lesson, one that relates to the communicative effect of practice – the mimetic force of doing compared to saying – but even more so to the multiplicity of possible registers of participation in a musical experiment. Indeed, it is all about the continuity of these positions, rather than a binary opposition between those who would be fans and participants and those who would be non-fans and distant: we did not become fans of techno, losing at a stroke all critical sense, renouncing any analysis in the pleasure taken. No, thanks to the mediation of a new system, we simply went through a series of intermediate positions together. We allowed ourselves a kind of delight by proxy, which engaged us truly, though only for a limited time and in a certain place, in the position of the fan. Even the production of this 'us', with its provisional and fragile status, is an effect of the meeting. As one of us says, 'The principal result of the meeting for me will not be to make me like techno more on a personal level, but to understand that it *can* be liked'. While it is being played, we are sensitive to the work on 'samples', to this emphasis on overexploiting a dimension of sound – work that, after all, very much resembles that which, employing more diverse parameters (from the sounds of natural instruments to the voice, from polyphony to rhythmic devices), can be found in many musical practices that pre-date techno.

A specific point seems to hold in the technical production of this music: there is no distance between the gesture that makes the music and the music that is made. Admittedly, to a certain extent, sight supports sound this way in any performance: watching executants is helpful when paying attention to their artistic technique. It is said, in fact, that spectators themselves play a little, too, by making imitative gestures with their bodies, such as swaying to the rhythm of the music they hear being played. However, the gap between the gesture made on an instrument and the music that is produced remains important. The visual and sonorous references coincide on secondary parameters (rhythm, intensity and so on), but rarely on melody and harmony, which cannot be 'seen' so directly. There is, by contrast, a striking immediacy between the gestures of the DJ and the sonorous effect produced – the speed-shifting of discs, the move from one disc to another, the rise or fall of the volume, all is heard immediately. Techno operates through the manipulation of music already made, and this interval in which the pre-existing material becomes transformed and mixed has, as a curious consequence, an extreme legibility, an easy and instantaneous passage between gesture and sound that helps it to be perceived very clearly.

We wonder if the rule that requires DJs to be invisible on techno nights and, instead of being positioned as instrumentalists, to officiate without being seen, is not a means of compensating for this excessive visibility of their actions; the device of having music diffused by the sound system and coming from who knows where, accords with this idea and is perhaps, in this second form, aimed at giving dancers another interpretation of the music – one suggestive of interior vagueness, of something lacking a place in which to show itself. Within the framework of our meeting, this visual element contributes strongly to the success of the experiment. For music such as this, which merges with the gestures of its own making, to show is to explain; the tactic adopted was perfectly adapted to that end. We even relativize our initial doubts regarding the definition of subgenres of techno by their tempo alone: in practice, it is striking to see how far this aspect – the work on a throbbing 'boom-boom' and on the very mechanics of the rhythmic repetition of an evolving sound – is, in effect, largely determined by tempo.

Sociology 'of' Techno, Sociology 'of' Rap

The concluding discussion relates to social milieu, the sociality of techno fans, the market forms of this music: the disc is its original material (the DJ's vinyl) at the same time as it is one of the end-products; but a good share of techno reality breaks free of the recording in much the same way as it does from orthodox visual media – nevertheless, that said, it is also listened to at home and is sold in the form of commercial recordings. Finally, if a part of the activity is semi-clandestine and displays an underground and anti-commercial character, the other part could not be more overt, installed, as it is, in the world of nightclubs and subject to the strong internal divisions carved out in a predictable manner among enthusiasts for this dance music and followers of rave parties.

From here, of course, the debate could bounce back and the comparison with rap recommence. It seems that the sociology of techno is played out elsewhere, in a form somewhat removed from the classical opposition between a 'pure' origin and the commercial success to which rap aspires – a form that more closely resembles that of avant-garde or 'underground' movements in that the development of a common taste and practice gradually produces the new identity of a group, then around it, if this is successful, a 'generation' arises, produced and expressed in that same gesture. It is on location, while going to the clubs, the dance nights and the rave parties, that, in line with ethnological practice (and in the manner achieved by works on rock by Frith or Hebdige 30 years earlier) one will begin to 'feel' one's way towards a sociology of techno, and the starting-point will be techno's capacity to engender a collective.

In the case of rap there is constant reference to lifestyle, to 'social problems' (misery and injustice, affairs and scandals), to the imaginary universe of the media which rappers are part of (animated drawings, gangster or kung-fu films, TV news) or to the record market and television networks. This is a long way from the usual split between musicians who take a purely musical view of their production and sociologists who come along to reveal what truly determines it (despite the resistance that producers and fans are supposed to marshal against such revelations). Here, instead, it is the producers who ensure that sociology is at the forefront in registering the manufacture and interpretation of their music. This is what makes the sociology of rap problematic: the comments made by specialists give the impression of merely repeating – in a heavier and over-serious fashion – the analyses of rappers themselves. The sociologist, being used to dealing with the aesthetic opinions and blithely anti-sociological comments of fans, is caught on the back foot by an explicitly sociological discourse. His discipline has become a central resource of the actors he observes, and his own analyses compete with theirs: the sociology 'of' rap is both something that rap itself puts to work and what sociologists make of it.

Finally, in this context, and in a symmetrical way, the question of the sociologist's own taste weighs once more upon him: 'Hey you! Aren't you a bit of a fan, too? What drives you to write on the sociology of this music?' It is not that being reflexive implies that you can only study what you like and that yesterday's prohibition should become today's imperative (the sociologist engaging his tastes in his work, instead of making an abstraction of his 'subjectivity' and adopting a pose of benevolent neutrality), but an account of how the analyst relates musically to the music that is being analysed ought to be added to the analysis as another level of reflexivity – one bearing on the tastes and reactions of the sociologist and showing how he is affected by what he hears in the capacity of listener or fan.

Conclusion: Towards Reflexivity, Reflexivity and More

When compared, the two methods of presentation can be seen as putting to the test the tacit assumptions that each presenter holds about the music they are dealing with: the first envisages it as an object captured on tape, ready to be dissected; the second thinks that the only way to put the music across is to produce it live, trusting in the gestures it makes and the sonic events it propels into being. The latter was a choice crowned with success, at least in the local circumstances provided by our comparative exercise. The fact that Paul hardly speaks does not mean that his activity does not 'speak'. It speaks because, even without words (or almost without), he shows how the activity relates to itself in the course of its realization. Through his hardware, his gestures, his attentiveness to our reactions, his effort to make the progressive and hesitant production of a sound world emerge before us and within us, Paul presents his music to us by offering us a grasp of something the non-initiated can seize for themselves. In response to his work, we do not take a distant and objective stance but, rather, our bodies are engaged in the experiment, the body being one of the experiment's variables in two meanings of the term: a changing element, not fixed or given, and one with reactions to be measured. 'Seek out the reflexive, the reflexive and more!'

The method we had imagined – music to be heard, music to be seen – was completely redundant in the case of techno and, in contrast, incoherent when it came to rap. Rap is full of demands, of setting in context, of provocation, and these social registers call for a response or reaction that quite naturally maps itself around the same issues. The last and most important level of reflexivity is revealed here:[13] music is not an inert object, but rather an animated project that already proposes its own interpretations. It calls for certain reactions and often constructs and evolves itself as a genre as a result of those reactions. It is for that reason that a genre's history becomes part of the genre itself; it participates in the collective work to isolate relevant features and to characterize what needs to be done. This it achieves even if it means that some features become solidified, either musically, as over-rigid formulas (following the tendency of music that is easy to identify but difficult to revitalize, such as the tango and rockabilly), or socially, as is the danger with rap, resulting in a 'posture' of revolt or a quickly stereotyped social gesture, even if the desire was to be seen as a genuine protester.

These elements can be linked to musical features, but also to much else besides: to ways of doing things or being together, to practices or ritualized signs, to age groups and various social or ethnic identities. It is not for us to sort them out. A very particular analytical interest concerning these present-day musical styles comes precisely from the co-construction of these features among themselves. Their contemporary character enables us to assist in this process 'live', before music history solidifies them into musical genres. Analysis consists partly of recognizing these criteria, rather than imposing criteria from without.

Thus, ultimately, this double meeting invited us to participate in a lesson on reflexivity. There is no middle-of-the-road position in this matter. The sociologist may feel able to take his leave, discrediting the spontaneous sociologies of the actors he has observed and emphasizing the distance between his own critical and scientific analyses and their partial and interested accounts, but we would argue that he does not actually 'leave' at all. On the contrary, he dives right into the problem: he accepts the need to take issue with the totality of accounts given about a certain type of music, his own included. This is not to say that he abandons all critical direction when situating himself in, and playing with, this mass of lay opinion, but, instead, that he goes along with all the little differences of perception which may be described as the variable series of effects and adjustments that the friction of reflexivities involves. This ranges from his own questions, as a sociologist, about what is occurring before him and in him (as much sensory as cognitive), to the words of actors who, far from lacking categories in which to think about their practice, do not differentiate between musical activity in itself and the activity of drawing a framework around it.[14]

---

13 Anoine Hennion, 'Those Things That Hold Us Together: Taste and Sociology', *Cultural Sociology* 1/1, ed. D. Inglis and R. Wagner-Pacifici (2007): 97–114.

14 It is clear that the concept owes much to ethnomethodology; see Harold Garfinkel, *Studies in Ethnomethodology* (Englewood Cliffs, NJ, 1967). For classical presentations of what is at stake in reflexivity, see James Clifford and George E. Marcus (eds), *Writing Culture: The Poetics and Politics of Ethnography* (Berkeley, CA, 1986); Steve Woolgar, *Knowledge and Reflexivity* (London, 1988); Malcolm Ashmore, *The Reflexive Thesis: Wrighting [sic] Sociology of Scientific Knowledge* (Chicago, 1989); and Ulrich Beck *et al.*, *Reflexive Modernization* (Cambridge, 1994).

PART 6
Reception and Scenes

Absolute Beginners:
The Evolution of a British
Popular Music Scene

Ian Inglis

But the great thing ... is that no one, not a soul, cares what your class is, or what your race is, or what your income, or if you're a boy, or girl, or bent, or versatile, or what you are – so long as you dig the scene. The result of all this is that you meet all kinds of cats, on absolutely equal terms, who can clue you up in all kinds of directions – in social directions, in culture directions, in sexual directions, and in racial directions ... in fact, almost anywhere, really, you want to go to learn.[1]

Introduction

Material and cultural histories of the postwar development of popular music in Britain have largely tended to focus on the star performers, their achievements and the music they created. However, the research considered in this chapter demonstrates that its growth can only be properly comprehended through an equal consideration of the fans, listeners and audiences who effectively established Britain's first popular music scene in the late 1950s and early 1960s.

Within popular musicology, a 'scene' is a site within and across which the production and consumption of popular music are performed, discussed, refined, adapted and assessed. These activities are practised in collaboration, rather than in seclusion. The sites are not static, but always in motion. Above all, they are dynamic; those who engage in them are active agents rather than passive customers.

In this sense, there was little evidence of a popular music scene in the UK through much of the 1950s. Popular music and many of its associated practices were essentially US imports. The charts were dominated by US performers and

---

1   Colin MacInnes, *Absolute Beginners* (London, 1959), p. 64.

records (or their British imitators); TV and radio paid little attention to popular music broadcasting, apart from a few weekend programmes; there were relatively few performance venues, professional circuits or specialist retail outlets. Overall, popular music was routinely perceived as one small sector of the entertainment industry or 'show business', and its audiences dismissed as youngsters whose musical appreciation was irrational and transitory.

However, towards the end of the decade there occurred what might be termed a 'positional shift' or 'switch', in which music-making rather than music-listening became, for many young people, a plausible social activity. Encouraged by the 'do-it-yourself' ethic of skiffle and the example of Lonnie Donegan, many hundreds of professional or semi-professional groups emerged in London, Liverpool, Birmingham, Newcastle, Manchester and other British cities. These groups – and, crucially, their immediate audiences – constituted the beginnings of an authentic popular music scene, whose members were knowledgeable, discerning and committed enthusiasts. They brought to their consumption of popular music levels of awareness that had previously been confined to the consumption of jazz music in the UK. Although still heavily reliant on US styles, the particular inflections through which the music was re-presented were matched by the growth and expansion of significant populations for whom music was a key signifying practice. Musical knowledge, involvement, expertise and – above all – collective participation became important providers of (sub)cultural capital, mapped out new work and leisure opportunities, and thus enabled the growth of Britain's first popular music scene.

Theorizing Scenes

A key task facing the researcher is to determine and justify the terminology used – in this case, the terminology used to describe and define these musical populations. Bennett has suggested that the meaning of 'scene' has been transformed from 'an everyday term used to describe a cluster of musicalized practices situated in a particular urban or rural location ... to encompass local, trans-local and even virtual activities'.[2] However, this recent recasting has been dependent on the commercial and technological expansion of popular music and its modes of production, delivery and reception. Subject to the decisions of a popular music industrial hierarchy based exclusively in London, overlooked by the actions of an indifferent popular music press and lacking the apparatus of rapid transport and communication (conventional, electronic or virtual), the fledgling scenes that began to appear in the late 1950s were effectively restricted to the local and, as a result, were often defiantly independent.

---

2   Andy Bennett, 'Subcultures, Scenes and Tribes' in Andy Bennett, Barry Shank and Jason Toynbee (eds), *The Popular Music Studies Reader* (London, 2006), pp. 95–97, at p. 96.

In what ways is 'scene' the correct label with which to refer to these sites of musical activity? What nuances of meaning does the term possess that make it a preferable option to others with similar, overlapping meanings? Many of these alternative concepts have been characterized by repeated processes of interrogation, reconstruction and, in some cases, redefinition, as revealed in a substantial range of theoretical and substantive literature that considers their generic and musical applications. They include 'community',[3] 'taste group' or 'taste culture',[4] 'network',[5] 'tribe' or 'neo-tribe',[6] 'peer group',[7] 'movement'[8] and 'subculture'.[9]

Successfully imported into the discourse of popular music and popular musicology at specific times, these terms contain, to a greater or lesser extent, implicit suggestions of stability, continuity or consensus in terms of the typical activities and approved memberships through which they are constituted. By contrast, the notion of a 'scene' signals the presence of a broader range of opportunities for musical mutation and permutation, which may be innovative, idiosyncratic, transformative or disruptive, but which, at the same time, may work to produce a 'collective consciousness' or common purpose. Cohen's discussion of the Liverpool rock scene in the mid-1990s – 'a local rock scene dominated by men

---

3   Ronald Frankenberg, *Communities in Britain* (Harmondsworth, 1966); Scott Alarik, *Deep Community: Adventures in the Modern Folk Underground* (Cambridge, MA, 2003); Graham Day, *Community and Everyday Life* (London, 2006).

4   Herbert J. Gans, *Popular Culture and High Culture: An Analysis and Evaluation of Taste* (New York, 1974); Karl F. Schuessler, *Musical Taste and Socio-Economic Background* (Manchester, NH, 1981); Pierre Bourdieu, *Distinction: A Social Critique of the Judgement of Taste* (Cambridge, MA, 1984).

5   Lesley Milroy, *Language and Social Networks* (Oxford, 1980); Patricia A. Stokowski, *Leisure and Society: A Network Structural Perspective* (New York, 1994); John Cotterell, *Social Networks and Social Influences in Adolescence* (London, 1996).

6   Michel Maffesoli, *The Time of the Tribes: The Decline of Individualism in Mass Society*, trans. Don Smith (London, 1996); Kevin Hetherington, *Expressions of Identity: Space, Performance, Politics* (London, 1998); Tom Cox, *The Lost Tribes of Pop* (London, 2006).

7   Hesh Joseph McLean, *Under the Influence: Friends, Peer Groups, Music, TV and Movies* (Colorado Springs CO, 1991); Patricia Adler and Peter Adler, *Peer Power* (Piscataway, NJ, 1998); Jeffrey A. McLellan and Mary Pugh (eds), *The Role of Peer Groups in Adolescent Social Identity* (Hoboken, NJ, 2006).

8   Stephen Stuempfle, *The Steelband Movement: The Forging of a National Art in Trinidad and Tobago* (Philadelphia, PA, 1996); Paul Byrne, *Social Movements in Britain* (London, 1997); S. Craig Watkins, *Hip-Hop Matters: Politics, Popular Culture and the Struggle for the Soul of a Movement* (Boston, MA, 2005).

9   Milton Gordon, 'The Concept of the Subculture and its Application', *Social Forces* 26/1 (1947): 40–42; Stuart Hall and Tony Jefferson (eds), *Resistance Through Rituals: Youth Subcultures in Post-War Britain* (London, 1975); Dick Hebdige, *Subculture: The Meaning of Style* (London, 1979); Ken Gelder and Sarah Thornton (eds), *The Subcultures Reader* (London, 1997); Chris Jenks, *Subculture: The Fragmentation of the Social* (London, 2005); Rupa Huq, *Beyond Subculture: Pop, Youth and Identity in a Postcolonial World* (London, 2006).

and by certain types of masculinity'[10] – presents it as a contested concept, variously defined in ways that give more or less weight to its characteristic activities, its creative essence, its physical and emotional properties and its particular sound. A similar conclusion is presented in Shank's ethnography of the rock 'n' roll scene in Austin, Texas, during the 1980s: 'a situated swirling mass of transformative signs and sweating bodies, continually reconstructing the meaning of a communion of individuals in a primary group'.[11] In an important contribution to the literature, Straw has asserted that:

> ... a musical scene is that cultural space in which a range of musical practices coexist, interacting with each other within a variety of processes of differentiation, and according to widely varying trajectories of change and cross-fertilization. The sense of purpose ... within a musical scene is articulated within those forms of communication through which the building of musical alliances and the drawing of musical boundaries take place.[12]

Such a perspective is well suited to analyses of the process of scene formation and the contribution it made to the remarkable shift in the status and significance of popular music in Britain. Within a few years it energetically metamorphosed from its position as one minor branch of the domestic entertainment business to a place at the centre of much of the world's commercial and creative musical activity. One of the first writers to explicitly draw attention to this change of direction was Harker:

> More research needs to be done on this important 'moment' ... we have to recognise that the commercially dead period around 1960 was one of the most potent and creative times for British adolescent working-class musical culture.[13]

Following Harker's appeal, much more research was done – not only into the history of that specific period but also, more generally, into the impact that time and place can have on all forms of music and music-related practices. Indeed, two decades later, Hesmondhalgh and Negus were able to note that:

> Much work had reported on the particular ways in which music cultures related to nations or particular locations and this emphasis continued into the

---

10   Sara Cohen, 'Men Making a Scene: Rock Music and the Production of Gender' in Sheila Whiteley (ed.), *Sexing the Groove: Popular Music and Gender* (London, 1997), pp. 17–36, at p. 34.
11   Barry Shank, *Dissonant Identities: The Rock 'n' Roll Scene in Austin, Texas* (Hanover, NH, 1994), p. 128.
12   Will Straw, 'Systems of Articulation, Logics of Change: Communities and Scenes in Popular Music', *Cultural Studies* 5/3 (1991): 368–88, at 373.
13   Dave Harker, *One for the Money: Politics and Popular Song* (London, 1980), p. 75.

*1990s ... there was an increasing emphasis on the way in which music helped
to constitute a sense of place as well as how it reflected local identities.*[14]

Approaching History

Historical investigations of any kind inevitably encounter obstacles and problems:
the unreliability of memory, the partiality of authors, the status of facts. Writing
more than 100 years ago, John Baker Hopkins offered the advice that 'in history,
only names and dates are trustworthy, and the former are frequently corrupted
and the latter are frequently wrong'.[15] Even when such mistakes are avoided or
corrected, it remains notoriously difficult to approach any historical account with
confidence: 'Every perception is a construction; the simplest observation is already
a theory. Facts are never neutral; they are impregnated with value judgements.'[16]

Indeed, historians such as E.H. Carr have argued that we should jettison any
faith in the absolute autonomy of history: 'The belief in a hard core of facts existing
objectively and independently of the interpretation of the historian is a preposterous
fallacy.'[17] Carr's judgement is based on three inescapable facts of historiographic
practice: the necessity for selection and interpretation; the need for some sort of
contact or imaginative understanding with those about whom the historian is
writing; and the constraints imposed on the historian by present conditions and
circumstances.

Yet Carr insists that these are not barriers to historical research: interpretation,
imagination and invention are 'the life-blood of history'[18] without which sensitive
investigations of the past – or, more accurately, the remnants and records of the
past – are impossible: attention to facts alone generates little more than the sterile
compilation of lists. Discussions about tensions between the aims and objectives
of the historian-as-archivist and the historian-as-author have been continued by,
for example, Tosh[19] and Jenkins,[20] both of whom recognize that what historical
research produces can only ever be a *version* of history.

These points are as relevant for investigations of popular music's history as they
are for any other branch of history; attempts to describe and assess the events,
conditions and contexts that surrounded the emergence of a popular music scene
in Britain several decades ago need to be tempered with an appreciation of the
constraints involved in such research, and of the manner in which they might

14   David Hesmondhalgh and Keith Negus (eds), *Popular Music Studies* (London, 2002),
     p. 207.
15   Valerie E. Chancellor, *History for Their Masters* (Bath, 1970), p. 10.
16   Peter Gay, *Style in History* (London, 1975), p. 195.
17   E.H. Carr, *What Is History?* (London, 1961), p. 12.
18   Ibid., p. 28.
19   John Tosh, *The Pursuit of History* (London, 1984).
20   Keith Jenkins, *On 'What Is History?'* (London, 1995).

shape its conclusions. One interesting exploration of the divergent strategies, routes and verdicts open to popular musicologists has been provided in a comparative analysis of explanations offered for the removal of Pete Best from The Beatles, and his replacement by Ringo Starr, in 1962. The observation that 'to the question, "what is the true story of Pete Best and the Beatles?", the answer must be that it does not exist'[21] is not a complaint about the inadequacy of such research, but a recognition that the past – even the recent past – rarely survives in a form that allows for complete understanding.

Nonetheless, attempts to understand this particular period can make use of evidence from a variety of sources. They include: formal histories of popular music and popular culture; social histories of postwar Britain; biographies and autobiographies of the key performers, producers and entrepreneurs of that time; novels, such as Colin MacInnes's *Absolute Beginners*, which provided the title (and epigraph) for this chapter; contemporary ethnographies; journalistic commentaries; 'insider' accounts; oral and personal histories. Many of these are discussed below. Taken together, they provide a composite picture of a vital period in British popular music history which, while it has often been noted, has seldom been thoroughly explored with any systematic intent. Relevant investigation may also refer, perhaps surprisingly, to academic research findings from elsewhere that may help to illuminate and organize themes in the area under investigation. I have in mind David Riesman's classic study of the emergence of a minority music scene in the United States in the late 1940s/early 1950s. One of its most important discoveries was that the dynamics of interaction within the scene were not limited to the purely musical, but extended into a whole range of actions and attitudes, including the politics of race, gender and consumerism: 'By learning to talk about music, one also learned to talk about other things.'[22]

The Jazz Scene in Postwar Britain

The nature of the jazz scene in Britain through the late 1940s and 1950s was largely determined by an intermeshing of three factors. The first of these was the reorientation in its approach to jazz music by the BBC (whose radio network was by far the largest single provider of music for public consumption in prewar and immediate postwar years). In 1933, Christopher Stone, the BBC's first disc jockey, felt able to dismiss jazz as a 'primitive din' that lowered the station's standards; yet by 1937, when the BBC re-classified its popular music output into music for dancing, music for entertainment and music for the connoisseur, jazz was

---

21   Ian Inglis, 'Pete Best: History and his Story', *Journal of Popular Music Studies* 11/12 (2000): 103–24, at 121.

22   David Riesman, 'Listening to Popular Music', *American Quarterly* 2/4 (1950): 359–71, at 369.

included in the last category.[23] The aesthetic and commercial repercussions of the transformation of texts from 'popular entertainment' into 'high culture' and vice versa, have been extensively examined in recent years.[24] In terms of the audience for jazz, a major impact was undoubtedly on the audience's perceptions of its own cultural and political identity, structured along the twin axes of 'outsidership' and 'connoisseurship'.

Second, attitudes to jazz were irrevocably shaped by the presence in Britain during the Second World War of many tens of thousands of US servicemen and the styles of music, dance and fashion they brought with them. Furthermore, tours by some of the leading US bands (notably those led by Glenn Miller and Artie Shaw/ Sam Donahue) only served to emphasize the contrast between their 'powerhouse big band' style and the 'effete ... filigreed phrases and virtuoso playing' of their British contemporaries,[25] and did much to undermine any ideas that the kind of domestic music produced in Britain could present a tenable alternative to that created and enjoyed in the distant, and infinitely more glamorous, settings of New Orleans, Kansas City, Chicago and New York.

Third, the 1950s witnessed the generation and circulation of perceptions of a bohemian lifestyle that was derived from romanticized media images of North America. Loosely clustered around attitudes to music, art, drugs, race, sexuality and work, it seemed to offer a dramatic and exciting substitute to the austerity of postwar Britain. It was exemplified in films such as *The Man with the Golden Arm* (dir. Otto. Preminger, 1955) and *Shadows* (dir. John Cassavetes, 1959); in novels like Jack Kerouac's *On the Road* (1957) and William S. Burroughs's *The Naked Lunch* (1959); in television series such as *Peter Gunn* (1958) and *Johnny Staccato* (1959), both set in an urban underworld of gangsters, nightclubs and crime; in the 'beat poetry' of Gregory Corso and Allan Ginsberg; in the photography of Robert Frank and William Klein; and in the paintings of Jackson Pollock and Robert Rauschenberg. It was also a perception supported by research – notably, that undertaken by Becker in the late 1940s and early 1950s – which repeatedly emphasized the gulf between the 'hip' world of jazz and the 'square' world of the conventional citizen:

> This attitude is generalized into a feeling that musicians are different from and better than other kinds of people ... The feeling of being a different kind of person who leads a different kind of life is deep-seated ... [and] behavior which flouts conventional social norms is greatly admired.[26]

The cumulative effect of these three issues – the status of jazz, the geography of jazz and the politics of jazz – was to produce, in postwar Britain, a musical site

23   Simon Frith, *Music for Pleasure* (Cambridge, 1988), pp. 45–63.
24   Harriet Hawkins, *Classics and Trash* (Hemel Hempstead, 1990); Jim Collins (ed.), *High-Pop: Making Culture into Popular Entertainment* (Oxford, 2002).
25   Sid Colin, *And the Bands Played On* (London, 1977), p. 129.
26   Howard Becker, *Outsiders: Studies in the Sociology of Deviance* (New York, 1963), pp. 86–87.

or scene that was distinguished by a high degree of self-segregation, a specialist musical knowledge, a tacit refusal to acknowledge the validity of conventional cultural (including racial) barriers and an acute sense of collective membership.

Much, although not all, of the music produced and consumed within this scene was 'revivalist' jazz – a reaction against the commercially successful swing or big band styles of the 1940s and a return to the traditional jazz forms associated with New Orleans. The postwar period has been described as 'Britain's first real jazz age ... hundreds of clubs, operating in pub back rooms, working men's institutions, drill halls and palais were formed to accommodate the legion of revivalists and their following'.[27] Alongside it, from the early 1950s onwards, were elements of what was termed 'be-bop' – modern jazz, derived from the improvisational styles of musicians like Dizzy Gillespie, Charlie Parker, Miles Davis and Thelonious Monk. In London, venues like Club 11 (1947), the Flamingo Jazz Club (1952), the Marquee Jazz Club (1958) and Ronnie Scott's (1959) presented bands led by Humphrey Lyttleton, Ken Colyer, Johnny Dankworth, Chris Barber among others that defined their approach to musical authenticity through their approximation of US styles. Although British in location, the scene was, therefore, largely American in outlook. This is an important, if not unexpected, point; in his survey of the performing history of jazz, Berendt commented that 'European jazz musicians have been spellbound by the great American players as long as jazz has existed. Thus, of necessity, they created a "second-hand" music.'[28]

In an account of social and cultural activities in London's Soho district (where many of the city's jazz clubs were located) in the 1950s, the following description is offered:

> At 7.30 p.m. at 100 Oxford Street, the doors opened into a large, ugly, smoke-filled basement where dancers twisted and turned to Humphrey Lyttleton's London Jazz Club Band with a frenzied discipline, until they were joined by Humph's ex-Etonian friends who jitterbugged and jived with the total lack of rhythm of the English upper classes ... the atmosphere was that of uninhibited enjoyment, an ecstasy of dripping faces and distorted bodies reaching a climax with the final scream from the trumpet.[29]

A study of the composition of the British jazz fan base in 1958 noted the relatively high proportion of students, office workers, skilled workers and technicians, and the relatively low numbers of unskilled, semi-skilled and factory workers. It concluded: 'Jazz enthusiasts as a group are distinctly above the national average in education, skill and technical qualification, and abnormally well represented in the characteristic occupations of the twentieth century.'[30]

---

27   Jim Godbolt, *A History of Jazz in Britain 1919–1950* (London, 1984), p. 268.
28   Joachim Berendt, *The Jazz Book* (Westport, CT, 1975), p. 403.
29   Daniel Farson, *Soho in the Fifties* (London, 1987), p. 72.
30   Francis Newton, *The Jazz Scene* (New York, 1960), p. 287.

The personal significance attached to participation in this milieu is revealed in an interview with British composer/musician (and founding member of Soft Machine) Robert Wyatt:

> It all started for me in the fifties when I was a jazz fan. I still am. That was my underground. That was the life I discovered outside the prescribed life. The place where culture and politics seemed to meet for me was always centred around black music. Jazz in the fifties ... that's the romantic period for me.[31]

Transitions and Transformations

In his analysis of the social and cultural changes that distinguished Britain in the 1950s and 1960s, Booker made a key observation:

> Of course, no great social transformation takes place overnight, without giving signs and omens of its approach for many years before. Any process of social change takes place round certain focal points; around groups or individuals which, as it were, catch the infection of change before the majority, and from which the new mood and ideas fan out into society at large.[32]

The jazz scene of the 1950s was one such 'centre of change'; in its provision of a focal point for the enjoyment and evaluation of music, and in its constituency of groups and individuals for whom these activities were central rather than peripheral concerns, it indicated routes along which unprecedented ideas about the significance of popular music would expand in the early 1960s.

This assessment is shared by many commentators. Melly has argued that 'it was in the jazz clubs of the late 1940s that what might be considered the dry-run for a pop explosion first took place';[33] Marwick has affirmed that 'the advent of rock-based pop had been preceded by a jazz revival';[34] and Longhurst has traced the persistent connections between art, jazz and rock: 'from the late 1940s and early 1950s, when they connected to, and bred a mode of appreciation of, black American jazz, [British] art schools went on to attract and produce a significant number of the most important and influential rock musicians of subsequent decades.'[35] While there may be general agreement on the centrality of the postwar jazz scene to the

31   Jonathon Green, *Days in the Life: Voices from the English Underground* (London, 1988), p. 9.
32   Christopher Booker, *The Neophiliacs: The Revolution in English Life in the Fifties and Sixties* (London, rev. edn 1992), p. 33.
33   George Melly, *Revolt into Style* (London, 1970), p. 21–22.
34   Arthur Marwick, *Culture in Britain since 1945* (Oxford, 1991), p. 99.
35   Brian Longhurst, *Popular Music and Society* (Cambridge, 1995), p. 61.

development of a pop/rock scene, it is, perhaps, necessary to clarify the precise nature of the transition.

The general condition of cultural and intellectual life in Britain during the early and mid-1950s has been widely depicted as one of inertia and conservatism: one contemporary commentator noted 'the apathy, the complacency, the idealistic bankruptcy'[36] and Shils later referred to its 'extraordinary state of self-satisfaction'.[37] It is, therefore, all the more surprising that the later years of the decade provided the impetus for a series of events and developments that would, in combination, redirect the nation along an entirely new trajectory:

> Out of this comparative placidity, Britain suddenly entered on a period of upheaval ... above all, a new spirit was unleashed – a new wind of essentially youthful hostility to every kind of established convention and traditional authority, a wind of moral freedom and rebellion.[38]

The events themselves included the rapid growth of television, the increasing availability of contraception, the emergence of the affluent society, the market invention of the 'teenager', the abolition of conscription, the expansion of higher education, the influx of West Indian immigrants to the UK and (via the establishment of CND) the growth of the anti-nuclear movement. The developments to which they led included a restructuring of family and domestic life, increased sexual freedom, a growth in discretionary spending, the identification of a novel and unique identity, an awareness of alternative choices in work and leisure, an increase in the student population, an introduction to unfamiliar and 'exotic' cultures and a willingness to engage in social and political confrontation.

The bohemian world of the jazz club provided an obvious and early location where the intersections of these separate strands could be assembled, tested and explored. They quickly coalesced into a style which, while specifically British, was informed by its receptivity to US and black conventions,[39] that set it apart from, and issued a challenge to, the mainstream pop entertainments offered to UK audiences by Cliff Richard, Adam Faith, Craig Douglas, Tommy Steele, Billy Fury and others. When jazz performers, critics, journalists and audiences within this expanding scene began to explore the overlapping genres of blues and gospel, and the oppositional values embedded within them, notions of 'resistance' or 'rebellion' quickly emerged as explicit components:

> This group, with its 'margin for rebellion', looks to new musical sources, notably in black American rhythm and blues, many aspects of which are predisposed to connotations clustered around feelings of 'oppression' on the

---

36   Tom Maschler (ed.), *Declaration* (London, 1957), p. 3.
37   Edward Shils, *The Intellectuals and the Powers* (Chicago, 1972), p. 139.
38   Booker, *The Neophiliacs*, pp. 32–33.
39   Hebdige, *Subculture*, pp. 46–51; Iain Chambers, *Urban Rhythms: Pop Music and Popular Culture* (London, 1985), pp. 50–83.

one hand, and relatively non-alienated use of the body (potentially subversive of capitalist work disciplines) on the other.[40]

The (apparently) contradictory relationship between young, white, British audiences and traditional Afro-American musical formations provided important possibilities for audience members to develop and demonstrate an ideological alliance that brought with it a certain kind of distinction. And in his history of the postwar British folk music scene, Brocken has further emphasized the explicitly political role attached to a range of parallel musical practices:

> *Many British jazz, folk and blues traditionalists were deeply rooted in the politics of the far Left, and romanticized images of the 'vulnerable yet noble' working classes of the USA (black and white alike) were inspirational, not only musically but also socially and politically.*[41]

Such associations are not uncommon. The concept of 'radical chic' employed by Wolfe[42] to explain the links between white liberal intellectuals and black militants in the 1960s and Frith's account of the 'homologous' attractions to some Western listeners in the 1980s of music and musicians from the Third World [43] describe very similar congruences.

It has, of course, been frequently noted that these (largely) middle-class groups have been far less prominent (at least, in numerical terms) in postwar Britain than their (largely) working-class equivalents. But it is easy to overstate this. The assertion that 'only a handful of the more intellectual youth was involved in the English counterpart to the Beat movement'[44] is a typical oversimplification of the complex and rapidly shifting cultural environment of the 1950s. As several observers[45] have testified, while the conservative and rigid structures of postwar Britain did not vanish overnight, dynamic patterns of social and cultural realignment began to be recognized and adopted by substantial numbers of young men and, to a lesser extent, women. Coming in the wake of the 1944 Education Act (which increased social mobility rates for some working-class children) and the establishment of the welfare state in 1948, and organized around notions of 'freedom' rather than 'responsibility', they found a particularly appropriate site at many of Britain's universities – including newly chartered institutions, such as Nottingham (1948), Southampton (1952), Hull (1954), Exeter (1955), Leicester (1957), Keele (1962)

---

40   Richard Middleton, *Studying Popular Music* (Milton Keynes, 1990), p. 15.
41   Mike Brocken, *The British Folk Revival 1944–2002* (Aldershot, 2003), p. 70.
42   Tom Wolfe, *Radical Chic and Mau-Mauing the Flak Catchers* (London, 1971).
43   Simon Frith (ed.), *World Music, Politics and Social Change* (Manchester, 1989), pp. 71–72.
44   John Clarke, Stuart Hall, Tony Jefferson and Brian Roberts, 'Subcultures, Cultures and Class' in Hall and Jefferson, *Resistance Through Rituals*, pp. 9–74, at p. 61.
45   Liz Heron (ed.), *Truth, Dare or Promise: Girls Growing up in the Fifties* (London, 1993); Miriam Akhtar and Steve Humphries, *The Fifties and Sixties: A Lifestyle Revolution* (London, 2002); Pete Frame, *The Restless Generation* (London, 2007); Peter Hennessey, *Having It So Good: Britain in the Fifties* (London, 2007).

– where, for many, education became an expressive, rather than an instrumental, choice, and in which opportunities for exposure to new or unfamiliar musical forms and the formation of student-centred scenes were common.

The willingness to expand and extend their original interest in jazz was not limited to students. Alerted, via skiffle, to the songs of Woody Guthrie, Big Bill Broonzy and Huddie 'Leadbelly' Ledbetter, and encouraged by the first visits to Europe of performers like Josh White (1950), Lonnie Johnson (1952), Otis Spann, Muddy Waters, Joe Turner, Sonny Terry and Brownie McGhee (1958), Champion Jack Dupree (1959), Willie Dixon, Memphis Slim (1960), Little Walter, John Lee Hooker (1962), Victoria Spivey, Big Joe Williams, Sonny Boy Williamson, Bo Diddley (1963), groups of young or potential performers began to adopt blues, rather than jazz, as their principal musical expression. They included Alexis Korner's Blues Incorporated, Cyril Davies's All Stars, and John Mayall's Powerhouse Four/Blues Syndicate/Bluesbreakers. The complex associations between many of these competing/complementary musical scenes are well illustrated by Chambers:

> *The blues, urban r & b, and contemporary soul music initially found their early audiences on the fringes of the folk and, more importantly, jazz club world. These musical interests were often intersected by an art school bohemia, an area that was particularly important for preserving the musical exotica of the blues in Britain after the collapse of trad jazz.*[46]

In his account of the history of popular music in Britain from the mid-1950s to the mid-1960s, Bradley has used the term 'codal fusion' to refer to the way in which separate musical styles, or codes, constantly merge, emerge and re-merge.[47] While he contends that this pattern has characterized virtually all musical development since the 1930s, its significance in the period under study is that the fusion occurred across traditional social barriers to create the kind of democratized scene described at the start of this chapter. Concurrent with this transition was a change in terminology. Stemming from the popular music industry's desire to establish a marketing category that would conveniently cover all styles of music created by black performers and popular with black audiences, the label of 'rhythm 'n' blues' had been successfully introduced in the US in the late 1940s;[48] a decade later, it began to be used in the same way in Britain to describe the increased popularity of those styles and their musical influence:

> *A picture emerges of … the more purist, romantic version of that influence remaining largely, though certainly not exclusively, a middle-class phenomenon. But a process of advancing and consolidating codal fusion was clearly proceeding very widely among young music-makers and music-*

---

46   Chambers, *Urban Rhythms*, p. 69.
47   Dick Bradley, *Understanding Rock 'n' Roll: Popular Music in Britain 1955–1964* (Buckingham, 1992).
48   Charlie Gillett, *The Sound of the City* (London, 1971), pp. 135–36.

*listeners, and proceeding across the class boundaries. Certainly, one cannot
pair off class backgrounds with musical preferences in any simple way.*[49]

Galvanized by that fusion, the growth of activity around the production and
consumption of rhythm 'n' blues irrevocably established the foundations for a
type of musical culture that had not existed in Britain before. However, just as the
jazz scene was invariably divided into traditional and modern camps, there also
existed comparable divisions in the emerging rhythm 'n' blues sector; as identified
by Melly, there were initially three parallel schools – prewar country blues, postwar
urban blues, and 'soul' blues.[50]

One immediate repercussion of these musical trajectories was observed in
the changing policies of music venues – principally in London, but also in other
metropolitan areas. Under pressure from performers and audiences, clubs
previously restricted to jazz, such as Soho's Marquee and Flamingo, Liverpool's
Cavern (1957) and Twickenham's Eel Pie Island (1958) began to include one or all
of these blues-derived musics in their regular schedules. Indeed, it is revealing
to note that the Cavern, now known as the home of The Beatles, opened as a jazz
club in 1957 and had presented jazz musicians like Humphrey Lyttleton, Ronnie
Scott, Tubby Hayes, Ken Colyer and Acker Bilk, alongside blues performers such
as Big Bill Broonzy, Rosetta Tharpe, Sonny Terry and Brownie McGhee, Champion
Jack Dupree and Speckled Red, long before The Beatles made their debut there in
February 1961.[51] In addition, there were newly created clubs devoted exclusively to
rhythm 'n' blues, including Richmond's Crawdaddy (1962), the Club-A-Go-Go in
Newcastle (1962) and London's Ad Lib, Pickwick and Scene clubs (1963). The full
significance of the opportunities that these venues provided to rapidly expanding
audiences was noted in Wolfe's account of the 'noonday underground' at Tiles in
Oxford Street:

> *Tiles has the usual 'beat club' sessions on at night, with name groups up on
> the bandstand, and it packs them in, like a lot of other places, the Marquee,
> the Flamingo, the Ramjam, the Locarno Ballroom and so forth. But it is
> the lunchtime scene at Tiles, the noonday underground, that is the perfect
> microcosm of The Life of working-class teenagers in England. It all goes on
> within a very set style of life, based largely on clothes, music, hair-dos and a
> super-cool outlook on the world ... that makes them unique.*[52]

Of course, while these venues provided settings for music, they did not constitute
musical scenes in themselves. One of the important contributors to scene formation
has always been the specialist media who, in supplying a formal site for news and
comment, enable the informal exchange of observations and opinions which, in

49   Bradley, *Understanding Rock 'n' Roll*, pp. 78–79.
50   Melly, *Revolt into Style*, pp. 88–90.
51   Phil Thompson, *The Best of Cellars* (Liverpool, 1994).
52   Tom Wolfe, *The Pump House Gang* (New York, 1968), p. 80.

turn, informs the construction of a 'fan culture' or scene. In Britain, the first popular music weekly to provide such a forum was *Melody Maker*. Since its first publication in 1926, it had concentrated on serving an informed jazz community; however, conscious of the growing number of club-based performers and audiences, it began to promote an analytical and critical approach to diverse musical styles that would characterize its editorial policy throughout the decade:

> *As growing audiences of middle-class kids and a heavy input of art ideology began to invest sixties rock with ambitions surpassed so far only by jazz, the phenomenon demanded more serious attention ... this registers a decisive turning point in the development of British rock criticism.*[53]

However, its change of emphasis was gradual. When *Melody Maker* gave The Beatles their first cover story (headlined 'Is Liverpool Britain's Nashville? The Beat Boys') on 23 March 1963, its other front-page news items were about Sarah Vaughan, Dizzy Gillespie, Stan Kenton and a forthcoming weekend of jazz in Paris.[54]

The manner in which the popular music media's output was incorporated into the structures and cultures of the developing scene is indicated in Fiske's general account of elements in the cultural economy of fandom:

> *It selects ... narratives or genres and takes them into the culture of a self-selected fraction of the people. They are then reworked into an intensely pleasurable, intensely signifying popular culture that is both similar to, yet significantly different from, the culture of more 'normal' popular audiences.*[55]

As he explains, this 'reworking' requires the capacity to engage in discrimination and distinction, regular involvement in productivity and participation (semiotic, enunciative and textual), and the practice of (cultural and material) capital accumulation.[56] In all of these activities, the ability to employ information, ideas and images from a relevant media, and to communicate them to others, were critically important factors in the expression of musical performance and consumption.

---

53 Gestur Gudmundsson, Ulf Lindberg, Morten Michelson and Hans Weisethaunet, 'Brit Crit: Turning Points in British Rock Criticism 1960–1990' in Steve Jones (ed.), *Pop Music and the Press* (Philadelphia, PA, 2002), pp. 41–64, at p. 41.

54 Nick Johnstone, *Melody Maker History of Twentieth Century Popular Music* (London, 1999), p. 119.

55 John Fiske, 'The Cultural Economy Of Fandom' in Lisa A. Lewis (ed.), *The Adoring Audience: Fan Culture and Popular Media* (London, 1992), pp. 30–49, at p. 30.

56 Ibid., pp. 34–45.

Conclusion

It is against this shifting background of transition and transformation in the late 1950s and the early 1960s that the birth of Britain's first authentic popular music scene needs to be situated. What has often been depicted as a sudden, unprecedented and irresistible overthrow of domestic and international musical tastes – initially by groups from Liverpool (The Beatles, Gerry and the Pacemakers, the Searchers, the Swinging Blue Jeans) followed by performers from London (the Rolling Stones, the Yardbirds, Georgie Fame and the Blue Flames, Manfred Mann), Manchester (the Hollies, Wayne Fontana and the Mindbenders), Birmingham (the Spencer Davis Group, the Moody Blues) and Newcastle (the Animals) – was, in fact, the public outcome of several years' collaborative exploration of jazz, blues, folk, skiffle and rhythm'n'blues traditions within a range of localized, but related, scenes across Britain. While rock 'n' roll and pop had been given very visible roles in popular music's architecture, these heterogeneous forms constituted an 'underground' alternative, whose distance from dominant musical practices reflected, and contributed to, its sense of exclusiveness. John Lennon's recollection that 'we felt very exclusive and underground in Liverpool listening to all those old time records … nobody was listening to any of them except Eric Burdon in Newcastle and Mick Jagger in London'[57] is an apt illustration of the perceived status of this fragmented community.

Indeed, one simple, but revealing, indication of the allegiances expressed by many of these performers lay in their chosen nomenclature. The Rolling Stones took their name from Muddy Waters' 1948 song 'Rollin' Stone'; the Pretty Things from Bo Diddley's 1956 song 'Pretty Thing'. The Yardbirds' name was a homage to Charlie 'Yardbird' Parker; Pink Floyd were named after two blues musicians from Carolina, Floyd Council and Pink Anderson.

Permeating from the bohemian world of the jazz club and the intellectual world of the art school/university, the scene grew to accommodate increasing numbers of (mainly) young people from outside those settings, whose levels of knowledge and enthusiasm elevated it far above a mere choice of entertainment. When, in 1963 and 1964, the apparently novel sounds of British 'beat' (as it was quickly labelled) supplanted much of the perennial pop styles of previous years, it was not a new musical option, but a part of a new identity that had been taking shape in a radically different cultural location 'which lay hidden beneath the straight world against which it was ostensibly defined … beyond the limited experiential scope of the bosses and teachers'.[58]

Examples of this musical opposition were evident on the early records of the Rolling Stones. The group's first single, released in June 1963, coupled Chuck Berry's 'Come On' and Willie Dixon's 'I Want To Be Loved'; and their first album, *The Rolling Stones* (April 1964) included cover versions of songs by Jimmy Reed ('Honest I Do'), Slim Harpo ('I'm a King Bee'), Chuck Berry ('Carol'), Willie Dixon ('I Just Want To

---

57 Jann Wenner, *Lennon Remembers* (London, 1971), p. 14.
58 Hebdige, *Subculture*, p. 53.

Make Love To You'), Bo Diddley ('I Need You Baby') and Rufus Thomas ('Walking the Dog'). And although The Beatles quickly eschewed the practice of featuring cover versions (apart from some Brill Building and Motown compositions) on their singles and albums, their early performing career routinely included songs by Joe Turner ('Honey Hush'), Arthur 'Big Boy' Crudup ('That's Alright Mama'), Leadbelly ('Rock Island Line'), Ray Charles ('I Got a Woman', 'Hallelujah I Love Her So', 'What'd I Say'), Bo Diddley ('Road Runner'), Fats Waller ('Your Feet's Too Big'), Little Willie John ('Leave My Kitten Alone') and Chuck Berry ('Johnny B. Goode', 'Roll over Beethoven', 'Little Queenie', 'Rock and Roll Music', 'Sweet Little Sixteen', 'Too Much Monkey Business'). The readiness with which these and other songs were accepted by eager British audiences demonstrated a prior knowledge that, as the aspiring entrepreneur Joe Boyd has recalled in his account of the British scene in the early 1960s, was quite unique:

> I decided I would live in England and produce music for this audience. America seemed a desert in comparison. These weren't the privileged elite, they were just kids ... and they knew who John Lee Hooker was! No white person in America in 1964 – with the exception of me and my friends, of course – knew who John Lee Hooker was.[59]

While the mainstream market for popular music had been manipulated and monitored by an entrenched industrial hierarchy, content to retain and exploit prevailing patterns, the developing scene, overlooked and unpublicized, had worked to acquaint its growing membership with the songs, history and styles of quite different musical traditions. The resulting impact produced a critical point of cultural transformation: 'Now the rhetoric of a previously restricted enclave, and its social, moral and political disaffiliation, begins to enter popular culture.'[60]

It has often been suggested, by American writers, that the remarkable impact of the 'British invasion' in the mid-1960s was due to its re-assembly of older forms: 'The British accomplished this in part by resurrecting music we had ignored, forgotten or discarded, recycling it in a shinier, more feckless and yet more raucous form ... much of this music had been written and performed by American blacks.'[61] However, what has been less often recognized is that the fusion of traditional US genres and contemporary British interpretations took place in a specific and distinctive popular music scene that developed in the late 1950s and early 1960s. Although largely derived from US jazz and blues styles, the scene's persistent disregard for rigid musical divisions and the importance granted to innovative repositionings of conventional boundaries were crucially maintained by an enthusiastic and informed cohort of performers and listeners. Not only did

---

59   Joe Boyd, *White Bicycles: Making Music in the 1960s* (London, 2006), p. 68.
60   Chambers, *Urban Rhythms*, p. 67.
61   Lester Bangs, 'The British Invasion' in Anthony DeCurtis and James Henke (eds), *The Rolling Stone Illustrated History of Rock 'n' Roll* (London, 1992), pp. 199–208, at p. 199.

this cohort fashion the immediate context within which 'beat' music was created and consumed, but it undoubtedly contributed to the emergence of a 'serious' or 'rock' culture that would characterize the dominant discourses of popular music throughout the rest of the decade and into the 1970s.

Studying Reception and Scenes

Adam Krims

Studying musical reception and scenes tends to take scholars outside the field of musicology proper. Of course, there is no reason why this need be so, except that musicology was shaped, and is still largely so, by a model which separates works out from their circulation and inflection in the social world. More than enough ink has been spilled on that point, and yet scholars who study music reception and scenes still by and large tend to do so in disciplines such as sociology, cultural studies, communications, gender (or area) studies and ethnomusicology (although this last rarely deals with Western musics). Thus, an investigation into the post-production social life of popular music (which, of course, will also precede more production in important mechanisms of feedback – discussed later) necessarily treads an uneven road of disciplines, approaches, theories and priorities, all nevertheless united by a series of recurring concerns. This chapter will first trace those concerns, visiting significant monuments and byways along the path; it will then turn to the related literature on 'scenes', investigating their sometimes vague definitions and meanings. Finally, the chapter will advance an argument that the developing literature on scenes points to an important dynamic too often missing from discussions of music reception.

I have elsewhere referred to Theodor Adorno's celebrated writings on mass culture and the culture industry (a term he himself coined) as a foundational trauma for popular-music scholars.[1] Although Adorno did not confine his scenario of regression in listening to popular music (or jazz, as he called it –later attributing similar properties to rock), he certainly saw jazz as epitomizing a dark moment in the history of capitalism, in which the history of music played only a part (a point that almost all examinations of Adorno-as-musicologist miss). That moment was, of course, the industrial-monopoly stage of capitalism, one which remained relatively stable for some four decades or so after his first publications on jazz. Of course, what offends the vast majority of popular-music scholars, about Adorno's nightmare of mass production and centralized control is the monolithic

---

1   Adam Krims, 'Marxist Music Analysis without Adorno: Popular Music and Urban Geography' in Allan F. Moore, *Analyzing Popular Music* (Cambridge, 2003), pp. 131–57.

meanings that he attributed to jazz: if the music's meaning is sealed at the point of production, then its manipulative effects seem inevitable. Here, 'meanings' are really something more abstract than the everyday understanding of the word: the music works through idiotic repetition, working its effects through constrained form, dulling the mind and, famously, forming and reinforcing its regression. Yes, naturally – this being Adorno after all – music's meaning here *is* its formal properties, and to speak of inflecting meaning, in the days before digital manipulability could hardly have made much sense. While those in communications and media studies have most begrudged Adorno his unwavering insistence on the fixity of meaning, which renders reception irrelevant by its predetermination, it could also be argued that Adorno's real error was in not accounting for mediation itself: the music itself carried its meanings, its poisonous effects not being manipulable but, rather, self-actualizing. If Adorno's strategy had been, instead, to allow capital to shape meanings through its flow throughout the entire social body, then he could have allowed for mediation while still constraining the possible social effects of music within the flows of capital. But this had never been Adorno's approach to music, and if Beethoven's music worked its effects directly on listeners, then there is really no reason that jazz should behave any differently. Reception for Adorno is passive, just as the music itself entrains passivity; scenes, if he had conceived of them, could have been little more than collective hypnosis.

Not surprisingly, perhaps, the studies of popular music's meanings that followed in the decades after Adorno fell not far from the notion of collective hypnosis – or, if not hypnosis strictly speaking, then some kind of social malady. But even in the early days of studying popular-music reception, notions of active audiences, and even the beginnings of a notion of a 'scene' (though very much *avant la lettre*) can be traced. Thus, an early study by David Riesman (originally published in 1950) drew a distinction between a majority group whose listening did not stray far from Adorno's passivity and a minority group whose listening was more critical.[2] That minority group developed their own technically informed standards for differentiating artists and invested much of their approval in more obscure, less commercially successful artists (and, with the latter, at least thus arguably became the model for every self-conscious teenage consumer of popular music in the industrialized world). While Riesman did clearly recognize the existence of critical listening, and while his active minority provides a distant glimpse of the notion of a 'scene' (at least, an audience scene), his majority remains very much a passive audience that is a little less mesmerized than that of Adorno himself.

The Birmingham School is most often seen as the turning-point at which the meanings of popular music came to be treated agonistically, the battle now involving audiences. Now, and with the cultural studies movement that followed, audiences become increasingly active, defining and redefining music and appropriating its social values and force. At its best, the work that came from this new approach charted the circulation and transformation of meanings in exciting ways that painted society's complexity in vivid colour. The transformation of Madonna by

2   David Riesman, 'Listening to Popular Music', *American Quarterly* 2/4 (1950): 359–71.

adoptive gay audiences, the gradual 'outing' of k.d. lang by lesbian audiences and the policing of hip-hop 'realness' by young white males – all of these critically important currents of culture (and, to some extent, politics) could not have been modelled and analysed without some conception of an at least dialogic relationship between audiences and the music that they consume.[3] A simple and utterly uncritical conception of supply and demand, borrowed straight from Adam Smith, could have suggested something similar, of course, except that Smith's model was one of accommodation and balance, whereas the cultural-studies approach was one of duelling priorities, of dominant and subaltern identities. Now reception became a way in which the oppressed could speak back, in which the presumably compliant products of corporate music (under Adorno's conception) could be remoulded as liberation; of course, a certain populist spirit bolstered such studies, and it is perhaps not surprising that North America, in particular the United States, became the place where such analyses have traditionally thrived. One will still find many examples of this model of meaning in popular-music studies, including among some quite well-respected scholars of popular music.

With the notion of 'scenes', though, the idea of active audiences became more geographically determinate – although, as will be argued presently, an even more precise determination might be helpful. Communications scholar Will Straw published the article which popularized the notion of 'scenes' in academic popular-music studies, although, of course, the term had already long existed in popular parlance.[4] Having had that existence in the informal speech of fans, 'the scene' came with a pre-formed meaning which may, in retrospect, have been something of a liability. Perhaps because it was easy to believe that one already knew what a scene is, Straw never quite defines it. Of course, a strict definition might arguably be inconsistent with the 'common sense' that scenes are informal, flexible and constantly in flux – which, of course, as human formations, they are. But then again, without a formal definition of a scene – its geographic parameters, in particular – the reader is left with a somewhat elusive or nebulous object to analyse. What constitutes a 'scene'? Are there ever situations in which one has musical artists, musical audiences, musical venues, but not a 'scene'? Is there a minimum number of (say) genres, or artists, that one must find in order to declare something a 'scene'? Are there limits to a 'scene', such that some musical activities (defined in whichever way) may lie outside of it? Are there multiple 'scenes' in any given place, or is everything defined as within it (in which case, a 'scene' is little more than a geographic locality in which some musical activity takes place)? In the case of the former, how does one draw boundaries between the different scenes, such that one can analyse them properly? Straw's theorization, as helpful as it was in opening up the question of a musical 'scene', does not offer any determinate answers to these rather basic questions. Nobody (as far as I know) doubts that scenes, whatever they may be, shape both the production and reception of popular

---

3   Keith Negus, *Popular Music in Theory: An Introduction* (Cambridge, 1996), pp. 130–33.
4   Will Straw, 'Systems of Articulation, Logics of Change: Communities and Scenes in Popular Music', *Cultural Studies* 5.3 (1991): 368–88.

musics, and just about anybody can name her/his favourite historical scene (be it the Merseybeat scene at the beginning of the 1960s or the Seattle grunge scene that may have ranged from the mid-1980s to the mid-1990s, depending on what ones calls a 'scene' – there, again, is our problem). But, leaving aside production for the moment, precisely how do scenes work to shape reception? The concept of a 'scene' would become far more useful, if scholars could trace that process. In fairness, it should be said that in later essays, Straw recognizes the 'fluidity' of the concept of a scene and tackles the problem in critically informed and helpful ways.[5]

Straw actually offers readers something of a clue to this in an essay that he published some two decades after his initial foray.[6] By that time, much of his work concerned specifically urban culture, and he offers the helpful observation that scenes are primarily associated with cities: he quotes Christopher Hume of the *Toronto Sun*, asserting that '[p]ut simply, the city provides the crucial mix of people and power, attention and anonymity, money and markets, necessary to generate a genuine cultural scene. It is content and context, cause and effect, creator and destroyer.'[7] That is indeed simply put and perhaps a bit overstated, but it does underline the urban context that is normally assumed, which in turn could be used as a key to expanding Straw's observations and outlining more specifically how scenes work to help shape reception.

The aforementioned cultural-studies approach to popular music's meanings entailed different (and sometimes conflicting) inflections of both artists and audiences. But a focus on the urban context of scenes permits scholars to bring in another figure often involved in shaping meanings, namely the *cultural intermediary*. Cultural intermediaries were first defined by sociologist Pierre Bourdieu as people who shape the reception of goods and services – normally people working in marketing, advertising, fashion, journalism, public relations and design.[8] While Bourdieu himself makes no such suggestion, the concept may be usefully extended to embrace electronic and print media, whose shaping of reception would seem sufficiently pervasive and definitive for inclusion as cultural intermediaries. Sociologist Mike Featherstone has extended Bourdieu's idea to suggest the rise of 'new cultural intermediaries' in post-Thatcher Britain, who, among other things, '[seek] to legitimate the intellectualization of new areas of expertise such as popular music, fashion, design, holidays, sport, popular culture, etc., which increasingly are subject to serious analysis'.[9] While Featherstone sees such legitimization as

---

5   Will Straw, 'Scenes and Sensibilities', *Public* 22–23 (2002): 245–57.

6   Ibid.

7   Ibid., p. 250.

8   Pierre Bourdieu, *Distinction: A Social Critique of the Judgement of Taste* (London, 1984). The last item suggests, of course, that cultural intermediaries may sometimes be involved in the production of goods and services too, effacing the difference between them and producers in a way that might ultimately be helpful.

9   Mike Featherstone, *Consumer Culture and Postmodernism* (London, 1990), p. 91. David Hesmondhalgh, *The Cultural Industries* (London, 2002), p. 54, asserts that Featherstone misunderstands Bourdieu in equating the new cultural intermediaries with the new petite bourgeoisie. Hesmondhalgh seems to be correct, although Featherstone's error

part of a tactic for the educated bourgeoisie to establish themselves, the notion of 'new cultural intermediaries' also suggests a mutation in the amount and kinds of input that popular-music consumers receive; part of urban socialization, now, may include not only newspaper or website reviews of new albums, but also aesthetically weighted discussions of popular music in design-intensive bars. Such a setting for popular-music consumption suggests something often hidden in academic discussions – namely, precisely the urban setting that Will Straw in his later work calls 'scenes', but here the scenes are specifically urban and involve the kinds of design intensity that are specific to recent urban production.[10]

Because they leave their imprint on both how music is produced and how it is judged, it is important to bear in mind who these cultural intermediaries are. In particular there are two characteristics to consider, since they will return in the ensuing discussion. First, by and large, these professions are populated by relatively well-educated people, holding at least a Bachelor's degree and sometimes more, who are cosmopolitan in outlook and versed in the liberal values normally propagated in higher-educational contexts. Of course, working (and, as Derek Wynne and Justin O'Connor argue, often living) in cities, such people are regularly confronted with a range of people of differing backgrounds, ethnicities and genders in professional and social situations, thus reinforcing the cosmopolitanism and tolerance developed in educational contexts.[11]

Second, those cultural intermediaries who work in or around the popular-music industry are also, as Keith Negus and others have pointed out, by and large avid *consumers* of popular music, so that an elaborate feedback loop develops between their leisure and their production.[12] Their own consumption, along with their production, of music is *reflexive* not only in the sense that they reflect on their choices and preferences, but also in the sense that they regard the music as reflecting something important about them. Highly self-conscious and often prioritizing remaining 'in the loop' about music, these particular intermediaries develop complex mixtures of commercial and aesthetic senses that are difficult to disentangle (and often fetishized as equivalent). Most important for our current purposes, these musical actors move principally within a contained, predominantly urban, educated social community and are consistently engaged with the design-intensive urban environment in which they live, shop, socialize, consume and produce.

Reinstating this urban context restores an element to many kinds of reception that, surprisingly, often seems to be missing from (although often implicit in) many of the analyses already published, and the remainder of this discussion will review and contextualize those analyses in such urban, cosmopolitan contexts. In

---

does not invalidate his quite helpful observations about the former.

10   I discuss those developments and their significance for recent music in Adam Krims, *Music and Urban Geography* (New York, 2007).

11   Derek Wynne and Justin O'Connor, 'Consumption and the Postmodern City', *Urban Studies* 35/5–6 (1998): 841–64.

12   Keith Negus, *Popular Music in Theory*, p. 31.

many cases, analyses of popular-music consumption rely on the binary notion of resistant versus dominant (or 'hegemonic') representations, a legacy (if sometimes oversimplified) of cultural studies. In such analyses, hegemonic representations are almost invariably negative ones that misrepresent a category of people in a way that is socially damaging; thus, for example, the hegemonic representation of women as passive or cruel (for instance, in Bob Dylan's 'Like A Rolling Stone' or in the Rolling Stones' 'Under My Thumb', two frequently invoked examples) might be countered by more 'resistant' interpretations of women as powerful and sympathetic. The idea is that the relationship between these different kinds of portrayal is agonistic: the hegemonic representations reinforce relationships of domination and exploitation, while the resistant ones promote (at least potentially) liberating discourses that in some ways either neutralize or at least complicate the symbolic forms of domination that help to sustain domination. Of course, mapping resistant musical practices will normally involve at least some kind of implicit favouring of such forms – would any rational person of goodwill consciously side with domination? – and different scholars do so with varying degrees of explicitness. And equally important, scholars may locate 'resistance' at just about any point along music's journey from production through consumption (although, interestingly, almost never at the point of distribution). Thus there may be songs portrayed as being inherently resistant or songs that only become resistant as they are (re)interpreted by audiences.

To illustrate, it will be useful to turn to one of the more sophisticated and successful such analyses, that of Frances Aparicio in her *Listening to Salsa: Gender, Latin Popular Music, and Puerto Rican Cultures*.[13] A Latino-studies scholar, Aparicio analyses discourses of both gender and ethnicity, and she does so at the level of both the music as produced (although she confines her approach to that of analysing lyrics, rather than engaging musical style and form), as well at the level of audience articulation. The latter she infers from discussions with 26 informants, finding acts of resistance in both listening (including practices such as changing misogynistic lyrics) and dancing. Salsa thus becomes 'a public as well as a personal space in which to argue our male–female relations in Latino/a societies'.[14] Indeed, Aparicio offers compelling and convincing evidence, from salsa lyrics, essays written on salsa by various Latino/a men and women, and her informants, that salsa does indeed play a significant role in forming, and re-forming, gender roles, sometimes in desirable and sometimes in less desirable ways. Aparicio is refreshingly open about her commitment to denouncing the racism and misogyny that pervade some salsa music and its reception; she is also quite open in affirming the value of salsa dancing, dubbing it, at one point, a 'cultural reaffirmation that wholly constitutes cultural resistance'.[15] That a practice like dancing might amount to 'cultural resistance' highlights the degree to which personal action and public

---

13   Frances R. Aparicio, *Listening to Salsa: Gender, Latin Popular Music, and Puerto Rican Cultures* (Hanover, NH, 1998).
14   Ibid., p. 156.
15   Ibid., p. 91.

discourses mix and become entangled in this kind of modelling of popular music and consumption. Dancing here becomes simultaneously personal and political, a way of embracing and supporting a (positive) model of Latino/a existence; it is not only consumption of popular music (although most certainly it is this), but also a politically effective act that asserts Latino/a identity.

Thus Aparicio, in her study, discusses both songs (that is, primary 'texts' – almost literally, since she discusses lyrics alone, a common drawback to many scholars' work, particularly those in the literary disciplines) and practices of reception, seeing possibilities for compliance and resistance in both. The possibilities are weighted, however: there are compliant songs but not compliant dancing practices (of course, to assess things in such blunt terms projects them as crude processes, but these are the terms set by her discussion, only stated more bluntly here). What is notable, however, is how the resistance predominantly seems to lie in reception, rather than in production (or, if the reader prefers, in 'the music itself'), and this tendency is by no means confined to Aparicio's work. One would be hard-pressed to find studies of popular music that examine consumption practices in significant detail and assess them as strictly compliant; on the contrary, those popular-music studies that examine popular-music consumption, almost unfailingly tend to model the latter as resistant, whatever the music and whatever the consumption practice might be. It may be suspected – and examining the studies would tend to confirm – that such a consistent assessment of consumption as resistant reflects a methodological bias: could it really be the case that people are constantly rebelling against domination when listening (or in Aparicio's case, dancing) to popular music? If resistance is that widespread, how is it that the hegemonic representations remain so robust? As far as I know, nobody has formalized the scale of popular-music consumption beyond the potentially misleading terms of phonogram sales, but anybody who has lived in the developed world surely has noticed that an enormous number of people consume popular music. If consumption were as resistant to domination on the scale that Aparicio (among many others) projects, would not the social effects of such a widespread tendency have been noticed outside the relatively contained academic field of cultural studies? Would it not indeed be a movement of massive proportions?

The rhetorical questions above are not intended to discredit entirely the idea that popular-music consumption might resist symbolic domination under certain conditions and in certain contexts; rather, they represent a call for those theorizing popular music and its meanings to situate the processes analysed in contexts that are broader than a sheer textual analysis of either the music or consumption practices like dancing, listening or mouthing lyrics (the last of these another of Aparicio's resistant practices). A return to the notion of 'scenes' and their urban context should help clarify the stakes and offer a refreshed and broader view of popular-music consumption and its relation to those scenes.

In particular, the cultural intermediaries mentioned earlier can offer a way of broadening the ideas of compliant and resistant meaning already circulating in cultural-studies analyses of popular music's meaning.[16] As previously discussed, cultural intermediaries tend to live and work in cities, and their socialization and consumption of popular music tends to occur in quite specific urban contexts. Of course, with enough digging, we could find any number of rural or (more likely) suburban cultural intermediaries, but by and large, the people who shape reception via advertising, marketing and the like are aggregated in cities.[17] The reasons for this have been much studied by geographers and economists, but, briefly and informally put, the skills and knowledge that people in these industries need professionally are often learned and shared in surprisingly informal contexts.[18] This can be understood by thinking about it quite straightforwardly: as the term 'cultural intermediaries' implies, the jobs of these workers are culturally saturated, replete with the kinds of knowledge that are transmitted in social relationships. Marketers (to take one example) must know what is 'cool' and stylish, what kinds of designs and 'lifestyles' prospective consumers tend to embrace, and also what kinds of music appeal to specific kinds of listeners. Those kinds of culturally saturated forms of knowledge can certainly be, and definitely are, conveyed in the formal context of the workplace – in meetings, papers, e-mails and prospectuses – but are also developed in nightclubs, bars, restaurants, stores, house parties and other public, informal and social contexts. While pushing the principle to its extreme may appear to be a rationalization, it is nevertheless true that a marketer learns part of her/his job while in social contexts, consuming the visual style of a fashionable restaurant with friends or, indeed, listening to music at a dance club with a partner. Since these professions tend to be urban-based, and since the trend since the 1980s has been for such urban workers to live in the city centre, the sites for relevant consumption also happen to be urban; we are thus talking about urban restaurants, converted loft spaces, design-intensive bars – in short, design-intensive city-centre environments.[19] It is thus difficult, if not impossible, to separate out the work environment of these intermediaries from the play environment, as both are saturated with social values and information that inform both production and leisure.

Although one cannot, of course, assume a full transmission of all values, styles and ideas in any one environment, the design- and information-intensive urban context, together with the continuity of work and leisure, suggest an important point that is directly relevant to popular-music reception. Popular music, as a common locus of leisure and socialization, may well, as cultural-studies analyses

---

16   I offer a somewhat differently formulated alternative to a cultural-studies approach in *Music and Urban Geography*, pp. 27–60.

17   Mohammed Arzaghi, 'Quality Sorting and Networking: Evidence from the Advertising Agency Industry', *Ideas*, at: <http://ideas.repec.org/p/cen/wpaper/05-16.html> (accessed 5 June 2008).

18   Allen J. Scott, *The Cultural Economy of Cities* (London, 2000), pp. 16–29.

19   E.L. Glaeser and J. D. Gottlieb, 'Urban Resurgence and the Consumer City', *Urban Studies* 43/8 (2006): 1275–99. I discuss design-intensive city environments and their significance for music in *Music and Urban Geography*, pp. xxii–xxxviii and pp. 127–62.

suggest, impart and inform social values, but it tends to do so in very specific social contexts in which values are shared and developed in particular ways. In the case of urban cultural intermediaries, the music's meanings will be developed in the context of relatively highly educated workers in the most cosmopolitan context that exists anywhere in the world, namely that of cities. And while it is certainly true that many, if not most, cities of the developed world retain a significant amount of ethnic and 'racial' segregation, the circumstances of living and working in a major city of the developed world nevertheless brings an individual into contact with people from an unparalleled variety of backgrounds.[20] This means that one can now state more precisely that popular music is experienced and shared, through work and leisure, among relatively well-educated and culturally sophisticated listeners, in a relatively cosmopolitan environment. Having (again, by and large) a background in higher education, the cultural intermediaries will have had the liberal values of tolerance and equality inculcated in university courses such as literature, sociology – and cultural studies, of course. And although there are certainly plenty of highly educated bigots and sexists, the values of tolerance and diversity tend to be embraced ideologically in the hippest and most 'creative' urban environments.[21]

All of this suggests that, for urban cultural intermediaries, the kinds of issues that haunt Aparicio's study of salsa may not carry the same weighty import. In the social environment being considered here, the equality of sexes and ethnicities is shared as a social value and policed through morality and ideology (which is, of course, not necessarily to say that it is taken to heart).[22] It also suggests that the issues of dominant and 'resistant' discourses may play out quite differently in the particular urban environment being considered here. Of course, neither Aparicio nor most other cultural-studies scholars specify urban cultural intermediaries as their chosen audiences – but this, of course, is precisely the issue. Audiences have their own geographies, and, without a consideration of those geographies and their social aspects, reading domination and resistance from musical texts, or even from delineated audiences (as in the case of Aparicio), may not always suffice.

---

20   Ronald van Kempen, 'Ethnic Segregation in Cities: New Forms and Explanations in a Dynamic World', *Urban Studies* 35/10 (1998): 1631–56.

21   The notion of the 'creative city' embraces a number of sometimes disparate theories, promoted by consultants and academics like Charles Landry and Richard Florida. For our present purposes, it suffices to say that the kinds of work/socialization 'synergies' mentioned here fall under the rubric of the broad, and sometimes frustratingly vague, notion of the 'creative city'.

22   One possible counterargument to the line of thought here is that music communicates values more intimately than other media or forms of discourse, and thus it speaks precisely 'to the heart', so to speak. While there is probably some legitimacy to this, it also most likely relies on an uncritical embrace of long-held ideologies concerning music's intimacy and ineffability. David Gramit discusses the latter in 'The Roaring Lion: Critical Musicology, the Aesthetic Experience, and the Music Department', *Canadian University Music Review* 19/1 (1998): 19–33.

All this brings us back to the notion of scenes, this time with a much more specific and developed idea of what that term might mean. The 'scene' in question here is not only an urban one (as Straw already specified in his later essay), it is also a design-intensive scene, cosmopolitan, often fast-paced, and self-consciously 'hip' world in which the packaging and interpretation of goods and services (including popular music, of course) are sustained and developed. For this reason, this particular 'scene' retains a special importance in the reception of popular music: cultural intermediaries play a key role in defining, judging and interpreting cultural goods. This, of course, is one reason for Bourdieu's and Featherstone's interest in these people. In particular, it may make sense to focus on the music journalist, the arbiter of taste who helps shape the media response to newly released recordings and artists' performances. While it has been widely observed (and is obvious enough, in any case) how crucially music journalists affect the reception of popular music, the world of popular-music scholarship has been surprisingly mute about precisely the urban context being considered here, in which most of them live and work. This neglect continues even though most of the best-known popular-music journalists are strongly associated with a particular urban publication, and – notwithstanding the force and greater geographic dispersal of the Internet – the opinion of publications like *Rolling Stone* (Manhattan, previously San Francisco), *The Source* (also Manhattan) and *New Musical Express* (London) tend to set the tone for larger public discussions of various popular musics. While this short essay cannot do much to correct that oversight, it can at least suggest ways in which scholars can correct it, while still engaging with the main currents of scholarship on music reception and scenes.

Maintaining a focus on the urban centrality of popular-music reception can be squared with studying scenes – that much is already evident – but it can also be squared with cultural-studies approaches, if one prefers the latter. While what was said above concerning the generally socially liberal culture of urban cultural intermediaries may be seen as weakening the force of Aparacio's study, it certainly does not entirely invalidate it. Any cultural milieu, no matter how liberal its standards and ideologies, would need to reinforce its better tendencies, especially given the more widespread racism and sexism that remains in the advanced Anglophone world. No part of the United States, Canada the United Kingdom or any other area of the world that English-language popular music touches is exempt from the dominant ideologies so steadfastly denounced in cultural studies, no matter what ideological engagements or standards; of course, the hypocrisies and double standards of self-described anti-racists and feminists are well enough known (although they often turn out as little more than sticks with which to beat any attempt to combat racism and sexism). More important, the workings of ideology, according to many, if not most, cultural-studies analyses are such that the explicit ideological engagements of musical listeners may well be somewhat beside the point; the representations of expressive culture (including music) present themselves less as explicit assertions, of course, than as 'the world itself' – that is precisely what is so pernicious and ideologically loaded (not to mention powerful) about representation. It can, in a sense, short-circuit our reasoning about the things that we see, suggesting that we are seeing the world *'wie es eigentlich gewesen'* (to borrow the famous formulation of historian E.H. Carr).[23] In that sense, one could argue that situating reception geographically, as I have suggested here, may not be so crucial, and that ideologically loaded representation – be it dominant or resistant – may always enjoy a performative force, regardless of the social situation or ideological stance of the audience. However, to rely heavily on this stance would be equivalent to seeing a clean split between ideology and representation, which would certainly undermine the value of the latter.

Musical representations, then, travel through all kinds of social locations, assigning value to them by their very nature; to be sure, Aparicio does not do this, but it is a fairly common practice in, especially, some of the more literary- or even musicologically-focused approaches to musical reception.[24] While representations that are mass-produced may have mass effects that transcend social geographies, at a minimum, some of the more helpful treatments of musical reception consider, or at least reveal, the social locations in which their exegeses are based. Aparicio herself does this, and whatever the limitations of her mainly urban and/or university-student sample, her readers at least are aware of their social location. This is perhaps why it is suggestive that the most influential subcategory of reception research, the study of scenes, seems to have melded with a study of urbanism per se, as it has in Straw's work. It is, after all, cities that have the capacity to support scenes: they offer the agglomeration of capital, sites of performance and purchase – in short, the sheer scale in which something that could be called a 'scene' may develop. But, equally importantly, as Scott's and others' work has underlined, cities offer the kinds of proximity and informal interactions in which scenes develop; after all, a 'scene', to be a scene, must involved something shared, whether it be a musical style, fashion or political attitudes.[25] Many scenes, of course, are about musical styles (as well as other things), such as the aforementioned grunge scene of Seattle, and the local spread of such styles is often accomplished through the drifting of musicians between bands, the developing enthusiasm of audiences for new approaches, or even some musicians cravenly copying what appears to be a successful formula. On the parts of audiences, too, the developing momentum of a scene often depends on a set of venues that they may visit regularly, word

---

23 E.H. Carr, *What is History?* [1961] (London, 1990). Carr, it should be noted, was not endorsing the notion of history as *'wie es eigentlich gewesen'* ('how it actually was'), but rather, was criticizing the notion, which he was attributing (some say wrongly) to the nineteenth-century Leopold van Ranke, who himself was reacting to moralistic historiography.

24 To take only one of many possible examples, one can look at Ellie Hisama, 'Postcolonialism on the Make: The Music of John Mellencamp, David Bowie, and John Zorn', *Popular Music* 12/2 (1993): 91–104.

25 It should be noted that Straw's definition of a 'scene' is broader in Straw, 'Scenes and Sensibilities'; he also includes such things as national 'scenes' disseminated by electronic media and geographically scattered. However, tellingly, after allowing for such a possibility, he then spends the rest of the article focusing exclusively on urban local scenes and their urbanity.

of mouth about new bands and styles, or simply seeing the cool clothes, styles and attitudes projected by the hippest music fans around. Non-musical venues can play crucial roles in developing urban scenes as well, with certain bars, restaurants, bookstores, clothing stores – not to mention universities – often providing crucial loci of socialization for shared musical values and preferences. Scenes, after all, do not end or freeze in time when music clubs close; they continue through the activities and social interactions of artists, intermediaries and audiences, together and separately, as they develop their attitudes, styles and preferences in all kinds of urban contexts. Of course, such non-musical venues exist outside of cities, but rarely on the scale, and with the proximity, capable of producing and sustaining a scene. And what is more, cities tend to attract the kinds of people who engage in scenes, generally younger, single or at least childless workers, who are self-conscious about creating and maintaining identities. While one should probably be sceptical about all of the commercial (and academic) discourse surrounding the 'creative city', it remains (and has long been) true that cities attract people eager to create identities and lifestyles through socialization and leisure, including through music.[26] Thus, cities provide not only the venues, but also the kinds of people who seek and support scenes – people who value innovation and style and tend to develop relatively well-engaged allegiances to scenes. This is another reason to maintain an urban context for the notion of a scene.

But the even broader reason for maintaining the character of cities in mind returns us for the last time to those pivotal figures, the urban cultural intermediaries. For while a great number of claims have been made for the democratizing of information through the Internet, the central dissemination of opinions and attitudes through the major print and electronic media remains a fact of cultural life, notwithstanding that ideas are formed and inflected through the Internet. Urban cultural intermediaries, in other words, retain their central position in the dissemination of musical taste and judgement. And it is the world of these intermediaries – the city centres, the most highly stylized and design-intensive parts of the larger cities – that is changing the most quickly and thus most calls for attention from scholars.[27] The quickly changing and style-conscious world of neighbourhoods like Southwark (London), Williamsburg (New York City) and SoMa (San Francisco) are often the crucibles in which new ways of receiving popular music are forged, although such cutting-edge tastes inevitably change on translation and distribution through the media that the intermediaries create and disseminate.

And, of course, that dissemination guarantees the relevance of these urban areas even to those most interested in the rural, or suburban, consumption of popular music. While movements certainly originate, and take unique forms, in rural and suburban areas, they cannot remain untouched by the mass-media forms that are centred and controlled in the large cities, and, what is more, those kinds of popular-music reception that do develop in the suburbs and rural areas only reach mass distribution through their appearance on the urban stage. So while it

---

26   Wynne and O'Connor, 'Consumption and the Postmodern City', pp. 857–61.
27   Krims, *Music and Urban Geography*, pp. 127–62.

would not do to dismiss rural and suburban reception entirely, by focusing on the urban character of scenes and mass-disseminated reception, scholars can capture essential cultural aspects of reception whose impact transcends the locality of origin and becomes generalized, long after its urban birth has been forgotten. And, of course, re-remembering the urban birth of popular-music reception may be one key way to understand its character, the social (not necessarily cultural) forces that then, in popular memory, become thinned out simply to become 'scenes' or become naturalized as placeless reception *tout court*.

So Straw's shift in focus, between his earlier and later essays on scenes, towards the character of 'the urban' was based on an important insight, and, if not inevitable, it is at least productive and helpful that more and more studies of popular reception move likewise towards a focus on urban culture and production. The word 'production' is used here in a purposefully broad sense, encompassing not just the production of expressive culture, but also what is usually treated as more 'purely' economic production; for while cities are indeed, as just mentioned, places to which younger people flock in order to establish identities, they are also, more basically, the hothouses of economic production in any capitalist society, as well as in mixed societies, like China. Although most of that production may appear, at first glance, only distantly relevant to popular-music reception and the other cultural practices that flourish in cities, the two worlds are far closer together than scholars may often assume. As economic activity in the advanced capitalist world becomes increasingly focused on the production of symbols and information, especially in the larger cities, the dividing line between economic production and cultural production becomes ever harder to draw with any clarity.[28] Cities are constantly in a process of restructuring for the production of capital, and their shifting for the production of information and symbols in the so-called 'post-industrial' economy has been nothing short of dramatic; thus, the transformation of urban environments in the past few decades or so has had everything to do with production that is simultaneously economic and cultural.[29]

While the products of urban work are becoming more cultural and information-saturated, the workplaces of urban workers are also becoming even more culturally saturated characterized by 'flexible' job roles and specialized, project-oriented organization.[30] In this way, urban economic production has become 'culturalized' and urban culture has become 'economized'; just as the lives of the

---

28 Scott Lash and John Urry, *Economies of Signs and Space* (London, 1994), pp. 17–30, 193–222.

29 Sharon Zukin, 'Urban Lifestyles: Diversity and Standardisation in Spaces of Consumption', *Urban Studies* 35/5–6 (1998): 825–938.

30 Edward A. Lenz, 'Flexible Employment: Positive Work Strategies for the 21st Century', *Journal of Labor Research* 17/4 (1996): 555–66, provides a somewhat disturbingly uncritical view of these new workplace practices; John Garrick and Robin Usher, 'Flexible Learning, Contemporary Work, and Enterprising Selves', *Electronic Journal of Sociology* 5/1 (2000), at: <http://scholarlyexchange.sociology.org/content/vol005.001/garrick-usher.html> (accessed 2 June 2008), provide a more critically informed view of the same developments.

urban cultural intermediaries blur the division between work and leisure, so does even the production of those outside that social group undermine the division between work and culture. With culture and economic production blending so intensively at the cutting edge of urban life, it should not be surprising to find that cities' accommodation of production bears tremendous cultural force. Of course, this has always been true; Walter Benjamin's Arcades Project had addressed how Paris's nineteenth-century built environment (namely, the arcades themselves) simultaneously sold goods to urban consumers and created new forms of leisure and sociality.[31] Thinking of urban change as simultaneously economic and cultural – rather than of the economic dimension as somehow 'causing' the cultural dimension or vice versa – may help scholars to stop worrying about reductionism and look at change holistically. But on a less lofty level, it is enough simply not to worry about what is cultural and what is economic in urban developments; it is far more crucial to understand that popular-music reception and scenes are the spaces in which these things are shaped, and the new social forms in which they unfold. Such an understanding will afford the popular-music scholar a way of contextualizing how people interpret and judge the music; not all popular-music reception occurs in cities, and not all scenes occur in cities (although most of them do, at least initially). But in the sense outlined above, all of them are, at least in a mediated fashion, urban.

---

31   Walter Benjamin, *The Arcades Project* (Cambridge, MA, 1999).

Interpretation: So What?[1]

Allan F. Moore

The Beach Boys' original recording of 'Good Vibrations' employs a striking double transformation. The song opens with a stepwise harmonic descent from E minor and repeats this move, before shifting to the relative major for the chorus. Carl Wilson's voice gives way to Mike Love's, who sings of being *in receipt* of 'good vibrations', over a harmonic pattern which moves upward, from G to A to B in readiness for the second verse.[2] The vector is clear: a gradual upward motion of harmonic roots coincides with activity in the relationship by his partner, towards him. This link is merely associative, but, once made, it becomes an operative force (at least within this single track). In the centre of the song the texture slims remarkably, down to organ and shakers, a change which coincides with the singer's dawning realization of his culpability – he's 'Gotta keep those … vibrations / A happenin' with her' - that is, he has to become active in the relationship himself. Thereafter, the 'good vibrations' hook is sung over the same pattern, but now transposed in the reverse direction, from B to A, to G. Now that 'he' has become active in the relationship a new, smoother, coda melody enters, is repeated transposed from G to A to B, and finally back to A, thereby finishing mid-way between the outer reaches of this pattern. The original G–A–B sequential motion is thus first reversed and then combined with its reversal to provide a conclusion. This transformation thus enables a reading of the future history of the protagonist, himself identified through his lyric, as one in which he will enjoy a probably successful relationship, resulting from the 'emotional work' he has implicitly agreed to undertake. What is the status of this reading?

---

1   Research for this paper was partially supported by an AHRC grant: it is the first output from a project, 'The Meanings of Spatialization in Popular Music Recordings', run at the University of Surrey.
2   Some listeners hear the track as based in G, others as G♭. The actual pitch is between the two, and the difference is not material to my argument – I refer to G simply for ease of presentation.

This chapter began as a presentation at an SMA day,[3] whose *raison d'être* was encompassed by the assertion that, in recent analytic work, 'one common goal has been to seek out a productive synthesis between contextual interpretive and formal analytical approaches' and that 'popular music provides a particularly relevant context in which to do this'.[4] I have been publishing analytically informed work on popular song for some 15 years now and have constantly worried about how well it passes what I call the 'so what?' test – that is, how well it moves from analysis to useful, and usable, interpretation. At first, I was content that the analysis of large areas of the repertoire, if necessarily somewhat superficial because of its scope, brought important understandings in terms of common practices, or 'style', helping to reinstate that concept as one worthy of consideration – indeed, I maintain that without an understanding of the style which *organizes* a particular performance, we cannot properly understand the details of that performance. More recently, I discovered that other key questions, particularly for me those of 'authenticity' and of 'intertextuality', could be addressed by analytic means. However, I have been unable to convince myself that such analysis of individual tracks always, as a matter of course, passes the 'so what?' test. It is this doubt which lies at the root of this chapter – a doubt I shall attempt to assuage.

The work which first convinced me there was a fruitful path to tread here was Philip Tagg's work on what he calls 'sign typology', whereby he identifies four types of sign recognized across a range of musics: style gestures, the topic which was, in effect, what I had largely been working on; episodic markers; genre synecdoches; and various types of anaphone.[5] One reason why Tagg's work provides a particularly strong starting-point is the experimental basis of his findings. Three years ago I published an article which attempted to ask how the relationship between a persona and that persona's environment was modelled in popular song, following in particular some related work by Tagg and a separate line of inquiry by Eric Clarke.[6] It is in that article that my view of 'Good Vibrations' appears.[7] This was a specific attempt on my part to provide a 'what' to the 'so what?' test. What I did not attempt in that article was to understand the bases on which Tagg and Clarke erected their respective dualities. To undertake this means, in practice, a return to some principles of semiotics; Tagg's sign typology is semiotically-

---

3   Allan F. Moore, keynote address at the Society for Music Analysis Autumn Study Day, 'Analysing Popular Music in Context', University of Liverpool, 16 November 2007. I am also grateful to colleagues at both Surrey and the Open Universities for insightful comments on subsequent versions.

4   Giles Hooper, e-mail communication.

5   Philip Tagg, 'Introductory Notes to the Semiotics of Music', Version 3 (July 1999), at: http://www.tagg.org/xpdfs/semiotug.pdf (accessed 18 June 2008). See <http://tagg.org/ articles/ptgloss.html> for a brief guide to Tagg's terminology and neologisms.

6   Eric F. Clarke, 'Subject-Position and the Specification of Invariants in Music by Frank Zappa and P.J. Harvey', *Music Analysis*, 18/3 (1999), pp. 347–74.

7   Allan F. Moore, 'The Persona/Environment Relation in Recorded Song', *Music Theory Online* 11/4 (2005), at: <http:www.music-theory.org/mto/issues/mto.05.11.4/ mto.05.11.4.moore_frames.html>.

derived, after all. However, because I have always found the rather hermetic world of Saussurian semiotics unsatisfactory for the discussion of music, I have followed the rehabilitation of Peirce's semiotic scheme with some interest, particularly as formulated by Thomas Turino in his 1999 article 'Signs of Imagination, Identity and Experience'.[8] My initial interest in this article came from his promise of a different approach to the understanding of authenticity, another topic which concerns me. Here, however, I ignore that line of argument, noting instead that Turino's article explicitly readdressed Peirce's semiotics in an (additional) attempt to escape the pull of the symbolic in musicological discourse. Peirce's thought is, of course, multifaceted, and he cannot really be described as presenting a *stable* theory. However, key to Peirce's middle-period approach at least are the concepts of 'firstness', 'secondness' and 'thirdness', which arise from different combinations of sign, reference and interpretant. In Turino's formulation, firstness refers to things in and of themselves, secondness is the realm of actual experience, and thirdness that of abstraction. What interests Turino are those musical experiences wherein the process of moving through these three realms is thwarted prior to reaching the last. Another way of seeing this is to say that Turino is interested in the operation of icons (signs which operate through resemblance) and indices (signs which operate through experiential proximity) rather than symbols (signs operating through the use of language). To return to my beginning, what is the status of my reading of the change of direction of the 'Good Vibrations' sequence as meaningful? It should surely be possible to understand it as semiotic in some way, if we accept that semiotics encompasses all processes of signification.

According to Peirce's scheme, it would at first appear to be symbolic. There is no resemblance obtaining between this musical transposition and a referent. The 'meaningfulness' of the changed direction of the sequence, B–A–G is only actualized because we were initially presented with an 'original' direction, G–A–B. What we have here is a typical case of meaning attendant purely on structuralist semiotic difference. The downward sequence carries meaning because it moves in the opposite direction to the sequence we have already encountered. Moreover, we can only know how to read this oppositional pair because of the coexistence of the sung lyric: the realm of signification of the directed sequence is only fixed by the lyric, and the opposition between the two directions only makes sense once that realm is identified. Following this, it is the second lyric (that of the bridge), where the protagonist's reversal of his position is made explicit, which permits, and confirms the grounds for, the musical reading I am making. So, having realized this, we see that it does, after all, operate indexically, in two ways, although in neither does it index something outside the track itself. First, the reversed order points back to the original order of the sequence, and transforms it. Second, the sequence coexists with the lyric. But, if it is indexical, how can it also be symbolic?

---

8   Thomas Turino, 'Signs of Imagination, Identity and Experience', *Ethnomusicology* 43/2 (1999): 221–55. A fuller exploration of Peirce's scheme for music can be found in Naomi Cumming: *The Sonic Self* (Bloomington, IN, 2000), pp. 73–104, but the differences do not seem material to my argument.

It is crucial here to recall that, for Peirce, the interpretant is an indispensable term. To unpack the archaeology of my own understanding of this track, I was aware of discussions such as that of Daniel Harrison where, in formal, structural terms, this change of direction is literally inexplicable.[9] Gradually, over the years, I became aware of the change of position occupied by the persona (after all, the lyrics of popular songs are not there to be attended to unless one goes out of one's way to make the effort!), and became fascinated by this feature, since so few songs in the repertoire trace such a change. I was also aware that the change of direction seemed 'right', without being able to put my finger on why that should be so (and one should never forget the power of simple repetitive familiarity in such cases). It was only once I started asking myself questions about the relationship between persona and environment that I suddenly saw how to make sense of what was happening here.[10] To reiterate, the change of direction appears pertinent, and there is at least one line of lyric that anchors it in the environment to which we can respond, just as we could respond to an interlocutor.

In his essay Turino argues that 'humans need distinct realms of practice which foreground the different semiotic levels of iconicity, indexicality, and symbolism to achieve subjective integration of the "whole" person', a need which explains the persistence of pre-symbolic systems such as music in the face of the presence of language.[11] But rather than accept Turino's total bracketing off of the symbolic, can (should?) we not discover such integration in the union of music and language – that is, in song? In order to address this question, I turn to another track which has fascinated me for years, the Kinks' 'See My Friend'. As an adolescent in the late 1960s I was unable to afford records, and so contented myself both with the illusion that playing pop songs from memory at the piano was 'as good as' owning the record (it wasn't, quite) and, eventually, with others' cast-offs in the shape of secondhand 45s, of which this was one of my first, scratches and all. Indeed, I'm convinced I re-create some of that ethereality whenever I listen to a remastered version such as that available on *The Ultimate Collection*, although I'm also aware that its sound-world somehow lacks focus for many listeners. At this point I am simply going to describe some of the features of this track which are at the forefront of my listening experience (refer to Table 22.1).

---

9   Daniel Harrison, 'After Sundown: The Beach Boys' Experimental Music' in John Covach and Graeme Boone (eds), *Understanding Rock: Essays in Musical Analysis* (New York, 1997), pp. 33–58, at pp. 42–44.

10   Luke Windsor recounts a similar anecdote, in a paper which traverses a similar direction to my own, but within a very different stylistic locus, that of electro-acoustic music. See W. Luke Windsor, 'An Ecological Approach to Semiotics'; *Journal for the Theory of Social Behaviour* 34/2 (2004): 179–98.

11   Turino, 'Signs of Imagination, Identity and Experience', p. 244.

Table 22.1   'See My Friend': identification of Peircean classes of sign [12]

Class of sign	Appearance in 'See My Friend'	Explanation/justification
Iconic rheme (qualisign)	OBS1; OBS2	The very quality of the timbre and of the groove, which acts as a Taggian episodic marker
Rhematic iconic sinsign	OBS3	The emptiness of the texture at this specific point represents the emptiness caused by 'her' lack of presence, simply to be observed
Rhematic indexical sinsign	OBS4	The lyric points to a possible riverbank
Dicent indexical sinsign	OBS5; OBS6	'She' is actually absent, in the narrative of the song; Davies' 'sneer' results from his observation of that absence
Rhematic iconic legisign	OBS7	The urgency is signified by this (conventional) episodic marker
Rhematic indexical legisign	OBS8	'Loss' as a quality of phenomena
Dicent indexical legisign	OBS9	The decision to accept such a representation
Rhematic symbolic legisign	OBS10	Accepted representation of 'her', as LSD, in interpretations of this track
Dicent symbolic legisign	OBS11	Lightness represented by that particular, contextualized, D♯
Argument	OBS12	The decision to make these immediate interpretations public

Note, first, the nasal quality of the opening timbres, both instrumental and vocal, which recall a contemporaneous infatuation with the sitar (an observation I shall identify as OBS1).[13] Note also the way the groove slides off the first beat (OBS2) – indeed, there is initial doubt as to where the beat is. The very substance of this quality identifies the beginning of the track – it would be out of place appearing later on. Recall if you will the lyrics' focus on the 'she' who is 'gone', 'gone' which is acted out by the change of texture (OBS3), as its centre literally

---

12   See note 4.
13   The sitar reference is explored by Jonathan Bellman, 'Indian Resonances in the British Invasion, 1965–68' in Jonathan Bellman (ed.), *The Exotic in Western Music* (Boston, MA, 1998), pp. 292–306.

vanishes. Prior to her leaving, she was 'playing 'cross the river'. I cannot avoid conjuring up here (OBS4) any number of riverbanks across which I have looked, and could easily imaginatively locate her. But it is a specific absence which is sung about, 'hers' (OBS5), and in Ray Davies' voice which has a distinct smiling quality to it, but perhaps with a sneer (OBS6). His is a voice which is notably absent over the track's last 30 seconds or so, where the intensity is achieved by rising pitch and dynamic, signifying urgency (OBS7). And yet, perhaps the textural absence refers only to itself, to 'absence', or 'loss', as a quality (OBS8). This makes sense if a listener refers (OBS9) it to the song's conventional connotation, as a drug-induced vision, where 'her' absence is adequately recompensed by the presence of LSD (OBS10).[14] If you have the track to hand, listen again to the wonderful lightness as we reach the point of 'absence'. Not only does the texture thin as we lose the cymbal haze which has surrounded the track hitherto, but the bass rises to an f♯ and then drops to a dominant b, but so weakly within the texture that the low d♯ in the guitar dominates, moving up to a tonic beneath a IV–I [in E] cadence, matched by Davies' wonderful smiling mouth shape. It's that guitar d♯ which really draws attention to the textural lightness (OBS11). Finally, I am drawn to put into words (OBS12), to justify the 'rightness' of this track, how it all conspires together to create a consistent sound-world within which activity takes place – not in order to conjure up an interpretation, but to put into words one which is already nascent in my experience of the track.

Now this may seem a rather heterogeneous collection of interpretive comments to make but, of course, I have an ulterior motive. Peirce's theory foregrounds ten possible classes of sign, a logically constrained collection of his three trichotomies: signs; relations; interpretants; moving from 'firstness' through 'secondness' to 'thirdness'. Turino's discussion argues that most musical signs fall into three categories: rhematic iconic legisigns; rhematic indexical legisigns and dicent indexical legisigns – in other words, conceptual signs of potential resemblance and proximity, or actualized proximity. However, by combining some musical details of this track with the lyric, and the way this actualizes Ray Davies' persona within the song, it seems to me possible to discover all ten of Peirce's classes, as I have just done. The details of this analytical categorization appear in Table 22.1. Is it possible that this is why listening to such a track is such a rich experience? Recall Turino's comment '… humans need distinct realms of practice which foreground the different semiotic levels of iconicity, indexicality, and symbolism to achieve subjective integration of the "whole" person'.[15] Is it possible to find all classes in any particular performance? One reason for beginning this essay with 'Good Vibrations' is that this is a track in which I have been unable to do so.

However, while this exercise seems useful (and not only in that it forces attention away from preconceived categories of features – structure, melodic outline and so on) to me, it doesn't seem to capture my experience of the track. Indeed, although

---

14   We must note that Davies' own view was that the song was about homosexuality, but this view was not publicly accepted. See Bellman, *The Exotic*, p. 303.,

15   Turino, 'Signs of Imagination, Identity and Experience', p. 244.

much of my interpretive work has been described as semiotic,[16] I have never felt easy with such a description since the insistence in critical discourse on music on concepts of 'encoding' and 'decoding' seems to me to misrepresent what musicians do. Indeed, exactly what is to be gained from the sort of tick-box approach I have endeavoured to demonstrate here? In my reading of his essay, Turino is trying to use this version of Peirce's semiotics to get at the *immediacy*, the *non-symbolic* nature of some musical experiences. In Eric F. Clarke's recent book, *Ways of Listening*, the model of ecological perception initially introduced by J.J. Gibson is used to achieve very much this aim – indeed to argue that the assumption of static, or fixed, interpretations of signs is misleading.[17] The key process in Clarke's work is threefold and can be summarized in the phrase: invariants afford through specifications. An ecological approach identifies *invariants* which are perceived in the environment, constants such as the flowing of water (which we identify as a river), a bounded slab of metal with a sharp edge (which we identify as a knife) or a high-pitched squeak. It observes what actions these invariants *afford*. A river, for example, affords both swimming and drowning. A knife affords both cutting and stabbing. A high-pitched squeak is more complex, without identifying precisely what invariants it has, but such a squeak might afford flight if it sounds like a mouse, inquiry if it sounds like a squeaking door, or contemplation if it sounds like (or even is) the opening to an electro-acoustic piece. Whichever of these responses we choose will depend on the particular source, for us, that the sound *specifies*. These affordances arise, as can be seen, not only from the environment, but also from the perceiver operating within a particular cultural environment. It is for the perceiver to either swim or drown, for example; that specific environment does not determine his/her swimming abilities. Bearing the example of the squeak in mind, I quote from Clarke: '[the ecological perspective on musical meaning discusses how] sounds specify their sources and in so doing afford actions for the perceiver'.[18] Invariants operate at different levels. In music, it is certainly possible to identify those constants which remain necessary to the performance of a particular song, and which remain present from one performance to another. Indeed, I have elsewhere insisted on a distinction between three categories – *song*, *track* and *performance* – and, at one extreme, invariants seem to be those very characteristics which define a particular *song*. At the opposite extreme,[19] the binary metre of both 'Good Vibrations' and 'See My Friend', or their tonal centres, operate as invariants against which the constant change of individual durations, or of individual pitches, creates meaning, so that invariance can work both externally and internally to a track. Most of my discussion here concentrates on its external operation.

I return for a while to 'See My Friend'. Notice again the nasal quality of those opening timbres, that richness of the upper partials which, for a perceiver with

---

16   Christian Kennett, 'Is Anybody Listening?' in Allan F. Moore (ed.), *Analyzing Popular Music* (Cambridge, 2003), pp. 196–217, at p. 199.
17   Eric F. Clarke, *Ways of Listening* (New York, 2005).
18   Ibid., p. 126.
19   My thanks to Eric Clarke on this point.

the right experience, specifies the sound-world of the sitar as associated with psychedelia. Notice again how the groove slides off that first beat. That sliding seems to specify a certain pleasurable somatic instability, not by way of the coining of the word 'sliding', but prior to it, the word identifying a feeling already there. Think again of the focus in the lyric on the 'she' who is gone: its acting out in the texture is more potent in its co-occurrence with 'and now there's no-one left'. Note how the guitar provides support to Davies' persona throughout by doubling his line, except at "Cept my friend' (and during the bridge), while a second voice adds to that support on 'she is gone'. The riverbank on which she is presumably playing is identified only in the lyric – there is no non-verbal sound which specifies it. The quality of Davies' voice in singing about it, however, does indicate the attitude of his persona towards the event; there is clear equanimity specified here until the middle eight, when we can perhaps perceive a sense of loss, but the recovery of the verse, and of his 'friend', seems to be sufficient compensation. The song's concluding rising pitch and dynamic level would function, outside the song, as specifying an object coming towards the perceiver. The increase of dynamic level seems particularly to be a feature of the greater presence of the bass, as it comes to emphasize every beat of the bar and is what gives rise, I believe, to the specification of urgency, a raising of the emotional level and an indication that some evasive action is required (in order to evade the oncoming object). To return to the textural absence, it works analogically, not directly, and it requires the intervention of the verbal medium to interpret this absence as 'loss' rather than as 'shedding unnecessary accoutrements'. for example. I'll recall just one other instance I referred to earlier, that lightening of tone with the d♯ in the guitar. That this is identified with the comment "Cept my friend' turns around the negative implied by the strong f♯ chord through the middle 8 to a positive, identified with the major, and a wonderfully balanced, nuanced one, identified with the first inversion. Compare three (E) sequences: ii–V–IV–I; ii–V–IVc–I; ii–Vb–IVc–I. They seem to me to become progressively less assertive, more accommodating; less forceful, more delicate. Since the only real variant feature here is the bass, I suggest this as the source of that change, if the sense is shared. You can see the procedure I am undertaking here. Each of the events that are describable by one of Peirce's classes of sign is also describable as specifying a sonic source, even if that source is the lyric which Ray Davies sings and which therefore requires interpretation of its sphere of reference (since the song forms an aspect of the listener's environment no less than do features external to the song, references within the song to itself are equally environmental). All these events carry meaning because they specify something perceived in the environment that works analogically to these details.

So much for one example. Can we make sense of 'Good Vibrations' from this perspective? In some respects, we certainly can. The opening to the track is unusually assertive. No introduction, simply the announcement of the singer's almost breathless identity, 'I', followed by an empty bar before we find out what this 'I' is about. The 'I' specifies a source, an individual speaker, whom we encounter unplanned (because of that lack of introduction), suddenly, in a way (I would suggest) that will always be with some measure of apprehension. As an immediate, encountered object, it can also be described as a dicent-index, and the immediacy of the encounter is dependent on the metaphorical space which surrounds the 'I'. What about that opening descending sequence? Perhaps its most immediate function is intertextual, in the reminiscence it permits of stylistically similar tracks such as the Turtles' 'Happy Together', a track whose lyric takes up a similar (although less nuanced) position. As such, it acts as an iconic rheme – the tracks resemble each other in their bass lines, but without imposing a necessity of interpretation on the act of recognition. The delicacy of the bass line also acts intertextually, reminding us, as it does, of Paul McCartney's upper-register playing. Here, the historical location of 'Good Vibrations', as part of the attempt to upstage The Beatles' *Sgt. Pepper* is inescapable. The theremin line, on which some of the track's notoriety is based, is perhaps best understood via Tagg's category of 'genre synecdoche', whereby the pure, slightly ethereal quality of its tone calls to mind the entire genre of science-fiction movies, although whether it brings with it (as Tagg would suggest) all the connotations of B-movie status (cheap effects, poor plots, the emphasis on wonder) attendant on the sound-world is moot.[20] Various other aspects of the track ask for this sort of treatment – in the competing melodic lines at the end, for example, we are given a choice as to which to identify with. Perhaps most importantly, we can choose to switch our identification from one time to another. Do we exult in the vibrations ('good, good, good vibrations'), or do we keep an eye on the relationship ('she's giving me...')? And this is where the bridge works so well since, in jettisoning everything from the texture (at about 2'15"), an important stage in the plot is reached – this is surely preparation for a greater level of attention that we are asked to give, and it is in that moment that the change happens. The sequence which becomes reversed, though, and – key to my interpretation of the track – seems peculiarly inert. Many another sequence, and an alternative set of transposition levels, would have signified in exactly the same way, since it is only the relative levels, conjoined as they are to the lyric, that carry the signification. This would suggest that an ecological perspective is not all-explanatory, but that where conscious interpretation is necessary, we may need to talk in terms of symbolic reference.

What about the revised version of 'Good Vibrations', which Brian Wilson issued as part of the finally completed *Smile* project? The first obvious difference lies in the main voice. It is, of course, older. It is more worn. With our knowledge of Brian Wilson's personal history, it is hard not to hear in it the scars of that history. That also makes it harder to hear the protagonist as someone inexperienced in personal relationships, to whom the necessity of proactivity comes as a revelation. One of the key constituents of ecological perception is that it promotes activity. What activity is promoted by this recognition? A reorientation of our attitude towards

---

20 Milton Mermikides has reminded me that, for some contemporaneous listeners, the theremin's electronic nature adequately represented the idea of 'pickin' up' vibrations from the ether, particularly since it is sounded without physically touching it. While this is undoubtedly true, this seems to me (and to a few others to whom I have spoken) to have been a less recognized reference than that of the sci-fi film.

one of sympathy, perhaps, by Wilson's voice, closely followed by one of suspicion if the song is what we have known for nearly four decades (by the time of the release of *Smile*).[21] There are some subtle differences. The rewritten first verse moves away from simply observing 'her', to considering the effect she is having on the singer – is this evidence of greater maturity, or of greater self-absorption (or both)? The lead into the chorus ('And I'm pickin' up') is new and, to my ears, adds nothing to the song. The second verse continues the self-absorption theme, but this does permit Wilson to ask 'I wonder what she's pickin' up from me?'. This is a question which only occurred to Carl Wilson much later in the course of the original version of the song. Here, one wonders whether it will promote an earlier change in the course of this version, but it doesn't. (Indeed, that it is immediately followed by the 'And I'm pickin' up' does seem to be a lamentable inattention to detail – switching back to the needless pick-up gives the lie to his asserted sense of 'wonder'.) This alone appears as evidence that the interpretation I have developed here is not one that occurred to Wilson, despite the many thousands of hours he must have spent with this material over the years. For some readers, to be sure, this will invalidate my interpretation. For others, it will simply confirm that we are not the authors of the consequences of our actions (and, of course, I find myself in this group). Two other new perspectives are worth noting, the theremin trill in the new version (which sounds a little more mechanical, as if the required effect is now well known, and is therefore too precisely achieved), and the interpolation ('dum be dah', at around 3') before the final section, which puts off the resolution. This seems masterly; in a track of this sort of length (only 4½ minutes), almost any delay of final resolution will intensify its effect, and where it literally enacts the words 'gotta keep those vibrations happening', its presence is almost too good to be true.[22] This diversion demonstrates that such an interpretation is an interpretation of the *track*, of the reality of what it is that we hear, rather than an interpretation of the *song*, the abstract identity which gives rise to a performance, and which can be realized in a large number of ways. It is the track which provides meaning.

Let me look at a range of other tracks from this perspective. The first is The Beatles' track 'With a Little Help from my Friends' and, in particular, the use on this track of the tambourine. I have recently realized why this is so effective, and it is to do with the strange pacing of its shuffle rhythm. Because of the speed at which one needs to move a tambourine to get a decent rattle of the jingles 'in real life', the particular speed of this tambourine sounds just too slow (particularly in the chorus preceding the final bridge). It seems to me that this helps portray Ringo Starr's awkwardness, perhaps reluctance, to admit his dependence in that final bridge, and I note that this realization is dependent on the way this sound specifies the movement of a tambourine in natural surroundings – the speed with which a tambourine moves in reality is an invariant feature of its construction.

---

21   A change of attitude is quite a profound activity to achieve.
22   Although, as Laura Leante pointed out to me, if you hear this as referencing 'Wimoweh' (which is very plausible), your reaction will be very different.

This is only one among very many examples I could cite. Another is John Lennon's 'Imagine'. Here, the moment which most interests me is the point at which melodic tonic and harmonic tonic first coincide, after a number of near-misses. This first happens on the word 'dreamer', and this observation seems to back up Lennon's uncertain ideology – the oft-noted position that he was 'all talk and no action'. However, it is harder to suggest that harmonic/melodic closure specifies closure in some other realm. Here, I'm taking it as specifying secure affirmation, specifically of the stance occupied by 'dreaming' rather than 'doing', taking the accompanying lyric as key. It may be that we can only understand this move through Peirce's symbolic category,[23] rather than directly ecologically, and here I'm reminded of two other positions. The first is Luke Windsor's argument that even using the ecological model, 'thirdness' is always necessary, that the symbolic 'interpretation' of a sign is a necessary stage.[24] The second is David Sless's insistence, in his critique of semiotics, that interpretation is not simply, or even mostly, the decoding of a message, but is marked initially by a quality Sless calls 'letness' – one begins from the creative act of allowing something, in one's own experience, to stand for something else.[25] Both of these critiques imply that at the root of interpretation is a creative act, but it is not an act built out of nothing. It is this bounded position which seems so well addressed in an ecological manner – the meanings I have been discussing are not encoded in the music in such a way that they permit only one 'decoding', but nor are they simply flights of fancy, in that they all start from sources specified in the recordings.

Like 'Good Vibrations', Cilla Black's singing of the Bacharach/David classic 'Alfie' is also a song which marks a change of position. Black's persona is at first rather cowed by this Alfie, a man who holds it 'wise to be cruel', a position that corresponds to the way she pronounces his name, with the stress always on the first syllable, as if she were pleading with him to come to an accommodation (the contrast with her 'Step Inside, Love' could hardly be more dramatic). However, after a bridge which threatens to challenge the harmonic world of the opening, her enquiries become an assertion: 'I believe in love'. A chromatic bass then moves us into a formally new area – what started as the third verse veers off somewhere new – an area where she insists that 'without true love we just exist, Alfie', stressing for the first time the last syllable of his name. Against the invariant of her approach to her lover, this moment specifies our perception of her inner change – a change which in everyday life is often marked by a difference of facial expression and which is modelled here by the shift in harmonic language and the transgression of normative formal practice. It thus affords us the possibility of extending our understanding of how an individual may respond under the pressures her persona is portrayed to have endured. Indeed, in the earlier article of mine to which I have referred,[26] I argued that the environment in which the persona moves is specified (to

---

23 Cumming, *The Sonic Self*, p. 103.
24 Windsor, 'An Ecological Approach'.
25 David Sless, *In Search of Semiotics* (London, 1986).
26 Clarke, 'Subject-Position and the Specification of Invariants'.

use ecological language) by three musical domains: the textural matters normally considered under the heading 'accompaniment'; the harmonic setting, including the modal/tonal vocabulary; and the formal setting or narrative structure – that is, the order in which its events take place, and the patterns of repetition within this order.

Jimi Hendrix's 'If Six was Nine' depends for its understanding on that title itself – a title which posits the ludicrous suggestion that our very understanding of reality is based on an insecure foundation. And a popular song can do little else, of course; it certainly cannot mount an argument for its case. So what does Hendrix's track do? Initially, of course, it simply refuses to play the game – Hendrix asserts his right 'not to care', and is happy to put off any debate until (as he puts it in 'Voodoo Chile') he'll 'meet you in the next world …'. So, what of this is open to an ecological interpretation? The first of three key moments in the track occurs when Hendrix switches from inhabiting what has seemed to be a space to a rather more intimate space[27] (condensing his vocal space[28] on the words 'white-collar conservatives …'). Hitherto, he has been singing at full volume to cut through the sound of his guitar (particularly during the last four bars of the 12-bar blues sequence). The shift of space coincides with his sharing with his listeners more particular details of his experience. This moment then gives way to his waving his 'freak flag high' as the guitar shoots from one side of the sound-box to the other; and the kit becomes less disciplined. The source specified here seems to be his own psyched-out space. Having mapped out the terrain, so to speak, at 'fall, mountains' he no longer needs to raise his voice over the kit, because we (his listeners) have become 'tuned in' to his intimate space. And then, as he gets more confidential still, 'when it's time for me to die', it is as if he has all but swallowed the microphone; we are almost privileged to have access to this peculiar vision. And this all works only because we have experience of that very difference between social and intimate spaces.

As in 'If Six was Nine', Billy Bragg's recording of 'The Home Front' relies for its force on a bald presentation detail, which seems particularly notable for a character like Bragg whose name is founded on his integrity, on his live performance. Bragg sings this rather equivocal song about English identity, accompanying himself on electric guitar, with a full brass band behind him. The band, however, is bathed in reverberation. At one point, Bragg sings of nostalgia being the 'opium of the age'. Bearing in mind that the production on the band sounds so strongly reminiscent of similar writing behind a track like Roy Harper's 'When an Old Cricketer Leaves the Crease', and bearing in mind also the association such bands have with a then almost-past, and now dead, mining culture, it seems to me that this glorious band sound reeks of that very nostalgia. Perhaps this is why Bragg's vocal is so dry; the visual image is perhaps akin to the contemporary use of black and white newsreel footage, as a backdrop to a talking head. Bragg isn't part of that world;

---

27   This distinction I owe to Edward T. Hall, *The Hidden Dimension* (London, 1969), pp. 110–18.

28   This concept I borrow from Dai Griffiths, 'From Lyric to Anti-lyric: Analyzing the Words in Pop Song', in Moore, *Analyzing Popular Music*, pp. 39–59.

they live in separate spaces – one resonant, one dry. So what of the track's strange ending, as a heavily compressed recording of 'Jerusalem' intrudes on the band's gentle exit? Surely to sing 'Jerusalem' is simply to evoke that very nostalgia Bragg is uncomfortable with? But that was not his intention: '*Jerusalem*, I think, should be the national anthem. I think it's the most powerful statement of pride in what the socialist tradition in Britain is about.'[29] In the article, 'The Taxman's Poet', he does go on to explain, but what is important here is, first, the way in which this ultimate expression is treated. It does not sound as if it is coming from either Bragg's or the brass band's world. At first appearance, it sounds as if it might be coming from under water, enacting the sinking that Jerusalem – that is, Britain – seemed, to the Left, to have endured under Thatcher. Simultaneously, it situates the narrative somewhere in the 1940s, since this sonic modulation also specifies the typical sound of interference as on a contemporaneous radio broadcast. And yet 'Jerusalem' is not swamped by the sound-world it finds itself in: it remains recognizable – perhaps the possibility of survival is made apparent. Bragg is also actually demonstrating the necessity of interpretation in that he himself offers an interpretation which was certainly at odds with what was the 'normative' (jingoistic) reading of the song in 1986. Can he, though, escape from the nostalgia which hearing such a song inevitably evokes in so many minds? And, in presenting it to us so problematically, is he not implicating us in that nostalgia too? These thoughts, to which there is no unequivocal answer, only arise from noticing what sound sources appear specified in the last half-minute of the track.

And what about tracks that do not have such an overt reference to the world? The Vapors' 'News at Ten' does for me what 'Ohio' does for Turino in his article: 'upon hearing only the opening chords of Crosby, Stills, Nash and Young's song "Ohio" on the radio I had a strong emotional reaction as well as a physical response … that was totally incommensurate with my feelings about the song when it was popular … I am still not sure of all that was being indexed by the opening chords … but this is precisely why the music was able to produce such a strong affective response.'[30] What is specified by the opening bass line of 'News at Ten'? First of all, of course, a guitar itself. The harmonic sequence is G–D/F♯–C/E – D/F♯. The descending bass line cannot continue further because of the (normal) tuning of an electric guitar, bass string E. The line thus returns on itself. The best way of conceiving the import of this is, I think, through a couple of Johnson's image schemata, the balance and the cycle:[31] the line is beautifully balanced between its outer points (G and E), swinging constantly via the F♯; but it also cycles around this unending sequence, each time a little further into the narrative of the song, but not having gained any wisdom from the encounter the lyrics narrate until much later in the song (as noted below). Indeed, I suspect a link between these schemata and an ecological view could be extremely productive for the interpretation of songs, but

29   Billy Bragg and Ian A. Anderson, 'The Taxman's Poet', *Folk Roots*, 42 (1986): 26–29, at 27.
30   Turino, Signs of Imagination, Identity and Experience, pp. 243–44.
31   Mark Johnson, *The Body in the Mind* (Chicago, 1987), pp. 74–96 and 119–21.

that is an exercise for another day. But then there is also the treble-rich modulation, as if the line is partially hidden, an awkwardness picked up by the subsequent continuation of the sequence to root position C (the F♯–C move executed quite unselfconsciously, it seems). The song concerns generational non-communication ('still I can't hear you' repeated *ad infinitum* to the end) and leads to a climax (which in the context of these lyrics, in most adults' experience will specify one or more adolescent arguments). The tension grows over that initial sequence and, when the high point is reached, a bass guitar G–F♯–E–D comes to the fore (it had been heard earlier, but not in a prominent position). This finally completes its path down through C–B–A–G, this downward scale neatly signalling the close of the track (another 'episodic marker' which could be viewed in terms of a Johnsonian 'path' schema). The attraction of this line is such as to encourage desire for such non-communication, for the communality offered by such overt opposition; the environment outlined here is a historical one, but a probably inevitable aspect of adolescent experience in UK culture.

So, these examples are intended to demonstrate simply that the perceptual approach – which I think explains why 'See My Friend' is so engaging, more successfully than does my attempted semiotic explanation – also addresses some of those other songs which are part of my own inner life. My assumption is that such an approach will act congruently for my readers, insofar as I am a normal listener. The concluding question is again, of course, how this matters. In other words, if we have a methodology which enables greater understanding, do we need an adequate theory to underpin it? I have to admit that I am no longer convinced of the necessity, although this is perhaps simply a matter of ideology. One of the things which is vital to note here, though, is that what is dominating my entire essay, and the assumptions behind it, is a realist aesthetic. In other words, in my work, in Clarke's, in Tagg's and in Turino's, one-to-one correspondences are being observed between musical details and life experience. In the case of the ecological explanation, this is overt, since such experiences are, by definition, the matter of our experiential reality. If invariants specify sources, they are not inventions of fantasy: as Cornelia Fales, says, 'the inclination to hear sources in sound constitutes a perceptual schema',[32] before arguing that, in ambient music, such an inclination is overridden. And it can only be overridden (if her argument convinces) because it is there in the first place. In other words, what I would understand as either a modernist, or a postmodernist, aesthetic position, cannot be interpretatively relevant here. One of the reasons why I prefer (most) popular song to (most) concert music is that it speaks to where I am, rather than where I might like to be (a moral issue, then); it addresses the real world of my experience, rather than evading it. Attention to the affordances specified by the assumed sources of the sounds of music we hear enables concentration on that facet, providing understanding. So what? *So this.*

---

32   Cornelia Fales, 'Short-Circuiting Perceptual Systems: Timbre in Ambient and Techno Music' in Paul D. Greene and Thomas Porcello (eds), *Wired for Sound* (Middletown, CT, 2004), pp. 156–80, at p. 165.

Discography

Beach Boys, 'Good Vibrations', *Greatest Hits* (EMI, 1966).

The Beatles, 'With a Little Help from my Friends', *Sgt. Pepper's Lonely Hearts Club Band* (Parlophone, 1967).

Cilla Black, 'Alfie', *Bacharach and David Songbook* (Connoisseur Collection, 1966).

Billy Bragg, 'The Home Front', *Victim of Geography* (Cooking Vinyl, 1986).

Jimi Hendrix, 'If Six was Nine', *Axis: Bold as Love* (MCA, 1967).

Jimi Hendrix, 'Voodoo Chile (slight return)', *Electric Ladyland* (MCA, 1968).

Kinks, 'See My Friend' *The Ultimate Collection* (Sanctuary, 1965).

John Lennon, 'Imagine', *Legend* (EMI, 1971).

Brian Wilson, 'Good Vibrations' *Smile* (Nonesuch, 2004).

Beyond the Master Narrative of Youth: Researching Ageing Popular Music Scenes

Nicola Smith

Popular music has consistently been tied to youth. Stemming from the Chicago School studies of urban existence and delinquency, music has been highlighted as a component in gang formation. Thus the entry of popular music into sociological study was contextualized in relation to urban youth formations, deviant behaviour and the social – as opposed to psychological – reasons for, and implications of, subcultural participation.[1] Subsequent Birmingham School subcultural studies focused more directly on popular music, yet continued to define music-related activity as a form of resistance and rebellion, but also exclusively for the young.[2] The aim of academic popular music investigation has thus been contained within seeking to achieve an understanding of societal problems led by youth and to map deviant behaviour and alternative (that is, non-mainstream, non-adult) style. In critique of the Birmingham School Centre for Contemporary Cultural Studies (CCCS) this chapter moves beyond notions of (youth) activity as fixed, spectacular and contained within the temporality of the cultural fad to enable recognition of active and meaningful *adult* scene participation.[3]

---

1   Robert K. Merton, *Social Theory and Social Structure* (London, 1957); David Matza and Gresham M. Sykes, 'Juvenile Delinquency and Subterranean Values', *American Sociological Review* 26/5 (1961): 712–19; Howard S. Becker, *Outsiders: Studies in the Sociology of Deviance* (New York, 1963).

2   Stuart Hall and Tony Jefferson (eds), *Resistance Through Rituals: Youth Subcultures in Post-War Britain* (London, 1976); Dick Hebdige, *Subculture: The Meaning of Style* (London, 1979).

3   Here the use of the term 'scene' is not tied to scene theory as explored by, for example, Will Straw, 'Systems of Articulation, Logics of Change', *Cultural Studies* 5/3 (1991): 368–88. The choice of terminology instead reflects the Northern Soul participants' own use of the term to describe their cultural world. This is more akin to Erving Goffman's use of the term 'making a scene' in *The Presentation of Self in Everyday Life* (London, 1959).

In response to the prioritization of the master narrative of youth within popular music studies this chapter explores how post-subcultural theorizations possess the potential to examine ageing popular music practice. Several post-subcultural frameworks currently exist,[4] yet it is the suitability of the neo-tribal paradigm that is discussed here in terms of its potential to embrace ageing participation and scene longevity. Here music is theorized as pleasure, as an aspect of everyday life and as a component for the construction of identity. Via an examination of the effect of time on a music scene, it can be argued that the appeal of participation is not dependent on age nor does it derive solely from a desire for community or a resistance to mundane existence, but is instead tied to identity formation and reflexive agency. As such, the self of youth constructed in relation to scene affiliation need not diminish with age.

While the notion of a popular music scene shelf-life has been repeatedly implied in media representations, via music industry marketing strategies and by fans keen to experience the 'next big thing', the instances of continuing music scenes are more common than we might first assume.[5] However, examples of continuing scenes with the same body of *continuing participants* are less frequent. The case of Northern Soul offers one such example. Northern Soul is a British dance-oriented music culture primarily located in the Midlands and north of England. The scene originated in the late 1960s, reaching its heyday in the 1970s and continuing to the present day. The music of choice is 1960s black American soul. The 45rpm vinyl records that are fanatically collected and passionately danced to are predominantly rare, non-chart hits from often unknown artists and minor record labels. Still attracting the same body of fans to all-night dancing events, Northern Soul highlights the need for a theoretical paradigm that bridges the gap between the frivolity and temporality of postmodern experience and the static, homogeneous subcultural collective. I present my typology of the scene with longevity with this aim, emphasizing the postmodern fluidity of, and the complexities inherent in, performing continued fandom within a continuous scene in adulthood. From this we can focus on the self within a collective and unpick the significance of identity performance, thus being able to focus on ageing (and the related issues of subjective constructions of self and nostalgia). The passage of time is relevant to music scenes in two ways: first, in terms of the ageing of a scene and, second, in relation to the complexities of ageing participation. In other words, theorizations of a scene *and* theorizations of the participants must be explored.

---

4 Post-subcultural theorizations stem from Steve Redhead, *The End-of-the Century Party* (Manchester, 1990) and David Muggleton, 'The Post-subculturalist' in Steve Redhead, Derek Wynne and Justin O'Connor (eds), *The Clubcultures Reader: Readings in Popular Cultural Studies* (Oxford, 1997). Alternative approaches include scene theory, neo-tribes, lifestyles and numerous reworked versions of subcultural theory.

5 For example goth, punk and heavy metal.

Ageing Scenes

The aim of this section is to highlight the potential for post-subcultural theory to recognize ageing music cultures. Music participation is not about spectacular existence but everyday life; it can be conducted beyond the fad. With a nod to postmodern conditions of cultural consumption, participation is also not about fixed, static routines as the CCCS implied. However, postmodern fluidity need not mean engagement without celebration of specificity; there is a middle ground. This middle ground demonstrates that music cultures have the potential to possess lasting appeal for participants and a level of depth that enables identity synthesis yet is fluid enough to be maintained throughout a participant's cultural career in an everyday sense. The need for fluidity *and* specificity leads us to post-subcultural theory.

The issues and flaws evident in the CCCS approach are well documented,[6] so it is not necessary to recount the limitations of this body of work. It is sufficient to note that subcultural theory overstated the difference *between* groups and also the internal homogeneity *within* groups. It neglected women, ethnic and racial minorities and, I argue, the non-youth. With post-subcultural theory there is acknowledgement that postmodernity allows for movement between identities, eroding the suggestion of a homogeneous collective and diluting the resistance reading of subcultures. To break away from the CCCS approach is to eradicate the unreflexive, passive subcultural participant. It is the potential for reflexive, active engagement in cultural practice that is relevant to post-subcultural theory and, as we shall see, to ageing scenes. A task of locating scenes with longevity, such as Northern Soul, within post-subcultural theory therefore involves understanding how performing within specific guidelines of scene membership is an expression of fluidity and how one individual's expression of specificity can occur alongside another's ephemeral experience.

Post-subcultural Scenes

The passion, commitment and community constructed around Northern Soul by fans of the music are testament to the importance of communal interaction (sociality) as stressed by Maffesoli.[7] The idea that a 'will to live' (*puissance*) and a human desire for belonging influence sociocultural participation are valid in relation to our understanding of the *initial* aspiration to become a member of a cultural group. However this, I believe, is not sufficient an explanation as to why people *continue* as members of a particular cultural group. In a postmodern world of choice, with ease of access and the frequency of movement in and out of cultural worlds, how can

---

6   See Andy Bennett and Keith Kahn-Harris (eds), *After Subculture: Critical Studies in Contemporary Youth Culture* (Basingstoke, 2004), pp. 6–11.
7   Michel Maffesoli, *The Times of the Tribes: The Decline of Individualism in Mass Society*, trans. Don Smith (London, 1996).

we explain individuals opting to remain as members of one collective for extended periods of time?

Northern Soul is embroiled in desires for and methods of identity-construction. Individuals acquire an aspect of self via scene participation. The space of social interaction is a zone in which participants can perform displays of knowledge, thus exhibiting passion and competency within that scene. By demonstrating to fellow participants the extent and proficiency of their membership, participants can perpetuate and improve their construction of personhood and, as such, affect their creation of selfhood.[8] Individuals become someone specific because of their involvement with(in) a scene. This presents an initial explanation as to why people continue to desire scene participation. But how does this intercept with post-subcultural (postmodern) constructions of frivolous, temporal and fluid cultural consumption? To answer this we must turn to the concept of the *tribus*.

With an aim of moving beyond positioning popular music as a study of deviant gangs and alternative collective practice for the disillusioned mass, and in an attempt to demonstrate postmodern characteristics of popular music consumption, many post-subcultural theses overtly foreground the individual and the frivolity, temporality and multiplicity of interaction.[9] In response to this and in recognition that consumer choice and individualism may produce a loss of shared sentiment of interaction, the Maffesoli's Durkheimian focus centralizes the collective, thus challenging the isolated, selfish, ironic individual of postmodernity. The collective is the site in which the creation and maintenance of self is achieved. It is thus the individual's awareness of this and the subsequent desire for the continuation of the collective that neo-tribal theory must address in the example of Northern Soul and, arguably, in the case of all scenes with longevity.

Northern Soul is competitive; it is constructed around the acquisition of identity, status and prestige as demonstrated by the overt and spotlighted performance of competency, skill and connoisseurship. As such, the pleasure of belonging of which Maffesoli speaks is tainted by the drive to construct selfhood derived from scene membership. To address this we can follow Sweetman's conclusion that we can entwine the reflexive process of identity-construction and neo-tribal sociality.[10] Sociality therefore can be considered in relation to the pleasure derived *because of what it can offer self* rather than simply the pleasure of belonging within a collective. As Bauman states, neo-tribes for him are formed 'by the multitude of individual acts of *self-identification*'.[11] While examples of continuous and long-running scenes contradict Bauman's pessimistic view that an individual moves between neo-tribes because of frustration with the unrealized promise of cultural affiliation, it is true

---

8   Richard Jenkins, *Social Identity* (London, 1996), p. 30, makes a distinction between selfhood ('private experience') and personhood ('what appears publicly').

9   For example, David Chaney, *Lifestyles* (London, 1996).

10   Paul Sweetman, 'Tourists and Travellers? "Subcultures", Reflexive Identities and Neo-tribal Sociality' in Bennett and Kahn-Harris, *After Subculture*, pp. 79–93, at pp. 88–89.

11   Zygmunt Bauman, *Intimations of Postmodernity* (London, 1992) p. 136, original emphasis.

that in Northern Soul participants do *dance alone, together*. Is this an example of the greyness of postmodern isolated practice? This is arguably not the case if the centralization of self is read not as a display of isolation or disengagement, but as a method of maintaining the purpose of collective interaction. The individual is celebrated within the collective and thus perpetuates the need for the collective.

While this postmodern approach to ageing scenes may provide a platform from which to explain the significance of an individual's understanding of their cultural participation, the temporality and fragility of neo-tribes does not immediately lend itself to an examination of scenes with longevity. Nor does the multiplicity of tribal engagement suggest the option of remaining within *one* cultural group. How does this temporality and fragility intersect with the commitment and longevity of the Northern Soul scene? As Hodkinson queries in relation to goth, the fluidity and ephemerality of neo-tribes is problematic.[12] However to place this fluidity and ephemerality in context, neo-tribes are fluid if we compare them to the prescriptive, fixed, social background-specific forms of affiliation exhibited within traditional anthropological tribes (in which membership is ascribed, not achieved). However, membership in *neo*-tribes is a choice – one option from an array of cultural groupings selected by an individual. What complicates matters further is that the fluidity and ephemerality with which Hodkinson takes issue is based on a comparison with the fixity of subcultures. It is subcultural fixity and associated values that Hodkinson desires to keep when theorizing goth. A *tribus* is fluid and, as such, the freedom to move in and out of neo-tribes dilutes, for Hodkinson, the depth of engagement attainable through cultural interaction and therefore does not accurately represent the commitment evident in the goth scene. To remedy such neo-tribal fluidity Hodkinson gives us 'subcultural substance': a reworked version of subcultural theory. With empathy for Hodkinson's concerns, I agree that it is paradoxical to classify a scene with longevity as solely constructed around frivolous engagement. Yet subcultural theory (even if reworked) does not present sufficient scope to present the participants as reflexively engaged in their own scene-derived identity-construction. Not all participants may desire fixity, just as Hodkinson recognizes that not all goth participants desire fluidity. In response, I think it is vital that we highlight the distance between the concepts of frivolity and fluidity. I suggest that all post-subcultural practice is fluid (but not necessarily frivolous). No fixed boundaries exist as participants can freely move between neo-tribes as, when and – importantly – *if* desired. Participants can consistently return to a particular cultural group just as easily as they can participate in many. Individuals may opt to engage with frivolity or with specificity (or substance as Hodkinson terms it) or with any degree of both.[13] For me, however, to engage with

---

12   Paul Hodkinson, *Goth Identity, Style and Subculture* (Oxford, 2002).
13   This potential to perform with a fusion of frivolity and substance reflects the postmodern experience and is thus distinct from Sweetman's fixed categories of Tourist *or* Traveller. Mine is a post-subcultural option; Sweetman's a depiction of both subcultural and post-subcultural activity occurring alongside one another. See Sweetman, 'Tourists and Travellers?', p. 80.

substance is not akin to spectacular displays to symbolize transgression, resistance and '"traditional" notions of stylistic unity and cohesion that have consistently been associated with the notion of subculture.'[14] Such specificity is instead 'post-subcultural subcultural play'.

Post-Subcultural Subcultural Play[15]

If variety of consumer choice and reflexivity are aspects of contemporary cultural practice why, then, can a participant not engage with cultural practice in a manner reminiscent of subcultural affiliation despite the absence of subcultures? Put simply, if every other option is available in postmodernity, why not the option to perform with 'subcultural' intentions? Individuals knowingly opt for, and consciously engage in, whatever level of cultural activity they desire/deem necessary. For some there is a desire to perform *as if* in a subculture. Importantly however, this performative form of engagement is devoid of the possibility of magical solution: it is *playing the subcultural game*.[16] That the method of cultural interaction can be specific to a cultural activity creates – at least from an external perspective – the *illusion* of subcultural interaction – situated in terms of rules, rituals and preferred modes of performance. Participants will knowingly interact with the pretence of subcultural specificity in order to create an identity, but are aware that 'subcultural' persistence, fixity and all-encompassing exclusivity are not essential (but can be performed, if desired). This is not subcultural as it is an option to repeatedly return to *one* scene. The links with longevity are evident here in relation to consistency of participation: a welcome alternative to the overarching postmodern post-subcultural presumption of ephemerality.

To perform with post-subcultural subcultural play is to perform seriously while knowing the limits of that performance (in terms of what that performance can

---

14   Bennett and Kahn-Harris, *After Subculture*, p. 17.

15   The use of term 'subculture' in the current post-subcultural climate is frowned upon. Yet I have opted to use the phrase 'post-subcultural subcultural play' in a paradoxical manner as this highlights the recognition of the inappropriateness of the term; just as the post-subcultural subcultural players are reflexively aware of the limitations of such play, post-subcultural theorists are reflexively aware of the rhetorical limitations of subcultures.

16   A useful analogy is that of a church wedding for a non-religious couple. This is a desire to perform a marriage ceremony under the guise of what is expected of a wedding, yet with full awareness of the illusion of religiosity as no belief system is in place. This is 'playing the wedding game'. This is not ironic or carnivalesque since this would disrupt the impact of the ceremony, but the significance of this experience is merely one of choice, one of aesthetics and one of doing what is desirable. Yet getting married in a church may generate a sense of appropriateness, correctness and depth of engagement, and the ceremony, the day (and indeed the marriage) may gain additional meaning/ kudos from this. The appeal is to hold a wedding in a traditional sense but not in relation to the symbolism of faith. Many thanks to Derek Scott for this analogy.

achieve). Awareness of the illusory quality of cultural participation is not expressed as ironic or carnivalesque. Such play is not frivolous either, but an expression of agency: it is 'playing at' rather than 'playing with'.

Highlighting the reflexive potential of postmodern practice and drawing upon Sweetman's instructive fusion of the reflexive modernization thesis and neo-tribal sociality,[17] engagement with cultural commodities involves a *knowing use* of these commodities. To have a choice (to achieve a form of cultural involvement rather than to have it ascribed) situates the individual as reflexive. Those playing the subcultural game are aware of the limitations of participation, how they can mould their form of engagement and that subcultures are not solutions. This may appear to be a rhetorical method of overcoming CCCS theory while explaining Northern Soul's subcultural elements, but I must stress that the unique feature is that the participants are aware that 'subcultural' affiliation is an illusion – they are not, as the CCCS would have proposed – using Northern Soul as a magical solution or rebellious resistance to the conditions of existence; this is instead pleasure, play and resultant identity-construction. For this reason, Maffesoli's religiosity thesis fails to step far enough beyond the idea that cultural practice is a solution. He sees the *tribus* as a solution to the disenchantment of contemporary society. This rather sanguine perspective fails to acknowledge that postmodern participants are (and arguably always have been) aware of the limitations of play and, because of this, are able to find a function of play that is not characterized as a sociocultural solution. In essence, the central feature of post-subcultural subcultural play is reflexivity:[18] it relies on the individual knowing that this is a substitute for the traditional community now lost. That said, knowing this does not dilute the passion for the rituals performed. If anything, performing with subcultural play heightens the Maffesolian insistence that it is part of the human condition – especially within postmodernity – to desire belonging.

Post-subcultural subcultural play depends on three factors: an individual's passion for the neo-tribe (implicit in Maffesoli's thesis); the reflexive intention of an individual; and a similar response from fellow tribal members (as it makes little sense to behave with post-subcultural subcultural play alone). You brush against people in the collective, feeling the pleasure of belonging implicit in the need to perform. This need to demonstrate self within the collective thrusts the intention of interaction beyond the basic appeal of togetherness (while still embracing it). It is worthy of note that it is not surprising that performing for each other and finding pleasure in this sociality creates networks (friendships). Yet this only occurs if performance translates into familiar interaction. Perhaps the only prerequisite for this is *prolonged interaction*. There is something paradoxical about Maffesoli's insistence of belonging and the ephemerality of the *experience* of belonging. Ultimately, to talk of belonging should not exclude the potential for longevity.

---

17   Sweetman, 'Tourists and Travellers?', pp. 79–93.
18   It is worth noting that the postmodernity versus reflexive modernity debate, while not pivotal here, is discussed in detail by Sweetman in 'Tourists and Travellers?', pp. 80–85.

It could be assumed that, as the 'sole *raison d'être* [of the neo-tribe] is a preoccupation with the collective present',[19] longevity and constancy of neo-tribal association is irrelevant. Yet if the moments of aesthetics, shared sentiments and sociality are experienced as the here-and-now, this does not eradicate the potential for continuous enjoyment of that 'now', arguably lasting for many years. The subcultural adage of 'living for the weekend' persists for as long as the working week does. Similarly, the need for the pleasure of being together fades only when the alienating conditions of (post)modernity cease. As Maffesoli notes, the solution to the isolation of contemporary existence is the solidarity of the neo-tribe.

So why should we assume that participants always leave? Participants may and do move in and out and between neo-tribes, but the need for a neo-tribe – in whatever form and in whatever quantity – does not necessarily cease. The thirst for solidarity can be quenched by experiencing a multitude of neo-tribes, but this can also be achieved via sustained commitment to *one* scene. This is not exclusive affiliation but sustained interaction. Individuals within scenes with longevity desire not to have to keep moving and to invest effort into re-creating the sentiment of belonging with each fad. They take the search for the sentiment of belonging and togetherness to the point at which the knowing individual plays at a more grounded, less ephemeral version of neo-tribal association. The postmodern choice can be to remain active within adulthood and to do so within one music scene. This, however, produces a problem, as not everyone engaged in a scene will treat that scene in the same way as those participating with post-subcultural subcultural play. Some will participate within scenes such as Northern Soul with frivolity – and this has a significant impact. Types of participant are therefore relevant and are examined below, but, first, it is necessary to place ageing participation in context.

Ageing Participation

The connection between popular music and identity-construction is often portrayed as solely a youth act.[20] Popular music is considered one method of separation, distinction and freedom from adult control and thus aids the life-course development from child to adult. As Sardiello states, 'adolescents and youths become emotionally involved with their music as a way of distinguishing themselves from adults and from each other'.[21] I do not refute this. However, little attention is paid to the *adult*

---

19 Maffesoli, *The Time of the Tribes*, pp. 74–75.
20 I am defining 'youth' as simply as Bennett defines it: 'a specific age group, typically 15 to 25 years old'. See Andy Bennett, *Cultures of Popular Music* (Buckingham, 2001) p. 152. Discussion of the complexity of terms, such as 'youthful' which consider youth an entity beyond age, is not pivotal here.
21 Robert Sardiello, 'Identity and Status Stratification in Deadhead Subculture' in Jonathon S. Epstein (ed.), *Youth Culture: Identity in a Postmodern World* (Malden and Oxford, 1998), p. 123.

use of music cultures as the role of music scene involvement is rarely considered beyond this adolescent usage. Brake hints at the justification for the concentrated focus on *youth* practices:

> The relation of subculture and age is important, because adolescence, and the period of transition between school and work, and work and marriage is important in terms of secondary socialisation ... actors enter into subcultural interpretations of the dominant hegemony, which presents them with a different perspective of social reality, or sometimes a different social reality. ... They introduce the values of the world outside work and school. ... Youth culture emphasises a relation of unattachment, dislocation from the confinements of work and committed relationships, a genuine experiment with 'free time'. ... The attraction of subculture is its rebelliousness, its hedonism, its escape from the restrictions of work and home.[22]

However, such hedonistic exploration and the use of leisure to inform self and to achieve imagined escape do not necessarily have to cease as a consequence of maturity. The explorative necessity may become exhausted in adulthood, yet the identity acquired via this initial youthful exploration informs and continues to inform selfhood and personhood, if allowed. The continuing Northern Soul scene does allow for this, as the behaviours practised within the scene are largely the same today as they have always been. What we are therefore presented with are youth actions, originally considered as distinct from adult society, being performed by adults.

There is a misguided assumption that adulthood brings about a rejection of, disinterest in, or even an inability to participate in a music scene. For example, Andes states with reference to the punk scene:

> Individuals must become punk and they must also, in most cases, cease to be a punk eventually. There are very few participants in the subculture who are older than their early twenties. Those who do stay actively involved in the subculture into their late twenties and beyond are people who are somehow involved at a more organizational level or creative level: musicians, promoters, fanzine writers, artists, etc. Most ... people ... eventually leave behind their punk identities.[23]

This implies a lasting rejection of identities achieved via pleasure-only participation. Yet identity is multifaceted and dynamic, with the most appropriate cultural identity becoming salient as and when required. Maturing fans who have moved away from scenes with longevity do not necessarily lose or discard their scene-derived identity, but can opt to put these identities on hold. Other sociocultural identities

---

22   Michael Brake, *Comparative Youth Culture: The Sociology of Youth Cultures and Youth Subcultures in America, Britain and Canada* (London, 1985), pp. 15–17 and p. 191.
23   Linda Andes, 'Growing Up Punk: Meaning and Commitment Careers in a Contemporary Youth Subculture' in Epstein, *Youth Culture*, pp. 218–19.

may become salient as marriage, children and further life commitments occupy an individual's primary focus in place of music scene participation. Equally, a loss of interest in scene participation can cause an individual to put their identity on hold. However, if a music scene remains in existence, the non-active fan can return to a scene, and scene-derived identity can be recalled.

Participants have control over how, where and when they perform. This occurs throughout the life-course. The question is: if a scene ages, do the attitudes of the participants remain static? Do intentions of scene participation alter with age? Arguably, they do if they have to. The conditions causing this alteration include the presence of newcomers who disrupt the illusion of scene stasis and physicality (actually being unable to perform as you did in youth).[24] Problems arise when a participant is unable to achieve the expected level of status via displays of fandom as a result of age. If all participants were maturing at an equal rate, competitive displays of membership would be unmarred because the reduction in competency because of age would be relative. It is the presence of *young* newcomers to a scene that causes tensions of competitive competency; hence the conflict noted below. For those ageing participants who have no issue with young newcomers, age may still be an issue, but in terms of an internal struggle with self to overcome the limitations of ageing in the context of the physicality and endurance inherent in music scene participation. If the scene were changed to accommodate age, so too would the original context of belonging. The self-taught displays of competency and knowledge would lose meaning if the context of participation changed, and thus the celebration of the specificity of a scene would be placed under threat. The definition of the scene therefore does not change, and individual capacities to perform within this definition become a personal quest or, conversely, an expression of self.

As exemplified by Northern Soul, it is clear that attempts to recover scene-derived identity in adulthood are pursued and also that ageing individuals do not have to eradicate music scene participation if continuation is possible. Some ageing fans have continuously remained active in Northern Soul whereas others have returned. So what is the appeal of continued participation in a 'youth scene' in adulthood? The answer is quite simple: the appeal of participation is the same in adulthood as it was in youth – to possess an identity and a form of cultural involvement that results in the achievement of scene-specific status, personhood and subsequent selfhood. The recognition of what scene-derived identity offered a participant in youth should be considered a major factor in the reasons why participants have returned to, or persisted with, a scene. A participant is aware of what cultural affiliation can offer them and they have experience of achieving this via past scene participation. Returning, or persistent participants, are using their return to, or persistence with, the scene as a process of regaining or maintaining a strand of self, just as newcomers to a scene seek initial identity formation.

The adults within the current Northern Soul scene are not aiming to be deviant, rebellious or in opposition to the mainstream per se. It could be argued that

---

24   This was a theme repeatedly addressed by ageing Northern Soul fans in a scene in which dancing is central to the majority of participants' experience.

ageing participants are trying to relive their youth, as opposed to directly resisting society. The realization of this does not need to be an extreme one. Reliving one's youth through involving oneself in a pastime once undertaken in youth can be understood as a method of maintaining and supporting the aspects of your personhood and selfhood informed and constructed via music scene involvement. Despite identifying the appeal of adult scene participation as beyond desires for achieving rebellion, this identity *does* stand in opposition to the norm. The adult is being alternative, but unwittingly so, by re-initiating or continuing a form of youth identity. Participants can still be received as deviant irrespective of intention simply because they are no longer young. Holland discusses the act of 'policing oneself' as an ageing, alternative female in terms of choice of dress and behaviour in reference to perceived appropriateness.[25] She situates the act of dying your hair pink at the age of 50 as more outrageous than doing this at a younger age. The older woman, via this alternative act, is not simply defying social norms, but refuting the idea of women becoming less visible as they age. As Holland states, '[she] becomes far more visible than a young woman with the same'.[26] Could it be that the act of membership within a music scene in adulthood is a greater form of supposed sociocultural rebellion than it was in youth? It is arguably regarded as socially less acceptable – or at least less expected – to be part of an underground dance scene at 50 as opposed to at the age of 18,. Therefore, a form of rebellion exists in adult-frequented scenes irrespective of whether it is intended by the participant or not. Looking again at the example of Northern Soul, the next section investigates the complexities of ageing participation.

Ageing Northern Soul

For every Northern Soul fan who ever attended a Wigan Casino all-nighter, the haunting Tobi Legend phrase 'Time Will Pass You By' will be all too familiar.[27] During the 1970s the warning of a fleeting present and the nostalgic consideration of the past that the song suggests was perhaps nothing more than a sentimental musical method of wrapping up a Northern Soul dance event. However, listening to this record in the twenty-first century has altered its relevance. For present-day Northern Soul fans – many of them now in their 40s, 50 and 60s – the realization of a past youth reverberates with different sentiments. Much of what is written about

---

25   Samantha Holland, *Alternative Femininities: Body, Age and Identity* (Oxford, 2006).
26   Ibid., p. 26.
27   Tobi Legend, 'Time Will Pass You By' (Gomba Music Inc. (BMI) 8453, 1968). A popular Northern Soul record; one of the 'three before 8' at the Wigan Casino club (the three tracks played at the end of every Casino all-nighter). The Wigan Casino was arguably the most celebrated and popular of all Northern Soul nightclubs. It ran all-nighters (all-night dance events from 8 pm to 8 am) from 1973 to 1981 in Wigan, a town in north-west England.

Northern Soul concentrates on the 1970s scene. This limited focus is somewhat predictable as this was the decade in which a definition of Northern Soul was cemented. This was the era during which the unique dance styles, 'classic' records and majority of fans entered the scene. Over the scene's history the arrival and departure of fans is to be expected. To discuss present-day Northern Soul is therefore to discuss the complexities of the fan dynamic in light of the continuous arrival of new fans and the manner in which existing, consistent fans respond to both the presence of newcomers and their own mode of performing Northern Soul fandom while ageing. Persistent, long-term Northern Soul fans have to cope with altered subjective constructions of selfhood and personhood induced because of age.

Longevity alters the participant dynamic: it matures the existing fan-base while simultaneously allowing a steady stream of new participants to discover the scene. Longevity and the different stages of fandom create an interesting and, at times, conflicting scene dynamic. To give an idea of some of the difficulties created because of scene longevity and the relevance this could have in terms of wider post-subcultural theorization, I present the 'scene with longevity participant typology' (Table 23.1). To surpass subcultural theorization this typology acknowledges cultural fluidity, the variations in modes of cultural membership and the individual – as well as collective – significance of such variations.

Table 23.1   Typology of participants in a scene with longevity

Non-established participants		Established participants	
Non-members	**Members**		
Passer-by Day-tripper Potential member	**Newcomer** *Mature* • Access via friend/ sibling/spouse • Access via complementary music scene • Access via affiliation after 'passing by' *Young* • Access via parent(s) (soul children) • Access via friend/ sibling/spouse • Access via complementary music scene • Access via affiliation after • 'passing by'	**Returning participant** Progressive Nostalgic	**Constant participant** Progressive Nostalgic

The typology in Table 23.1 illustrates the potential for sociality in terms of offering wider modes of postmodern cultural fluidity and choice while also recognizing the possibility of specific scene involvement. Each participant-type is dependent on two factors: when and how the participant found the scene and also the intentions of that participation. So to briefly explain each participant-type, the passer-by embraces the postmodern fluidity of cultural involvement. The passer-by experiences the fluidity of cultural affiliation, but will be disinterested in or unable, at this stage, to experience Northern Soul membership.

After experiencing a scene as a passer-by, the individual may respond to the scene in one of three ways: they may reject the scene, adopt the role of a day-tripper[28] or aim to be a potential member. The day-tripper desires merely to socialize in a club venue without any pursuit of membership and thus celebrates the possible insincerity of consumer selection and therefore the opportunity to compile dynamic collages of neo-tribal experience. The specificity of post-subcultural subcultural play would be unappealing to the day-tripper who regards too highly the frivolity and multiplicity of postmodern cultural consumption. So, although the boundaries between participant-types are permeable, the choice remains with the participant, and there is no guarantee that non-members will progress into the membership stage.

The potential member has a curiosity about the scene in response to participating from the margin.[29] To achieve membership,[30] the potential member alters his or her intentions of cultural involvement by learning to perform to achieve peer acceptance and by displaying commitment to the scene (by increasing personal experience longevity). Such commitment will be embroiled in reflexive awareness of this performance of post-subcultural subcultural play.

Newcomers are those who have chosen to pursue an affiliation with a scene; they are learning about membership, but are not yet established participants. This can occur via potential member status, or if an understanding of a scene has been granted via a friend, sibling, spouse or parent, or via a complementary music scene. The issue of age becomes relevant here. *Young* newcomers possess additional pressures in terms of performing fandom to achieve in-crowd acceptance (to become established). Such difficulties include the pressure from protective existing fans, especially those experiencing subjective disruption of cultural identity due to the presence of newcomers and the possible internal conflict of ageing. *Mature* newcomers are less visible because they 'fit in' in terms of age and thus experience fewer problems of access since their appearance does not incite existing fans to question how suitable their own adult participation in the current scene is, as young newcomers potentially do. Aware of this, young newcomers may resort to retro performances of Northern Soul in an attempt to display their understanding of

---

28   This is the term used by Northern Soul fans for those participants who visited the scene in response to the heyday peak in popularity.

29   Interestingly, this is often the position of the non-fan researcher at the initial stages of participant observation.

30   To move from column 1 to 2 of Table 23.1.

the history of the scene and to counter the issue of youth. However, this somewhat paradoxically places the young newcomer as visibly separate to the constant (progressive) participant, who no longer dresses or dances in what has become a stereotypical fashion. *Returning* participants have quite obviously left the scene at some point and have decided to return. *Constant* participants have remained active on the scene. Returning and constant participants can be either progressive or nostalgic. *Nostalgics* are committed to reliving and maintaining scene involvement, as well as protecting the specifics of Northern Soul. *Progressives* are committed to exploration, discovery and development within the scene. Progressives and nostalgics are ideal-types; they are extremes of experience. The majority of established participants will identify more strongly with one rather than the other type, but may exhibit characteristics representative of that other type.[31] This reflects the idea that cultural identity is open to choice (at least in terms of intention).

The young newcomers are adventuring into the unknown by participating in something that not many of their peers are doing while also experiencing an adult world in everyday terms. This is an escape from childish things into something that 'the adults do'. The potential for Northern Soul to create distance between youth and parental authority – a trait often considered evident in youth cultural activity – is problematic for the soul children, however. The rebelliousness of partaking in cultures unknown to parents is severely limited for the soul child, especially if their parent(s) remain active on the scene. Perhaps parental firsthand knowledge of the deviant aspects of the scene and the heightened comprehension of scene specificity is rewarding, but ultimately being unable to create a cultural identity beyond parental influence may hinder the appeal of Northern Soul once it has been explored, understood and exhausted of the uniqueness that initially presented itself as an identity construct beyond that available to their peers. Living in a post-subcultural age aids the ease with which soul children can opt out of Northern Soul, with many looking to the nu-soul, Modern Soul, funk and acid jazz scenes for potential music membership that embraces the specificity of Northern Soul but without parental presence.

A survey of self-identified Northern Soul fans showed that 49.5 per cent of participants in 2005–06 were aged 46–55 years.[32] No participants were over 65 or under 18. One participant was aged 18–25 years (the daughter of a returning participant) and 95 per cent of all survey participants were over 36, clearly illustrating that the current scene is adult-frequented. When asked in which year the fans originally participated in the scene, the highest number of people questioned entered the scene in 1973 (12.3 per cent); 16 per cent first participated in the scene in the 1960s; 66.7 per cent in the 1970s; 8.6 per cent in the 1980s;

---

31   For example, those who consider themselves progressives may have a fondness for a classic (nostalgic) record, although this will not shape their weekly experience of the scene.

32   Author's PhD findings: 81 quantitative questionnaires were completed by self-identified Northern Soul fans in the UK, 2005–2006. Pilot questionnaire results are not considered.

3.7 per cent in the 1990s; and 4.9 per cent discovered Northern Soul post-millennium. Notably, 16 per cent of people discovered Northern Soul in the 1960s and are still participating today. As expected, the 1970s saw the majority of these participants join the scene.. As nostalgics tend to attend events with little routine and only when the opportunity arises (major events), it is interesting to note that 44.4 per cent of people attend on an infrequent basis, with 7.4 per cent of people attending events once or twice a year as opposed to 56.8 per cent attending current events regularly.[33] This supports the thesis of a divide on the scene between the nostalgics and the progressives while also demonstrating that Northern Soul is, for the majority, still an active (as opposed to a retro) scene.

Conflicting Fandom: An issue of Age

Age-related conflict within Northern Soul is twofold. First, there is the internal conflict between the identity of the participant in youth and of that participant, still on the scene, having to rectify the contradictions inherent in an *aged* youth identity. The concept of nostalgia is relevant here. Second, there is the conflict between the established, older participant (either returning or constant) and the young newcomer. While such age-related conflict is not a condition of *all* participant experience it is a noticeable and talked-about aspect of the current scene. As Sean, a 19-year-old Northern Soul DJ, told me:

> *Northern Soul's a scene that's very much stuck in its ways because obviously it's an older generation and although there's a lot that are accommodating to younger people there's a lot who aren't and jealousy rears its head. It's like it's always 'oh he's only so young, what's he doing?' It's extremely difficult. … From the majority of people you'll get support and encouragement but from the minority you won't and it's very elitist … you have all these records and you can put a set together better than anybody else could but because of your age it doesn't seem relevant.*[34]

Self is context-specific and develops through monitoring our own behaviour and by making social comparisons. Established participants are forced to re-evaluate personhood and selfhood in relation to Northern Soul, based on comparisons they make between themselves and the young newcomers to 'their' scene. This re-evaluation comes as an unexpected downside especially as the initial appeal of returning to, or persisting with, the current scene involves the assumption that past participants would not need to reassert themselves in an alien social context to experience a music scene in adulthood. The fears that younger participants

---

33 Infrequent attendance is defined as those attending less than 12 times in one year (less than monthly). Regular attendance is defined as those attending Northern Soul events monthly, fortnightly, weekly or several times a week.

34 Interview with author, Salford, 3 November 2005.

produce among some existing participants has caused conflict to arise. The fact that older newcomers are not experiencing this level of conflict supports my claim that this tension is *age*-related rather than simply being an issue of commitment and exclusivity. This conflict exists, I believe, because young newcomers are problematizing the merits of ageing competitive display, thus complicating the achievement of status and resultant personhood and selfhood for older, existing participants. This is combined with fears of losing ownership of the scene and subsequently losing what informs this strand of a participant's selfhood.

Current older fans, either constant or returning, have conflicting identifications as participants. This is a result of possessing (memories of) selfhood based in a youthful past and simultaneously possessing personhood on the present-day scene. This internal conflict of cultural identity is evident in the participant who has to re-evaluate because of the arrival of new, younger fans. Moreover, this is further complicated by feelings of reminiscence and the subsequent separation of then and now – in other words, by nostalgia. Nostalgia is relevant to the conflict of age in Northern Soul as it creates a unique subjectivity for the older participant that the newcomer cannot possess.[35] Beyond this separation, nostalgia impacts on the subjective identity of the older participant. The older participant compares youth-derived selfhood with the adult scene personhood that is now being applied to them, both from without and from within. The emotive response from existing fans to young newcomers, cumulating in conflict, mediates the personal relevance of nostalgia in relation to the formation of personhood and selfhood, as Tannock explains:

> Nostalgia ... invokes a positively evaluated past world in response to a deficient present world. The nostalgic subject turns to the past to find/construct sources of identity, agency, or community, that are felt to be lacking, blocked, subverted, or threatened in the present ... Invoking the past, the nostalgic subject may be involved in escaping or evading, in critiquing, or in mobilizing to overcome the present experience of loss of identity, lack of agency, or absence of community.[36]

Tannock goes on to say that nostalgia typically manifests itself within an 'underlying suggestion that ... sources are not available in the present' and that 'that was then, and this is now'.[37] However, this is not true in the case of Northern Soul because the scene continues to exist. It follows, therefore, that participants are not nostalgic about the scene but about the loss of the youth experience of the scene. Nostalgia is thus an internal sense of separation; it divides what informs a

---

35 This begs the question: are newcomers entering the scene for Northern Soul of today or in response to the golden age of the scene? Are young newcomers nostalgic for the myth of Northern Soul? The answers may well be unique for each participant, so narrative analysis would be a useful tool here.

36 Stuart Tannock, 'Nostalgia Critique', *Cultural Studies*, 9/3 (1995): 453–64, at 454.

37 Ibid., p. 456.

fan's sense of cultural self by categorizing the source of that self as discontinued. Conclusively, therefore, it seems that while a scene may experience longevity and appear unchanged, the type of participant and the reality of participant experience do alter with the passage of time. With such complex networks of subjective identity-construction and the age-derived conflict evident in the scene the methodology implemented to observe and record such scenes with longevity requires careful consideration.

Researching Ageing Participation

As identity is central within Northern Soul it is essential to involve ethnographic methods to investigate the current scene and to access personal understandings of self expressed by the participants. The techniques of participant observation, focus groups and interviews grant access to participant interpretations of and involvement in, a scene. Ethnographic methodology can thus penetrate the specifics of cultural participation, yet the necessary inclusion of participant observation is complicated in light of the fact that access is problematic due to the visible distinction of age that potentially situates the researcher outside of the subject group.[38] Fans assume that a young researcher, on account of the age difference, could not possibly have gained firsthand experience of a scene with longevity and that they do not understand what has occurred throughout the history of the scene under study. To tackle the issue of 'not knowing what went before', access to the scene and to fan accounts of the scene is essential. It is impossible to conduct research covertly because of the visibility of age, yet it is essential for the overt researcher to demonstrate some understanding of the scene to gain acceptance and thus access. Efforts should be made to locate gatekeepers to enable access to the present scene and to gain information from constant fans about the past. Data from the latter is open to narrative analysis.

Arguably, the forced overt position of the young researcher is not such a hurdle for the researcher who complements the age of the subject group, and acceptance may be more easily achieved as the possibility of 'knowing the scene' exists. Interestingly the problems of gaining access and 'not knowing what went before' are eradicated if the researcher is a fan of the scene under study. However a fan-turned-researcher may potentially fix investigative research within (biased) fan discourses and, while they may know the scene, they must consciously keep a check on subjective interpretations. To separate personal comprehension derived from the experience of being a fan from the information gained via ethnographic research may be impossible. Moreover, the fact that fan-researchers have to deal with the ethics of recording a scene consisting of their peers for academic gain is not easily dealt with. Of course, scholars cannot choose their researcher position:

---

38   There is a barrier between older researchers and their access to (new) youth cultures and also between younger researchers attempting to conduct ethnographic explorations of cultural groups frequented by notably older participants.

they are either fans of the scene under study or not. If the fan-researcher can successfully and in an unbiased manner manage their duality, then the consequent data will have depth of historical understanding. The researcher new to a scene has to learn the rules of behaviours and, as such, does not have access to comparative experience of then and now. However, they do possess details of the experience of gaining access to a scene. They can tell the illuminating story of the process of becoming a fan.[39]

The issues inherent in ethnographic research of scenes with longevity are thus:

- access for the researcher who belongs to an age group visibly distinct from the group under study
- interpretation of participant observation when the subjective issue of identity is central to such investigations
- not knowing what went before, because researching a scene with longevity means missing aspects of that scene
- the complexities of recording biographies of all participant-types
- coping with the duality of a fan-researcher position.

In response to such issues, the technique of narrative analysis offers the researcher of ageing music scenes an insight into a fan's scene career with scope to span all eras of participation and include issues of subjective identity-construction, nostalgia and sentiments towards self and others without having to delve into discussions of scene politics and value judgements. The implicit innocence and personal sentiment of one's own story-telling dilutes the need for the researcher to openly and directly probe sensitive areas of cultural involvement. This – for a scene in which members continue to participate in and have participated in for many years – is a welcome method of qualitative analysis.[40]

Concluding Thoughts

The fact that Northern Soul consumption centres upon already-aged vinyl records means that the passage of time has not impacted on this scene to the extent that we might witness in live (as opposed to record-based) music scenes. The lack of relevance of the performing artist, chart positioning or major industry input has enabled Northern Soul to continue for five decades without being pushed to 'move with the times'. But while all else remains in stasis, the fans still age. In fact, the only

---

39 Drawing from personal experience, I consider my initial outsider status to Northern Soul as an advantage because I experienced firsthand the issue of gaining access to a scene shrouded in exclusivity. I was able to better understand the issues involved in joining a music scene as a younger newcomer.

40 Amanda Coffey and Paul Atkinson explain the merits of narrative analysis in *Making Sense of Qualitative Data: Complementary Research Strategies* (London, 1996), pp. 56–57.

visibly ageing dimension of the scene is the fans. This would not be such a pertinent issue if it were not for the constant arrival of younger participants, highlighting the passage of time and, as a result, disrupting the illusion of stasis: reliving one's youth through Northern Soul has became more difficult. Age and scene longevity have altered the subjective conceptualization of being a Northern Soul fan for continuous and returning older participants. This has initiated a confusion of identification and expectations of the role of fan when performed in adulthood. The presence of young newcomers to the contemporary scene has forced older participants to question the appropriateness of performing youth-derived actions in adulthood and also acted as a reminder of past youth.

The fact that we do not have a term in popular music for an adult-frequented music culture is very telling. Even apparently innocuous terms such as 'music scene' imply youth association. The adult scene I recognize in Northern Soul is not independent of the original youth culture, but serves to give recognition to adult participation. The prioritization of the master narrative of youth in popular music studies can therefore be placed into question and subsequently age – *not merely youth* – should be considered a relevant element within the construction of popular music identities.

PART 7
The Music Industry
and Globalization

Music and the Creative Knowledge Economy

Geraldine Bloustien

*The creation and consumption of music is a personal, cultural experience and
the technology of the Internet changes the mode of consumption in a way that
is both appealing and threatening – and certainly disruptive.*[1]

*A relationship has slowly been developed, albeit a sometimes dysfunctional
one, in which social actors and technology, specifically Internet technologies,
have altered the course of how this one art form, music, is created, produced,
consumed, worshipped and ultimately perceived.*[2]

The Creative Context: Ideas, Innovation and Enterprise

As a significant, deeply integrated element of the cultural and entertainment
industries, popular music in the twenty-first century is marked by discernible
synergies, unexpected convergences and innovative uses of technology. One of
the main forces behind these changes and resultant growth is the extraordinarily
fast development of technological change in multimedia and telecommunications
that has occurred globally in the past 15 years, particularly in the areas of digital
technology and related new media. In turn, these changes have facilitated and
encouraged new channels of dissemination and distribution. Industries and
individuals have responded by creating and providing a greater variety of creative
products to the market. In the (post)industrialized world, as real incomes have
risen, consumers have demanded, and were encouraged to demand, more products
along with new expressions of cultural consumption, which led to sustained

---

1   Martin Mills, 'Introduction' in Department of Culture Media and Sport, *Consumers Call
     the Tune: The Impact of New Technologies on the Music Industry* (London, 2000), p. 5.
2   Michael D. Ayers (ed.), *Cybersounds: Essays on Virtual Music Culture* (New York, 2006),
     p. 2.

growth in this creative sector of the wider economy.[3] By 2005 creative industries were contributing 3–6 per cent of the GDP.[4] This was confirmed several years later in the UN 2008 report on creative industries:

> *Recent estimates collated by OECD for member countries indicate that the creative industries in France and the United States made up about 3 per cent of gross value added in 2002–2003 and almost 6 per cent of gross value added in the United Kingdom.*[5]

While this is particularly so in (post)industrialized societies, it has been also increasingly becoming so in the developing nations – although, clearly, differences in the industrial and export capabilities of each country results in greater hurdles and diversity, despite their rich cultural heritage. It also varies according to whether the nations themselves have recognized the necessity, and been able to realize the potential, of the creative sector through new policies. The recent United Nations report cited above, notes the particularly obvious example of the case of African music where the majority of its industry is based on live performance. Because developing countries like Africa lack the institutional structure and resources to manage copyright, the musicians and artists frequently leave to pursue overseas' financial and professional opportunities overseas. On the other hand, in Asian countries such as Korea and Singapore, innovation in new media, computer and video games and mobile technologies is 'formulating urban development strategies with a strong emphasis on cultural and creative activities',[6] which in turn drives the rapid production of related cultural industries such as local music-based enterprises as well as the take-up and interconnectivity of these types of businesses and opportunities overseas.[7] Similarly in the states of South America, while it is Jamaica that is particularly concentrating on its music industry,[8] the burgeoning film industry in Mexico also provides new opportunities for development and distribution of its music products and enterprises through screen scores, advertising revenue and related merchandising.

---

3   UNCTAD/UNDP, *Creative Economies Report 2008: The Challenge of Assessing the Creative Economy Towards Informed Policy Making* (Geneva, 2008). This is a detailed study of the global impact of creativity on cultural, social and economic well-being and development.

4   John Hartley (ed.), *Creative Industries* (Oxford, 2005).

5   UNCTAD/UNDP, *Creative Economies Report 2008*, p. 203.

6   Ibid.

7   Ian Collinson, '"Dis is England's New Voice": Anger, Activism and the Asian Dub Foundation' in Gerry Bloustien, Margaret Peters and Susan Luckman (eds), *Sonic Synergies: Music, Technology Community and Identity* (Aldershot, 2008), pp. 105–14.

8   Julian Henriques, 'The Jamaican Dancehall Sound System as a Commercial and Social Apparatus' in Bloustien, Peters and Luckman, *Sonic Synergies*, pp. 125–40.

Music in the New Global Economy: Defining Creativity

So what exactly is the creative knowledge economy and why does it affect contemporary music production, consumption and distribution so profoundly? It is a very different type of economic and political context, which has been recognized and described initially as 'the knowledge economy',[9] 'the networked society',[10] and then variously as 'the cultural economy',[11] 'the creative economy'[12] and 'the creative knowledge economy'.[13] It can be understood as a kind of material and virtual marketplace – a vehicle for the ways in which ideas are generated and disseminated at the level of formal and informal corporate and private industries, not-for-profit and non-government organizations and government-run and funded bodies. It is also the means through which new ways of knowing and acting upon knowledge, aesthetics and affect are generated and consolidated, where risk-taking, new enterprises and intangible assets evolve and are established.[14] While clearly stemming from economic discourse, the term 'creative knowledge economy' extends our understanding of the creative industries into everyday potentially acts, performances and artefacts that can attract copyright and licensing – and therefore it is a particularly pertinent context for the development of new forms of music. This is an economy where capitalism is being transformed to a system from an 'older corporate centred system defined by large companies to a more people driven one'.[15]

Although there is no simple definition of creativity, it has been argued that it involves artistic, scientific and economic processes and that all of these involve technological creativity. Creativity, knowledge and access to information are thus increasingly understood as the central catalysts behind economic growth and development in a globalizing world: The UN *Creative Economies Report*, outlined above, brought together the perspectives of five relevant organizations: the United Nations Conference on Trade and Development (UNCTAD), the United Nations Development Programme (UNDP), the United Nations Educational, Scientific and Cultural Organization (UNESCO), the World Intellectual Property Organization (WIPO) and the International Trade Centre (ITC). Its findings argued that, while

---

9   Peter Drucker, *The Age of Discontinuity: Guidelines to Our Changing Society* (New York, 1969).

10   Manuel Castells, *End of Millennium: Information Age, Economy, Society and Culture*, Vol. 3 (Oxford, 2nd edn 2000).

11   Paul Du Gay and Michael Pryke (eds), *Cultural Economy: Cultural Analysis and Commercial Life* (London, 2002).

12   John Howkins, *The Creative Economy: How People Make Money from Ideas* (London, 2001); Terry Flew, 'Creative Economy' in John Hartley (ed.), *Creative Industries* (Oxford, 2005), pp. 344–60.

13   Bloustien, Peters and Luckman, *Sonic Synergies*.

14   Flew, 'Creative Economy'.

15   Richard L. Florida, *The Rise of the Creative Class: And How It's Transforming Work, Leisure, Community and Everyday Life* (New York, 2002), p. 6, cited in Flew, 'Creative Economy', p. 345.

every culture has a rich, sometimes untapped, resource of creativity 'associated with originality, imagination, inspiration, ingenuity and inventiveness',[16] there is a now a growing awareness that these aspects of cultural capital can also be the drivers of economic growth. In developing countries an understanding of the ways in which the creative industries can underpin economic growth and a developing creative economy is more recent, however. Initiatives such as a symposium held in Nagaur, India in 2005, organized by UNESCO, stressed the importance of local artistic and cultural activity for economic empowerment and the alleviation of poverty, recognizing 'that creativity and human talent, more than traditional production factors such as labour and capital, are fast becoming powerful engines of sustainable development'.[17]

In other words, the creative industries are now acknowledged as the drivers behind the process of creation, production and dissemination of goods and services that use intellectual and creative capital as their primary input. They require the convergence of traditional industrial output and service-oriented industries and so include, and frequently foreground, music in festivals, folk art, books, exhibitions, performing arts, as well as industries requiring more technological input – such as the film industry, radio, television, mobile technologies broadcasting, digital animation and video games. Such developments indicate a broader shift in economic activity 'from goods to services, from producers to consumers'.[18] Analyses of the ways in which cultural products such as music are being affected by new economic developments described above, now tend to refer to 'value chains'[19] in order not only to understand the steps in the creative process, but also to understand more clearly the role that creativity plays in innovation and enterprise development.[20] The term 'value chain' describes the ways in which products gain symbolic and economic value as they pass along all the processes from creation to consumption, producing a final artefact that is greater than the sum of its parts and also clearly indicating that previous romantic notions of 'the concentration on individual talent and the separation of innovation from the processes that precede and follow it, are what creativity is not'.[21]

Such a focus stresses the importance of the structure of the production processes for creative goods and services which, in the case of the music industry, means both individual musicians and large transnational record companies. Yet, if we look even more closely, we can now see the importance of small and medium-sized enterprises (SMEs), including the not-for-profit sector,[22] in the creative knowledge

---

16 UNCTAD/UNDP, *Creative Economies Report 2008*, p. 3.
17 Ibid., p. 8.
18 Hartley, *Creative Industries*, p. 20.
19 See Michael E. Porter, *Competitive Advantage* (New York, 1985); and 'What is Strategy?', *Harvard Business Review* (November/December 1996): 61–78.
20 Chris Bilton, *Management and Creativity: From Creative Industries to Creative Management* (Malden, MA, 2007).
21 Ibid., p. 11.
22 Gerry Bloustien, 'Up the Down Staircase: Grassroots Entrepreneurship in Young People's Music Practices' in Bloustien, Peters and Luckman, *Sonic Synergies*, pp. 195–

economy – enterprises that are particularly relevant in many developing countries. In many cases these enterprises offer the best opportunities for new musicians to gain access to resources to develop their skills and achieve some form of economic revenue. Indeed, many argue that the SMEs have become 'the cornerstone of locally based strategies for sustainable development of the creative industries, enhancing the economic, cultural and social life of the community'.[23]

These aspects point, as the two extracts that head this chapter suggest, to both a sense of euphoria and excitement, but simultaneously to tensions and disruptions – opportunities for greater creativity and innovation perhaps, but also ongoing concerns about copyright, licensing and intellectual property,[24] including new concerns and debates about who is controlling or gatekeeping the production and dissemination of the globally disseminated cultural and entertainment industries.[25] Such thinking forms the basis for the kind of British initiatives as the Music Manifesto, launched in 2004,[26], Young Enterprise Quickstart Music[27], and the new free online resource, Sound Rights, for educators and young people wanting to know more about song creation, copyright and the music business.[28] It is clearly a time not only of limitless possibilities and new opportunities, but also of new anxieties and uncertainties about exploitation.

As Luckman points out, for many young musicians hoping to capitalize on their talent, most will find themselves 'negotiating a complex new workplace environment and its problematic refashioning not only of the producer–consumer, but also of the work–life, divide'.[29] A growing critique argues that, in the new-economy cultural industries, such as music, 'precarious labour' is 'underpinned … by the self-taught, modders and unpaid'.[30] Leadbeater was one of the first to note that, despite his enthusiasm for the new creative economy, such a precarious economic context, would not benefit everyone and that 'advances in knowledge

210; Margaret Peters, 'Risky Economies: Community-Based Organizations and the Music-Making Practices of Marginalized Youth' in Bloustien, Peters and Luckman, *Sonic Synergies*, pp. 161–84.

23   UNCTAD/UNDP, *Creative Economies Report 2008*, p. 204.

24   Fiona Macmillan (ed.), *New Directions in Copyright Law*, Vol. 6 (Cheltenham, 2007); Danny Butt and Axel Bruns, 'Digital Rights Management and Music in Australasia', *Media & Arts Law Review* 10/4 (2005): 265–78; Axel Bruns, 'Futures for Webcasting: Regulatory Approaches in Australia and the US' in Bloustien, Peters and Luckman, *Sonic Synergies*, pp. 17–26.

25   Richard E. Caves, *Creative Industries: Contracts Between Art and Commerce* (Cambridge, MA, 2000); Bilton, *Management and Creativity*; Bruns, 'Futures for Webcasting'.

26   <http://www.musicmanifesto.co.uk.

27   <http://www.young-enterprise.org.uk/qsmusic/home/htm>.

28   <http://www.soundrights.org.uk>.

29   Susan Luckman, '"Unalienated Labour" and Creative Industries: Situating Micro-Entrepreneurial Dance Music Subcultures in the New Economy' in Bloustien, Peters and Luckman, *Sonic Synergies*, pp. 185–94, at p. 191.

30   Ibid.

improve our lives but only at the cost of creating uncertainties, risks and dilemmas'.[31] The structural limitations of race, class, ethnicity and gender mean that some young people are able to develop their dreams and ambitions far more than others; invisible boundaries prevent many from being able to formulate such dreams in the first place.[32] Other critiques of the new creative knowledge economy[33] focus on its tendency to replace one form of marginalization with another, making the individual who 'opted for this kind of unstable career choice'[34] more vulnerable and open to exploitation for 'maybe there can be no workplace politics when there is no workplace, i.e. where work is multi-sited'.[35]

So the creation, consumption and distribution of music in the new global economy is quite a different beast from what it was just 20 years ago. With their focus particularly on the growing significance of the creative, entertainment and service industries, accounts and analyses of such an economic and political system point to at least four interrelated phenomena that have changed the ways in which businesses and organizations operate:

- Markets and products have focused on the global rather than the local, and yet, at the same time, the smaller, micro-businesses or smaller medium-sized enterprises have become key players in the realization of creative enterprises.
- Production depends on information, communication skills and creativity rather than on more traditional forms of knowledge, with nearly 80 per cent of the workforce in all developed countries now engaged in service, rather than industrial, industries.
- Geographic distance is largely irrelevant as the Internet brings people and their networks easily together – although how the local and the global interrelate in this new marketplace is far from simple and will be discussed in more detail below.
- Creative practices interweave and converge as, for example, the ways in which music and music-related activities now demonstrably and overtly

---

31 Charles Leadbeater, *Living on Thin Air: The New Economy* (London, 1999), p. 123.
32 Gerry Bloustien, *Girl Making: A Cross-Cultural Ethnography on the Processes of Growing Up Female* (Oxford, 2003); Lawrence Grossberg, *Caught in the Crossfire: Kids, Politics and America's Future* (Boulder, CO, 2005).
33 Angela McRobbie, *In the Culture Society* (London, 1999); 'Clubs to Companies: Notes of the Decline of Political Culture in Speeded up Creative Worlds', *Cultural Studies* 16/4 (2002): 516–31; 'From Holloway to Hollywood: Happiness at Work in the new Cultural Economy?' in Du Gay and Pryke, *Cultural Economy*, pp. 97–114; Charles Leadbeater and Kate Oakley, *The Independents: Britain's New Cultural Entrepreneurs* (London, 1999); Toby Miller, 'A View from a Fossil: The New Economy, Creativity and Consumption – Two or Three Things I Don't Believe In', *International Journal of Cultural Studies* 7/1 (2004): 55–65.
34 McRobbie, 'Clubs to Companies', p. 521.
35 Ibid., p. 522.

thread through and underpin fashion, games, film, television production and new mobile media technologies.

The creation and consumption context is also one where the products themselves now become less important than the experience and the ways in which the products can be linked to ongoing services or other experiences – that is, their 'symbolic values' are more important than their material qualities.[36] Chris Bilton and Ruth Leary summarize the importance of symbolic values and the ways in which these become integrated into the products themselves:

> 'Creative industries' produce 'symbolic goods' (ideas, experiences, images) where value is primarily dependent upon the play of symbolic meanings. Their value is dependent upon the end user (viewer, audience, reader, consumer) decoding and finding value within these meanings ; the value of 'symbolic goods' is therefore dependent upon the user's perception as much as on the creation of original content, and that value may or may not translate into a financial return.[37]

Perhaps even more importantly for the focus of this chapter, music itself has clearly become more overtly fundamental in the value chain of the ever-increasing 'culturalization of economic life',[38] for its production is now even more easily occurring at the grassroots – highlighting the blurring of production and consumption, creator and consumer, aesthetics and affect.

So where does this leave music now, intricately entwined, as it is, in the heart of new creative industries and the knowledge economy? Many would argue that music underpins the formation of new business ventures in the creative industries where 'personal and consumer tastes have led to new publics'.[39] The concept of sonic synergy[40] becomes particularly useful here as the ways in which music interacts with and on other cultural forces, particularly technology, identity and community – all catalysts of change within the new creative knowledge economy – together create an entity that is bigger than the sum of the parts.

To understand the particular significance of synergy, creativity and innovation, following this broad overview of the creative knowledge economy, it is valuable to consider some recent research and specific case studies. I now focus on three aspects of this economic, political and cultural climate that have particularly impacted on

---

36 J. Rifkin, *The Age of Access: How the Shift from Ownership to Access is Transforming Economic Life* (London, 2000).

37 Chris Bilton and Ruth Leary, 'What Can Managers do for Creativity? Brokering Creativity in the Creative Industries', *International Journal of Cultural Policy* 8/1 (2002), p. 50, cited in Flew, 'Creative Economy', p. 345. See also John Allen, 'Symbolic Economies: The "Culturalization" of Economic Knowledge' in Du Gay and Pryke, *Cultural Economy*, pp. 39–58.

38 Scott Lash and John Urry, *Economies of Signs and Space* (London, 1994).

39 Hartley, *Creative Industries*, p. 108.

40 Bloustien, *et al.*, *Sonic Synergies*.

the way in which contemporary music is produced, consumed and disseminated: first, the kinds of places and spaces that enable creative and innovative music practices to occur and flourish; second, by examining what Hartley calls 'creative identities',[41] I consider how new forms of subjectivity emerge in this climate where human imagination, experience, creative labour and consumption underpin the creative knowledge economy and new forms of music-related creative enterprises. Third, I explore how this relates to innovative forms of creative practice, including new concepts of citizenship and social entrepreneurship.[42] First, then, I take a closer look at the specific physical and geographic climates in which contemporary music develops and flourishes.

Music without Borders? Rejuvenating the Local in a Global Context

> Economic globalization, the rise of the knowledge-based economy, and the rapid growth of the internet have, perhaps paradoxically, placed a renewed focus upon why geographically mobile capital and skilled workers choose to locate in some cities and regions in preference to others.[43]

Place has always been an important factor in the ways in which music is created, consumed and marketed.[44] In recent years, however, with the globalization of music and the development of new forms of communication technologies which might suggest that geographical distance is largely irrelevant in the 'weightless economy',[45] a new paradox has arisen. A complex interaction between the global and the local has become increasingly highlighted so that, far from the local music industry and local identities being eroded or disappearing in the global marketplace, the dynamic between the global and local flows of information, products, trade and culture have arguably become more complex, reaffirming old meanings while simultaneously

---

41   Hartley, *Creative Industries*, p. 106.

42   Charles Leadbeater, *The Rise of the Social Entrepreneur* (London, 1996); Joanna Mauir, Jeffrey Robinson and Kai Hockerts, *Social Entrepreneurship* (London, 2006).

43   Terry Flew, 'Music, Cities and Cultural and Creative Industries Policy' in Bloustien, Peters and Luckman, *Sonic Synergies*, pp. 7–16, at p. 7.

44   Sara Cohen, *Rock Culture in Liverpool: Popular Music in the Making* (Oxford, 1991); Martin Stokes, *Ethnicity, Identity and Music: The Musical Construction of Place* (Oxford, 1994); Andy Bennett, 'Music, Media and Urban Mythscapes: A Study of Canterbury Sound', *Media, Culture and Society*, 24/1 (2002): 107–20; Andy Bennett, 'Popular Music, Media and the Narrativisation of Place' in Bloustien, Peters and Luckman, *Sonic Synergies*, 69–78; Peter Dunbar-Hall and Christopher Gibson, *Deadly Sounds, Deadly Places: Contemporary Music in Australia* (Sydney, 2004).

45   Diane Coyle, *The Weightless World: Thriving in a Digital Age* (London, 1999).

creating new connotations and transforming local spaces.[46] In this context, cities all over the world have become catalysts and signifiers of innovation – urban sites where changes in social, economic and cultural processes can be mapped and observed. Indeed, recent research by cultural geographers, cultural studies scholars and ethnomusicologists suggest that there is no support for the 'popular argument that geography, or specifically place and distance no longer matters'.[47] Such work has examined the role of social networks,[48] the concept and development of creative cities or hubs,[49] creative clusters and networks.[50] The concept of creative clusters or cultural 'hot spots' which has been realized in many cities around the world is one where the old infrastructures created during industrialization have been deliberately rejuvenated for the redevelopment of industry and business enterprises through culture. Charles Landry, the founder of Comedia, Europe's leading cultural planning organization, describes the importance of a successful creative milieu in such cities. Such a context for innovation, he argues, needs to combine what he calls 'hard infrastructure' (the network of facilities, buildings, transport, institutions and communications structures) with 'soft infrastructure' (social networks, human resources and interactions).[51] Such thinking has been behind the development of British 'music cities' such as Liverpool, Glasgow and London, and particular areas in cities such as the Cultural Industries Quarter (CIQ) in Sheffield and the Northern Quarter (NQ) in Manchester.[52] It lay behind Tony Blair's somewhat less successful 'Cool Britannia' campaign.[53] It also underpins recent attempts to enhance and market the music industries of Austin (Texas), Chicago and such urban sites elsewhere, such as Brisbane in Australia.[54]

---

46 Stokes, *Ethnicity, Identity and Music*; Dunbar-Hall and Gibson, *Deadly Sounds, Deadly Places*; Jinna Tay, 'Creative Cities' in Hartley, *Creative Industries* (Oxford, 2005), pp. 220–32.

47 Andy C. Pratt, 'New Media, the New Economy and New Spaces', *Geoforum* 31 (2000): 425.

48 Ibid.

49 Leadbeater and Oakley, *The Independents*; Adam Brown, Justin O'Connor and Sara Cohen, 'Local Music Policies within a Global Music Industry: Cultural Quarters in Manchester and Sheffield', *Geoforum* 31/4 (2000): 437–51; Charles Landry, 'London as a Creative City', paper presented at Cultures of World Cities Central Policy Unit, Hong Kong, 31 July 2001; Flew, 'Creative Economy'; Flew, 'Music, Cities and Cultural and Creative Industries Policy'.

50 Michael E. Porter, 'Location, Competition and Economic Development: Local Clusters in a Global Economy', *Economic Development Quarterly* 14/1 (2000): 15–34.

51 Charles Landry, *The Creative City: A Toolkit for Urban Innovators* (London, 2000); Landry, 'London as a Creative City'.

52 Brown *et al.*, 'Local Music Policies'.

53 Angela McRobbie, 'Fashion as a Cultural Industry' in S. Bruzzi and P.C. Gibson (eds), *Fashion Cultures: Theories, Explorations and Analysis* (London, 2000), pp. 253–63; Nityanand Deckha, 'The Cool Britannia Effect and the Emergence of the Creative Quarter', *M/C: A Journal of Media and Culture* 5/2 (2002), at: <http://www.media-culture.org.au/0205/britspace.php> (accessed 20 August 2008).

54 Stephen Cox, Abraham Ninan, Greg Hearn, Simon Roodhouse and Stuart Cunningham,

On a more micro level, many writers, such as Keith Kahn-Harris[55] and Ian Maxwell[56] draw on their own ethnographic music research to critique studies of what they see as the 'strangely disembodied concept'[57] that decontextualizes music from its local source of production.[58] They emphasize the need for a more nuanced look at the significance of specific places in the creation of contemporary music. So, for example, Ian Maxwell draws on his work with the contemporary hip-hop band in Sydney, Def Wish Cast, to argue that while place names are used to 'brand' musical products, to identify and market styles of music in this way, as described above, 'as markers of distinction for the user',[59] it is also important to recognize the significance of place in contemporary popular music as the 'the social imaginary'. This is, Maxwell argues, the embodied realization of sound 'a place unified in – resounding in – rather than simply represented by, the music'.[60]

The examples described above both in their macro- and micro-analyses particularly highlight the importance of the 'night-time economy'[61] to the economic and cultural sustainability of new musics. This is the reorganization of city centres around consumption rather than production – night-clubs, dance clubs, music festivals, live performances – with a greater awareness that 'this invitation to transgression, marginal to the Fordist city of work, is now central to contemporary consumerism'.[62]

Queensland Music Industry Basics: People, Businesses and Markets (Brisbane, 2004); Ian Rogers, Abraham Ninan, Greg Hearn, Stuart Cunningham and Susan Luckman, *Queensland Music Industry Value Web: From the Margins to the Mainstream* (Brisbane, 2004); Flew, 'Music, Cities and Cultural and Creative Industries Policy'.

55 Keith Kahn-Harris, '"Roots"? The Relationship Between the Global and the Local within the Global Extreme Metal Scene', *Popular Music* 19/1 (2000): 13–30 – also in A. Bennett, B. Shank and J. Toynbee (eds), *The Popular Music Studies Reader* (London, 2006), pp. 128–36; and '"I Hate This Fucking Country": Dealing with the Global and the Local in the Israeli Extreme Metal Scene', *Critical Studies 19: Music, Popular Culture, Identities* (2002): 133–51..

56 Ian Maxwell, *'Phat Beats, Dope Rhymes': Hip Hop Down Under Comin' Upper* (Indianapolis, 2003); and 'There's No There There' in Bloustien, Peters and Luckman, *Sonic Synergies*, pp. 79–90.

57 Maxwell, 'There's No There There', p. 89.

58 Andre Pinard and Sean Jacobs, 'Building a Virtual Diaspora: Hip Hop in Cyberspace' in Ayers, *Cybersounds*, pp. 83–106.

59 Maxwell, 'There's No There There', p. 83.

60 Ibid., p. 89.

61 Franco Bianchini, 'Night Cultures, Night Economies', *Planning Practice and Research* 10/2 (1995): 121–6; Alan Lovatt and Justin O'Conner, 'Cities and the Night-Time Economy', *Planning Practice and Research* 10/2 (1995): 127–33; Hartley, *Creative Industries*; Flew, 'Creative Economy'; Flew, Music, Cities and Cultural and Creative Industries Policy'.

62 Lovatt and O'Connor, 'Cities and the Night-Time Economy', p. 133.

Music and New Technologies: Place, Space and Embodiment

Related to the complex concepts of space and place is the development of new media technologies for production, consumption and dissemination of new musics. For, if music is concerned with the boundaries of the local, material body in particular geographical locales, it is, of course, also concerned with the mobile, moving 'out of body' to blur historical and geographical boundaries. Because music is able to transcend the local to be in several places at the same time, simultaneously transforming physical and social space, it becomes a way of appropriating and distinguishing space. On another level, it explains the ubiquitous popularity of radios, the walkman and personal radio, tape and CD players in contemporary life.[63] As each new technology develops, new ways of creating, consuming and marketing music produce marked effects on the meanings understood to emanate from all of its forms. In turn, this results in new ways of recognizing a particular style and its attendant cultural forms and meanings.

The advent of electronic media and new technologies has other implications, too. It affects what is understood as the perceived 'authenticity' of the performer and consumer of that music. It means that the performance and consumption of music can be undertaken far from the original place of origin and endlessly repeated. As Jody Berland reminds us, '[m]usic is now heard mainly in technologically communicated form, not live, and its circulation through these spaces (in connection with that of its listeners), along with its assimilation to and appropriation of previous contexts for musical performance, is part of the elaboration of its forms and meanings'.[64] Music, in other words, has become completely mobile not only moving with us from room to room, country to country, and from work to leisure, but also moving us emotionally, as from depression to elation. In these ways, contemporary practices of engaging with music particularly through new technologies, through ever-evolving 'mimetic machinery',[65] can blur our sense of time and space.

However, as these cultural contexts have become even more complex with the advent of new ways of performing, producing and listening to music, the very categories of 'producer' and 'consumer' are collapsing in on one another as digital content travels rapidly around the globe.[66] New technologies, for example, have

---

63   Shuhei Hosokawa, 'The Walkman Effect', *Popular Music* 4 (1984): 165–80; Shuhei Hosokawa and Hideaki Matsuoka, 'On the Fetish Character of Sound and the Progression of Technology: Theorising Japanese Audiophiles' in Bloustien, Peters and Luckman, *Sonic Synergies*, pp. 39–50; Sarah Thornton, *Club Cultures: Music, Media and Subcultural Capital* (Cambridge, 1995).

64   Jody Berland, 'Angels Dancing: Cultural Technologies and the Production of Space' in Lawrence Grossberg, Carey Nelson and Paula Treicher (eds), *Cultural Studies* (New York, 1992), pp. 38–50, at p. 39; and Berland, 'Postmusics' in Bloustien, Peters and Luckman, *Sonic Synergies*, pp. 27–38.

65   Michael Taussig, *Mimesis and Alterity: A Particular History of the Senses* (New York, 1993), p. 20.

66   Bloustien, 'Up the Down Staircase'; Flew, 'Creative Economy'; Flew, 'Music, Cities and Cultural and Creative Industries Policy'.

brought about particular changes in the way we engage with music. The music we hear is affected by the choices we make on the turntable, the dial, the mixer. In the dance clubs and rave scenes, the DJ and MC who skilfully mix and sample the prerecorded sounds to create new music have become revered artists since the 1990s. Just as the advent of the VCR affected television watching, so, too, have the CD players and burners, the walkman, MP3 players, iPods and now the computer terminals affected music audiences. Consumers can now produce, rearrange and re-create the kind of music they listen to. The lines between consumption and production, between the original and the copy, become blurred.[67] In other words, like those ephemeral self-identities that we struggle to 'fix', music itself has become a process of becoming, something we now experience as fragmented and unstable.[68] MP3 devices mean the end of the set order list of the album; each user becomes more and more his/her own DJ, customizing aural space and experience. Driven from the grassroots upwards, the culture of file-sharing has emerged out of the shadows of underground or bedroom knowledge and expertise and into the mainstream of global music distribution.[69] Although initially slow to respond and distrustful of the market demand for MP3 music downloads, the major record labels have been forced to accept that they need to fundamentally reconfigure their preferred business models in order to keep pace with the future of music consumption technologies. This is especially so as mobile MP3 devices are emerging as a powerful force as part of convergent technologies, especially those embedded in mobile telephones:

> As MP3 technology becomes embedded in all sorts of consumer items, it remains to be seen how long this market leadership will continue and what may emerge to take its place as the music accessory de jure.[70]

Feel the Vibe: Experience, Symbolic Capital and Creative Practices

The technological, together with the interrelated cultural and economic, change in the creative knowledge economy is having a profound effect on individuals and

---

67   Elizabeth A. Buchanan, 'Deafening Silence: Music and the Emerging Climate of Access and Use' in Ayers, *Cybersounds*, pp. 9–20.

68   Shuhei Hosokawa, *The Aesthetics of Recorded Sound* (Tokyo, 1990); Berland, 'Angels Dancing'; Berland, 'Postmusics'.

69   See Andrew Whelan, 'Do U Produce? Subcultural Capital and Amateur Musicianship in Peer to Peer Networks', in Ayers, *Cybersounds*, pp. 57–82.

70   Gerry Bloustien, Susan Luckman and Margaret Peters, '"Be not Afeard; the Isle is full of Noises": Reflections on the Synergies of Music in the Creative Knowledge Economy' in Bloustien, Peters and Luckman, *Sonic Synergies*, pp. xxi–xxviii, at p. xxvi.

groups, both producers and consumers of music. One of the central paradigms currently at play is that of 'openness' – works are created and organized to offer a multitude of possibilities in performance, interpretation and reception. Brad Haseman particularly notes the application of Umberto Eco's[71] philosophy to so many contemporary cultural products where 'their internal mobility of form sets up the possibility of a dialog [sic] or interaction between author, performer and audience'.[72] Such a concept seems particularly apt for considering the changes in the music industry, in the innovative forms of production and content of new digital musical forms, with their flow of sampling and peer-to-peer networking. John Hartley calls this kind of process 'redaction'[73] a kind of playful restructuring whereby the editing process of creativity – a reclaiming and re-forming from diverse sources and contexts – becomes all-important across the whole spectrum of cultural forms, but perhaps particularly music. Such a process expands the possibilities of meaning and interpretation 'through the use of fragmentation, appropriation and intertextuality'.[74] My own research found many examples of such redactive creativity in Australia, Europe, Britain and the USA,[75] as many young and gifted performers, DJs, rappers and break-dancers sought, selected, adapted, rearranged, remixed and created new pieces of music for their own purposes.

It is a framework that is also particularly apt for consideration of collaborative production, file-sharing and what Ayers describes as 'bedroom' or '(cyber)activism' – a context 'where politics, creativity and Internet technology meet and create highly visible grassroots campaign'.[76] Elsewhere, I have discussed the ways in which the young people in my own research used their virtual networks and their music to advocate for particular causes. Using their music lyrics, event publicity and website forums as vehicles of protest, the young people often raise social issues including racism, poverty, corporate greed, homelessness and ecology. Alicia (aged 24), the co-founder of an Australian event management organization Patterns in Static[77] is campaigning against the incorporation of local music by the professional music industry. She wages her battles under the umbrella of an organization called 'Really Good in Theory'. The 'homemade' press release is headed:

---

71   Umberto Eco, *The Open Work* [1962], trans. Anna Cancogni (London, 1989).
72   Brad Haseman, 'Creative Practices' in Hartley, *Creative Industries*, p. 162.
73   John Hartley, 'Communicative Democracy in a Redactional Society: The Future of Journalism Studies', *Journalism* 1/1 (2000): 39–47.
74   Haseman, 'Creative Practices', p. 165.
75   Gerry Bloustien, '"Wigging People Out": Youth Music Practice and Mediated Communities', *Journal of Community & Applied Social Psychology* 17 (2007): 446–62; Bloustien, 'Up the Down Staircase'.
76   Michael D. Ayers, 'The Cyberactivism of a Dangermouse' in Ayers, *Cybersounds*, p. 128.
77   Previously at <http://www.patternsinstatic.net.au>, now Alicia's website is to be found at <http://www.patternsinstatic.com> and at <http://www.aviatorlane.com.au>.

ADELAIDE MUSIC UNITED AGAINST PROFESSIONALISM

What's really good in theory? – a chance to celebrate and unite Adelaide's rock 'n' roll cottage industrialists … What's really good in theory is a corner shop for the local music neighbourhood, where everyone knows everyone, you look after each other's kids, and nah, we cannot sell you the ice-cream scoop, but you can borrow it for the weekend. It is that kind of spirit – spiked with the necessary rock 'n' roll bravado and art school affectation. That is really good in theory.[78]

Similarly, DJ Shep (aged 28) and his crew, also in Australia, are passionate about the role of hip hop and rap in providing a voice for young people at risk. He is not only a well-known Adelaide DJ, rapper and inline skater in the hip-hop scene, but is increasingly becoming known as a young entrepreneur through his integrated media business, Da Klinic,[79] consisting of a retail outlet, skills workshops and an event management business. It is also, as indicated above, concerned with social justice and helping others in his community and beyond:

We do everything from jails, kids in lock ups to regional schools, kids who obviously aren't in lock up. We do different programs, same programs we do with the kids in schools are the same as we do in jail. We teach them how to rap – so they might write lyrics. We teach them how to breakdance. We teach them how to Graph. We teach them how to DJ. So for us they're just the names of the things that we do but to break it down – DJing is music Breakdancing is a form of dance rapping is poetry and Graffiti art is Art.[80]

Shep's comments also point to another aspect of contemporary music in the global economy – the centrality of the experiential activities and their relationship to new forms of subjectivity. What this means is that, again, the role of the experience, as part of both production and consumption, is far more important in the creative knowledge economy than the material products created. Florida pointed this out, arguing that 'the Creative Class lifestyle comes down to a passionate quest of experience … a creative life packed full of intense, high quality, multidimensional experiences'.[81]

---

78   See <http://www.junkcentral.com> for more information about RGIT and other related projects.
79   <http://www.daklinic.com>.
80   A. Shepherd, interview on *Australia Wide*, ABC 2, 2 May 2006. Available at: <http://www.abc.net.au/tv/australiawide/stories/s1628585.htm> (accessed 12 November 2006). Information also acquired through many personal conversations.
81   Florida, *The Rise of the Creative Class*, p. 166.

Music and Creative Identities

The creative lifestyle – the creation and consumption of experiences – is thus central not only to engagement with music in the global marketplace, but also to the ways in which individuals and groups perceive their way of being in the world, where personal and consumer tastes have led to new publics',[82] new forms of democracy and new social movements 'using the very formats of consumer commercialism to critique the political philosophies that underpin them'.[83] Leadbeater noted that in the creative economy the consumer no longer receives knowledge, but shares in its production:

> *In a knowledge-driven economy, consuming will become more a relationship than an act; trade will be more like a replication than exchange; consumption will often involve reproduction, with the consumer as the last worker on the production line; exchange will involve money, but knowledge and information will flow both ways as well.*[84]

Is this too celebratory a vision of the new creative economy? Many would argue that it is, but anyone working with young people, particularly those involved in music, hears the same arguments and claims on a daily basis. DJ Shep, introduced briefly above, echoed these positive sentiments to me just recently. He works around the clock to maintain his vision of a hip-hop scene that allows him not only to do the things that he loves and earn a living through his networks, his technical know-how, his music and related business, and his imagination, but also to help others by, for example, running workshops for Aboriginal youths in custody.[85] 'Today young people can do anything', he stated with his customary excitement as he told me about his latest ventures and ideas. 'You just have to want to do it and be prepared to try.'[86]

Conclusion: Music, Citizenship Creative Identities

While the central role of creativity and innovation within the new economy has been recognized as its most valued currency, empirical and ethnographic accounts of the nature of that creativity, particularly in terms of everyday experience of music-making and consumption are still emerging in academic literature. The post-industrial, increasingly globalized system of wealth production depends on

---

82   Hartley, *Creative Industries*, p. 108.
83   Ibid., p. 109.
84   Leadbeater, *Living on Thin Air*, p. 30.
85   See Bloustien, 'Wigging People Out'; Bloustien, 'Up the Down Staircase'; and <http://www.daklinic.com>.
86   Personal conversation with the author, 24 August 2008.

complex, often informal networks within which music-related artefacts are inspired, produced, circulated and consumed. Within such a dynamic environment, small-scale local production takes on a new importance, often leading to the development of fresh initiatives by the young, working by necessity from the margins of their societies. On these margins, with their blurring of production and consumption, as noted above, problems arise over issues of ownership of copyright and intellectual property – increasingly in developing countries[87] and in indigenous and diasporic ethnic communities around the globe. As Andreas Rahmatian points out in his discussion of the protection of traditional cultural expression in both non-Western and European traditional music and copyright:

> One should not forget that, for example, the seemingly simple and ordinary art category of 'music' does not exist as such in sub-Saharan African musical cultures the rough equivalents of music are complex performance phenomena, which westerners would describe as a music/dance/movement combination (for example in Kiswahili named 'ngoma') but also as a celebration, feast, theatre (play) song and the like.[88]

On the positive side, the types of initiatives mentioned above in turn generate and reimagine new communities of practice that tap into broader international networks. In so doing, such do-it-yourself creativity lies at the forefront of creative industries' discourses about innovation, but therefore also points to some of the tensions implicit in 'top-down' approaches to innovation as they intersect with grassroots synergies of production and consumption. In attempting to mobilize cultural production as a cornerstone of the twenty-first-century creative knowledge economy, issues of respecting the place of creativity and the conditions of its production come to the fore. For example, as Sheila Whiteley argues in a discussion of young people and their music practices and performances, shifting commercial and policy environments impact on how individual producers themselves can be exploited and abused – especially in the case of very young performers.[89] Similarly, we need to protect the sustainability of local cultures in a globalized creative marketplace – for example, by ensuring access to affordable rental premises while simultaneously encouraging critical mass and the synergistic development of creative clusters. In encouraging potential economic 'winners' in the evolving music industries, care needs to be taken to ensure that the 'second tier' (grassroots or more informal parts of the cultural industries) continues to have space to grow and

---

87 See Bruns, 'Futures for Webcasting'; Joseph Savirimuthu, 'P2P @software(e).com: Or the art of Cyberspace 3.0.' in Macmillan, *New Directions in Copyright Law*, Vol. 6, pp. 247–78.

88 Andreas Rahmatian, 'Universal Norms for a Globalised Diversity: On the Protection of Traditional Cultural Expressions', in Macmillan, *New Directions in Copyright Law*, Vol. 6, p. 200.

89 Sheila Whiteley, 'Use, Misuse and Abuse: Problems Surrounding Popular Music and its Young Performers' in Bloustien, Peters and Luckman, *Sonic Synergies*, pp. 145–56.

innovate. It is an exciting time – a time that is impacting on our very perceptions of reality and self and on the ways in which we shape and create new forms of culture through and in diverse forms of musical expression.

The Transnational Music Industry

Andreas Gebesmair

Introduction

During the twentieth century the culture and media industries became a dominant force in modern life. In providing information and entertainment they not only fulfil important functions for democracies, but also regulate access to the global diversity of cultural expressions. With an annual turnover of some US$ 100 billion dollars, the business contributes substantially to what was called the global informational economy.[1] Certainly, the music industry is only one of the smaller sectors of the culture and media business. Nevertheless, it shows the same characteristics:[2] the largest share of revenues is gained by a handful of corporations, which are often part of huge media conglomerates with subsidiaries all over the world.

Central to all cultural industries are those technologies which allow the big corporations to target a mass market: audio recordings can be duplicated as often as one wants for almost no cost, broadcasting and satellite technologies enable radio and TV stations to reach large portions of the population, and via the Internet even small producers can address a global audience. Thus far, the history of the music industry can be told as a history of its core technologies. Certainly, the nineteenth century's dance halls, pleasure gardens and music halls offered popular music for profit wherever industrialization brought an audience of sufficient size to the thriving towns, and even a kind of transnational distribution occurred some years before the first record was made when European musicians like Henry Russell, Joseph Gung'l, and the younger Johann Strauss toured the United States.[3] But it was

---

1   Manuel Castells, *The Rise of the Network Society* (Malden, MA, 1996).
2   For a good overview of cultural industries in general see, for instance, David Hesmondhalgh, *The Cultural Industries* (London, 2002); Peter S. Grant and Chris Wood, *Blockbusters and Trade Wars: Popular Culture in a Globalized World* (Vancouver, 2004); and Daya Kishan Thussu, *International Communication: Continuity and Change.* (London, 2nd edn 2006).
3   Cf. Andrew Lamb and Charles Hamm, 'Popular Music' in Sadie Stanley (ed.), *The Grove*

not before 1877 when Thomas A. Edison applied for a patent on his phonograph that a technological basis for industrial mass production was available.[4] Edison himself marketed his invention as a 'Talking Machine' employable in modern bureaucracies since its sound qualities were too poor for recording music. But, after some technological improvements, the recording industry began to prosper. The most decisive improvement was that of Emile Berliner, who replaced Edison's cylinder with a disc whose grooves were not engraved during the recording process but reproduced from a zinc master. This technology allowed the production and distribution of recordings on a huge scale and proved to be a veritable goldmine. Only in the 1920s and 1930s when radio stations worldwide began to broadcast music did the recording industry face a serious decline in revenue. After the Second World War it recovered quickly, and selling music on discs became the core business of the music industry until the advent of the Internet in the 1990s.

Interestingly, the main features of the music industry were already fully developed in the first decades of the twentieth century: the market was dominated by a small number of so-called major labels which ran subsidiaries in almost all parts of the world and which were integrated step by step into larger conglomerates embracing a broad range of commercial activities within and beyond the culture and media industries. An important prerequisite of commercial success was a legal framework that vested in artists and record producers the right to profit from their productions. Artists and especially publishers were already protected by copyright long before the rise of the recording industries, but regulations had to be adapted to the emerging technologies during the twentieth century. The whole system of copyright protection was recently challenged by the advent of new digital devices for copying discs and the possibility of sharing music files with others via the Internet, which led some people to question copyright legislation altogether.[5] The problem of how to protect music in a digital environment may be controversial; nevertheless, a strong legal framework was crucial to the development of an industry which basically rested on the exploitation of rights.

The four main characteristics of the music industry, its dependence on copyright regulations – the high concentration of markets, the vertical integration of firms and their transnationalization – will be discussed in greater detail in the second part of this chapter. As we will see, there are also forces which counterbalance these general tendencies.

Dictionary of Music and Musicians (London, 1980), pp. 87–121.

4   The early history of the phonographic industry is described in Roland Gelatt, *The Fabulous Phonograph 1877–1977* (New York, 2nd edn 1977); Oliver Read and Walter L. Welch, *From Tin Foil to Stereo: Evolution of the Phonograph* (Indianapolis, IN, 2nd edn 1976); Russell Sanjek and David Sanjek, *Pennies from Heaven: The American Popular Music Business in the Twenties Century* (New York, 1996); and Pekka Gronow and Ilpo Saunio, *An International History of the Recording Industry* (London, 1998).

5   Cf. Joost Smiers, 'The Abolition of Copyright: Better for Artists, Third World Countries and the Public Domain', *Gazette* 62 (2000): 379–406.

In the first part I will touch on four theoretical positions which deal with the music industry from four different perspectives.[6] These approaches derive from different social science traditions and they differ not only in their theoretical foundation, but also in their methodologies. However, we have to take into account that these theoretical positions are not as clear-cut as the following overview suggests. Some writers take up insights and methods from different traditions that cannot easily be assigned to just one of these approaches. Furthermore, most of them were not applied mainly to the music industry but to the culture and media industries in general. Therefore, some references have to be made to other areas of the industrial production of culture.

Understanding the Music Industry: Four Approaches

Marxist Traditions

Among the first in the academic world to deal with the culture industries were sociologists and philosophers from, and associated with, the Frankfurt School. Although some, such as Walter Benjamin, regarded the new production technologies as revolutionary, since they, in his view, undermined the bourgeois forms of art perception, most of them criticized the new industrial sectors and their products for perpetuating existing inequalities and the system of capitalistic exploitation. This kind of critique reached its classical form when Max Horkheimer and Theodor W. Adorno published their *Dialektik der Aufklärung* in 1944 during their exile years in the United States.[7] They coined the term 'culture industry' for these new industrial forms of entertainment and elaborated on their critique which regarded its products as mass deception. Some thoughts had already been developed in earlier articles by Adorno, who was mostly interested in music. For instance, in his radio lecture 'On Popular Music'[8] he describes the high degree of standardization in popular music as a strategy of the industry to increase the potential market. In order to satisfy as many listeners as possible, producers aim at the lowest common denominator. At the same time, the competing suppliers try to distinguish their products by offering special features and superficial effects. In Adorno's view, the

---

6   For an overview of theories see also Roy Shuker, *Understanding Popular Music* (London and New York, 1994); and David Hesmondhalgh and Keith Negus (eds), *Popular Music Studies* (London, 2002).

7   Max Horkheimer, Theodor W. Adorno and Gunzelin Schmid Noerr, *Dialectic of Enlightenment: Philosophical Fragments, Cultural Memory in the Present* (Stanford, CA, 2002).

8   Theodor W. Adorno, 'On Popular Music' in Theodor W Adorno., *Essays on Music; Selected, with Introduction, Commentary, and Notes by Richard Leppert; New Translations by Susan H. Gillespie* (Berkeley, CA, 2002), pp. 437–69.

customers of the music industries pay more and more attention to characteristics of the music that fulfil merely marketing functions. Borrowing from Marx, he called this 'commodity fetishism'.[9] But how does this depreciation of musical forms contribute to the stabilization of capitalism?

Adorno's and Horkheimer's theoretical position is often misunderstood as a critique of the industry's manipulative power. But they do not accuse the industry mainly of spreading 'false consciousness', but rather of providing a kind of pleasure that makes people feel reconciled with the world. We cannot fully understand this argument unless we take into account the tremendously pessimistic assessment of history which both intellectuals presented in their *Dialektik der Aufklärung*. In their view, a human being obtained his/her autonomy only at the cost of oppressing the inner and outer nature. Therefore the process of enlightenment is permanently threatening to turn into tyranny. The atrocities of the Nazi regime proved to be a final confirmation of this verdict. Against this background all the colourful promises made by the culture industries have to be regarded as mass deception.[10]

Contrary to the opinion of many of Adorno's critics, he does not simply offer classical music as an escape from this process. Certainly he believes that we could catch a glimpse of a better life from its finest examples and contrasts them with popular music which, from his perspective, lacks this potential. But he regards the live performance of bourgeois music, with all its opera stars and celebrity conductors, as affected in similar ways by the logic of the culture industries. Only the most advanced musical works may resist the process of commodification and hence retain their utopian character.

In the 1960s and 1970s Marxist theoreticians, as well as political activists, took up some of these ideas, but shifted their focus from matters of musical form and reception to the economic structures of the industry. Early adherents of the so-called cultural imperialism thesis as Herbert I. Schiller and Armand Mattelart provided critical analyses of single-media products and denounced the global spread of consumerism.[11] But these questions were increasingly neglected for the benefit of a thorough analysis of corporate power. The discussion about global inequalities in the production and distribution of culture and information was fuelled when the first commercially run information satellite was put into operation in 1965, and less developed countries feared the weakening of their national communication policies. UNESCO, especially, became the battleground for the debate on the New World Information and Communication Order, as it was called then.

---

9   Theodor W Adorno, 'On the Fetish-Character in Music and the Regression of Listening' in Adorno, *Essays on Music*, pp. 288–317.

10   The alleged subversive politics of pleasure, which later generations of cultural theoreticians referred to, appear from this perspective as an even more perfidious means of oppression.

11   Herbert I. Schiller, *Mass Communications and American Empire* (Boston, MA, 1969); Armand Mattelart, *Multinational Corporations and the Control of Culture: The Ideological Apparatuses of Imperialism* (Brighton, 1979).

Radical political economists of both sides of the Atlantic[12] remain in a Marxist framework of analysis insofar as they try to show how large corporations utilize their media platforms, as well as direct connections to national elites, in order to guarantee a political and legal environment which serves their interest. This holds true also for those authors who apply this kind of criticism to the music industry: in their classical study from 1977 Steve Chapple and Reebee Garofalo provided a detailed description of the gradual integration of music production into larger and larger conglomerates as well as its interconnection with the military complex and the political elites of the United States.[13] Furthermore, they feared, in the course of this process, a loss of rock music's critical potential, although they conceded that in the 1960s and 1970s this very industry contributed substantially to the diffusion of a liberal and even leftist world-view worldwide. It is this kind of contradiction within the industry that has led many music industry researchers to abandon an orthodox Marxist stance.

Production-of-Culture Perspective

The production-of-culture perspective differs from the Marxist tradition insofar as corporate interests are only seen as one among many forces within the production system. While Marxists exclusively focus on the effects of an economic basis on a so-called superstructure, representatives of the production-of-culture perspective look also at technology, law, organizational structure, markets or occupational roles as independent factors of cultural production.[14] In addition, they not only provide case studies or illustrative examples to support their arguments, but strive to systematically test their hypotheses. In an article from 1975 Richard A. Peterson and David G. Berger, for instance, challenged Joseph Schumpeter's assumption that large corporations have more potential and incentives to innovate than small companies.[15] Using data from singles hit-parades over several decades, they could show that innovation, and hence musical diversity was highest, when more and

---

12   Herbert I. Schiller, Noam Chomsky, Robert McChesney, Edward Herman in the USA, the Chilean-Belgian Armand Mattelart, Bernard Miège in France, Dieter Prokop in Germany, Nicolas Garnham, James Curran, Peter Golding and Graham Murdock in the UK, to name just a few.

13   Steve Chapple and Reebee Garofalo, *Rock 'n' Roll is Here to Pay: The History and Politics of the Music Industry* (Chicago, 1977).

14   The production-of-culture perspective should not be regarded as an academic tradition in its own right. Rather, it summarizes some tendencies of cultural sociology in the USA of the 1970s and 1980s. Richard A. Peterson, who coined the term, identified several constraints of production processes that can be studied in different cultural fields. See Richard A. Peterson, 'Five Constraints on the Production of Culture: Law, Technology, Market, Organizational Structure and Occupational Careers', *Journal of Popular Culture* 16 (1982): 143–53.

15   Richard A. Peterson and David G. Berger, 'Cycles in Symbol Production: The Case of Popular Music', *American Sociological Review* 40 (1975): 158–73.

more small independent labels entered the record market during the 1950s. This process was supported by changes in the industrial environment as, for example, the authorization of local radio stations which depended mostly on recorded music in contrast to the large networks.

In an earlier paper Peterson and Berger applied some concepts from organization theory to the music industry.[16] They asked how organizations change with their environment. Contemporary theories expected that, the less predictable demand is, the more organizations tend to form semi-autonomous departments which can flexible adapt to changes. When competition increased in the 1950s major labels began to hire artist and repertoire managers who had much more autonomy than people in marketing departments, but could be quickly laid off.

Organization theory generally proved to be extremely stimulating for the production-of-culture perspective. Paul Hirsch explained how cultural production firms cope with uncertainties by maintaining close relationships with people from the media and the press. Lopes described major labels as open systems which are able to quickly integrate new musical styles. And, in a recent contribution, Anand and Peterson took up the concept of organizational sense-making to show how methods of processing sales data change the perception of markets within an industry.[17]

Another testimony of what a sociological approach can contribute to the understanding of industrial production of music is Simon Frith's detailed analysis of rock music.[18] The British researcher describes the different roles within the industry and how they interact in the process of music production and marketing. Frith's work is usually not subsumed under the production-of-culture category, and its scope is much broader than the studies of his US-American counterparts. Nevertheless, he takes up many ideas from his US-American predecessors who are equally sceptical of simplistic Marxist critiques of culture industries.

Neoclassical Economics

Sociological approaches are sometimes accused of lacking a theoretical foundation that enables the researcher to explain why effects occur under certain circumstances.

---

16 Richard A. Peterson and David G. Berger, 'Entrepreneurship in Organizations: Evidence from the Popular Music Industry', *Administrative Science Quarterly* 16 (1971): 158–73.

17 Paul M. Hirsch, 'Processing Fads and Fashions: An Organization-Set Analysis of Cultural Industry Systems', *American Journal of Sociology* 77 (1972): 639–59; Paul D. Lopes, 'Innovation and Diversity in the Popular Music Industry 1969 to 1990', *American Sociological Review* 57 (1992): 56–71; N. Anand and Richard A. Peterson, 'When Market Information Constitutes Field: Sensemaking of Markets in the Commercial Music Industry', *Organization Science* 11 (2000): 270–84. See also Timothy J. Dowd, 'Concentration and Diversity Revisited: Production Logics and the U.S. Mainstream Recording Market, 1940–1990', *Social Forces* 82 (2004): 1411–55.

18 Simon Frith, *Sound Effects: Youth, Leisure, and the Politics of Rock 'n' Roll* (New York, 1981).

Musical diversity, for instance, is said to depend on technological change, market form, organizational structure and so on, but it is not always clear why these factors have specific consequences. Economists give an easy all-embracing answer to this question: these factors change the cost and incentive structure of musical production. And since people in a market scrutinize costs in order to maximize their profit, affordable technologies provide small competitive producers with a strong incentive to target small innovative niches. Conversely, large corporations in an oligopolistic market with just four or five suppliers gain a maximum return when selling as many copies as possible of one record. Although these explanations have to be refined with additional suppositions, in their basic form they show how neoclassical economists approach the music industry: all phenomena have to be attributed to utility-maximizing market participants who weigh benefits against costs and invest as long as there is a marginal profit.

Until the 1980s popular music was a neglected area of research for neoclassical economists. In the 1960s the performing arts and its cost problems were analysed with tools from economics, and the effects of concentration of the media attracted the attention of neoclassical economists a decade later.[19] But it was not until 1987 that a highly formalized model was developed that explained diversity and innovation in the popular music industry from an economic perspective.[20] Interestingly, the authors confirmed their theory mostly with data provided by Peterson and Berger more than ten years before. New empirical evidence was offered by Peter J. Alexander who measured diversity by analysing the musical structure of some 100 hit singles between 1955 and 1988.[21] The more the pieces deviated from a standard form of popular music the more they contributed, in his opinion, to musical diversity. However one assesses the validity of this measure, the results are surprising, since, in contrast to sociological as well as economic models, diversity in the music industry seems to suffer not only from high concentration, but also from fierce competition. Diversity is greatest in phases of moderate media concentration.

A similar phenomenon was recently detected in the broadcasting industry.[22] Using airplay charts from format radio channels in the USA, Steven T. Berry and Joel Waldfogel could show that, in larger markets, format diversity even increased after radio stations had merged into larger corporations. They argued that large radio conglomerates differentiate their channels in order to prevent in-firm competition,

19   William J. Baumol and William G. Bowen, *Performing Arts, the Economic Dilemma: A Study of Problems Common to Theater, Opera, Music, and Dance* (New York, 1966); Michael Spence and Bruce Owen, 'Television Programming, Monopolistic Competition, and Welfare', *The Quarterly Journal of Economics* 91 (1977): 103–26.

20   Michael Black and Douglas Greer, 'Concentration and Non-Price Competition in the Recording Industry', *Review of Industrial Organization* 3 (1987): 13–37.

21   Peter J. Alexander, 'Product Variety and Market Structure: A New Measure and a Simple Test', *Journal of Economic Behavior & Organization* 32 (1997): 207–14.

22   Steven T. Berry and Joel Waldfogel, 'Do Mergers Increase Product Variety? Evidence from Radio Broadcasting', *Quarterly Journal of Economics* (2001): 1009–24.

whereas small competitors tend to concentrate on the mainstream in search for the largest market share.

Many students of popular music feel uncomfortable with economic analyses of the music industries. Indeed, measurements of diversity do not meet the criteria of contemporary popular music analysis. Furthermore, sociologists claim that people do not always behave as rationally as economists believe. Nevertheless, neoclassical economics brought more clarity to questions raised by sociologists and contributed substantially to debates about an appropriate regulation of cultural markets.

Cultural Studies of the Music Industry

People may strive to maximize their utility, but equally important to the understanding of social processes is the meaning they ascribe to their activities. Cultural studies from diverse origins have focused on popular music from this perspective for decades. Surprisingly, the industrial production of popular music was neglected by representatives of these approaches for a long time. Most of them concentrated on musical texts and their reception.[23] British Cultural Studies (usually capitalized to stand out against other cultural traditions) provided careful semiotic analysis of cultural products and detailed ethnographies of subcultures but hesitated to apply their analytical instruments to the production side of the cultural market. It wasn't until the 1990s that researchers in this vein developed a more inclusive understanding of the culture industries. The Sony Walkman served Paul du Gay and his colleagues as an example to illustrate how meanings circulate between different spheres of society through a circuit of culture.[24] Using a wide range of different materials the study group traces how Sony constructed specific images of its product and how these images are integrated in lifestyles by the customers. In one chapter they explicitly turned their attention to the corporation itself, which presents its history as a kind of epic with an almost mystical founding personality. But, despite the abundance of surprising insights, the study remains at the surface of cultural production processes.

A much more down-to-earth account of corporate culture is given by Keith Negus, who is interested not only in the self-presentation of firms, but also in everyday practices of those working within big corporations.[25] Comparing rap, country and world music departments of major labels he describes which criteria managers in the industry use to assess popular music and how they reconcile diverging demands during the working process. The departments differ considerably from each other

---

23 Questions of musical style and identity as well as amateur music production are certainly related to the music industry but excluded from this chapter, since they are discussed thoroughly in other contributions to this *Companion*. I focus solely on music production in an industrial environment.

24 Paul du Gay, Stuart Hall, Linda Janes, Hugh Mackay and Keith Negus, *Doing Cultural Studies: The Story of the Sony Walkman* (London, 1997).

25 Keith Negus, *Music Genres and Corporate Cultures* (London, 1999).

and develop individual strategies to cope with the peculiarities of their clientele. Negus calls corporate culture a myth which disguises existing inequalities between the actors within the industry and the hard facts of the market.

The study of inequalities is a principal cultural approach to the music industries. While Marxists concentrate on class relationships, younger representatives of British Cultural Studies draw attention to gender and race inequalities.[26] Questions of gender are a recurrent theme in Angela McRobbie's analyses of different culture industries, and race and cultural production is repeatedly discussed by Paul Gilroy,[27] but both are much more interested in products than in industrial production processes.

Beyond British Cultural Studies there are several researchers from different traditions who deal with the cultural dimension of production systems. They all have in common an interest in everyday practices in the music industry and how those are interpreted by the actors. Hence they prefer qualitative methodologies to statistical data analysis. Edward R. Kealy, who is usually subsumed under the production-of-culture category, analyses the symbolic interactions between those present in studios during recording sessions. He argues that musical recordings are the result of negotiations between at least three types of actors: producers, sound engineers and artists. In a similar way the French sociologist Antoine Hennion portrays producers as intermediaries who represent the world outside the industry during production processes. In a recent contribution Jarl A. Ahlkvist built a typology of different programming philosophies in the radio industry, which differ in the degree of commitment to different stakeholders in the industry. He shows under which industrial conditions these philosophies are most likely to flourish.[28]

All of these studies prove that cultural studies of the music industry provide valuable insights into production processes and that qualitative methods can be rewardingly applied to the prosaic world of business. Nevertheless, the studies are often accused of lacking theoretical persuasiveness and methodological precision. Interview material is often presented without looking at people's hidden motives and at external forces which constrain our practices in a way we do not fully understand without some reflexive distance.

---

26   This view is of course a simplification of research realities. Chapple and Garofalo also touched on the situation of women and African-Americans in the music industry and the founding fathers of British Cultural Studies were deeply rooted in Marxism and interested in class analysis. But in recent years interest in economic classes has receded in favour of a more general theory of exclusion.

27   For example, Angela McRobbie, *In the Culture Society: Art, Fashion, and Popular Music* (London, 1999); and Paul Gilroy, *The Black Atlantic: Modernity and Double Consciousness* (Cambridge, MA, 1993).

28   Edward R. Kealy, 'Conventions and the Production of the Popular Music Aesthetic', *Journal of Popular Culture* 16 (1982): 100–15; Antoine Hennion, 'An Intermediary between Production and Consumption: The Producer of Popular Music', *Science, Technology, & Human Values* 14 (1989): 400–24; and Jarl A. Ahlkvist, 'Programming Philosophies and the Rationalization of Music Radio', *Media, Culture and Society* 23 (2001): 339–58.

Structural Features of the Music Industry: Four Characteristics[29]

Market Concentration

All profit-oriented organizations strive to expand their market share, and industries where companies take advantage of so-called economies of scale tend to be highly concentrated. This holds true also for the transnational music industry. Almost all national markets except for some Asian countries are dominated by the big four: Universal, Sony BMG, EMI and Warner. They share about 80 per cent of the global market with recorded music. Radio and TV markets show similar degrees of concentration, although in many countries the corporate power is balanced by public broadcasting which is committed not just to profit, but also to public values.

As we have seen in the first part of this chapter, the effects of concentration and corporate power on innovation, diversity, critical content and the working conditions of artists are hotly debated in music industry research. Recent contributions have revealed that concentration does not always reduce diversity and innovation and it is not always size that suppresses critical voices.[30] In addition, entry barriers to production are low and the Internet opens up new opportunities for global distribution.[31] Therefore, at the fringes of the music market there are thousands of small entrepreneurs who offer an unprecedented diversity of music, although not all can make a living from it. Admittedly, big money is still made with a handful of superstars distributed mainly by the four major labels.

All these companies look back to turbulent histories which partly reach back to the first half of the twentieth century. Sony, a subsidiary of the Japanese electronic giant, and BMG, part of the German Bertelsmann conglomerate, which now form a

---

29 There are many practical guides to the music business that also introduce its structural features. Among the more academic depictions the following are recommended: R. Serge Denisoff and William L. Schurk, *Tarnished Gold: The Record Industry Revisited* (New Brunswick, NJ, 1986); Keith Negus, *Producing Pop: Culture and Conflict in the Popular Music Industry* (London, 1992); Michael Fink, *Inside the Music Industry: Creativity, Process, and Business* (New York, 1996), Robert Burnett, *The Global Jukebox. The International Music Industry* (London, 1996); Geoffrey Hull, *The Recording Industry* (Boston, MA, 1998); and Andreas Gebesmair, *Die Fabrikation globaler Vielfalt. Struktur und Logik der transnationalen Popmusikindustrie* (Bielefeld, 2008). Data and statistics are available from the International Federation of the Phonographic Industry (< http://www.ifpi.org >) which publishes an annual report titled *Recording Industry in Numbers*.

30 Lopes, 'Innovation and Diversity'; Berry and Waldfogel, 'Do Mergers Increase Product Variety?'; Gabriel Rossman, 'Elites, Masses, and Media Blacklists: The Dixie Chicks Controversy', *Social Forces* 83 (2004): 61–78.

31 Some observers of contemporary developments even predict a sharp increase of diversity due to technological innovations; cf. Chris Anderson, *The Long Tail: Why the Future of Business is Selling Less of More* (New York, 2006).

joint venture, became global players when they acquired the US labels CBS and RCA respectively in the 1980s. Those shaped the history of popular music production in the USA as well as abroad for decades and were led to success by large radio networks of the 1920s. EMI was created in 1931 as a result of a merger between the UK's Gramophone Company and the Columbia Graphophone Company. In the second half of the twentieth century it gradually expanded its interests and became, not least with The Beatles' recordings, one of the big players in the music markets. Warner is the youngest of the four major labels and came into existence when the big Hollywood Studio began to invest in music in the 1950s. It, too, pursued an aggressive acquisition policy in the following years.

The major labels and their precursors dominated the market for almost the whole history of the music industry, and they still do. But the market itself is shrinking. The graph in Fig. 25.1 shows sales of recordings from 1991 to 2004 in the top five markets of Europe. All countries have faced a serious decline since the end of the millennium. Although some markets are slightly recovering, and digital music sales are becoming a lucrative alternative (now representing about 15 per cent of the global music market), the dramatic loss in revenues led to cutbacks in corporations all over the world.

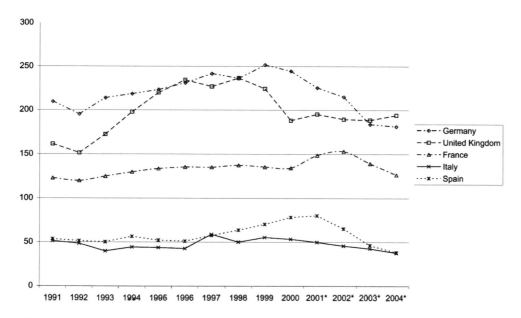

Figure 25.1 Sales of recordings, including DVDs and videos, in the top five European markets in million units. Source: IFPI (2005).

Industry representatives usually attribute the decline to peer-to-peer file-sharing via the Internet, private copying and commercial piracy. In addition, the music industry faces increasing competition from other branches of the entertainment industry like the video and game business, which cater to similar customers. Critics often point to the fact that the CD market came up against natural limits since eventually most people replaced their vinyl collections with CDs. Furthermore, they accuse the industry of lacking attractive repertoire that could be sold globally.

Music business futurists like David Kusek and Gerd Leonhard predict that records and, to a certain degree, old media like radio and music TV will soon be replaced by new forms of music distribution and marketing.[32] Digital downloads, webcasting, satellite radio and cell phones are gaining territory and provide a sound basis for commercial interests. Whatever tomorrow's music business may look like, high marketing expenses and economies of scale will favour big companies. Hence we can expect high concentration, although large electronics, software or telecommunication firms may dominate the future music market instead of the existing major labels.

Vertical Integration

Nevertheless, the future industry has to fulfil two core functions which have been central to the music business for more than a century. On the input side personnel are needed to select from the myriad musicians, bands, songs and productions those that have the potential of being successful in certain markets. Record labels employ artist and repertoire managers (A&Rs) who entertain a tight network of contacts to local or national music scenes. They function not only as talent scouts, but also try to develop, together with marketing specialists, a whole trademark out of an artist. At best, A&Rs reconcile the aesthetic intentions of musicians with the demands and constraints of the commercial world. On the output side, promotion and marketing people struggle to get the artist known to potential buyers. Whereas in the traditional music industry radio and music TV played a central role in breaking new artists and new releases, the Internet offers new ways of promotion and direct marketing. Besides, music is increasingly marketed in combination with other media products like movies or computer games and consumer goods. Commercials became a tempting source of revenue which even artists of high integrity like Leslie Feist cannot resist.

The relationship between record labels, on the one hand, and the media, on the other hand, is of special interest to music industry researchers. Hirsch has pointed out different legal and illegal strategies to persuade media gatekeepers to promote one's own productions.[33] An efficient way of securing access to promotion and distribution channels is to integrate several stages of the production and distribution chain into one corporate framework. Economists call this kind of merger vertical integration. The music joint venture Sony BMG is connected through its corporate mothers not only to music publishers, CD manufactures and online shops, but also to radio and TV channels (RTL), Sony Pictures and the computer games business

---

32   David Kusek, Gerd Leonhard and Susan Gedutis Lindsay, *The Future of Music: Manifesto for the Digital Music Revolution* (Boston, MA, 2005).
33   Hirsch, 'Processing Fads and Fashions'.

(Playstation). The efficiency of vertical integration is often questioned by economists not least because anti-trust authorities try to prevent corporations from excluding smaller competitors. Obviously vertical integration serves more as a means to spread risk on as many different economic sectors as possible than to control all stages of the value chain.

Indeed, researchers have also observed a tendency to vertical disintegration in the culture industries since the 1950s.[34] Flexible specialization, as this trend was called, occurred not just in the music industry. The big Hollywood studios which, in their classical era, afforded a huge staff embracing scriptwriters as well as lighting technicians began to buy services from small specialized firms in the Los Angeles area. Now teams are formed for each production, although their composition does not change completely every time. A vertically disintegrated studio can react flexibly to changes of technology, movie formats and demand. The same is true for the music industries where independent music producers took on tasks formerly carried out by major labels themselves. Thus, we face two opposite trends in the history of the music industry: while major labels often became integrated into big media corporations, they themselves disintegrate production.

Globalization

Edison's phonograph and Berliner's gramophone changed the way music was experienced completely. It was the first time in history that music could be separated from the time and location of performance. Hence a tendency to leave its local context is inherent to all forms of mechanical reproduction. It is supported by economic considerations since distributing cylinders or discs is much cheaper than touring with a live band, and, where production costs are high compared to the costs of making a copy, people have an additional incentive to expand their market. From its beginning the music industry contributed enormously to the globalization of music. Opera singers like Enrico Caruso can even be regarded as the first global superstars, highly esteemed among those middle-class listeners around the world who could afford the new technology.

But there is also a countertendency in global music production: the very technology which enables companies to spread music all over the world reinforces local music production. In search for repertoire which could be added to the Gramophone catalogue, the early 'talent scouts' Fred and Will Gaisberg travelled around Europe and Asia and recorded local singers and musicians. Around 1910 the Victor Talking Machine Company ran agencies in all Latin American countries as well as in China, Japan and the Philippines. Local recordings were duplicated

---

34   Michael Storper, 'The Transition to Flexible Specialisation in the US Film Industry: External Economies, the Division of Labour, and the Crossing of Industrial Divides', *Cambridge Journal of Economics* 13 (1989): 273–305. David Hesmondhalgh, 'Flexibility, Post-Fordism and the Music Industries', *Media, Culture and Society* 18 (1996): 469–88.

centrally in large manufactures in the USA, Europe or India and redistributed to local markets.[35]

Another period of regionalization of production was triggered by the advent of the tape recorder as a cheap alternative to manufacturing discs in the 1960s. All over the world regional entrepreneurs began to market local repertoire for less affluent parts of the population.[36] In many countries new commercialized versions of local musical traditions were created, which proved to be extremely popular among the non-elite classes. Even in Austria a boom of so called *volkstümliche Musik* was set off, which rested solely on sales of cassettes in the beginning.

Radio, in its early years, was inherently a national medium. Due to the scarcity of frequencies and political considerations, in most countries highly regulated organizations were obliged to serve the national interest. Nevertheless, challenged by US-American military channels and commercial pirates, after the Second World War, public radio in Europe, as well as in other parts of the world, began to broadcast international pop music especially from the USA and later from the UK. With The Beatles and their followers, the 1960s witnessed the first global invasion by international superstars. They created a new musical language which was appreciated by young listeners everywhere. But, simultaneously, local popular music production began to flourish. Inspired by the global superstars, thousands of young people formed bands and created music which sometimes took up even local musical traditions. The sociologist Roland Robertson uses the term 'glocalization' to express the dialectic of globalization and localization.[37] He argues that globalization is actually a prerequisite of localization. It provides the tools to reformulate local experiences and traditions in a modern language which raises the awareness of distinctiveness. So-called musical hybrids which amalgamate global popular genres with local forms became a lucrative global market in itself when middle-class listeners, especially in Europe, got tired of international pop music and looked for musical inspiration at the margins.[38]

Nevertheless, we must not deny the fact that the major labels make the most money with their international superstars. So, how can we summarize the results of a critical assessment of globalization in the music industry?[39]

First, globalization does not necessarily mean Americanization. There are almost as many global acts from the UK as from the USA. Also, some smaller countries

---

35   Gronow and Saunio, *An International History*, pp. 11–31; Pekka Gronow, 'The Record Industry: The Growth of a Mass Medium', *Popular Music* 3 (1983): 53–75..

36   Roger Wallis and Krister Malm, *Big Sounds from Small Peoples: The Music Industry in Small Countries* (London, 1984), Peter Manuel, *Cassette Culture. Popular Music and Technology in North India* (Chicago, 1993).

37   Roland Robertson, 'Glocalization: Time-Space and Homogeneity-Heterogeneity', in Mike Featherstone, Scott Lash and Roland Robertson (eds), *Global Modernities* (London, 1995), pp. 25–44.

38   Timothy D. Taylor, *Global Pop: World Music, World Markets* (New York, 1997), Andreas Gebesmair and Alfred Smudits (eds), *Global Repertoires: Popular Music within and Beyond the Transnational Music Industry* (Aldershot, 2001).

39   Cf. Gebesmair, *Die Fabrikation globaler Vielfalt*.

like Canada, Australia, Sweden and Denmark have contributed substantially to global pop music. Second, peaks of high global homogenization are superseded by periods of strong regional production. The British invasion in the 1960s, the disco craze in the 1970s and the video superstars of the 1980s can be regarded as global phenomena. In between there was room for regional music production. Third, there are regions which resist global pop better than others, although within these regions there may be considerable exchange of repertoire between countries. South-east Asia, the Arabic world and Latin America form strong regional markets with a high degree of regional repertoire. Fourth, a high share of domestic repertoire does not necessarily mean diversity. From a local point of view, international repertoire can also balance the domination of regional music. Furthermore, regional or national markets show sometimes a high degree of concentration on local superstars at the expense of a more diverse local and global music production. Finally, specialized music production in niches itself becomes affected by globalization processes. Since the advent of the Internet, producers of music specialities can easily reach a global audience and thus enlarge their market.

All in all, we face a paradoxical situation: while mainstream markets show a substantial degree of regional differentiation, people have access to the same niche products all over the world. To put it bluntly, you can listen to Senegalese Mbalax in every small British village as well as in Buenos Aires or Seoul. But hit radio programming in the UK has little to do with that in Argentina and Korea.

Copyright

Copyright regulations are essential to the music market. Only when artists and producers are vested with the exclusive right to broadcast, duplicate and distribute their productions can they profit from an industrial reproduction of music. There are some exceptions to this right, such as fair-use rules that allow the use of music for some non-profit purposes and compulsory licences which are provided for a fee to everybody who applies for them. But, in general, broadcasting, copying and distributing music without permission from the copyright holders is prohibited.[40] Equally important are those societies which help copyright holders to assert their rights in every country of the world, to license use and collect fees. Usually there are separate societies for performing and broadcasting rights (as, for instance, ASCAP or PRS) and the right to mechanical reproduction (Harry Fox Agency, MCPS). In addition, publishers often represent the interest of artists and earn a considerable share of the licence fees. Hence, the publishing arms of major labels acquired, throughout the history of popular music, huge catalogues of protected songs which provide them an extra profit.

Copyright regimes basically do not favour established artists and producers over newcomers or the less popular. But in practice there are substantial inequalities in asserting one's claims. Roger Wallis and Krister Malm cite the example of the

---

40 I do not touch on performing since basically it is pre-industrial.

song 'Malaika', which was covered by dozens of artists from Harry Belafonte to Boney M. Most likely it was written by the Kenyan musician Fadhili William who never received a cent of licensing fees. Instead, almost every time it was recorded, another person claimed authorship.[41]

Nevertheless, collecting societies serve the interest of artists and usually provide a minimum compensation even for artists who have not signed with a major publisher. Furthermore, in many European countries a part of fees on blank discs and digital storage systems is used for social security and innovative productions. Unfortunately, this system of redistribution is increasingly threatened by corporate interests.[42] Since many licence agreements between artists and producers are reached within a corporate structure, the major publishers owned by the big four record companies regard collecting societies as inefficient and try to circumvent them. A loss of power of these societies has consequences for less established copyright holders who cannot afford lawyers to assert their rights.

While major labels and their publishing arms try to monopolize rights management, they themselves are threatened by piracy. For years they have been lamenting serious losses from illegal counterfeiting of their products. In its last piracy report the IFPI estimated that the trade of pirate discs was worth US$ 4.5 billion globally in 2005.[43] In some countries piracy even seems to exceed the legitimate market, although these figures are not easily to verify. Interestingly, especially in those countries which are most seriously affected by piracy, artists also see the positive aspects of illegal distribution. The Indian singer Pamela Singh points to the publicity effects of piracy:

> *Piracy has its advantages and disadvantages for the artist. The advantage is that you can reach more people. The disadvantage is that the quality is not good; people who have not really heard you [i.e. in person] might think that your quality is substandard. But really, the cassettes only help you get more concerts. They give you more popularity, but in terms of money, I don't think anyone makes recordings with the royalties in mind, because it's very hard to keep track of sales. But you can't have concerts without cassettes, because first people have to know about you.*[44]

There are artists and producers who think that such a phlegmatic view of copyright problems could serve as a model for the digital age. The Internet is regarded as a huge promotional platform where music can be downloaded for free. The future artist will make his living exclusively from live performance.

---

41   Wallis and Malm, *Big Sounds from Small Peoples*, pp. 182–85.
42   Roger Wallis, Charles Baden-Fuller, Martin Kretschmer and George Michael Klimis, 'Contested Collective Administration of Intellectual Property Rights in Music: The Challenge to the Principles of Reciprocity and Solidarity', *European Journal of Communication* 14 (1999): 5–35.
43   See <http://www.ifpi.org>.
44   Manuel, *Cassette Culture*, p. 86.

But this stance seems somehow naïve, since income from live entertainment will never compensate for losses from copyright infringement. Labels, as well as artists, earned substantially from selling discs, and there is no reason to do without this income stream in favour of the electronics industries, Internet service providers or the telecommunication business which depend on artistic content. Therefore we should not play down the piracy problem. Peer-to-peer networks do hurt not just the major industry, but also the small independent producers. And there are opportunities for copyright-holders to recoup their investments even in the Internet age. In contrast to the majors who struggle for an increasingly rigid system of control, which comes up against technological and political limits, music business experts see the future of music in collective and compulsory licensing models.[45] Without going into details, these models focus on flat fees for limited or even unlimited use of music charged to the subscribers' or the Internet service providers' accounts. Collecting societies could play an important role in such a copyright regime.

Conclusion

The transnational music industry is currently undergoing a fundamental change. Discs, the main musical commodity for more than a century, are rapidly vanishing from the scene. At present we cannot predict with certainty which technologies and which business models will replace the existing ones. But it is very likely that the structural features of music production will shape the future music market, too. There are signs of high concentration and vertical integration into media conglomerates as well as flexible specialization and network forms of production on the input side. Technologies will enable music to spread more and more rapidly all over the world and to simultaneously contribute to the awareness of local traditions. And copyright will play a crucial role in defining how money can be earned by artists and producers and how it is distributed among stakeholders.

As we have seen, research traditions provide useful tools for the assessment of these features and their consequences. They not only show how musical innovation and diversity are affected by different structural factors, but also contribute understanding how people in this industry interact, how they cope with uncertainties and constraints, and what meanings they attribute to their doings. All our detailed analyses and studies of single aspects of industrial music production should not blind us to the fact that the music industry is a part of the overall society, for which it serves certain functions. Early critics of the culture industries have insisted on a wider scope of analysis. Future debates will show if their approaches are still worth taking up.

---

45   Kusek, Leonhard and Lindsay, *The Future of Music*, pp. 130–35.

Pop Idol: Global Economy – Local Meanings

Tarja Rautiainen-Keskustalo

One of the most popular talent shows of the early twenty-first century has been the *Pop Idol* TV format. Very different kinds of records have been presented in the context of the show: it has been estimated that it has generated over 3.2 billion viewers over the past six years and broken viewer records everywhere. Moreover, the fourth *American Idol*, for example, was the biggest texting event in the world, with approximately 41 million SMS text messages sent.[1] It is particularly noteworthy that the format has been easily integrated into very different kinds of cultural contexts. Between 2001 and 2008 the format and its spin-offs have been broadcast in over 40 countries. It is almost easier, indeed, to say where the format has not been broadcast; among such countries are Japan and China, for example.

In a way, *Pop Idol* extends the historical continuum of talent shows. However, global cultural production – the new technology and the fact that the music industry is nowadays more and more integrated within the wider entertainment industry – establishes a special framework for this music format. Recent developments in television culture have been especially important. First, so-called 'reality TV' has established structures used by the format. Second, *Pop Idol* is, in many cases, broadcast through national, commercial TV channels having a multinational ownership or through cross-border channels which break the national boundaries.[2] Thus, media transnationalism is the key concept when debating the significance of the format.

In this chapter my aim is, then, twofold. First, I will debate how in *Pop Idol* the elements of talent shows and reality TV are combined with each other and what makes this combination successful. In particular, the emphasis on emotionality and

---

1   Allan F. Moore, 'The Fake Plastic Trees of Reality TV of Participatory Democracy in Close-up?', 1 October 2006, at: <http://smlxtralarge.com/archives/2006_10.php> (accessed 27 April 2008)..

2   Jean K. Chalaby, 'Towards an Understanding of Media Transnationalism' in Jean K. Chalaby (ed.), *Transnational Television Worldwide: Towards a New Media Order* (London, 2005), pp. 1–13.

authenticity during the show, and the focus on the process of becoming a star are discussed. Charles Fairchild defines *Pop Idol* as the construction of a celebrity brand which cannot be understood as a traditional venue for becoming a star, but as 'a series of text and events that exist in parallel to a related series of continuously available sites of consumption'.[3] Fairchild's perspective acts as my starting-point for analysing the characteristics of the format. However, in this chapter I will also highlight how the 'sites of consumption' are constituted in a local cultural context, –that is, how, for example, the notions of stardom, as well as the local history of popular culture and national culture, are articulated in these sites of consumption.

Therefore, my second angle deals with the way in which the format can be understood as a transnational musical phenomenon. As hinted above, the concept of transnationalism highlights the special dynamics between 'local' and 'global' in communication and social practices. Although the role and the efficacy of the boundary politics of nation-states is questioned in various ways in twenty-first-century culture, the idea and significance of national identity has not disappeared. National (local) and global are constantly negotiating with each other. This negotiation can be understood, as formulated by Japanese media researcher Koichi Iwabuchi, as 'interconnections and asymmetries that are promoted by the multidirectional flow of information and images, and by the ongoing cultural mixing and infiltration of these messages'.[4] *Pop Idol*, thus, seems to operate in this kind of mode: on the one hand, it represents global popular music culture, the global economy and media culture, but, on the other, local meanings are constantly connected with it.

The History and Structures of Tested Stardom

Talents shows, such as *Pop Idol*, are not new phenomena in popular music culture. They have been – above all – an essential part of American television culture. In the 1940s, for example, *Original Amateur Hour* and *Arthur Godfrey's Talent Scouts, Doorway to Fame, Paul Whiteman's TV Teen Club* and, in the 1950s, *Lights, Camera, Action* and *Chance of a Lifetime* were popular programmes. Many of them shared similar aspects with *Pop Idol*: a panel evaluated contestants, and viewers could vote for their favourites.

The American show *Making the Band*[5] launched the format which Jake Austen calls reality TV rock 'n' roll.[6] The show was made by the MTV team and was

---

3   Charles Fairchild, 'Building the Authentic Celebrity: The "Idol" Phenomenon in the Attention Economy', *Popular Music and Society* 30/3 (2007): 355–75, at 360.

4   Koichi Iwabuchi, *Recentering Globalization. Popular Culture and Japanese Transnationalism* (Durham, NC, 2002), pp. 16–17.

5   ABC, 2000–2001; MTV 2002.

6   Jake Austen, *TV a-Go-Go: Rock on TV from American Bandstand to American Idol* (Chicago,

based on a similar concept to the boy bands of the 1990s like Backstreet Boys and *NSYNC: stardom was strictly constructed and controlled by the manager. The next innovation was *Popstars*, formed by New Zealander producer Jonathan Dowling. The series first began in New Zealand in 1999 and was later sold to Australia and the UK, after which the format rapidly spread worldwide. *Popstars* was a talent show, where, after filtering out single contestants, boy and girl bands were formed. The programme was a source of inspiration for British manager and producer Simon Fuller, who invented the *Pop Idol* format. It debuted on British television on ITV1 in the autumn of 2001 and was based on the idea of finding a brilliant young star. What distinguishes *Pop Idol* from earlier talent shows is the manner in which the symbolic forms of stardom are produced and the contexts in which they are consumed. While the old American TV shows were 'local', being aimed at American viewers in the first place (although they were also popular elsewhere), *Pop Idol* is, above all, global. The premise is to circulate star images through a wide geographical space. Second, stardom in *Pop Idol* is connected with consumption culture in particular ways, especially via branding, as Fairchild, among others, points out.[7] These characteristics can also be found in *Popstars*, but I argue that in *Pop Idol* they are highlighted in special ways because its focus is on an individual's fame, which seems to speak to audiences in effective ways in the late capitalist age.

The *Pop Idol* format is owned by the international entertainment and drama producer Fremantle Media, and it is managed by 19 Entertainment. The record company, BMG, is closely tied with the format. The word 'pop' is not used in the titles of the spin-offs, because Fremantle Media does not want the format to be mixed with *Popstars*. Therefore, the words 'idol(s)' and 'superstar' are most frequently used in the local versions. The structure of the original format and its spin-offs are quite similar in different countries. The first auditions, which are arranged in local cities and towns, are based on separating 'talented singers' from 'poor singers'. There are also some rules which impose certain limits on the participants: generally the auditionee must be between 18 and 28 years old and he or she must not have an agreement with a publisher, manager or agent. In addition, the auditionees must agree that all material concerning the auditions is the property of the format producers and they have no legal rights to it.[8]

In the first auditions each auditionee must sing one *a capella* selection, which is judged by a jury consisting of three or four members. Very often two of them are men and one is a woman. They represent the music industry in various ways; they are, for example, producers, managers, composers, stylists, radio DJs or journalists. Gender conventions are highlighted in the way in which women most often seem to have the role of 'stylist', whereas men represent more often the 'serious' side of music production. Part of the idea of the format is that the jury does not stay faceless; members of the jury can achieve as much publicity as auditionees, or they

---

2007), p. 227.
7   Fairchild, 'Building the Authentic Celebrity'.
8   Ibid., p. 361.

may already be celebrities in some way. The reputation of the British *Pop Idol* judge, Simon Cowell is a good example of this. It seems to be typical of the format that at least one member of the jury is a formidable, plainspoken 'angry' man.

Emotionality and mockery are emphasized, as is typical of the TV reality show, especially at the beginning of the series. The emotions of the auditionees, the tears of disappointment or success, harsh criticism or praise from the jury are intensified through 'caught-on-tape' footage. Mockery is often presented by introducing the personalities of the contestants with their unrealistic dreams and hopes about success and stardom. After the first auditions the festival-like atmosphere gradually fades away, and the show focuses on the competition between the auditionees. At this point, viewer interactivity becomes a part of the show. In the first auditions the jury makes the decision about who will get through; in the later auditions the audience can vote by telephone, text message or via the official website.

It is difficult to cover the musical features of *Pop Idol* in brief. The primary object of the format is to find a star – musical characteristics in the terms of style and performance can vary greatly. Therefore, the format can be characterized as a cavalcade of different musical styles; typically, the episodes of the show are named as 'Elton John's' songs or 'The '80s hits' and so on. Contestants' ability to interpret different kind of styles is highly appreciated. However, the imitation per se does not guarantee success; on the contrary, the challenge of the format is to produce new, credible and authentic stars who, however, cannot be too original in case they fail to reach a wide audience. Therefore, the concept of mainstream can be connected with *Pop Idol*. However, the mainstream that the format generates is of a special kind: on the one hand, it circulates the most popular styles of Western pop and rock music, but, on the other, it allows, to a certain degree, room for local popular music styles. In this sense it represents the mainstream in the era of global networks.[9]

Pop Idol as a Brand Hybrid

The emergence of the *Pop Idol* format has been interpreted as a sign of crisis in the Western music industry. The music industry has become increasingly dependent on media publicity – the new advertising environment demands new ways of getting publicity – and its autonomy has decreased. The decreasing sale of compact discs as a consequence of Internet downloading has also been cited as a reason for the crisis; some people think the record industry is actually dying.[10]

It cannot be denied that the structures and strategies of the record industry have changed, and one indication of this is the increasing branding – of artist, records

---

9   Jason Toynbee, 'Mainstreaming, from Hegemonic Centres to Global Networks' in David Hesmondhalgh and Keith Negus (eds), *Popular Music Studies* (London, 2002), pp. 157–59.

10 David Kusek and Gerd Leonhard, *The Future of Music. Manifesto for the Digital Music Revolution* (Boston, MA, 2005).

labels and, in the case of *Pop Idol*, even an entire format. I call *Pop Idol* a brand hybrid, by which I mean that a cluster of complementary products and services are connected with it. They, in turn, constitute a meta-market which extends across a diverse set of industries and media, and, thus, are an example of the vertical integration of the music industry.

Complementary products and services constitute different kinds of unities. First, supranational brand names like Ford and Coca-Cola, for example, are integrated in the emotional world of the show in a special way. Coca-Cola plays an essential role in advertisements screened during the show. The brand also arranges a so-called 'red room' during the semi-finals and finals: this is a room where the contestants wait for their turn to perform or to hear their results. Ford, in turn, appears symbolically: a blue, oval sign right by where the performers stand is used in every location where the format is broadcast. Practices of this kind exemplify the product placement: the products are presented as a seamless part of the show. Second, some products have the role of a 'traditional' side-product, such as numerous shirts, fan magazines, ringtones, posters, books, baseball caps, diaries, package tours, computer games and even hair colours and toupees, which are marketed alongside the show. They are often introduced by means of product placement: for example, contestants use the same clothes that are advertised during the show, or the names of certain brands can be seen on signs or balloons among the audience.

Henry Jenkins's concept of the affective economy by can be used to understand this kind of marriage between music and the different kinds of goods.[11] For various business branches it is becoming more and more important to understand the way in which customers enjoy and experience a show, in order to address them when promoting goods. The traditional way of just offering goods is not enough; instead, companies must be able to speak *with* customers, to enter their life-worlds.

Authenticity after MTV

The role of television in popular music has not been sufficiently taken into consideration. As Simon Frith notes, television has been understood as an important medium in star-making and record promotion, but at the same time a television audience is rarely regarded as a music audience, and TV-made stars are often seen to lack musical credibility.[12] On the other hand, for example, the significance of MTV in popular music has been highlighted in the formation of a global pop music culture, but the research carried out by Andrew Goodwin represents one of few studies done in the field.[13]

---

11   Henry Jenkins, *Convergence Culture. Where Old and New Media Collide* (New York, 1992).

12   Simon Frith, 'Look! Hear! The Uneasy relationship of Music and Television', *Popular Music* 21/3 (2002): 277–89.

13   Andrew Goodwin, *Dancing in the Distraction Factory. Music Television and Popular Culture*

The success of the *Pop Idol* format, however, indicates that television truly is an important medium in twenty-first century popular music culture. As such, the format can be seen as a continuum of MTV: if MTV expanded the practices of the music industry by developing the promotion of pop music,[14] in *Pop Idol* the nature of promotion reflects the very complex media setting of the twenty-first century. The special characteristics of reality TV are a part of this setting; this is particularly so in the emphasis on 'real' and 'authentic', which establishes a new kind of framework for promoting music.

As Geoff King notes, impressions of the 'real' or the 'authentic' are valued in contemporary media forms, and often this 'incredible reality' is represented as a form of spectacle.[15] Engagement with the 'real' can be both a quotidian and intensely interpersonal engagement. Mark Andreijevic sees the reason for the boom in reality TV as the decline of symbolic order in Western societies because of urbanization, industrialization and secularization.[16] According to him, this gives rise to a need for individuals to find 'real', authentic experiences. Authenticity does not represent real objectivity, but the emphasis is on subjective identification, the closeness of feeling and sensation. In this light the popularity of the music competition as a reality TV format is not a surprise. Success both in creative work and stardom is associated in Western societies with qualities which are experienced subjectively: reasoned analysis rarely occurs when a person talks about his or her musical taste. In the history of popular music, on the other hand, authenticity refers to the question whether the performer is authentic or, in other words, whether the performer represents authenticity. How can he or she express the emotionality of the music, his or her own feelings, and can he or she do it in a credible way? Thus, the notion of authenticity here is historical and refers to romanticism and romantic notions of art.

Authenticity as a part of the *Pop Idol* spectacle is constructed in the process of 'experiencing the birth and rise of stardom'. This means revealing and narrating the process of becoming a star. The establishment of a legitimate pop star has traditionally been a linear process in popular music that, eventually, becomes reconstructed in biographies and memoirs. In *Pop Idol* the birth of stardom is a range of ups and downs that the contestants experience. (Over)emphasizing the emotions of contestants is an essential part of constructing the authenticity of the format.[17] Here, however, it is important to pay attention to how stardom is perceived and defined in *Pop Idol*. Generally the concept of 'celebrity', rather

---

(London, 1993).

14   Ibid., p. 187.

15   Geoff King, 'Introduction: The Spectacle of the Real' in Geoff King (ed.), *Spectacle of the Real: From Hollywood to Reality TV and Beyond* (Bristol, 2005), p. 13.

16   Mark Andreijevic, *Reality TV. The Work of Being Watched* (Oxford, 2004), p. 207.

17   This is done both by filming the reactions of auditionees at point-black range and also by the specific use of the background music. In the semi-finals of *2004 Pop Idol* in Finland, for example, the clips of weeping and disappointed contestants were put together and soundscaped with songs: Carpenter's 'Rainy Days and Mondays' for the losers and Robbie Williams 'Let Me Entertain You' for the winners.

than 'star', is connected with *Pop Idol* in academic research; 'celebrity' refers to 'light' pop music whereas 'star' implicates a more 'serious' attitude towards music-making. However, P. David Marshall emphasizes that the concept of celebrity can be used as a general and encompassing term, which represents 'the construction of individuality through ... mass public and audience', and thus embodies the definitions of individual worth and value.[18] On the other hand, the concept of celebrity is used almost exclusively when talking about today's media culture; celebrities are phenomena of the multimodal media world. In this context the concept of star is, for Marshall, a more specific category which is used when a persona is seen to have a special aura;[19] he or she has been seen as an autonomous person, whose fame rests, as it were, 'beyond' the media. The roots of this kind of approach are, again, in the romantic vision of artist and creativity, which have played a central role in Western rock music history.

In order to understand the characteristics of *Pop Idol* stardom it is important to consider both these aspects: first, historical notions about stardom and, second, how these notions are rearticulated in late modern media culture, because they overlap in the format. The new technologies and the mass market constitute a continual challenge to the romantic notion of authenticity and rearticulate it on new terrain, as the case of reality TV illustrates; authenticity is constituted in 'real' emotions. Thus, *Pop Idol* continually fluctuates between the notions of the traditional authentic star and the demands of the present-day music industry, where authenticity is more fragmentarily constituted. In this essay I name it the 'here and now' authenticity.

However, it is important to see that the construction of the mixed celebrity/stardom images I have sketched mediate the history of Anglo-American pop and rock culture. Therefore it is important to debate how the star/celebrity images are received and modified outside of the centres of Anglo-American popular music, such as, for example, in Africa, Arabic countries and India. In these countries Anglo-American popular music is an acculturated form of music: it is not indigenous but imported, and it can have a very complicated relationship with the local music culture.[20] Local music styles often mix with pop and rock influences, but the new genres can also arrive so quickly that their position remains more or less independent. Nabeel Zuberi, for example, notes how popular music in India lacks wide plurality, because MTV has so rapidly and massively introduced Western European and North American music culture.[21] I do not claim that popular culture in these countries is somehow less developed than in Europe and America, but that the history of popular music and popular culture is different: India, for example,

---

18 P. David Marshall, *Celebrity and Power: Fame in Contemporary Culture* (Minneapolis, MN, 1997), pp. 7–8.
19 Ibid., p. 7.
20 Lars Lilliestam, 'The Sounds of Swedish Rock' in Tarja Hautamäki and Tarja Rautiainen (eds), *Popular Music Studies in Seven Acts* (Tampere, 1996), pp. 23–54, at pp. 23–24.
21 Nabeel Zuberi, 'India Song: Popular Music Genres since Economic Liberalization' in David Hesmondhalgh and Keith Negus (eds), *Popular Music Studies* (London, 2002) pp. 238–50, at pp. 240–41.

does have a rich history of song contests.[22] In that sense, *Pop Idol* is not entirely a new phenomenon there.

Next, I will compare the Western meta-narrative of the concept of stardom/celebrity with examples from different cultures. As a reference point I will use Charles Fairchild's analysis of the *Australian Pop Idol* programme which highlights the construction of stardom/celebrity in the Western context very well.[23]

Pop Idol Stardom in a Transnational Context

Experiencing the Birth of Stardom

Based on his analysis of the *Australian Pop Idol* programme, Charles Fairchild calls the first auditions of *Pop Idol* a spectacle of the 'ordinary'.[24] These auditions well exemplify the basic characteristics of reality TV: a festival-like atmosphere is created by showing queuing, waiting, singing, crying and rejoicing performers. Although the spectacle of the 'ordinary' attempts to anchor the format to the present – and create a 'here and now' authenticity – the emphasis on the 'ordinary' encompasses features of the traditional stardom of popular music. The most evident of these is the 'rags to riches' myth, which is typical of Western popular culture. It is often used when introducing the contestants in Western countries: for example, a working-class background (a truck driver, a salesperson, a bus driver) seems to give the auditionee a special kind of credibility.

The efforts to create a 'here and now', 'happy time' spectacle also becomes evident in the various spin-offs of the format. Queuing young candidates and their happy faces after their successful performance are shown in auditions in European countries, as well as in Afghanistan and contests in West Africa. The impression of a 'here and now' spectacle is also created by showing a large, enthusiastic crowd surrounding the competition venue. Probably one of the most curious examples, from the perspective of a Western viewer, is the introduction to the Kandahar auditions of *Afghan Star*. 'Cool' Arabic pop is used as background music while showing street views in Kandahar, which is one of the most religiously conservative regions in the country.[25]

Alongside with the 'rags to riches' myth, the ethnic background of the contestants plays a significant role outside of the historical centres of Western popular music. Ethnic controversy arose, for instance, when Prashant Tamang, a contestant of

---

22   About popular music contests in India, see Asha Kasbekar, *Pop Culture India! Media, Arts and Lifestyle* (Santa Barbara, CA, 2006).

23   Fairchild, 'Building the Authentic Celebrity'.

24   Ibid., p. 361.

25   'Afghan Star Jalalabad/Kandahar Auditions 2', YouTube,, at: <http://www.youtube.com/watch?v=4q_5LUH6m5E&feature=related/> (accessed 15 May 2008).

Nepalese origin, won the title of *Indian Idol* during the third season in 2007. After racist jokes in the local radio against Tamang and Nepalese people in general, the singer's fans caused riots.[26] The ethnic or national background of the contestants is also highlighted in *Pop Idol* shows covering certain geographical areas. This could be regarded as self-evident, but in certain cases the manifestations of national identity contain special nuances. For example, when an Iraqi singer Shada Hassoun won the Arab *Pop Idol* in 2007, many saw her win as uniting Iraqis.[27]

Another important part of 'experiencing the birth of stardom' and creating the 'here and now' authenticity can be seen in the category of 'worst singers'. This practice has caused a lot of criticism in almost every country, but it has aroused the greatest confusion in cultures where a straightforward verbal insult is very unusual. In Ethiopia, for example, *Pop Idol* introduced this type of practice in the media, and it was a major reason for its popularity.[28]

Coaching Contestants

Fairchild critically points out that the first auditions, nonetheless, establish the aesthetic ideals for the contestants. Some of the ideals are explicit, such as the requirements for age, or amateur status (not valid contracts), but some are not explicated. For example, so-called 'producer auditions' are often organized, which are not shown to the television audience and which every potential participant must pass. Fairchild also emphasizes the significance of the so-called 'art talk', which the jury uses when judging auditionees.[29] He considers it a strategic practice which materializes the values of the music industry. This art talk is typically vague but pervasive: it consists of aesthetic judgements concerning musical aspects as well as the contestant's clothes and *habitus*.

It is astonishing how well this 'art talk' has been adapted to very different kinds of cultural contexts: coaching the contestant with the means of art talk is a part of the show everywhere. A good example of this is the discussion which Nigerian Timi Dakolo, winner of West-African Idol 2007, had with jury member Dene Mabiaku on a morning TV show.[30] In the show Dakolo first explained how he 'was able to define who he was' during the show. Mabiaku, in turn, characterized Dakolo in the following way: 'You are begun to get into character. It is a continuum.

26   Liberal India, 'The Backlash for an Offensive Joke against Indian Idol Winner', at: <http://liberalindia.com/2007/10/01/rioters-riot-60-injured-the-backlash-for-an-offensive-joke-against-indian-idol-winner> (accessed 9 June 2008).
27   'Iraqi Singer Wins Arab "Pop Idol"', Aljazeera.net, at: <http://english.aljazeera.net/NR/exeres/A8DB97F3-F70D-4E15-8F2D-63158CA74788.htm> (accessed 27 May 2008).
28   Shawn Lindseth, 'Idol Franchise Set to Destroy Ethiopia', 9 January 2006, at: <http://www.hecklerspray.com/idol-franchise-set-to-destroy-ethiopia/20061948.php> (accessed 26 May 2008).
29   Fairchild, 'Building the Authentic Celebrity', pp. 356–57.
30   'YouTube, Idols West African Extension', at: <http://www.youtube.com/watch?v=9GrZaOkgpCI&feature=related> (accessed 2 June 2008).

Give Supreme His chance to put you in that character when that time comes. For now you begin to getting into it, trust me.' The reason why art talk plays a central role is partly related to the importance of the jury. Their judgements constitute an essential discourse of the show, which the audience looks forward to and which is often a topic in the local media. In the same talk show, Mabiaku, who was the 'angry' man of the jury, justifies his way of acting.

What kind of relationship, then, has the art talk with the local popular music culture and its history? As I have noted above, the aesthetic ideals of the music performed in the show are based on Western mainstream pop and rock music; the characteristics of the art talk are also mainly derived from there. However, in non-Western countries, the freedom of action of the contestants seems to be slightly broader, at least on paper. For example, in *West-African Idol* auditionees can sing, according to the webpage: 'Traditional, Western, English, Nigerian, African, Pop, Reggae, R 'n' B and rock, though the Idols entrant should be aware that the show is looking for a pop star.'[31] Yet, when listening to the singing style of winner Timi Dakalo it is easy to hear Anglo-American popular music influences – late 1970s soul music (especially Al Green) in this case.

Local music influences have apparently maintained their place in the best way in India and in Arabic countries. In India the local genres of popular music, Hindi pop and Bollywood music are so powerful that Western pop and rock music do not dominate the performances very much. The same holds true for the Arabic spin-offs: the music performed in these countries can be labelled as Arabic pop. Perhaps the most unique of the spin-offs, when considering singing style, is the *Afghan Star*, where the contestants can also perform their own songs in the auditions.[32]

Branding Stardom

In the last rounds of the show, also called the *Theatre Auditions*, the emphasis is on the 'construction' of the star/celebrity. According to Fairchild, the process is based on the idea that participants are seen as talented, yet 'not ready'.[33] This discourse is constructed through art talk. The performances of the auditionees are judged over and over again, and the jury aims to direct them, for example, by impugning the aesthetic choices made by the auditionees. Fairchild therefore stresses that the process of constructing a star has already gone far by the time the viewer/audience can vote in the semi-finals. Sometimes the ambitions of the music industry can be seen very clearly. In the first season of the Finnish *Idols*, for example, one of the male contestants was chiefly promoted because he presented a pop genre that had not had a significant role in Finnish popular music markets at that time. In

---

31   'Idols West Africa Comes To Nigeria', at: <(http://www.nairaland.com/nigeria/topic-33091.0.html> (accessed 2 June 2008).

32   'Afghan Star Jalalabad/Kandahar Auditions 2', at: <http://www.youtube.com/watch?v=4q_5LUH6m5E&feature=related> (15 May 2008).

33   Fairchild, 'Building the Authentic Celebrity', p. 362.

other words, the format took part in establishing this genre on the Finnish music market.

During the semi-finals and the so-called 'wild card round', the branding of the contestants continues, and coaching – of vocal and choreographic skills, make-up and wardrobe enhancement – becomes increasingly important. The Final 12 is, according to Fairchild, the finishing touch for the branding.[34] In addition to the actual show, associated programmes (*Idol House Party*, *Up Close and Personal*) and popular magazines introduce the star candidates, and many of them soon become media celebrities. Again, these characteristics also appear in the spin-offs. For example, coaching contestants on their make-up and wardrobe is part of the format even in countries where the cultural climate is conservative, as in Afghanistan and Ethiopia. However, the future success of those who have done well in the show is another story. Some, such as the American Kelly Clarkson and British Will Young, have had successful careers. What seems to be typical is that some participants become celebrities, whose life is followed by the tabloid press looking for scandals. However, stardom does not always fulfil a winner's expectations. Timi Dakolo, for example, did not release an album after winning the competition; for some reason, BMG did not fulfil the contract.[35] The fact that Lima Sahar, the successful female contestant of *Afghan Star*, has faced threats from religious groups can be seen as an example of clashing value systems.[36]

Articulating a Post-capitalist Ethos and National Identity

When summing up the basic characteristics of *Pop Idol*, the central notion is that the format can be rooted easily in very different kinds of cultural contexts. However, I do not argue that the format, as such, is an example of how a global format can 'colonialize' the local music culture. Although this kind of tendency could be seen, as a whole the effects of the format are very complex. In order to understand the significance of the format, we need to see how different kinds of musical, historical and social worlds overlap when the format is broadcast in the different cultures. The concept of transnationalism aptly describes this overlapping, because in *Pop Idol* it is possible to see the 'multidirectional flow of information and images and their cultural mixing', as Iwabuchi defines the concept.[37] In more concrete terms, this means that, in the current media world, new influences spread very rapidly,

---

34   Ibid., p. 364.
35   'Scandal Rocks Idols West Africa', 26 January 2008, at: <http://thelongharmattan season.blogspot.com/2008/01/scandals-rocks-idols-west-africa-by.html> (accessed 16 June 2008).
36   Jason Straziuso, 'Afghanistan Clerics Upset as Woamn Makes Final of "Pop Idol"', 14 March 2008 at: <http://news.scotsman.com/latestnews/Afghanistan-clerics-upset -as-woman.3878336.jp> (accessed 15 June 2008).
37   Iwabuchi, *Recentering Globalization*, pp. 16–17.

but these influences constantly collide with elements from the local culture. This collision – or, if anything, negotiation – is a continuous balancing act (or struggle) between the local music culture and the global music industry. In other words, the significance of *Pop Idol* must be interpreted in a locally contextualized manner. In the following I will sketch this negation and struggle by illustrating the basic characteristics of both poles: first, the global music industry and, second, what the special contextual factors are under which the format has been adapted in different cultures.

As I have explained, the *Pop Idol* format can be seen as a model example of how the music industry is nowadays integrated with the larger entertainment industry. Media transnationalism – for example, cross-border channels – establishes the global frames for the format that cross the borders of the traditional music industry. In addition, in the format, the stardom and the authenticity of stardom is constructed by means of reality-TV practices (spectacle, mockery, art talk), which create a specific 'here and now' type of authenticity. How this changes the characteristics of stardom in the long run is difficult say, but it can be argued that the format tends to simultaneously create disposable media celebrities and act as a springboard for more traditional types of stardom.

It is possible to claim that as a whole the format and the extensive branding (establishing a brand hybrid) connected with it may, in the long run, transform the character of the music industry, because branding gives rise to a process by which music (as a traditional musical text) may lose its essence as a distinct commodity product (the value of the music based on artist, song, genre and so on), and be replaced with a kind of 'experience industry', where priority is given to experiences that the commodity product arouses and to the web of commodities and experiences it is connected with.[38]

Although attempts to establish a brand hybrid and create new kind celebrity stardom in popular music are evident also in the spin-offs of the format, some of their characteristics can be regarded as examples of 'empowering' articulations. Those elements that the format offers as a manifestation of national identity or contemporary youth culture are especially important. A good example of the importance of manifesting national identity was the win of Iraqi Shada Hassoun in *Arab Idol*. It was interpreted in the press as a sign that Iraqis, Sunnies and Shiites could become a unified nation. Of course, this kind of manifestation must be understood in the context of the political situation of the country.

However, the question of national identity is also raised in special ways in such countries where the political situation is more stable. For example, a 14-year-old auditionee of *Ethiopian Idols* noted that the format was '[a] good start for Ethiopian society – we are too timid, we are afraid of out talent'.[39] While one may hardly

---

38   Tarja Rautiainen-Keskustalo, 'Rocking the Economy: On the Articulations of Popular Music and the Creative Economy in Late Modern Culture, *Popular Musicology Online*, at: <http://www.popular-musicology-online.com>.

39   Abdirahman Koronto, '"Pop Idol" Fever Sweeps Ethiopia', 26 January 2006, at: <http://news.bbc.co.uk/2/hi/africa/4648208.stm> (accessed 15 June 2008).

imagine a European contestant speaking like this, this kind of ethos seems be a part of many non-European spin-offs. It can be argued that this kind of idea represents a new articulation between the late-capitalist ethos and national identity: the construction of national identity is now a question of developing a talent or a person; it is no longer a symbol – for example, a flag or a song. This aspect is, however, also related to the position of youth cultures in these countries. In Ethiopia, as in many other non-Western countries, rapidly diffused Western media have caused the young generations to live in different kind of culture than their parents. In this situation the international format can offer elements for constructing a new, flexible identity which connects the young people of Ethiopia to global youth culture.

Yet, the question of constructing a new national identity is not without problems. As I noted earlier, the success of Lima Sahar in *Afghan Star* caused much criticism; Lima's idea for improving the status of women was not eventually accepted. In Afghanistan, at the beginning of 2008, Taliban fighters launched several attacks against Western popular culture and went so far as to explode bombs in shops where Western movies and music were sold. This last example shows, in extreme form, the consequences of clashes between deeply contradictory value systems that may be brought into confrontation via transnational popular culture forms.

Bibliography

'1978 3M Digital Audio Mastering System', *Mix Magazine*, 1 September 2007, p. 112

Abbott, Kingsley, *The Beach Boys Pet Sounds: The Greatest Album of the Twentieth Century* (London: Helter Skelter Publishing, 2001).

Abercrombie, Nick and Brian Longhurst, *Audiences: A Sociological Theory of Performance and Imagination* (London: Sage, 1998).

Adams, Rachel and David Savran, 'Introduction' in *The Masculinity Studies Reader* (Oxford: Blackwell, 2002), pp. 1–8.

Adler, Patricia and Peter Adler, *Peer Power* (Piscatawy, NJ: Rutgers University Press, 1998).

Adorno, Theodor W., *Essays on Music; Selected, with Introduction, Commentary, and Notes by Richard Leppert; New Translations by Susan H. Gillespie* (Berkeley: University of California Press, 2002).

——, *Introduction to the Sociology of Music*, trans. E.B. Ashton (New York: Continuum, 1976).

——, 'On Popular Music' in Adorno, *Essays on Music*, pp. 437–69.

——, 'On the Fetish Character in Music and the Regression of Listening', *The Culture Industry: Selected Essays on Mass Culture* (London: Routledge 1991), pp. 26–52.

——, 'On the Fetish-Character in Music and the Regression of Listening' in Adorno, *Essays on Music*, pp. 288–317.

——, 'Types d'attitude musicale', *Introduction à la sociologie de la musique* (Genève: Contrechamps, 1994), pp. 7–25.

Adorno, Theodor W. and Hanns Eisler, *Composing for the Films* (London: Athlone, 1994).

'Afghan Star, Jalalabad/Kandahar Auditions 2, YouTube, at: http://www.youtube.com/watch?v=4q_5LUH6m5E&feature=related (accessed 15 May 2008).

Ahlkvist, Jarl A., 'Programming Philosophies and the Rationalization of Music Radio', *Media, Culture and Society* 23 (2001): 339–58.

Akhtar, Miriam and Steve Humphries, *The Fifties and Sixties: A Lifestyle Revolution* (London: Boxtree, 2002).

Alarik, Scott, *Deep Community: Adventures in the Modern Folk Underground* (Cambridge, MA: Black Wolf, 2003).

Alexander, Peter J., 'Product Variety and Market Structure: A New Measure and a Simple Test', *Journal of Economic Behavior & Organization* 32 (1997): 207–14.

Allen, John, 'Symbolic Economies: The "Culturalization" of Economic Knowledge', in Du Gay and Pryke, *Cultural Economy*, pp. 39–58.

Amico, Stephen, '"I Want Muscles": House Music, Homosexuality and Masculine Signification', *Popular Music*, 20/3 (2001): 359–78.

Amos, Tori. and Ann Powers, *Tori Amos, Piece by Piece* (London: Plexus, 2005).

Anand, N. and Richard A. Peterson, 'When Market Information Constitutes Field: Sensemaking of Markets in the Commercial Music Industry', *Organization Science* 11 (2000): 270–84.

Anderman, Joan, 'Of Course She Should Go to Rehab: But Like the Troubled Talents Who Came before her, Amy Winehouse Made her Pain Part of her Artistry', *Boston Globe*, 16 December 2007.

Anderson, Chris, *The Long Tail: Why the Future of Business is Selling Less of More* (New York: Hyperion, 2006).

Andes, Linda, 'Growing Up Punk: Meaning and Commitment Careers in a Contemporary Youth Subculture' in Jonathon S. Epstein (ed.), *Youth Culture: Identity in a Postmodern World* (Oxford: Blackwell, 1998).

Andreijevic, Mark, *Reality TV. The Work of Being Watched* (Oxford: Rowman & Littlefield Publishers, 2004).

Apache Indian, 'Music has no Colour, no Barriers'. *The Rediff Chat*, 1 August 2001, at: <http://www.rediff.com.E:\Books\Bhangra\Bhangra\Artist\AZ\Apache\ indian\rediff_com.Chat\Transcript\Apache Indian.htm> (accessed 11 August 2008).

Aparicio, Frances R., *Listening to Salsa: Gender, Latin Popular Music, and Puerto Rican Cultures* (Hanover, NH: Wesleyan University Press, 1998).

Appleford, Steve, *The Rolling Stones: It's Only Rock 'n' Roll: The Stories Behind Every Song* (London: Carleton, 1997).

Arzaghi, Mohammed, 'Quality Sorting and Networking: Evidence from the Advertising Agency Industry', *Ideas*, at: <http://ideas.repec.org/p/cen/ wpaper/05-16.html> (accessed 5 June 2008).

Ashmore, Malcolm, *The Reflexive Thesis: Wrighting Sociology of Scientific Knowledge* (Chicago: Chicago University Press, 1989).

Attali, Jacques, *Noise* (Minneapolis: University of Minnesota Press, 1985).

Auslander, Philip, 'I Wanna Be Your Man: Suzi Quatro's Musical Androgyny', *Popular Music* 23/1 (2004): 1–16.

——, *Liveness: Performance in a Mediatized Culture* (London: Routledge, 2nd edn 2008).

——, 'Musical Personae', *The Drama Review* 50/1 (2006): 100–19.

——, 'Performance Analysis and Popular Music: A Manifesto', *Contemporary Theatre Review* 14/1 (2004): 1–13.

——, *Performing Glam Rock: Gender and Theatricality in Popular Music* (Ann Arbor: University of Michigan Press, 2006).

Austen, Jake, *TV a-Go-Go: Rock on TV from American Bandstand to American Idol* (Chicago: Chicago Review Press, 2007).

Averill, Gage, *Four Parts, No Waiting: A Social History of American Barbershop Harmony* (New York: Oxford University Press, 2003).

Ayers, Michael D., 'The Cyberactivism of a Dangermouse', in Ayers, *Cybersounds*, pp. 127–36.

Ayers, Michael D. (ed.), *Cybersounds: Essays on Virtual Music Culture* (New York: Peter Lang, 2006).

'Backing Vocalist', *Wikipedia*, at: <http://en.wikipedia.org/wiki/Backing_vocalist> (accessed 11 July 2008).

Balfour, Ian, 'Queer Theory: Notes on the Pet Shop Boys' in Roger Beebe, Denise Fulbrook and Ben Saunders (eds), *Rock Over the Edge: Transformations in Popular Music Culture* (Durham, NC: Duke University Press, 2002), pp. 357–70.

Ballantyne, Tony, *Between Colonialism and Diaspora: Sikh Cultural Formations in an Imperial World* (Durham, NC: Duke University Press, 2006).

'Bally Sagoo', *Wikipedia: The Free Encyclopedia*, at: <http://en.wikipedia.org/wiki/ Bally_Sagoo> (accessed 11 August 2008).

Banerji, Sabita, 'From Ghazals to Bhangra in Great Britain', *Popular Music* 7/2 (1981): 207–14.

Banerji, Sabita and Gerd Bauman, 'Bhangra 1984–8: Fusion and Professionalization in a Genre of South Asian Dance Music' in Paul Oliver (ed.), *Black Music in Britain: Essays on the Afro-Asian Contribution to Popular Music* (Milton Keynes: Open University Press, 1990), pp. 137–53.

Bangs, Lester, 'The British Invasion', in Anthony DeCurtis and James Henke (eds), *The Rolling Stone Illustrated History of Rock & Roll* (London: Plexus, 1992), pp. 199–208.

Bannister, Matthew, 'Dark Side of the Men: Pink Floyd, Classic Rock and White Masculinities' in Russell Reising (ed.), *'Speak To Me': The Legacy of Pink Floyd's The Dark Side of the Moon* (Aldershot: Ashgate, 2005), pp. 43–55.

——, '"Loaded": Indie Guitar Rock, Canonism, White Masculinities', *Popular Music* 25/1 (2006): 77–95.

——, *White Boys, White Noise: Masculinities and 1980s Indie Guitar Rock* (Aldershot: Ashgate, 2006).

Barber, Benjamin R., *Jihad vs McWorld: How Globalism and Tribalism are Reshaping the World* (New York: Random House, 1995).

Barthes, Roland, 'The Grain of the Voice', in Stephen Heath (ed. and trans.), *Image-Music-Text* (London: Fontana, 1977), pp. 179–89.

Batten, Joe, *The Joe Batten Book – Story of Sound Recordings* (London: Rockliff, 1956).

Battino, David and Kelli Richards, *The Art of Digital Music* (San Francisco: Backbeat Books, 2005).

Baudelaire, Charles, *The Painter of Modern Life* [1863] (New York: Da Capo Press, 1964).

Baudrillard, Jean, 'The Precession of Simulacra' in *Simulacra and Simulation* (Ann Arbor: University of Michigan Press, 1995), pp. 1–42.

Bauman, Zygmunt, *Intimations of Postmodernity* (London: Routledge, 1992).

Baumann, Gerd, *Contesting Culture: Discourses of Identity in Multi-Ethnic London* (Cambridge: Cambridge University Press, 1996).

Baumol, William J. and William G. Bowen, *Performing Arts, the Economic Dilemma: A Study of Problems Common to Theater, Opera, Music, and Dance* (New York: Twentieth Century Fund, 1966).

Bayton, Mavis, 'Women and the Electric Guitar' in Whiteley (ed.), *Sexing the Groove*, pp. 37–49.

Bazin, Hugues, *La Culture hip hop* (Paris: Desclée de Brouwer, 1995).

Beadle, Jeremy J., *Will Pop Eat Itself? Pop Music in the Soundbite Era* (London: Faber, 1993).

Beck, Jay and Tony Grajeda (eds), *Lowering the Boom: Critical Studies in Film Sound* (Champaign, IL: University of Illinois Press, 2008).

Beck, Ulrich, Anthony Giddens and Scott Lash, *Reflexive Modernization* (Cambridge: Polity, 1994).

Becker, Howard S., *Outsiders: Studies in the Sociology of Deviance* (New York: Free Press, 1963).

——, 'The Professional Dance Musician and his Audience', *American Journal of Sociology* 57/2 (1951): 146–54.

Beller, Jonathan, *The Cinematic Mode of Production: Attention Economy and the Society of the Spectacle* (Lebanon, NH: University Press of New England, 2006).

Bellman, Jonathan, 'Indian Resonances in the British Invasion, 1965–68', in Bellman (ed.), *The Exotic in Western Music*, pp. 292–306.

Benjamin, Walter, *The Exotic in Western Music* (Boston, MA: Northeastern University Press, 1998).

——, 'Charles Baudelaire', cited at: <http://www.thelemming.com/lemming/dissertation-web/home/flaneur.html> (accessed 21 July 2008).

——, *The Arcades Project* (Cambridge, MA: Harvard University Press, 1999).

——, 'The Work of Art in the Age of Mechanical Reproduction' [1936] in Francis Frascina and Jonathan Harris (eds), *Art in Modern Culture: An Anthology of Critical Texts* (London: Phaidon Press, 1992), pp. 297–307.

——, 'The Work of Art in the Age of Mechanical Reproduction', in *Illuminations* [1936], trans. Hannah Arendt, ed. Harry Zohn (New York: Harcourt, Brace and World, 1968), pp. 217–51.

Bennett, Andy, 'Bhangra in Newcastle: Music, Ethnic Identity and the Role of Local Knowledge', *Innovation: The European Journal of the Social Sciences* 10/1 (1997): 107–16.

——, *Cultures of Popular Music* (Buckingham: Open University Press, 2001).

——, 'Music, Media and Urban Mythscapes: A Study of Canterbury Sound', *Media, Culture and Society* 24/1 (2002): 107–20.

——, *Popular Music and Youth Culture: Music, Identity and Place* (Basingstoke: Macmillan, 2000).

——, 'Popular Music, Media and the Narrativisation of Place', in Bloustien, Peters and Luckman, *Sonic Synergies*, pp. 69–78.

——, 'Subcultures or Neo-Tribes? Rethinking the Relationship Between Youth, Style and Musical Taste', *Sociology* 33/3 (1999): 599–617.

——, 'Subcultures, Scenes and Tribes', in Bennett, Shank and Toynbee, *The Popular Music Studies Reader*, pp. 95–97.

Bennett, Andy and Keith Kahn-Harris, (eds), *After Subculture: Critical Studies in Contemporary Youth Culture* (Basingstoke: Palgrave Macmillan, 2004).

Bennett, Andy and Richard A. Peterson (eds), *Music Scenes: Local, Translocal, and Virtual* (Nashville, TN: Vanderbilt University Press, 2004).

Bennett, Andy, Barry Shank and Jason Toynbee (eds), *The Popular Music Studies Reader* (London: Routledge. 2006).

Berendt, Joachim, *The Jazz Book* (Westport, CT: Lawrence Hill and Company, 1975).

Berger, John, *Ways of Seeing* (London: Penguin, 1972).

Bergman, David, 'Introduction', in David Bergman (ed.), *Camp Grounds: Style and Homosexuality* (Amherst: University of Massachusetts Press, 1993), pp. 3–16.

Berland, Jody, 'Angels Dancing: Cultural Technologies and the Production of Space', in Lawrence Grossberg, Carey Nelson and Paula Treicher (eds), *Cultural Studies* (New York: Routledge, 1992), pp. 38–50.

——, 'Postmusics' in Bloustien, Peters and Luckman, *Sonic Synergies*, pp. 27–38.

Berlyne, Daniel E., *Aesthetics and Psychobiology* (New York: Appleton-Century-Crofts, 1971).

Bernstein, Arthur, Naoki Sekine and Dick Weissman, *The Global Music Industry: Three Perspectives* (New York: Routledge, 2007).

Berry, Steven T. and Joel Waldfogel, 'Do Mergers Increase Product Variety? Evidence from Radio Broadcasting', *Quarterly Journal of Economics* (2001): 1009–24.

Béthune, Christian, *Le Rap: une esthétique hors la loi* (Paris: Editions Autrement, 1999).

Bhabha, Homi K., *The Location of Culture* (London: Routledge, 1994).

Bhachu, Parminder, *East African Sikh Settlers in Britain* (London: Tavistock Publications, 1985).

Bianchini, Franco, 'Night Cultures, Night Economies', *Planning Practice and Research* 10/2 (1995): 121–26.

Biddle, Ian and Freya Jarman-Ivens, 'Introduction' in Jarman-Ivens, *Oh Boy!*.

Bijsterveld, Karin, '"What Do I Do with My Tape Recorder … ?" Sound Hunting and the Sounds of Everyday Dutch Life in the 1950s and 1960s', *Historical Journal of Film, Radio and Television* 24/4 (2004): 613–34.

Bilton, Chris, *Management and Creativity: From Creative Industries to Creative Management* (Malden, MA: Blackwell, 2007).

Bilton, Chris and Ruth Leary, 'What Can Managers Do for Creativity? Brokering Creativity in the Creative Industries', *International Journal of Cultural Policy* 8/1 (2002): 49–64.

Björnberg, Alf, 'Probing the Reception History of Recording Media: A Case Study', *Papers from CHARM Symposium 1*, 2005, at: <http://www.charm.rhul.ac.uk/content/events/s1Bjornberg.pdf> (accessed 1 October 2008).

——, 'Structural Relationships of Music and Images in Music Video' in Richard Middleton (ed.), *Reading Pop: Approaches to Textual Analysis in Popular Music* (Oxford: Oxford University Press, 2000), pp. 347–78.

Black, Michael and Douglas Greer, 'Concentration and Non-Price Competition in the Recording Industry', *Review of Industrial Organization* 3 (1987): 13–37.

Bloustien, Gerry, *Girl Making: A Cross-Cultural Ethnography on the Processes of Growing Up* Female (Oxford: Berghan, 2003).

——, 'Up the Down Staircase: Grassroots Entrepreneurship in Young People's Music Practices', in Bloustien, Peters and Luckman, *Sonic Synergies*, pp. 195–210.

——, '"Wigging People Out": Youth Music Practice and Mediated Communities', *Journal of Community & Applied Social Psychology*, 17 (2007): 446–62.

Bloustien, Gerry, Susan Luckman and Margaret Peters, '"Be not Afeard; the Isle is full of Noises": Reflections on the Synergies of Music in the Creative Knowledge Economy', in Bloustien, Peters and Luckman, *Sonic Synergies*, pp. xxi–xxviii.

Bloustien, Gerry, Margaret Peters and Susan Luckman (eds), *Sonic Synergies: Music, Technology Community and Identity* (Aldershot: Ashgate, 2008).

Bly, Robert, *Iron John: A Book About Men* [1990] (New York: Vintage Books, 1992).

Bocquet, José-Louis and Philippe Pierre-Adolphe, *Rap ta France* (Paris: Flammarion, 1997).

Bohlman, Philip V., *World Music: A Very Short Introduction* (Oxford: Oxford University Press, 2002).

Bolter, Jay David and Richard Grusin, 'Remediation', *Configurations* 3 (1996): pp. 311–58.

Booker, Christopher, *The Neophiliacs: The Revolution in English Life in the Fifties and Sixties* (London: Pimlico, rev. edn 1992).

Borwick, John, *Microphones: Technology and Technique* (London: Focal Press, 1990).

Boschi, Elena, '"Please, Give Me Second Grace": A Study of Five Songs in Wes Anderson's The Royal Tenenbaums' in Cooper, Fox and Sapiro, *CineMusic?*, pp. 97–110.

——, 'Radiofreccia: A New Direction for Italian Film Music?', paper given at the Sound, Music and the Moving Image Conference, Institute of Musical Research, London, 10–12 September 2007.

Boucher, Manuel, *Rap expression des lascars: significations et enjeux du rap dans la société française* (Paris: L'Harmattan, 1998).

Bourdieu, Pierre, *Distinction: A Social Critique of the Judgement of Taste* [1979], trans. Richard Nice (Cambridge, MA: Harvard University Press, and London: Routledge and Kegan Paul, 1984).

——, *The Field of Cultural Production: Essays on Art and Literature*, ed. Randal Johnson (Cambridge: Polity Press, 1993).

Bowman, Rob, 'The Determining Role of Performance in the Articulation of Meaning: The Case of "Try a Little Tenderness"' in Moore, *Analyzing Popular Music*.

Boyd, Joe, *White Bicycles: Making Music in the 1960s* (London: Serpent's Tail, 2006).

Boyd, Todd, *Am I Black Enough For You? Popular Culture From the 'Hood and Beyond* (Bloomington: Indiana University Press, 1997).

Brackett, David. 'Elvis Costello, the Empire of the E Chord, and a Magic Moment or two', *Popular Music* 24/3 (2005): 357–67.

——, '(In Search of) Musical Meaning: Genres, Categories and Crossover' in Hesmondhalgh and Negus, *Popular Music Studies*.

——, *Interpreting Popular Music* [1995] (Berkeley: University of California Press, 2000).

Bradby, Barbara, 'Sampling Sexuality: Gender, Technology and the Body in Dance Music', *Popular Music* 12/2 (1993): 155–76.

Bradley, Dick, *Understanding Rock 'n' Roll: Popular Music in Britain 1955–1964* (Buckingham: Open University Press, 1992).

Bragg, Billy and Ian A. Anderson, 'The Taxman's Poet', *Folk Roots* 42 (1986): 26–29.

Brake, Michael, *Comparative Youth Culture: The Sociology of Youth Cultures and Youth Subcultures in America, Britain and Canada* (London: Routledge, 2nd edn 1995).

Braudy, Leo. 'Afterword: Rethinking Remakes' in Andrew Horton and Stuart Y. McDougal (eds), *Play it Again, Sam: Retakes on Remakes* (Berkeley: University of California Press, 1998).

Bray, Roger and Vladimir Raitz, *Flight to the Sun: The Story of the Holiday Revolution* (London: Continuum, 2001).

Brett, Philip, Elizabeth Wood and Gary C. Thomas (eds), *Queering the Pitch: The New Gay and Lesbian Musicology* (New York: Routledge, 1994).

Brisbane, Robert, *Black Activism: Racial Revolution in the United States, 1954–1970* (Valley Forge, PA: Judson, 1974).

Brittan, Francesca, 'Women Who "Do Elvis": Authenticity, Masculinity, and Masquerade', *Journal of Popular Music Studies* 18/2 (2006): 167–90.

Brocken, Mike, *The British Folk Revival 1944–2002* (Aldershot: Ashgate, 2003).

Brooks, Daphne, *Grace* (New York: Continuum, 2005).

Brooks, Tim, 'Columbia Records in the 1890s: Founding the Record Industry', *Association for Recorded Sound Collections Journal* 10/1 (1978): 5–36.

Brophy, Philip, *100 Anime* (London: BFI, 2006).

——, 'Body Mats and Super Slams: Sport, Sound and Violence', paper given at the Fourth Cinesonic International Conference on Film Scores and Sound Design, Melbourne, 2001.

Brown, Adam, Justin O'Connor and Sara Cohen, 'Local Music Policies within a Global Music Industry: Cultural Quarters in Manchester and Sheffield', *Geoforum* 31/4 (2000): 437–51.

Brown, Lee B., 'Documentation and Fabrication in Phonography', *Twentieth World Congress of Philosophy, Boston*, 1998, at: <http://www.bu.edu/wcp/Papers/Aest/AestBrow.htm>.

Brown, Royal S., *Overtones and Undertones: Reading Film Music* (Berkeley, CA: University of California Press, 1994).

Brown, Scot, 'A Land of Funk: Dayton, Ohio' in Tony Bolden (ed.), *The Funk Era and Beyond* (New York: Palgrave Macmillan, 2008), pp. 73–88.

Bruns Axel, 'Futures for Webcasting: Regulatory Approaches in Australia and the US' in Bloustien, Peters and Luckman, *Sonic Synergies*, pp. 17–26.

Buchanan, Elizabeth A., 'Deafening Silence: Music and the Emerging Climate of Access and Use' in Ayers, *Cybersounds*, pp. 9–20.

Buhler, James, Caryl Flinn, and David Neumeyer (eds), *Music and Cinema* (Hanover, NH: Wesleyan University Press, 2000).

Burnett, Robert, *The Global Jukebox. The International Music Industry* (London: Routledge, 1996)

Butler, Judith, *Gender Trouble: Feminism and the Subversion of Identity* [1990] (London: Routledge, 1999).

——, 'Performative Acts and Gender Constitution: An Essay in Phenomenology and Feminist Theory' in Sue-Ellen Case (ed.), *Performing Feminisms: Feminist Critical Theory and Theatre* (Baltimore, MD: Johns Hopkins University Press, 1990), pp. 66–67.

Butt, Danny and Axel Bruns, 'Digital Rights Management and Music in Australasia', *Media & Arts Law Review* 10/4 (2005): 265–78.

Byrne, Paul, *Social Movements in Britain* (London: Routledge, 1997).

Byrnside, Ronald, 'The Formation of a Musical Style: Early Rock' [1975], in Moore, *Critical Essays*, 217–50.

Cachin, O., *L'Offensive rap* (Paris: Gallimard, 1996).

Camille, 'Bhangra is our Common Link?' *The Langar Hall » Blog Archive*, 1 February 2008 – 08:40, at: <http://thelangarhall.com/archives/111>. (accessed 11 August 2008).

Carlson, Marvin, *Performance: A Critical Introduction* (New York: Routledge, 2004).

Carr, E.H., *What is History?* [1961] (London: Penguin, 1990).

Castells, Manuel, *End of Millennium: Information Age, Economy, Society and Culture*, Vol. 3 (Oxford: Blackwell, 2nd edn 2000).

——, The Internet Galaxy: Reflections on the Internet, Business and Society (Oxford: Oxford University Press, 2001).

——, *The Rise of the Network Society* (Malden, MA: Blackwell Publishers, 1996).

Caughie, John, *Theories of Authorship: A Reader* (London: Routledge, 1981).

Caves, Richard E., *Creative Industries: Contracts between Art and Commerce* (Cambridge, MA: Harvard University Press, 2000).

Chalaby, Jean K., 'Towards an Understanding of Media Transnationalism' in Jean K. Chalaby (ed.), *Transnational Television Worldwide: Towards a New Media Order* (London: I.B. Tauris, 2005).

Chambers, Iain, *Urban Rhythms: Pop Music and Popular Culture* (London: Macmillan, 1985).

Chanan, Michael, *Repeated Takes: A Short History of Recording and Its Effects on Music* (London: Verso, 1995).

Chancellor, Valerie E., *History for Their Masters* (Bath: Adams and Dart, 1970).

Chandler, Kim, 'Backing Up', *The Singer* (2004): 21–22.

Chaney, David, *Lifestyles* (London: Routledge, 1996).

Chapple, Steve and Reebee Garofalo, *Rock 'n' Roll is Here to Pay: The History and Politics of the Music Industry* (Chicago: Nelson-Hall, 1977).

Chartier, Roger, *Lecture et lecteurs dans la France d'Ancien Régime* (Paris: Seuil, 1987).

—— (ed.), *Pratiques de la lecture* (Paris: Payot, 1993).

Chester, Andrew, 'Second Thoughts on a Rock Aesthetic: The Band' [1970] in Moore, *Critical Essays*, pp. 111–18.

Chion, Michel, *Pierre Henry* (Paris: Fayard, 2003).

Chop, Max, 'Ergänzungsfragen für die Sprechmaschinen-Literatur', *Phonographische Zeitschrift*, 10/4 (1909): 75–78.

Clarke, B. Paul, '"A Magic Science": Rock Music as Recording Art' in Richard Middleton and David Horn (eds), *Popular Music. Vol. 3: Producers and Markets* (Cambridge: Cambridge University Press, 1983), pp. 195–214.

Clarke, Eric F., 'Subject-Position and the Specification of Invariants in Music by Frank Zappa and P.J. Harvey', *Music Analysis* 18/3 (1999), pp. 347–74.

——, *Ways of Listening* (New York: Oxford University Press, 2005).

Clarke, Eric F. and Nicola Dibben, 'Sex, Pulp and Critique', *Popular Music* 19/2 (2000): 231–41.

Clarke, John, Stuart Hall, Tony Jefferson and Brian Roberts, 'Subcultures, Cultures and Class' in Hall and Jefferson, *Resistance Through Rituals*, pp. 9–74.

Clawson, Mary Ann, 'Masculinity and Skill Acquisition in the Adolescent Rock Band', *Popular Music* 18/1 (1999): 99–114.

Clayton, Martin 'Communication in Raga performance' in Dorothy Miell, Raymond MacDonald and David J. Hargreaves (eds), *Musical Communication* (New York: Oxford University Press, 2005), pp. 361–81.

Clifford, James and George E. Marcus (eds), *Writing Culture: The Poetics and Politics of Ethnography* (Berkeley: University of California Press, 1986).

Clough, Patricia Ticineto, *The Affective Turn: Theorizing the Social* (Durham, NC: Duke University Press, 2007).

Coates, Norma, 'Elvis from the Waist Up and Other Myths: 1950s Music Television and the Gendering of Rock Discourse' in Roger Beebe and Jason Middleton (eds), *Medium Cool: Music Videos from Soundies to Cellphones* (Durham, NC: Duke University Press, 2007) pp. 226–51.

Coffey, Amanda and Paul Atkinson, *Making Sense of Qualitative Data: Complementary Research Strategies* (London: Sage, 1996).

Cogan, Jim and William Clark, *Temples of Sound: Inside the Great Recording Studio*, (San Francisco, CA: Chronicle Books, 2003).

Cohan, Steven, *Incongruous Entertainment: Camp, Cultural Value, and the MGM Musical* (Durham, NC: Duke University Press, 2005).

Cohen, Sara, 'Men Making a Scene: Rock Music and the Production of Gender' in Whiteley, *Sexing the Groove*, pp. 17–36.

——, *Rock Culture in Liverpool: Popular Music in the Making* (Oxford: Clarendon Press, 1991).

Cohen, Stanley, *Folk Devils and Moral Panics: The Creation of the Mods and Rockers* [1972] (London: Routledge, 3rd edn 2002).

Colin, Sid, *And the Bands Played On* (London: Elm Tree, 1977).

Collins, Jim (ed.), *High-Pop: Making Culture into Popular Entertainment* (Oxford: Blackwell, 2002).

Collins, Karen, 'An Introduction to the Participatory and Non-linear Aspects of Video Games Audio' in John Richardson and Stan Hawkins (eds), *Essays on Sound and Vision* (Helsinki University Press/Yliopistopaino, 2007), pp. 263–98.

Collinson, Ian, '"Dis is England's New Voice": Anger, Activism and the Asian Dub Foundation' in Bloustien, Peters and Luckman, *Sonic Synergies*, pp. 105–14.

Connell, John and Chris Gibson, *Sound Tracks: Popular Music, Identity and Place* (London: Routledge, 2003).

Connell, Raewyn W., *Masculinities* (Berkeley: University of California Press, 1995).

——, 'The Sociology of Masculinity', in Stephen M. Whitehead and Frank J. Barrett (eds), *The Masculinities Reader* (Cambridge: Polity, 2001), pp. 30–50.

Connolly, Harold X., *A Ghetto Grows in Brooklyn* (New York: New York University Press, 1977).

Cook, Nicholas, *Analysing Musical Multimedia* (Oxford: Oxford University Press, 1998).

Cooper, David, Christopher Fox, and Ian Sapiro (eds), *CineMusic? Constructing the Film Score* (Newcastle: Cambridge Scholars Publishing, 2008).

Cotterell, John, *Social Networks and Social Influences in Adolescence* (London: Routledge, 1996).

Countryman, Matthew J., *Up South: Civil Rights and Black Power in Philadelphia* (Philadelphia: University of Pennsylvania Press, 2006).

Covach, John and Graeme Boone (eds), *Understanding Rock: Essays in Musical Analysis* (Oxford: Oxford University Press, 1997).

Cowan, Jane, 'Greece', in *The Garland Encyclopedia of World Music. Vol. 8: Europe*, ed. Timothy Rice, Christopher Goertzen and James Porter (New York: Garland Publishing, 1998), pp. 1007–28.

Cox, Stephen, Abraham Ninan, Greg Hearn, Simon Roodhouse and Stuart Cunningham, *Queensland Music Industry Basics: People, Businesses and Markets* (Brisbane: Creative Industries Research and Applications Centre, 2004).

Cox, Tom, *The Lost Tribes of Pop* (London: Portrait, 2006).

Coyle, Diane, *The Weightless World: Thriving in a Digital Age* (London: Capstone, 1999).

Cranny-Francis, Anne, *et al.*, *Gender Studies: Terms and Debates* (New York: Palgrave Macmillan, 2003).

Crary, Jonathan, *Suspensions of Perception* (Cambridge, MA: MIT Press, 1999).

Cumming, Naomi, *The Sonic Self* (Bloomington: Indiana University Press, 2000).

Cunningham, Mark, *Good Vibrations. A History of Record Production* (London: Sanctuary, 2nd edn 1998/Chessington: Castle Communications, 1st edn 1996).

Darling-Wolf, Fabienne, 'SMAP, Sex, and Masculinity: Constructing the Perfect Female Fantasy in Japanese Popular Music', *Popular Music and Society* 27/3 (2004): 357–70.

Daston, Lorraine and H. Otto Sibum, 'Introduction: Scientific Personae and Their Histories', *Science in Context*, 16/1–2 (2003): 1–8.

Davidson, Jane W., '"She's the One": Multiple Functions of Body Movement in a Stage Performance by Robbie Williams' in Anthony Gritten and Elaine King (eds), *Music and Gesture* (Aldershot: Ashgate, 2006), pp. 208–25.

——, 'The Role of the Body in the Production and Perception of Solo Vocal Performance: A Case Study of Annie Lennox', *Musicae Scientiae* 5/2 (2001): 235–56.

Davies, Helen, 'All Rock and Roll is Homosocial: The Representation of Women in the British Rock Music Press', *Popular Music* 20/3 (2001): 301–19.

Davis, George and Glegg Watson, *Black Life in Corporate America: Swimming in the Main Stream* (Garden City, NY: Anchor Press/Doubleday, 1982)

Davis, Robert, 'Who Got Da Funk? An Etymophony of Funk music from the 1950s to 1979', PhD diss. (Université de Montréal, 2005).

Davison, Annette, 'Copyright and Scholars's Rights', *Music, Sound, and the Moving Image* 1/1 (2007): 9–14.

——, *Hollywood Theory, Non-Hollywood Practice: Cinema Soundtracks in the 1980s and 1990s* (Aldershot: Ashgate, 2004).

Dawe, Kevin, 'Between East and West: Contemporary Grooves in Greek Popular Music (*c*.1990–2000)' in Goffredo Plastino (ed.), *Mediterranean Mosaic: Popular Music and Global Sounds in the Mediterranean Area* (New York: Routledge/Garland Publishing, 2003), pp. 221–40.

——, *Music and Musicians in Crete: Performance and Ethnography in a Mediterranean Island Society* (Lanham, MD: Scarecrow Press, 2007).

——, 'Regional Voices in a National Soundscape: Balkan Music and Dance in Greece', in D. Buchanan (ed.), *Balkan Popular Culture and the Ottoman Ecumene: Music, Image, and Regional Political Discourse(s)* (Lanham, MD: Scarecrow Press, 2007).

Day, Graham, *Community and Everyday Life* (London: Routledge, 2006).

Day, Robin, *Day by Day: A Dose of My Own Hemlock* (London: Kimber, 1975).

——, *The Case for Televising Parliament* (London: Hansard Society for Parliamentary Government, 1964).

Day, Timothy, *A Century of Recorded Music: Listening to Musical History* (New Haven, CT: Yale University Press, 2000).

Debord, Guy, *Society of the Spectacle* [1967] (London: Rebel Press, 2004).

Deckha, Nityanand, 'The Cool Britannia Effect and the Emergence of the Creative Quarter', *M/C: A Journal of Media and Culture*, 5/2 (2002), at: <http://www.media-culture.org.au/0205/britspace.php> (accessed 20 August 2008).

DeCordova, Richard, *Picture Personalities: The Emergence of the Star System in America* (Chicago: University of Illinois Press, 1990).

Denisoff, R. Serge and William L. Schurk, *Tarnished Gold: The Record Industry Revisited* (New Brunswick, NJ: Transaction Books, 1986).

DeNora, Tia, "Music as a Technology of the Self", *Poetics*, 26 (1999): 1–26.

——, *Music in Everyday Life* (Cambridge: Cambridge University Press, 2000).

Dent, David J., *In Search of Black America: Discovering the African-American Dream* (New York: Simon and Schuster, 2000).

Derrida, Jacques, *Writing and Difference*, trans. Alan Bass (London: Routledge, 1978).

Desse, S.B.G., *Freestyle* (Paris: Massot et Millet, 1993).

Dibben, Nicola, *Björk*, (London: Equinox Press, forthcoming).

——, 'Subjectivity and the Construction of Emotion in the Music of Björk', *Music Analysis* 25/1–2 (2006): 171–97.

Dickinson, Kay, '"Believe"? Vocoders, Digitalised Female Identity and Camp', *Popular Music* 20/3 (2001): 333–47.

——, 'Music Video and Synaesthesic Possibility' in Roger Beebe and Jason Middleton (eds), *Medium Cool: Music Videos from Soundies to Cellphones* (Durham, NC: Duke University Press, 2007), pp. 13–29.

DJ Ritu, 'Bhangra/Asian Beat: One-way Ticket to British Asia' in Simon Broughton, Mark Ellingham and Richard Trillo (eds), *World Music: The Rough Guide Volume 1* (1999). Available at: <http://www.ulme-mini-verlag.de/CR.HTM> (accessed 11 August 2008).

Donnelly, K.J., *Film and Television Music: The Spectre of Sound* (London: BFI, 2008).

Doss, Erika, *Elvis Culture: Fans, Faith, and Image* (Lawrence: University Press of Kansas, 1999).

Douglas, Mary, *Purity and Danger: An Analysis of the Concepts of Pollution and Taboo* (London: Routledge, 1966).

Dowd, Timothy J., 'Concentration and Diversity Revisited: Production Logics and the U.S. Mainstream Recording Market, 1940–1990', *Social Forces* 82 (2004): 1411–55.

Doyle, Peter, *Echo and Reverb: Fabricating Space in Popular Music Recording, 1900–1960*, (Middletown, CT: Wesleyan University Press, 2005).

Drucker, Peter, *The Age of Discontinuity: Guidelines to Our Changing Society* (New York: Harper and Row, 1969).

Du Gay, Paul and Michael Pryke (eds), *Cultural Economy: Cultural Analysis and Commercial Life* (London: Sage, 2002).

Du Gay, Paul, Stuart Hall, Linda Janes, Hugh Mackay and Keith Negus, *Doing Cultural Studies: The Story of the Sony Walkman* (London: Sage, 1997).

Dudrah, R.K., 'British Bhangra Music and the Battle of Britpop: South Asian Cultural Identity and Cultural Politics in Urban Britain', *Migration: A European Journal of International Migration and Ethnic Relations*, 39/40/41 (2002): 174–93.

——, 'Cultural Production in the British Bhangra Music Industry: Music-Making, Locality, and Gender?', *International Journal of Punjab Studies* 9/2 (2002): 219–51.

——, 'Drum N Dhol: British Bhangra Music and Diasporic South Asian Identity Formation', *European Journal of Cultural Studies* 5/3 (2002): 363–83.

Duffett, Mark, 'Caught in a Trap? Beyond Pop Theory's "Butch" Construction of Male Elvis Fans', *Popular Music* 20/3 (2001): 395–408.

Dunbar-Hall, Peter and Christopher Gibson, *Deadly Sounds, Deadly Places: Contemporary Music in Australia* (Sydney: University of New South Wales Press, 2004).

Durant, Alan, *Conditions of Music* (Albany, NY: State University of New York Press, 1985).

Dyer, Richard, *Heavenly Bodies: Film Stars and Society*, (London: Macmillan, 1987).

——, 'In Defense of Disco' [1979], in Frith and Goodwin, *On Record*, pp. 410–18.

——, *The Culture of Queers* (London: Routledge 2002).

Dyson, Michael Eric, *Holler If You Hear Me: Searching for Tupac Shakur* (New York: Basic Civitas Books, 2001).

Eagleton, Terry, *The Illusions of Postmodernism* (Oxford: Blackwell, 1996).

Eco, Umberto, *The Open Work* [1962], trans. Anna Cancogni (London: Hutchinson Radius, 1989).

'Edison Snares Soul of Music', *New York Tribune*, 29 April 1916, p. 3.

Ehrenreich, Barbara, Elizabeth Hess and Gloria Jacobs, 'Beatlemania: Girls Just Want to Have Fun', in Lisa A. Lewis (ed.), *The Adoring Audience: Fan Culture and Popular Media* (London: Routledge, 1992), pp. 84–106.

Eidsheim, Nina Sun, 'Voice as a Technology of Selfhood: Towards an Analysis of Racialized Timbre and Vocal Performance', PhD diss. (University of California, San Diego, 2008).

Eisenberg, Evan, *The Recording Angel: Explorations in Phonography* (New York: McGraw-Hill, 1987, pub. Harmondsworth: Penguin 1987, with subtitle *The Experience of Music from Aristotle to Zappa*).

——, *The Recording Angel: Music, Records and Culture from Aristotle to Zappa* (New Haven, CT: Yale University Press, 2005).

Ekman, Paul and Wallace V. Freisen, 'The Repertoire of Nonverbal Behaviour: Categories, Origins, Usage and Coding', *Semiotica* 1 (1969): 49–98.

Ellis, John, *Visible Fictions* (London: Routledge, 1992).

Ellis, Katharine, 'Rocks and Hard Places', *Herchel Smith Intellectual Property Futures*, (Cheltenham, forthcoming).

Emerick, Geoff, *Here, There and Everywhere. My Life Recording the Music of The Beatles*, (New York: Gotham, 2006).

Eno, Brian, 'Pro Session: The Studio as Compositional Tool', *Down Beat* 50 (1983): 65–67.

Erlewine, Stephen Thomas, '*All The Right Reasons*', at: <http://www.allmusic.com> (accessed 9 July 2008).

Everett-Green, Robert 'Familiar Tunes, Surprising Angles', review of Robert Plant and Alison Krauss at the Molson Amphitheatre, Toronto, 14 July 2008, *The Globe and Mail*, 16 July 2008, at: <http://www.theglobeandmail.com/servlet/story/RTGAM.20080716.wplant16/BNStory/Entertainment/home> (accessed 17 July 2008).

Fabbri, Franco, 'A Theory of Musical Genres: Two Applications' in David Horn and Philip Tagg (eds), *Popular Music Perspectives* (Göteborg and Exeter: IASPM, 1982), pp. 52–81.

——, 'Browsing Music Spaces: Categories and the Musical Mind' [1999], in Moore, *Critical Essays*, pp. 49–62.

Fairchild, Charles, 'Building the Authentic Celebrity: The "Idol" Phenomenon in the Attention Economy', *Popular Music and Society*, 30/3 (2007): pp. 355–75.

——, *Pop Idols and Pirates: Mechanisms of Consumption and the Global Circulation of Popular Music* (Aldershot: Ashgate, 2008).

Fales, Cornelia, 'Short-circuiting Perceptual Systems: Timbre in Ambient and Techno Music' in Greene and Porcello, *Wired for Sound*, pp. 156–80.

Farida, Syeda, 'Pioneer in Bhangra Pop', *The Hindu*, Metro Plus Hyderabad, 18 June. 2002.

Farinella, David John, *Producing Hit Records. Secrets from the Studio* (New York: Schirmer, 2006).

Farson, Daniel, *Soho in the Fifties* (London: Michael Joseph, 1987).

Fast, Susan, '"Girls! Rock Your Boys:" The Continuing (Non)History of Women in Rock Music', Annette Kreutziger-Herr and Katrin Losleben (eds), *History/ Herstory: Alternative Musikgeschichten*, (Köln: Böhlau, 2008).

——, *In the Houses of the Holy: Led Zeppelin and the Power of Rock Music* (New York: Oxford University Press, 2001).

Featherstone, Mike, *Consumer Culture and Postmodernism* (London: Sage Publications, 1990).

——, *Global Culture: Nationalism, Globalization and Modernity* (London: Sage, 1994).

Feigenbaum, Anna, '"Some Guy Designed This Room I'm Standing In": Marking Gender in Press Coverage of Ani DiFranco', *Popular Music* 24/1 (2005): 37–56.

Feist, Leslie, at: <http://www.el-oso.net/blog/archives/2005/08/11/feist/11> (accessed 26 May 2008).

Feld, Stephen, *Sound and Sentiment: Birds, Weeping, Poetics, and Song in Kaluli Expression* (Philadelphia: University of Pennsylvania Press, 1982).

Fernando, S.H. Jr, *The New Beats: Culture, musique et attitudes du hip hop* (Paris: Kargo, 2000).

Fetterley, Leanne, 'Hey, Hey, I Wanna be a Rock Star: Nickelback, Sincerity and Authenticity', paper presented at the annual meeting of IASPM-Canada, 2008, at Brock University.

Fine, Sidney, *Violence in the Modern City: Race Relations, Cavanagh Administration, and the Detroit Race Riots of 1967* (Ann Arbor: University of Michigan Press, 1989).

Fink, Michael, *Inside the Music Industry: Creativity, Process, and Business* (New York: Schirmer Books, 1996)

Fink, Robert, *Repeating Ourselves: American Minimalism as Cultural Practice* (Berkeley: University of California Press, 2005).

Fiske, John, 'The Cultural Economy of Fandom' in Lewis, *The Adoring Audience*, pp. 30–49.

Fiske, John and John Hartley, *Reading Television* (London: Routledge, 2003).

Flew, Terry, 'Creative Economy' in Hartley, *Creative Industries*, pp. 344–60.

——, 'Music, Cities and Cultural and Creative Industries Policy', in Bloustien, Peters and Luckman, *Sonic Synergies*, pp. 7–16.

Flinn, Caryl, *Strains of Utopia: Gender, Nostalgia, and Hollywood Film Music* (Princeton, NJ: Princeton University Press, 1992).

Florida, Richard L., *The Rise of the Creative Class: And How It's Transforming Work, Leisure, Community and Everyday Life* (New York: Basic Books, 2002).

Ford, Charles, 'On Music and Masculinity' in Scott, *Music, Culture, and Society*, pp. 77–82.

Forman, Murray, 'Television Before Television Genre: The Case of Popular Music', *Journal of Popular Film and Television* 31 (Spring 2003): 5–17.

Foucault, Michel, *The History of Sexuality. Vol. 1: An Introduction* [1976], trans. Robert Hurley (Harmondsworth: Penguin, 1990).

Fox, Aaron A., *Real Country: Music and Language in Working-Class Culture* (Durham, NC: Duke University Press, 2004).

——, 'White Trash Alchemies of the Abject Sublime: Country as "Bad" Music', in Christopher J. Washburne and Maiken Derno (eds), *Bad Music: The Music We Love To Hate* (New York: Routledge, 2004), pp. 39–61.

Frame, Pete, *The Restless Generation* (London: Rogan House, 2007).

Frankenberg, Ronald, *Communities in Britain* (Harmondsworth: Penguin, 1966).

Frazier, Edward Franklin, *The Black Bourgeoisie* (New York: Collier Books, 1962).

Freeman, Richard B., *The Black Elite* (New York: McGraw-Hill, 1976).

Frere-Jones, Sasha, 'A Paler Shade of White', *The New Yorker*, 22 October 2007, at: <http://www.newyorker.com/arts/critics/musical/2007/10/22/071022crmu_music_frerejones?currentPage=1> (accessed 18 July 2008).

Friedman, Jonathan, 'Global Crises, The Struggle for Cultural Identity and Intellectual Porkbarrelling: Cosmopolitans versus Locals, Ethnics and National in an Era of De-hegemonisation' in Pnina Webner and Tariq Modood (eds), *Debating Cultural Hybridity: Multi-cultural Identities and the Politics of Anti-Racism* (London: Zed Books, 2000), pp. 70–89.

Frith, Simon, 'Art Versus Technology: The Strange Case of Popular Music', *Media, Culture & Society* 8/3 (1986): 263–79.

——, 'Look! Hear! The Uneasy relationship of Music and Television', *Popular Music* 21/3 (2002): 277–89.

——, *Music for Pleasure* (Cambridge: Polity Press, 1988).

——, *Performing Rites: Evaluating Popular Music* (Cambridge, MA: Harvard University Press, and Oxford: Oxford University Press, 1996).

——, *Sound Effects: Youth, Leisure and the Politics of Rock 'n' Roll* [1981] (London: Constable, 1983).

——, 'The Industrialization of Popular Music' in James Lull (ed.), *Popular Music and Communication* (London: Sage, 1992), pp. 49–74.

——, '"The Magic That Can Set You Free": The Ideology of Folk and the Myth of the Rock Community', in *Popular Music. Vol. 1: Folk or Popular? Distinctions, Influences, Continuities* (Cambridge: Cambridge University Press, 1981), pp. 159–68.

——, 'Towards an Aesthetic of Popular Music' in Richard Leppert and Susan McClary (eds), *Music and Society: The Politics of Composition, Performance and Reception* (Cambridge: Cambridge University Press, 1987), pp. 133–49.

——(ed.), *World Music, Politics and Social Change* (Manchester: Manchester University Press, 1989).

Frith, Simon and Andrew Goodwin (eds), *On Record: Rock, Pop and the Written Word* (London: Routledge, 1990).

Frith, Simon and Angela McRobbie, 'Rock and Sexuality' [1978] in Frith and Goodwin, *On Record*, pp. 371–89.

Gaisberg, Frederick W., *The Music Goes Round* (New York: Macmillan, 1942).

Gaither, Edmund B. '"Hey! That's Mine": Thoughts on Pluralism and American Museums' in Ivan Karp, Christine Mullen Kreamer and Steven D. Lavine (eds.), *The Politics of Public Culture: Museums and Communities* (Washington, DC: Smithsonian Institution Press, 1992), pp. 56–64.

Gans, Herbert J., *Popular Culture and High Culture: An Analysis and Evaluation of Taste* (New York: Basic Books, 1974).

Garber, Marjorie, *Vested Interests: Cross-Dressing and Cultural Anxiety* (New York: Routledge, 1997).

Garcia, Luis-Manuel, 'On and On: Repetition as Process and Pleasure in Electronic Dance Music', *Music Theory Online*, 11/4 (2005): sections 1.1–7.4, at: <http://www.societymusictheory.org/mto/issues/mto.05.11.4/mto.05.11.4.garcia.html>.

Garfinkel, Harold, *Studies in Ethnomethodology* (Englewood Cliffs, NJ: Prentice Hall, 1967).

Garofalo, Reebee, *Rockin' Out! Popular Music in the USA* (Boston: Allyn and Bacon, 1997).

Garrick, John and Robin Usher, 'Flexible Learning, Contemporary Work, and Enterprising Selves', *Electronic Journal of Sociology*, 5/1 (2000), at: <http://scholarlyexchange.sociology.org/content/vol005.001/garrick-usher.html> (accessed 2 June 2008).

Gay, Peter, *Style in History* (London: Jonathan Cape, 1975).

Gebesmair, Andreas, *Die Fabrikation globaler Vielfalt. Struktur und Logik der transnationalen Popmusikindustrie* (Bielefeld: Transcript, 2008).

Gebesmair, Andreas and Alfred Smudits (eds), *Global Repertoires: Popular Music within and beyond the Transnational Music Industry* (Aldershot: Ashgate, 2001).

Gelatt, Roland, *The Fabulous Phonograph 1877–1977* (London: Macmillan, 2nd edn 1977).

Gelder, Ken and Sarah Thornton (eds), *The Subcultures Reader* (London: Routledge, 1997).

Geyrhalter, Thomas, 'Effeminacy, Camp and Sexual Subversion in Rock: The Cure and Suede', *Popular Music* 15/2 (1996): 217–24.

Giddens, Anthony, *New Rules of Sociological Method: A Positive Critique of Interpretative Sociologies* (Cambridge: Polity Press, 2nd edn 1993).

Gilbert, Jeremy, 'White Light/White Heat: *Jouissance* Beyond Gender in the Velvet Underground', in Andrew Blake (ed), *Living Through Pop* (London: Routledge, 1999), pp. 31–48.

Gilbert, Roger, 'The Swinger and the Loser: Sinatra, Masculinity, and Fifties Culture', in Leonard Mustazza (ed.), *Frank Sinatra and Popular Culture: Essays on an American Icon* (Westport, CT: Praeger, 1998), pp. 38–49.

Gill, Gerald R., *Meanness Mania: The Changed Mood* (Washington, DC.: Howard University Press, 1980).

Gillespie, Marie, *Television, Ethnicity, and Cultural Change* (London: Routledge, 1995).

Gillett, Charlie, *The Sound of the City* (London: Sphere, 1971).

Gilroy, Paul, *Against Race: Imagining Political Culture Beyond the Color Line* (Cambridge, MA: Belknap Press of Harvard University Press, 2000).

——, *The Black Atlantic: Modernity and Double Consciousness* (Cambridge, MA: Harvard University Press, and London: Verso, 1993).

Glaeser, E.L. and J.D. Gottlieb, 'Urban Resurgence and the Consumer City', *Urban Studies* 43/8 (2006): 1275–99.

Godbolt, Jim, *A History of Jazz in Britain 1919–1950* (London: Quartet, 1984).

Goffman, Erving, *Frame Analysis: An Essay on the Organization of Experience* [1974] (Boston, MA: Northeastern University Press, rev. edn. 1986).

——, *The Presentation of Self in Everyday Life* [1959] (London: Penguin, 1990).

Goldberg, Rose Lee, *Performance Art: From Futurism to the Present* (London: Thames & Hudson, 1988).

Goldin-Perschbacher, Shana, '"Not with You but of You": "Unbearable Intimacy" and Jeff Buckley's Transgendered Vocality' in Jarman-Ivens, *Oh Boy!*, pp. 213–34.

Goldmark, Daniel, *Tunes for 'Toons: Music and the Hollywood Cartoon* (Berkeley: University of California Press, 2005).

Goldrosen, John, *The Buddy Holly Story* (New York: Quick Fox, 1979).

Goodwin, Andrew, 'Sample and Hold: Pop Music in the Digital Age of Reproduction' in Frith and Goodwin, On Record, pp. 258–73.

——, *Dancing in the Distraction Factory. Music Television and Popular Culture* (London: Routledge, 1993).

Goody, J., *La raison graphique. La domestication de la pensée sauvage* (Paris: Minuit, 1979).

Gopinath, Gayatri, 'Bombay, U.K., Yuba City: Bhangra Music and the Engendering of Diaspora,' *Diaspora* 4/3 (Winter 1995): 303–21.

Gorbman, Claudia, 'Auteur Music' in Daniel Goldmark, Lawrence Kramer and Richard Leppert (eds), *Beyond the Soundtrack* (Berkeley: University of California Press, 2007), pp. 149–62.

——, 'Ears Wide Open: Kubrick's Music' in Robynn Stilwell and Phil Powrie (eds), *Changing Tunes: The Use of Pre-existing Music in Film* (Aldershot: Ashgate, 2006), pp. 3–18.

——, *Unheard Melodies: Narrative Film Music* (Bloomington: Indiana University Press, and London: BFI, 1987).

Gordon, Milton, 'The Concept of the Subculture and its Application', *Social Forces* 26/1 (1947): 40–42.

Gorman, Paul, *The Look: Adventures in Pop and Rock Fashion* (London: Sanctuary Publishing, 2001).

Graakjaer, Nikolai and Christian Jantzen (eds), *Music in Advertising: Commercial Sounds in Media Communication and Other Settings* (Aalborg: Aalborg University Press, 2009).

Gracyk, Theodore, *Rhythm and Noise: An Aesthetics of Rock* (Durham, NC: Duke University Press, and London: I.B. Tauris, 1996).

Graham, Lawrence Otis, *Our Kind of People: Inside American's Black Upper Class* (New York: Harper Collins, 1999).

Gramit, David, 'The Roaring Lion: Critical Musicology, the Aesthetic Experience, and the Music Department', *Canadian University Music Review* 19/1 (1998): 19–33.

Granata, Charles L., *I Just Wasn't Made for These Times: Brian Wilson and the Making of Pet Sounds* (London: Unanimous, 2003).

Grant, Peter S. and Chris Wood, *Blockbusters and Trade Wars: Popular Culture in a Globalized World* (Vancouver: Douglas & McIntyre, 2004).

Grebowicz, Margaret, 'Introduction: After Lyotard' in Margaret Grebowicz (ed.), *Gender After Lyotard* (Albany, NY: State University of New York Press, 2007), pp. 1–12.

Green, Jonathon, *Days in the Life: Voices from the English Underground* (London: Heinemann, 1988).

Green, Lucy, *How Popular Musicians Learn: A Way Ahead for Music Education* (Aldershot: Ashgate, 2001).

——, *Music, Informal Learning and the School: A New Classroom Pedagogy* (Aldershot: Ashgate, 2008).

Greene, Paul D. and Thomas Porcello (eds), *Wired for Sound: Engineering and Technologies in Sonic Cultures* (Middletown, CT: Wesleyan University Press, 2005).

Greenwald, Andy, *Nothing Feels Good: Punk Rock, Teenagers, and Emo* (New York: St Martin's Griffin, 2003).

Gridley, Mark C., 'Cool Jazz', *Grove Music Online*, at: <http://www.grovemusic.com/shared/views/article.html?section=jazz.100900> (accessed 15 March 2008).

Griffiths, Dai, 'From Lyric to Anti-lyric: Analyzing the Words in Pop Song' in Moore, *Analyzing Popular Music*, pp. 39–59.

——, 'The High Analysis of Low Music' [1999], in Moore, *Critical Essays*, pp. 63–109.

Gronow, Pekka, 'The Record Industry: The Growth of a Mass Medium', *Popular Music* 3 (1983): 53–75.

Gronow, Pekka and Ilpo Saunio, *An International History of the Recording Industry* (London: Cassell, 1998).

Grossberg, Lawrence, *Caught in the Crossfire: Kids, Politics and America's Future* (Boulder, CO: Paradigm Publishers, 2005).

——, 'The Media Economy of Rock Culture: Cinema, Post-Modernity and Authenticity' in Simon Frith, Andrew Goodwin and Lawrence Grossberg (eds), *Sound & Vision: The Music Video Reader* (London: Routledge, 1993), pp. 185–209.

——, *We Gotta Get out of This Place* (London: Routledge, 1992).

Grynzpan, E., *Bruyante Techno* (Nantes: Mélanie Séteun, 1999).

Gudmundsson, Gestur, Ulf Lindberg, Morten Michelson and Hans Weisethaunet, 'Brit Crit: Turning Points in British Rock Criticism 1960–1990' in Steve Jones (ed.), *Pop Music and the Press* (Philadelphia, PA: Temple University Press, 2002), pp. 41–64.

Guins, Raiford and Omayra Zaragoza Cruz, *Popular Culture: A Reader* (London: Sage, 2005).

Habermas, Jürgen, *The Structural Transformation of the Public Sphere: An Inquiry Into a Category of Bourgeois Society*, trans. Thomas Burger with the assistance of Frederick Lawrence (Cambridge: Polity Press, 1989).

——, *The Theory of Communicative Action. Vol 2: Lifeworld and System: A Critique of Functionalist Reason*, trans. Thomas McCarthy (Cambridge: Polity Press, 1987).

Haenfler, Ross, *Straight Edge: Clean-Living Youth, Hardcore Punk, and Social Change* (New Brunswick, NJ: Rutgers University Press, 2006).

Halberstam, Judith, 'An Introduction to Female Masculinity: Masculinity Without Men' [1998] in *The Masculinity Studies Reader* (Oxford: Blackwell, 2002), pp. 355–74.

——, *Female Masculinity* (Durham, NC: Duke University Press, 1998).

——, *In a Queer Time and Place* (New York: New York University Press, 2005).

——, 'Queer Voices and Musical Genders' in Jarman-Ivens, *Oh Boy!*, pp. 183–95.

——, 'What's That Smell? Queer Temporalities and Subcultural Lives', in Whiteley and Rycenga, *Queering the Popular Pitch*, pp. 3–26.

Hall, Edward T., *The Hidden Dimension* (London: The Bodley Head, 1969).

Hall, Stuart, 'New Ethnicities' in A. Rattansi and J. Donald (eds), *Race, Culture and Difference* (London: Sage, 1992), pp. 252–59.

Hall, Stuart and Tony Jefferson (eds), *Resistance Through Rituals: Youth Subcultures in Post-War Britain* (London: Hutchinson, 1975).

Hamilton, Jaimey, 'The Way We Loop "Now": Eddying in the Flows of Media', *Invisible Culture: An Electronic Journal for Visual Culture* 8 (2004): 1–24.

Hamm, Charles, Bruno Nettl and Ronald Byrnside (eds), *Contemporary Music and Music Cultures* (Englewood Cliffs, NJ: Prentice-Hall, 1975).

Harcourt, Nic, 'One Man Band', *Smithsonian Magazine*, October 2007, at: <http://www.smithsonianmag.com/arts-culture/10036476.html> (accessed 31 July 2008).

Hare, Nathan, *The Black Anglo-Saxons* (New York: Marzani & Munsell, 1965).

Harker, Dave, *One for the Money: Politics and Popular Song* (London: Hutchinson, 1980).

Harrigan, Jinni, 'Proxemics, Kinesics and Gaze' in Jinni Harrigan, Robert Rosenthal and Klaus R. Scherer (eds), *The New Handbook of Methods in Nonverbal Behaviour* (New York: Oxford University Press, 2005), pp. 137–98.

Harris, John, *Britpop! Cool Britannia and the Spectacular Demise of English Rock* (London: Da Capo Press, 2004).

Harrison, Daniel, 'After Sundown: The Beach Boys' Experimental Music' in John Covach and Graeme Boone (eds), *Understanding Rock: Essays in Musical Analysis* (New York: Oxford University Press, 1997), pp. 33–58.

Hartley, John, 'Communicative Democracy in a Redactional Society: The Future of Journalism Studies', *Journalism* 1/1 (2000): 39–47.

——, (ed.), *Creative Industries* (Oxford: Blackwell, 2005).

Harvith, John and Susan Edwards Harvith, *Edison, Musicians, and the Phonograph. A Century in Retrospect* (New York: Greenwood Press, 1987).

Haseman, Brad, 'Creative Practices' in Hartley, *Creative Industries*, pp. 158–76.

Hatch, David and Stephen Millward, *From Blues to Rock: An Analytical History of Pop Music* (Manchester: Manchester University Press, 1987).

Hatschek, Keith, *The Golden Moment. Recording Secrets from the Pros* (San Francisco, CA: Backbeat Books, 2005).

Hawkins, Harriett, *Classics and Trash* (Hemel Hempstead: Harvester Wheatsheaf, 1990).

Hawkins, Stan, 'Feel the Beat Come Down: House Music as Rhetoric' in Moore, *Analyzing Popular Music*, pp. 80–102.

——, 'Perspectives in Popular Musicology: Music, Lennox, and Meaning in 1990s Pop', *Popular Music* 15/1 (1996): 17–36.

——, 'Prince: Harmonic Analysis of "Anna Stesia"', *Popular Music* 11/3 (1992): 325–36.

——, *Settling the Pop Score: Pop Texts and Identity Politics* (Aldershot: Ashgate, 2002).

——, 'The Pet Shop Boys: Musicology, Masculinity and Banality' in Whiteley, *Sexing the Groove*, pp. 118–34.

——, '[Un]*Justified*: Gestures of Straight-Talk in Justin Timberlake's Songs' in Jarman-Ivens, *Oh Boy!*, pp. 197–212.

Hebdige, Dick, *Subculture: The Meaning of Style* (London: Methuen, 1979/London: Routledge, 1988).

Heckman, Don, 'The Backup Singers: High Reward for a Privileged Few', *High Fidelity and Musical America* 28 (1978): 120–22.

Hennessey, Peter, *Having It So Good: Britain in the Fifties* (London: Penguin, 2007).

Hennion, Antoine, 'An Intermediary between Production and Consumption: The Producer of Popular Music', *Science, Technology, & Human Values* 14 (1989): 400–24.

——, 'L'Ecoute à la question', *Revue de musicologie* 88/1 (2002): 95–149.

——, 'Listen!', *Music and Arts in Action* 1/1 (2008): 39–45. Also available at: <http://musicandartsinaction.net/index.php/maia/article/view/listen>.

——, 'Musiques, présentez-vous!', *French Cultural Studies*, 16/2 (2005): 121–34.

——, 'Those Things That Hold Us Together: Taste and Sociology', *Cultural Sociology* 1/1, ed. D. Inglis and R. Wagner-Pacifici (2007): 97–114.

Henriques, Julian, 'The Jamaican Dancehall Sound System as a Commercial and Social Apparatus', in Bloustien, Peters and Luckman, *Sonic Synergies*, pp. 125–40.

Heron, Liz (ed.), *Truth, Dare or Promise: Girls Growing up in the Fifties* (London: Virago, 1993).

Hesmondhalgh, David, 'Flexibility, Post-Fordism and the Music Industries', *Media, Culture and Society* 18 (1996): 469–88.

——, 'Subcultures, Scenes or Tribes? None of the Above', *Journal of Youth Studies* 8/1 (2005): 21–40.

——, *The Cultural Industries* (London: Sage Publications, 2002).

Hesmondhalgh, David and Keith Negus (eds), *Popular Music Studies* (London: Arnold, 2002).

Hetherington, Kevin, *Expressions of Identity: Space, Performance, Politics* (London: Sage, 1998).

Hill, Mike (ed.), *Whiteness: A Critical Reader* (New York: New York University Press, 1997).

Hilmes, Michele (ed.), 'In Focus', *Cinema Journal* 48/1 (2008).

——, 'Television Sound: Why the Silence?' in Beck and Grajeda, *Lowering the Boom*.

Hirsch, Paul M., 'Processing Fads and Fashions: An Organization-Set Analysis of Cultural Industry Systems', *American Journal of Sociology* 77 (1972): 639–59.

Hisama, Ellie, 'Postcolonialism on the Make: The Music of John Mellencamp, David Bowie, and John Zorn', *Popular Music* 12/2 (1993): 91–104.

Hockney, David, *Secret Knowledge – Rediscovering the Lost Techniques of the Old Masters* (London: Thames & Hudson, 2006).

Hodkinson, Paul, *Goth: Identity, Style and Subculture* (Oxford: Berg, 2002).

Hoffert, Paul, *Music for New Media* (Boston, MA: Berklee Press, 2007).

Holbrook, Morris B., 'Ambi-Diegetic Music in Films as a Product Design and Placement Strategy: The Sweet Smell of Success', in *Marketing Theory* 4/3 (2004): 171–85.

Holland, Samantha, *Alternative Femininities: Body, Age and Identity* (Oxford: Berg, 2004).

Holmes, Su, 'Reality Goes Pop! Reality TV, Popular Music, and Narratives of Stardom in Pop Idol', *Television and New Media* 5/2 (2004): 147–72.

Holmes, Thom, *Electronic and Experimental Music: Technology, Music and Culture* (New York: Routledge, 3rd edn 2008).

Holt, Fabian, *Genre in Popular Music* (Chicago: University of Chicago Press, 2007).

hooks, bell, 'Eating the Other: Desire and Resistance' in Meenakshi Gigi Durham and Douglas M. Kellner (eds), *Media and Cultural Studies: Key Works* (New York: Blackwell, 2001), pp. 424–38.

Horkheimer, Max, Theodor W. Adorno and Gunzelin Schmid Noerr, *Dialectic of Enlightenment: Philosophical Fragments, Cultural Memory in the Present* (Stanford, CA: Stanford University Press, 2002).

Hornby, Nick, *High Fidelity* (New York: Riverhead Books, 1995).

Horrocks, Roger, *Masculinity in Crisis: Myths, Fantasies and Realities* (New York: St Martin's Press, 1994).

Hoskyns, Barney, *Glam! Bowie, Bolan and the Glitter Rock Revolution* (New York: Pocket Books, 1998).

Hosokawa, Shuhei, *The Aesthetics of Recorded Sound* (Tokyo: Keisó Shobó, 1990).

——, 'The Walkman Effect', *Popular Music* 4 (1984): 165–80.

Hosokawa, Shuhei and Hideaki Matsuoka, 'On the Fetish Character of Sound and the Progression of Technology: Theorising Japanese Audiophiles' in Bloustien, Peters and Luckman, *Sonic Synergies*, pp. 39–50.

Housee, Shireen and Mukhtar Dar, 'Remixing Identities: "Off" the Turntable' in Sharma, Hutynk and Sharma, *Disorienting Rhythms*, pp. 81–104.

Howkins, John, *The Creative Economy: How People Make Money from Ideas* (London: Allen Lane, 2001).

Hull, Geoffrey, *The Recording Industry* (Boston, MA: Allyn and Bacon, 1998).

Huntington, Samuel, *The Clash of Civilizations and the Remaking of World Order* (New York: Simon & Schuster, 1996).

Huq, Rupa, *Beyond Subculture: Pop, Youth and Identity in a Postcolonial World* (London: Routledge, 2006).

Huron, David, *Sweet Anticipation: Music and the Psychology of Expectation* (Cambridge, MA: MIT Press, 2006).

Hutnyk, John, *Critique of Exotica: Music, Politics and the Culture Industry* (London: Pluto Press, 2000).

Huyssen, Andreas, 'Mass Culture as Woman: Modernism's Other' in *After the Great Divide: Modernism, Mass Culture, Postmodernism* (Bloomington: Indiana University Press, 1986), pp. 44–62.

Idols West African Extension, at: <http://www.youtube.com/watch?v=9GrZaOkgp CI&feature=related/>.

Inglis, Ian, 'Pete Best: History and His Story', *Journal of Popular Music Studies* 11/12 (2000): 103–24.

'Iraqi Singer Wins Arab "Pop Idol"', Aljazeera.net, at: http://www.youtube.com/ watch?v=4q_5LUH6m5E&feature=related (accessed 27 May 2008).

Isherwood, Christopher, *The World In The Evening* (New York: Noonday Press, 1954).

Iwabuchi, Koichi, *Recentering Globalization. Popular Culture and Japanese Transnationalism* (Durham, NC: Duke University Press, 2002).

Jagose, Annamarie, 'An Extract from "Queer Theory"', *Australian Humanities Review* 4 (December 1996). Available at: <http://www.australianhumanitiesreview.org/ archive/Issue-Dec-1996/jagose.html> (accessed 23 August 2008).

Jameson, Fredric, 'Notes on Globalization as a Philosophical Issue' in Fredric Jameson and Masao Miyoshi (eds), *The Cultures of Globalization* (Durham, NC: Duke University Press, 1996), pp. 54–77.

——, *Postmodernism, or, the Cultural Logic of Late Capitalism* (Durham, NC: Duke University Press, 1991).

Jarman-Ivens, Freya, '"Don't Cry, Daddy": The Degeneration of Elvis Presley's Musical Masculinity' in Jarman-Ivens, *Oh Boy!*, pp. 161–80.

——, 'Oh Boy! Making Masculinity in Popular Music' in Jarman-Ivens, *Oh Boy!*, pp. 1–20.

—— (ed.), *Oh Boy! Masculinities and Popular Music* (London: Routledge, 2007).

——, 'Queer(ing) Masculinities in Heterosexist Rap Music' in Whiteley and Rycenga, *Queering the Popular Pitch*, pp. 199–219.

Jazz at Lincoln Center, 'The Architecture', at: <http://www.jalc.org/fprh/architecture. html> (accessed 23 September 2005).

Jenkins, Henry, *Convergence Culture. Where Old and New Media Collide* (New York: New York University Press, 1992).

Jenkins, Keith, *On 'What Is History?'* (London: Routledge, 1995).

Jenkins, Richard, *Social Identity* (London: Routledge, 1996).

Jenks, Chris, *Subculture: The Fragmentation of the Social* (London: Sage, 2005).

Johnson, James H., *Listening in Paris: A Cultural History* (Berkeley: University of California Press, 1995).

Johnson, Mark, *The Body in the Mind* (Chicago: University of Chicago Press, 1987).

Johnson-Grau, Brenda, 'Sweet Nothings: Presentation of Women Musicians in Pop Journalism', in Steve Jones (ed.), *Pop Music and the Press* (Philadelphia, PA: Temple University Press, 2002), pp. 202–18.

John-Steiner, Vera, *Creative Collaboration* (Oxford: Oxford University Press, 2000).

Johnstone, Nick, *Melody Maker History of Twentieth Century Popular Music* (London: Bloomsbury, 1999).

Jones, Diem, *#1 Bimini Road: Authentic P-Funk Insights* (Oakland, CA: Sufi Warrior Publishing, 1996).

Jones, Nicholas, *Sultans of Spin: Media and the New Labour Government* (London: Gollancz, 2000).

Jones, Steve, *Rock Formation: Music, Technology and Mass Communication* (London: Sage, 1992).

Jouvenet, Morgan, '"Emportés par le mix": les DJ et le travail de l'émotion', *Terrain* 37 (September 2001): 45–60.

Jung, Carl, G., *Psychological Reflections: An Anthology of his Writings 1905–1961*, ed. Jolande Jacobi (London: Routledge and Kegan Paul, 1971).

Kahn-Harris, Keith, '"I Hate This Fucking Country": Dealing with the Global and the Local in the Israeli Extreme Metal Scene', *Critical Studies 19: Music, Popular Culture, Identities* (2002): 133–51.

——, '"Roots"? The Relationship Between the Global and the Local within the Global Extreme Metal Scene', *Popular Music* 19/1 (2000): 13–30; reprinted in Bennett, Shank and Toynbee, *The Popular Music Studies Reader*, pp. 128–36.

Kalinak, Kathryn, *Settling the Score: Music and the Classical Hollywood Film* (Madison: University of Wisconsin Press, 1992).

Kalra, Virinder S. and John Hutnyk, 'Visibility, Appropriation and Resistance', *Seminar* 503 (2001). <http://www.india-seminar.com> (accessed 11 August 2008).

Kaplan, E. Ann, *Rocking Around the Clock: Music Television, Postmodernism, and Consumer Culture* (London: Methuen, 1987).

Kasbekar, Asha, *Pop Culture India! Media, Arts and Lifestyle* (Santa Barbara, CA: ABC-Clio, 2006).

Kassabian, Anahid, *Hearing Film: Tracking Identifications in Contemporary Hollywood Film Music* (New York: Routledge, 2001).

——, 'Popular' in Bruce Horner and Thomas Swiss (eds), *Key Terms in Popular Music and Culture* (Oxford: Blackwell, 1999), pp. 113–23.

——, 'The Sound of a New Film Form' in Ian Inglis (ed.), *Popular Music and Film* (London: Wallflower Press, 2003), pp. 91–101.

——, *The Soundtracks of Our Lives: Ubiquitous Musics and Distributed Subjectivities* (Los Angeles: University of California Press, forthcoming).

Katz, Mark, *Capturing Sound: How Technology has Changed Music* (Berkeley: University of California Press, 2004).

Katz, Michael B. (ed.), *The 'Underclass Debate': Views from History* (Princeton, NJ: Princeton University Press, 1993).

Kealy, Edward R., 'Conventions and the Production of the Popular Music Aesthetic', *Journal of Popular Culture* 16 (1982): 100–15.

Keast, James, 'Exclaim: Sigur Rós – 20,000 Icelanders Can't be Wrong', *Eighteen Seconds before Sunrise*, at: <http://www.sigur-ros.co.uk/media/articles/exclaim0.php> (accessed 22 May 2008).

Keightley, Keir, 'Reconsidering Rock' in *The Cambridge Companion to Pop and Rock* (Cambridge: Cambridge University Press, 2001), pp. 109–42.

——, '"Turn it Down!" She Shrieked: Gender, Domestic Space, and High Fidelity, 1948–59', *Popular Music* 15/2 (1996): 149–77.

Keil, Charles and Feld, Steven, *Music Grooves* (Chicago: University of Chicago Press, 1994).

Keller, Hans, *Functional Analysis: The Unity of Contrasting Themes* (Vienna: Peter Lang, 2001).

Kelley, Robin D.G., 'The Black Poor and the Politics of Opposition in a New South City', in Katz, *The 'Underclass' Debate*, pp. 293–333.

——, Yo' Mama's DisFunktional! Fighting the Cultural Wars in Urban America (Boston, MA: Beacon Press, 1977).

Kempen, Ronald van, 'Ethnic Segregation in Cities: New Forms and Explanations in a Dynamic World', *Urban Studies* 35/10 (1998): 1631–56.

Kennett, Christian, 'Is Anybody Listening?' in Allan F. Moore (ed.), *Analyzing Popular Music* (Cambridge: Cambridge University Press, 2003), pp. 196–217.

Kenney, William H., *Recorded Music in American Life: The Phonograph and Popular Memory, 1890–1945* (New York: Oxford University Press, 1999).

Kerman, Joseph, *Contemplating Music: Challenges to Musicology* (Cambridge, MA: Harvard University Press, 1985); published in the UK as *Musicology* (London: Fontana, 1985).

Kilpiö, Kaarina, 'The Use of Music in Early Finnish Cinema and TV Advertising' in Lotte Yssing Hansen and Flemming Hansen (eds), *Advertising Research in the Nordic Countries* (Copenhagen: Samfundslitteratur, 2001) pp. 68–76.

Kimmel, Michael, *Manhood in America: A Cultural History* (Oxford: Oxford University Press, 2005).

Kindlon, Dan and Michael Thompson, *Raising Cain: Protecting the Emotional Life of Boys* (New York: Ballantine Books, 2000).

King, Geoff, 'Introduction: The Spectacle of the Real' in Geoff King (ed.), *Spectacle of the Real: From Hollywood to Reality TV and Beyond* (Bristol: Intellect Books, 2005), pp. 13–21.

Kittler, Friedrich A., *Gramophone, Film, Typewriter*, trans. Geoffrey Winthrop-Young and Michael Wutz (Stanford, CA: Stanford University Press, 1999).

Klein, Bethany, *As Heard on TV: Popular Music in Advertising* (Aldershot: Ashgate, 2008).

Korner, Anthony, 'Aurora musicalis' (An interview with Brian Eno), *Art Forum* 24/10 (1986): 76–79.

Koronto, Abdirahman, '"Pop Idol" Fever Sweeps Ethiopia', 26 January 2006, at: http://news.bbc.co.uk/2/hi/africa/4648208.stm (accessed 15 June 2008).

Kotz, Liz, 'The Body You Want: Liz Kotz interviews Judith Butler', *Artforum* 31/3 (1992): 82–89.

Krims, Adam, 'Marxist Music Analysis without Adorno: Popular Music and Urban Geography' in Moore, *Analyzing Popular Music*, pp. 131–57.

——, *Music and Urban Geography* (New York: Routledge, 2007).

——, *Rap Music and the Poetics of Identity* (Cambridge: Cambridge University Press, 2000).

Kristeva, Julia, *Powers of Horror: An Essay on Abjection* [1980], trans. Leon S. Roudiez (New York: Columbia University Press, 1982).

——, *Revolution in Poetic Language* [1974], trans. Margaret Waller (New York: Columbia University Press, 1984).

Kurosawa, Kaori and Jane W. Davidson, 'Nonverbal Behaviours in Popular Music Performance: A Case Study of the Corrs', *Musicae Scientiae*, 9 (2005): 111–37.

Kusek, David, Gerd Leonhard and Susan Gedutis Lindsay, *The Future of Music: Manifesto for the Digital Music Revolution* (Boston, MA: Berklee Press, 2005).

Lacan, Jacques, *Ecrits: A Selection*, trans. Alan Sheridan (London: Routledge, 1977).

Lacasse, Serge, 'Intertextuality and Hypertextuality in Recorded Popular Music' [2000] in Moore, *Critical Essays*, pp. 147–70.

——, '"Listen to My Voice": The Evocative Power of Vocal Staging in Recorded Rock Music and other Forms of Vocal Expression', PhD diss. (University of Liverpool, 2000), at: <http://www.mus.ulaval.ca/lacasse/texts/THESIS.pdf> (accessed 28 May 2008).

——, 'Persona, Emotions and Technology: The Phonographic Staging of the Popular Music Voice', CHARM Symposium 2: The Art of Record Production, University of Westminster, London, 2005.

Laing, Dave, 'A Voice without a Face: Popular Music and the Phonograph in the 1890s', *Popular Music* 10/1 (1991): pp. 1–9.

——, *One Chord Wonders: Power and Meaning in Punk Rock* (Milton Keynes: Open University Press, 1985).

Lamb, Andrew and Charles Hamm, 'Popular Music' in Sadie Stanley (ed.), *The Grove Dictionary of Music and Musicians* (London: Macmillan, 1980), pp. 87–121.

Lamont, Michèle and Marcel Fournier (eds), *Cultivating Differences: Symbolic Boundaries and the Making of Inequality* (Chicago: University of Chicago Press, 1992).

Landry, Bart, *The New Black Middle Class* (Berkeley: University of California Press, 1987).

Landry, Charles, 'London as a Creative City', paper presented at Cultures of World Cities Central Policy Unit, Hong Kong, 31 July 200, at:. <http://www.cpu.gov.hk/english/documents/conference/e-landry.rtf> (accessed 24 August 2008).

——, *The Creative City: A Toolkit for Urban Innovators* (London: Earthscan, 2000).

Langlois, Tony, 'Pirates of the Mediterranean: Audiovisual Bricolage in Moroccan Music Video' in Miguel Mera (ed.) 'Prequels/Sequels/Translations/Re-Invention', special issue of *Music, Sound, and the Moving Image* (forthcoming).

Lapassade, George and Philippe Rousselot, *Le Rap ou la fureur de dire* (Paris: Loris Talmart, 1990).

Lash, Scott and John Urry, *Economies of Signs and Space* (London: Sage Publications, 1994).

Laughey, Dan, *Music and Youth Culture* (Edinburgh: Edinburgh University Press, 2006).

Lawson, Steven F., *Running for Freedom: Civil Rights and Black Politics in America Since 1941* (New York: McGraw-Hill, 2nd edn 1977).

Leadbeater, Charles, *Living on Thin Air: The New Economy* (London: The Penguin Group, 1999).

——, *The Rise of the Social Entrepreneur* (London: Demos, 1996).

Leadbeater, Charles and Kate Oakley, *The Independents: Britain's New Cultural Entrepreneurs* (London: Demos, 1999).

Lehman, Peter, *Roy Orbison: The Invention of an Alternative Rock Masculinity* (Philadelphia, PA: Temple University Press, 2003).

Lemann, Nicholas, *The Promised Land: The Great Black Migration and How It Changed America* (New York: Alfred A. Knopf, 1991).

Lenz, Edward A., 'Flexible Employment: Positive Work Strategies for the 21st Century', *Journal of Labor Research* 17/4 (1996): 555–66.

Leonard, Marion, *Gender in the Music Industry: Rock, Discourse and Girl Power* (Aldershot: Ashgate, 2007).

Lewis, Lisa A. (ed.), *The Adoring Audience: Fan Culture and Popular Media* (London: Routledge, 1992).

Liberal India, 'The Backlash for an Offensive Joke against Indian Idol Winner', 10 January 2007, at: <http://liberalindia.com/2007/10/01/rioters-riot-60-injured-the-backlash-for-an-offensive-joke-against-indian-idol-winner> (accessed 9 June 2008).

Liberatore, Paul, 'An Incredible Journey for Band's New Frontman', *Marin Independent Journal*, 27 December 2007, at: <http://www.marinij.com//ci_7826224?IADID=Search-www.marinij.com-www.marinij.com> (accessed 30 July 2008).

Lilliestam, Lars, 'The Sounds of Swedish Rock' in Tarja Hautamäki and Tarja Rautiainen (eds), *Popular Music Studies in Seven Acts* (Tampere: Department of Folk Tradition/Institute of Rhythm Music, 1992), pp. 23–54.

Lindseth, Shawn, 'Idol Franchise Set to Destroy Ethiopia', 9 January 2006, at: <http://www.hecklerspray.com/idol-franchise-set-to-destroy-ethiopia/20061948.php> (accessed 26 May 2008).

Lipovetsky, Gilles with Sébastien Charles, *Hypermodern Times*, trans. Andrew Brown (Cambridge: Polity Press, 2005).

Lipsitz, George, *Dangerous Crossroads: Popular Music, Postmodernism and the Poetics of Place* (New York: Verso, 1994).

——, *The Possessive Investment in Whiteness: How White People Profit from Identity Politics* [1999] (Philadelphia, PA, Temple University Press, rev. edn 2006).

Livingstone, Sonia and Lunt, Peter, *Talk on Television: Audience Participation and Public Debate* (London: Routledge, 1994).

London, Kurt, *Film Music: A Summary of the Characteristic Features of its History, Aesthetics, Technique, and Possible Developments* (London: Faber, 1936).

Longhurst, Brian, *Cultural Change and Ordinary Life* (Maidenhead: Open University Press/McGraw-Hill Education, 2007).

——, *Popular Music and Society* [1995] (Cambridge: Polity Press, 2nd edn 2007).

Lopes, Paul D., 'Innovation and Diversity in the Popular Music Industry 1969 to 1990', *American Sociological Review*, 57 (1992): 56–71.

Louw, Eric, *The Media and Political Process* (London: Sage Publications, 2005).

Lovatt, Alan and Justin O'Connor, 'Cities and the Night-Time Economy', *Planning Practice and Research* 10/2 (1995): 127–33.

Luckman, Susan, '"Unalienated Labour" and Creative Industries: Situating Micro-Entrepreneurial Dance Music Subcultures in the New Economy' in Bloustien, Peters and Luckman, *Sonic Synergies*, pp. 185–94.

Lull, James, *Popular Music and Communication* (London, Sage Publications, 1992).

Lundberg, Dan, Krister Malm and Owe Ronström, *Music, Media, Multiculture: Changing Musicscapes*, trans. Kristina Radford and Andrew Coulthard (Stockholm: Svenskt Visarkiv, 2003).

Lutyens, Elisabeth, *A Goldfish Bowl* (London: Cassell, 1972).

Lyotard, Jean-François, *The Postmodern Condiction: A Report on Knowledge* [1979], trans. Geoff Bennington and Brian Massumi (Minneapolis: University of Minnesota Press, 1984).

Maasø, Arnt, 'Designing Sound and Silence', at: <http://www.nordicom.gu.se/common/publ_pdf/242_maaso_1.pdf> (accessed 2 October 2007).

MacInnes, Colin, *Absolute Beginners* (London: MacGibbon and Kee, 1959).

McClary, Susan, *Conventional Wisdom: The Content of Musical Form* (Berkeley, CA: University of California Press, 2002).

——, *Feminine Endings: Music, Gender, and Sexuality* (Minneapolis: University of Minnesota Press, 1991; rev. edn 2002).

McCoy, Heath, 'Critics Be Damned, Nickelback Rawks', *Calgary Herald*, 15 November 2003, ES.01.F; cited in Fetterley, 'Hey, Hey, I Wanna be a Rock Star'.

McDonald, Chris, *Rush, Rock Music and the Middle Class: Dreaming in Middletown* (Bloomington, IN: Indiana University Press, forthcoming).

McGinn, Robert, 'Stokowski and the Bell Telephone Laboratories: Collaboration in the Development of High-Fidelity Sound Reproduction', *Technology and Culture* 24/1 (1983): 38–75.

McLean, Hesh Joseph, *Under the Influence: Friends, Peer Groups, Music, TV and Movies* (Colorado Springs, CO: Navpress, 1991).

McLellan, Jeffrey A. and Mary Pugh (eds), *The Role of Peer Groups in Adolescent Social Identity* (Hoboken, NJ: Wiley, 2006).

McLeod, Kembrew, 'Authenticity within Hip-Hop and Other Cultures Threatened With Assimilation', *Journal of Communication* 49/4 (1999): 134–50.

McLeod, Kembrew, 'Between Rock and a Hard Place: Gender and Rock Criticism' in Steve Jones (ed), *Pop Music and the Press* (Philadelphia, PA: Temple University Press, 2002), pp. 93–113.

McLuhan, Marshall, *Understanding Media* (London: Routledge, 1964).

Macmillan, Fiona (ed.), *New Directions in Copyright Law*, Vol. 6 (Cheltenham: Edward Elgar, 2007).

McRobbie, Angela, 'Clubs to Companies: Notes of the Decline of Political Culture in Speeded up Creative Worlds', *Cultural Studies* 16/4 (2002): 516–31.

——, 'Fashion as a Cultural Industry' in S. Bruzzi and P.C. Gibson (eds), *Fashion Cultures: Theories, Explorations and Analysis* (London: Routledge, 2000), pp. 253–63.

——, 'From Holloway to Hollywood: Happiness at Work in the new Cultural Economy?', in Du Gay and Pryke, *Cultural Economy*, pp. 97–114.

——, *In the Culture Society: Art, Fashion, and Popular Music* (London: Routledge, 1999).

——, 'Settling Accounts with Subcultures: A Feminist Critique', *Screen Education* 34 (1980): 37–49.

Maffesoli, Michel, *The Time of the Tribes: The Decline of Individualism in Mass Society*, trans. Don Smith (London: Sage Publications, 1996).

Magoun, Alexander Boyden, 'Shaping the Sound of Music: The Evolution of the Phonograph Record, 1877–1950', PhD diss. (University of Maryland, College Park, 2000).

Maitland, Sara (ed.), *Women Fly When Men Aren't Watching* (London: Virago, 1993).

Manning, Marable, *Race, Reform, and Rebellion: The Second Black Reconstruction in America, 1945–1990*, (Jackson: University Press of Mississippi, rev. 2nd edn 1991).

Manuel, Peter, *Cassette Culture. Popular Music and Technology in North India* (Chicago: University of Chicago Press, 1993).

——, *Popular Music of the Non-Western World: An Introductory Survey* (Oxford: Oxford University Press, 1988).

Marshall, Lee, *Bootlegging: Romanticism and Copyright in the Music Industry* (London: Sage, 2005).

Marshall, P. David, *Celebrity and Power: Fame in Contemporary Culture* (Minneapolis: University of Minnesota Press, 1997).

Martin, Christopher, 'Traditional Criticism of Popular Music and the Making of a Lip-synching Scandal', *Popular Music and Society* 17/4 (1993): pp. 63–81.

Martin, George, *Summer of Love: The Making of Sgt Pepper* (London: Pan Books, 1995).

Marwick, Arthur, *Culture in Britain since 1945* (Oxford: Blackwell, 1991).

Maschler, Tom (ed.), *Declaration* (London: MacGibbon and Kee, 1957).

Massey, Howard, *Behind the Glass. Top Record Producers Tell How They Craft Their Hits* (San Francisco, CA: Backbeat Books, 2000).

Mattelart, Armand, *Multinational Corporations and the Control of Culture: The Ideological Apparatuses of Imperialism* (Brighton: Harvester Press, 1979).

Matza, David and Gresham M. Sykes, 'Juvenile Delinquency and Subterranean Values', *American Sociological Review* 26/5 (1961): 712–19.

Mauir, Joanna, Jeffrey Robinson and Kai Hockerts, *Social Entrepreneurship* (London: Palgrave Macmillan, 2006).

Maultsby, Portia K., 'Funk' in Mellonee V. Burnim and Portia K. Maultsby (eds), *African American Music: An Introduction* (New York: Routledge, 2006), pp. 305–306.

——, 'Funk' in Ellen Koskoff (ed.), *The Garland Encyclopedia of World Music. Vol 3: The United States and Canada* (New York: Garland, 2001), pp. 75–81.

——, 'Funk Music: An Expression of Black Life in Dayton, Ohio and the American Metropolis', in Hans Krabbendam, Marja Roholl, and Tity de Vries (eds),

The American Metropolis: Image and Inspiration (Amsterdam: Vu University Press, 2001), pp. 198–213.

Maus, Fred E., 'Glamour and Evasion: The Fabulous Ambivalence of the Pet Shop Boys', *Popular Music* 20/3 (2001): 379–93.

——, 'The Disciplined Subject of Musical Analysis' in A. Dell'Antonio (ed.), *Beyond Structural Listening: Postmodern Modes of Hearing.* (Berkeley: University of California Press, 2004), pp. 13–43.

Maxwell, Ian, *'Phat Beats, Dope Rhymes': Hip Hop Down Under Comin' Upper* (Indianapolis, IN: Wesleyan Publishing House, 2003).

——, 'There's No There There' in Bloustien, Peters and Luckman, *Sonic Synergies,* pp. 79–90.

Mazullo, Mark, 'Revisiting the Wreck: PJ Harvey's *Dry* and the Drowned Virgin-Whore', *Popular Music* 20/3 (2001): 431–47.

Meintjes, Louise, *Sound of Africa! Making Music Zulu in a South African Studio* (Durham, NC: Duke University Press, 2003).

Mellers, Wilfrid, *Twilight of the Gods: The Beatles in Retrospect* (London: Faber, 1973).

Melly, George, *Revolt into Style* (London: Allen Lane, 1970).

Mera, Miguel, *Mychael Danna's The Ice Storm: A Film Score Guide* (Lanham, MD: Scarecrow Press, 2007).

Mera, Miguel and David Burnand (eds), *European Film Music* (Aldershot: Ashgate, 2006).

'Merry Clayton', <http://www.soulwalking.co.uk/Merry%20Clayton.html> (accessed 11 August 2008).

Merton, Robert K., *Social Theory and Social Structure* (New York: Free Press, 1957).

Meyer, Moe, 'Introduction: Reclaiming the Discourse of Camp' in Moe Meyer (ed.), *The Politics and Poetics of Camp* (London: Routledge, 1994), pp. 1–22.

Middleton, Richard, '"Last Night a DJ Saved My Life": Avians, Cyborgs and Siren Bodies in the Era of Phonographic Technology', *Radical Musicology* 1 (2006), at: <http://www.radical-musicology.org.uk/2006/Middleton.htm>.

——, 'Mum's the Word: Men's Singing and Maternal Law' in Jarman-Ivens, *Oh Boy!,* pp. 103–24.

——, 'Popular Music Analysis and Musicology: Bridging the Gap' in Middleton, *Reading Pop,* pp. 104–21.

——, (ed.), *Reading Pop: Approaches to Textual Analysis in Popular Music* (Oxford: Oxford University Press, 2000).

——, *Studying Popular Music* (Milton Keynes: Open University Press, 1990).

Miller, Toby, 'A View from a Fossil: The New Economy, Creativity and Consumption – Two or Three Things I Don't Believe In', *International Journal of Cultural Studies* 7/1 (2004): 55–65.

Mills, Martin, 'Introduction' in Department of Culture Media and Sport, *Consumers Call the Tune: The Impact of New Technologies on the Music Industry* (London: Department of Culture Media and Sport, 2000) at: <http://www.culture.gov.uk/reference_library/publications/4677.aspx> (accessed 23 August 2008).

Milroy, Lesley, *Language and Social Networks* (Oxford: Blackwell, 1980).

'Mister E', at: <http://www.cbc.ca/arts/music/story/2008/07/08/nickelback-deal. html#articlecomments> (accessed 9 July 2008).

Mockus, Martha, 'Queer Thoughts on Country Music and k.d. lang' in Brett, Wood and Thomas, *Queering the Pitch*, pp. 257–74.

Mook, Richard, 'White Masculinity in Barbershop Quartet Singing', *Journal of the Society for American Music* 1/4 (2007): 453–83.

Moore, Allan F., (ed.), *Analyzing Popular Music* (Cambridge: Cambridge University Press, 2003).

——, 'Authenticity as Authentication', *Popular Music* 21/2 (2002): 209–23.

——, 'Categorical Conventions in Music Discourse: Style and Genre', *Music and Letters* 82/3 (2008): 432–42.

—— (ed.), *Critical Essays in Popular Musicology* (Aldershot: Ashgate, 2007).

——, 'The Persona/Environment Relation in Recorded Song', *Music Theory Online* 11/4 (2005), at: <http:www.music-theory.org/mto/issues/mto.05.11.4/ mto.05.11.4.moore_frames.html>.

——, 'Pop Idol: The Fake Plastic Trees of Reality TV of Participatory Democracy in Close-up?', 1 October 2006, at: <http/:www.smlxtralarge.com/archives:000363. php> (accessed 20 June 2008).

——, *Rock – The Primary Text: Developing a Musicology of Rock* [1993] (Aldershot: Ashgate, 2nd edn 2001).

——, *The Beatles: Sgt. Pepper's Lonely Hearts Club Band* (Cambridge: Cambridge University Press, 1997).

Moore Allan F. and Ruth Dockwray, 'The Establishment of the Virtual Performance Space in Rock', *Twentieth Century Music* (forthcoming).

Moore, Jr, William and Lonnie H. Wagstaff, *Black Educators in White Colleges* (San Francisco, CA: Jossey-Bass Publishers, 1974).

Moorefield, Virgil, *The Producer as Composer: Shaping the Sounds of Popular Music* (Cambridge, MA: MIT Press, 2005).

Morgan, Joan, *When Chickenheads Come Home to Roost: My Life as a Hip-Hop Feminist* (New York: Simon & Schuster, 1999).

Morrow, Mary Sue, *Concert Life in Haydn's Vienna: Aspects of a Developing Musical and Social Institution* (Stuyvesant, NY: Pendragon Press, 1989).

Morton, David L., *Sound Recording: The Life Story of a Technology* (Baltimore, MD: Johns Hopkins University Press, 2006).

Moylan, William, *Understanding and Crafting the Mix: The Art of Recording* (Amsterdam: Elsevier, 2007).

Muggleton, David, *Inside Subculture: The Postmodern Meaning of Style* (Oxford: Berg, 2000).

——, 'The Post-subculturalist' in Steve Redhead, Derek Wynne and Justin O'Connor (eds), *The Clubcultures Reader: Readings in Popular Cultural Studies* (Oxford: Blackwell, 1997).

Muggs, Joe, 'The Family That Plays Together', *The Word* 63 (May 2008): pp. 50–51.

Mullin, John T., 'Creating the Craft of Tape Recording', *High Fidelity* (1976): 62–67.

——, 'Magnetic Recording for Original Recordings', *Journal of the Audio Engineering Society* 25/10–11 (1977): 696–701.

Mulvey, Laura, *Visual and Other Pleasures* (Bloomington: Indiana University Press, 1989).

Murphy, John, 'Nickelback: *All the Right Reasons*', at: <http://www.musicomh.com/albums/nickelback-2_1005.htm> (accessed 9 July 2008).

Murrells, Joseph, *Million Selling Records from the 1900s to the 1980s: An Illustrated Directory* (London: Batsford, 1984).

Naughtie, James, *The Rivals: The Intimate Story of a Political Marriage* (London: Fourth Estate, 2001.)

Negus, Keith, *Music Genres and Corporate Cultures* (London: Routledge, 1999).

——, *Popular Music in Theory: An Introduction* (Cambridge: Polity Press, 1996)

——, *Producing Pop: Culture and Conflict in the Popular Music Industry* (London: Arnold, 1992)

Negus, Keith and John Street (eds), 'Music and Television', special issue of *Popular Music* 21/3 (2002).

Nettl, Bruno, *The Western Impact on World Music: Change, Adaption, and Survival* (New York: Schirmer, 1985).

Newton, Francis, *The Jazz Scene* (New York: Monthly Review Press, 1960).

Niblock, Sarah, 'Prince: Negotiating the Meanings of Femininity in the Mid-1980s', PhD diss. (Middlesex University, 2005).

'Nickelback signs 3-album deal with Live Nation', at: <http://www.cbc.ca/arts/music/story/2008/07/08/nickelback-deal.html> (accessed 8 July 2008).

Nyman, Michael, *Experimental Music: Cage and Beyond*, (Cambridge: Cambridge University Press, 2nd edn 1974).

Nyre, Lars, *Fidelity Matters. Sound Media and Realism in the 20th Century* (Bergen: Haugen, 2003).

Oakes, Jason Lee, 'The Filth and the Fury: An Essay on Punk Rock Heavy Metal Karaoke', Current Musicology 85 (2008): 73–112.

——, 'Queering the Witch: Stevie Nicks and the Forging of Femininity at the Night of a Thousand Stevies' in Whiteley and Rycenga, *Queering the Popular Pitch*, pp. 41–54.

O'Hare, Peter, 'Approaching Sound: A Sonicological Examination of the Producer's Role in Popular Music', MPhil thesis (University of Glasgow, 2008).

Olsen, Eric, Paul Verna and Carlo Wolff, *The Encyclopedia of Record Producers* (New York: Watson-Guptill, 1999).

O'Meara, Caroline, 'The Raincoats: Breaking Down Punk Rock's Masculinities', *Popular Music* 22/3 (2003): 299–313.

Oppenheimer, Daniel, 'Gladiator: Matt Haimovitz Fights the War on Terror with an Unlikely Weapon', *Valley Advocate*, 25 March 2004, at: <http://www.valleyadvocate.com/gbase/Arts/content.html?oid=oid:59415> (accessed 10 January 2005).

O'Reilly, Karen, *The British on the Costa del Sol: Transnational Identities and Local Communities* (London: Routledge, 2000).

Palmer, Gareth, 'Bruce Springsteen and Masculinity' in Whiteley, *Sexing the Groove*, pp. 100–17.

Pappademas, Alex, 'Foolish, Foolish Throat: A Q&A with Steve Perry', Men.style. com, 29 May 2008, at: <http://men.style.com/gq/blogs/gqeditors/2008/05/foolish-foolish.html> (accessed 29 July 2008).

——, 'He Didn't Stop Believin'', *GQ Magazine*, June 2008, at: <http://men.style.com/gq/features/full?id=content_6818&pageNum=11> (accessed 30 July 2008).

Pareles, Jan and Patricia Romanowski, *The Rolling Stone Encyclopedia of Rock & Roll* (New York: Rolling Stone Press, 1983).

Patterson, Sylvia, 'I'm a Robbing Gypsy Bastard' (KT Tunstall interview), *The Word* 37 (March 2006): 74–78.

Paul, Les, 'Multitracking: It Wasn't Always This Easy…' in G. Petersen (ed.), *Modular Digital Multitracks* (Emeryville, CA: Mix Books, 1997), pp. 1–7.

Pennanen, Risto Pekka, 'The Development of Chordal Harmony in Greek Rebetika and Laika Music, 1930s–1960s', *British Journal of Ethnomusicology* 6 (1997): 65–116.

——, *Westernisation and Modernisation in Greek Popular Music* (Tampere: University of Tampere, 1999).

Peraino, Judith, 'PJ Harvey's "Man-Size Sextet" and the Inaccessible, Inescapable Gender', *Women & Music* 2 (1998): 47–63.

Perry, Imani, *Prophets of the Hood: Politics and Poetics in Hip Hop* (Durham, NC: Duke University Press, 2004).

Peters, Margaret E., *Dayton's African American Heritage* (Virginia Beach, VA: The Doninng Company, 1995).

——, 'Risky Economies: Community-Based Organizations and the Music-Making Practices of Marginalized Youth' in Bloustien, Peters and Luckman, *Sonic Synergies*, pp. 161–84.

Peterson, Richard A., 'Five Constraints on the Production of Culture: Law, Technology, Market, Organizational Structure and Occupational Careers', *Journal of Popular Culture* 16 (1982): 143–53.

Peterson, Richard A. and David G. Berger, 'Cycles in Symbol Production: The Case of Popular Music', *American Sociological Review* 40 (1975): 158–73.

—— and David G. Berger, 'Entrepreneurship in Organizations: Evidence from the Popular Music Industry', *Administrative Science Quarterly* 16 (1971): 158–73.

Peterson, Richard A. and Roger M. Kern, 'Changing Highbrow Taste: From Snob to Omnivore', *American Sociological Review* 61 (1996): 900–907.

Peterson, Richard A. and Albert Simkus, 'How Musical Taste Groups Mark Occupational Status Groups' in Lamont and Fournier, *Cultivating Differences*, pp. 152–86.

Philip, Robert, *Performing Music in the Age of Recording* (New Haven: Yale University Press, 2004).

Pillsbury, Glenn, Damage Incorporated: Metallica and the Production of Musical Identity (New York: Routledge, 2006).

Pinard, Andre and Sean Jacobs, 'Building a Virtual Diaspora: Hip Hop in Cyberspace', in Ayers, *Cybersounds*, pp. 83–106.

'Pink Floyd: Pink Floyd Singer Wins Settlement from Band', *ContactMusic.com* 13 April 2005, at: <http://www.contactmusic.com/new/xmlfeed.nsf/mndwebpages/

pink%20floyd%20singer%20wins%20settlement%20from%20band>(accessed19 July 2008).

Pollack, William, *Real Boys: Rescuing Our Sons from the Myths of Boyhood* (New York: Owl Books, 1999).

Polychronakis, Ioannis, 'Anna Vissi: The Greek "Madonna"?', paper from the Conference 'Inter: A European Cultural Studies Conference in Sweden', Advanced Cultural Studies Institute of Sweden, 2007. Available at: <http://www.ep.liu.se/ecp/025/>.

Pop, Iggy, 'The Immortals – The Greatest Artists of All Time: 20) Bo Diddley', *Rolling Stone* 946 (15 April 2004).

Porter, Michael E., *Competitive Advantage* (New York: Free Press, 1985).

——, 'Location, Competition and Economic Development: Local Clusters in a Global Economy', *Economic Development Quarterly* 14/1 (2000): 15–34.

——, 'What is Strategy?', *Harvard Business Review* (November/December 1996): 61–78.

Potter, John, *Vocal Authority: Singing Style and Ideology* (Cambridge: Cambridge University Press, 1998).

Powers, Ann, 'The Male Rock Anthem: Going all to Pieces', *The New York Times*, 1 February 1998, at: <http://query.nytimes.com/gst/fullpage.html?res=9E07E4D81 73AF932A35751C0A96E958260&sec=&spon=&pagewanted=print> (accessed 15 July 2008).

Pratt, Andy C., 'New Media, the New Economy and New Spaces', *Geoforum* 31 (2000): 425–36.

Prendergast, Roy M., *Film Music: A Neglected Art* (New York: Norton, 2nd edn 1992).

Proust, Marcel, 'Sur la lecture' ('On Reading'), Preface to *Sésame et les Lys* (*Sesame and Lilies*) by John Ruskin, trans. Marcel Proust (Paris: Editions Complexe, 1987).

Pruter, Robert, *Doowop: The Chicago Scene* (Urbana: University of Illinois Press, 1996).

Quinn, Eithne, *Nuthin' But A 'G' Thang: The Culture and Commerce of Gangsta Rap* (New York: Columbia University Press, 2005).

Quiñones, Marta García, 'Escucha Ambiental y Tradición Musical: Cuando las emisoras de música clásica programan para el oyente distraído', in Marta García Quiñones (ed.), *La música que no se escucha* (Barcelona: Orquestra del Caos, 2008).

Rahmatian, Andreas, 'Universal Norms for a Globalised Diversity: On the Protection of Traditional Cultural Expressions', in Macmillan, *New Directions in Copyright Law*, Vol. 6, pp. 199–231.

Railton, Diane, 'The Gendered Carnival of Pop', *Popular Music* 20/3 (2001): 321–31.

Randall, Annie, *Dusty! Queen of the (Post) Mods* (New York: Oxford University Press, 2008).

Rautiainen-Keskustalo, Tarja 'Rocking the Economy: On the Articulations of Popular Music and the Creative Economy in Late Modern Culture, *Popular Musicology Online*, at: <http://www.popular-musicology-online.com>.

Raykoff, Ivan, 'Concerto con amore', *ECHO*, 2/1 (2000). Available at <http://www.echo.ucla.edu/Volume2-Issue1/raykoff/raykoff-article.html> (accessed 28 August 2008).

Read, Oliver and Walter L. Welch, *From Tin Foil to Stereo: Evolution of the Phonograph*. (Indianapolis: H.W. Sams, 2nd edn 1976).

Redhead, Steve, *The End-of-the Century Party: Youth and Pop Towards 2000* (Manchester: Manchester University Press, 1990).

Regev, Motti, 'The "Pop-rockization" of Popular Music' in Hesmondhalgh and Negus, *Popular Music Studies*, pp. 251–64.

Reynolds, Simon and Joy Press, *The Sex Revolts: Gender, Rebellion, and Rock 'n' Roll* (Cambridge, MA: Harvard University Press, 1995).

Richardson, John, '"The Digital Won't Let Me Go": Constructions of the Virtual and the Real in Gorillaz' "Clint Eastwood"', *Journal of Popular Music Studies* 17/1 (2005): pp. 1–29.

——, *Singing Archaeology: Philip Glass's* Akhnaten (Hanover, NH: Wesleyan University Press, 1999).

Riemann, Hugo, *Ideen zu einer 'Lehre von den Tonvorstellungen'* in *Jahrbuch der Musikbibliothek Peters* (Leipzig, 1914/15), pp. 1–26.

Riesman, David, 'Listening to Popular Music', *American Quarterly* 2/4 (1950): 359–71.

Rifkin, J., *The Age of Access: How the Shift from Ownership to Access is Transforming Economic Life* (London: Penguin, 2000).

Rimé, Bernard and Loris Schiaratura, 'Gesture and Speech' in Robert S. Feldman and Bernard Rimé (eds), *Fundamentals of Nonverbal Behaviour* (Cambridge: Cambridge University Press, 1991), pp. 239–81.

Robertson, Pamela, *Guilty Pleasures: Feminist Camp from Mae West to Madonna* (London: I.B. Tauris, 1996).

Robertson, Roland, 'Glocalization: Time-Space and Homogeneity-Heterogeneity' in Mike Featherstone, Scott Lash and Roland Robertson (eds), *Global Modernities* (London: Sage, 1995), pp. 25–44.

Robinson, Peter, 'The Next Worst Thing', *Guardian*, 9 February 2008. Available at: <http://www.guardian.co.uk/theguide/music/story/0,2253822,00.html> (accessed 9 July 2008).

Roche, John P., *The Quest for the Dream: The Development of Civil Rights in Human Relations in Modern America* (New York: Macmillan, 1963).

Rodger, Gillian, 'Drag, Camp and Gender Subversion in the Music and Videos of Annie Lennox', *Popular Music* 23/1 (2004): 17–29.

Rogers, Holly, 'Acoustic Architecture: Music and Space in the Video Installations of Bill Viola', *Twentieth Century Music* 2/2 (2005): 197–220.

Rogers, Ian, Abraham Ninan, Greg Hearn, Stuart Cunningham and Susan Luckman, *Queensland Music Industry Value Web: From the Margins to the Mainstream* (Brisbane: Creative Industries Research and Applications Centre, 2004).

Rojek, Chris, *Celebrity* (London: Reaktion, 2001).

Rosenbloom, Stephanie, 'Selling a Concept with a Song', *New York Times*, Real Estate, 5 August 2007.

Ross, Andrew, 'Uses of Camp' in David Bergman (ed.), *Camp Grounds: Style and Homosexuality* (Amherst: University of Massachusetts Press, 1993), pp. 54–77.

Rossman, Gabriel, 'Elites, Masses, and Media Blacklists: The Dixie Chicks Controversy', *Social Forces* 83 (2004): 61–78.

Rowbotham, Sheila, 'Dreams and Dilemma' in Maitland, *Women Fly When Men Aren't Watching*.

Rowland, Steve, 'Live Commentary on "Profile of George Clinton, the Master of Funk"', *Weekend Edition*, National Public Radio, 6 February 1994.

Roy, Anjali Gera, 'Who is Dancing to the Bhangra?', *Phalanx: A Quarterly Journal for Continuing Debate* 1 (2006), at: <http://www.phalanx.in/pages/article_i001_dancing_bhangra.html> (accessed 11 August 2008).

Ruby, Jennie, 'Women's "Cock Rock" Goes Mainstream', *Off Our Backs*, 35/7–8 (July 2005): 42–44.

Ryan, Kevin and Brian Kehew, *Recording the Beatles. The Studio Equipment and Techniques Used to Create Their Classic Albums* (Houston, TX: Curvebender Publishing, 2006).

Rycenga, Jennifer, 'Endless Caresses: Queer Exuberance in Large-Scale Form in Rock' in Whiteley and Rycenga, *Queering the Popular Pitch*, pp. 233–47.

Sabaneev, Leonid, *Music for the Films* (New York: Arno, 1978).

Sagoo, Bhagwant, 'Bhangra: The Best Asian Beats from the Streets', at: <http://www.unionsquaremusic.co.uk/titlev4.php?ALBUM_ID=351&LABEL_ID=2> (accessed 17 April 2009).

Said, Edward, *Culture and Imperialism* (New York: Alfred A. Knopf, 1993).

Salmon, Barry, 'Music in Recent Car Advertisements on Television', paper given at the Twelfth Biennial IASPM International Conference, Montreal, 3–7 July 2003.

Sampson, Jim, 'Genre', *Grove Music Online*, ed. Laura Macy, at: <http://www.grovemusic.com.libaccess.lib.mcmaster.ca> (accessed 3 July 2008).

Sanjek, Russell and David Sanjek, *Pennies from Heaven: The American Popular Music Business in the Twenties Century* (New York: Da Capo Press, 1996).

Sardiello, Robert, 'Identity and Status Stratification in Deadhead Subculture' in Jonathon S. Epstein (ed.), *Youth Culture: Identity in a Postmodern World* (Oxford: Blackwell, 1998).

Savirimuthu, Joseph, 'P2P @software(e).com: Or the art of Cyberspace 3.0.', in Macmillan, *New Directions in Copyright Law*, Vol. 6, pp. 247–78.

'Scandal Rocks Idols West Africa', 26 January 2008, <http://thelongharmattanseason.blogspot.com/2008/01/scandals-rocks-idols-west-africa-by.html> (accessed 16 June 2008).

Scannell, Paddy, *Radio, Television and Modern Life* (Oxford: Blackwell, 1996).

Schade-Poulsen, Marc, *Men and Popular Music in Algeria: The Social Significance of Raï* (Austin: University of Texas Press, 1999).

Schiller, Herbert I., *Mass Communications and American Empire* (Boston, MA: Beacon Press, 1969).

Schloss, Joseph Glenn, *Making Beats: The Art of Sample-Based Hip-Hop* (Middletown, CT: Wesleyan University Press, 2004).

Schuessler, Karl F., *Musical Taste and Socio-Economic Background* (Manchester, NH: Ayer, 1981).

Schwarz, K. Robert, 'Steve Reich: Music as a Gradual Process, Part 1', *Perspectives of New Music* 19 (1981): pp. 374–92.

Schwarzkopf, Elisabeth, *On and Off the Record* (Boston, MA: Northwestern University Press, 1992).

Scott, Allen J., *The Cultural Economy of Cities* (London: Sage, 2000).

Scott, Derek B. (ed.), *Music, Culture, and Society: A Reader* (Oxford: Oxford University Press, 2000).

——, *Sounds of the Metropolis: The 19th-Century Popular Music Revolution in London, New York, Paris, and Vienna* (New York: Oxford University Press, 2008).

Sedgwick, Eve Kosofsky, *Epistemology of the Closet* (Berkeley: University of California Press, 1990).

Shank, Barry, *Dissonant Identities: The Rock 'n' Roll Scene in Austin, Texas* (Hanover, NH: Wesleyan University Press, 1994).

Shapiro, Peter, *Turn the Beat Around: The Secret History of Disco* (London: Faber, 2005).

Sharma, Ashwani, 'Sounds Oriental: The (Im)possibility of Theorising Asian Musical Cultures' in Sharma, Hutnyk and Sharma, *Disorienting Rhythms*, pp. 1–11.

——, 'South Asian Diaspora Music in Britain', *South Asian Diaspora Literature and Art Archive*, at: <http://www.salidaa.org.uk/salidaa/docrep/docs/sectionIntro/music/docm_render.html?dr_page_number=1> (accessed 11 August 2008).

Sharma, Sanjay, 'Noisy Asians or "Asian Noise"?' in Sharma, Hutnyk and Sharma, *Disorienting Rhythms*, pp. 32–57.

Sharma, Sanjay, John Hutnyk and Ashwani Sharma (eds), *Disorienting Rhythms: The Politics of the New Asian Dance Music* (London: Zed Books, 1996).

Shils, Edward, *The Intellectuals and the Powers* (Chicago: University of Chicago Press, 1972).

Shuker, Roy, *Understanding Popular Music* (London and New York: Routledge, 1994).

Simmons, Sylvie, *Serge Gainsbourg: A Fistful of Gitanes* (Cambridge: Da Capo, 2002).

Simons, David, *Studio Stories* (San Francisco, CA: Backbeat Books, 2004).

Simpson, Mark, *Male Impersonators: Men Performing Masculinity* (London: Cassell, 1994).

——, *Saint Morrissey: A Portrait of This Charming Man by an Alarming Fan* (New York: Simon & Schuster, 2005).

Singh, Channi, *The Guardian*, 'Weekend', 13 March 1993, p. 32.

Singh, Harneet, 'All Jazzed up!', *The Times of India*, 22 November 2002, at: <http://timesofindia.indiatimes.com/articleshow/29091271.cms> (accessed 11 August 2008).

Skeggs, Beverley, *Class, Self, Culture* (London: Routledge, 2004).

Sless, David, *In Search of Semiotics* (London: Croom Helm, 1986).

Slobin, Mark, 'Ethnomusicology' in *Continuum Encyclopaedia of Popular Music. Vol. 1: Media, Industry, Society* (London: Continuum, 2003), pp. 72–74.

Small, Christopher, *Musicking: The Meanings of Performing and Listening* (Hanover, NH: Wesleyan University Press, 1998).

Smalley, Denis, 'Space-Form and the Acousmatic Image', *Organised Sound* 12/1 (April 2007): 35–58.

Smiers, Joost, 'The Abolition of Copyright: Better for Artists, Third World Countries and the Public Domain', *Gazette* 62 (2000): 379–406.

Smith, Jeff, *The Sounds of Commerce: Marketing Popular Film Music* (New York: Columbia University Press, 1998).

Smith, Patricia J., *The Queer Sixties* (London: Routledge, 1999).

Smith,Graham. 'Rapper Snoop Dogg under Fire for "Culturally Insensitive" Bollywood Video' at:, <http://www.dailymail.co.uk/tvshowbiz/article-1040509/Rapper-Snoop-Dogg-culturally-insensitive-Bollywood-video.html> (accessed 11 August 2008).

Solie, Ruth, 'Gender, Genre, and the Parlor Piano', *The Wordsworth Circle* 25 (1994): 53–56.

—— (ed.), *Music and Difference: Gender and Sexuality in Music Scholarship* (Berkeley: University of California Press, 1993).

Solomon-Godeau, Abigail, 'Male Trouble' in Maurice Berger, Brian Wallis and Simon Watson (eds), *Constructing Masculinity* (New York: Routledge, 1995), pp. 69–76.

Somervell, D.C., 'The Visual Element in Music', *Music & Letters*, 24/1 (1943): 42–47.

Sontag, Susan, 'Notes on "Camp"' [1964] in Fabio Cleto (ed.), *Camp: Queer Aesthetics and the Performing Subject – A Reader* (Edinburgh: Edinburgh University Press, 1999), pp. 53–65.

Spence, Michael and Bruce Owen, 'Television Programming, Monopolistic Competition, and Welfare', *Quarterly Journal of Economics* 91 (1977): 103–26.

Spicer, Mark, '(Ac)cumulative Form in Pop-Rock Music', *Twentieth-Century Music* 1/1 (2004): 29–64.

Spiller, Henry, 'Negotiating Masculinity in an Indonesian Pop Song: Doel Sumbang's "Ronggeng"' in Jarman-Ivens, *Oh Boy!*, pp. 39–58.

Stefani, Gino, 'A Theory of Musical Competence' [1987] in Moore, *Critical Essays*, pp. 19–34.

Stephens, Vincent, 'Pop Goes the Rapper: A Close Reading of Eminem's Genderphobia', *Popular Music* 24/1 (2005): 21–36.

Sterne, Jonathan, *The Audible Past: Cultural Origins of Sound Reproduction* (Durham, NC: Duke University Press, 2003).

Stevens, Sufjan, 'John Wayne Gacy Jr.', *Illinois* (Asthmatic Kitty, 2005).

Steward, Sue, 'Bhangra Spreads Its Empire', *Observer Music Monthly*, 14 October 2007, at: <http://www.guardian.co.uk/music/2007/oct/14/urban)> (accessed 11 August 2008).

Stewart, Rowena, 'Bringing Private Black Histories to the Public' in Janet W. Solinger (ed.), *Museums and Universities: New Paths for Continuing Education* (New York: Macmillan for National University Continuing Education Association, 1990).

Stilwell, Robynn J., 'The Fantastical Gap Between Diegetic and Non-diegetic' in Daniel Goldmark, Lawrence Kramer and Richard Leppert (eds), *Beyond the Soundtrack* (Berkeley: University of California Press, 2007).

Stockfelt, Ola, 'Adequate Modes of Listening' in David Schwarz and Anahid Kassabian (eds), *Keeping Score: Music, Disciplinarity, Culture* (Charlottesville, VA: University Press of Virginia, 1997), pp. 129–46.

Stokes, Martin, *Ethnicity, Identity and Music: The Musical Construction of Place* (Oxford: Berg, 1994).

——, 'Talk and Text: Popular Music and Ethnomusicology' in Moore, *Analyzing Popular Music*, pp. 218–39.

Stokowski, Patricia A., *Leisure and Society: A Network Structural Perspective* (New York: Continuum, 1994).

Stone, Ruth and Verlon Stone, 'Event, Feedback, and Analysis: Research Media in the Study of Music Events', *Ethnomusicology* 25/2 (1981): 215–25.

Storper, Michael, 'The Transition to Flexible Specialisation in the US Film Industry: External Economies, the Division of Labour, and the Crossing of Industrial Divides', *Cambridge Journal of Economics,* 13 (1989): 273–305.

Storr, Anthony, *Music and the Mind* (London: Harper Collins, 1997).

Stras, Laurie, 'Voice of the Beehive: Vocal Technique at the Turn of the 60s' in Laurie Stras (ed.), *She's so Fine: Whiteness, Femininity, Adolescence and Class in 1960s Music* (Farnham: Ashgate, forthcoming).

Straw, Will, 'Scenes and Sensibilities', *Public* 22–23 (2002): 245–57.

——, 'Sizing Up Record Collections: Gender and Connoisseurship in Rock Music Culture' in Whiteley, *Sexing the Groove*, pp. 3–16.

——, 'Systems of Articulation, Logics of Change: Communities and Scenes in Popular Music', *Cultural Studies* 5/3 (1991): 368–88.

Straziuso, Jason, 'Afghanistan Clerics Upset as Woman Makes Final of "Pop Idol"', 14 March 2008, at: <http://news.scotsman.com/latestnews/Afghanistan-clerics-upset-as-woman.3878336.jp (accessed 15 June 2008).

Stuempfle, Stephen, *The Steelband Movement: The Forging of a National Art in Trinidad & Tobago* (Philadelphia: University of Pennsylvania Press, 1996).

Sugrue, Thomas J., *The Origins of the Urban Crisis: Race and Inequality in Postwar Detroit* (Princeton, NJ: Princeton University Press, 1996).

Sweetman, Paul, 'Tourists and Travellers? "Subcultures", Reflexive Identities and Neo-Tribal Sociality' in Bennett and Kahn-Harris, *After Subculture*, pp. 79–83.

Swift, Jacqui, 'Wine, Woman and Song', *Sun*, 27 October 2006.

Tagg, Philip, 'An Anthropology of Stereotypes in TV Music?', *Swedish Musicological Journal* (1989): 19–42. Available at: <http://www.tagg.org/articles/xpdfs/tvanthro.pdf> (accessed June 2008).

——, 'Analysing Popular Music: Theory, Method, and Practice', in Middleton, *Reading Pop*, pp. 71–103.

——, '"Black Music," "Afro-American Music," and "European Music"', *Popular Music* 8 (1989): 285–98. Reprinted in Moore, *Critical Essays*, pp. 5–18.

——, *Fernando the Flute* (Liverpool: Institute of Popular Music, 1991).

——, 'From Refrain to Rave: The Decline of Figure and the Rise of Ground', *Popular Music* 13/2 (1994): pp. 209–22.

——, 'Introductory Notes to the Semiotics of Music', Version 3, July 1999, at: <http://tagg.org/xpdfs/semiotug.pdf> (accessed 18 June 2008).

Tagg, Philip and Bob Clarida, *Ten Little Title Tunes: Towards a Musicology of Mass Media* (New York and Montreal: The Mass Media Musicologists' Press, 2003).

Talbot, Michael (ed.), *The Musical Work: Reality or Invention?* (Liverpool: Liverpool University Press, 2000).

Tan, Shzr Ee, '"My Humping" the Prime Minister: Mash-up Podcast Politics in a Singaporean Context', paper given at the Sound, Music and the Moving Image Conference, London, 10–12 September 2007.

Tannock, Stuart, 'Nostalgia Critique', *Cultural Studies* 9/3 (1995): 453–64.

Taussig, Michael, *Mimesis and Alterity: A Particular History of the Senses* (New York: Routledge, 1993).

Tay, Jinna, 'Creative Cities', in Hartley, *Creative Industries*, pp. 220–32.

Taylor, Timothy D., *Global Pop: World Music, World Markets* (New York: Routledge, 1997).

——, *Strange Sounds: Music, Technology and Culture* (New York: Routledge, 2001).

——, 'Territoires du hip hop', *Art Press*, Hors Série (December 2000).

Théberge, Paul, *Any Sound You Can Imagine: Making Music/Consuming Technology* (Hanover, NH; Wesleyan University Press and University Press of New England, 1997).

——, 'The "Sound" of Music: Technological Rationalization and the Production of Popular Music', *New Formations* 8 (1989): 99–111.

Thompson, Emily A., 'Machines, Music, and the Quest for Fidelity: Marketing and the Edison Phonograph in America, 1877–1925', *Musical Quarterly* 79 (1995): 131–71.

——, *The Soundscape of Modernity. Architectural Acoustics and the Culture of Listening in America, 1900-1933*, (Cambridge, MA: MIT Press, 2002).

Thompson, Phil, *The Best of Cellars* (Liverpool: Bluecoat Press, 1994).

Thompson, William Forde, Phil Graham and Frank A. Russo, 'Seeing Music Performance: Visual Influences on Perception and Experience', *Semiotica* 156/1–4 (2005): 203–27.

Thornton, Sarah, *Club Cultures: Music, Media and Subcultural Capital* (Cambridge: Polity Press, 1995).

Thussu, Daya Kishan, *International Communication: Continuity and Change* (London: Hodder Arnold, 2nd edn 2006).

Tosh, John, *The Pursuit of History* (London: Longman, 1984).

Toynbee, Jason, 'Mainstreaming, from Hegemonic Centres to Global Networks' in Hesmondhalgh and Negus, *Popular Music Studies*, pp. 149–63.

——, *Making Popular Music: Musicians, Creativity and Institutions* (London: Arnold, 2000).

Tragaki, Dafni, *Rebetiko Worlds: Ethnomusicology and Ethnography in the City* (Newcastle: Cambridge Scholars Publishing, 2007).

Traister, Bryce, 'Academic Viagra: The Rise of American Masculinity Studies', *American Quarterly* 52/2 (2000): 274–304.

Joe William Trotter, Jr, 'Blacks in the Urban North' in Katz, *The 'Underclass' Debate*, pp. 55–81.

——, *River Jordan: African American Urban Life in the Ohio Valley* (Lexington: The University of Kentucky Press, 1998).

Trotter, Jr, Joe William and Eric Ledell Smith (eds), *African Americans in Pennsylvania: Shifting Historical Perspectives* (University Park: Pennsylvania State University Press, 1998).

Turino, Thomas, 'Signs of Imagination, Identity and Experience', *Ethnomusicology* 43/2 (1999): 221–55.

Turner, Victor, *From Ritual to Theatre: The Human Seriousness of Play* (New York: PAJ Publications, 1982).

——, 'Liminal to Liminoid, in Play, Flow, and Ritual', in Carlson, *Performance*, pp. 56–78.

UNCTAD/UNDP, *Creative Economies Report 2008: The Challenge of Assessing the Creative Economy Towards Informed Policy Making* (Geneva: United Nations Conference on Trade and Development, 2008).

Van der Merwe, Peter, *Origins of the Popular Style: The Antecedents of Twentieth-Century Popular Music* (Oxford: Clarendon Press, 1989).

Verevis, Constantine, *Film Remakes* (Edinburgh: Edinburgh University Press, 2006).

Vernallis, Carol, 'The Aesthetics of Music Video: An Analysis of Madonna's "Cherish"' [1998] in Moore, *Critical Essays*, pp. 443–75.

Vincent, Rickey, *Funk: The Music, the People, and the Rhythm of the One* (New York: St Martin's Griffin, 1996).

Wagner Naphtali, 'Psychedelic Classicism and Classical Psychedelia' in Olivier Julien (ed.), *Sgt. Pepper and the Beatles: It Was Forty Years Ago Today* (Aldershot: Ashgate, 2008), pp. 75–90.

Waksman, Steve, 'Every Inch of My Love: Led Zeppelin and the Problem of Cock Rock', *Journal of Popular Music Studies* 8 (1996): 4–25.

——, *Instruments of Desire: The Electric Guitar and the Shaping of Musical Experience* (Cambridge, MA: Harvard University Press, 1999).

Wallis, Roger and Krister Malm, *Big Sounds from Small Peoples: The Music Industry in Small Countries* (London: Constable, 1984).

Wallis, Roger, Charles Baden-Fuller, Martin Kretschmer and George Michael Klimis, 'Contested Collective Administration of Intellectual Property Rights in Music: The Challenge to the Principles of Reciprocity and Solidarity', *European Journal of Communication* 14 (1999): 5–35.

Walser, Robert, 'Popular Music Analysis: Ten Apothegms and Four Instances', in Moore, *Analyzing Popular Music*, pp. 16–38.

——, 'Prince as Queer Poststructuralist', *Popular Music and Society* 18/2 (1994): 79–89.

——, *Running with the Devil: Power, Gender and Madness in Heavy Metal Music* (Hanover, NH: Wesleyan University Press, 1993).

Warburton, Dan, 'A Working Terminology for Minimal Music', *Intégral*, 2 (1988): 135–59.

Warner, Tim, 'Narrating Sound: The Pop Video in the Age of the Sampler' in Phil Powrie and Robynn J. Stilwell (eds), *Changing Tunes: The Use of Pre-existing Music in Film* (Aldershot: Ashgate, 2006).

——, *Pop Music – Technology and Creativity* (Aldershot: Ashgate, 2003).

Wartofsky, Alona, 'What's Shakin'? Bhangra. Big Time. Take Traditional Punjabi Music, Add Drum Machines – and Hip-Hop to It', Special to *The Washington Post*, 13 May 2001 at: <http://www.washingtonpost.com/ac2/wp-dyn?pagena me=article&node=&contentId=A14732-2001May11> (accessed on 11 August 2008).

Warwick, Jacqueline, '"And the Colored Girls Sing": Backup Singers and the Case of the Blossoms' in Steven Baur, Raymond Knapp and Jacqueline Warwick (eds), *Musicological Identities: Essays in Honor of Susan McClary* (Aldershot: Ashgate, 2008), pp. 63–77.

——, *Girl Groups, Girl Culture: Popular Music and Identity in the 1960s* (New York: Routledge, 2007).

Waterman, Christopher Alan, *Jùjú·: A Social History and Ethnography of an African Popular Music* (Chicago: University of Chicago Press, 1990).

Watkins, S. Craig, *Hip-Hop Matters: Politics, Popular Culture and the Struggle for the Soul of a Movement* (Boston, MA: Beacon Press, 2005).

Weber, William, 'Did People Listen in the 18th Century?', *Early Music* (November 1997): 678–91.

Wechsler, Robert, 'Artistic Considerations in the Use of Motion-tracking with Live Performers: A Practical Guide' in Susan Broadhurst and Josephine Machon (eds), *Performance and Technology: Practices of Virtual Embodiment and Interactivity* (Basingstoke: Palgrave Macmillan, 2006), pp. 60–77.

Weinstein, Deena, *Heavy Metal: A Cultural Sociology* (New York: Lexington, 1991).

Weis, Liz and John Belton, *Film Sound: Theory and Practice* (New York: Columbia University Press, 1985).

Wellman, David, 'Minstrel Shows, Affirmative Action Talk, and Angry White Men: Marking Racial Otherness in the 1990s', in Ruth Frankenberg (ed.), *Displacing Whiteness: Essays in Social and Cultural Criticism* (Durham, NC: Duke University Press, 1997), pp. 311–32.

Wenner, Jann, *Lennon Remembers* (London: Penguin, 1971).

Whelan, Andrew, 'Do U Produce? Subcultural Capital and Amateur Musicianship in Peer to Peer Networks' in Ayers, *Cybersounds*, pp. 58–82.

Whitburn, Joel, *Joel Whitburn's Top R & B Billboard Singles 1942–2004* (Menomonee Falls, WI: Record Research Inc., 2004).

Whiteley, Sheila (ed.), *Christmas: Ideology and Popular Culture* (Edinburgh: Edinburgh University Press, 2008).

——, 'Little Red Rooster v. The Honky Tonk Woman: Mick Jagger, Sexuality, Style and Image' in Whiteley, *Sexing the Groove*, pp. 67–99.

——, *Mindgames* (Lulu.com, 2008).

—— (ed.), *Sexing the Groove: Popular Music and Gender* (London: Routledge, 1997).

——, 'The Killing Fields of Popular Music' in Sue Holmes and Sean Redmond (eds), *Framing Celebrity: New Directions in Celebrity Culture* (New York: Routledge, 2006), pp. 329–42.

——, *The Space Between the Notes: Rock and the Counter-culture* (London: Routledge, 1992).

——, *Too Much Too Young: Popular Music, Age and Gender* (London: Routledge, 2005).

——, 'Use, Misuse and Abuse: Problems Surrounding Popular Music and its Young Performers', in Bloustien, Peters and Luckman, *Sonic Synergies*, pp. 145–56.

——, 'Which Freddie? Constructions of Masculinity in Freddie Mercury and Justin Hawkins' in Jarman-Ivens, *Oh Boy!*, pp. 21–37.

——, *Women and Popular Music. Sexuality, Identity and Subjectivity* (London: Routledge, 2000).

Whiteley, Sheila and Jennifer Rycenga (eds), *Queering the Popular Pitch* (London: Routledge, 2006).

Whiteley, Sheila, Andy Bennett and Stan Hawkins (eds), *Space and Place: Popular Music and Cultural Identity* (Aldershot: Ashgate, 2004).

Wicke, Peter, *Rock Music: Culture, Aesthetics, Sociology*, trans. Rachel Fogg (Cambridge: Cambridge University Press, 1990).

Williams, Raymond, *Television: Technology and Cultural Form* [1974] (New York: Schocken, 1975).

Williams, Sarah F. '"A Walking Open Wound": Emo Rock and the "Crisis" of Masculinity in America' in Jarman-Ivens, *Oh Boy!*, pp. 145–60.

Willis, Paul E., *Profane Culture* (London: Routledge and Kegan Paul, 1978).

Wilson, Carl, 'The Trouble with Indie Rock', *Slate.com*, <http://www.slate.com/id/2176187> (accessed 21 July 2008).

Windsor, W. Luke, 'An Ecological Approach to Semiotics', *Journal for the Theory of Social Behaviour*, 34/2 (2004): 179–98.

Wise, Sue, 'Sexing Elvis' [1984] in Frith and Goodwin, *On Record*, pp. 390–98.

Wishart, Trevor, *On Sonic Art* (York: Imagineering Press, 1985).

Wittgenstein, Ludwig, *Lectures and Conversations on Aesthetics, Psychology, and Religious Belief*, ed. Cyril Barrett (Berkeley: University of California Press, 2007).

Wolfe, Tom, *The Pump House Gang* (New York: Farrar, Strauss and Giroux, 1968), pp. 75–87.

——, *Radical Chic and Mau-Mauing the Flak Catchers* (London: Michael Joseph, 1971).

Woolgar, Steve, *Knowledge and Reflexivity* (London: Sage, 1988).

Wright, H. Stephen, 'The Materials of Film Music: Their Nature and Accessibility' in Clifford McCarty (ed.), *Film Music 1* (New York, Garland, 1989).

Wring, Dominic, 'The New Media and the Public Relations State' in Patrick Dunleavy, Richard, Heffernan, Phillip Cowley and Colin Hay (eds), *Developments in British Politics 8* (Basingstoke: Palgrave Macmillan, 2006), pp. 231–50.

Wynne, Derek and Justin O'Connor, 'Consumption and the Postmodern City', *Urban Studies* 35/5–6 (1998): 841–64.

Yano, Christine, 'The Floating World of Karaoke in Japan', *Popular Music and Society* 20/2 (1996): 1–18.

Young, Greg, '"So Slide Over Here": The Aesthetics of Masculinity in Late Twentieth-Century Australian Pop Music', *Popular Music* 23/2 (2004): 173–93.

Young, Robert J. C., *Colonial Desire: Hybridity in Theory, Culture and Race* (London: Routledge, 1995).

Zak III, Albin J., *The Poetics of Rock: Cutting Tracks, Making Records* (Berkeley: University of California Press, 2001).

Zuberi, Naabel, 'India Song: Popular Music Genres since Economic Liberalization' in Hesmondhalgh and Negus, *Popular Music Studies*, pp. 238–50.

Zukin, Sharon, 'Urban Lifestyles: Diversity and Standardisation in Spaces of Consumption', *Urban Studies* 35/5–6 (1998): 825–938.

Index

To avoid this index becoming unwieldy, song titles have been omitted. Please check under the relevant artist, composer, or producer. Rock music has been listed by subgenre (arena rock, heavy metal, punk, and so forth). The footnotes have been indexed only when they hold pertinent information in addition to citation of sources.